VALUABLE VINTAGE

VALUABLE VINTAGE

THE INSIDER'S GUIDE TO PRICING AND COLLECTING IMPORTANT VINTAGE FASHIONS

Elizabeth Mason
The Paper Bag
Princess

THREE RIVERS PRESS
NEW YORK

The author is in no way associated with or endorsed by Robert Munsch, author of *The Paper Bag Princess*, or Annick Press Ltd., publisher of *The Paper Bag Princess*.

Special note: Actress Maria Bello donated her entire appearance fee for this publication to Dream Yards Los Angeles, an organization that brings art into the lives of underprivileged children.

Published by Three Rivers Press, New York, New York.
Member of the Crown Publishing Group, a division of Random House, Inc.

www.randomhouse.com

THREE RIVERS PRESS and the Tugboat design are registered trademarks of Random House, Inc.

Printed in the United States of America

Design by Caitlin Daniels Israel

Front cover and insert photography by David Blank
Makeup by Carter Bradley; hair by Sean James, Hair at Fred Segal; styling by "B"

Back cover photograph by Peggy Sirota

Library of Congress Cataloging-in-Publication Data
Mason, Elizabeth.
Valuable vintage : the insider's guide to pricing and collecting important vintage fashions / by Elizabeth M. Mason.
1. Vintage clothing—Collectors and collecting—United States.   I. Title.
GT610 .M37 2001
687'.075—dc21   2001023958

ISBN 0-609-80703-X

10 9 8 7 6 5 4 3 2 1

First Edition

ONTENTS

FOREWORD

In the Beginning

I was lucky enough to be a young adult in the early 1970s, "a baby boomer." Through the political explosion of the 1960s came the revolution in fashion. The strict codes evaporated overnight and it was a time when street fashion turned into runway chic. All of a sudden, the designers were looking at what people were wearing in the street, otherwise known as "hippie chic." I was living in London then where it was not uncommon that women were wearing incredible Victorian undergarments as daywear. I was unfamiliar with the history of fashion at the time, but simply being around the atmosphere of high-quality textiles helped me to develop an appreciation of what I considered a new art form and my future.

I started buying costumes and antique textiles from the markets in London, from embroidered shawls to elaborate gilt-metal-embroidered caftans, assembling a large and representative collection. The industry was much more developed in the early seventies in London because of the great historical wealth of objects and works of art, including costumes and textiles, found there because of England's unique global history.

After returning to New York and joining Condé Nast Publications in the mid-seventies, and then eventually working for David Bowie as well as other rock artists, I found myself drawn to what had been my hobby of vintage clothing. It developed into my passion and ultimately my career by the end of the seventies.

I was very fortunate to be in the right place at the right time and took a chance by opening Trouve, a vintage clothing boutique, on the second floor of a Lexington Avenue and 82nd Street commercial building. I tried to create a "salon" along with my partner Caroline Rennolds Milbank. The atmosphere was eclectic and fun and we attempted to introduce a "new" product in a contemporary way. It was important to us to educate our clients to appreciate the idea of vintage clothing, which had not been considered by the mainstream consumers before.

In America, the emphasis throughout the twentieth century had been new house, new car, and new clothes. There were only a handful of collectors and dealers who had a passion for vintage clothing at the time. Our hope was to introduce to our own generation the incredible craftsmanship of couture and designer vintage garments that was fading away in the rush to buy "ready-to-wear." Every item in Trouve was uniquely special, and the fun of our relationship was that I looked at the fashion aspect and wearability of the couture dresses and Caroline never let us forget their important historical significance and value.

In the early 1980s I approached my friend Bill Doyle of William Doyle Galleries, who was handling famous estate sales, and together we decided to not only sell the entire celebrity estate, but to include for the first time the clothing and accessories as well. Gloria Swanson, Ruth Gordon, and socialite Hope Hampton were just a few of our early estates. In the beginning it was easier for the public to grasp fashion at auction through the notoriety of a celebrity name.

Through those experiences, we realized that the clientele who were buying fashion at auction were completely different from those who were buying from our other estates, so we decided to spin off and have sales uniquely for couture. Today the sales have drawn buyers from museums all over the world, including Japan, Europe, South America, and Australia. New York is a mecca for all "fashionistas," and major international designers, celebrities, and fashion students all either attend our live auction viewing, our couture sales at Doyle, or review it on the Internet. The exciting thing about vintage couture collecting is that every item is unique and will never be seen again, and the auctions offer a tremendous wealth of information through the more than 700 items that Doyle offers up at auction twice a year.

In my opinion, vintage designer and couture collecting is here to stay. Film stars, socialites, and fashionable ladies alike of every age understand it, want it, and compete very passionately for it!

—Linda Donohue
Executive Director
of Costume and Textiles,
William Doyle Galleries

Part One
VINTAGE
INFORMATION

INTRODUCTION

"That an article of clothing, made from a mere yard or two of fabric, could be recognizable as the work of a specific individual is a relatively new idea in the history of fashion. It has only been for the past one hundred and thirty years—since Charles Frederick Worth built an international business out of dictating style to his customers. Worth was the first dressmaker whom we would not hesitate to call a couturier. He was the first to put his signature on the clothes he made for his clients—both literally on a label and metaphorically, by creating clothes that were readily attributed to him."

—FROM *COUTURE*, BY CAROLINE RENNOLDS MILBANK

"Romance makes me giddy and insecure, work is both thrilling and fraught with anxiety, but shopping—specifically shopping for vintage clothing—is, for me, pure pleasure."

—LYNN HIESCHBERG

"Once seen mainly as a personal statement of style and considered a luxury, fashion has now become an object of collecting and display, and is viewed as an eloquent cultural expression."* Over the last few decades the collection of vintage couture and designer-made clothing has become an important trend in the antiques industry. Major auction houses from New York to Paris have taken notice by adding couture and designer-made auctions to their calendars; never before in the history of vintage clothing sales has the industry seen such a lucrative market as it is experiencing today.

The William Doyle Galleries in New York are now in their second very successful decade of presenting their "Couture and Textiles" auction to a full house. Their attendees range from some of the world's most celebrated designers to museum buyers, celebrities, and fashionistas as well as hobby vintage fashion collectors.

---

* Lisa Koenigisberg, Director, Programs in Arts at New York University.

There are more than ten thousand nonprofit thrift stores in North America, many offering vintage clothing sections, and across the country on any given weekend there are hundreds of antiques shows which attract hordes of collectors. There are now also important antique events, such as the "Vintage Fashion Expo" in Los Angeles and San Francisco, and "The New York Vintage Fashion & Antique Textile Show," which focus on vintage clothing, accessories, and textiles.

In November of 1998, New York University (NYU) hosted a two-day conference entitled "Fashion, The New Art." Again in November of 1999, NYU hosted another two-day conference on "The Ascendancy of American Fashion," and in November 2000, "The Globalization of Fashion." These events featured some of the world's most notable fashion and antique authorities whose primary focus was to debate fashion as the newest collectible.

Vintage couture and ready-to-wear boutiques are cropping up across the globe and auction websites such as eBay.com, sothebys.com, amazon.com, and firstauction.com offer live, online auctions of vintage fashions 24 hours a day, seven days a week!

It is not a surprise that there is such a frenzy for vintage fashion when you consider the prices some of these items can command. Who could have imagined that a Charles James ball gown would sell for $49,450 in April 1996, at the auction of William Doyle Galleries in New York? It was bought by Cora Ginsberg, a vintage clothing dealer who reportedly purchased it for a prominent international couture collector. In 1978, Charles James died of pneumonia, penniless in his two-room apartment at the Chelsea Hotel in New York. Prices like that put the great couturiers like James on par with some of the great artists, who worked in more traditional media, like paint or photography.

It is truly only the most informed collector who knows which works of art or which pieces of a specific designer's oeuvre are the most valuable and therefore command the greatest prices. That is what inspired me to write *Valuable Vintage*, the definitive guide to the identification and value of collectible couture and designer-made ready-to-wear vintage clothing.

In this book I demystify the vintage couture industry by defining the elements of style and design that enable the user to identify specific designers at a glance. The information considers both the historical and cultural impact a specific designer has and how this affects the values of those garments in today's collectibles market.

Having an eye on current trends in the contemporary fashion market will ultimately set you ahead of the pack in vintage couture collecting. If you are able to forecast the future of this emerging market by having your finger on the pulse of rising fashion stars, and have insight into their influences from the fashion past, then you will become adept at knowing when to save, or sell, valuable designer pieces.

Understanding the vintage designer market can be as baffling as diving headfirst into the New York Stock Exchange armed with nothing more than your local paper. It is important to understand what elements cause a flux in the market. Developing an awareness of what to watch for, and which designers you should look to the future with will enable you to ride the crest of emerging trends. It is this ebb and flow that can mean the difference between a savvy, successful investment and one which will simply clog the closet.

This book is your guide to the buying and selling of vintage couture and designer-made clothing in the sophisticated world of auction houses, vintage boutiques, and online auctions. If you are simply a novice collector or have inherited some wonderful pieces, yet have no idea of their true value, the price guide in this book is the reference for you. If you are already a collector with a moderate grasp of this fast-paced, ever-changing industry, you too will find this book a valuable resource.

Although it's not exactly the average consumer who is shelling out tens of thousands of dollars at auctions of important vintage couture pieces, you will be surprised at who is choosing vintage over the pick of the litter on the contemporary fashion runways. Supermodels like Shalom Harlow and Kate Moss are opting for a fabulous vintage 1960s Yves Saint Laurent ensemble or a sleek 1970s Rudi Gernreich fishtail gown that would rival anything Tom Ford of Gucci has sent down the runway recently. It is time to sit up and take notice when you consider they could be the muse of virtually any notable designer, and wear at whim their top couture, contemporary designs.

While it is true that many celebrities are choosing designer vintage clothing and that this trend has definitely grabbed the mainstream media's attention, it is not reserved simply for the privileged class. Designer vintage collecting has a strong hold on the average style-conscious consumer as well. In the 1980s, style was about "flash and trash" and how much you spent, then we saw the 1990s move toward savvy shoppers who would flaunt with pride just how little they paid for something fabulously secondhand. Shopping in thrift stores is no longer reserved simply for the budget-minded consumer. If you are willing to roll up your sleeves and really dig in, treasures abound!

Why would you want to brave the frosty early morning hours, or an aggressive elbow to the ribs that may be thrown your way in a not-always-friendly, highly competitive arena of vintage couture collecting? One answer in part is simple economics; there is serious money to be made if you know what you're doing. The other reason is that the garments you will find while shopping for vintage will most certainly be of better quality and workmanship then most contemporary items. There is no question in anyone's mind that it is very difficult to find high-quality contemporary garments or accessories today without an enormous price tag attached to them, and even still, corners have been cut. It is simply too cost-restrictive today to produce the type of craftsmanship which was quite common practice in the past.

It is true today that it is becoming harder and harder to find a fabulous cache of incredible, never-worn Rudi Gernreich garments as I did in the mid-1990s. There are many of us who would scream out in a thrift store, from high atop a bale of clothing, "Get out of here, I found it first!" I must admit I have broken into a full gallop at a flea market in order to reach a particular dealer's booth before the hundreds of others who were pressed up against the front gate before the opening bell at 6:00 A.M. You can't help but hear a voice announcing, "And they're OFF!"

ONE
What Is Vintage?

The wonderful thing about vintage is that it doesn't get old, it just gets older, and to a vintage collector this is a good thing, because the older it gets, the more valuable it becomes. Often, after a contemporary garment has been purchased it continues to get old and less desirable until it becomes vintage.

Many are confused by the very term vintage and there are varying responses to the question of just how old "vintage" is. Vintage does not mean antique, which is an industry standard that normally refers to an item that is one hundred years old or older. Any garment or accessory which was made earlier than the 1920s, such as Victorian, Turn-of-the-Century, or Edwardian, is referred to as antique. Nor does vintage simply mean something that is not new. The time frame for vintage clothing mainly refers to items dating from the 1920s and, until recently, up to the 1970s; for our purposes, that definition has been expanded.

Although there is a tremendous following for Victorian clothing and many museums are greatly interested in garments which predate Victorian times—reaching back to the beginnings of people's fascination with clothing and personal ornamentation—this book will mainly be referring to 20th-century clothing, 1920s through the 1980s, and in some cases may refer to various important items from the 1990s.

We have had to adjust our attitudes toward the limitations of this time frame theory due to the latest demand for the iconic designer looks of the early 1980s. Up until recently, no one referred to garments from the 1980s as vintage; they were simply referred to as secondhand garments which you would expect to find mainly in contemporary resale boutiques. Suddenly, clothing from the 1980s is considered vintage and feverishly sought after by collectors. In the fall of 2000, the Guggenheim Museum in New York presented a retrospective of the designs by Azzedine Alaïa which focused on his work through the early 1980s. It is precisely this type of media attention which encourages the public demand for certain designer pieces, as well as for the era from which the items are noted.

It appears that almost any designs from only yesterday are now being referred to as "vintage." Contemporary fashion is moving at such a frenzied pace today that it is difficult to stay ahead of it. The fashion media is constantly comparing a designer's latest collection to their last, and their seminal collections. They analyze what the designers did then, in comparison to now. In many cases with new young designers, the difference between then and now may only be just a few years. Yet already the media uses the term vintage when referring to the collections which are only a few years old.

It is true that the media plays a very important role in influencing trends in the vintage clothing industry. They broadcast news about the trends and the changes, but where do the influences come from? Who starts the trends? Why are we always looking back in self-examination? There is much speculation as to where it all begins. It seems that the act of looking just 20 years back in fashion for influencing trends continues to be an important factor in vintage collecting. This is played out in other influential cultural trends such as time settings for a particular novel, film, or television series. Often it is a matter of the particular professional's career ascent. A designer or writer reaches a point of success in their career at which they are embraced by their respective industry. Their breakthrough film or fashion collection's romantic references are usually drawn from their years of struggling up the ladder of success. This, in most cases, is about 20 years back, or when they first started to really respond to their sensibilities. It was a carefree period, where the artists were freer to explore ideas with an experimental, untethered hand.

One of the inherent problems with understanding vintage is to know how to recognize when something is old and from which time period it came. Often a client will bring something for me to appraise, assuming it was from a specific time period, only to discover it was in fact from a more recent time, only reflecting the style of an older period. With all the designers glancing backwards for influence, they have made it very difficult for the lay person to accurately date a particular item.

The 1970s saw designers borrowing heavily from the 1940s with their long hippie-chic styling, taking many of the elements of style from the glamorous 1930s and 1940s, incorporating them into their designs. This is not unlike contemporary designers such as Mark Jacobs, Miuccia Prada, or

Gucci. It is important to know what elements to look for when determining which vintage era a piece is from, and not to be fooled by the copycat designs of later years.

I will define most of the important elements in the following chapters and this will assist you in determining the vintage of particular items, as well as the value of the pieces when these are compared to the data in the price guide section of this book.

Two
Vintage Designer Ready-to-Wear versus Vintage Haute Couture

The term "Couture" refers to a garment that is ordered specifically by one client from a design house, which is then constructed exclusively by hand for that particular client. It was only the top design houses of the past, such as Dior, Chanel, Balenciaga, Yves Saint Laurent, Cardin, Worth, Jean Dessès, Vionnet, or Charles James who produced haute couture garments for their private clientele. Today you can expect to find true haute couture coming out of only such design houses as Versace, Valentino, Dior, Chanel, Yves Saint Laurent, John Galliano, and the like.

The term "vintage haute couture" has been widely misused by many vintage clothing dealers over the last few years, mainly due to the booming demand in the vintage clothing industry and the sellers' desire to add cachet to their merchandise. Very few pieces that are truly haute couture make their way into the mainstream vintage market. It is more likely that a client who purchased such an expensive item understands its value and would not dispose of it through a resale outlet or by donating it (although this has certainly been known to happen).

Occasionally, those fortunate few who are in a tax bracket that supports the need for a large tax write-off may donate an expensive couture item to a specific charity, which is able to appraise its value and issue an appropriate write-off for the donor. Some may choose to have an item appraised by a third party prior to donating it in order to ensure the highest possible tax write-off. Others may choose to give their very expensive couture items to a museum which houses a costume and textile department.

In many cases some charities have relationships with either high-end vintage dealers or auction houses to which they sell or consign important couture items in order to receive the best possible prices. People who choose to donate a couture item to a particular charity's resale outlet probably have a personal relationship with it, either through patronage of its foundation or as a volunteer. Rarely do they give something away blindly. Most who could originally afford expensive garments ranging in price from $5,000 to $20,000, are not about to throw such valuable items away without considering the financial consequences. With all the information available today, it has become even less likely that they would make that mistake.

Therefore, in the present vintage industry climate you can expect to find most of the real haute couture items only through the important auction houses, or very high-end vintage clothing boutiques. It would be wise to scrutinize items coming from most other sources.

Ready-to-wear vintage garments are much more common and easily located for the obvious reason: more were produced. Ready-to-wear designer garments or prêt-a-porter, as the French say, are garments which were manufactured by a particular design house and distributed for the mass consumer through department stores or specialty boutiques. Most of what you will find in the high-end vintage boutiques and auction venues is ready-to-wear designer vintage.

Ultimately it is a couture garment which will demand the highest price. That is not to say however that there aren't extremely valuable ready-to-wear vintage items that will command unheard-of prices, such as important design pieces like an original wrap dress by Claire McCardell or a topless swim suit by Rudi Gernreich. Who could have predicted the demand for vintage Emilio Pucci garments and accessories? Many of Emilio Pucci's vintage pieces are selling today for as much or more than the design house's contemporary pieces. I have personally seen customers fighting to pay thousands of dollars for a 1970s suede or leather Gucci coat, or a 1960s Courrèges ensemble. It is always so surprising to see a ready-to-wear item go for so much more than what you would expect a couture garment to command. This phenomenon is usually swayed by media hype and the subsequent consumer demand. This is why it is important to always stay ahead of the media in its predictions. I think it is probably fair to say that we have all, at one time or another in our lives, fallen prey to media hype and reflected on our purchase with regret.

THREE
Identifying Important Haute Couture and Designer Ready-to-Wear Vintage Garments

"Vintage fashion is avidly collected today, because more and more people appreciate the historic and artistic significance of period couture garments. A Schiaparelli jacket from the 1930s, for example, is not just an object of beauty, it is also a piece of fashion history. Schiaparelli was an artist who worked in the medium of fabric, but even ordinary vintage fashions, such as period sweaters and blouses, are often far more interesting and attractive than contemporary examples. Certainly, in many cases the quality of the workmanship greatly surpasses all but the most expensive contemporary couture. In addition, many people enjoy the pleasure of the hunt, and the thrill of finding unique objects."

—DR. VALERIE STEEL, CURATOR, THE MUSEUM AT THE
FASHION INSTITUTE OF TECHNOLOGY

A haute couture garment will usually have an inventory number on a small label located either next to or just behind the designer's label. Often the numbers on these small labels may have faded over time because they were handwritten with ink. They may also be difficult to discern because of their handwritten nature. Also the numbers may be written a little differently due to the fact that they were written by a European. This series of numbers is like a vehicle identification number (VIN) on a car and will lead you straight back to the original owner. Most top design houses keep fairly accurate client files and the numbers found on the label should correspond with the account of the person for whom it was originally ordered. This account information contains the client's name, all of their precise measurements, and a log of their orders with the house.

Identifying a garment which is truly haute couture is not always as easy as locating a numbered label. As mentioned in the last chapter, oftentimes the customer removed a label from a garment if they traveled extensively abroad so that they would not find themselves held up at a customs office with the fear of having to pay duty every time they traveled in and out of the country with the garment.

You need to use more sophisticated construction details to determine the quality and therefore the value of a garment. In performing your due diligence and detective work you should look for exquisite fabrics, fine silk or rayon linings, intricate hand-stitching, bead or embroidery work, hand-picked tailoring, French seams, great buttons, hand-bound buttonholes, tiny fabric-covered snap fasteners, delicate metal zippers set in by hand, quality in craftsmanship, and distinguished overall design and construction. These types of details will only be found in very expensive garments and can certainly point to a more sophisticated and demanding design house. A lesser garment may have unfinished seams and heavier zippers in place of finer zippers which are more aesthetically pleasing. In a fine couture garment you find entire bodices beaded by hand; by contrast you find machine applied beadwork in ready-to-wear.

Beadwork and embroidery are telltale signs of either a couture garment or a ready-to-wear piece. Hand-done work will have slight irregularities. By turning the garment to the reverse, you will find that the stitching will have defined beginnings and hand-knotted endings, whereas machine-applied embroideries or beading will not have the same finishes. It is much more difficult to see where machine-done work begins and ends. There is a continuous flow to machine work, not the constant start and stop of handwork.

A good tip on knowing the difference between hand-done beadwork and machine work is to know your beads. The more expensive the beads the stronger the potential for haute couture origins. Beautiful glass beads are preferred over plastic beads by the better design houses. They are more expensive to produce and their look is much more dramatic and pleasing to the eye. Their colors are more vibrant and often the shapes are more refined. You will find that the faceted, cut glass, or crystal beads have sharper edges, and the plastic beads which appear to be similar will have small seams in them where the molds have met in the manufacturing process. The plastic beads will have smoother edges because they were molded rather than hand-cut.

It is also easy enough to know when you have a garment with glass beads, simply by the sheer weight of the garment, because glass is usually twice as heavy as plastic. If you are still not sure, a simple test is to tap one of the beads against your teeth. The difference between the sensation of a glass bead and a plastic one will be something you will come to appreciate with trial and error. Glass is also cold to the touch, whereas the plastic will not have a true sensation of temperature.

You can determine whether you have a hand-embroidered garment or a machine-applied one by examining the thread. The more expensive the embroidery thread, the more likely it is a hand-embroidered piece. Fine silk threads are used in hand-embroidered garments and in the exquisite Eastern examples you frequently find the use of silver and gold threads.

The smaller the stitch the better the work because the use of fine thread contrasted with thicker thread is a sure sign of fine workmanship. This is true with lovely petit point work on handbags and accessories as well. The smaller, more delicate the stitch, the more refined the craftsmanship. You may need to use a magnifying glass to examine and discern the stitch closely because it is often difficult to tell if you cannot examine the reverse side of an item in order to spot the hand-knotted ends to the stitching. The hand-knotted ends will, as mentioned, be a true indication of handwork over machine work when it comes to small delicate work such as petit point.

One of the best ways to determine if you have a fine handmade, couture item is to turn the garment inside out to examine the finish to it. French seams are a clear indication that you have an example of refined craftsmanship. The seams are turned in, or under, as the garment is being constructed, and when each piece is stitched together the end result will show no selvage edge to the fabric. In other words the entire garment is completely finished on the inside and there are no raw or unfinished edges. A French seam requires more time to construct and for this reason is more cost-restrictive in the manufacturing of a ready-to-wear item. Garments of lesser quality have their seams finished with an over-locking zigzag stitch that simply keeps them from fraying. This use of the machine-applied zigzag or over-locking stitch harkens back to when manufacturers and couture design houses would over-lock all the raw inside seams with this type of stitch by hand.

Hand-finished linings are lovely to behold. I absolutely adore turning a garment inside out to find that a fine silk lining has been placed in a garment by hand. To discover whether a lining has been placed in by hand you only need to look for the small stitches which run around the perimeter of the entire lining of the garment. Often the lining may have been initially placed in by machine and then stitched over with very small stitches known as tailor's tacks or hand-picked stitching. These stitches are approximately ⅛ to ¹⁄₁₆ of an inch in length. Better tailoring of men's suits has this type of stitch on the outside of the garment, particularly around the lapels of a jacket or edge of a trouser or jacket pocket. This fine work ensures that the garment edges will remain flat. The refinement of this stitch is found only in more expensive garments due to the extensive labor required to produce the effect.

It is also very important to familiarize yourself with various notable designer labels and look for the labels which are made of fine woven silk. Oftentimes the department store label will be the most prominent; however, you should search for the designer's label inside the garment, because it may be hidden underneath the lining of a dress, or on the side seam of a jacket, rather than located directly at the neckline of the garment. It is true, however, that some department stores and specialty shops remove the designer's label altogether and simply add their own. This practice still occurs today when a specialty boutique will purchase the collection of a lesser known designer and remove their label, then insert the boutique's own label and present the garment as a sort of "house brand" offering.

Another common occurrence was that a department store may have viewed the collection of a particular design house in Paris and purchased a garment only to bring it back to their design team to have it copied stitch for stitch. This is why many items come up at auction and the catalog description may say that the garment is "Attributed to" a particular design house, yet has no label or proof of authenticity. This is where you need to have done your homework. If it is not important to you that the garment be haute couture, but simply in the style of, then these "Attributed to" garments are a less expensive alternative, just as they were at the time when they were first manufactured.

All in all, identifying a haute couture or designer ready-to-wear garment at a glance takes plenty of trial and error. The more you handle a garment, the more you investigate workmanship, the better you will become. It is advisable that you spend some time simply browsing the vintage clothing and haute couture markets. Be open to the opportunity when a merchant shares with you some incredible detail about a garment and listen closely as to why that element fascinates them. Explore the contemporary markets as well. Visit the high-end designer sections at your local department stores and specialty boutiques. Get up close and personal with the workmanship. It is all this information that fills your personal database from which you draw upon later, and enables you to buy that wonderful estate piece with confidence.

How Important Is a Label?

There is no question that a label speaks volumes about the item. A label on a garment is not unlike a signature on a fine work of art; if the label is missing then the value is seriously compromised. Oftentimes a label is removed from a garment by a customer when they bought an item overseas and were hoping to avoid an import customs charge. I never understood why they did not simply mail the labels home to themselves and sew them back on once they were safely on home turf. It baffles me when someone proudly pronounces that they remember when their mother once traveled abroad and clipped all the labels out of her original Christian Dior garments. I will never understand the reasoning behind defacing the garment by removing the label in the hopes that the customs' officials will buy their story that the lovely gown was really something they picked up at the local department store.

There is also the consideration that a consumer purchased a copy of a particular garment by a private manufacturer and the history of that item is translated down through the years as an original design. This is often referenced by vintage sellers as **attributed to** (means that the item was made in the style of, or as a replica of the original garment or by a noncredited designer working for a design house at the time of the garment's creation, like Yves Saint Laurent at The House of Dior or Donna Karan at Anne Klein). (See Terms, page 348.) Occasionally a customer would order one dress from a haute couture design house and then have a less expensive seamstress or tailor make an exact copy of it.

There are a few designers or fashion houses who have chosen to incorporate the word "couture" in their label to give it some weight; however, that does not mean that the garment is in fact a haute couture, handmade piece. More often, it really means that the designer has chosen to represent this particular line of their designs as being in the style of haute couture. It may be that this was a piece from their more expensive collection and that should certainly be taken into consideration when assessing its value. All that said, use your common sense; if you can see telltale signs that a garment has been mass-produced such as a union label, size tag, and machine-finished seams, then it is probably safe to say that the garment is not haute couture, no matter what the label says.

An unusual and interesting trend that always seems to amuse people was when the designers would insert their labels upside down at the neck of a garment. This was most commonly done in expensive fur coats; however, this practice can be found in less expensive designer wear as well. The theory was that when you took your coat off and laid it over the back of a chair in a fine restaurant or theater, or perhaps just haphazardly had it thrown over your arm, the label to the admiring onlooker would then appear right side up. This way proper credit and admiration could be read and appreciated.

*F*OUR
The Most Important Vintage Designers to Collect

You have to buy what you love. Do not allow yourself to be seduced by a designer's name just because you heard somewhere that it was important or collectible. Designers are not infallible; they have been known to make mistakes too. Not every garment from a single designer is worth considering. The piece must have a real *look* to it, something that sets it apart. Understanding what that look should be is a sense that you will develop with experience. The bottom line is that *you* need to truly adore the piece before you buy it.

Although it is true that we can never be absolutely sure where the next trend will come from, there are many designers from the past who have already earned their stripes as the most valuable on the auction block. As you become familiar with the price guide in this book it will be very clear which designers reign supreme. Designers who are the treasured talents from the past are the Americans: Pauline Trigère, Irene Lentz, Gilbert Adrian, Rudi Gernreich, James Galanos, Norman Norell, Charles James, Mainbocher, Roy Halston, Bonnie Cashin, Claire McCardell; and the Europeans: Charles Federick Worth, Coco Chanel, Ossie Clark, Mary Quant, Paco Rabanne, Pierre Cardin, Christian Dior, Cristobal Balenciaga, Madeleine Vionnet, Paul Poiret, Mariano Fortuny, Mme. Alix Grés, Jean Dessès, and Yves Saint Laurent who are among the top performers at auction. You should also seriously consider many important vintage items from design houses such as Hermès, Gucci, Louis Vuitton, and Prada.

It is the quality of the workmanship that sets one designer above another, the painstaking attention to fine details, the luxurious fabrics, as well as the beauty in the design. James Galanos said recently, "Couture is laughable in America today," and I tend to agree with him. Very few American designers are truly producing couture garments today, with few exceptions such as Maggie Norris, Richard Tyler, or Geoffrey Beene.

Gone are the American designers like Gilbert Adrian, Ceil Chapman, Norman Norell, Irene Lentz, Mainbocher, Claire McCardell, Bonnie Cashin, or Anne Klein. It is a difficult task to explain just why a designer becomes so collectible. To understand it fully you have to examine each designer's body of work as a whole and I simply do not have the pages available to me here. What I can tell you is that the top collectible designers of today were the stars of yesterday. They were the designers who stole our hearts and kept us hooked until they were gone. Designers like Adrian, who almost single-handedly carved out the look of American women in the 1930s and 1940s through his gorgeous work as a costume designer in film, then moved on to create his own clothing collections. Or Claire McCardell, who in the late 1930s and 1940s redefined a woman's role in society by creating women's activewear. The simplicity of her designs set women free from the restrictions of formal dressing. It is the risk takers such as McCardell who dominate the pages of fashion history and consequently hold our attention and ultimately become very collectible.

Look to the designers who changed the face of fashion and created an entirely new barometer of popular demand. These are the designers who sent shock waves throughout the fashion world, and it is these collections that had staying power and larger-than-life iconic theme pieces, which have become the Holy Grail to search for today. If a designer's collection inspired other contemporaries to follow their lead, as Christian Dior did in the postwar years with the "New Look," or Rudi Gernreich with his unisex dressing and infamous "Topless Swimsuit," then these are the front page stories of the past which drive the retrospectives of today and consequently ignite a demand for their garments.

When considering which designers might be the most desirable, look to those who historically had important breakthrough collections and created a look which was undeniably theirs, but which everyone scrambled to emulate. Examples of designers who illustrate these qualities are: Paco Rabanne with his futuristic metal disc designs, and André Courrèges with his minimalist modern approach to tailoring. Yves Saint Laurent also changed the face of fashion when he took over designing for the house of Christian Dior the year after Dior's death in 1958. Particularly noteworthy was Charles Worth, who in making single garments for his customers created the "Look of Worth" by being the first designer to put his name on a label in his creations.

Coco Chanel's rise to fame and fall into scandal, then subsequent resurrection and rebirth was a widely publicized one, so it is a little easier for us to understand the popularity of her vintage designs today. Although in some cases it does make a difference if a designer's vision is carried forward by the design house that they founded, this doesn't necessarily define the reason behind its desirability. Chanel has defined the term "staying power"; however, a Chanel design may be just as sought after as a vintage design from Rudi Gernreich, who stopped designing in the mid-1970s and did not leave behind a design house to carry on his vision.

However, if a particular designer did leave behind a design house or the designer's name was picked up and bought much in the way Halston has seen a rebirth, or the house of Gucci and Dior and more recently Balenciaga and Worth, then it stands to reason that there would be renewed interest in those particular designers. Another good example of this is the house of Yves Saint Laurent, who is stronger than ever now with Yves Saint Laurent stepping back from his house with its acquisition by Gucci and the appointment of Tom Ford as head designer for ready-to-wear.

Most of the prized vintage couture pieces are the work of designers who are long gone. Their particular designs will never be produced again, and since in their lifetime, they may have produced only a limited number of garments—as in the case of Charles James or Gilbert Adrian—then it stands to reason that their pieces will be much more valuable. The designer Irene produced exquisite work which mirrored that of Adrian. Unfortunately, her career and consequently the amount of work that she produced were cut tragically short by her suicide in 1962. Today her designs are very collectible. Some collectors even prefer Irene's designs over Adrian's.

It is a little-known industry secret that both Irene and Adrian shared the same design director, Chris Ghiatis, who specialized in the expert tailoring for which both designers were renowned. Chris Ghiatis only just retired in the spring of 2000 and presently resides in Los Angeles. Chris confided in me once that the intricate detailing that was the look of Adrian's tailored suits was not so much the result of design genius; the complicated tailoring details were designed to deter copycats. They kept making the designs more and more complicated which made replication of the patterns too cost-restrictive.

The onset of the AIDS epidemic in late 1970s and early 1980s claimed the lives of many of the fashion world's brightest stars such as Scott Barrie, Roy Halston, and Rudi Gernreich, all of whom are highly collectible today. The fact that we lost some of these truly brilliant designers so tragically when they still had so much more to offer has made their work much more valuable. The serious collector knows that the work of the designers who rise to the top of the pop chart in vintage collecting, have designs which stand on their own merit. To recognize the quality of these designs you don't need to know who originally created them; you just know they are great!

Although certain designers or design houses are highly collectible, not everything that bears these designer labels is great and valuable to collect. You need to take into consideration the fact that there were many designers, especially those in the 1970s and 1980s who sold licenses to their names. Halston, Cardin, and Dior are prime examples of this. Although some of their licensed products certainly are collectible, such as the logo bags which have ruled the collectibles market for the last five years or so, the licensed clothing lines usually are substantially less expensive than the designer's house couture and ready-to-wear designs.

When looking to the future and considering designers to preserve for your collection, consider again designers who have had important breakthrough collections like John Galliano and his early work for Christian Dior as well as Karl Lagerfeld for Chanel, Tom Ford for Gucci and Yves Saint Laurent for Christian Dior, Nicolas Ghesquière for Balenciaga, Stella McCartney for Chloé, Azzedine Alaïa, Miuccia Prada, Thierry Mugler, Jean-Paul Gaultier, Vivienne Westwood, Martin Margiela, Comme des Garçons, Fendi, Ann Demeulemeester, and Dolce & Gabbana, as well as Alexander McQueen and Christian Lacroix, both of whom had turbulent careers.

FIVE
Prices Realized in Varying World Markets

The price of a garment may vary greatly depending on the venue where you purchase it. It stands to reason that there would be a sliding scale in price ranges from low to high. The low comprises markets such as thrift stores, flea markets, or estate sales. Do not expect to pay the same rate when buying in the high markets such as designer vintage boutiques, online auctions, or at important auction houses.

Over the last five years or so, many of the larger thrift stores' chains have started to train their staff to sort out the better merchandise and price it higher. Many of them have set up special sales or boutique departments in their shops which offer the pre-selected high end vintage items. Some thrift chains, such as Goodwill with ShopGoodwill.com, are even offering pre-selected items around the clock on their websites. Others such as the National Council of Jewish Women's thrift shops in Los Angeles are joining the Internet bandwagon and offering selected items for sale online at eBay.com.

Many feel that gone are the days of finding an amazing gown just hanging from a nail on the wall at your local thrift haunt. This considered, there is something to be said for educating the thrift industry. Primarily, the thrift businesses are taking greater care with the vintage clothing that they receive. This means you are less likely to find a price tag which has been recklessly applied with a tagging gun, pierced straight through the body of a garment, or a wonderful beaded gown thrown into a bin like a discarded memory from a 1960s prom better left forgotten. It is also fair to mention that the good intention of these charity thrift stores is to make money; therefore, you should not be upset that they are beginning to catch up with current trends and reap some of the benefits as well.

The more hands a garment passes through, the more selected and expensive it may become. It could start out as a donation to a thrift shop, be snapped up by a **picker** (someone who combs resale locations for items to sell at a higher price to a **dealer** or private party), sold to a dealer (a person who may resell privately or own a retail shop which deals in used, vintage, or antique merchandise), who may pass it over to an auction house, which then sells it to the highest bidder. The price could start as low as ten dollars and with a final blow of the hammer, end well into the thousands! (See Terms, page 348.)

Contemporary consignment shops are beginning to cash in on things as well. In the past they may not have carried any merchandise which was more than a few years old; however, today you are just as likely to see a specialty rack in those same shops offering selected vintage garments for sale. Depending on whether or not a particular consignment shop is up to date on the latest trends and the going prices of various vintage collectibles, you may still find that the prices in these establishments are still considerably lower than in a strictly vintage boutique.

Geography plays an important role in determining prices as well. Certain items may be of greater interest in different areas of the world. Things that sell well on the West Coast are not necessarily always in demand in New York. For example, a heavy cotton velvet Emilio Pucci outfit may sell for a much higher price due to its demand in the New York market, simply because one might not consider wearing so much fabric on the sunny West Coast. Supply and demand—and therefore prices—also fluctuate in the foreign markets. London and Paris seem to be more interested in European designers, whereas the Japanese buyers really love pop culture, American designers, or image-driven items such as Gucci, Roberta di Camerino, Pierre Cardin, and most recently (due to the reinvention of the Dior logo), anything with the Christian Dior logo on it.

The Japanese have always been very instrumental in creating popular demand. They seem to be one step ahead at all times and it is very important to watch their buying patterns. Their passion for a particular vintage designer can virtually change overnight without warning! Where just yesterday they couldn't seem to get enough vintage Gucci or Pucci, today they are snapping up iconic 1980s looks by Chanel, Yves Saint Laurent, and Azzedine Alaïa.

The Japanese youth couture love American pop culture and all that vintage designer items represent, emblems of wealth and success. One of the ways that the Japanese establish a position in their couture's fashion society is to acquire an item which is difficult to find and much sought after, such as a vintage designer item.

To some degree, the Japanese spending patterns have fueled the vintage market today. A Japanese journalist who has been covering Japanese popular culture for many years speculated about the misconception that because of their wealth, the Japanese are conspicuous consumers. It is not that they have so much money, rather it is a matter of how they choose to spend the money they have. They do not have an option to spend a great deal on a large home and fancy furnishings; there simply isn't room in Japan for this type of expenditure of income. Consequently, they choose to spend their money on fashion, and more specifically on fashion that will set them apart from the masses. Many have decided that the best way to do this is with designer vintage.

Auctions are without question the most reliable venue to consider if you are ever unsure of the value of an item. Important houses such as William Doyle, Drouot Hôtel des Ventes, and Sotheby's have also played major roles in establishing values for designer-associated vintage garments. The knowledgeable auction house may place a substantial **reserve price** (the price under which the auction house will not sell any item). Ultimately it is the buyer who will establish the **realized price** (the final bid on an item that may include the buyer's premium which is an amount above the **hammer price** or final bid price, charged to the buyer by auction houses). You should always consider that you will be responsible for paying a buyer's premium when bidding on an item when the hammer finally comes down with the last bid. (See Terms, page 348.)

Some of the larger auction houses are moving toward presenting their auctions both as a live auction as well as on the Internet. Sotheby's has recently decided to offer its vintage couture auctions solely online over a two-week period. Many believe that this decision will affect the popularity of Sotheby's vintage auction by taking away the live experience, and limiting its audience to those who have online capabilities. However, the auction house's choice to go online is much more cost-effective because they will not have to incur the cost of producing an expensive glossy catalog or hosting the live event and they feel that going online will open the auctions up to a greater world market.

There is already a thriving online vintage clothing business well known to those who buy and sell on any of the many online auction sites, most notably eBay.com. These sites offer a variety of vintage merchandise and are available to the consumer at the click of a mouse, twenty-four hours a day, seven days a week. The online auction sites have opened up a world of possibilities to the vintage novice, and to Mom-and-Pop storeowners who prior to these venues would not have been able to sell off their inherited items, or better vintage items, with much success, or add to a personal collection without living in the proximity of a high-end shop or auction house.

Like the live auction houses, the online auctions can dictate the value of an item in a world market by virtue of its very competitive nature. I have found overall that important designer vintage will fetch high prices online, but other lesser known items can be acquired at almost wholesale prices. Many of the mass-produced items such as "Emilio Pucci for Formfit Rogers," a loungewear line from the famed Emilio Pucci, will tend to sell for about half of what it would sell for in a vintage boutique.

It is very important to note that while it may be very safe to bid on an auction item over the Internet when it is being offered by a reputable auction house, it is difficult to have a guarantee on the quality of merchandise when dealing with some of the strictly online venues such as eBay. The online industry for the most part is left to police itself. There have been tremendous advancements in establishing professional decorum online in recent years; however, just like the service you may get in a less than reputable bricks and mortar business, you may run into problems. One main problem seems to be that this online venue has opened up the industry to a number of amateurs who may not understand the meaning of a proper condition report on an item. Therefore it is advisable that you ask as many questions as possible about the item's condition prior to bidding on it.

Although many will claim that the vintage clothing markets are saturated and picked over, I strongly believe that there is still uncharted territory and great finds to be had if you are prepared to know what to look for. You just may need to roll your sleeves up a little higher. This is what makes a true vintage enthusiast a great champion. It is true that the increased interest in the designer vintage clothing market has had measurable consequences and the industry as a whole has seen a tremendous depletion of resources. It has, however, forced the emergence of a small number of truly great vintage clothing purveyors who have excelled in establishing a much more refined market worldwide.

$\mathcal{S}$IX
Emerging Trends in the Designer Vintage Clothing Market

From the beginning the press has always played an important role in contemporary fashion and today they play an integral part in dictating emerging style trends by what they publish and thereby propel the values of vintage designer wear. When we have renowned fashion writers and editors such as Lynn Hirshberg at *Vanity Fair* or Hamish Bowles at *Vogue* magazine who are passionate vintage couture collectors themselves, then it is no wonder the stories on vintage collecting remain in the spotlight.

There is no question that the more the public sees a celebrity wearing vintage the more they want to emulate that look. You must factor in the power that the media wields when they show a photograph of Julia Roberts accepting the Academy Award in 2001 wearing a spectacular vintage couture Valentino gown, or Wynona Ryder wearing a vintage Pauline Trigère gown from Lily et Cie in Beverly Hills at the 2000 Academy Awards, as well as new fashion trendsetters on the vintage scene like Chloé Sévigny, who adores older Yves Saint Laurent and Balenciaga. It doesn't take long after the press runs a photograph of Brooke Shields in vintage Emilio Pucci for things to get all fired up again over Pucci.

After Nicole Kidman appeared on the cover of *Esquire* magazine (August 1999) in a vintage outfit by Georgio of Beverly Hills, and wore it to the premiere of her film, *Eyes Wide Shut*, I received calls from all over the world when it was publicized that the fashion stylist Jonathan Skow had purchased it for her from my boutique, The Paper Bag Princess. The outfit engendered an entire movement toward backless halter tops that summer.

Actress Maria Bello came into my boutique, The Paper Bag Princess, after she had been to all the best designers, looking for a special gown to wear to the Golden Globe Awards. After days of searching, she fell in love with a sexy 1960s gown from my boutique which was completely beaded with clear rhinestones and silver bugle beads. The gown had no designer label attached to it, yet it mirrored what Marilyn Monroe had in mind when choosing her now infamous dress by Jean Louis to wear while singing, "Happy Birthday to You," to President John F. Kennedy. It was reminiscent of an era of lost glamour, not to mention breathtakingly gorgeous! We did do some major updating of the overall style of the gown to give it a sleek contemporary look while still maintaining the integrity of the original design. The dress truly cried out for a deep backless cut and thigh-high back slit. Maria is a perfect example of a visionary who recognizes the potential in an incredible vintage piece and expresses her passion for the glamour and craftsmanship of an era.

It is difficult to say who started it all and where the credit should be given. Is it the celebrity like Maria Bello who has a strong independent vision, or the powerful Hollywood stylists like L'ren Scott, Jonathan Skow, Lori Goldstein, Patty Wilson, Jessica Pastor, Philip Block who will be paid handsomely to dress the celebrity? Personally, I think it is a little bit of both. The stylist may steer the celebrity in a certain direction, but ultimately it is the individual who makes the decision to walk down that red carpet in a chosen gown.

This passion for vintage is crossing over into major mainstream fashion editorials as well. It has become commonplace to see the page credits for any number of the top fashion publications commingle the latest hot designer wear with some of the great designers of the past. Internationally renowned fashion stylist Lori Goldstein has been very influential in brilliantly cross-merchandising exceptional vintage garments and accessories with contemporary designs for important fashion layouts photographed by Steven Meisel. With such major influences, it is not a wonder that fashion enthusiasts the world over are clamoring for vintage designs.

In the late 1990s the industry felt a surge in demand for vintage Halston, Versace, and Gucci designs. This was due mainly to the revitalization of Gucci by Tom Ford, whose inaugural collection borrowed heavily from previous Gucci designs and Halston looks of the 1970s. Also, the unfortunate death of Gianni Versace in 1998 had an immediate impact on the value of his couture designs. All of this sent collectors scouring the markets for originals, causing prices to soar. More recently, the vintage industry has seen a renewed interest in Versace due to Donetella Versace and her incredible design team now heading the house of Versace. The more popular a contemporary designer is, the greater the demand there is for their vintage pieces.

In the fall of 2000 at the conference on fashion at NYU, Norma Kamali revealed that she had been stockpiling pieces from her collections over the last 20 years of her business. She announced that she was going to reintroduce certain popular vintage designs of hers, as well as release some of her collection to the retail marketplace. She had also just launched her first website. All of this was terrific news for vintage collectors, because this tells us that there will most certainly be an increased interest in her earlier pieces once the media starts to pick up on these announcements. Granted, she has long been a favorite of many vintage and contemporary fashion enthusiasts; however, this will certainly fire things up a little more.

It is not just contemporary designers who set the pace. Museum curators who are moved to present a retrospective of a particular fashion designer from the past can catch the market completely by surprise. Suddenly we are awakened with the inspirations of designers such as Bonnie Cashin, Claire McCardell, or Koos Van Den Akker. This can have a powerful impact on the vintage industry. The domino effect happens when designers see an exhibit, then incorporate the influences they've seen, and those influences transcend their new collections. Those of us who understand the derivations of their influences, hit the streets and hunt down the original designs. It is advisable if you are becoming more serious about your vintage clothing collecting, that you get on the mailing lists of all the important museums and fashion institutions in your area, or if you are planning a trip to a major city, that you check in advance as to which venues may be presenting a fashion retrospective exhibit. If you are not able to attend a particular exhibit, check to see if the venue has published the retrospective or look for any books on a particular designer that is on exhibit. The more information you can acquire, the more knowledgeable your purchases will become.

This theory of the retrospectives influencing buying trends proved itself in the fall of 2000 when the Guggenheim Museum in New York presented an exciting retrospective of Azzedine Alaïa's work. There had already been substantial renewed interest in this designer. Many stylists for editorial publications started borrowing Alaïa's pieces from vintage boutiques to augment their layouts in major fashion publications, and supermodels started showing up at important events clad in their sexy vintage Alaïa ensembles. *Harper's Bazaar* published an in-depth story on Alaïa earlier in 2000 and this proved to truly ignite the interest in his early work. Since Alaïa remains an independent designer today, producing only a small amount of work, the scarcity of his garments make him a rare find in the vintage market.

Similar phenomena occur at couture auctions around the world. There may be a curator, collector, or designer who for a myriad of reasons will do battle over a particular garment which comes before the auction block. This will send the whispering onlookers to frantically speculate, not wanting to be on the outside, looking in. Consequently, this may artificially drive up interest in a particular designer. The media may then pick up on the adrenaline in the room and before you know it, a new and influential vintage star is born.

SEVEN
Condition Rating and Its Impact on Values

One of the most important factors in establishing the value of a particular designer vintage garment or accessory is its condition. The rules are subjective depending on the period of an item. The industry is much more forgiving of an item if it is very old, such as an antique of 100 years plus, and the condition is a direct reflection of its age and not simply misuse or handling over the years. Often the value of an antique item will not be contingent on its condition and hold strong simply because of its rarity. This is usually true with items which are sought after by museums or designers who may wish to have the piece solely for display or design inspiration.

It is not advisable to purchase an item if it is not in **good** (a condition rating given to an item which would normally indicate that the item is not in perfect condition, and may in fact have some damage to it, although the item is still considered to be in a salable condition) to **excellent** (a condition rating given to an item which would normally indicate that the item is in perfect condition, without flaws or damage. This is the optimum condition to purchase, unless you are in a position to restore the item, or you have access to a skilled resource for restoration). It is advisable to understand the terms which refer to the condition of the item, for example, **excellent** condition is considered optimum. **Good** indicates that the item has some problems yet is still considered acceptable by industry standards, depending on the specific requirements of the item. **Fair** is a condition rating given to an item which would normally indicate that the item is not without some problems and may need some restorations. This condition is considered to be less desirable than "Good" condition, while still being acceptable. **Fair to Good** is a condition rating given to an item which would normally indicate that the item is better than "Fair," but not considered to be an advisable purchase unless you are well aware of the flaws in the item and are prepared to restore it or use it as is. It may be best avoided. **Poor** is the lowest condition rating given to an item and would normally indicate that the item is very badly flawed and not advisable to purchase unless you are well aware of the flaws in the item and are prepared to restore it or use it as is. It may also be best avoided. Poor condition would rarely be offered in an upscale sale and would suggest that you should avoid this item entirely. (See Terms, page 348.)

A simple example of how condition can play a significant role in the value of an item is a 1920s beaded handbag which may have some minor-to-major bead loss. It may seem simple to replace the missing beads if you had access to someone who was competent at doing the re-beading, but consider the fact that you may not be able to locate the right beads for replacement in the marketplace today. They may no longer be producing this particular bead in a specific color or style. Your only hope may be to find another 1920s beaded bag with similar beads and marry the two together by using one to repair the other. I would warn you that this is a difficult task, unless you have the type of access to the quantities of bags that a dealer might be able to locate.

Likewise, if a beautiful vintage Christian Dior wool ensemble has a multitude of moth holes in the garment, is it really worth what a perfect condition ensemble by the same designer is? The answer is quite obviously "no" once you consider the cost of the re-weaving which could run into the hundreds of dollars.

EIGHT
The Contemporary Designer's Influences on the Vintage Clothing Industry

It is no longer a secret that contemporary designers gather some of their design influences from vintage designer pieces. Many would say that the high-end purveyors of designer vintage clothing are very instrumental in moving contemporary designer trends by stocking unique vintage merchandise from the past which is snapped up by the contemporary designers of today. Many major design houses have teams of stylists and vintage clothing buyers who regularly shop the world over for that one fantastic piece which will direct a new collection. I have relationships with many internationally renowned designers who regularly look to my business to supply them with various vintage items that reflect a collection they are working on. This is not unlike the designers of the past who simply turned to archival renderings to reinvent new designs. Just look at the pages of any major fashion publication and you will see the influences that the designers of today have borrowed from the past.

A prime example of this would be the collections by Tom Ford in the early 1990s for Gucci which were very reminiscent of Rudi Gernreich's and Halston's work in the 1970s. Another example is a featured leather jacket from Balenciaga's fall 2000 collections which was almost stitch per stitch a replica of a vintage leather jacket from East West leather from the 1970s which the designer Nicolas Ghesquière was said to have found at the vintage boutique Resurrections in New York.

The unfortunate thing about contemporary designers borrowing from the past is that oftentimes they cannot reproduce a specific design element in today's costly labor market. Therefore, many wonderful elements are eliminated from an item in order to make the manufacturing of that item more cost-effective. Consequently the newer versions are lacking in most of the elements that made them so wonderful to begin with. This is a major reason why so many consumers are opting to buy lovely original vintage items instead of their lesser contemporary versions. For the most part the quality is simply not there today.

Because many contemporary designers are so focused on looking back, the vintage industry as a whole is plagued by the riddle of "What Came First?" Many younger, less informed consumers are simply drawn to a contemporary designer's piece because they love it. Others may be enticed to buy it because it is reminiscent of a happy time in their past. Also, there are those who are watching fashion trends as closely as the designers who are creating them, and hitting the vintage venues for the original versions of the items which are inspiring the present. Confused yet? I find it amusing when a client comes into my boutique and discovers a wonderful vintage garment and proclaims with surprise that it is just like the new collection by Dolce & Gabbana!

Design houses such as Ralph Lauren have long understood the importance of significant vintage influences and have cross-merchandised selected vintage garments successfully in their boutiques for years. Many important department stores such as Barneys and Henri Bendel in New York and Maxfields Fred Segal in Los Angeles are now adding designer vintage departments. All of this is a healthy and profitable force behind the vintage clothing industry. The market is undeniably driven by the contemporary designer's resurrections from the past.

NINE
Turning Your Collecting Passion into a Profitable Business

In previous chapters I taught you primarily how to buy for your own personal use. Here I hope to lead your passion and love for vintage fashion, through an enjoyable hobby, into what just might reward you with a handsome profit. Armed with all you have learned so far and with the price guide in this book you should be able to enter any vintage clothing venue and know when you are getting a good buy for your money. You will be in a position to make knowledgeable decisions on what items to buy and what you should expect to pay for them. If you recognize when an item is a significant piece and has a great asking price, you should be able to buy right and realize a profit when you sell it in a higher resale market. The idea, of course, is to always buy low and sell high.

Once you have an established relationship with your chosen sales venue you can begin to refine your merchandise and tailor it to their market. It is important to develop strong relationships with your vendors and stay on top of what their customers' demands are so that you can cater to them.

Building Your Inventory

The easiest and perhaps most cost-effective way to start building your inventory is to purchase items from estate and garage sales, thrift stores, flea markets, as well as online auctions. With all of the information in this book you should be well prepared to unearth some wonderful bargains if you are prepared to do the work. I would encourage you to start off slowly and gradually move up into more expensive items as you see your items selling and realizing a profit. You may need to move out of the realm of personal preferences in order to cater more precisely to public demands.

Buying at Auction

Once you have honed your buying skills at the flea market, you may wish to venture out into the auction arena or high-end boutiques. There are many important auction houses which I have mentioned previously, such as William Doyle, Sotheby's, Christie's, as well as Skinner in Boston and D. & J. Ritchie and Drouot Hôtel des Ventes in Toronto, which offer designer vintage clothing and accessories auctions.

There are a few things you should consider when buying at auctions, such as the condition of a garment. I discussed earlier in the book the importance of the condition of a vintage item, and whether it is a garment or accessory, you should always strive to find things in the best possible condition. If you are unable to attend a scheduled preview prior to the auction to inspect the garment personally, do not rely solely on the catalog description. Damage can occur to an item after it was described for a catalog listing. Occasionally an item is mishandled after it has been examined for description and condition reporting in a catalog. Likewise, damage can be overlooked at the time of first inspection and unless you yourself are examining the item, it will be your sad folly if you purchase the item sight unseen.

It is within proper auction decorum when you are not able to attend the auction preview, yet you are still interested in bidding on some items, to contact the appropriate representative at the auction house and ask them for specific condition reports on the items you are considering. It is for this reason that I would impress upon you the value of establishing a personal relationship with the specialists of important auction houses if you intend to become serious about your collecting.

Auctions can be a wonderful source for better designer vintage items. Like the high-end vintage boutiques, auction houses are very selective and therefore the items are generally much better than what you might expect to find through online auctions or local vintage shops. Because they have limited space and time in which to present a particular auction, there is a concentration of good-quality merchandise being offered at the same time. Most of the better houses may attempt to have a general theme to a particular auction which may focus on a certain time period or a specific collection of items from one major estate or designer.

Most of the items at auction come from consignors. These consignors may be individuals who owned the item originally, or they may have inherited it. Dealers also put some of their more important designer vintage through an auction house if they feel that using this venue will realize the highest price. It may be that a vintage dealer or boutique owner has acquired a piece which is not necessarily the focus of their business or in demand by their clientele. It makes good business sense for them to turn the sale of that item over to another venue such as an auction house.

Another thing to be aware of at auction is the competition factor. It is best to check your ego at the counter and keep a cool head. There is a tremendous amount of competition out there and you don't want to be caught up in an auction frenzy and end up paying far more than an item is worth, and certainly more than what you could realize a profit on.

You also need to calculate into the **hammer price** (this is the final price an item sells for at auction, excluding the "buyer's premium") the **buyer's premium** (the percentage of the hammer price you are obligated to pay as the buyer, which is added to the "hammer price" by the auction house, and goes directly to the auction house; in most cases it is approximately 15 percent). The buyer's premium is added to the auction house's total gross on a particular item. So if the commission which they charge to the consignor is approximately 25 percent and they receive an additional 15 percent from the buyer in the form of a "buyer's premium," then the auction house receives approximately 40 percent. (See Terms, page 348.)

The most important thing to consider when buying at auction is: If you are buying strictly for your own personal collection and not for resale, then set your own limit as to what you are willing to spend on a particular item. Do your research and go into the auction with a clear understanding of the item's value. If you are planning to resell an item you purchase at an auction, you better be sure you can realize a profit above their selling price, because for the most part you are going to pay top dollar at auction.

Buying at High-End Vintage Clothing Boutiques

If you want to try your hand at buying at high-end designer vintage boutiques, many of the same principles apply as with buying at auction. The items are normally priced at the highest level and unless you have a very specific client who may be willing to pay an additional premium for you to locate an item for them, you will rarely be able to sell an item for more than you paid for it.

If you have an established relationship with a boutique you may be able to do some trading of merchandise for a specific piece you are after. This is a common practice and can be beneficial to both parties. If you have merchandise which you have bought well, at a low price, and the boutique is interested in that merchandise and sees the potential profit in trading your merchandise for theirs, then this can be a potentially lucrative way for you to trade-up your merchandise.

It only stands to reason if you have a relationship with a particular vintage boutique and by this I truly mean, if you have established yourself as a real player by stepping up to the counter and spending some serious money; then and only then, can you honestly expect the owner of an establishment to take you seriously and consider giving you any form of discount. In truth, there is nothing worse than the buyer who simply thinks they should be granted a discount for no other reason than the fact that this is their first time in your establishment and they want you to cut them a deal. There must be a reciprocal arrangement. If you have something to offer a vintage boutique in exchange for their consideration, then perhaps they will be more inclined to accept your offer.

As with buying at auction houses, you really need to know what you are doing. When you buy at high-end vintage boutiques, it is much more difficult to uncover a reasonably priced bargain than when you forage through the thrift stores, flea markets, estate, tag, and garage sales across the country.

All this said, the high-end vintage boutiques are the best places for a collector to find an incredible item. You can simply walk into the boutique and everything is pre-selected for you. The owner has done all the looking for you. They have peered under every stump, visited every flea market across the country at 5:00 A.M., and unearthed the very best designer vintage there is to offer, and for their work you must accept that you will pay a premium.

Buying Online

I enjoy buying online, but to be fair, I am a seasoned professional. If you truly know what you are doing, it can be a wonderful way to augment your sources for merchandise. Although my intention is not to promote one online auction site over another, I personally have had the best success on **eBay.com, Amazon.com,** and **Sothebys.com.**

The online auction arenas have given back some of the power to the consumers because when buying online, it is the buyers who ultimately decide the value of something. Therefore the prices of items are closer to their true value.

When buying on a reputable website such as Sothebys.com, you have an impressive company reputation standing behind the merchandise that is offered. That said, there are certainly things to be aware of such as fraud and poorly described merchandise when dealing with some of the other online auction sites that are self-regulated by the buyers and sellers.

In the present online auction scene you should be prepared for one out of twenty items to be a disappointment. Oftentimes one seller's idea of a "flaw" is not someone else's. I can recall when a seller from eBay shipped me a beaded 1940s dress that they had described as having only a few beads missing from the shoulder area. When I received the dress I discovered that an entire portion of the shoulder was missing the beads, rendering the dress worthless. The seller's response to me was, "It was an old dress and old things are supposed to look old, and have damage. What do you expect?" Unfortunately, this person did not understand proper decorum, business ethics, and even more unfortunately they did not have a true appreciation for vintage clothing. After a multitude of e-mails back and forth the seller finally agreed to issue me a refund on the garment and I returned the dress. Some may not be as lucky.

It is important to ask questions. Ask as many questions as you can prior to placing your bid. If the pictures the seller has offered up are out of focus or don't reveal the necessary details, then e-mail them and request additional photos. Inquire about the garment's condition, even if they state the item is in good condition.

If the seller has not offered a picture of the label on a garment, be sure that you request one. There may be a reason they have not offered this. An honest seller understands the value in the item's label and will offer a photograph of it when possible.

A good example to consider as to when it is advisable to ask a seller some pointed questions prior to placing your bid might be when you are bidding on a vintage silk jersey Emilio Pucci dress. You should be sure to ask the seller if there are any stains on the dress. Often with patterned silk jersey dresses stains go unnoticed until subjected to closer scrutiny. The stains may have been on the garment for years without the owner ever really noticing them. Likewise the stains may have been undetectable when they first occurred; however, over time the stains may have manifested into something quite disastrous. Although the seller may not have noticed any staining on the garment when they hung it in their closet some 20 years earlier, there is a good chance that the stains have aged over time and unfortunately have become permanent. Have the seller check under the arms for perspiration stains. If this is their own personal possession, one of the last things they ever want to admit is that it has flaws, let alone that they may have perspired in it. However, take it from an expert, the underarms are the first places I look for damage on an Emilio Pucci dress.

If you are dealing with a forthright seller then they should have no problem in honestly responding to your questions. Also, if they guarantee in writing that the garment or article is without the specific flaws you are concerned about, then you will have a powerful recourse if you need to return the item.

Always check out the seller's **feedback** in the online **feedback forum**. (On most reputable online auction sites such as eBay, the buyers and sellers can voice their opinions and experiences with each other. You can place either positive, negative, or neutral feedback on the seller or buyer if you have completed a transaction through the auction site with them. This forum is designed to regulate the professional decorum of both the buyer and the seller.) (See Terms, page 348.)

Another very important tip when buying online is to view the other items a seller has for sale. If the rest of their merchandise is of the same caliber as the item you are interested in, then it is probably safe to say that they know what they are doing and you can rest assured that you are dealing with a more experienced seller. On the other hand, if you discover that aside from the one wonderful item, the seller is offering completely unrelated items, then you may want to ask even more questions.

Dealing with an uninformed online seller can also be in your favor. They may not know the true value of a particular item if they have not spent the time and exercised due diligence. They may not have placed an appropriate reserve price on the item or used the right descriptive words to attract buyers, so you may be able to run away with the item for a low price.

It is up to the seller to place on an item a title description which will attract a buyer. If they have not used the best descriptive words to attract the buyers, such as the designer name or appropriate style or era of the piece, then the item may go unnoticed in the auction.

A trick that I have heard a few savvy buyers like to employ is to search for designer items by spelling the name just a little off. Oftentimes a novice seller will mistakenly misspell an item and again in this instance the item will go undetected by buyers. If you happen to come across these misspelled items you may be able to pick them up for a very low price.

When searching for designer items on an online auction venue such as eBay, you should consider certain terms which are meant to be misleading. One practice employed by some sellers which is discouraged by the powers that be at eBay and other online auction services, is to use a specific designer's name when describing an item in the title description. The words in the title description are the words that will trigger a search for a particular item with the auction's search engine. For example, if sellers list an item which wasn't a designer item, yet they wished to attract potential buyers to that item, they may attempt to use a popular designer name in the title such as Gucci or Dior. They may attempt to get around the rules by describing something as "in the style of," or "like" Gucci or Prada. The best advice is always read the description of an item very carefully, and look for the photo of the label if it is described as a designer item.

Many buyers complain about the practice of using unrelated designer names in the title description for another reason. When the seller uses an unrelated name in describing an item and you are searching for an authentic designer piece, you can become overwhelmed by the volume of unrelated items which may come up on your screen when you search for a specific designer. This is very frustrating and damages the online market for everyone.

I do not recommend shopping online to the novice collector, because there are so many variables. If you have not had a great deal of experience buying vintage designer items, you may find yourself buying things which you will regret. You need to consider that you can't try things on and most sellers' terms are "All Sales Final." Returns are usually not possible. Sizing can be a problem if you are not familiar with the variances in sizing with vintage garments. For example, a vintage Emilio Pucci dress whose label indicates a size 12, in today's size scale, is approximately a size 8 to 10. This is something you will come to know only with experience. So if you are not sure, then the best advice is to ask the seller for precise measurements before you bid.

Always read the seller's terms and conditions. If you are not interested in paying for the item under the terms offered by the seller, you need to make that decision before you bid. Some sellers only accept money orders and will not accept personal or company checks. In most cases when they accept checks, they will hold an item for ten days to two weeks to ensure that your check clears prior to sending your item out. Depending on the mail service and the form of shipping you have requested, this could amount to almost a month before you receive your item from the seller.

Most online auctions run for seven to ten days, so it is important if you are truly serious about buying an item that you monitor the auction if you intend to win it. Online auctions have a system of e-mails which automatically notify you if you have been outbid on an item; however, if you are not checking your e-mail frequently enough, you may miss this information and consequently miss the close of the auction as well. Check the items you are bidding on frequently, especially if you are bidding on more than one online auction.

There are many techniques you can use when you get really good at bidding online to ensure that you win a particular auction. The most notorious technique is called "sniping." There are numerous sites on the web which will take you through a step-by-step sniping procedure which, if employed correctly, will guarantee your success. In short, sniping entails opening up two browser windows simultaneously and continuing to re-load a particular auction as it is about to close on one browser, all the while you are poised with your other browser window with your final bid which you are careful to ensure is always higher than the highest bid just 10 to 30 seconds prior to the auction closing; thus the term "sniping." You basically snipe all other potential bidders by being the highest and last one to bid.

Many of the online auction sites are now offering alternative forms of payment in an attempt to counter the effects of credit card fraud and delayed deliveries from sellers who require that a check be held for clearance. One service is known as PayPal and it is a very efficient way to handle fast transactions.

eBay introduced a new tool to their auction site in the fall of 2000 called "Buy It Now." This is an option open to both the bidder and the seller, and is set by the seller. The seller will set a price which they will be willing to accept as a final price and if a buyer selects this option then the transaction is final and the auction then closes prior to the regular set term of the auction. This is a terrific way for the buyer to guarantee that they will get an item for a set price and not have to run the risk of losing the auction item at the last moment to a higher bidder. The only drawback for the seller is that the item has the potential to go higher than their reserve and their "Buy It Now" price if the bidding is highly competitive.

All of this said, I have had hundreds of successful online transactions. I suggest you try the online auction experience provided you are aware, ask the right questions prior to bidding, and do your homework before you make your final winning bid.

Resale License, Seller's, or Vendor's Permit

No matter at what level you intend to go into the vintage clothing business the first thing you want to do is acquire a **resale license,** also referred to as a **seller's permit** or **vendor's permit.** You are required by law in North America to have a resale license and vendor's permit regardless of the venue you choose to do business in, including online sales. You can acquire a license in the United States by applying to your local office of the State Board of Equalization, or in Canada to the Ministry of Revenue. You will need to acquire a separate license for every location (event) or state where you intend to sell. In most states your permanent residence must appear on your original license as your *Principal Location*; in California, for example, a separate form known as a BT-530-B must be attached with the address of any temporary location (flea market, etc.) where you plan to sell. Check with your local offices for the appropriate form in your state.

Temporary location permits are often made available at the office of the flea market where you are selling, but do not depend on it. It is advisable that you acquire the proper permit from your local State Board of Equalization prior to the event. If you do intend to acquire one at the event on the day of the sale, be sure to have your valid **Principal Location seller's permit** with you at that time. The venue operators are required by law to ask to see your permit, and are often subjected to state inspection, and can face up to a $1,000 penalty for each unverified rental. It is advisable to have your permits with you at all times.

There are no fees for these temporary permits as long as you are in good standing. If you have had a problem with a permit in the past or owe money, you may be required to post a bond to ensure that your taxes will be paid in the future. This amount could be substantial so try to remain in good standing and file your taxes appropriately. All you need do is keep your books up to date and send in the sales tax you have collected on any of the merchandise sold in that quarter. It is that simple.

When selling at a swap meet or flea market in many states you will also be required to complete a **Swap Meet Seller's Information Report.** According to business and professional codes, you are required to report all property offered or displayed for sale or exchange on these forms to assist in tracing and recovering stolen property and detecting sales tax evasion.

You may also be required by local regulations to acquire a **Secondhand Dealer's License** when selling vintage clothing and accessories. You should apply to your local police department where you will be required to submit to a background check and have your fingerprints taken. These regulations vary from state to state and it is advisable that you check with both your local and federal authorities, as well as the State Board of Equalization. Additional licenses are required if you intend to sell antique and estate jewelry and accessories which contain precious gemstones and are made from fine metals such as gold and platinum.

Choosing a Seller's Venue to Suit You

Choosing the right venue is usually a trial-and-error game. A market that may work for someone selling used Levi's may be the wrong market for someone selling high-end designer vintage clothing. It's always wise to shop the venue prior to booking the space for your sale. Do some research. This way you can assess for yourself what type of merchandise is being sold, its range of prices, and the demographics of the consumers who are shopping a particular venue.

There are many levels which you may choose from to initiate yourself into the business of selling designer vintage clothing. The ones I'm describing are the most common venues, although new ideas are cropping up all the time. There really are no hard-and-fast rules and you should be completely open to creating your own way.

Selling to Other Vintage Clothing Dealers

If you choose to sell directly to a vintage dealer who sells strictly through vintage clothing shows, or to a vintage clothing boutique, you need to understand the term **wholesaler** (someone who sells to a dealer or boutique owner at a volume discount; this term can also be interchangeable with the terms "Picker" or "Dealer"). (See Terms, page 348.) As a wholesaler, you must offer your merchandise to a vendor at a price at which they can increase and realize a profit, so you need to buy your merchandise at a very low price and be willing to release it to someone else who will earn a considerable profit on it. After all they are the ones who will be incurring the overhead cost to present that merchandise at a higher level through either their boutiques, or the rental of a show space. Just because something may retail in a shop for a high dollar amount does not mean that it is worth the same on a wholesale level. You must factor in that the item's price is qualified by hanging next to like items, so that a consumer is granted a selection in a comfortable up-scale environment where they can consider their purchase.

Considering Consignment

If something is truly a unique piece, I prefer to buy it outright from the wholesaler. However, I also offer consignment terms which allow for greater profit sharing on an item. If both the seller and the buyer are willing to consider consignment and can agree on the terms, then it will be a win-win for both parties. The buyer doesn't have to risk their capital by owning the item and the seller is rewarded a higher dollar amount by opting for consignment terms rather than selling outright. The only drawback is that you as the seller must wait for the item to sell, which in some cases could be a lengthy time.

Consignment terms vary depending entirely on a particular shopowner and how they prefer to structure their terms. For some newcomers to the consignment business, it is truly a matter of trial and error. There are some simple basics to consider. The company with which you choose to consign must have a contract for you to read and sign, which states all of their terms and conditions. This contract states in full the length of your contract—with a pickup date for unsold items—and most importantly details the consignment split. The consignment split simply means how much of the sale price you will be getting and how much is kept by the shop. You are issued an account number, and all your items which you have entrusted with the particular business are described in detail on an inventory listing. It is important for the business to issue an adequate description for a few reasons, mainly so that your item is given the credit it is due. If it is made by a designer, then that designer name should be in the description. The designer name will ultimately add to its value. The other reason for a detailed inventory listing is that if your item doesn't sell and you return to the business to retrieve it, the business needs to have an adequate description to facilitate the staff in locating the item in a shop full of garments.

Always pay close attention to a consignment contract's pickup date. If your contract expires after 60 days, then certainly consider checking with the business prior to the expiration of the contract, otherwise you may discover that the company has disposed of your unsold items at a local charity thrift shop. Most consignment businesses have a clause in their contract which states that all unsold items which are left after the termination of the contract may be donated at their discretion. This practice discourages consignors from leaving their unsold items for long periods of time, thinking that the company will simply hold and store them. Most businesses do not have the room to do this. There is also the risk that in that time period the item may become damaged or stolen, which in most cases is not covered in the consignment terms.

Most consignment businesses offer a 40 percent commission to the seller, although some may go as high as 50 to 60 percent, depending on the particulars of that business. If they were to buy outright, they may offer only approximately 20–30 percent of what the item will retail for in their shop. Considering all the pros and cons, I always advise a seller to choose consignment terms whenever possible or an outright sale if they are looking to move a particular item immediately.

You must be aware of when payment on sold items is scheduled to be issued by a consignment business. My company issues checks on the 15th of the following month of the sale. In this way, we have ample time to take into consideration possible returns, as well as assuring our bookkeeping department adequate time to perform an accurate review of the accounts prior to issuing final statements and checks for the previous month.

Selling at Auction

You may also decide to sell your very best designer vintage through an auction house such as William Doyle, Sotheby's, Christie's, Skinner, or D. & J. Ritchie. One of the drawbacks of putting something up for auction is that the auctions take place only at certain times of the year, and often the auction houses are only looking for items which fall into certain categories, themes, or time periods. If you miss the deadline for submission, then you will have to wait until your item is considered for the next appropriate auction.

If you want to sell through an auction house you should consider the cost involved. There are many different expenses associated with submitting an item to an auction house, including listing fees, photographs in the catalog, commissions, as well as shipping, and insurance. With items which sell for under $500, you might consider another more cost-effective venue. On the other hand, if you have an exceptional piece to sell, then an auction house represents your best interest in realizing the greatest price, because of the level of consumers who attend auctions and the competitive bidding of the auction venue.

Selling on the Internet

If you are experienced with computers you may wish to try your hand at listing your merchandise on one of the numerous online auction sites. The sites have become very user friendly over the last few years and almost anyone with a computer can list an item for sale without much difficulty. They have easy and informative step-by-step procedures for both selling and buying items online. Buying and selling on the Internet is fast becoming commonplace in the average business and household around the world, often taking the place of traditional bricks-and-mortar businesses.

Selling on the Internet through the auction sites does require almost as much initial start-up capital as a traditional business if you intend to do things right. You will need a computer, a regular 35 mm camera, a scanner or a digital camera, as well as various software which is designed specifically to upload your photo images onto the auction websites.

Your largest expenditure will be the cost of building and maintaining a website. You are very fortunate if you have the experience to do this yourself. If you must rely on an outside service to build one for you, then you will need to do some serious shopping around before you contract someone. Unfortunately in my experience, the types of web designing companies which you may be able to afford in the beginning are not necessarily the most professional. Web design is a relatively new industry and it certainly is feeling its growing pains. It seems that anyone with just a little knowledge and a decent computer is offering their services as a web design company. He or she may have great creative skills, yet absolutely no business acumen and simply can't seem to run a professional business.

My advice is to explore the competition which is already on the Internet. Contact the web master (the person who either built the site or manages it for the company) of a particular site that you consider professional and esthetically pleasing. Ask them if they are available to build your site, what their rates are, as well as for some references to other sites they may have built. Whomever you choose, be sure to draw up an agreement which spells out the terms; what they are to design, how long they will take, and what the maintenance costs will be. Oftentimes a company will give you a great start-up price to build your site and then charge you through the roof to do any type of updating and maintenance. The fees for updating a site could range between $50 and $150 an hour. You need to choose your web designer as carefully as you would the architect or contractor you would hire to build or renovate your home.

You can also choose to sell on the Internet simply through an online auction service without having a website for your company; however, I strongly believe in having an important presence on the Internet which will back up the reputation of your company as well as its merchandise. Selling online through auction venues is a terrific way to attract new customers to your personal website and in this way increase your sales potential.

There are numerous online companies which offer image hosting and online auction management tools for a fee. One of the most popular of these service companies is **AuctionSubmit.com.** They manage your online auctions for you by timing when you wish to start a particular auction so that it finishes at a more convenient time for the buyers, and in this way ensures the best possible exposure for your item. They also send buyer notifications and payment terms to the bidder who has placed the highest bid at the close of the auction.

Bear in mind that selling on the Internet requires a lot of effort communicating back and forth with people through e-mail and can be very time consuming. You need to establish your business terms and conditions of sale, as well as strong company policies. Be forthright in revealing those policies in your auction listings, otherwise you will run into many problems.

There are multitudes of companies that offer an online seller the option of accepting credit cards on the Internet. This service is unquestionably one that does not come cheap. These companies charge you a hefty premium to use their merchant card services so that you can accept credit card payments for your business. If you have a healthy relationship with your personal bank, it is much more advisable to set up your own merchant card services account with your bank. The fees you pay vary depending on the volume your company is selling; the more you sell, the lower the fees will be. A first-time merchant card account holder is required to pay a processing fee for every credit card transaction they accept, ranging anywhere from 2.5 percent on up.

There are many rules which you must follow to the letter when accepting credit cards over the Internet, and I would sincerely advise you to read the merchant card service agreement very carefully because the power really is given to the credit cardholder who is purchasing an item from you. Even if your terms and conditions are clearly stated on your auction or website, unless you have an imprint of the cardholder's credit card which has been signed by the cardholder and clearly states on the form the terms of your sale, regarding whether your sales are final or what your return policy is, then the cardholder always has the right, should they choose to exercise it, to return the item to you for any reason and receive a full refund. The same policy applies with any mail-order business you do. The best way to ensure that you protect yourself from this clause is to send out the manual credit card form to the consumer, with their credit card number clearly written on it in the appropriate place, as well as the expiration date of the card. Then you must clearly write out the terms of the sale in the description space provided (above where the cardholder signs) and have them sign the form and return it to you by mail prior to your shipping the item to them.

You must also check with your merchant card services to confirm that the credit card number you have taken over either the Internet or the telephone matches both the shipping and billing address of the cardholder. Never ship an item to a buyer whose information does not match, unless authorized by your merchant services. There are the rare occasions when for private banking or personal reasons, a cardholder may have special concessions set up with their bank to have variables in their billing and shipping addresses. The bottom line is to always use common sense when making the decision with special circumstances, remembering it is ultimately your risk, not the cardholder's.

There are online dealers who for a fee will list your items for you; however, I suggest that you research these dealers first. Check out their other auctions and view their **feedback forum** (an area on eBay's online auction site where the buyers and sellers can voice their opinions and experiences with each other. This is where you can place either positive, negative, or neutral feedback on the seller or buyer if you have completed a transaction through eBay with them. This forum is designed to regulate the professional decorum of both the buyer and the seller to see whether or not they have any negative feedback and what their seller's reputation is like). (See Terms, page 348.) I have heard numerous reports from people who entrusted very expensive merchandise to an online dealer only to find that they never received payment from the seller once their merchandise was sold. In one unfortunate case an acquaintance of mine lost over $18,000 to an online dealer who offered to sell their merchandise but never paid them for the merchandise once they sold it.

Selling at Flea Markets

If you choose to sell at a flea market you need to be prepared for some very hard work and early morning hours. It is extremely difficult to purchase a vendor's space at some flea markets, such as the Rose Bowl in Pasadena, California, one of the largest in the world. Many of the dealers who hold the prime selling spaces there have held them for decades. There is no denying that flea market sellers are hardy folks. Every Saturday evening across the country they are loading up their trucks and stealing an hour or so of sleep before they join the long caravans of other flea market sellers as they slowly wind their way into the flea market location.

It is a continual ballet of items being loaded, unloaded, set up, taken down, sold, not sold, traded, and so on. There are many variables that can make or break a seller's day at a flea market, such as unpredictable weather conditions, seasonal shift in consumer demand, who shows up that day, and whether they want to buy your merchandise. There's no guarantee that even after all that hard work you will sell a thing.

Selling at a flea market is particularly hard on delicate vintage garments. There is the ever-present threat of sun-bleaching damage, even if your space is somewhat covered, and there is the problem of the multitude of general public who will be pawing over your items. The more an item is handled, the greater risk there is for irreparable damage.

But perhaps the greatest drawback for selling at a flea market is that overall it is considered by the vintage clothing industry to be more of a wholesale market, and so you should not expect to receive full retail value on high-end designer vintage, unless someone just falls in love with your item and is willing to pay the high price. The bulk of your merchandise will have to be offered at discounted prices. If you are selling in quantity you may do well with the high-end vintage dealers who use flea markets as a good source for reasonably priced merchandise.

Selling at Garage Sales

Even when choosing to hold your own yard, garage, or tag sale, you may wind up with some unfortunate surprises, such as a very poor turnout, or a customer base that simply does not understand the value of your merchandise. Some neighborhoods do not get the type of "drive-by shoppers" that others do. The idea of taking a friend up on an offer to have your sale at their home which may be in a more upscale location can prove to be very profitable. You should always take into consideration the income level of the neighborhood where you are selling. You might think you could make an absolute killing by holding your sale in an upscale area like Beverly Hills, but beware! Most people who live in such an area are not necessarily your early Saturday morning garage salers in search of a fabulous designer vintage garment. There are also certain restrictions in holding a garage or estate sale in many of the upscale neighborhoods across the country. As a whole, garage sale offerings of your designer vintage clothing is not your best choice of sales venue.

If you do plan on having your vintage clothing business kick off by holding a garage sale, it is very advisable that you distribute invitations to your event. Your invitation can be as simple as a flyer, which you distribute to other vintage clothing venues such as independent dealers, vintage clothing boutiques, and costume houses which may be in the market to increase their stock. The most important thing is to get the buyers to your sale however you can.

Garage Sale, Yard Sale, Tag Sale, Estate Sale, Flea Market, Swap Meet; What's the Difference?

There are many different venues where you can begin your vintage clothing business. The most common are **garage sales, yard sales, tag sales, estate sales, flea markets, swap meets,** or professional **antiques and vintage clothing markets** that are either monthly, quarterly, or annually. Many people have asked me what the difference is between a flea market and a swap meet. It has been my experience that many swap meets will sell predominantly new merchandise—more specifically, a large percentage of knock-off or fake merchandise from the Far East—whereas a true flea market will sell mainly collectibles and antiques. The terms are certainly interchangeable, though, and can vary from state to state.

There is really no difference between a **garage sale** and a **yard sale,** except that one is often held in a garage and the other is held in the front or backyard. A **tag sale** is a term used in place of garage or yard sale in the Northeastern United States. More often than not, the person holding the sale has simply opted for one name over the other, not really considering any difference.

An **estate sale** is held to sell off the possessions of a deceased person. Estate sales are often a good source for vintage clothing; however, the items offered for sale will undoubtedly be as varied as the people who originally owned them.

Garage Sale Regulations in Your Neighborhood

You may find that you can get away with the occasional garage sale on your own property without acquiring a resale license, seller's, or vendor's permit. You should check the regulations on holding garage sales in your residential area with your City Hall, local police authority, State Board of Equalization, or Ministry of Revenue in Canada. Some local governments allow you to hold a private sale of personal belongings only two to four times a year and require you to acquire the necessary permits to do so. If you do not have the necessary permits and licenses, your local police department may enforce those regulations, and without warning close your sale down. Many local retail businesses are opposed to the independent vendor and feel that garage sales and flea markets cut into their retail profits.

You need to also check on the regulations for posting signs to advertise your sale in local areas. Many municipalities have strict regulations against it.

Why Not Just Open a Shop?

After owning my shop, The Paper Bag Princess, for over seven years I can honestly say that you should think long and hard if you really want the commitment of such a full-time business. It started off slowly and then it began to grow, and grow, and grow. Today, I put in on average twelve- to fourteen-hour days, six days a week and am up at the crack of dawn *every* Sunday morning, because there is a wonderful flea market to scour in every corner of the world! It is a very personal business which will devour all of your time to run it successfully. There are no half measures in this industry if you want to reach the top.

You may not be ready to jump straight into the full-time responsibility of owning and operating a shop. Holding private sales or renting space at a particular venue is a great way to get your feet wet without a great deal of financial risk. You will not have the overhead or the overwhelming responsibilities that are involved in operating a full-time business. In this way you can feel the industry out gradually, and take your time deciding if selling designer vintage is really for you. While you decide, you can build your inventory, hone your bartering skills, and develop an eye for buying right.

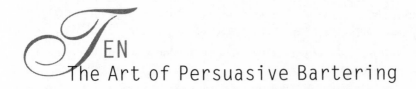

Ten
The Art of Persuasive Bartering

If you are ever to succeed in the designer vintage clothing business, or if you simply want to receive the best possible price when buying an item for your personal collection, one of the most important things you need to learn is the fine art of negotiating. You will need to apply this skill to both buying and selling. Understanding how to cut the best deal on an item will also help you to counter someone's offer when they attempt to purchase your merchandise. Having a well-honed bartering banter will quickly establish you as a professional dealer and you will find that it commands both respect from other dealers and ultimately the best possible price on any merchandise you want to buy.

The Object of the Game

Remember that for many, bartering and bargaining are forms of mutual entertainment. In some cultures sellers are offended if you *don't* attempt to bargain with them. You are buying from dealers as your business grows so it is wise to hone your skills early. The object of the game is to get the *best possible price*. Many people are tremendously apprehensive or shy about asking for a better price or discount. Under certain circumstances you may be justified in asking for a discount, based on an item being flawed or damaged in some way. The damage may require a cost in restoration and therefore, if the seller is fair, they may consider the cost of repair when factoring an appropriate discount on the item.

There is absolutely no reason why you should not ask for a reduced price simply because you would like to pay less for that item and need to realize a profit on it once you go to resell it. It may be that you think the item is slightly overpriced, or you may be inclined to believe, as I do, that you're not worth your salt unless you get something knocked off! Many dealers take this into consideration when they price an item, understanding that they may need to reduce the price by 10 percent or so, if requested.

How do you get the best price? It is always best to *go straight to the top* and find the dealer, owner, or manager of the venue. They will ultimately be the one whom the sales staff turns to to get the authorization anyway. *Be direct.* Know what you're willing to pay for that item and be willing to buy it if they do give you their best price. There is nothing worse for a future relationship with a particular seller than if you ask for their best price, they give it to you, and then you decide *not* to buy it!

I have had it suggested to me that it is wise to *dress down* when shopping at flea markets or thrift stores, so that the dealer won't size you up and allow their price to reflect what they think you can afford to pay. In fact, I once had an amusing conversation with a dealer whom I had bought from on several occasions. They remarked that the reason they did not recognize me from the other times we had done business, was that I had dressed down, in disguise, hoping to get a better deal. My response to them was "I could approach you dripping in diamonds and I would still walk away paying the price I want to pay for an item. It's not what you wear or who you are, *it's how you crack the deal!*"

Industry, Dealers, or Members of the Trade

If you are a professional dealer you may request a dealer price or industry discount when making a purchase from other dealers or professional businesses. Most will give you a standard 10 percent off the listed price. Some may give you as much as 40 percent off if you are purchasing large quantities. The amount of a discount may also be contingent on how desirable a particular item is. Obviously, if the dealer has had it for a long time they may be more inclined to let it go at a more substantial discount.

Often a vintage clothing dealer will offer special discounts to stylists and costume designers when they are purchasing large quantities for a film or television show. The customer usually has a restrictive budget, yet needs to purchase a multitude of items which may span a long time frame for the character in the role. I have found that when you offer a courtesy discount, you will have a loyal customer for life. Word of mouth in the film and television industry can be worth its weight in gold when you have a satisfied customer.

If you are a dealer or a member of the trade, and are in the possession of a valid resale license, you may request that you *not* pay sales tax on a particular item if you intend to resell it. The reason for this is that you are not the *end* user. Your business will be selling that item to the ultimate end user and charging them the sales tax at the time of their purchase. People have been known to abuse this system to avoid paying the sales tax on their personal purchases. It is not, however, a wise decision. The government is really cracking down on this. If the IRS finds an item reported by the seller that did not have sales tax recorded, and that item does not show up on your books that year as being sold with a sales tax charge, then you may face some rather grave charges (i.e., tax fraud, sales tax evasion) and a tax audit to boot!

You may wish to request a discounted price if you pay cash instead of using a check or credit card. Both banks and credit card companies charge the seller a percentage of the total sale in order to process the transaction through their merchant services. This fee can range anywhere from 2 percent to 5 percent, depending on the discounted volume a seller is putting through their merchant services. For this reason only, it is within the realm of appropriate decorum to ask for a discounted price if you were to pay with cash. It is not acceptable to ask for a discount by paying cash and then request to not pay the sales tax on top of it if you are not purchasing the item for resale. That is in fact asking the seller to break the law.

My Own Approach

I prefer to identify myself as a dealer to a new vendor after I have asked for my best prices. If I think they are offering fair prices, I will leave it at that. If I think I am still receiving normal retail prices, I will open the negotiations up to the fact that I am a professional dealer and would need to receive a greater discount in order for me to purchase the selected items in volume.

Never tell the dealer what you are willing to pay for an item first, even if the item has a price tag on it. Once you have told them, you may feel obligated to buy that item and pay more for it than what the seller is willing to take. I like to ask, as I browse, what the dealer is willing to sell an item for. The dealer may offer to sell the item to you for a lot less than what you were prepared to offer. You have no way of knowing what the particular item's variables are. They may be thrilled that someone has finally shown interest in an item that they may have carted around to numerous flea markets and are happy to see it finally go. The key is to never tip your hand until they do.

I may even ask for the price of an item I am not seriously interested in. By doing this you create a type of buying power. You will then be in a position to gauge if the dealer is offering you a consistent discount on items. If the dealer sees that you are considering buying a number of items, they may quote you a more favorable price on each item in the hopes that you will purchase all of them.

When I am at the cash desk, I make sure I ask for a price on each item separately. Once I have been given *the best price* on each item individually, I will then ask for the best price if I took all of it. In this way you indicate that there is potential for you to buy it all, but only if the seller gives you a further reduction.

Some dealers may give you both the discount on the individual item and an additional amount off the total—but don't count on it. Dealers are at least as sharp as buyers are and, after all, they are in the business to maximize their profit. You will gain bargaining leverage by having a large amount to purchase when attempting your best price. By the same token, if you are shopping with a friend, consolidate your purchases at the counter and designate one of you to negotiate the deal as one purchase. The more you buy, the better the discount.

Remember to be courteous. You want the seller on your side. Be respectful. If something is truly priced fairly, don't ask for the discount. Ask only once, if it is not priced to your liking, then let it go. There is nothing worse than a buyer who badgers the seller. This advice will always play in your favor with future transactions. It is inevitable that you will pass that way again and you do not want the proprietor thinking, "Here comes that stingy cheapskate again!" Don't kid yourself: they remember a "cheapskate" just as clearly as a "big spender"! They know if you were willing to pay an honest price for things, or if they wanted to throw you out of their shop for pleading for a discount. No one likes a pushy person.

Above all, once you receive the bottom line price from the dealer who assumes you will be taking everything, do not remove items from your pile of considerations and expect to still get the same volume discount on the few items you ultimately decide to purchase. This is a practice that doesn't go over well in anybody's business. This is simply deceptive and you will find that the next time you attempt to do business with that dealer you will be paying full price.

Find the approach that works best for you. Be straight, fair, and honest. Both parties will walk away feeling satisfied that they have made a good, fair deal. A win-win situation is best for both the buyer and the seller!

Just Ask!

The following are some phrases that I have found work well and are acceptable approaches by most professional dealers around the world. These will help you to open the floor to negotiating and help you to receive a discount or better price. You may wish to use a combination of these phrases or find the one that best suits your personal style and approach to bargaining:

"What is your best price?"

"Can you do any better on this price?"

"Are your prices firm?"

"What is the best you can do on this?"

"Will you come down any on this?"

"Why don't we split the difference?" (Between the price you want to pay and what the seller hopes to get.)

"Would you take (and quote a price) for this?"

"What if I take all of it?"

"Do you offer an industry or to-the-trade discount?"

ELEVEN
How to Research the Provenance

Researching the **provenance** of a designer vintage garment can be very important when establishing its value. Often when a piece has an important history—for instance, if it was owned by a celebrity or notable personality—then it may have added value and demand. A great example of this are the "ruby slippers" that were worn by Judy Garland in *The Wizard of Oz*, or the beautiful Jean Louis sequined gown that Marilyn Monroe wore onstage while singing her rendition of "Happy Birthday to You," to President John F. Kennedy. It could also be a item that represents a breakthrough design by a specific designer, which was well documented by the press in fashion history, in publications such as *Harper's Bazaar, Vogue,* or *Women's Wear Daily* to name a few. There are also numerous books available that profile a great number of important designers and are of tremendous use in researching a time period of a particular designer.

We are fortunate because of the reference materials that are available to us for much of the designer garments from the 20th century. You can start with any number of fashion publications which are available in many reference libraries, as well as in the archives of many museums' costume and textile departments. Simply narrow down the time period of a garment by its style and design elements and begin with any articles relating to the designer of that item in the particular time period.

The Internet is another good resource at your fingertips. There are so many vintage companies with websites today who will offer informative help when you contact them about a particular garment. Many of the major museums which have costume and textile departments have e-mail and web contact information which will certainly expedite your research.

Most of the major design houses such as Chanel, Yves Saint Laurent, or Dior have extensive archives which can provide information if you write to their head offices and include accurate photographs of an important designer piece. I suggest contacting any of the major design houses only if you have what you perceive to be a very important and historical garment.

You can also do your research simply by getting as many answers as possible from the source where you acquire the item. I like to get as much information from the source as possible. I have found that my customers truly enjoy hearing as much history as I can uncover on a garment when they purchase it. This adds to the romanticism of the garment and is a delightful and treasured selling point.

TWELVE
The Preservation of Your Vintage Clothing

Not everything you find at the various venues you shop will be in perfect condition. After all, oftentimes the reason it was donated or sold in the first place might be due to some type of damage or imperfection. It is up to you to bring it back to life and keep it healthy for many years to come. There are many special needs of vintage textiles that I will share with you which will make the transformation and preservation of your wonderful piece of designer vintage much easier.

If you are truly serious about developing an important and valuable designer vintage clothing collection I would suggest that you look into becoming a member of The Costume Society of America, 55 Edgewater Drive, P.O. Box 73, Earleville, MD 21919, (410) 275-1619; or the Canadian Conservation Institute, 1030 Innes Road Ottawa, Ontario Canada K1A 0M5, (613) 998-3721. The information they have available for their members is extremely beneficial and a tremendous resource. You may also wish to contact your local museums as many have a department for the preservation of costumes and textiles.

I could not possibly teach you everything you will need to know about preserving your antique and vintage fashions in this short section but I will attempt to give you some very helpful tips:

• Wash your hands thoroughly before handling your fine vintage garments and when at all possible trim your nails and remove nail polish. Polish can transfer onto buttons or zippers.

• Remove all rings, necklaces, broaches, watches, or bracelets which could catch on fine fabrics.

• Use clean white cotton gloves (available at photographic supply stores) when handling all your delicate fabrics. Gloves will keep the oils from your hands from being transferred to your garments. The oils will eventually stain and damage the fabric.

• Do not smoke anywhere near your garments and most of all do not eat or drink near them.

• If taking notes near your garments, never use an ink pen or marker; use a pencil to avoid any devastating accidents.

• Whenever possible do not wear makeup when putting on or trying on your valuable vintage garment. It is best to put the garment on first and carefully apply your makeup afterwards, rather than risk a makeup smear from pulling a garment on over your head. Be sure to place tissue around a neckline as you apply your makeup. If you are to put your garment on while wearing makeup, I would suggest using a silk head cover to ensure you don't transfer any makeup to the garment.

• Be sure to wear dress shields with all your vintage garments. Older fabrics do not stand up well to the newer chemicals found in deodorants and the chemicals can be very damaging to fine fabrics.

• Take extra care when trying on delicate beaded or fragile, fine fabric garments and whenever possible have a second person to assist you in supporting a heavily beaded garment, especially as you attempt to put them on over your head.

• Never use wooden hangers unless you have covered them with *needle-punched polyester batting*, surrounded by *unbleached cotton muslin*. You can use this batting to cover the tips of a clip hanger to avoid clip-pinch damage. Wood contains lignin, a polymer that functions as a natural binder and support for the cellulose fibers of woody plants. Lignin breaks down and forms an acid that will drastically damage your vintage clothing over time. Therefore, all the expensive cedar closets and accessories that are on the market should be considered a hazard to your valuable antique and vintage clothing. You can avoid damage from lignin by sealing the wood on these hangers with an acrylic emulsion or acid-free tissue paper. Wooden hangers, if used properly, are your best choice because they can be easily cut to fit a garment. This is especially true when hanging a child's garment.

• The needle-punched polyester batting, surrounded by unbleached cotton muslin can also be used to stuff a hat, shape a collar, or fill out a sleeve.

• Fasten all buttons, zippers, and snaps. This will ensure that the garment hangs properly and will help to avoid unwanted creases. Replace all necessary fasteners before storing when required to ensure proper hanging of the garment.

• It is best to cover all hung garments with loose-fitting cotton garment bags which will not only keep dust off the garment, but also allow it to breathe. If you do not have proper cotton garment bags, use clean old cotton sheets draped over the garment. You can snip a hole in the center and slip your hanger through the hole.

• Always remove all dry-cleaning bags immediately. Not only do the dry-cleaning bags trap damaging toxic gases from the dry-cleaning solvents in your garment, but those chemical fumes are also toxic to humans and household pets.

• Do not store your garments in plastic garment bags because they have the potential to trap moisture that will ultimately damage your garment. If you must use a plastic garment bag always leave it open so that moisture can escape and air can circulate freely to allow the garment to breathe. You may wish to tag the outside of the garment bag with a photograph for quick identification.

• Do not hang garments in an area which is overfilled. It is important not to cramp the garments or they will become crushed. Be careful not to allow garments to rub up against or catch on each other.

• Avoid prolonged exposure of the items to direct sunlight as well as artificial light, as it will bleach the color and destroy the fabric over time. You may wish to cover lights with ultraviolet (UV) filters or place black felt over windows and skylights where you are storing your valuable vintage garments.

• Do not hang a beaded garment as the weight of the beading can tear the garment under its own weight. Store your beaded and bias-cut garments flat, wrapped in *acid-free tissue paper*, in the largest *acid-free box* available. If the garment is too large for the box, then roll it rather than folding it. Folding the garment is to be avoided at all cost, as older fabrics become brittle and can crack and break on fold lines. You may wish to wad up or roll some acid-free tissue to support the position of the garment as well as various design details or required folds.

• Use buffered acid-free materials when storing jute, cotton, flax, or linen fabrics and unbuffered acid-free when storing furs, silks, or woolens.

- It is always best to store only one garment per box. However, if space is at a premium, take into consideration the weight of one garment before placing it on top of another. For example, you will have disastrous results if you place a heavy beaded garment on top of a fine velvet fabric. The weight of the beaded fabric will create indentations on the velvet below from the beadwork, which may be irreversible. The same principle should be considered when packing a garment for travel.

- Be careful when hand-washing older sequined garments. The older sequins are made of a gelatin substance which may dissolve in water, and they will most certainly lose their color in water.

- Vintage silks should never be folded because they will eventually break on the fold lines. They should be rolled and stored in acid-free tissue paper.

- Do not use moth balls or moth cakes to protect the garments from moths. Moth balls are extremely toxic to both moths and humans, as well as beloved household pets. They also leave a permanent odor in the garment which is nearly impossible to remove. There are herbal alternatives that work equally well, such as **MothAway,** which is available at The Paper Bag Princess, Bed Bath & Beyond, or your local health food or hardware stores. You can also place boric acid in all the cracks and crevices of your closets and drawers, which is where the moths like to lay their larvae. It is the larvae that perpetrate the damage on your garments. You may also wish to consider the use of sticky moth traps which are an added weapon in the battle against the moth.

- Avoid washing or dry-cleaning at all cost. Washing will expand and contract fibers, a process that will eventually weaken the fibers.

- Natural bleach is safer on fine fabrics than chlorine bleach.

- Vacuuming your garment is a more advisable method of removing superficial dirt. Place a light nylon screen over the garment and use the soft brush adaptation of your vacuum. It is not advisable to use this method on fine, delicate, or beaded fabrics.

- There is a fine wire lint brush that I have made available in my boutique for years. It is manufactured by the industry of the Society for the Blind and is the best lint brush on the market. It is wonderful for lifting the nap on heavier wool and cashmere fabrics and is truly miraculous at removing years of dust which may have settled deep into a fabric. The lint brush is also the best I could possibly ever hope to find at dusting any fine vintage hats.

• Do not store any vintage garments in a damp basement. Even the best storage closet will eventually grow mold and mildew which can soil and destroy a fabric, as well as leaving an odor that is next to impossible to remove. Keep the silica gel packages from your vitamin bottles and toss them into your storage area, the more the better. This will help to dissipate the moisture.

• The optimum storage temperature should be moderated to approximately 65 ° with 50 percent relative humidity.

• It is a wise idea to periodically check on the garments you have stored to ensure that they are undisturbed by the surrounding elements as well as moth-free.

• If dry-cleaning is necessary, it is always best to consult with the owner of your chosen dry-cleaning establishment to discuss the individual garment for any potential problem that might arise due to the age or fragility of the garment.

Cleaning Fine Vintage Garments by Hand

There is a wonderful book on the market, Clean & Green by Annie Berthold Bond that you can order by calling (845) 679-5573. In it you will find a tremendous amount of information on common household alternatives that can be used as cleansing products, as well as many environmentally friendly commercially manufactured products, too numerous to mention here. Whatever the fiber content, when it comes to cleaning a garment by hand there are plenty of tricks. Some ideas have been passed down for many generations and I cannot guarantee that all will work; I always suggest that you test a small and undetectable area of a garment first before proceeding. Here are several tips:

• Creases can be removed from hems of some garments by rubbing them with a solution of white vinegar and water and then pressing.

• You can remove makeup stains by rubbing them with a slice of white bread.

• A sticky zipper can run smoothly again after running a bar of soap over it; however, take care not to damage the fabric next to the zipper in the process.

• White chalk is said to absorb oils from a soiled collar.

• Make a paste from either baking soda or table salt and water and rub into a perspiration stain. (First be sure that the fabric is colorfast.)

• Cream of tartar will work well on various stains when applied as a paste mixed with water. (First be sure that the fabric is colorfast.)

• One-fourth cup of table salt added to a final rinse will keep clothes from freezing if you are line-drying fine cotton in the winter.

• Hair spray is said to remove ink from washable fabrics.

• Ice works well at removing chewing gum.

• Never apply water without detergent to a grease stain, as this will only cause the grease stain to set.

• A few tablespoons of Epsom salts works well as a fabric brightener. (First be sure that the fabric is colorfast.)

• Lemon juice works well as a bleaching agent in conjunction with exposing the rinsed garment to direct sunlight to dry.

Some Good Cleaning Solvents

There are various spot remover products on the market. The best ones are sold in the notions department of fabric stores or in businesses such as Bed Bath & Beyond. These products include: Rit Fabric Whitener® and Rust Remover®, Zout®, Whink®, Bleach Stick®, white vinegar, lemon juice, baby shampoo, toothpaste, salt, packaged dry-cleaning solvent, diluted hydrogen peroxide, diluted ammonia, and glycerin. Considering most of your vintage garments were probably made with fabrics prior to these products being on the market, it is necessary to use common sense when choosing the product most suitable for your fabric. It is critically important to spot-check any garment to make sure that it is colorfast, especially if the product you are using has any bleach in it.

I have not had a great deal of success with using vinegar and/or salt, but what does work well on protein or blood stains is toothpaste. This is a good trick if you are traveling and do not have your regular cleaning supplies with you. Use a paste rather than a gel, one that doesn't have all the fancy colors or additives. Simply take a small amount of the toothpaste and rub it gently into the stain, then rinse the item thoroughly and you should see some immediate results as the stain lifts away. Although the environmentally safe detergents and bleaches may not be as tough on dirt and stains as some of the leading brands, I encourage you to use them whenever possible.

Tips for Dry-Cleaning Fine Vintage Garments

I would like to start by encouraging you not to dry-clean your garments, because the chemicals used in the process are indoor air pollutants, suspected carcinogens, and are highly toxic to both humans, household pets, and the environment. If you must dry-clean I should point out how important it is that you develop a strong relationship with a very good dry cleaner. Be sure to express to them that you are presenting a vintage garment to them which may not react the same to their chemicals as more contemporary fabrics might. The item should be given special handling instructions and perhaps cleaned completely by hand.

A large percentage of dry cleaners never pre-spot anything. They simply toss everyone's garments into one big communal drum where they are left to tumble around. That is why you often get your garment back with that piece of chocolate you sat on at the movie theater still stuck to the seat of your trousers!

It is advisable to remove all vintage buttons before dry-cleaning because oftentimes they crack or chip in the process. If you don't want to remove all of the buttons, then at the very least, cover the buttons completely with aluminum foil to protect them. Many of the older jeweled buttons will shed their jewels which have been glued in, due to the heat and tumbling of the dry-cleaning process, and for this reason should be removed completely prior to dry-cleaning.

When dropping your cleaning off always point out to the attendant the stain(s) you want removed. Often, they will have little stickers you can indicate the spot with. Oh, they hate me! I will stand there and place stickers everywhere, so they have no choice but to pre-spot. Also, you should check your garments when you pick them up. If they're not done right, have them do them again. After all, you are paying for this. While you're at it, if you are running many of your garments through their service, it's not a bad idea to ask for a special deal. They are usually quite accommodating and many have memberships or discount cards.

The Textile Conservation Workshop, which has been in business for over 21 years, is a wonderful organization located at 3 Main Street, South Salem, NY 10590, (914) 763-5805. They have state-of-the-art equipment which can remove stains from almost anything from a small christening dress to a fabulous vintage ball gown. They give free on-site estimates or you can telephone them and arrange to ship your item by mail. They will send you a proposed treatment report for a fee of $75. An important vintage garment may cost between $300 to $500 to clean and store in acid-free tissue paper.

Dyeing Fine Vintage Garments

You can often revive a vintage garment by dipping it into a bath of Rit® Fabric Dye. You may find that stripping the original color with Rit Color Remover® first will make the new color adhere better to the fabric. I have found that wool and cashmere sweaters are a dream to dye and that natural fabrics will take the dye much better than synthetics. You will also find that even if the garment is made from a natural fiber, it may have been constructed with a synthetic thread. Unfortunately, most synthetic thread will not take the new color you are attempting to add and the difference in the thread will be a telltale sign that the garment has been re-dyed. Carefully remove all labels from the garment prior to dyeing it, otherwise the label will also become dyed. Replace the labels only after the garment is completely dry.

Dissolve the dye in a small amount of hot water first, then add the cold water. The instructions on the package will tell you to use hot water when dyeing a garment, but many of the fabrics you will be dyeing will shrink if placed in hot water. I have found that the dyeing works equally well in cold water. Be sure to immerse the entire garment and force any trapped air out of the garment. It is best to oscillate the garment in the dye as much as possible.

I have heard of some people soaking the dyed item in a bath of salt water (a solution of regular table salt and tap water), after they have dyed it. This apparently helps the dye to set into the garment.

Call me frugal, but I always save the dye solution by pouring it through a funnel back into a large bottle for future dyeing. If you choose to do this as well, it is advisable that you do your dyeing in a large container rather than a sink or washing machine.

You can also have garments dyed professionally; however, you will truly need to shop around to find a good, affordable dry cleaner who will offer this service in your area.

Alterations

I purchase many garments that may require some type of alteration or restoration. Many things are disposed of because they either became damaged, outdated, or too small. Resurrecting a particular garment can be as simple as altering a hemline. It always baffles me when I find a perfectly good skirt that simply needs a few inches taken off the bottom, or a hem let back down. If you are talented and know what you are doing, I suggest you do the basic alterations yourself. However, if you are busy or all thumbs with a needle and thread, you may prefer to out-source your restorations and alterations. It certainly does help if you know what you are doing, or at the very least, what you hope to accomplish in your alteration so that you can properly direct your specialist.

I am not opposed to altering a vintage garment so that it sets pace with present fashion trends, as long as it is not an important vintage designer piece which will lose its value if it has been altered in any way. If you have purchased a garment strictly for your own pleasure and have no intentions of reselling it, then use your best judgment. You should keep in mind however, that if the garment is to stay in the family and be passed down to future generations, you may want to keep your alterations to a minimum.

Finding a talented re-weaver for holes can be worth its weight in cashmere. There is an excellent one in New York, **French American Re-Weaving,** (Manager Ron Moore, 119 West 57th Street, Suite 1406, New York, NY 10019, (212) 765-4670) or Lamb's Invisible Weaving, 1624 Montana Avenue, Santa Monica, CA, (310) 828-7748. The companies can repair moth holes and cigarette burns, as well as a tear in the fabric. The average cost of repairing a small-to-medium hole usually runs between $25 to $45.

Re-creations

I have become quite well known by my customers for my wonderful re-creations that my team of designers do. I recommend this practice whole-heartedly to anyone who has a vivid imagination. If you ever played dress-up, I think you will understand. Throw caution to the wind, because this is a fashion you create oftentimes from just a single element of a vintage garment. I cannot possibly describe here all that is required in re-creating something special because every garment is different; however, I can help expand your imagination with the possibilities.

First you need to start with a fabulous garment. I mainly work with exciting vintage beaded pieces. Many wonderful beaded garments came from Hong Kong in the 1950s and 1960s and have no specific designer attached to them, so I do not feel as strongly about maintaining their original shape. The present fashion trend is to find something from the 1960s or 1970s and bring it forward to today's fashion esthetics.

If you find a garment that has something wonderful about it, such as a fabulous jeweled neckline, but something else that just doesn't cut it—then do just that, cut it away! You would be surprised how lovely the beaded bodice on a dress can look when it has been liberated and converted into a blouse.

A "re-creation" can be as simple as removing old vintage buttons on a great 1940s suit and replacing them with something more contemporary. Or it can be as elaborate as something I created by cutting a 1960s beaded gown to pieces and turning it into half a dozen sexy little halter tops. I am never opposed to cutting off out-dated sleeves, or tapered A-lines on dresses or skirts.

I realize that some of the ideas I'm describing here may seem too difficult for some of you who do not sew. I suggest that you find a good, fast, affordable tailor or seamstress whom you can direct.

Part Two

CURRENT PRICE GUIDE TO THE WORLD'S MOST COLLECTIBLE VINTAGE DESIGNERS

HIRTEEN
Current Values

À LA PENSÉE, HENRY

EVENING ENSEMBLE, 1930s
Gold, silver, and purple lamé with fitted camisole bodice, straight skirt, and jacket.
est. $400–$600 sold: $373
William Doyle Galleries 11/16/1999

SWEATER, 1950s
Black wool sweater with embroidered and appliquéd cigarettes and lighter.
est. $200–$300 sold: $632
Sotheby's 9/30/1999

ADOLFO

COAT, 1960s
Black marabou, cardigan-style with high round neck, three-quarter-length sleeves.
est. $200–$300 sold: $258
William Doyle Galleries 5/6/1998

EVENING GOWN, 1970s
Printed strapless silk with red and white roses outlined in black, bias cut with train.
est. not available sold: $895
The Paper Bag Princess 8/1/2001

EVENING SUIT, 1980
Black knit with white mink collar, cuffs, and skirt hem, jeweled buttons.
est. $100–$150 sold: $402
William Doyle Galleries 11/10/1998

HAT, 1950s
Black velvet with black egret plumes.
est. $60–$80 sold: $115
William Doyle Galleries 9/30/1993

HAT, 1960s
Lacy green straw sewn overall with violet, white, and gray blossoms.
est. $75–$100 sold: $201
William Doyle Galleries 4/12/1995

HAT, 1970
Brown mink fedora.
est. not available sold: $175
The Paper Bag Princess 12/13/1999

HAT, 1970s
Cream fur felt cowboy style with large pheasant feathers.
est. not available sold: $295
The Paper Bag Princess 1/1/2000

SKIRT, 1960s
Black net sewn with colored silk flowers.
est. $200–$300 sold: $316
William Doyle Galleries 5/12/1999

STOLE, 1960s
Triangle of brown mink bordered with double row of silver fox.
est. $200–$400 sold: $1035
William Doyle Galleries 11/16/1999

SUIT, 1960S
Three-piece suit, skirt, jacket, and matching purse, brown and rust plaid fabric; with brown mink trim on cuffs.
est. not available sold: $895
The Paper Bag Princess 9/15/2000

ADRIAN

CAPE, 1950S
Black crepe sewn with horizontal bands of black silk fringe.
est. $800–$1200 sold: $1380
William Doyle Galleries 5/12/1999

COAT, 1940S
Black wool crepe, collarless, cape-like front contrasts with straight-line back, bands of gold, crystal and silver beads, heart-shaped sequins.
est. $600–$900 sold: $977
William Doyle Galleries 6/11/1997

COAT, 1950S
Back and sleeves of black ribbed wool, front of black-and-white-striped wool panels sewn together in geometric patterning, asymmetrically folded collar.
est. $600–$900 sold: $1380
William Doyle Galleries 6/11/1997

COCKTAIL DRESS, 1940S
Lavender and peach silk satin pieced in asymmetric curves, sleeveless on one side, cap sleeve on other.
est. $600–$900 sold: $7187
William Doyle Galleries 4/12/1995

COCKTAIL DRESS, 1940S
Silk crepe, bodice draped as a scarf, seamless and unshaped, slit sleeves, skirt gathered at one side, black crepe printed with tropical print.
est. $300–$400 sold: $1955
William Doyle Galleries 6/11/1997

COCKTAIL DRESS, 1940S
Black silk faille woven with oversized stripes of green satin, camisole bodice, full skirt.
est. $600–$900 sold: $2300
William Doyle Galleries 4/24/1996

COCKTAIL DRESS, 1940S
Blue satin, bodice has square neckline with fan-shaped pleated detail, three-tiered skirt.
est. $1500–$2000 sold: $1955
William Doyle Galleries 6/11/1997

COCKTAIL DRESS, 1940S
Black crepe with long sleeves, V neck, skirt gathered into drape and further sewn with draped panel, one sleeve sewn midway with self ties.
est. $200–$300 sold: $1495
William Doyle Galleries 5/6/1998

COCKTAIL DRESS, 1940S
Gray velvet cut to pewter taffeta in a pattern of Chinese rondels, halter neckline asymmetrically draped to one side, skirt with pleats on other side.
est. $300–$500 sold: $2185
William Doyle Galleries 12/5/1996

COCKTAIL DRESS, 1940S
Gray satin woven with Japanese-inspired falling leaves, strapless bodice with cummerbund pleats, full skirt gathered at waist.
est. $300–$500 sold: $402
William Doyle Galleries 6/11/1997

COCKTAIL DRESS, 1950S
Black net with strapless sweetheart bodice, full skirt with double tier of black Chantilly-style lace, separate apron creating a third front tier.
est. $500–$700 sold: $690
William Doyle Galleries 5/12/1999

COCKTAIL DRESS, 1950S
Black taffeta with sheer black silk and lace yoke.
est. $200–$300 sold: $1035
William Doyle Galleries 4/27/1994

COCKTAIL DRESS, 1950S
Black crepe de chine with sweetheart neckline, taffeta upper bodice and short wing sleeves, skirt with taffeta peplum waist, back with tiered panels.
est. $600–$800 sold: $517
William Doyle Galleries 6/11/1997

Cocktail Dress, 1950s
Black lace sweetheart strapless bodice, lace neck strap, skirt of black crepe sewn with tiers of taffeta ruffles at the sides.
est. $300–$500 sold: $747
William Doyle Galleries 11/12/1997

Cocktail Dress, 1950s
Black crepe, bodice sewn with dolman sleeves, central sheer chiffon and lace panel revealing flesh pink underbodice, skirt with full front gathers.
est. $200–$400 sold: $488
William Doyle Galleries 11/12/1997

Cocktail Jacket, 1940s
White wool, collarless, front cut-away in curves, padded confronting S's at each side.
est. $200–$400 sold: $805
William Doyle Galleries 11/10/1998

Cocktail Suit, 1950s
Black wool with black bugle bead accents.
est. $2000–$3000 sold: $1725
Sotheby's 9/30/1999

Dress, 1940s
Black crepe with round neck, padded shoulders, appliquéd at the yoke with red, navy, and green gingham, and other plaid cottons.
est. $300–$500 sold: $3450
William Doyle Galleries 4/24/1996

Dress, 1940s
Black faille with black velvet collar, fastens down front with teardrop rhinestone buttons.
est. $500–$750 sold: $2300
William Doyle Galleries 4/24/1996

Dress, 1940s
Silk printed with large brown discs on black ground, knee-length with short sleeves, draped cowl neck.
est. $300–$500 sold: $172
William Doyle Galleries 11/16/1999

Ensemble, 1950s
Two-piece ivory silk crepe, the bodice with wide shoulders; sewn variously sized white sequined spots ringed with bright pink and long straight skirt.
est. $500–$700 sold: $575
William Doyle Galleries 5/2/2000

Evening Ensemble, 1950s
Sheath dress with sweetheart neckline, wide self straps, center bodice tucking, skirt draped at center front and back, with a cut-away jacket.
est. $600–$800 sold: $920
William Doyle Galleries 5/2/2000

Evening Gown, 1940s
Ombré chiffon in russet, slate, green, and smoke with coral accents at shoulder and waist, one shoulder bodice asymmetrically draped with chiffon.
est. $1500–$2000 sold: $2760
William Doyle Galleries 6/11/1997

Evening Gown, 1940s
Black crepe, two-piece, hip-length strapless bodice embroidered band of foliate pattern with sequins, pearls, and beads, labeled: Adrian Original.
est. $800–$1200 sold: $6900
William Doyle Galleries 11/2/2000

Evening Gown, 1940s
Brown crepe two-piece, peplum bodice with high neck, cap sleeves extending into long looped streamers attached at back edge of peplum, flared skirt.
est. $700–$900 sold: $1495
William Doyle Galleries 11/16/1999

Jacket, 1940s
Charcoal wool, single-breasted with curved and folded appliqué in front, wide teardrop appliqué in back.
est. $300–$500 sold: $2530
William Doyle Galleries 4/24/1996

Jacket, 1940s
Alternating yellow and black chevron striped wool sewn together in geometric patterns on sleeve and back yoke, large black buttons.
est. $400–$600 sold: $402
William Doyle Galleries 6/11/1997

A

JACKET, 1940s
Pola Stout fabric, brown striped, inset with partially crisscrossed bands extending around back on a slant, repeated on one arm.
est. $500–$700 sold: $287
William Doyle Galleries 11/16/1999

JACKET, 1940s
Gray and green double-faced wool partially lined in green silk.
est. $300–$500 sold: $258
William Doyle Galleries 12/6/1995

JACKET, 1940s
Finely striped gray wool, jacket pieced at shoulder to create geometric patterns with stripes, wide-pointed collar, square mottled gray buttons.
est. $500–$700 sold: $1035
William Doyle Galleries 11/10/1998

SHIRT, 1950
Navy embroidered eyelet short sleeves edged with contrasting band of white eyelet, mother-of-pearl buttons.
est. $100–$150 sold: $258
William Doyle Galleries 6/11/1997

SHIRT, 1950s
Navy silk shantung, bee buzzing out of the pocket and looping across the back.
est. $150–$200 sold: $575
William Doyle Galleries 11/12/1997

SUIT, 1940s
Brown wool, jacket with small round collar, ties at neck and waist, square tabs protruding from seams, straight skirt.
est. $800–$1200 sold: $1840
William Doyle Galleries 11/10/1998

SUIT, 1940s
Pink wool, fitted hip-length jacket applied with semicircular bands at front and back of yoke, mother-of-pearl buttons overlapping gilt metal mounts.
est. $400–$600 sold: $316
William Doyle Galleries 6/11/1997

SUIT, 1940s
Black wool, collarless jacket with four buttons geometrically spaced, skirt slightly flared with kick pleat.
est. $500–$700 sold: $345
William Doyle Galleries 6/11/1997

SUIT, 1940s
Pink and wine narrow stripes, jacket with crossed inset bands, one band forming collar, slit pockets at shoulders, flared skirt.
est. $500–$700 sold: $632
William Doyle Galleries 11/16/1999

SUIT, 1940s
Taupe wool, single-breasted jacket with small shawl collar and paddle shape appliquéd detail.
est. $100–$150 sold: $115
William Doyle Galleries 4/12/1995

SUIT, 1940s
Black wool, hip-length jacket applied with curved and straight intersecting bands extending from front to back of yoke, straight skirt.
est. $300–$500 sold: $402
William Doyle Galleries 6/11/1997

SUIT, 1940s
Two-piece, short coat dress, decorative strips and loops at shoulder and waist, pearl buttons, skirt silk crepe, lamé tarnished, labeled: Adrian Original.
est. $800–$1200 sold: $2070
William Doyle Galleries 11/2/2000

SUIT, 1940s
Black wool woven with flecks of anthracite thread, inset coral wool tabs on single-breasted jacket.
est. $600–$800 sold: $2185
William Doyle Galleries 12/6/1995

SUIT, 1940s
Black gabardine, jacket defined at waist and midsection with horizontal self bands, pointed collar and pockets with like bands crisscrossed, skirt.
est. $200–$300 sold: $1610
William Doyle Galleries 5/6/1998

SUIT, 1940s
Navy rayon faille, jacket has small shawl collar and smoky mother-of-pearl buttons.
est. $200–$300 sold: $345
William Doyle Galleries 4/12/1995

SUIT, 1940s
Black wool, jacket with signature ties at throat and waist, sleeves sewn with extra flaps to create stepped geometric pattern.
est. $800–$1200 sold: $690
William Doyle Galleries 11/16/1999

SUIT, 1940s
Wool woven with mauve stripes, jacket sewn with bands ending in loops oriented on the horizontal, skirt has three inverted pleats.
est. $500–$700 sold: $287
William Doyle Galleries 5/12/1999

SUIT, 1940s
Navy wool with triangular folded flaps, flat navy buttons.
est. $200–$300 sold: $460
William Doyle Galleries 9/30/1993

SUIT, 1948
Changeable wool twill woven in stripes of plum, green, and taupe, self ties on jacket at neck and waist.
est. $600–$900 sold: $2185
William Doyle Galleries 12/6/1995

SUIT, 1950s
Black wool, short bolero-style jacket with velvet collar, two large mother-of-pearl buttons set in silver, full skirt with wide top-stitched waistband.
est. $300–$500 sold: $316
William Doyle Galleries 6/11/1997

SUIT, 1960s
Jacket hip-length, left side closure, asymmetrical cutout collar, accented with large mother-of-pearl buttons, straight skirt, labeled: Adrian Original.
est. $300–$500 sold: $6325
William Doyle Galleries 11/2/2000

AGHAYAN, RAY AND MACKIE, BOB

EVENING GOWN, 1967
Sleeveless ivory crepe, skirt suspended below midriff held by lattice straps with gold scalloped paillettes and turquoise beads. Angie Dickinson, 1967 Academy Awards.
est. not available sold: $9775
Christie's Oscar Dress Auction 3/18/1999

ALAÏA, AZZEDINE

BODY SUIT, 1980s
Sheer black lace with velvet over bust, thong bottom.
est. not available sold: $295
The Paper Bag Princess 3/2/2001

BODY SUIT, 1980s
Black stretch lace with long sleeves, scoop-neck, thong bottom.
est. not available sold: $295
The Paper Bag Princess 3/2/2001

DRESS, 1980s
Black sheer knit with ruffle at back and spaghetti straps.
est. not available sold: $495
The Paper Bag Princess 3/2/2001

DRESS, 1980s
Body-hugging and short, white stretch wool woven with pink and blue stripes
est. $200–$300 sold: $400
William Doyle Galleries 5/2/2000

GOWN, 1980s
Black woven rayon viscose, with mesh knit fluted sleeves, mesh knit band around bottom, plunging scooped neckline.
est. not available sold: $664.98
eBay Online Auctions 2/24/2001

JACKET, 1980s
Black leather motorcycle style with silver zipper pockets and laces up the back, buckle strap in back.
est. not available sold: $695
The Paper Bag Princess 3/2/2001

ALIX

DRESS, 1930s
Black crepe with slit neck and long sleeves, narrowly pleated from shoulder to hem, midriff sewn with bands of black tape.
est. $100–$150 sold: $143
William Doyle Galleries 4/24/1996

ALLARD, ISABELLE

COCKTAIL DRESS, 1980s
Black taffeta with sweetheart neckline and gathered bodice, fitted to knees, skirt then flares out to floor, three center bows and detachable sleeves.
est. $300–$500 sold: $230
Skinner 12/16/1999

AMIES, HARDY

COAT, 1950s
Black textured wool, double-breasted jacket, pockets and pocket flaps of skirt trimmed in gray braid.
est. $125–$175 sold: $316
William Doyle Galleries 4/24/1996

SUIT, 1940s
Brown-and-charcoal-checked wool, brown velvet collar on jacket, long skirt.
est. $300–$500 sold: $460
William Doyle Galleries 9/30/1993

SUIT, 1940s
Brown silk, fitted jacket, long skirt.
est. $300–$500 sold: $287
William Doyle Galleries 9/30/1993

SUIT, 1940s
Black wool, padded hip jacket with black velvet collar, skirt with inverted front pleat and velvet band hem.
est. $300–$500 sold: $575
William Doyle Galleries 6/11/1997

ANN, LILLI

COAT, 1950s
Printed silk satin below-the-knee coat with black silk trim at collar, closure front patch pockets and cuffs.
est. $300–$500 sold: $345
Skinner 9/14/2000

COAT, 1960
Coral wool with silver fox fur collar and cuffs, tie belt, swing skirt.
est. not available sold: $595
The Paper Bag Princess 10/10/1998

COCKTAIL SUIT, 1940s
Nubbly black and white weave, peplum jacket, left side extending into diagonal self strap anchored with rhinestone buckle, straight skirt.
est. $150–$250 sold: $517
William Doyle Galleries 5/6/1998

COCKTAIL SUIT, 1940s
Black gabardine, broad-shouldered jacket sewn with curved bands of crystal beads, straight skirt.
est. $100–$150 sold: $316
William Doyle Galleries 5/6/1998

COCKTAIL SUIT, 1940s
Black wool, single-breasted fastening with rhinestone buttons, yoke of bunched wool studded with rhinestones.
est. $150–$200 sold: $373
William Doyle Galleries 6/11/1997

COCKTAIL SUIT, 1940s
Black velvet, jacket trimmed with square rhinestone-set buttons, two fringed, triangular flaps at sides, flared skirt.
est. $300–$500 sold: $402
William Doyle Galleries 11/10/1998

JACKET, 1950s
Navy crepe with front pleating on one side that arcs midway to the other shoulder, collarless with high V neck.
est. $150–$200 sold: $632
William Doyle Galleries 5/12/1999

Suit, 1940s
Navy wool with silver Lurex threads woven throughout fitted jacket and matching skirt.
est. not available sold: $595
The Paper Bag Princess 5/1/1999

ANNE-MARIE OF FRANCE

Handbag, 1940s
Reims Champagne, white leather handbag with gold trim and plastic ice.
est. $1000–$1500 sold: $1150
Sotheby's 12/9/1998

Handbag, 1940s
White leather telephone handbag with gold-toned frame and dial, white leather strap attached to handset.
est. $500–$700 sold: $2415
Skinner 9/14/2000

APONTE, LAURA

Cardigan, 1950s
Hand-knit sapphire blue wool with blue sequins, three-quarter-length sleeves.
est. not available sold: $325
The Paper Bag Princess 1/1/2001

Cardigan, 1950s
Hand-knit black wool with black sequins, short sleeves with V-neck.
est. not available sold: $325
The Paper Bag Princess

Evening Sweater, 1950s
Cardigan with black sequins sewn in wool knit mesh with round collar.
est. $200–$300 sold: $460
William Doyle Galleries 11/10/1998

Evening Sweater, 1950s
Cardigan with black sequins sewn in wool knit mesh.
est. $150–$200 sold: $575
William Doyle Galleries 5/12/1999

ARDEN, ELIZABETH

Cocktail Dress, 1950s
Ivory crepe de chine satin with black, charcoal, and gray blossoms, strapless bodice sewn in narrow panels that release at waistline into full skirt.
est. $100–$150 sold: $920
William Doyle Galleries 5/12/1999

Cocktail Dress, 1950s
Strapless, aquamarine mousseline draped at the bodice with aquamarine satin.
est. $200–$300 sold: $517
William Doyle Galleries 4/24/1996

Handbag, 1940s
Black crocodile.
est. not available sold: $495
The Paper Bag Princess 11/1/1996

Suit, 1960s
Pink and red floral printed linen box cut jacket with Peter Pan collar, hand-painted plastic buttons, with matching knee-length skirt.
est. not available sold: $225
The Paper Bag Princess 11/1/1999

ARMANI, GIORGIO

Evening Gown, 1995
Short jacket of ivory silk georgette with beads and sequins, bordered in ivory silk jersey, silk crepe wrap skirt with off-center button closure. Emma Thompson, 1995 Academy Awards.
est. not available sold: $6900
Christie's Oscar Dress Auction 3/18/1999

ARMANI, GIORGIO, VALENTINO, AND THE GAP

Cocktail Dress, 1995
Black silk crepe trumpet skirt by Valentino, black silk velvet coat by Armani, black stretch T-shirt by The Gap. Sharon Stone, 1995 Academy Awards.
est. not available sold: $9775
Christie's Oscar Dress Auction 3/18/1999

AUSTIN, ALAN

JACKET, 1970s
Rust-colored water snake blazer, single-breasted.
est. not available sold: $345
The Paper Bag Princess 5/10/2000

AZZARO, LORIS

CATSUIT, 1978
One-piece catsuit embroidered with blue sequins, V neckline and thin shoulder straps. Raquel Welch, 1978 Academy Awards.
est. not available sold: $6325
Christie's Oscar Dress Auction 3/18/1999

COCKTAIL DRESS, 1970–1975
Black silk jersey, halter top bodice has triangular cut-out bust area and V-shaped square back.
est. $2000–$3000 sold: $2300
Sotheby's 4/8/1998

COCKTAIL DRESS, 1970–1975
Brown jersey sheath with wrapped halter bodice and bronze metal chains at midriff area.
est. $800–$1200 sold: $3162
Sotheby's 4/8/1998

COCKTAIL DRESS, 1970–1975
Black jersey with eight rows of fringe, bateau neckline with fringe creating sleeve effect.
est. $1000–$2000 sold: $1150
Sotheby's 4/8/1998

ENSEMBLE, 1970s
Silver crocheted top with attached silver chain fringe, fitted with low V neck and center front snap closure, long chain sleeves. Matching purse.
est. $300–$500 sold: $805
Skinner 12/16/1999

ENSEMBLE, 1970s
Gold crocheted top with attached gold-toned chain fringe imitating chain mail, fitted bodice with bateau neck, chain sleeves, evening purse to match.
est. $300–$500 sold: $690
Skinner 12/16/1999

EVENING GOWN, 1989
Black georgette dress with long tunic bodice that is draped and gathered, flowing skirt. Lili Zanuck, 1989 Academy Awards.
est. not available sold: $4600
Christie's Oscar Dress Auction 3/18/1999

BABANI

DRESS, 1920s
Sleeveless and tubular, pink lamé embroidered at center with two large bouquets of flowers.
est. $600–$800 sold: $690
William Doyle Galleries 11/10/1998

DRESS, 1930s
Sleeveless, neck and armholes bound with self-edging, extending into ties at back of neck, blue satin waist sash.
est. $400–$600 sold: $2645
William Doyle Galleries 5/2/2000

BADGLEY MISCHKA

EVENING GOWN, 1996
Sleeveless asymmetrical dress with lime-colored slip under jet-beaded Chantilly lace overlay, with dense beading. Jennifer Lopez, 1996 Academy Awards.
est. not available sold: $6325
Christie's Oscar Dress Auction 3/18/1999

EVENING GOWN, 1997
Butterscotch silk with sleeveless bodice quilted with metallic cord and beading, long straight skirt. Elisabeth Shue, 1997 Academy Awards.
est. not available sold: $6325
Christie's Oscar Dress Auction 3/18/1999

BAL MASQUE

Cocktail Dress, 1958

American copy of Yves Saint Laurent design, strapless, dropped waist, bell-shaped skirt, outer layers of net, satin bows, overlaying understructure.
est. $500–$700 sold: $977.50
William Doyle Galleries 11/2/2000

BALENCIAGA

Ball Gown, 1950

Full skirt of ruby velvet fastening down front with buttons, bodice and sleeve poufs of black mousseline over beige silk.
est. $1000–$1500 sold: $920
William Doyle Galleries 4/12/1995

Blouse, 1945

Oyster silk satin embroidered with looped colored beads densely at shoulders then less so overall.
est. 300–500 pounds sold: 437 pounds
Sotheby's London 11/25/1998

Cape, 1950s

Red silk enveloping bell form with wide sweeping cape collar, three-quarter-length, with bracelet-length sleeves.
est. 1200–1800 pounds sold: 2875 pounds
Sotheby's London 11/25/1998

Coat, 1950

Black wool flared coat with wide shawl/cape collar.
est. $300–$500 sold: $1725
William Doyle Galleries 12/5/1996

Coat, 1950

Black silk taffeta with wide shawl collar that drapes over elbow-length sleeves, wrapped bodice and short pleated skirt.
est. $4000–$5000 sold: $4600
Sotheby's 4/8/1998

Coat, 1950s

Black faille silk with simple collar and fabric gathered into a yoke at front and back
est. 500–800 pounds sold: 920 pounds
Sotheby's London 11/25/1998

Coat, 1950s

Red ribbed wool, cocoon silhouette, roll collar, elbow-length sleeves.
est. $400–$600 sold: $287
Skinner 12/16/1999

Coat, 1950s

Reversible wool three-quarter-length coat with gray and white houndstooth on one side, camel on the other. Boxy silhouette, sloped shoulders.
est. $400–$600 sold: $546
Skinner 12/16/1999

Coat, 1950s

Camel wool knee-length coat with raglan sleeves, welt seam detail at collar, hem, and pockets.
est. $400–$600 sold: $431
Skinner 12/16/1999

Coat, 1957

Fuchsia silk velvet, fabric gathered into yoke at the back shoulders, low-cut full sleeves, opening center front with large pleated folds.
est. 1000–1500 pounds sold: 2185 pounds
Sotheby's London 11/25/1998

Coat, 1959

Black leather applied with random-shaped patches of leather.
est. 400–600 pounds sold: 437 pounds
Sotheby's London 11/25/1998

Coat, 1960

Pink satin, four pockets with flaps, gathered yoke back.
est. $800–$1200 sold: $1150
William Doyle Galleries 9/30/1993

Coat, 1960s

Black silk satin, single-breasted with black bead cluster buttons.
est. $600–$900 sold: $575
William Doyle Galleries 11/17/1994

Coat Dress, 1948

Brown changeante faille figured with pin dots and applied with black plush passementerie, full flared skirt.
est. $1500–$2000 sold: $9487
William Doyle Galleries 6/11/1997

B

Coat Dress, 1950

Black silk irregularly ribbed, fitted sheath, buttons down front.
est. $600–$900 sold: $460
William Doyle Galleries 11/17/1994

Cocktail Dress, 1940s

Black silk with long sleeves, plunging V neck with collar, hip sewn with wide sashes tying in a bow over gathered front panel.
est. $300–$500 sold: $1955
William Doyle Galleries 11/12/1997

Cocktail Dress, 1940s

Strapless black silk, button-front bodice, long skirt draped into swag at one side.
est. $1000–$1200 sold: $3220
William Doyle Galleries 12/6/1995

Cocktail Dress, 1948

Black taffeta with matching capelet.
est. $3500–$4000 sold: $3450
Sotheby's 9/30/1999

Cocktail Dress, 1949

Black wool with green taffeta.
est. $2000–$3000 sold: $7820
William Doyle Galleries 9/30/1993

Cocktail Dress, 1950s

Short dress of iridescent brown/black silk taffeta, jacket of brown Chantilly lace embroidered with beads, black satin ribbon sash.
est. $750–$1000 sold: $1265
William Doyle Galleries 12/6/1995

Cocktail Dress, 1950s

Cream silk twill printed with multicolored roses, one-shoulder dress cut in one piece to wrap around fastening at shoulder.
est. $500–$750 sold: $747
William Doyle Galleries 12/6/1995

Cocktail Dress, 1950s

Black sheer wool, scarf bodice draped in a cowl in front forming cap sleeves continuing around and tying at the low back.
est. $500–$750 sold: $2530
William Doyle Galleries 12/6/1995

Cocktail Dress, 1950s

Pink tulle over satin floor-length strapless dress, tulle embroidered with sequins and stones.
est. $2000–$3000 sold: $1035
William Doyle Galleries 9/30/1993

Cocktail Dress, 1950s

Black Chantilly lace with applied organza ribbon detailing.
est. $600–$800 sold: $1265
Sotheby's 9/30/1999

Cocktail Dress, 1950s

Pink silk taffeta draped over a hooped petticoat with dropped bodice, bodice and hem trimmed with scalloped tiers of embroidered organdy.
est. $1500–$2000 sold: $920
William Doyle Galleries 5/12/1999

Cocktail Dress, 1950s

Black lace re-embroidered with wool made as a narrow strapless dress with attached black sheer silk scarf forming a rounded neck.
est. $400–$600 sold: $402
William Doyle Galleries 4/12/1995

Cocktail Dress, 1950s

Strapless, ivory satin with coin dots.
est. $750–$1000 sold: $690
William Doyle Galleries 11/17/1994

Cocktail Dress, 1960

Black silk crepe, sleeveless with gathered neckline.
est. $600–$800 sold: $632
William Doyle Galleries 12/6/1995

Cocktail Dress, 1960s

Pink and silver fabric embroidered with pink sequins and beads, silver sequins, attached at one shoulder with a pink ostrich boa.
est. $600–$900 sold: $345
William Doyle Galleries 4/24/1996

Cocktail Dress, 1960s
Black silk chiffon, sleeveless with additional panel attaching at shoulders to form cowl hood.
est. 400–600 pounds sold: 690 pounds
Sotheby's London 11/25/1998

Cocktail Dress, 1960s
Black silk slip dress with separate cape.
est. $1000–$1500 sold: $1265
William Doyle Galleries 9/30/1993

Cocktail Dress, 1963
Pink and white floral silk gazar, draped strapless bodice, gathered long skirt, two self bows at back of the bodice.
est. $600–$900 sold: $1495
William Doyle Galleries 4/24/1996

Cocktail Dress, 1965
Black lace strapless sheath with boned bodice, black silk underdress and matching knee-length scallop-edged cape and ribbon tie.
est. 300–500 pounds sold: 805 pounds
Sotheby's London 11/25/1998

Cocktail Ensemble, 1950s
Black brocaded silk straight skirt and sleeveless top, jacket with three-quarter-length sleeves and shawl collar.
est. $300–$500 sold: $575
Skinner 12/16/1999

Cocktail Ensemble, 1951
Satin two-piece, strapless bodice can be worn with detachable Chantilly lace over, magenta silk satin ribbon over bodice, ballet-length skirt.
est. $1500–$2000 sold: $3737
Sotheby's 10/29/1997

Cocktail Ensemble, 1960s
Black wool crepe trimmed with white mink, A-line shift suspended by straps sewn from center of bodice, jacket cut away in wide curve.
est. $300–$500 sold: $2070
William Doyle Galleries 5/6/1998

Cocktail Ensemble, 1960s
Blue velvet woven with a small checkerboard, fitted jacket with blue jeweled buttons, chemise dress with V back and neckline.
est. $200–$300 sold: $373
William Doyle Galleries 4/12/1995

Cocktail Suit, 1960
Jacket and skirt of dress in red chenille-ribbed purple silk, strapless bodice of dress has long fringe of cream silk.
est. $500–$750 sold: $1265
William Doyle Galleries 4/24/1996

Dress, 1950s
Black wool, short-sleeved top with three buttons.
est. $150–$250 sold: $402
William Doyle Galleries 12/6/1995

Dress, 1950s
Double-faced navy cotton with small paisleys.
est. $200–$400 sold: $345
William Doyle Galleries 9/30/1993

Dress, 1950s
Navy, sleeveless, self bow.
est. $500–$750 sold: $920
William Doyle Galleries 11/17/1994

Dress, 1950s
Charcoal loosely woven wool, pullover top with boat neck, bracelet-length sleeves, pleated skirt.
est. $200–$300 sold: $1150
William Doyle Galleries 4/12/1995

Dress, 1960
Black, double-breasted with notched lapels closing into V neck, three-quarter-length sleeves, straight skirt.
est. $300–$500 sold: $632
William Doyle Galleries 5/6/1998

Dress, 1960s
Yellow gazar, strapless short underdress with sleeveless overdress, self bow.
est. $1500–$2000 sold: $2300
William Doyle Galleries 9/30/1993

ENSEMBLE, 1950s
Tweed, sleeveless dress with low V neckline with two scarf tabs, single-breasted, short jacket.
est. $300–$400 sold: $517
William Doyle Galleries 4/12/1995

ENSEMBLE, 1951
Black silk collarless and sleeveless jacket and straight skirt to the knee, sleeveless blouse of ivory linen fastening on the side with four buttons.
est. 600–1000 pounds sold: 1725 pounds
Sotheby's London 11/25/1998

ENSEMBLE, 1957
Wool knit dress, rounded shoulders, slit neckline, slash pockets in below-knee straight skirt, "Balenciaga, Avenue Georges V Paris," 101360 in ink.
est. $600–$800 sold: $1380
Skinner 9/14/2000

ENSEMBLE, 1960
Red-orange linen, sleeveless chemise dress with suede leather belt and jacket with large buttons sewn with twisted braid.
est. $500–$750 sold: $977
William Doyle Galleries 6/11/1997

EVENING CLOAK, 1950s
Black silk faille, cardigan style, stand-up collar, bracelet-length sleeves.
est. $600–$900 sold: $1150
William Doyle Galleries 11/17/1994

EVENING ENSEMBLE, 1960s
Chocolate brown crinkled silk, short skirt, long skirt, pullover bodice, sleeveless shell and silk slip.
est. $750–$1000 sold: $1092
William Doyle Galleries 12/6/1995

EVENING GOWN, 1950s
Peach silk faille, wide V neck, back has fringed bustle panels over slight train.
est. $750–$1000 sold: $575
William Doyle Galleries 11/17/1994

EVENING GOWN, 1950s
Pink chiffon sewn onto satin, sleeveless sheath embroidered with paillettes shaped like shells and flowers, pearls, rhinestones, and sequins.
est. $1300–$1500 sold: $1150
William Doyle Galleries 11/12/1997

EVENING GOWN, 1950s
Two shades of ocher shantung and organza, strapless bodice twists into a swag.
est. $500–$750 sold: $1265
William Doyle Galleries 12/6/1995

EVENING GOWN, 1950s
Ivory satin embroidered with scrolls, sewn with crystal beads and rhinestones, scoop neckline, elbow-length sleeves, slight fishtail train on skirt.
est. $750–$1000 sold: $1265
William Doyle Galleries 12/6/1995

EVENING GOWN, 1950s
Strapless dress, black silk faille, bodice has gathered panels coming together in a bow.
est. $800–$1200 sold: $1380
William Doyle Galleries 11/17/1994

EVENING GOWN, 1950s
Black silk faille with portrait neckline, fitted bodice, and full skirt, pleats/darted waist with floor-length hem in back, exposing ankles in front.
est. not available sold: $5600
The Paper Bag Princesss 9/14/2001

EVENING GOWN, 1950s
White tulle embroidered with rhinestones, sequins, camisole bodice.
est. $750–$1000 sold: $747
William Doyle Galleries 9/30/1993

EVENING GOWN, 1950s
Silver floral brocade and lamé gown and matching jacket, sleeveless bodice with jewel neckline, bow at waist.
est. $800–$1000 sold: $747
Skinner 12/16/1999

EVENING GOWN, 1950S
Silver floral brocade and lamé evening gown with matching jacket, sleeveless fitted bodice with jewel neckline, low round back, boxy jacket.
est. $800–$1000 sold: $748
Skinner 12/16/1999

EVENING GOWN, 1960
Strapless, wool embellished with scrollwork, vinery, fleurs-de-lis, and other plant forms in black velvet appliqué and beads, separate capelet.
est. $800–$1200 sold: $2530
William Doyle Galleries 11/16/1999

EVENING GOWN, 1960
Pink silk taffeta applied with stemmed flowers of padded gold kid centered with marquise rhinestones, strapless bodice.
est. $1500–$2000 sold: $1495
William Doyle Galleries 11/10/1998

EVENING JACKET, 1960S
Above-the-waist boxy jacket of white organza embroidered with pearlized gold sequins, rhinestones, snowflake paillettes, crystal lozenges, pearls.
est. $700–$900 sold: $690
William Doyle Galleries 5/2/2000

HAT, 1950S
Black satin pillbox with fringe of large silk bobbles and jet beads.
est. $200–$300 sold: $1955
William Doyle Galleries 12/6/1995

HAT, 1950S
Brown chenille sewn with chenille-edged net ruffles.
est. $75–$100 sold: $460
William Doyle Galleries 12/6/1995

JACKET, 1950S
Black wool, double-breasted with cut-away hem.
est. $400–$600 sold: $747
William Doyle Galleries 12/6/1995

JACKET, 1950S
Black, double-breasted with notched lapel collar.
est. $500–$750 sold: $862
William Doyle Galleries 4/27/1994

JACKET, 1959
Red/purple bouclé tweed trimmed at the neck, down the front, and around the hem with self-piping loops, buttons with purple rhinestones.
est. $150–$200 sold: $460
William Doyle Galleries 6/11/1997

SCARF, 1960S
Abstract landscape design.
est. $40–$60 sold: $172
William Doyle Galleries 9/30/1993

SUIT, 1940
Navy shantung, jacket embroidered at the shoulders inside the slit collar and down the front with silk ribbon flowers in pink, turquoise, and purple.
est. $800–$1200 sold: $3105
William Doyle Galleries 4/12/1995

SUIT, 1940S
Black wool single-breasted jacket and straight knee-length skirt.
est. not available sold: $795
The Paper Bag Princess 6/1/1995

SUIT, 1940S
Navy wool skirt and double-breasted boxy-style crop jacket.
est. not available sold: $495
The Paper Bag Princess

SUIT, 1950
Black cashmere and wool, single-breasted, bracelet-length sleeves.
est. $500–$750 sold: $862
William Doyle Galleries 4/27/1994

SUIT, 1950S
Oatmeal tweed, single-breasted jacket.
est. $300–$500 sold: $345
William Doyle Galleries 11/17/1994

SUIT, 1950S
Gray tweed, single-breasted jacket.
est. $100–$125 sold: $431
William Doyle Galleries 12/6/1995

B

Suit, 1950s

Black bouclé wool, fitted tunic-style top fastening with press studs at left shoulder, mid-calf-length skirt with silk satin ribbon at the waist.
est. 400–600 pounds sold: 402 pounds
Sotheby's London 11/25/1998

Suit, 1960

Gray tweed skirt and double-breasted jacket with a white tweed wool blouse, short-sleeved and trimmed with a row of three buttons at each side.
est. $300–$500 sold: $345
William Doyle Galleries 11/10/1998

Suit, 1960

Gray flannel, double-breasted jacket set with eight shimmering metal filigree dome buttons, straight skirt gathered at waist.
est. $400–$600 sold: $920
William Doyle Galleries 11/10/1998

Suit, 1960

Red chine silk strewn with stemmed flowers and overwoven with self florets, two-button jacket, skirt slightly flared.
est. $300–$400 sold: $575
William Doyle Galleries 6/11/1997

Suit, 1960

Peach bouclé wool, double-breasted jacket with fold-over collar, straight skirt slightly gathered at waist.
est. $300–$500 sold: $373
William Doyle Galleries 6/11/1997

Suit, 1960s

Mustard wool tweed, single-breasted jacket with cut-away hem and straight jacket.
est. $100–$125 sold: $517
William Doyle Galleries 12/6/1995

Suit, 1960s

Boxy jacket, notched lapel, two front flap pockets, straight knee-length skirt, silk-lined, "Balenciaga Avenue Georges V Paris," 69999 on tape in back.
est. $400–$600 sold: $862.50
Skinner 9/14/2000

Suit, 1960s

Two tops, one sleeveless orange twill, other silk twill printed in an orange, green, and blue plaid, single-breasted jacket and skirt.
est. $100–$125 sold: $345
William Doyle Galleries 12/6/1995

Suit, 1960s

Black silk twill printed with green dots, short cardigan jacket and skirt edged with a ruffle.
est. $250–$400 sold: $258
William Doyle Galleries 4/12/1995

Suit, 1960s

Brown and white striped wool double-breasted jacket.
est. $300–$500 sold: $920
William Doyle Galleries 4/27/1994

Suit, 1960s

Light blue tweed with single-breasted jacket.
est. $100–$125 sold: $862
William Doyle Galleries 4/24/1996

Suit, 1960s

Aqua and white tweed, double-breasted jacket with bracelet-length sleeves.
est. $100–$125 sold: $402
William Doyle Galleries 4/24/1996

BALENCIAGA, EISA

Blouse, 1962

Silk twill, white dots against navy background.
est. $300–$500 sold: $115
William Doyle Galleries 9/30/1993

Hat, 1950s

Seven close-fitting hats: blue wool turban; camel wool bowler; black bowler; velvet riding cap; brown suede cap; navy draped cloche; mustard circular hat.
est. $100–$200 sold: $103.50
Skinner 12/16/1999

BALMAIN, PIERRE

COAT, 1960
White trapunto effect silk damask with V neck, self-tie closure at bust and three-quarter-length sleeves.
est. $600–$800 sold: $690
Sotheby's 4/8/1998

COAT, 1960S
A-line coat, wide lapel collar, double-breasted closure, welted seam detail, two side slash pockets, red silk lining, # 155387, Pierre Balmain Paris.
est. $600–$800 sold: $920
Skinner 9/14/2000

COAT, 1960S
Wool A-line coat with wide lapel collar, double-breasted closure, welted seam detail, and two side slash pockets.
est. $600–$800 sold: $920
Skinner 9/14/2000

COCKTAIL DRESS, 1950S
Black taffeta mid-length dress, fitted sleeveless bodice with low round neckline and full crinolined skirt with eight layers of ruffles at hem.
est. $400–$600 sold: $633
Skinner 12/16/1999

COCKTAIL DRESS, 1950S
Strapless, ivory lace re-embroidered with white sequins, beads, and rhinestones, swag of silk taffeta.
est. $500–$750 sold: $316
William Doyle Galleries 12/6/1995

COCKTAIL DRESS, 1950S
Black silk velvet floor-length dress with fitted silhouette and sweetheart neckline with spaghetti straps, silk velvet extends to knees, flaring skirt.
est. $300–$500 sold: $546
Skinner 12/16/1999

COCKTAIL DRESS, 1950S
Ivory satin hand-embroidered with pastel flowers in silk and chenille and sprinkled with iridescent stones, sleeveless with low scooped neckline.
est. $500–$700 sold: $920
William Doyle Galleries 5/6/1998

COCKTAIL DRESS, 1950S
Black taffeta and point d'esprit lace, sleeveless bodice, satin cummerbund, full skirt with eight layers of ruffles at hem.
est. $400–$600 sold: $632
Skinner 12/16/1999

COCKTAIL DRESS, 1950S
Gathered black net dress with V neck, cap sleeves, and taffeta waistband, center front button closure, tulle petticoat.
est. $500–$700 sold: $546.25
Skinner 9/14/2000

COCKTAIL DRESS, 1956
Horizontally draped black satin comprises bodice, thin belt at waist, attached skirt, windowpane-patterned satin net over yellow satin underskirt.
est. $750–$1000 sold: $4025
Sotheby's 4/8/1998

COCKTAIL DRESS, 1960
Strapless, short, composed of cancan ruffles of pleated white or aqua net with cummerbund of white satin and full skirt.
est. $750–$1000 sold: $1150
William Doyle Galleries 6/11/1997

COCKTAIL DRESS, 1960
Brown silk crepe, bodice has V neck and corded satin trim at bustline and waist, skirt has trumpet hem with corded satin trim on flounces.
est. $750–$1000 sold: $1380
Sotheby's 4/8/1998

COCKTAIL DRESS, 1960S
Sleeveless shift, small straps, high waist, straight skirt, black net decorated with flowering branches, chenille, rhinestones, and metallics.
est. $600–$800 sold: $862.50
William Doyle Galleries 11/2/2000

Cocktail Dress, 1960s

Black silk, sleeveless with scoop neck, double flat straps and wide brown waistband, bolero jacket trimmed with jet ball passementerie.
est. $200–$300 sold: $1955
William Doyle Galleries 5/6/1998

Cocktail Dress, 1960s

Black chiffon, bodice is a draped overblouse, waist encircled with wide velvet band, gathered skirt highlighted with velvet ball fringe at hem.
est. $300–$500 sold: $1380
William Doyle Galleries 5/6/1998

Cocktail Dress, 1960s

Brown, beige, and white silk jersey with draped halter bodice, velvet cut-out at midriff, pleated skirt of alternating bands of brown, beige, and white.
est. $750–$1000 sold: $920
Sotheby's 4/8/1998

Cocktail Dress, 1960s

Black chiffon, draped overblouse bodice, waist encircled with velvet band, gathered skirt with velvet ball fringe at hem.
est. $200–$300 sold: $517
William Doyle Galleries 5/12/1999

Cocktail Dress, 1970

Black silk chiffon with detachable rose at neckline, short-sleeved bodice, pleated skirt with matching silk crepe petticoat.
est. $600–$800 sold: $690
Sotheby's 4/8/1998

Dress, 1960

Multicolored silk taffeta in pastel print, strapless bodice has tucks, self bow at bust and waist, tulip skirt in signature "infanta" style.
est. $800–$1200 sold: $920
Sotheby's 10/29/1997

Ensemble, 1960s

Taupe wool fitted sheath, zips up front, pocket at each hip, small chevron quilt pattern, matching jacket with white mink trim, both silk lined.
est. not available sold: $695
The Paper Bag Princess

Evening Ensemble, 1956

Bodice composed of horizontally draped black satin and thin shoulder straps, satin belt, full-pleated taffeta skirt with two black satin petticoats.
est. $1000–$1500 sold: $4025
Sotheby's 4/8/1998

Evening Ensemble, 1960s

Coral brocade silk two-piece ensemble, ankle-length tunic with long sleeves, gold cuffs, matching slim pants.
est. $600–$800 sold: $460
Skinner 12/16/1999

Evening Gown, 1950s

Strapless, ivory taffeta chine with charcoal dots, narrow underskirt.
est. $600–$900 sold: $402
William Doyle Galleries 11/17/1994

Evening Gown, 1950s

Gold, white, and pink brocaded silk, flowers with appliquéd details, "Watteau" back with two detachable velvet bows.
est. $1000–$1500 sold: $4025
Sotheby's 4/8/1998

Evening Gown, 1950s

Tricolored, draped silk, off-the-shoulder straps.
est. $1500–$2500 sold: $2300
William Doyle Galleries 9/30/1993

Evening Gown, 1950s

Sheath dress of ivory satin embroidered in gold bullion, beads, sequins, and rhinestones in floral pattern dense on bodice, scattered on skirt.
est. $2000–$3000 sold: $3450
William Doyle Galleries 5/6/1998

Evening Gown, 1957–1958

Ivory satin with blue satin back panel and bow, Lesage floral embroidery in ivory, blue, pink, and silver with diamantes and beads.
est. $3000–$5000 sold: $11,500
Sotheby's 4/8/1998

EVENING GOWN, 1960
Black tulle over sheer black silk over heavy silk, sleeveless, embroidered with horizontal stripes of beads and sequins.
est. $300–$500 sold: $258
William Doyle Galleries 4/12/1995

EVENING GOWN, 1960
Strapless bodice in mustard faille extending into side streamers and wrapped in black velvet, black brocade skirt with gold and silver chrysanthemums.
est. $300–$400 sold: $977
William Doyle Galleries 11/12/1997

EVENING GOWN, 1961
White tulle with gold sequins sewn on strapless bodice and skirt, long pheasant feathers with bands of taffeta painted to resemble pheasant feathers.
est. $1000–$1500 sold: $2185
William Doyle Galleries 4/24/1996

EVENING GOWN, 1961
White tulle with gold sequins sewn on strapless bodice and skirt, long pheasant feathers with bands of taffeta painted to resemble pheasant feathers.
est. $1000–$1500 sold: $4312
William Doyle Galleries 6/11/1997

EVENING GOWN, 1962
Princess-line strapless gown of ivory satin, gold lamé and printed pink flowers, skirt flat in front and gathered in full folds at back.
est. $300–$500 sold: $316
William Doyle Galleries 5/2/2000

EVENING GOWN, 1965
Alençon-style lace, strapless bodice with low curved back, pink satin sash at waist, full skirt with layers of organza and tulle petticoats.
est. $400–$600 sold: $230
William Doyle Galleries 5/2/2000

HAT, 1970
Black and white dot tweed, jacket, sleeveless shell with cut-out detail, hat shaped like a helmet.
est. $150–$200 sold: $230
William Doyle Galleries 4/24/1996

BARISH, PAMELA

EVENING GOWN, 1995
Forest green cut velvet in floral motif with draped back and slightly flared hem. Kathleen Quinlan, 1995 Academy Awards.
est. not available sold: $4025
Christie's Oscar Dress Auction 3/18/1999

BAROCCO

EVENING COAT, 1980S
Three-quarter-length coat of black silk with metallic green, gold, and purple brocade, padded shoulders, full skirt, front closures, black fur trim.
est. $400–$600 sold: $230
Skinner 12/16/1999

BATTILOCCHI FOR SORELLE FONTANA

COCKTAIL ENSEMBLE, 1950S
Pale pink chiffon skirt and bodice with beading of pale pink bead fringe with rhinestones, fitted bodice with halter straps, straight skirt.
est. $500–$700 sold: $288
Skinner 12/16/1999

BEENE, GEOFFREY

CHEMISE, 1980S
Straight chemise with kimono-cut sleeves of heather wool honeycomb-weave overlaid with gold and silver metallic lace.
est. $200–$300 sold: $345
William Doyle Galleries 11/12/1997

COAT, 1960S
Red and white check with prominent white pocket and front zippers.
est. $150–$200 sold: $373
William Doyle Galleries 6/11/1997

COAT, 1960S
Wool felt cardigan pieced with reverse and applied appliqué, front stripes of black, green, orange, and yellow, back in tile-pattern grid.
est. $400–$600 sold: $805
William Doyle Galleries 11/16/1999

COCKTAIL DRESS, 1960s
Gray flannel with jewel neck, long sleeves, bodice sewn with rhinestones in diaper pattern and delineated front and back with rhinestone bands.
est. $300–$500 sold: $345
William Doyle Galleries 5/12/1999

COCKTAIL DRESS, 1960s
Wool jersey studded with rhinestones, jewel neck, short sleeves, bodice and hem defined with bands of round and square rhinestones.
est. $300–$500 sold: $1380
William Doyle Galleries 5/6/1998

COCKTAIL DRESS, 1960s
Gray wool twill, sleeveless, belt with rhinestone buckle.
est. $150–$250 sold: $575
William Doyle Galleries 11/12/1997

COCKTAIL DRESS, 1964
Gray felted wool A-line accented with four rows of rhinestones along the neck, sleeves, and hem.
est. $500–$700 sold: $1035
Sotheby's 4/8/1998

COCKTAIL DRESS, 1970s
Taupe silk jersey, sleeves that zip at wrists, hem edged with brown and white ostrich and quail feathers.
est. $150–$250 sold: $1265
William Doyle Galleries 11/17/1994

COCKTAIL DRESS, 1980
Shirt bodice of brown and white pin-striped cotton, midriff embroidered with sequins, charcoal and white striped gazar, taffeta bolero jacket.
est. $150–$250 sold: $287
William Doyle Galleries 12/6/1995

DRESS, 1960s
Maize silk, loose-fitting, falls straight from shoulders, long sleeves, side and back seams and hem topstitched, others outlined with silver lamé.
est. $100–$150 sold: $632
William Doyle Galleries 6/11/1997

DRESS, 1960s
Green linen, sleeveless, high waist, A-line skirt pleated at sides.
est. $100–$125 sold: $431
William Doyle Galleries 4/24/1996

DRESS, 1960s
Short brown silk, sleeveless, empire waist with bow, covered buttons down front, large patch pockets, labeled: Geoffrey Beene Boutique.
est. not available sold: $325
The Paper Bag Princess 8/10/2001

DRESS, 1960s
Pink with black trim silk, black pattern, bow at neck, black patent leather belt, full skirt, covered buttons, labeled: Geoffrey Beene Boutique.
est. not available sold: $495
The Paper Bag Princess 7/1/1998

DRESS, 1970s
Gold and cream lace appliquéd with curved and straight panels of gold-stitched, pleated silk, trimmed with floral silk, self obi sash and beige slip.
est. $200–$300 sold: $1092
William Doyle Galleries 4/24/1996

DRESS, 1970s
Green wool tweed with matching jacket, dress has square neckline, raglan sleeves, circular skirt, bolero jacket with ruffled hem.
est. $300–$500 sold: $287
Skinner 12/16/1999

ENSEMBLE, 1960s
Double-breasted flared coat of purple and navy/black gingham wool faced at the collar to match the dress of purple/black and white floral printed knit.
est. $100–$125 sold: $460
William Doyle Galleries 4/24/1996

ENSEMBLE, 1960s
Pink and brown horizontally striped wool cardigan coat with wooden buttons, short-sleeved shell and straight skirt.
est. $200–$300 sold: $977
William Doyle Galleries 5/12/1999

ENSEMBLE, 1980s
Black satin, pullover top with two gray quilted patches, wide leg trousers gathered at harem-style waistband, edged with gold braid.
est. $200–$250 sold: $373
William Doyle Galleries 11/12/1997

ENSEMBLE, 1989
Salt and pepper matte rayon and jersey bolero and long dress, dress has sheer gray silk bodice showing silver sequined bustier underbodice.
est. $200–$250 sold: $1840
William Doyle Galleries 12/5/1996

EVENING ENSEMBLE, 1963
Sleeveless chiffon bodice embroidered with black and ivory paillettes, black satin bow at dropped waist, two ivory silk skirts and jacket.
est. $1500–$2500 sold: $4312
Sotheby's 4/8/1998

EVENING ENSEMBLE, 1983
Black wool jersey, floor-length, long-sleeved straight sheath and loose bolero jacket with quilted appliqué, sleeve ends decorated in satin.
est. $700–$900 sold: $1265
William Doyle Galleries 5/2/2000

EVENING GOWN, 1964
Gray wool flannel falling straight from shoulder, trimmed with bands of rhinestones at collar and down each side.
est. $300–$500 sold: $920
William Doyle Galleries 11/10/1998

EVENING GOWN, 1980s
Sleeveless with high neck, white in front and back, black at sides, white satin ribbon belt.
est. $400–$600 sold: $431
William Doyle Galleries 11/10/1998

EVENING GOWN, 1980s
Black jersey with quilted silver sleeveless bodice and silver trim at hem.
est. not available sold: $1295
The Paper Bag Princess 2/1/2001

EVENING GOWN, 1990
Black column dress with slit center panel fitted with blue velvet and lamé, matching opera gloves in velvet. Glenn Close, 1990 Academy Awards.
est. not available sold: $3450
Christie's Oscar Dress Auction 3/18/1999

JACKET, 1970s
Black satin with flared skirt, bodice with low décolletage and straps crisscrossing in back, trimmed with rhinestones.
est. $200–$300 sold: $488
William Doyle Galleries 11/12/1997

SUIT, 1970s
Oatmeal tweed, jacket with welt seaming, cut in two points at front, open V collar with lapels, full skirt from gathered waist.
est. $300–$500 sold: $345
William Doyle Galleries 11/16/1999

BENDEL, HENRI

DRESS, 1920s
Ivory chiffon embroidered with flame design emanating from intertwined bands in silver and gold sequins, white beads and rhinestones.
est. $300–$500 sold: $373
William Doyle Galleries 12/5/1996

BENNIS, SUSAN AND EDWARDS, WARREN

CLUTCH BAG, 1980s
Brown alligator envelope sewn in geometric patchwork with detachable shoulder strap.
est. $300–$500 sold: $690
William Doyle Galleries 11/12/1997

BERGDORF GOODMAN

EVENING ENSEMBLE, 1950s
Three-piece black silk with topographical pattern, coat with rhinestone buttons, halter top with rhinestone strap.
est. $100–$150 sold: $345
William Doyle Galleries 11/17/1994

EVENING GOWN, 1967
Grecian-style white crepe with silver bugle bead stripes, sleeveless wrap bodice with V neck and back, beaded faux belt and pleated skirt.
est. $150–$250 sold: $448
Skinner 12/16/1999

BERIN, HARVEY

COCKTAIL DRESS, 1950s
Silk taffeta with overall vermicelli embroidery, fitted bodice with rounded neckline, elbow-length sleeves, three-quarter-length skirt fitted over hips.
est. $300–$500 sold: $172.50
Skinner 9/14/2000

BERLYN, TINA

COCKTAIL DRESS, 1950s
Black silk crepe dress with allover beading of green rhinestones and bugle bead fringe, fitted silhouette with camisole bodice and knee-length skirt.
est. $300–$500 sold: $632.50
Skinner 12/16/1999

BES-BEN

HAT, 1940s
White satin hat in the shape of clasped hands, hands have red painted fingernails, a large gold-toned faux pearl and rhinestone cocktail ring.
est. $500–$700 sold: $2530
Skinner 9/14/2000

HAT, 1940s
Fitted hat composed of large red teardrop faux gemstones, green plastic leaves, and red net.
est. $300–$500 sold: $345
Skinner 9/14/2000

HAT, 1940s
Black felt spiral with a line of gilt beetles marching upwards, gold balls sprinkled throughout on net.
est. $600–$800 sold: $920
William Doyle Galleries 11/16/1999

HAT, 1940s
Black velvet curving base set with people of various nationalities worked in leather.
est. $200–$300 sold: $977
William Doyle Galleries 5/12/1999

HAT, 1940s
Green felt base with raised back set with six champagne bottles worked in leather with gilt paint tops.
est. $200–$300 sold: $3220
William Doyle Galleries 5/12/1999

HAT, 1940s
Curving base of gray felt topped with miniature plastic chairs, bookcase, and piano, inhabited by a pigtailed girl and her spotted furry friend.
est. $200–$300 sold: $2300
William Doyle Galleries 5/12/1999

HAT, 1940s
Plastic smiling Santa Claus faces attached to holly leaf sprigs, set on green felt base.
est. $200–$300 sold: $977
William Doyle Galleries 5/12/1999

HAT, 1940s
Close-fitting velvet and net headpiece adorned with papier-mâché yellow bananas and green leaves with gold leaf embellishment.
est. $300–$500 sold: $546
Skinner 12/16/1999

HAT, 1940s
Curving base of green burlap with brown and green leather grasshoppers and one toad.
est. $200–$300 sold: $1725
William Doyle Galleries 5/12/1999

HAT, 1950
Small crown shape covered with red silk jersey, trimmed with a multiplicity of miniature black records with red and green labels.
est. $800–$1200 sold: $4312
William Doyle Galleries 11/16/1999

HAT, 1950s
Head-hugging bands set with faux carved ivory and coral flowers, bands outlined with pearls and sprinkled throughout with pearls and rhinestones.
est. $300–$500 sold: $1265
William Doyle Galleries 11/16/1999

HAT, 1950s
Gray felt, cut-out crescent shapes, black and white leather skunks, each smelling a bouquet of felt flowers, labeled: Bes-Ben/Made in Chicago.
est. $500–$700 sold: $632.50
William Doyle Galleries 11/2/2000

HATS, 1950s
First, a shaped head-hugging form of black velvet sewn with six lizards at center point; the other with felt sewn pipe cleaner skunks running around.
est. $300–$500 sold: $2875
William Doyle Galleries 11/2/2000

HATS, 1950s
Each a plastic coil, the first, yellow with bees, the other, blue and green with balls. Each labeled.
est. $400–$600 sold: $431.25
William Doyle Galleries 11/2/2000

HAT, 1950s
Silk printed with chips and playing cards and a 3-D five-card hand fanned out at one side. Very good condition, tear to veil.
est. $500–$700 sold: $977.50
William Doyle Galleries 11/2/2000

HAT, 1950s
Black pillbox sewn with black, white, and red fabric penguins marching along perimeter, labeled: Bes-Ben/Made in Chicago, very good condition.
est. $400–$600 sold: $517.50
William Doyle Galleries 11/2/2000

HAT, 1950s
Padded velvet ivory hands with applied red plastic fingernails, large pearl and gilt metal ring and pearl bracelets. Labeled.
est. $800–$1200 sold: $1380
William Doyle Galleries 11/2/2000

HAT, 1950s
Green and brown leather grasshoppers and one green toad, labeled.
est. $500–$700 sold: $2587.50
William Doyle Galleries 11/2/2000

HAT, 1950s
Pearlized snail shells with straw bodies crawling amidst spikey grasses, labeled, excellent condition.
est. $1000–$1200 sold: $3162.50
William Doyle Galleries 11/2/2000

HAT, 1950s
Round ivy-covered crown with embroidered owls arranged around perimeter, labeled, excellent condition.
est. $400–$600 sold: $460
William Doyle Galleries 11/2/2000

HAT, 1950s
Coiled yellow plastic cord swarming with bees.
est. $150–$200 sold: $805
William Doyle Galleries 11/10/1998

HAT, 1950s
White straw bowler applied with white fuzzy cats holding green balls of yarn.
est. $150–$200 sold: $546
William Doyle Galleries 11/10/1998

HAT, 1950s
Ring of large gem-set rhinestone flowers arranged on a small black base, black veil sprinkled with rhinestones.
est. $600–$800 sold: $575
William Doyle Galleries 11/16/1999

BIBA, BY BARBARA HULANICKI

ENSEMBLE, 1970S
Long jacket with low V neck, patch pockets and square buttons, flared skirt, worked in cable knit pattern in shades of gray, black, and white.
est. $200–$300 sold: $258.75
William Doyle Galleries 5/2/2000

PANTS, 1968
Wide-cuffed, tan and gold knit with black spots.
est. $300–$500 sold: $460
William Doyle Galleries 11/16/1999

BIENEN-DAVIS

HANDBAG, 1950S
Brown alligator, cylindrical.
est. $100–$150 sold: $287
William Doyle Galleries 4/12/1995

BLASS, BILL

COCKTAIL DRESS, 1950S
Flesh-colored and metallic gold lace dress with gold sequins, floral pattern, scalloped neckline, open back, below-the-knee skirt with crinoline.
est. $400–$600 sold: $517.50
Skinner 9/14/2000

COCKTAIL ENSEMBLE, 1960S
Black silk sleeveless dress with matching jacket, dress has round neckline, A-line skirt, jacket with long sleeves and wide tab collar.
est. $150–$250 sold: $488
Skinner 12/16/1999

COCKTAIL SUIT, 1980S
Sequined jacket and pants, long-sleeved jacket with three broad stipes of yellow, red, and black. Pants black-sequined with black satin.
est. $1000–$1500 sold: $632
Skinner 12/16/1999

DRESS, 1960S
Multicolor velvet, fitted bodice, long-sleeved, with multicolored hand-painted feather hemline, above-the-knee length skirt.
est. not available sold: $1895
The Paper Bag Princess 4/5/2001

ENSEMBLE, 1960S
Black silk knee-length sleeveless cocktail dress with matching jacket; dress with round neck, A-line skirt; long-sleeved jacket with side pockets.
est. $150–$250 sold: $489
Skinner 12/16/1999

EVENING TRENCHCOAT, 1970S
Full-length, trenchcoat-style and belt, allover sequins, labeled: Bill Blass for Bond Street. Excellent condition.
est. $700–$900 sold: $977.50
William Doyle Galleries 11/2/2000

BOHAN, MARC

COAT, 1962
Black sheer silk cardigan with bracelet-length sleeves.
est. $100–$150 sold: $258
William Doyle Galleries 6/11/1997

COCKTAIL DRESS, 1961
Orange silk brocaded in gold with stylized design, long sleeves, knee-length skirt, colored bow in back.
est. 500–700 pounds sold: 977 pounds
Sotheby's London 11/25/1998

COCKTAIL DRESS, 1961
Black zibeline, long sleeves, V neck wrap-over bodice, full skirt with stiffened petticoat, interchangeable belts of fabric or black velvet with bow.
est. 400–600 pounds sold: 2300 pounds
Sotheby's London 11/25/1998

COCKTAIL DRESS, 1963
One-shouldered mint green silk matte jersey, rose at shoulder, pouf, and a floating panel to the floor.
est. $300–$500 sold: $373
William Doyle Galleries 6/11/1997

COCKTAIL DRESS, 1965
Strapless silk chiffon simple sheath form
draped with satin-edged chiffon panels.
est. 300–500 pounds sold: 368 pounds
Sotheby's London 11/25/1998

COCKTAIL DRESS, 1967
Purple gown falling to the floor from
round monastic-style front yoke extending
to wide back-baring straps, skirt with folds
at center with bow.
est. $300–$400 sold: $460
William Doyle Galleries 5/6/1998

COCKTAIL DRESS, 1968
Short, black silk jersey, round neck, long
sleeves, full skirt, sewn at cuffs and hem
with black ostrich fronds, belt sewn at ends
with beads.
est. $200–$250 sold: $690
William Doyle Galleries 6/11/1997

COCKTAIL ENSEMBLE, 1961
Black silk chiffon shell top fastening at the
back, slip dress beneath with multilayered
skirt of pleated chiffon, satin sash at the hips.
est. 400–600 pounds sold: 920 pounds
Sotheby's London 11/25/1998

DRESS, 1960s
Short and straight with square-cut armholes, melon silk faille applied with African
motif pattern worked in beads, faux shells,
Mylar, and sequins.
est. $400–$600 sold: $460
William Doyle Galleries 11/10/1998

ENSEMBLE, 1966
A-line ivory dress with pleated navy hem,
matching navy blue A-line double-breasted
jacket.
est. $600–$800 sold: $1725
Sotheby's 4/8/1998

ENSEMBLE, 1968
Sleeveless dress with camel bodice and
black/brown tweed skirt, double-breasted
tweed coat with mink-trimmed band collar
and pockets, tie belt.
est. $150–$200 sold: $316
William Doyle Galleries 11/12/1997

EVENING GOWN, 1963
Pink silk full-length gown with cap sleeves
and V décolletage, bodice densely applied
with colored pastes.
est. 300–400 pounds sold: 747 pounds
Sotheby's London 11/25/1998

EVENING GOWN, 1963
Multilayered skirt of pink organza,
overblouse worked in pink ribbon-work
rosebuds sewn with beads, trimmed with
beaded fringe, sleeveless bolero.
est. $300–$400 sold: $1725
William Doyle Galleries 5/6/1998

EVENING GOWN, 1973
Black crepe, low V neck plunging to meet
high waistband, full skirt sewn with trumpet gores, transparent chiffon jacket
trimmed with marabou.
est. $300–$500 sold: $747
William Doyle Galleries 11/10/1998

SUIT, 1961
Black and white tweed, double-breasted
jacket with separate self scarf, underdress
with black silk bodice and A-line tweed
skirt.
est. $200–$300 sold: $632
William Doyle Galleries 6/11/1997

SUIT, 1965
Black bouclé wool long-sleeved jacket,
sleeveless vest in off-white silk crepe, black
bouclé skirt.
est. $600–$800 sold: $1265
Sotheby's 4/8/1998

BON TON

HANDBAG, 1930s
Brown crocodile box bag with gold-toned
hardware and short crocodile handle,
brown satin lining.
est. $200–$300 sold: $316.25
Skinner 12/16/1999

BONWIT TELLER

HANDBAG, 1960s
Black crocodile handbag with circular crocodile handle and two exterior side pockets.
est. $1500–$2500 sold: $2185
Sotheby's 12/9/1998

BOTTEGA VENETTA

MESSENGER BAG, 1970s
Black, rust, square leather with snap-on shoulder strap attached to gold-tone ring hardware.
est. not available sold: $295
The Paper Bag Princess 1/26/2001

BOUÉ SOEURS

BED JACKET, 1920s
Tan pleated tulle trimmed with panels of peach organdy embroidered in cream with ribbon roses.
est. $60–$90 sold: $230
William Doyle Galleries 4/24/1996

DRESS, 1920s
Jumper shape, turquoise lawn, embroidered.
est. $1000–$1500 sold: $977
William Doyle Galleries 9/30/1993

BROOKS, DONALD

COAT, 1960s
Broadtail, double-breasted with black jeweled buttons, bottom portion of horizontal black mink bands, flat mink collar.
est. $1000–$1500 sold: $575
William Doyle Galleries 11/16/1999

COAT DRESS, 1960s
Brown, cream, and rust tweed, double-breasted with brown leather buttons.
est. $125–$175 sold: $258
William Doyle Galleries 4/24/1996

COCKTAIL DRESS, 1970s
Black-feathered full-length dress, black satin shoulder straps have bows in front and back.
est. $800–$1000 sold: $1495
Sotheby's 9/30/1999

DRESS, 1960s
Black silk jersey, halter style with long black silk ribbon belt that wraps around body in a Grecian style and ties at the waist.
est. not available sold: $325
The Paper Bag Princess 2/5/2001

BRUNO

COCKTAIL DRESS, 1940s
Black silk crepe, padded shoulders, embroidered down one side with gold bullion.
est. $200–$300 sold: $230
William Doyle Galleries 12/6/1995

BUGNAND, BOB

COAT, 1960s
Fuchsia with floral pattern, wide flat collar, high waistband tied in bow at front.
est. $500–$700 sold: $316
William Doyle Galleries 5/12/1999

COCKTAIL DRESS, 1958
Blue chine, strapless with bouffant skirt, fabric gathered at waist in cummerbund effect, accented at side with silk flowers.
est. $500–$700 sold: $373
William Doyle Galleries 5/12/1999

DRESS, 1960s
Yellow sleeveless chiffon with plunging neckline, jeweled rhinestone waistband and full layered chiffon skirt.
est. not available sold: $895
The Paper Bag Princess 1/9/1998

ENSEMBLE, 1959
Ivory and gold Indian silk brocade with pattern of elephants, lions, and birds, overblouse with long sleeves and peg leg pants, beaded bands on edges.
est. $400–$600 sold: $1725
William Doyle Galleries 5/12/1999

Evening Suit, 1960s
Wool houndstooth, navy and blue pattern studded with rhinestones.
est. $500–$700 sold: $460
William Doyle Galleries 5/12/1999

BURKE-AMEY

Cocktail Dress, 1960s
Red, olive, ivory, pink, lilac, gold, and taupe sequined dress, long sleeves, jewel neckline, floor-length, taupe silk lining, back zipper closure.
est. $300–$500 sold: $230
Skinner 12/16/1999

Dress, 1960s
Floor-length black silk empire-waisted sleeveless dress with low, round neckline and center front buttons that extend from neck to hem.
est. $300–$500 sold: $287.50
Skinner 9/14/2000

BURROWS, STEPHEN

Dress, 1970s
Silver panne velvet mid-calf-length wrap dress, short sleeves and signature zigzag topstiching on sleeves, neckline, hem.
est. $100–$200 sold: $373
Skinner 12/16/1999

Halter Top
Silver metal mesh with silver leather ties.
est. not available sold: $395
The Paper Bag Princess 3/1/1997

Pantsuit, 1970s
Black silk tunic and pants ensemble printed with pink, green, and blue feathered pattern, loose tunic, accordion collar, full sleeves, pleated cuffs.
est. $200–$400 sold: $345
Skinner 12/16/1999

Pantsuit, 1972
Pale yellow and red wool jacket and pants printed in bowling ball pattern. V neck, snap closure, long sleeves, patch pockets, wide-legged pants.
est. $200–$400 sold: $517
Skinner 12/16/1999

CALEM

Handbag, 1940s
Rectangular black quilted snakeskin handbag with "tortoise" Bakelite closure, quilted snail design, camel calfskin lining with two pockets.
est. $200–$300 sold: $258.75
Skinner 12/16/1999

CALLOT SOEURS

Cape, 1920
Seafoam silk taffeta edged with flat wide bands of taffeta and trimmed with fluted self bands and tiers of black Chantilly lace.
est. $750–$1000 sold: $977
William Doyle Galleries 4/12/1995

Cape, 1927
Beige net worked with iridescent blue-green sequins and gold metal thread in Egyptian wing design.
est. $400–$600 sold: $1150
William Doyle Galleries 11/12/1997

Chemise, 1926
Black silk crepe woven with gold lamé bands, skirt sewn with horizontal panel draping in two points in front.
est. $200–$300 sold: $1092
William Doyle Galleries 5/6/1998

Cocktail Dress, 1905
Peach chiffon, pouched bodice with pleated waistband, sleeves trimmed with gold lace, three-tiered skirt, two trimmed with gold lace, third velvet.
est. $1500–$2000 sold: $1725
William Doyle Galleries 11/10/1998

COCKTAIL DRESS, 1922
Sleeveless tubular chemise of ivory silk brocaded in gold metallic with Japanese-inspired floral and block pattern, outlined with pearls, train.
est. $2000–$3000 sold: $3450
William Doyle Galleries 11/16/1999

DRESS, 1920s
Black satin with gold lamé Art Deco foliate pattern, low-waisted blouson bodice, dangling jet bead ornaments at bodice front and side of hip.
est. $300–$500 sold: $805
William Doyle Galleries 5/6/1998

DRESS, 1920s
Cream linen, linen bobbin lace insets running vertically around the edges, linen underslip.
est. $400–$600 sold: $2760
William Doyle Galleries 11/16/1999

DRESS, 1927
Tubular, sleeveless ivory chiffon embroidered in ivory silk floss and pearls with flowers, inset lace panels.
est. $300–$500 sold: $977
William Doyle Galleries 5/6/1998

DRESS, 1927
Green chiffon with floral design worked in small pearlescent beads and gold thread, skirt sewn in two layers.
est. $300–$500 sold: $805
William Doyle Galleries 11/12/1997

DRESS, 1927
Tubular and sleeveless ivory chiffon embroidered in ivory silk floss and pearls with Chinese-inspired flowers.
est. $300–$500 sold: $517
William Doyle Galleries 11/12/1997

EVENING GOWN, 1905
Pink chiffon bodice with pintucked tulle, embroidered garlands of pastel flowers from shoulders to waist, pink jeweled ornaments at front and back.
est. $1000–$1200 sold: $3450
William Doyle Galleries 5/12/1999

EVENING GOWN, 1930s
Fitted, floor-length brown silk and metallic gold striped dress with silk roses and flowers adorning neckline, spaghetti strap bodice, bias-cut skirt.
est. $400–$600 sold: $690
Skinner 9/14/2000

CAPPUCI, ROBERTO

COCKTAIL DRESS, 1980s
Slubbed silk, bottom third of shift is flared and applied with multiple triangular pieces, forming fan shapes at each side, very good condition.
est. $400–$600 sold: $2070
William Doyle Galleries 11/2/2000

EVENING GOWN, 1964
Silk in three shades of pink, sewn on top with four triangular panels varying in length, back panel forms train, skirt embroidered with flowers.
est. $3000–$5000 sold: $2070
William Doyle Galleries 11/16/1999

CAR, BETH

SHOES, 1960s
Clear vinyl appliqué with racing car motifs.
est. $500–$700 sold: $316
William Doyle Galleries 9/30/1993

CARDIN, PIERRE

COAT, 1951
Black ribbed silk, single-breasted.
est. $500–$750 sold: $575
William Doyle Galleries 11/17/1994

COAT, 1960s
A-line, knee-length, large round side pockets, welted seams, band collar fastens to side with gold/silver button, black wool jersey lining.
est. $500–$700 sold: $632.50
Skinner 9/14/2000

Coat Dress, 1959
Plum wool fastening down the front to waistline with maroon buttons, gently gathered skirt with oversized pockets.
est. $200–$300 sold: $316
William Doyle Galleries 4/12/1995

Cocktail Dress, 1960s
Cloque ombré from lavender/blue to silver/bronze, collar embroidered with sequins, beads, and rhinestones.
est. $500–$750 sold: $632
William Doyle Galleries 4/24/1996

Cocktail Dress, 1960s
Overdress of cream silk crepe with long sleeve on one side, fold draped to hem in lieu of sleeve on other side, underdress of black silk.
est. $400–$600 sold: $460
William Doyle Galleries 4/24/1996

Cocktail Dress, 1969
Pink silk crepe sheath with tabard that wraps in back, beaded diamond-shaped motifs around the neck and tabard.
est. $750–$1000 sold: $920
Sotheby's 10/29/1997

Cocktail Dress, 1970
Short, white checkerboard jacquard, sheath dress under a one-shouldered tunic with diagonal hem edged with white ostrich.
est. $300–$500 sold: $431
William Doyle Galleries 4/24/1996

Cocktail Dress, 1970s
Black velvet, body and hem in shape of a chasuble, satin underslip, with long sleeves and high band neckline.
est. $300–$400 sold: $575
William Doyle Galleries 5/12/1999

Cocktail Dress, 1970s
Red silk chiffon draped and layered, sleeveless underdress has knife-pleated ruffle around hem, overdress attached to V neckline and falls in cowl.
est. $800–$1200 sold: $920
Sotheby's 10/29/1997

Cocktail Dress, 1976
Black silk georgette, four flared bias-cut tiers on the skirt in the style of the 1930s.
est. $600–$800 sold: $460
Sotheby's 10/29/1997

Dress, 1960s
Bib front camisole dress of pink satin, the skirt gathered at waist front, Duchesse satin woven in fuchsia and pink blocks, silk rose ornaments.
est. $300–$400 sold: $805
William Doyle Galleries 11/12/1997

Dress, 1960s
Black wool crepe, large metal breastplate decorates the front opening of the dress.
est. $400–$600 sold: $2760
Sotheby's 9/30/1999

Dress, 1960s
Sleeveless shift of fawn leather with purple hip band accented with off-center green and purple disc.
est. $300–$500 sold: $517
William Doyle Galleries 5/12/1999

Dress, 1960s
Black crepe sleeveless chemise sewn with long self loops extending from bodice yoke to hem.
est. $500–$700 sold: $1150
William Doyle Galleries 11/16/1999

Dress, 1960s
Black crepe sleeveless chemise sewn with long self loops extending from bodice yoke to hem.
est. $400–$600 sold: $920
William Doyle Galleries 11/10/1998

Dress, 1960s
Brown wool A-line, sleeveless, with large white patent leather dots appliqué.
est. not available sold: $595
The Paper Bag Princess 1/1/2000

Dress, 1960s
Navy wool knit with synthetic white patent leather appliqués on collar, cuff, hem, and front of dress.
est. $600–$800 sold: $862
Sotheby's 9/30/1999

DRESS, 1960s
Boat neck, long sleeves, overlapping sequins in five colors, some losses to sequins, labeled: Pierre Cardin Boutique/Paris.
est. $400–$600 sold: $632.50
William Doyle Galleries 11/2/2000

DRESS, 1970
Black and white wool tweed with long sleeves, ribbed patent leather hem, neck and center front patch pocket.
est. $400–$600 sold: $546
William Doyle Galleries 11/16/1999

DRESS, 1980s
Gray flannel, double-breasted coatdress with two rows of black snap studs, three-quarter-length sleeves, lined in China silk.
est. $800–$1200 sold: $3162
Sotheby's 10/29/1997

ENSEMBLE, 1960s
Navy wool lined in ivory wool.
est. $100–$150 sold: $3680
William Doyle Galleries 9/30/1993

ENSEMBLE, 1969
Bare-midriff black wool top has four silver eyelets with wool lacing, black fringed leather skirt.
est. $1000–$2000 sold: $1150
Sotheby's 4/8/1998

HANDBAG, 1960s
Fan-shaped, sewn with small beads in arcs of gold, yellow, and silver gray, with gilt metal spherical thumbpiece, chain-link shoulder strap.
est. $100–$150 sold: $230
William Doyle Galleries 4/12/1995

HANDBAG, 1960s
White and lavender geometric motif, beaded, with chain strap and PC logo on long gold metal clasp.
est. not available sold: $395
The Paper Bag Princess 4/5/1999

JACKET, 1960s
Soft black leather with red ribbed collar, bottom, and trimmings, heavy chrome buckle, labeled: Pierre Cardin/Paris/New York/Made in France.
est. not available sold: $510
eBay Online Auctions 9/29/2000

JUMPER, 1960s
Yellow wool with appliqué of black vinyl.
est. $100–$150 sold: $402
William Doyle Galleries 12/5/1996

JUMPER, 1960s
Black leather trimmed around the neck, at the patch pockets, narrow band of red and purple leather.
est. $200–$300 sold: $920
William Doyle Galleries 4/27/1994

JUMPER, 1960s
Navy hip-hugger miniskirt suspended from red patent leather straps that button in back and converge in front to a concentrically quilted square.
est. $300–$400 sold: $1265
William Doyle Galleries 11/10/1998

SKIRT, 1960s
Black leather fringed hip-hugger skirt.
est. $100–$150 sold: $402
William Doyle Galleries 11/17/1994

SUIT, 1960s
Orange fitted ribbed wool jacket and short A-line skirt with large white plastic buttons.
est. not available sold: $595
The Paper Bag Princess 5/8/1999

TABARD, 1960s
Red double-knit wool with black patent circular geometric appliqué, each of two panels sewn as a tube and connected at bodice by two wide strips.
est. $300–$500 sold: $1035
William Doyle Galleries 5/6/1998

TURTLENECK, 1970s
Blue ribbed wool with long sleeves and silver logo pin on neck.
est. not available sold: $165
The Paper Bag Princess 1/5/1999

CARDINALI

PANTSUIT, 1960S
Black, tunic-style dress with center slit and matching flare-legged pants.
est. not available sold: $495
The Paper Bag Princess 5/6/1998

CARETTE, YVONNE

EVENING JACKET, 1930S
Green velvet, surplice neckline with ruffled collar and draped curved sleeves.
est. $200–$300 sold: $115
William Doyle Galleries 4/12/1995

CARNEGIE, HATTIE

CARDIGAN, 1950S
Cream embroidered with black sequins and beads.
est. $50–$75 sold: $201
William Doyle Galleries 11/17/1994

COCKTAIL DRESS, 1950S
Silk chiffon printed with leopard spots in brown, gray, and off-white, camisole bodice with double spaghetti straps, full skirt from dropped waistline.
est. $150–$250 sold: $402
William Doyle Galleries 4/12/1995

COCKTAIL DRESS, 1950S
Short, red satin woven with wide chine floral stripes in green and gray-blue.
est. $150–$250 sold: $546
William Doyle Galleries 4/12/1995

COCKTAIL DRESS, 1950S
Red faille with fitted sleeves, V neck, self bow at waist, hem and sash with fringed ends.
est. $100–$150 sold: $460
William Doyle Galleries 4/12/1995

COCKTAIL DRESS, 1950S
Short, aquamarine silk with fitted surplice front and full bubble skirt, sewn front, the back of the shoulders with wings of aquamarine with turquoise.
est. $125–$175 sold: $460
William Doyle Galleries 12/5/1996

COCKTAIL DRESS, 1955
Blue silk, sleeveless bodice with triangular cut-outs of blue beaded fringe, sheer silk over flesh-colored chiffon covers bust area.
est. $600–$800 sold: $690
Skinner 12/16/1999

COCKTAIL SUIT, 1950S
Lavender check, jacket padded at hip and with a peplum, checks embroidered at regular intervals with blue iridescent beads, flared skirt.
est. $300–$500 sold: $805
William Doyle Galleries 11/10/1998

DRESS, 1930S
Black crimped silk, bias-cut, sleeveless with high-waisted bodice sewn to skirt with central point, cowl neck, skirt flared at hem.
est. $200–$300 sold: $431
William Doyle Galleries 5/12/1999

DRESS, 1940S
Black silk jersey, sewn with purple and pink sequins, high front neckline dipping to bare diamond-shaped back.
est. $400–$600 sold: $977
William Doyle Galleries 11/12/1997

DRESS, 1950S
Black silk jacquard with white polka dots, sleeveless dress, wide Peter Pan collar, matching black cashmere cardigan trimmed with the dotted silk.
est. $100–$150 sold: $230
William Doyle Galleries 4/12/1995

DRESS, 1960S
Green satin with camisole bodice, wide straps extending to below the waist accented by bows at end.
est. $100–$150 sold: $632
William Doyle Galleries 5/12/1999

DRESS, 1950S–1960S
Pink silk, with fitted bodice, short cap sleeves, buttons down the entire front of dress with full skirt.
est. not available sold: $495
The Paper Bag Princess 4/1/1997

EVENING GOWN, 1955
Midnight blue silk floor-length dress, sleeveless fitted bodice, full bias-cut skirt, thin belt at waist.
est. $600–$800 sold: $690
Skinner 12/16/1999

GLOVES, 1940S
Pink silk pongee with black embroidered punched linen gauntlets.
est. $40–$60 sold: $287
William Doyle Galleries 11/12/1997

HAT, 1930S
Wide-brimmed, black straw with small funnel-shaped crown, long chin ties of black tulle.
est. $60–$90 sold: $258
William Doyle Galleries 4/12/1995

SKIRT, 1950S
Midnight blue silk taffeta skirt composed of panels of knife pleats turned at right angles to form "pineapple" effect, full skirt with front pockets.
est. $100–$200 sold: $258
Skinner 12/16/1999

SUIT, 1940S
Black wool tailored jacket with pleated poet sleeve, fitted waist, and matching straight skirt.
est. not available sold: $595
The Paper Bag Princess 4/1/1997

SUIT, 1950S
Gray flannel with diamond-shaped rhinestone buttons.
est. $100–$150 sold: $373
William Doyle Galleries 12/6/1995

CARTIER

CLUTCH BAG, 1930S
Gold metallic and ivory brocade worked in Viennese block pattern.
est. $200–$300 sold: $632
William Doyle Galleries 11/10/1998

HANDBAG, 1950S
Matte black lizard with 14k gold circle.
est. $300–$500 sold: $977
William Doyle Galleries 12/6/1995

HANDBAG, 1970S
Brown suede with inset panels of red silk adorned with multicolored floral embroidery.
est. $500–$700 sold: $920
Sotheby's 12/9/1998

TOTE BAG, 1970S
Tote of sang de boeuf leather, suede portfolio.
est. $150–$200 sold: $345
William Doyle Galleries 11/10/1998

CARVEN

COCKTAIL DRESS, 1950S
Black silk faille faux halter bodice that ties at neck with cap sleeves, glass bead button-back closure, tucks at hip to create full skirt.
est. $400–$600 sold: $1840
Sotheby's 10/29/1997

CASHIN, BONNIE

COAT, 1960S
Pink leather three-quarter-length car coat, collarless with white stitching, brass closures.
est. not available sold: $595
The Paper Bag Princess 11/23/2000

COAT, 1970S
Ivory cotton below-the-knee-length coat with detachable hood, white leather trim at closure, cuffs, and hem, attached white leather change purse.
est. $300–$500 sold: $345
Skinner 9/14/2000

HANDBAG, 1960S
Leather, orange and red, hinged handles of gold-toned metal, signature change purse pocket on side, lined with multicolored stripe fabric.
est. not available sold: $370
eBay Online Auctions 10/1/2000

JACKET, 1970s
Royal blue leather, mandarin collar, brass toggle closures, patch pockets in back.
est. not available sold: $212.50
eBay Online Auctions 9/8/2000

SUIT, 1960s
Bouclé tweed wool two-piece suit, herringbone weave, leather-trimmed mandarin collar, pockets, and edging, A-line skirt, inverted pleating, and belt.
est. not available sold: $327.99
eBay Online Auctions 9/10/2000

CASHIN, BONNIE FOR COACH

HANDBAG, 1960s
Red leather, multistriped interior, one center and two side compartments, gold chain handles, labeled: Coach Leatherware, a Bonnie Cashin Design.
est. not available sold: $202.50
eBay Online Auctions 9/24/2000

WRIST BAG, 1960s
Orange leather, flat, square-shaped, wrist bag with brass hardware.
est. not available sold: $595
The Paper Bag Princess 2/1/2000

CASSINI, OLEG

BATHING SUIT, 1960s
White one-piece entitled "Carousel" with multicolored satin streamers fluttering the full length from bodice top.
est. $200–$300 sold: $287
William Doyle Galleries 5/12/1999

COCKTAIL DRESS, 1950s
Black lace over nude bodice, cap sleeves, fitted knee-length skirt.
est. not available sold: $695
The Paper Bag Princess 1/1/1998

HALTER TOP, 1970s
Gold metal mesh with leather ties at back.
est. not available sold: $395
The Paper Bag Princess 2/1/1998

CASTILLO, ANTONIO DEL

COAT, 1960s
Black silk with flamenco sleeves of looped black silk satin ribbon.
est. $400–$600 sold: $632
William Doyle Galleries 12/6/1995

CHANEL

BACKPACK, 1994
Drawstring closure, flap with gold-toned double "C" logo and leather and gold-toned chain straps, black leather interior with zip pocket.
est. $300–$500 sold: $575
Skinner 12/16/1999

BELT, 1980s
Leather belt with assorted gold buckles all along belt.
est. not available sold: $895
The Paper Bag Princess 3/2/2001

BELT, 1980s
Large gold-toned circle links with double row in front. Dangling interlocking C's within a circle.
est. not available sold: $595
The Paper Bag Princess 3/2/2001

BELT, 1980s
Black leather with a large gold-toned metal plate with Chanel in black letters.
est. not available sold: $1995
The Paper Bag Princess 3/2/2001

CARDIGAN, 1980s
Hip-length cardigan with cream trim, center front Chanel insignia buttons, patch pockets.
est. $400–$500 sold: $550
Ritchie's 9/20/2000

COAT, 1960s
Red, black, and blue plaid bouclé wool lined with black jersey, single-breasted with black jersey and gilt metal buttons.
est. $250–$400 sold: $460
William Doyle Galleries 12/5/1996

COAT, 1960s

Yellow and faun mohair tweed, double-breasted with lion's-head buttons, mink collar and cuffs.
est. $400–$600 sold: $546
William Doyle Galleries 11/12/1997

COAT, 1960s

Black, white, and brown bouclé tweed with pocket trim and edging of blue chenille.
est. $300–$500 sold: $517
William Doyle Galleries 12/5/1996

COAT, 1960s

Cream wool tweed lined with Mongolian lamb, single-breasted, cream plastic and gilt metal buttons.
est. $300–$500 sold: $805
William Doyle Galleries 4/12/1995

COAT, 1980s

Fuchsia wool and mohair raglan coat with wide lapels, front pockets, silk band trim at collar, pockets, hem, and wrists.
est. $300–$500 sold: $431
Skinner 12/16/1999

COCKTAIL DRESS, 1925

Black silk lace, side closing belt accented with lace bow at hip.
est. $3000–$4000 sold: $5780
Sotheby's 9/30/1999

COCKTAIL DRESS, 1930s

Black tulle with sweetheart neckline, bodice and skirt decorated with Art Deco fountain design in black sequins.
est. $1000–$1500 sold: $18,400
William Doyle Galleries 5/12/1999

COCKTAIL DRESS, 1930s

Gray/blue horizontal bands of lace alternating with net, silk, and chiffon underslip with lace hem.
est. $500–$700 sold: $1840
William Doyle Galleries 6/11/1997

COCKTAIL DRESS, 1950s

Beige tulle printed in floral pattern of orange and brown, edged with gold braid and sequins.
est. $750–$1000 sold: $546
William Doyle Galleries 11/17/1994

COCKTAIL DRESS, 1960s

Camisole bodice, fitted waist set with grosgrain ribbon, slightly full skirt, chiffon overlaid with bands of sheer gold lamé, labeled: Chanel no. 40764.
est. $600–$800 sold: $1092.50
William Doyle Galleries 11/2/2000

COCKTAIL DRESS, 1970s

Sheer striped silk dress in pink and purple, sleeveless bloused bodice, with high ruffled collar, flowing two-layered skirt, lilac satin bow.
est. $400–$600 sold: $374
Skinner 12/16/1999

COCKTAIL DRESS, 1980s

Black below-the-knee-length silk taffeta dress, bugle-beaded and velvet-trimmed bodice with sweetheart neckline, spaghetti straps, full skirt.
est. $500–$700 sold: $287.50
Skinner 9/14/2000

COCKTAIL DRESS, 1980s

Black silk jersey trimmed with wide satin ribbon fringe at bustline and skirt, spaghetti strap bodice.
est. $800–$1200 sold: $2587
Sotheby's 4/8/1998

COCKTAIL ENSEMBLE, 1960s

Gold brocade, sleeveless dress with diagonal tucks at each side of waist, two-button jacket trimmed with gold metallic braid.
est. $200–$300 sold: $632
William Doyle Galleries 5/6/1998

COCKTAIL JACKET, 1930s

Blue, sewn with sequins in vermiculate pattern, ivory satin lining revealed at neck and cuffs.
est. $1000–$1500 sold: $920
William Doyle Galleries 11/16/1999

DRESS, 1920s

Comprised of bands of Alençon-style lace connected by hemstitching, skirt of solid lace, chiffon slip attached at bodice, sleeves button at wrists.
est. $700–$900 sold: $1840
William Doyle Galleries 5/6/1998

DRESS, 1920s
Beige dress with sheer yoke, long sleeves.
est. $800–$1000 sold: $920
William Doyle Galleries 12/6/1995

DRESS, 1930s
Blue spangled chiffon embroidered with
blue paillettes on bodice in patchwork effect, long chiffon sleeves, matching scarf.
est. $2000–$3000 sold: $10,925
William Doyle Galleries 11/12/1997

DRESS, 1960s
Peach and cream wool woven with silver
and pink foil, sewn at the edges at four
pockets of the jacket with rows of gilt.
est. $300–$400 sold: $747
William Doyle Galleries 6/11/1997

DRESS, 1960s
Black wool, Nehru collar, black and gilt
metal buttons.
est. $750–$1000 sold: $575
William Doyle Galleries 4/27/1994

DRESS, 1960s
Navy tweed with white removable linen
collar and cuffs, buttoning down the front
to the waist with chain-link and filigree-
centered navy buttons.
est. $200–$300 sold: $805
William Doyle Galleries 4/12/1995

DRESS, 1980s
Navy knit mini column dress with camisole
bodice with taupe straps, matching taupe
jacket, long sleeves. Navy wool hip-length
jacket with three pockets.
est. $300–$500 sold: $287.50
Skinner 12/16/1999

ENSEMBLE, 1960s
Wool tweed woven with yellow, green, russet, and gilt threads, knee-length coat and
skirt, edges bound with gilt, yellow, and
black.
est. $600–$800 sold: $3220
William Doyle Galleries 11/16/1999

ENSEMBLE, 1960s
Single-breasted coat of cream wool tweed
lined with civet in a banded diamond pattern, skirt of civet edged with a band of
cream braid.
est. $300–$500 sold: $1380
William Doyle Galleries 12/5/1996

ENSEMBLE, 1980
Cream silk crepe dress with pleating and
kimono sleeves, black wool crepe coat with
gold-toned buttons.
est. $1500–$2000 sold: $2875
Sotheby's 10/29/1997

ENSEMBLE, 1985
Red wool blanket jacket with two front
pockets, trim at collar, closure, pockets,
hem, cuffs. Sleeveless ivory satin vest extending to mid-thigh.
est. $400–$600 sold: $402.50
Skinner 12/16/1999

ENVELOPE BAG, 1980s
Red leather with gilt metal chain.
est. $125–$175 sold: $373
William Doyle Galleries 12/5/1996

ENVELOPE BAG, 1980s
Quilted navy jersey with burgundy calf
corners.
est. $100–$150 sold: $287
William Doyle Galleries 12/5/1996

ENVELOPE BAG, 1980s
Quilted brown suede, with gilt metal chain
handle.
est. $150–$250 sold: $345
William Doyle Galleries 12/5/1996

EVENING BAG, 1980s
Black-sequined with gilt metal and black
leather tassel.
est. $200–$300 sold: $402
William Doyle Galleries 12/5/1996

EVENING BAG, 1980s
Black quilted satin with shoulder strap of
black braid through gilt metal link.
est. $150–$250 sold: $431
William Doyle Galleries 11/17/1994

C

EVENING BAG, 1980S
Black satin gathered onto a black lizard frame with a gilt metal chain.
est. $150–$250 sold: $402
William Doyle Galleries 12/5/1996

EVENING BLOUSE, 1960
Nude, sheer silk embroidered with small pearlescent nude sequins.
est. $500–$750 sold: $575
William Doyle Galleries 4/27/1994

EVENING GOWN, 1930S
Black lace with sweetheart neckline trimmed with grosgrain ribbon ending in back center bow, flared skirt.
est. $1500–$1700 sold: $5750
William Doyle Galleries 6/11/1997

EVENING GOWN, 1930S
Sleeveless body-hugging sheath with bloused bodice, cowl neck, low V back of silk chiffon, with cut-out self appliqués on skirt.
est. $6000–$8000 sold: $3450
William Doyle Galleries 5/2/2000

EVENING GOWN, 1980
Simple sheath with plunging V back, embroidered to the knee with black sequins, flaring gently with shaped band of white sequins forming fishtail hem.
est. 300–500 pounds sold: 345 pounds
Sotheby's London 11/25/1998

EVENING GOWN, 1980
Full-length gown with high neck trimmed with black satin bow, skirt with flamenco-style lace and bow-trimmed ruffled layers.
est. 200–300 pounds sold: 437 pounds
Sotheby's London 11/25/1998

EVENING GOWN, 1980S
Ivory silk chiffon floor-length gown, white-and-gold-sequined empire-waisted bodice with cap sleeves and round neckline, ivory silk lining.
est. $600–$800 sold: $345
Skinner 9/14/2000

EVENING JACKET, 1950S
Silk brocade woven in gold and cream with an abstract design, trimmed at pockets with gilt thread, lined in pink silk crepe.
est. $150–$250 sold: $345
William Doyle Galleries 4/12/1995

EVENING SUIT, 1970
Yellow and gold brocaded silk three-piece suit with gold braid trim, jacket, skirt, and sleeveless top.
est. $1000–$1500 sold: $3450
Sotheby's 4/8/1998

HANDBAG, 1980S
Black quilted leather with shoulder chain of gilt metal run through with black leather.
est. $150–$200 sold: $431
William Doyle Galleries 12/5/1996

HANDBAG, 1980S
Quilted navy jersey outlined with red braid, handle of red braid run through gilt metal links.
est. $200–$300 sold: $402
William Doyle Galleries 12/5/1996

HANDBAG, 1980S
Natural straw trimmed with black patent leather, gilt metal chain.
est. $125–$175 sold: $431
William Doyle Galleries 12/5/1996

HANDBAG, 1980S
Burgundy leather gathered onto a burgundy lizard frame, with gilt metal chain.
est. $100–$150 sold: $460
William Doyle Galleries 12/5/1996

HANDBAG, 1980S
Quilted beige fabric with beige leather trim, chain handle run through with leather.
est. $100–$150 sold: $345
William Doyle Galleries 6/11/1997

HANDBAG, 1980S
Black leather gathered onto a black lizard frame, gilt metal chain.
est. $100–$150 sold: $632
William Doyle Galleries 12/5/1996

Handbag, 1980s

Navy calf, rectangular with fold-over flap, interlocking "C" logo clasp, red cord edging, gilt metal chain run through with red cord.
est. $150–$200 sold: $575
William Doyle Galleries 5/12/1999

Handbag, 1980s

Black leather with exterior and interior fold-over flaps, interlocking gilt metal "C" logo gilt metal chain run through with leather.
est. $300–$400 sold: $805
William Doyle Galleries 5/6/1998

Handbag, 1990s

Rectangular handbag with double "C" clasp and leather and gold-toned chain-link strap, burgundy leather lining.
est. $400–$600 sold: $575
Skinner 12/16/1999

Jacket, 1930s

Ivory satin, slightly tapered at the waist, wide pointed collar, long sleeves puffed and shaped.
est. $600–$800 sold: $1150
William Doyle Galleries 6/11/1997

Pants, 1980s

Soft black leather pants, tapered leg with zipper bottoms, excellent condition, with logo on pocket.
est. not available sold: $895
The Paper Bag Princess 11/15/2000

Scarf, 1950s

Wool yarn stitched to beige China silk in abstract pattern in blue, rust, red, and ocher, long sleeves, button-down front bodice, metal chain at waist.
est. $200–$250 sold: $575
William Doyle Galleries 6/11/1997

Shoulder Bag, 1980s

Quilted pink satin with gold chain run through with self fabric.
est. $100–$150 sold: $373
William Doyle Galleries 6/11/1997

Suit, 1950s

Nubby white wool, jacket with patch pockets, welt side seams on straight skirt, short-sleeved black taffeta blouse, faux blouse cuffs at sleeve ends.
est. $400–$600 sold: $805
William Doyle Galleries 5/6/1998

Suit, 1960s

Pink tweed, jacket with band collar, sleeveless shirt, cuffs and waistband of pink, green, yellow, and blue plaid silk, straight skirt.
est. $600–$800 sold: $2990
William Doyle Galleries 11/16/1999

Suit, 1960s

Navy wool, Eisenhower-style jacket, molded gold buttons with slightly flared gored skirt.
est. $500–$700 sold: $402
William Doyle Galleries 11/10/1998

Suit, 1960s

Wool woven with wool yarns in horizontal stripes of purple, gold, and charcoal with jeweled buttons, jacket has Nehru collar, short hip-hugger skirt.
est. $600–$800 sold: $575
William Doyle Galleries 11/10/1998

Suit, 1960s

Cream tweed edged with rope-twisted yarn.
est. $100–$150 sold: $373
William Doyle Galleries 12/6/1995

Suit, 1960s

Boxy jacket to waist, flat collar, two patch pockets, gold lion's-head buttons, slightly flared skirt, labeled: Chanel, Estate of Mary McCarthy.
est. $700–$900 sold: $1265
William Doyle Galleries 11/2/2000

Suit, 1960s

Cream tweed woven with flecks of green and beige, edged at collar, pockets, and sleeves with green twisted yarn, cuffs of green silk.
est. $100–$150 sold: $632
William Doyle Galleries 12/6/1995

Suit, 1960s
Gold matelasse and pink silk, cardigan jacket with collar and cuffs of pink silk, sleeveless blouse with top-stitched neckband.
est. $200–$300 sold: $373
William Doyle Galleries 6/11/1997

Suit, 1960s
Blue tweed lined with matching silk, jacket with trim and toggle loops of blue wool braid, gilt metal filigree buttons, shell blouse.
est. $200–$300 sold: $460
William Doyle Galleries 6/11/1997

Suit, 1960s
Pink, cream, and black wool tweed, wrap shell blouse and lining of pink silk cloque, cardigan jacket with band collar.
est. $300–$400 sold: $575
William Doyle Galleries 6/11/1997

Suit, 1960s
Black basket-weave wool, single-breasted jacket with four pocket flaps of black satin applied and quilted with strips, skirt with satin waistband.
est. $300–$400 sold: $690
William Doyle Galleries 6/11/1997

Suit, 1960s
White shantung, cardigan jacket trimmed with white grosgrain, cuffs, inside and side pleat of skirt trimmed with navy grosgrain.
est. $200–$300 sold: $460
William Doyle Galleries 6/11/1997

Suit, 1960s
Cream bouclé wool, jacket showing pink raw silk lining at the collar, interlocked "C" buttons, wrap skirt with pink silk waistband, pink silk blouse.
est. 300–500 pounds sold: 782 pounds
Sotheby's London 11/25/1998

Suit, 1960s
Orange, cream, pink, and green plaid tweed, single-breasted jacket with pleated ruffle collar, skirt with box pleats at hem.
est. $150–$250 sold: $373
William Doyle Galleries 12/5/1996

Suit, 1960s
Black knit, single-breasted jacket with silk cord trim, gold-toned filigree buttons and cuff links, flared skirt.
est. $400–$600 sold: $345
William Doyle Galleries 11/12/1997

Suit, 1960s
Black wool, double-breasted Eisenhower-style jacket with black grosgrain bow at neck.
est. $250–$350 sold: $230
William Doyle Galleries 12/5/1996

Suit, 1960s
Mohair tweed woven in plaid pattern in mustard, green, camel, and gray, beige silk blouse figured with interlocking "C" logo, straight skirt.
est. $400–$600 sold: $747
William Doyle Galleries 11/12/1997

Suit, 1960s
Red tweed woven with fuchsia and olive mohair and black narrow tape, black buttons, red/fuchsia wool braid trim, quilted red lining.
est. $200–$300 sold: $373
William Doyle Galleries 12/5/1996

Suit, 1963
Ivory silk, sewn at collar, pockets, and skirt with self bands, sleeveless blouse with removable French cuffs, white silk twill jacket.
est. $300–$500 sold: $690
William Doyle Galleries 6/11/1997

Suit, 1965
Ivory bouclé with wool braid trim, metal lion's-head buttons, knitted wool shell.
est. $750–$1000 sold: $805
William Doyle Galleries 9/30/1993

Suit, 1966
Black silk chenille with removable coq feather collar, jacket with lion's-head buttons and wrap skirt.
est. $750–$1000 sold: $2070
Sotheby's 4/8/1998

SUIT, 1968

Black two-piece suit, knee-length skirt, long-sleeved jacket with bow, button-down front, lined in black silk couture, numbered.
est. not available sold: $3800
The Paper Bag Princess 9/15/2000

SUIT, 1970

Aqua, black, and white tweed with dress bodice of gold and blue brocade, jacket with four pockets, lion's-head gold-toned and aqua buttons.
est. $400–$600 sold: $1150
William Doyle Galleries 5/12/1999

SUIT, 1970s

Tweed woven in purple, lavender, rose, and ivory, jacket with small stand collar and patch pockets, gilt lion's-head buttons, box-pleated skirt.
est. 300–500 pounds sold: 287 pounds
Sotheby's London 11/25/1998

SUIT, 1975

Boxy jacket with two patch pockets, band collar, interlocking buttons with "C" logo, white starched faux collar and cuffs, skirt pleated in front.
est. $300–$500 sold: $374
William Doyle Galleries 5/2/2000

CHAPMAN, CEIL

COCKTAIL DRESS, 1950s

Black jersey with Austrian-style draped bodice, sleeves, and skirt front, skirt stiffened and full at back.
est. $200–$400 sold: $373
William Doyle Galleries 5/12/1999

COCKTAIL DRESS, 1950s

Black crepe with sequins in vermicelli pattern, flared below-the-knee skirt.
est. $400–$600 sold: $1035
Skinner 12/16/1999

DRESS, 1940s

Black taffeta full skirt with shirred circles.
est. $400–$600 sold: $460
William Doyle Galleries 9/30/1993

DRESS, 1940s

Pink chiffon, strapless with gathered bodice and full multilayered knee-length skirt.
est. not available sold: $495
The Paper Bag Princess 3/1/1999

EVENING GOWN, 1950s

Fitted sheath of black crepe with camisole bodice, beaded in vermiculate design.
est. $100–$150 sold: $805
William Doyle Galleries 6/11/1997

EVENING PANTSUIT, 1960s

Black velvet decorated with silver beads, sequins, and rhinestones at neck and waist.
est. $400–$600 sold: $460
Sotheby's 9/30/1999

CHLOÉ

COCKTAIL DRESS, 1980s

Black crepe sheath, front embroidered with a sequined minidress hanging on a silver hanger, back bared in diamond shape.
est. $100–$150 sold: $2300
William Doyle Galleries 5/6/1998

DRESS, 1970s

Beige crepe de chine printed with Art Deco motifs in brown, edged with pleated ruffle.
est. $80–$120 sold: $172
William Doyle Galleries 12/6/1995

DRESS, 1975

Black hand-painted silk with multicolored flower bouquets and zigzags, kimono sleeves and pleated skirt.
est. $1000–$1500 sold: $1150
Sotheby's 4/8/1998

CLARK, OSSIE

COCKTAIL DRESS, 1970s

Black crepe, bodice with plunging slit, sewn on either side with triple pleats that extend the length of the skirt, tying at neck.
est. $400–$600 sold: $805
William Doyle Galleries 5/12/1999

DRESS, 1970s
Cream crepe wrap-around style with
slashed open back and deep V neck to
waist, extra-long sleeves puffed at the wrist
and finished with buttoned cuffs.
est. 100–150 pounds sold: 172 pounds
Sotheby's London 11/25/1998

DRESS, 1970s
Black crepe, floor-length, bodice slit at center front and cut to waist in back, long
sleeves with ruffles cut to expose shoulder
and upper arm.
est. $600–$800 sold: $460
William Doyle Galleries 5/2/2000

DRESS, 1970s
Black vertically crimped silk or rayon,
matte surface, pointed collar and cuffs in
satin, raglan sleeves gathered into dress
with wide cuffs.
est. $400–$600 sold: $230
William Doyle Galleries 5/2/2000

COLE OF CALIFORNIA

BATHING SUIT, 1940s
Strapless bathing suit with heart-shaped
neckline, elasticized fabric with allover sequin beading, back zipper closure.
est. $200–$300 sold: $316.25
Skinner 9/14/2000

COLLINS, ENID

HANDBAG, 1960s
Natural wood adorned with paint and
"gems."
est. $200–$300 sold: $690
Sotheby's 12/9/1998

COMME DES GARÇONS

ENSEMBLE, 1983
Sculptural composition of black and white
cotton pieces with overlapping raw seams,
oversized top, cowl neck, winged shoulders, full skirt.
est. $200–$300 sold: $1092.50
William Doyle Galleries 5/2/2000

ENSEMBLE, 1983
Unbleached tricot and muslin, oversized
top and gathered skirt, top sewn of large ir-
regular patches, skirt same with raw edges
and torn effect.
est. $200–$300 sold: $1150
William Doyle Galleries 5/2/2000

SHOES, 1980s
Clear plastic tie shoes with white top
stitching, air-vent holes.
est. $200–$300 sold: $230
William Doyle Galleries 11/16/1999

CONNOLLY, SYBIL

EVENING ENSEMBLE, 1950s
White, machine Irish-crocheted midriff top
and a blue floor-length skirt of shirred
linen.
est. $300–$500 sold: $345
William Doyle Galleries 11/16/1999

SUIT, 1950
Gray flannel, peplum jacket curving up in
front with slight padding at hips, black velvet band outlining collarless V neckline,
straight skirt.
est. $100–$150 sold: $517
William Doyle Galleries 11/10/1998

COPELAND, JO FOR PATTULLO

COAT, 1960s
Red wool with rhinestone buttons and
half-belt in back.
est. $100–$150 sold: $230
William Doyle Galleries 12/6/1995

COCKTAIL DRESS, 1940
Green satin embroidered with sequin fish.
est. $300–$500 sold: $172
William Doyle Galleries 9/30/1993

COCKTAIL DRESS, 1950s
Black silk sleeveless sheath with black
taffeta draped overskirt.
est. $200–$300 sold: $172
William Doyle Galleries 4/27/1994

COURRÈGES, ANDRÉ

Boots, 1963
White kid leather stamped in gold "Courrèges, Paris" with slightly squared toes, decorative center seam, stitched decoration and bow trimming.
est. 450–650 pounds sold: 437 pounds
Sotheby's London 11/25/1998

Coat, 1960s
Blue-checked, double-breasted, asymmetrically shaped patch pockets, back belt.
est. $300–$500 sold: $546
William Doyle Galleries 11/12/1997

Coat, 1960s
Cream silk, single-breasted with small stand-up shawl collar, quilted China silk lining.
est. $100–$150 sold: $201
William Doyle Galleries 12/6/1995

Coat, 1960s
Vinyl with yellow and white stripes superimposed with aqua grid, double-breasted, wide aqua leather belt.
est. $100–$150 sold: $373
William Doyle Galleries 6/11/1997

Coat, 1960s
Navy wool, single-breasted with silver-toned buttons, turned-up cuffs, back-buttoned belt.
est. $150–$200 sold: $402
William Doyle Galleries 6/11/1997

Coat, 1960s
Black wool, hooded, knee-length, with nylon trim.
est. not available sold: $981
Vintage Designs Ltd. 2/5/2001

Coat, 1960s
Black wool, knee-length with hood and synthetic leather trim.
est. not available sold: $980
What Comes Around Goes Around 2/20/2001

Coat, 1960s
Cream and beige double knit with plain cream front yoke, band collar, prominent buttoned vertical belt loops, repeated look at sleeve ends.
est. $600–$800 sold: $633
William Doyle Galleries 5/2/2000

Coat, 1960s
Cream wool twill, single-breasted with top-stitched seams.
est. $200–$300 sold: $517
William Doyle Galleries 6/11/1997

Coat, 1965
White leather, mid-calf with horizontal rectangular cut-outs joined in front by white leather tie.
est. $300–$500 sold: $805
Sotheby's 4/8/1998

Coat, 1970
Woven small, textured pattern, buttons at left, patch pockets, wide rounded flat collar, welt seaming at all edges, self belt, very good condition.
est. $800–$1200 sold: $1380
William Doyle Galleries 11/2/2000

Coat, 1970s
Green and white wool and acrylic blend three-quarter-length coat, long sleeves, pointed collar, center-front button closure.
est. $150–$250 sold: $920
Skinner 12/16/1999

Coat, 1970s
Fitted three-quarter-length, with four flap pockets, two slit pockets, welted seam detail, back slit with buttons, orange lining, # 17801 at neckline.
est. $300–$500 sold: $805.00
Skinner 9/14/2000

Coat, 1970s
Pink double knit, high-waisted with self belt, front and back welt seam, white patent leather buttons.
est. $150–$200 sold: $690
William Doyle Galleries 5/6/1998

COAT, 1971
Navy crinkle patent with front pockets,
front snap closures, self belt, white zippers
and Courrèges logo on front.
est. $800–$1200 sold: $1035
Sotheby's 4/8/1998

COCKTAIL DRESS, 1960s
Bands of black silk inset with bands of
sheer black silk revealing the beige silk lining, sleeveless with shoulder straps and
slightly flared skirt.
est. $200–$300 sold: $1035
William Doyle Galleries 12/5/1996

COCKTAIL DRESS, 1970s
Black floor-length A-line with high jumper
bodice, straps of black leather sewn with
bows at each join.
est. $500–$700 sold: $1495
William Doyle Galleries 11/16/1999

DRESS, 1960s
Cream wool A-line shift, long sleeves, deep
waist, tie belt.
est. not available sold: $495
The Paper Bag Princess 1/1/2001

DRESS, 1960s
Brown wool crepe maxidress tank-style
with matching belt at waist.
est. not available sold: $695
The Paper Bag Princess 9/10/2000

DRESS, 1960s
Orange cotton with puckered bib front,
straps buttoning at back waist.
est. $300–$400 sold: $517
William Doyle Galleries 5/12/1999

DRESS
Orange wool, can be worn with the sleeves
as a coat or without the sleeves as a dress.
est. not available sold: $512
eBay Online Auctions 11/24/1999

DRESS, 1965
Silver organza with woven silver circles.
est. $500–$750 sold: $575
William Doyle Galleries 9/30/1993

DRESS, 1965
Brown and white checked sleeveless A-line
shift with round neckline bordered in
brown, rounded patch pockets.
est. $200–$300 sold: $431
William Doyle Galleries 5/12/1999

DRESS, 1967
Baby-girl-style dress, ivory wool trimmed
with navy scallops.
est. $300–$500 sold: $431
William Doyle Galleries 9/30/1993

DRESS, 1968
White cotton piqué with scalloped yoke,
pockets of pink piqué.
est. $200–$300 sold: $460
William Doyle Galleries 12/6/1995

DRESS, 1970
Light pink cotton A-line with cap sleeves,
flower-shaped cut-outs at neckline have
gauze inserts with sequin centers.
est. $500–$700 sold: $8625
Sotheby's 4/8/1998

DRESS, 1970s
Short-sleeved with square neckline, empire
waist, below-knee-length skirt, white plastic buttons, white logo on chest. #
0054371 at neckline.
est. $200–$300 sold: $402.50
Skinner 9/14/2000

ENSEMBLE, 1960s
Double-weave camel wool woven in black
and brown check on the reverse, double-
breasted, hip-hugger skirt with checked belt.
est. $125–$175 sold: $345
William Doyle Galleries 11/12/1997

ENSEMBLE, 1960s
Orange wool sweater, with logo on chest.
est. not available sold: $295
The Paper Bag Princess 11/1/1996

ENSEMBLE, 1970s
Navy crinkle vinyl jacket with Courrèges
logo, wool ribbed sweater, and flat front
wool wide-legged pants.
est. not available sold: $795
The Paper Bag Princess 7/1/1997

HALTER TOP, 1960s
White sheer knit, halter neck with tie at waist.
est. not available sold: $185
The Paper Bag Princess 5/1/1999

HANDBAG, 1960s
Rectangular, with cutout white leather Courrèges insignia on front panel, shoulder strap, zippered top.
est. $100–$150 sold: $400
Ritchie's 9/20/2000

HANDBAG, 1970s
Navy patent leather shoulder bag with large white logo on front.
est. not available sold: $385
What Comes Around Goes Around 12/31/2000

JACKET
White crinkle vinyl with pockets and button-down front, logo on the breast.
est. not available sold: $295
The Paper Bag Princess 1/1/1997

JACKET, 1960s
Brown crinkle vinyl with snap closures and white crinkle vinyl Courrèges logo.
est. $100–$150 sold: $258
William Doyle Galleries 12/5/1996

JACKET, 1960s
Cropped green crinkle vinyl with Courrèges logo on breast.
est. not available sold: $595
The Paper Bag Princess 2/1/1997

JUMPER, 1970
Wool floor-length, sleeveless, square neckline, trim at seams, pockets, closure, #71547 at neckline.
est. $300–$500 sold: $747.50
Skinner 9/14/2000

SUIT, 1960s
Leopard wool trimmed with brown yarn fringe at collar and cuffs.
est. $600–$800 sold: $431
William Doyle Galleries 9/30/1993

SUIT, 1970s
Brown crinkle vinyl, cropped jacket fastening with white snaps, white logo inset with bell-bottom hip-hugger pants.
est. $150–$200 sold: $460
William Doyle Galleries 11/12/1997

SUNGLASSES, 1965
Off-white plastic with opaque slit lenses.
est. $100–$150 sold: $460
William Doyle Galleries 11/17/1994

SWEATER, 1960s
Yellow wool, ribbed, short-sleeved with small white logo on chest.
est. not available sold: $195
The Paper Bag Princess 2/5/2000

SWEATER, 1960s
Light green, ribbed wool with long sleeves and logo on the chest.
est. not available sold: $195
The Paper Bag Princess 2/5/2000

SWEATER, 1960s
Orange knit long-sleeved turtleneck with logo on chest.
est. not available sold: $250
What Comes Around Goes Around 1/25/2000

TURTLENECK, 1960s
Sheer blue wool blend knit body with wool turtleneck and cuffs.
est. not available sold: $225
The Paper Bag Princess 12/1/1997

CROSS, MARK

CASE, 1930s
Brown textured leather with beige and orange ribbed silk top stitched in diamond pattern, sterling mirror, brushes, cut-crystal containers.
est. $400–$600 sold: $258
William Doyle Galleries 12/5/1996

ENVELOPE BAG, 1970s
Tan grained leather with white top stitching.
est. $75–$100 sold: $230
William Doyle Galleries 6/11/1997

HANDBAG, 1960S
Black crocodile with ribbed gold button
closure.
est. $600–$800 sold: $1092
Sotheby's 12/9/1998

DACHÉ, LILLY

COCKTAIL DRESS, 1950S
Taupe mousseline with strapless draped
bodice and full ankle-length skirt.
est. $100–$125 sold: $230
William Doyle Galleries 12/5/1996

COCKTAIL DRESS, 1950S
Pewter knit crewel embroidered with gray
scrolls with accents of iridescent charcoal
beads, low V neck, elbow-length sleeves.
est. $100–$150 sold: $345
William Doyle Galleries 12/5/1996

DRESS, 1950S
Black satin with shawl collar.
est. $150–$250 sold: $230
William Doyle Galleries 4/27/1994

HAT, 1930S
Navy felt, wide brim rolled in front,
trimmed with red, yellow, and green
chevron ornament.
est. $150–$200 sold: $258
William Doyle Galleries 11/12/1997

HAT, 1940S
Taupe fur felt with small turned-back brim,
decorated with three pink silk roses, a
strand of pearls, and two-tone striped ostrich feathers.
est. $100–$150 sold: $920
William Doyle Galleries 11/16/1999

HAT, 1940S
Black wool sewn with iridescent sequins
and black soutache.
est. $75–$100 sold: $201
William Doyle Galleries 6/11/1997

HAT, 1950S
Large black fur felt with ostrich feather
brim.
est. not available sold: $295
The Paper Bag Princess 1/5/2000

HAT, 1950S
Black straw with fringe along the edge of
the wide brim.
est. not available sold: $265
The Paper Bag Princess 5/9/1999

DALÍ, SALVADOR

TIE, 1930S
"Gypsy Mandolin," depicting ethereal body
of a woman merged with emerging form
and suspended between two stringed in-
struments, ivory and cream on red.
est. $150–$175 sold: $258
William Doyle Galleries 6/11/1997

TIE, 1930S
White swans with looped necks sitting on
pink egg forms, each wearing a crown
with a candle on its head, red ground.
est. $150–$175 sold: $230
William Doyle Galleries 6/11/1997

TIE, 1930S
"The Olympiad," Olympic torches, the
flames of each merged with a double
image woman's profile in white, brown,
and green against swirling ground.
est. $150–$175 sold: $287
William Doyle Galleries 6/11/1997

TIE, 1930S
Black and white scrolling foliate bracket
supporting a candle, set against curvilinear
lilac and red forms.
est. $150–$175 sold: $230
William Doyle Galleries 6/11/1997

TIE, 1930S
Carousel horse and angel flying above, each
in white on yellow sections of curvilinear
yellow and rust forms set on brown
ground.
est. $150–$175 sold: $287
William Doyle Galleries 6/11/1997

TIE, 1930S
Red satin with diagonal gold stripe flanked
by two tongues of flame, each has woman's
face and flowing tresses emerging.
est. $150–$175 sold: $258
William Doyle Galleries 6/11/1997

TIE, 1930s
Ecru, red, and white stylized lilies drawn in black on red ground.
est. $150–$175 sold: $230
William Doyle Galleries 6/11/1997

TIE, 1930s
"Cinderella's Slipper," high-heeled pumps set on fabric unrolling from a bolt, peach and white on brown.
est. $150–$175 sold: $287
William Doyle Galleries 6/11/1997

TIE, 1930s
"The Paradise Wall," curvilinear red wall beyond which is a woman's head emerging from sea form.
est. $150–$175 sold: $258
William Doyle Galleries 6/11/1997

TIE, 1930s
Two stepped bridges each in the shape of a high-heeled shoe sprouting a tree, set on mauve and red geometric ground.
est. $150–$175 sold: $258
William Doyle Galleries 6/11/1997

DE GIVENCHY, HUBERT

BATHING SUIT, 1970s
White one-piece Lycra, V-neck with red G logos.
est. not available sold: $165
The Paper Bag Princess 6/6/1999

BOLERO JACKET, 1952
Rose velvet and mousseline petals with crystal dewdrops.
est. $750–$1000 sold: $1725
William Doyle Galleries 4/27/1994

COAT, 1950s
Red satin swing coat with jewel neckline, modified kimono sleeves and slanted pockets.
est. $300–$500 sold: $1035
William Doyle Galleries 6/11/1997

COAT, 1960
Chine matelasse with floral designs in fuchsia, red, yellow, and green against a black ground.
est. $150–$200 sold: $546
William Doyle Galleries 12/5/1996

COAT, 1960s
Green stretch wool knit, double-breasted with small fold-over collar, slanted pockets, curved shoulder yoke, angular sleeve seams.
est. $500–$700 sold: $517
William Doyle Galleries 11/16/1999

COAT, 1970s
Maxi-length spotted faux fur.
est. not available sold: $495
The Paper Bag Princess 12/1/1997

COCKTAIL DRESS, 1950s
Black silk taffeta, long-sleeved bodice sewn with low V moiré plastron extending into stand-away collar, bouffant skirt, multiple petticoats.
est. $700–$900 sold: $4312
William Doyle Galleries 11/10/1998

COCKTAIL DRESS, 1960s
Velvet cut to black satin in a pattern of leaves and flowers, sleeveless bodice.
est. $200–$300 sold: $488
William Doyle Galleries 4/12/1995

COCKTAIL DRESS, 1960s
Wool, long sheath with boat neck, back gathered in folds with black satin ribbon, rhinestone pavé flower.
est. $750–$1000 sold: $517
William Doyle Galleries 4/27/1994

COCKTAIL DRESS, 1960s
Underdress of orange silk gauze, bolero overbodice of gauze embroidered with beads and feathers in orange and yellow.
est. $500–$750 sold: $460
William Doyle Galleries 12/6/1995

Cocktail Dress, 1960s
Underdress of orange silk gauze, bolero overbodice of the gauze embroidered with beads and feathers in orange and yellow.
est. $500–$750 sold: $517
William Doyle Galleries 4/24/1996

Cocktail Dress, 1960s
Black velvet sheath, long sleeves of sheer black silk with rhinestones.
est. $750–$1000 sold: $632
William Doyle Galleries 4/27/1994

Cocktail Dress, 1960s
Embroidered with black paillettes and sewn at center of bodice with pink satin bow.
est. $400–$600 sold: $316
William Doyle Galleries 6/11/1997

Cocktail Dress, 1960s
Pink silk organdy sleeveless dress gathered at the waist, matching bolero vest with green, white, and gold beading.
est. $1000–$1500 sold: $1150
Sotheby's 4/8/1998

Cocktail Dress, 1961
Black satin with black velvet edges.
est. $750–$1000 sold: $517
William Doyle Galleries 9/30/1993

Cocktail Dress, 1965–1966
Fuchsia silk damask with two straps on either side of neck, bell-shaped skirt and bow at center front.
est. $1500–$2000 sold: $5175
Sotheby's 4/8/1998

Cocktail Dress, 1970s
Black gazar, sleeveless chemise dress sewn around the hem with a stiff flounce scalloped at the top in back.
est. $400–$600 sold: $1380
William Doyle Galleries 6/11/1997

Cocktail Dress, 1980s
Black silk velvet with paisley-patterned embroidery and black rhinestones, straps and bodice with bands of black sequins, beads and fringe.
est. $2000–$3000 sold: $1725
Sotheby's 10/29/1997

Cocktail Ensemble, 1960s
Black gazar appliquéd with black embroidered rondels sewn with black rhinestones and beads, hourglass-shaped sleeveless dress, single-breasted jacket.
est. $400–$600 sold: $1035
William Doyle Galleries 12/5/1996

Dress, 1950s
Navy silk with plain front bodice, short sleeves, bouffant skirt sewn at center with "double-breasted" panel.
est. $300–$500 sold: $1092
William Doyle Galleries 11/12/1997

Dress, 1970s
Sheer silk chiffon with long-cuffed sleeves, high round neck, pleated bodice, full skirt, self sash and separate scarf shawl.
est. $300–$500 sold: $1955
William Doyle Galleries 5/2/2000

Ensemble, 1960s
Black sleeveless dress with slightly gathered skirt and fitted jacket, silk quilted in diamond pattern.
est. $300–$500 sold: $1610
William Doyle Galleries 11/10/1998

Evening Coat, 1960s
Black and white wool, empire waist A-line dress, white bodice with wide straps buttoning at front, black skirt and bolero jacket with white lapels.
est. $200–$300 sold: $1380
William Doyle Galleries 11/10/1998

Evening Coat Dress, 1960s
Black bouclé wool with long black sequined sleeves.
est. $750–$1000 sold: $431
William Doyle Galleries 4/27/1994

Evening Ensemble, 1956
Tan wool tweed sheath with matching coat.
est. $2000–$3000 sold: $2760
Sotheby's 9/30/1999

Evening Ensemble, 1960s

Strapless, black wool grosgrain dress and jacket with notched lapels and elbow-length sleeves.
est. $400–$600 sold: $575
Sotheby's 10/29/1997

Evening Ensemble, 1960s

Strapless, yellow satin embroidered with rows of silver beads ending in silver loops, yellow satin jacket with mandarin collar to match.
est. $1500–$2000 sold: $1725
Sotheby's 10/29/1997

Evening Gown, 1950s

Russet/black changeante taffeta, strapless cuffed bodice, fan pleating at waist into full skirt, bustle effect in back.
est. $800–$1200 sold: $4140
William Doyle Galleries 11/12/1997

Evening Gown, 1960s

Printed chiffon, strapless bodice, one halter strap, wrapped with boned band at bare center back, skirt slightly gathered at waist, labeled: Givenchy.
est. $800–$1200 sold: $2300
William Doyle Galleries 11/2/2000

Evening Gown, 1960s

Strapless minimalist linen sheath with A-line skirt and wrap back, obi-style shoulder wrap.
est. $800–$1200 sold: $4025
William Doyle Galleries 5/2/2000

Evening Gown, 1960s

White silk organza printed in red with houndstooth and a grid, long-sleeved bodice and strapless underbodice, skirt with ruffle, shawl.
est. $200–$300 sold: $920
William Doyle Galleries 4/24/1996

Evening Gown, 1970s

Long with blue gazar skirt sewn to slip top, outer bodice is a middy-style blouse with low V front, very good condition.
est. $500–$700 sold: $1380
William Doyle Galleries 11/2/2000

Evening Gown, 1984

Blue and black polka dot silk faille, pouf bodice trimmed at waist with silk flower, skirt gathered into bow at back.
est. 400–600 pounds sold: 402 pounds
Sotheby's London 11/25/1998

D

Suit, 1950s

Coral wool jacket with small collar, bracelet-length sleeves, pocket flaps trimmed with colored ribbon, straight skirt.
est. 400–600 pounds sold: 437 pounds
Sotheby's London 11/25/1998

Suit, 1956

Black bouclé wool, jacket with petersham trim and hook-and-eye fastening, wrap-around skirt similarly trimmed.
est. 400–600 pounds sold: 402 pounds
Sotheby's London 11/25/1998

Suit, 1966

Gray and white wool herringbone fitted jacket with Bermuda collar, double back zipper on skirt.
est. $3000–$4000 sold: $10,350
Sotheby's 10/29/1997

Suit, 1970s

Green loden cloth single-breasted jacket trimmed with black velvet and faille, skirt of black velvet, blouse of green and black plaid silk.
est. $100–$150 sold: $402
William Doyle Galleries 12/5/1996

DE LA RENTA, OSCAR

Coat, 1980s

Full-length shearling, A-line coat with fur collar, center-front buttons, cuffed sleeves, welted seam detail.
est. $600–$800 sold: $345
Skinner 9/14/2000

Coat, 1980s

Pieced boiled wool full-length coat composed of pink, brown, green, blue, tan, and red panels in modified sunburst pattern.
est. $800–$1000 sold: $1380
Skinner 9/14/2000

Cocktail Dress, 1970s
Metallic gold, brown, and orange brocade floor-length dress, fitted bodice with square neckline and brown fur cap sleeves, A-line skirt, wide belt.
est. $300–$500 sold: $316.25
Skinner 9/14/2000

Cocktail Dress, 1980s
One-shouldered floor-length dress, white bodice with diagonal rows of white beads and rhinestones, black silk organza skirt with front bow.
est. $800–$1000 sold: $633
Skinner 12/16/1999

Dress, 1960s
Floor-length and strapless, trompe l'oeil bow in bugle beads at center front, labeled: Oscar de la Renta, excellent condition.
est. $300–$500 sold: $460
William Doyle Galleries 11/2/2000

Evening Jacket, 1960s
Black silk organza, knee-length, with nine rows of large ruffles, elbow-length ruffled sleeves.
est. $150–$200 sold: $431
Skinner 12/16/1999

Evening Jacket, 1980s
19th-century-inspired black wool jacket embroidered with black jet and silk cord in foliate pattern, open front, long sleeves, black fox fur trim.
est. $300–$500 sold: $1150
Skinner 12/16/1999

Evening Skirt, 1980s
Fuchsia, forest green, white, black, and orange sequined "plaid" knee-length skirt. Multicolored fringe at hem, black velvet belt.
est. $200–$400 sold: $316
Skinner 12/16/1999

Pantsuit, 1968
Black and white large, bold op art, poplin zip front, three-quarter-length top and full leg, lined slacks, never worn, with original tags.
est. not available sold: $750
The Way We Wore 10/1/1999

DE PARIS, LUCILLE

Case, 1950s
Black calf in the shape of a doctor's bag, with two handles.
est. $300–$500 sold: $747
William Doyle Galleries 5/12/1999

Evening Bag, 1960s
Black alligator with silver-toned metal frame enameled in black and set with rhinestones and marcasite.
est. $200–$300 sold: $431
William Doyle Galleries 12/5/1996

Handbag, 1940s
Red ostrich, box style with two handles and gold-toned clasp.
est. not available sold: $495
The Paper Bag Princess 5/1/1998

Handbag, 1940s
Large black crocodile.
est. not available sold: $695
The Paper Bag Princess 5/8/1999

Handbag, 1950s
Black alligator, trapezoidal with lift-up clasp.
est. $150–$200 sold: $316
William Doyle Galleries 11/12/1997

Handbag, 1950s
Black crocodile body and handle, gold-toned hardware, excellent condition.
est. not available sold: $675
The Paper Bag Princess 12/18/2000

Handbag, 1950s
Turquoise alligator, rounded shape with covered frame and handles.
est. $300–$500 sold: $632
William Doyle Galleries 5/6/1998

DE PARIS, ROSEMARIE

Headbands, 1950s
Set of three feathered headbands in black, white, and magenta with matching miniature hat boxes.
est. $200–$300 sold: $287
Sotheby's 9/30/1999

DE RAUCH, MADELEINE

ENSEMBLE, 1960S
Pearl gray wool, single-breasted coat with
wool exclamation points, silver braid, and
rhinestones, sleeveless flared dress.
est. $200–$300 sold: $143
William Doyle Galleries 11/17/1994

DENNIS, PAMELA

EVENING GOWN, 1996
Navy blue silk jersey, short sleeves, square
neckline with navy diamanté beading and a
cascading beaded floral motif. Bette Midler,
1996 Academy Awards.
est. not available sold: $5750
Christie's Oscar Dress Auction 3/18/1999

DESGRANGES, FERNANDE

HANDBAG, 1954
Navy alligator with watch-set carrying handle.
est. $300–$500 sold: $632
William Doyle Galleries 12/5/1996

DESSÈS, JEAN

BAL MASQUE COSTUME, 1960
Peasant blouse and scarf of turquoise silk
jersey, narrow below-the-knee skirt of
black satin.
est. $100–$125 sold: $575
William Doyle Galleries 6/11/1997

COAT, 1950
Black silk gabardine with blouson effect in
back, round collar and three-quarter-length
sleeves.
est. $400–$600 sold: $3450
Sotheby's 4/8/1998

COCKTAIL DRESS, 1950S
Brown silk chiffon draped into basket-
weave pattern.
est. $300–$500 sold: $3450
William Doyle Galleries 4/24/1996

COCKTAIL DRESS, 1960
Ivory silk chiffon printed with roses in orange, turquoise, beige, and brown, one-
shouldered, toga-style drapery.
est. $400–$600 sold: $575
William Doyle Galleries 6/11/1997

COCKTAIL DRESS, 1960
Black silk crepe, fitted boned bodice
shirred and sewn at back with a circular
cowl piece draped over the head to encircle
neck, gathered skirt.
est. $300–$500 sold: $345
William Doyle Galleries 5/2/2000

COCKTAIL DRESS, 1960S
Silk satin sleeveless dress with crossover
bodice, covered in floral sprays of crystal
bugle beads, pastel thread run through
each bead.
est. $1000–$1500 sold: $1150
Sotheby's 10/29/1997

COCKTAIL DRESS, 1960S
Pink faille with black-beaded mesh bodice
and fringe, bodice trimmed in same
beaded fringe that finishes skirt.
est. $1000–$1500 sold: $1380
Sotheby's 10/29/1997

COCKTAIL DRESS, 1960S
Cream silk with maillot-style bodice, dress
and belt covered with alternating rows of
sequins and beads, tulip skirt, boned inner
corset.
est. $1000–$1500 sold: $2587
Sotheby's 10/29/1997

DRESS, 1950S
Blue silk, bodice cut on the bias with kimono sleeves, skirt with pleated front panel
attached at center and spread to each side.
est. $150–$200 sold: $258
William Doyle Galleries 5/6/1998

EVENING GOWN, 1954
Sheath of black silk chiffon worked in scalloped tucks, layered chiffon train.
est. $1300–$1500 sold: $8625
William Doyle Galleries 6/11/1997

D

EVENING GOWN, 1960
Strapless, red silk chiffon edged around
bodice with matching satin, pouf above the
tulip. Hem sewn with satin bow.
est. $500–$750 sold: $6037
William Doyle Galleries 6/11/1997

EVENING GOWN, 1960
Chartreuse silk chiffon, narrow long skirt
with curved overskirt panel, starting at side
of bodice, looped drapery of chartreuse
and blue chiffon.
est. $600–$900 sold: $3450
William Doyle Galleries 6/11/1997

EVENING GOWN, 1960
Strapless, yellow silk chiffon, draped bodice
with drapery falling to the hem and continuing around the back hem in a U-line.
est. $500–$750 sold: $9200
William Doyle Galleries 6/11/1997

EVENING GOWN, 1960
Strapless, black silk chiffon, boned and
draped bodice with drapery falling to hem,
wrapping the body, pouf above the tulip.
Hem sewn with satin bow.
est. not available sold: $6895
The Paper Bag Princess 1/10/2001

EVENING GOWN, 1961
Pink silk chiffon with dark rose at hem to
pale pink bodice, clear and pink crystal
beading mirroring color gradation, silk
chiffon underdress.
est. $1500–$2000 sold: $4312
Sotheby's 10/29/1997

JACKET, 1950S
Short bolero jacket with elbow-length
sleeves and muff, covered with rayon or silk
plain and plush purple and lavender petals
with taffeta lining.
est. $200–$300 sold: $977.50
William Doyle Galleries 5/2/2000

SUIT, 1950S
Gray flannel, double-breasted jacket, wrap
skirt.
est. $300–$500 sold: $345
William Doyle Galleries 11/16/1999

SUIT, 1960S
Wool tweed, collarless jacket closing with
three buttons at a diagonal, extra scarf
draping down back, slim skirt and American hat.
est. $400–$600 sold: $977.50
William Doyle Galleries 11/2/2000

DI CAMERINO, ROBERTA

HANDBAG, 1960S
Black calf, turquoise enameled frame and
long red shoulder strap.
est. $100–$150 sold: $316
William Doyle Galleries 12/6/1995

HANDBAG, 1970S
Tote-style bag of faux felt, green and red
with buckle motif.
est. not available sold: $395
The Paper Bag Princess 11/1/1999

HANDBAG, 1970S
Multicolored, grid-patterned velvet in
rounded box shape, black leather handle.
est. $300–$400 sold: $1150
Sotheby's 4/8/1998

HANDBAG, 1970S
Raspberry and blue velvet and black calfskin with trompe l'oeil pockets and gold
metal handle/trim.
est. $400–$600 sold: $575
Sotheby's 12/9/1998

HANDBAG, 1970S
Black alligator rectangle with matching
"belt" encircling top edge, gold hardware
unsnaps from the top and is hinged at the
bottom.
est. $500–$700 sold: $1265
Sotheby's 4/8/1998

HANDBAG
Red, white, and black velvet.
est. not available sold: $400
eBay Online Auctions 4/18/2000

HANDBAG, 1971
Elongated bag with green, red, and blue
striped cut velvet back and fold-over top,
navy calf front, top handle and side gussets,
roomy compartments.
est. $500–$700 sold: $863
William Doyle Galleries 5/2/2000

SHOULDER BAG, 1970s
Green cut velvet shoulder bag with large
gold-tone metal keyhole hardware that re-
leases the clasp.
est. not available sold: $395
The Paper Bag Princess 1/1/1999

TOTE BAG, 1972
Ombre gray velvet with black leather trim
and handles.
est. $750–$1000 sold: $920
Sotheby's 12/9/1998

DICKERSON, DOROTHY

ENSEMBLE, 1950s
Brown jersey circle skirt strewn with velvet
flowers, with coordinating yellow cashmere sweater applied at neck with similar
velvet flowers.
est. $200–$250 sold: $316
William Doyle Galleries 11/10/1998

DIOR, CHRISTIAN

BALL GOWN, 1952
Black Chantilly lace over white faille.
est. $500–$750 sold: $402
William Doyle Galleries 4/27/1994

CLUTCH BAG
Envelope-style beige and cream monogrammed, gold-plated Christian Dior insignia, gold-plated chain shoulder strap,
brown leather lining.
est. $40–$60 sold: $130
Ritchie's 9/20/2000

COAT
Three-quarter-length, white marabou
feathers, with long sleeves and silk lining.
est. not available sold: $595
The Paper Bag Princess 5/10/1999

COAT, 1940s
Red wool with a small plaid in darker red
and green.
est. $500–$750 sold: $575
William Doyle Galleries 12/6/1995

COAT, 1950
Navy wool bodice, elbow-length sleeves.
est. $500–$750 sold: $460
William Doyle Galleries 11/17/1994

COAT, 1950s
Silk chine with gray thumbprint pattern,
wide flat collar, gray mother-of-pearl
buttons.
est. $400–$500 sold: $373
William Doyle Galleries 5/12/1999

COAT, 1950s
Three-quarter-length day coat, cocoon
shape, wide pointed collar, large center
buttons, slash pockets, removable nutria
lining, number illegible.
est. $600–$800 sold: $575
Skinner 12/16/1999

COAT, 1950s
Cardigan-style, melon velvet with three-
quarter-length sleeves, band collar, oversized patch pockets.
est. $300–$500 sold: $575
William Doyle Galleries 5/6/1998

COAT, 1952
Charcoal wool, single-breasted, hourglass
shape, padded shoulders.
est. $600–$900 sold: $862
William Doyle Galleries 11/17/1994

COAT, 1953
Black wool, single-breasted, hourglass shape.
est. $500–$750 sold: $460
William Doyle Galleries 11/17/1994

COAT, 1954
White silk faille, very full, styled with voluminous stand-up cape collar pleated at
neck and extending to hemline.
est. $300–$500 sold: $1380
William Doyle Galleries 5/6/1998

D

COAT, 1955
Black silk taffeta with portrait neckline,
sleeves give the illusion of an evening wrap.
est. $500–$700 sold: $3450
Sotheby's 10/29/1997

COAT, 1956
Flared cardigan coat of ivory satin embroidered in polychrome pastel silk floss with
flowers and sequin accents.
est. $2000–$3000 sold: $3680
William Doyle Galleries 11/12/1997

COAT, 1957
Short, black textured wool, flared with
Peter Pan collar and full sleeves with gath-
ered hems.
est. $500–$750 sold: $1495
William Doyle Galleries 6/11/1997

COAT, 1960s
Black and white zebra printed cotton twill,
button front, single-breasted car coat.
est. not available sold: $495
The Paper Bag Princess 11/1/1996

COAT, 1960s
Maxi-length, fitted bodice, A-line body,
golden and black Native American printed
motif.
est. not available sold: $1295
The Paper Bag Princess 4/7/2000

COAT, 1960s
White ermine with white fox border
at hem.
est. $700–$900 sold: $3737
Sotheby's 10/29/1997

COAT, 1970
Brown velvet, double-breasted, with wide
pointed, notched collar, embroidery on collar, cuffs, pockets, with four large buttons.
est. $200–$300 sold: $546
William Doyle Galleries 5/2/2000

COAT, 1970s
Brown suede double-breasted with brown
fur lining, collar, and cuffs.
est. $400–$600 sold: $546
Skinner 12/16/1999

COAT DRESS, 1950
Black, white, and charcoal wool houndstooth trimmed with flat black braid,
double-breasted jacket, skirt has two rows
of black buttons.
est. $400–$600 sold: $575
William Doyle Galleries 12/5/1996

COAT DRESS, 1950s
Ivory silk twill, white mink shawl collar extending in interior to hem, wide sash belt.
est. $200–$250 sold: $402
William Doyle Galleries 6/11/1997

COAT DRESS, 1962
White mohair tweed, single-breasted with
white buttons.
est. $200–$300 sold: $287
William Doyle Galleries 6/11/1997

COCKTAIL DRESS, 1950s
Ivory faille printed with black petit pois, V
neck, draped shoulders, cap sleeves.
est. $600–$900 sold: $517
William Doyle Galleries 11/17/1994

COCKTAIL DRESS, 1950s
Periwinkle blue silk taffeta with short
sleeves, full skirt, bow at front of bodice
with fringed ends hanging below waist.
est. $300–$500 sold: $690
Skinner 12/16/1999

COCKTAIL DRESS, 1950s
Cream silk ottoman chine with charcoal
flowers, high-draped waist and pleated
skirt.
est. $600–$900 sold: $431
William Doyle Galleries 4/24/1996

COCKTAIL DRESS, 1950s
Black ziberline with boat neckline, off-the-
shoulder short sleeves with bow trimmings, straight below-the-knee skirt.
est. 400–600 pounds sold: 345 pounds
Sotheby's London 11/25/1998

Cocktail Dress, 1954
Rose satin woven with velvet floral sprigs, camisole bodice with gathered full skirt and bowed self belt, jacket with short sleeves and shawl collar.
est. $1200–$1500 sold: $2300
William Doyle Galleries 5/6/1998

Cocktail Dress, 1954
Black silk faille, net underbodice with center faille panel and wide straps crossing in back, strapless dress with button front to reveal underbodice.
est. $100–$150 sold: $517
William Doyle Galleries 5/6/1998

Cocktail Dress, 1955
Ivory satin with black velvet dots, two-piece, bodice with short sleeves, straight skirt sewn with boned understructure.
est. $400–$600 sold: $460
William Doyle Galleries 11/16/1999

Cocktail Dress, 1955
Black grosgrain silk with black floral-shaped paillettes. Relief beading over entire dress, fitted boned bodice with interior corset and multilayered underskirts, one-inch shoulder straps and full knee-length skirt. Numbered and labeled: Christian Dior Automne-Hiver 1955, made in France.
est. not available sold: $12,000
The Paper Bag Princess 1/10/2001

Cocktail Dress, 1956
Black silk faille with off-the-shoulder half-puff sleeves, bodice has sash below the bustline, waist applied with folded V-shaped sash detail.
est. 800–1200 pounds sold: 1840 pounds
Sotheby's London 11/25/1998

Cocktail Dress, 1956
Green silk faille, fitted bodice with corset, full skirt, trained peplum-style attachment at back covering fringed bow, fringed stole.
est. 1000–1500 pounds sold: 2875 pounds
Sotheby's London 11/25/1998

Cocktail Dress, 1956
Red chiffon, fitted bodice with shoestring straps, full circular skirt designed with bow-trimmed puffed pleated flounces of chiffon.
est. 500–700 pounds sold: 1955 pounds
Sotheby's London 11/25/1998

Cocktail Dress, 1956
Black wool crepe, square neckline, short sleeves, self-tied belt.
est. $500–$750 sold: $431
William Doyle Galleries 11/17/1994

Cocktail Dress, 1959
Watermelon silk faille with off-the-shoulder neckline, straps sewn to interior corset, full skirt.
est. $1000–$1500 sold: $1955
William Doyle Galleries 11/17/1994

Cocktail Dress, 1961
Black silk shantung, A-line skirt sewn to a boned net corset, separate waist-length bodice with plunging notch sewn with self bow.
est. $200–$400 sold: $402
William Doyle Galleries 6/11/1997

Cocktail Dress, 1961
Black velvet with cock-feather trim at hem.
est. $2000–$3000 sold: $2990
Sotheby's 9/30/1999

Cocktail Dress, 1962
Woven in shades of gold and bronze with scrolling foliate design, sleeveless dress has jeweled neckline, waist-length jacket with sable shawl collar.
est. $100–$200 sold: $373
William Doyle Galleries 12/6/1995

Cocktail Dress, 1965
Strapless purple/pink silk crepe wrap-around sheath, metal thread and paste embroidered hem and border, bow to the back, semicircular shawl.
est. 200–400 pounds sold: 230 pounds
Sotheby's London 11/25/1998

D

COCKTAIL DRESS, 1968
Maize silk crepe A-line dress, geometric embroidered hem and sleeves with colored diamanté beading, floral vines and orchids worked in beads.
est. $800–$1200 sold: $690
Sotheby's 10/29/1997

COCKTAIL ENSEMBLE, 1952
Strapless bustier, pleated skirt and waist-length jacket in black silk faille.
est. $200–$300 sold: $1092
William Doyle Galleries 6/11/1997

COCKTAIL ENSEMBLE, 1956
Embroidered with gilt metal thread applied in a lattice design and embellished with glass droplets, vertical slash neckline, similarly decorated hat.
est. 1200–1800 pounds sold: 1610 pounds
Sotheby's London 11/25/1998

COCKTAIL ENSEMBLE, 1958
Black silk taffeta strapless dress with pleated, pegged skirt, jacket with shawl collar.
est. $1500–$2000 sold: $17,250
Sotheby's 10/29/1997

COCKTAIL ENSEMBLE, 1960s
Blue silk sleeveless mini shift with band of silver rhinestones, sequins, and metallic thread. Eastern-inspired embroidery at neck, Nehru collar.
est. $300–$500 sold: $1035
Skinner 9/14/2000

DRESS, 1949
Paper silk dress, fitted bodice with button detail, fitted wrist tie sleeves, fitted waist, voluminous below-the-knee skirt, patch pockets at sides of skirt.
est. $500–$700 sold: $1955
Skinner 9/14/2000

DRESS, 1950
Black wool, long-sleeved bodice fastening at a slant with black buttons, self-tie neck, cuffs lined with black moiré taffeta.
est. $200–$300 sold: $3450
William Doyle Galleries 4/24/1996

DRESS, 1950
Off-white embroidered organza, bodice has shawl collar and center-front button closure, full skirt with net petticoat.
est. $1500–$2500 sold: $4600
Sotheby's 4/8/1998

DRESS, 1950s
Gray wool hip-length overtunic with over-sized gauffered round collar, cut low to reveal bodice of silk underdress, skirt bubble-shaped at bottom.
est. $800–$1200 sold: $977
William Doyle Galleries 11/10/1998

DRESS, 1950s
Shirtwaist dress of black and brown gingham taffeta with black satin stripes, V neck blousy bodice with lapel collar, skirt with inverted pleating.
est. $400–$600 sold: $575
Skinner 12/16/1999

DRESS, 1950s
Red silk faille, straight-skirted sheath with portrait collar, long sleeves, separate full skirt with two unattached petal-like overlapping panels.
est. $300–$400 sold: $316
William Doyle Galleries 5/2/2000

DRESS, 1950s
Gray wool, long day dress with round neckline, sloped shoulders, elbow-length sleeves, fitted at waist, balloon skirt, center front bow.
est. $400–$600 sold: $316
Skinner 12/16/1999

DRESS, 1950s
Black faille, wrap bodice with short sleeves, flared skirt falls in panels, center fold inset with panel of black satin.
est. $300–$500 sold: $517
William Doyle Galleries 12/5/1996

DRESS, 1952
Navy blue wool, short-sleeved top with pointed collar and slit neckline, flared skirt.
est. $300–$500 sold: $460
William Doyle Galleries 4/12/1995

Dress, 1957

Cranberry wool, bodice with jewel neckline, three-quarter-length sleeves and faux patch pockets, full skirt with large box pleats.
est. $500–$700 sold: $690
William Doyle Galleries 11/16/1999

Dress, 1957

Black silk faille, sweetheart neckline, full-pleated skirt, three self roses at neckline.
est. $800–$1200 sold: $977
William Doyle Galleries 11/17/1994

Dress, 1957

Off-white chiffon embroidered with green and blue floral motifs, sleeveless bodice with V neck, pleated skirt.
est. $800–$1200 sold: $4600
Sotheby's 4/8/1998

Dress, 1960

Blue lace re-embroidered with chenille, elbow-length sleeves, skirt pleated into high-waisted, triangular stole.
est. $800–$1200 sold: $460
William Doyle Galleries 11/16/1999

Dress, 1960

Black net sewn with small sprigs worked in jet beads, neckline square and trimmed in black velvet, multiple tulle and silk petticoats.
est. $600–$800 sold: $345
William Doyle Galleries 11/16/1999

Dress, 1960

Silk printed with green dots, boat neck, green grosgrain bow at waist.
est. $200–$250 sold: $517
William Doyle Galleries 6/11/1997

Dress, 1960s

Ivory silk twill, princess line dress with tulip-shaped skirt and strapless bodice wrapping and fastening at side back.
est. $150–$200 sold: $316
William Doyle Galleries 11/12/1997

Dress, 1962

Black wool crepe, sleeveless, one armhole outlined by a self band run through a gathered channel, tied in a self bow.
est. $600–$900 sold: $2185
William Doyle Galleries 4/12/1995

Ensemble, 1948

Navy wool twill two-piece, bodice has col-montant collar, back button closure, skirt draped to left hip with abalone button.
est. $1500–$2000 sold: $16,100
Sotheby's 10/29/1997

Ensemble, 1950s

Black mohair sleeveless sheath with bubble hemline, jacket with four pompoms.
est. $1000–$1500 sold: $2300
William Doyle Galleries 11/10/1998

Ensemble, 1950s

Gray mohair collarless three-button jacket, skirt slightly gathered with four front buttons, attached black leather belt, detached tie for neck, muff.
est. $400–$600 sold: $1150
William Doyle Galleries 11/10/1998

Ensemble, 1954

Green, black, and blue herringbone dress, single-breasted jacket.
est. $150–$200 sold: $517
William Doyle Galleries 12/6/1995

Ensemble, 1956

Navy burlap-textured wool sheath dress with short sleeves, white cotton ottoman neckline, jacket with shawl collar and self bow.
est. $200–$300 sold: $258
William Doyle Galleries 4/12/1995

Ensemble, 1958

Jacket has bracelet-length sleeves and self belt, gathered skirt attached to black slip bodice.
est. $200–$300 sold: $517
William Doyle Galleries 4/27/1994

Ensemble, 1960

Blue silk faille, three-quarter-length sleeves, button front, self belt.
est. $300–$500 sold: $402
William Doyle Galleries 9/30/1993

Ensemble, 1960s

Scarlet wool sleeveless dress and fitted princess coat trimmed with gold lace.
est. $100–$150 sold: $258
William Doyle Galleries 12/6/1995

D

Evening Cape, 1968
Ivory silk flowing from gathers at shoulder, white mink hood.
est. $200–$300 sold: $977
William Doyle Galleries 11/12/1997

Evening Coat Dress, 1960s
Knee-length satin-weave fabric printed with Eastern-inspired pattern in pale aqua, blue, and orange, Nehru collar, fitted sleeves, aqua lining.
est. $300–$500 sold: $287.50
Skinner 9/14/2000

Evening Ensemble, 1948
Blue velvet and satin bodice, velvet skirt cut to reveal purple satin lining, silk satin cummerbund.
est. $1500–$2000 sold: $2875
Sotheby's 10/29/1997

Evening Ensemble, 1953
Black wool sleeveless sheath, bodice encrusted with gold metallic cord and rhinestones, collarless blouson jacket with panels tying at hip.
est. $800–$1200 sold: $977
William Doyle Galleries 5/12/1999

Evening Ensemble, 1960
Gold satin, camisole with wide straps, fastens in back with self buttons, narrow pants.
est. $100–$150 sold: $575
William Doyle Galleries 6/11/1997

Evening Gown, 1950s
Black velvet floor-length evening gown, strapless fitted bodice, with band around bust, then dropped at waistline with bow to left side, full skirt.
est. $400–$600 sold: $1150
Skinner 12/16/1999

Evening Gown, 1950s
Black silk taffeta, strapless.
est. $2000–$2500 sold: $3162
Sotheby's 9/30/1999

Evening Gown, 1950s
Strapless, yellow cotton velvet, fitted torso with fold-down top and full-pleated skirt.
est. $400–$600 sold: $460
William Doyle Galleries 12/6/1995

Evening Gown, 1950s
Black tulle dotted with velvet, strapless bodice scalloped at edge and open waist at back, multilayered tulle bouffant skirt, satin ribbon waist to hem.
est. $500–$700 sold: $1840
William Doyle Galleries 5/6/1998

Evening Gown, 1950s
Black cotton cloque with square neck, puffed sleeves, fitted bodice, and flared long skirt.
est. $600–$900 sold: $1840
William Doyle Galleries 4/24/1996

Evening Gown, 1953
Claret silk faille, princess-line, sleeveless with V front and back, bows at shoulder and back, bustle train in back.
est. $1000–$1200 sold: $2530
William Doyle Galleries 5/12/1999

Evening Gown, 1953
Strapless silk satin, self-covered buttons, long flared skirt.
est. $400–$600 sold: $345
William Doyle Galleries 11/17/1994

Evening Gown, 1955
Gray tulle embroidered with metallic silver thread over pink taffeta.
est. $500–$700 sold: $1035
Sotheby's 9/30/1999

Evening Gown, 1955
Gray silk satin two-piece, bodice with crossover neckline, bell-shaped skirt, floral garland and basket embroidery with beads.
est. $3000–$4000 sold: $2875
Sotheby's 10/29/1997

Evening Gown, 1956
Black chine taffeta patterned with gray blossoms, round neck, three-quarter-length sleeves, full skirt pleated at top.
est. $150–$200 sold: $920
William Doyle Galleries 11/12/1997

EVENING GOWN, 1956
Black faille ground applied overall with
tufted velvet spots, black velvet bands
adorned with faceted jet beads, tulle
petticoats.
est. 500–800 pounds sold: 460 pounds
Sotheby's London 11/25/1998

EVENING GOWN, 1956
Peach silk faille, halter neck, A-line skirt,
self knot at the midriff.
est. $750–$1000 sold: $2990
William Doyle Galleries 12/6/1995

EVENING GOWN, 1957
Strapless, changeante garnet/black taffeta
chine with roses in pink and green, long
train.
est. $1000–$1500 sold: $17,250
William Doyle Galleries 6/11/1997

EVENING GOWN, 1960s
Black chiffon flowing from strapless
bodice, two back floating panels fastened to
a jewel neckline, rhinestone ball accents.
est. $150–$200 sold: $1610
William Doyle Galleries 4/24/1996

EVENING GOWN, 1960s
Sapphire velvet long princess dress with
jewel neck, bolero jacket of sable with
elbow-length sleeves and sapphire velvet ties.
est. $200–$300 sold: $373
William Doyle Galleries 4/12/1995

EVENING GOWN, 1960s
White A-line sleeveless silk faille, scoop neck.
est. not available sold: $995
The Paper Bag Princess 7/1/1998

EVENING GOWN, 1961
White faille embroidered with pearlescent
horsehair ornaments, pearls, rhinestones,
pink satin sash.
est. $2000–$3000 sold: $1265
William Doyle Galleries 9/30/1993

EVENING JACKET, 1962
Ivory silk with gold brocade leaf pattern,
double-breasted with shawl collar and
buttons.
est. $150–$200 sold: $258
William Doyle Galleries 6/11/1997

GOWN, 1970s
Red silk brocade, sleeveless, with fitted em-
pire waist, and full A-line skirt, labeled:
Christian Dior, Holt Renfrew.
est. not available sold: $1200
The Paper Bag Princess 4/1/1997

HANDBAG, 1980s
Burgundy and cream canvas, logo print
speedy bag with zipper top, leather trim,
and two leather handles.
est. not available sold: $395
The Paper Bag Princess 12/13/2000

HAT, 1940s
1920s-style cloche, beige suede with veil.
est. not available sold: $495
The Paper Bag Princess 8/1/1997

HAT, 1950s
Black fur felt tall cone-shaped cylinder that
comes to a point at the top.
est. not available sold: $295
The Paper Bag Princess 1/1/1998

HAT, 1950s–1960s
Red and black cut velvet, turban style.
est. not available sold: $325
The Paper Bag Princess 11/1/1997

HAT, 1960s
Orange floppy-brimmed fur felt with band
of orange and black feathers.
est. not available sold: $225
The Paper Bag Princess 7/1/1998

HAT, 1960s
Green mesh turban style with multicolor
velvet strips sewn throughout.
est. not available sold: $165
The Paper Bag Princess 3/1/1999

HAT
Reddish brown felt hat with wide brim,
olive ribbon trim, labeled: Christian Dior
Chapeaux, England.
est. $50–$75 sold: $300
Ritchie's 9/20/2000

D

JACKET, 1960
Goldenrod silk damask woven with round
flowers, round neck, elbow-length sleeves,
edged at sleeves and waistline with fringe.
est. $200–$300 sold: $690
William Doyle Galleries 6/11/1997

JACKET, 1960s
Bolero of beige satin covered with gold
metal paillettes and large gray jewel clusters, sable cuffs.
est. $1200–$1500 sold: $690
William Doyle Galleries 11/16/1999

JACKET, 1960s
Cream tulle over cream silk embroidered
with flowers in mint silk floss, sequins,
faux pearls, and gold thread.
est. $300–$500 sold: $230
William Doyle Galleries 12/6/1995

SUIT, 1940s
Black silk faille, jacket with asymmetrical
collar, flat and pointed at one side, other
side gathered and crossing over to close.
est. $1500–$1800 sold: $2530
William Doyle Galleries 5/6/1998

SUIT, 1940s
Gray wool, jacket and long skirt.
est. $300–$400 sold: $287
William Doyle Galleries 11/17/1994

SUIT, 1948
Ivory and black striped wool, single-
breasted jacket slightly padded at shoulders
and hips, knife-pleated skirt.
est. $1500–$2000 sold: $5175
Sotheby's 4/8/1998

SUIT, 1953
Black silk faille double-breasted jacket and
slim skirt.
est. 600–1000 pounds sold: 632 pounds
Sotheby's London 11/25/1998

SUIT, 1965
Wool, woven in plaid of gray, peach, and
cream, single-breasted jacket and A-line skirt.
est. $200–$300 sold: $402
William Doyle Galleries 4/24/1996

TUXEDO SUIT, 1970s
Black satin, jacket fitted at the waist,
double lapels and French cuffs, faux vest
and straight skirt, labeled: Christian Dior-
New York Original.
est. $300–$500 sold: $402.50
William Doyle Galleries 11/2/2000

DIOR, CHRISTIAN/LIBRI, ALBERTO

EVENING GOWN, 1951–1952
Brown velvet strapless bodice embroidered
with gold sequins, brown silk net skirt embroidered in crescent pattern.
est. $600–$800 sold: $431
Skinner 12/16/1999

DOLCE & GABBANA

COCKTAIL DRESS, 1997
Bodice of corselet foundation overlaid with
black stretch tulle, transparent skirt gathers
to a train held with silk flowers. Susan
Sarandon, 1997 Academy Awards.
est. not available sold: $6325
Christie's Oscar Dress Auction 3/18/1999

DOREEN

SWEATERS, 1950s
Two black cashmere cardigan sweaters, one
with large embroidered rose, the other
with two front panels of beaded black lace
and black satin.
est. $150–$200 sold: $403
Skinner 12/16/1999

DRÉCOLL

EVENING GOWN, 1905
Ivory point d'esprit with whitework appliquéd lace and satin ribbon trim, bodice
has high collar and Renaissance sleeves,
skirt with tiered train.
est. $700–$900 sold: $402
William Doyle Galleries 5/12/1999

DUIZEND-GANS

EVENING BAG, 1940S
Black suede with gathered edge, held by
gold-toned and "amber" dumbbells.
est. $300–$400 sold: $747
Sotheby's 9/30/1999

DUKE, RANDOLPH FOR HALSTON

EVENING GOWN, 1997
Red jersey bias-cut full-length dress with
asymmetrical front drape and plunging
back, red fox stole and sandals. Minnie
Driver, 1997 Academy Awards.
est. not available sold: $16,100
Christie's Oscar Dress Auction 3/18/1999

EISENBERG

DRESS, 1940
Black rayon crepe embroidered diagonally
from one shoulder to the other hip in
green, gold, and red sequins with flowers
and scrolls.
est. $200–$300 sold: $172
William Doyle Galleries 4/12/1995

EMANUEL

ENSEMBLE, 1966
A-line short-sleeve dress with navy blue,
sky blue, and silver wool lamé chevrons,
matching double-breasted coat.
est. $1500–$2000 sold: $1725
Sotheby's 10/29/1997

EVENING COAT, 1970
Eisenhower-style jacket and skirt in black-
and-white-striped and dotted wool, jersey
blouse with black and red flowers.
est. $200–$300 sold: $287
William Doyle Galleries 9/30/1993

EVENING GOWN, 1988
Dyed black silk with asymmetrically
shirred bodice, ruffled off-the-shoulder
sleeves and full skirt. Melanie Griffith,
1988 Academy Awards.
est. not available sold: $5750
Christie's Oscar Dress Auction 3/18/1999

ESCADA

COCKTAIL DRESS, 1993
Collarless jacket with vest and trousers embroidered with blue and black sequins in
pinstripe and geometric designs. Shirley
MacLaine, 1993 Academy Awards.
est. not available sold: $2530
Christie's Oscar Dress Auction 3/18/1999

ESTÉVES, LOUIS

EVENING GOWN, 1960S
Tangerine silk faille, tabard style, halter
bodice, plunging neckline, copper bugle
beads with diamantes. Anne Jeffrey, Academy Awards.
est. not available sold: $2300
Christie's Oscar Dress Auction 3/18/1999

EVINS, DAVID

SHOES, 1957
Black satin with high-cut vamp, single
rhinestone button ornament.
est. $75–$125 sold: $138
William Doyle Galleries 11/17/1994

FARE, ROGER

GLOVES, 1950S
Gray kid faced with mustard suede edged
with plush fringe, one small and wrist-
length, the other long and flared.
est. $100–$150 sold: $172
William Doyle Galleries 12/6/1995

F

GLOVES, 1960s
Mustard suede gathered with cuffs
trimmed with piping and tassels of
turquoise suede.
est. $75–$125 sold: $575
William Doyle Galleries 12/6/1995

FARELL, JEAN

SUIT, 1936
Green tweed appliquéd at four pockets
with red suede.
est. $500–$750 sold: $1265
William Doyle Galleries 12/6/1995

FATH, JACQUES

CARDIGAN, 1970s
Baby blue three-ply cashmere cardigan.
est. not available sold: $195
The Paper Bag Princess 9/8/2000

COAT, 1950
Metallic evening coat trimmed with mink
fur at collar and sleeves, V neck buttoned
down left side.
est. $3000–$5000 sold: $3450
Sotheby's 4/8/1998

COAT, 1950s
Black satin, knee-length with high collar
buttoning to neck, double-breasted front
and cuffs sewn with black buttons and outlined with white stitching.
est. $300–$500 sold: $1265
William Doyle Galleries 5/12/1999

COAT, 1951
Black-and-white-check wool trapeze coat
with high velvet Peter Pan collar, wide
folded cuffs.
est. $1000–$1500 sold: $1955
Sotheby's 10/29/1997

COCKTAIL DRESS, 1950
Strapless, black taffeta with velvet band at
top and skirt edged with velvet.
est. $1000–$1500 sold: $1150
William Doyle Galleries 11/17/1994

COCKTAIL DRESS, 1950s
Black, gray, and white animal print strapless
dress with empire waist, fan-pleated bodice
and pleating in back of skirt.
est. $1500–$2000 sold: $1725
Sotheby's 10/29/1997

COCKTAIL DRESS, 1953
Gray printed organdy with pattern of pink,
green, and ivory floral bouquets, bodice
has cap sleeves, two bows, skirt is bias-cut
with slight bustle.
est. $750–$1000 sold: $3737
Sotheby's 4/8/1998

COCKTAIL SUIT, 1950s
Brown and white tweed wool with flecks
of green, red, and yellow.
est. $1000–$1500 sold: $1150
Sotheby's 9/30/1999

COCKTAIL SUIT, 1950s
Black-and-white-tweed wool, jacket has
five-button closure, skirt has side zipper.
est. $1000–$1500 sold: $1265
Sotheby's 9/30/1999

DRESS, 1950s
Charcoal silk/wool, low V neck, elbow-
length sleeves, black silk and horsehair underdress.
est. $800–$1200 sold: $4312
William Doyle Galleries 4/27/1994

ENSEMBLE, 1948
Candlelight faille taffeta, sleeveless dress,
side poufs over slit-front skirt, bodice embroidered with jeweled clusters, bolero
jacket.
est. $600–$900 sold: $345
William Doyle Galleries 4/24/1996

EVENING GOWN, 1950s
White cotton piqué with black dots, strapless, trimmed with black piping, matching
shoulder cape.
est. $5000–$7000 sold: $3450
William Doyle Galleries 4/27/1994

Evening Gown, 1950s

Peach silk satin embroidered with flowers, beads, and sequins, camisole bodice, ankle-length skirt.
est. $750–$1000 sold: $460
William Doyle Galleries 12/6/1995

Evening Gown, 1954

White organdy embroidered with small yellow flowers.
est. $2000–$3000 sold: $1150
William Doyle Galleries 9/30/1993

Evening Jacket, 1950s

Black silk velvet bolero jacket with white mink collar, satin bow closure with dia-manté-covered circular buckle and cuff or-naments.
est. $1500–$1750 sold: $3162
Sotheby's 10/29/1997

Scarf, 1955

Printed with figures of spring, summer, winter, and fall holding and wearing calen-dars listing the days of the saints for 1955.
est. $75–$100 sold: $143
William Doyle Galleries 4/12/1995

Suit, 1950

Black-and-white-flecked wool, double-breasted jacket with rounded shoulders, padded peplum sewn with pointed seam-ing at front and back waist.
est. $500–$700 sold: $1035
William Doyle Galleries 5/6/1998

Suit, 1950s

Checkerboard-weave wool, cape-style jacket, pleated collar, leather buttons, straight skirt, labeled: Jacques Fath/Paris/Made in France.
est. $800–$1200 sold: $2185
William Doyle Galleries 11/2/2000

Suit, 1950s

Navy wool, jacket round-shouldered, fitted and tied at back above waist, button-front straight skirt.
est. $300–$500 sold: $977
William Doyle Galleries 5/6/1998

FERRAGAMO, SALVATORE

Evening Shoes, 1950s

Spiked-heel sling backs, heel and strap of gold kid, vamp of black lace embroidered with flowers and outlined with beads in pink, coral, and green.
est. $200–$300 sold: $345
William Doyle Galleries 11/10/1998

Shoes, 1940s

Black suede and gold calf.
est. $200–$250 sold: $575
William Doyle Galleries 4/24/1996

Shoes, 1960

Sky blue, thigh-high stockings on leather soles.
est. $200–$300 sold: $402
Sotheby's 4/8/1998

FERRERAS, MIGUEL

Evening Gown, 1950

Taupe satin camisole bodice, changeante chartreuse/taupe silk skirt.
est. $200–$300 sold: $115
William Doyle Galleries 9/30/1993

FIORUCCI

Boots, 1980s

Cotton candy pink, plastic "Love" boots.
est. not available sold: $145
The Paper Bag Princess 12/1/1999

Shoes, 1970

Black patent leather.
est. $60–$90 sold: $184
William Doyle Galleries 11/17/1994

FOGARTY, ANNE

Dress, 1950s

Black taffeta, fitted bodice and waist, full swing skirt, back zip.
est. not available sold: $395
The Paper Bag Princess 11/1/1997

DRESS, 1970S
Maxi-dress with empire waist, red and navy paisley print, poet sleeves.
est. not available sold: $425
The Paper Bag Princess 10/1/1999

FONTANA

COCKTAIL DRESS, 1960S
Blue silk chiffon sewn with ribbon stripes and small lace and velvet florets embroidered with purple beads, jewel neck.
est. $100–$150 sold: $201
William Doyle Galleries 4/12/1995

FORTUNY

BOLERO JACKET, 1940
Coral velvet stamped in gilt with small design, short sleeves.
est. $500–$750 sold: $575
William Doyle Galleries 4/27/1994

CAFTAN, 1920S
Caramel peach silk velvet stenciled caftan with large tree-of-life pattern and scrolled border.
est. not available sold: $3500
The Way We Wore 9/1/1999

CAFTAN, 1920S
Green velvet stenciled in silver with pattern inspired by Renaissance and Turkish textiles, peach faille lining.
est. $3000–$5000 sold: $3910
William Doyle Galleries 11/12/1997

COAT, 1920
Black silk velvet stenciled with bronze foliate motifs.
est. $5000–$7000 sold: $9775
Sotheby's 4/8/1998

COAT, 1920S
Kimono-cut with V at back of neck, gold velvet stenciled with Persian-inspired patterns including leafy trees above foliate band at hem.
est. $1200–$1500 sold: $3680
William Doyle Galleries 5/6/1998

COAT, 1920S
Gold velvet cardigan coat with above-the-elbow sleeves, stenciled in gold Middle Eastern–inspired motifs around edges and down center back.
est. $1000–$1500 sold: $1495
William Doyle Galleries 6/11/1997

COAT, 1920S
Puce velvet stenciled with gold Renaissance pomegranate pattern with aqua rolled and padded edging and cuff bands, pink faille lining.
est. $2000–$3000 sold: $4600
William Doyle Galleries 11/12/1997

COAT, 1930
Bluish-green silk velvet with bronze stenciled foliate pattern, black and bronze velvet trim at cuffs, hem, and front, sleeveless brown velvet mantle.
est. $5000–$7000 sold: $9200
Sotheby's 4/8/1998

COAT, 1930S
Cardigan-style brown velvet stenciled in gilt with flowering vines, ties of black cord knotted with amber glass beads, lined with beige silk satin.
est. $4000–$6000 sold: $5175
William Doyle Galleries 4/24/1996

COAT, 1930S
Black velvet, cardigan-style with side pleats, stenciled in gold with pattern at hem and shoulders.
est. $800–$1200 sold: $1725
William Doyle Galleries 11/12/1997

DRESS, 1920S
Champagne pleated silk with Venetian glass beads.
est. $1800–$2000 sold: $2415
William Doyle Galleries 6/11/1997

DRESS, 1920S
Rose pleated silk, sleeveless with Venetian glass beads on silk cord at sides, stenciled belt.
est. $1000–$1500 sold: $1265
William Doyle Galleries 5/6/1998

DRESS, 1930s
Green pleated silk with short sleeves, green
and yellow Venetian glass beads at sides,
gold-leaf pattern stenciled belt.
est. $500–$700 sold: $517
William Doyle Galleries 11/12/1997

DRESS, 1930s
Black pleated silk with drawstring neck,
long vertically pieced sleeves, beige Venetian glass beads down each side.
est. $1500–$2000 sold: $7475
William Doyle Galleries 11/16/1999

DRESS, 1930s
Champagne silk with bateau neckline gathered on a silk cord, short sleeves open at
top and laced with silk cord strung with
milky Venetian glass beads.
est. $700–$900 sold: $1495
William Doyle Galleries 5/12/1999

EVENING GOWN, 1920s
Black velvet stenciled in gold and silver
with flowering branch pattern, pleated silk
side panels, Venetian glass beads.
est. $1500–$2000 sold: $4887
William Doyle Galleries 11/10/1998

EVENING GOWN, 1930s
Pleated black silk satin, sleeveless with
Venetian glass bead trim.
est. $6000–$8000 sold: $10,350
Sotheby's 4/8/1998

EVENING GOWN, 1930s
Jewel neckline, integral tunic, edges
trimmed with Venetian glass beads, with
black satin belt, some loosening of pleats at
back, labeled: Made in Italy.
est. $5000–$7000 sold: $9200
William Doyle Galleries 11/2/2000

EVENING GOWN, 1978
Crimson pleated silk, V-shaped bodice, tassels with Venetian glass beads. Lauren Bacall, 1978 Academy Awards.
est. not available sold: $19,550
Christie's Oscar Dress Auction 3/18/1999

JACKET, 1920s
Apricot velvet stenciled in gilt in Islamic
pattern, hip-length kimono-style with
short sleeves.
est. $3000–$5000 sold: $5462
William Doyle Galleries 4/24/1996

JACKET, 1930s
Multicolored stenciled velvet with 16th-
century Italian foliate and serpentine designs, eye closures with Venetian glass
beads at front.
est. $6000–$8000 sold: $6900
Sotheby's 4/8/1998

JACKET, 1940s
Apricot silk velvet stenciled in silver with
flowering trees and vines.
est. $200–$300 sold: $575
William Doyle Galleries 4/12/1995

TEA GOWN, 1920s
Gray silk satin sewn down sides with white
Venetian glass beads striped in red and
brown, in original box.
est. $3000–$5000 sold: $2415
William Doyle Galleries 4/12/1995

TEA GOWN, 1930s
Black, sewn down sides with amber, red,
and brown striped Venetian glass beads,
belt stenciled in silver and sewn with two
pairs of Venetian beads.
est. $5000–$7000 sold: $5750
William Doyle Galleries 4/12/1995

TEA GOWN, 1940
White silk satin edged with frosted, white-
striped Venetian glass beads, with original
box.
est. $5000–$7000 sold: $5750
William Doyle Galleries 11/17/1994

FOX, WILLIAM

EVENING GOWN, 1950s
Mid-length dress with seed bead embroidery, sleeveless bloused bodice with high
round neckline and fitted waist, straight
skirt, chiffon lining.
est. $300–$500 sold: $259
Skinner 12/16/1999

FREDERICK'S OF HOLLYWOOD

DRESS, 1940s
Black synthetic silk, V neck, elbow-length sleeves.
est. $100–$150 sold: $172
William Doyle Galleries 9/30/1993

GALANOS, JAMES

COAT, 1960s
Silk shantung dyed with horizontal stripes in blue, pink, magenta, and coral, cardigan-style with back double-inverted pleat.
est. $200–$300 sold: $632
William Doyle Galleries 6/11/1997

COAT, 1960s
Black brocade woven with abstract satin pattern, trimmed with bands of black satin.
est. $200–$300 sold: $230
William Doyle Galleries 12/6/1995

COAT, 1960s
Heavy wool, navy and white check coat, '20s style, navy belted waist, silk-lined with large double lapeled collar.
est. not available sold: $1295
The Paper Bag Princess 9/25/2000

COCKTAIL DRESS, 1950s
Strapless black velvet, long and narrow with swallowtail train.
est. $250–$400 sold: $632
William Doyle Galleries 12/5/1996

COCKTAIL DRESS, 1950s
Black chiffon, camisole bodice shirred in three sections with center extending into a high bib, satin straps crossing at back center nude panel.
est. $200–$300 sold: $287
William Doyle Galleries 5/12/1999

COCKTAIL DRESS, 1950s
Short, black satin, fitted bodice with curved V neck and full skirt.
est. $200–$300 sold: $345
William Doyle Galleries 4/12/1995

COCKTAIL DRESS, 1950s
Black silk linen, halter neck, with diamond cut-out bare back, bow over closure, fitted darted bodice with full swing skirt just below the knee.
est. not available sold: $5000
The Paper Bag Princess 1/10/2001

COCKTAIL DRESS, 1950s
Black wool with curved V neck and high waistline, gathered back with large flat buttons.
est. $250–$400 sold: $431
William Doyle Galleries 12/6/1995

COCKTAIL DRESS, 1950s
Black taffeta, bodice with square neckline and cap sleeves, full-pleated skirt.
est. $150–$200 sold: $373
William Doyle Galleries 6/11/1997

COCKTAIL DRESS, 1950s
Ivory satin printed with subtle chine flowers and woven with large yellow velvet iris accented with taupe.
est. $300–$500 sold: $373
William Doyle Galleries 11/16/1999

COCKTAIL DRESS, 1950s
Black chine taffeta woven with red and orange roses, high-waisted dress with inverted pleat skirt, pillbox hat.
est. $200–$300 sold: $546
William Doyle Galleries 4/12/1995

COCKTAIL DRESS, 1955
Black chiffon long-sleeved shirtwaist with round black satin collar, square-buckled belt, circular skirt composed of three layers of gossamer chiffon.
est. $300–$500 sold: $575
William Doyle Galleries 11/10/1998

COCKTAIL DRESS, 1959
Red, black, and green rose-patterned silk taffeta dress, sleeveless bodice, bubble skirt, matching grosgrain coat with fitted bodice.
est. $400–$600 sold: $2415
Skinner 9/14/2000

COCKTAIL DRESS, 1960

Green satin shirtwaist with Peter Pan collar, short sleeves, center tailored bow, bouffant skirt intricately pleated all around waist.
est. $500–$600 sold: $862
William Doyle Galleries 11/10/1998

COCKTAIL DRESS, 1960

Black peau de soie, low round décolletage, cap sleeves, skirt arranged with wide triple layer pleats, two at each side, one off front center.
est. $300–$500 sold: $373
William Doyle Galleries 11/10/1998

COCKTAIL DRESS, 1960

Black satin two-piece, sleeveless top embroidered in black cord, chenille, and jet beads with scrollwork and paisley motif, A-line skirt.
est. $700–$900 sold: $805
William Doyle Galleries 11/16/1999

COCKTAIL DRESS, 1960s

Satin chine in black and white with parallelograms, waistline raised in front with bow.
est. $125–$175 sold: $690
William Doyle Galleries 4/24/1996

COCKTAIL DRESS, 1960s

Bodice cut straight in manner of strapless style with upper portion composed of separate horizontal strips attached to solid back and jewel neckline.
est. $300–$500 sold: $373
William Doyle Galleries

COCKTAIL DRESS, 1960s

Straight shift covered from mid-bodice with black sequins and disc accents, long-sleeved bodice top of silk tulle sewn with sequined polka dots.
est. $500–$700 sold: $287
William Doyle Galleries 5/2/2000

COCKTAIL DRESS, 1960s

Black wool crepe, high-waisted, bodice front and crossed straps of marquise rhinestones and faux emeralds forming flowers.
est. $500–$750 sold: $632
William Doyle Galleries 11/17/1994

COCKTAIL DRESS, 1960s

Long, narrow skirt of black twill, transparent long-sleeved bodice of black lace sewn with a lattice of marquise, round, and oval rhinestones.
est. $300–$500 sold: $1150
William Doyle Galleries 4/24/1996

COCKTAIL DRESS, 1960s

Layers of silk chiffon flowing from empire-waist bodice, front black, back brown.
est. $200–$250 sold: $920
William Doyle Galleries 6/11/1997

COCKTAIL DRESS, 1970s

Green matte silk jersey, one-shouldered, inset at midriff with a self-piping-outlined band of sheer dark green silk.
est. $200–$250 sold: $1035
William Doyle Galleries 12/5/1996

COCKTAIL DRESS, 1970s

Paisley silk, halter bodice overlaid with black cordonnet lace sewn with beads, tying in a bow at bare back, skirt overlaid with black satin streamer.
est. $300–$500 sold: $977
William Doyle Galleries 11/10/1998

COCKTAIL DRESS, 1970s

Ivory silk chiffon woven with gold flowers, sleeveless slip dress with V neck, coat embroidered with gold braid, beads, sequins, and crystals.
est. $250–$400 sold: $575
William Doyle Galleries 4/24/1996

COCKTAIL ENSEMBLE, 1950s

Dress has black wool crepe bodice with black satin waistline, chiffon skirt, beige sleeveless bolero edged with black satin.
est. $300–$500 sold: $460
William Doyle Galleries 11/17/1994

COCKTAIL ENSEMBLE, 1960s

Tight-fitting gold moiré sheath under a tent dress of gauze sewn with gold lamé ribbons in lattice pattern, bottom with beads and crystals.
est. $800–$1200 sold: $805
William Doyle Galleries 5/6/1998

G

Dress, 1950s
Black faille short-sleeved bodice buttoning at one side, full skirt pleated into waistband.
est. $300–$500 sold: $632
William Doyle Galleries 11/16/1999

Dress, 1950s
Silk pongee with foliage print in green and black, sleeveless bodice, full skirt.
est. $200–$300 sold: $1380
William Doyle Galleries 5/12/1999

Dress, 1970s
Red silk with quilted stitch edges.
est. $200–$300 sold: $373
William Doyle Galleries 9/30/1993

Ensemble, 1950s
Black wool sleeveless dress outlined at boat neck with satin bands, half-belt of black satin, short flared jacket with four pockets.
est. $100–$150 sold: $287
William Doyle Galleries 4/24/1996

Ensemble, 1970s
Long-sleeved jacket with wide flat collar, sleeveless vest and wide-legged hip-hugger pants of heavy ivory guipure lace, with sheer chiffon.
est. $700–$900 sold: $1092.50
William Doyle Galleries 5/2/2000

Evening Coat, 1950s
Metallic gold, brown, gray floral three-quarter-length coat with fitted silhouette, three-quarter-length sleeves, notched lapel, brown silk lining.
est. $300–$500 sold: $316.25
Skinner 9/14/2000

Evening Ensemble, 1980s
Blouse of silk tulle with floral rhinestone and beadwork, long sheer sleeves, jewel neck, slim skirt of silk, released in knife pleats at hem.
est. $400–$600 sold: $1035
William Doyle Galleries 11/2/2000

Evening Gown, 1960s
Long white silk, halter style with red and blue polka dots, leather belt with red and blue stripes.
est. not available sold: $495
The Paper Bag Princess 1/8/1998

Evening Gown, 1960s
Sheath with silk faille skirt, long-sleeved black lace bodice encrusted with clusters of rhinestones set in lattice framework.
est. $800–$1200 sold: $575
William Doyle Galleries 11/10/1998

Evening Gown, 1960s
Bandeau bodice sewn with horizontal rows of yellow and blue bugle beads, attached only to skirt front, skirt of yellow/green crepe.
est. $300–$500 sold: $316
William Doyle Galleries 5/12/1999

Evening Gown, 1960s
Long white skirt straight in front and gathered in back under a black minidress with bib-front bodice and bare back, square rhinestone buttons.
est. $1000–$1500 sold: $1150
William Doyle Galleries 5/6/1998

Evening Gown, 1960s
Black chiffon shimmering with rhinestone and crystal discs arranged horizontally and graduated in size.
est. $1500–$2000 sold: $2990
William Doyle Galleries 11/10/1998

Evening Gown, 1960s
V neck sleeveless tunic of black wool knit, long, narrow skirt of black satin, black satin ribbon sash.
est. $250–$400 sold: $316
William Doyle Galleries 4/24/1996

Evening Gown, 1970s
Aubergine satin, bodice bare to waist at back, scarf ends tying at throat, edges trimmed with bands of black bugle beads, flared skirt of black satin.
est. $600–$800 sold: $575
William Doyle Galleries 11/16/1999

G

EVENING GOWN, 1997
Silk with blue and green foliate pattern, overlay of black lace studded with blue velvet pompoms. Jennifer Jones, 1997 Academy Awards.
est. not available sold: $2530
Christie's Oscar Dress Auction 3/18/1999

GALLENGA

CAPE, 1930S
Semicircular, quilted red border, stenciled interpretive Luccese pattern around top third section, red lining and edging, signed: Gallenga.
est. $2000–$3000 sold: $4312.50
William Doyle Galleries 11/2/2000

COAT, 1920S
Black velvet stenciled in gold and silver with historical animal and foliate pattern.
est. $1500–$2000 sold: $3680
William Doyle Galleries 11/12/1997

COAT, 1920S
Black silk velvet with stenciled gold and silver Medieval pattern.
est. $1000–$1500 sold: $690
William Doyle Galleries 4/27/1994

COAT, 1920S
Cardigan-style with long pointed Medieval sleeves, black velvet with Renaissance-inspired pattern stenciled in gold and silver.
est. $600–$800 sold: $2530
William Doyle Galleries 11/16/1999

EVENING SHAWL, 1920S
Brown velvet with gold stenciled design.
est. $400–$600 sold: $632
Sotheby's 9/30/1999

SHAWL, 1920S
Green, gray, aquamarine silk velvet with border of lilac silk, stenciled with dogs and birds, border stenciled with vines.
est. $200–$300 sold: $805
William Doyle Galleries 4/24/1996

SHAWL, 1930
Ivory silk chiffon stenciled in gold with small leafy vine pattern, sewn at each end with border of mango chiffon.
est. $100–$125 sold: $345
William Doyle Galleries 6/11/1997

GALLIANO, JOHN

COCKTAIL DRESS, 1980S
Slip dress in two layers, gold and black knit snakeskin pattern sheath overlaid with black net, plunging nude front and back bodice.
est. $800–$1200 sold: $460
William Doyle Galleries 11/16/1999

EVENING ENSEMBLE, 1997
Gray flannel "New Look" jacket with nipped waist and padded hips and Spanish shawl wrap skirt with knotted fringe. Excellent condition, unworn.
est. $1000–$1200 sold: $4312.50
William Doyle Galleries 11/2/2000

EVENING JACKET, 1990S
Black moiré silk, waist-length at front, shorter at back, cut full around the torso as a cape, fold-over collar, sleeves wide, flaring bell-shaped cuff.
est. $400–$600 sold: $1265
William Doyle Galleries 5/2/2000

GANEV, TZETZI

EVENING GOWN, 1985
Green crepe asymmetrical empire silhouette with shirred bodice and single dolman sleeve, left shoulder bare, skirt accented with kick pleat. Angelica Huston, 1985 Academy Awards.
est. not available sold: $3450
Christie's Oscar Dress Auction 3/18/1999

GARDINER, LIZZY

DRESS, 1994
Exact replica of the dress constructed of
171 American Express Cards, connected by
links, chain straps. Lizzy Gardiner, 1994
Academy Awards.
est. not available sold: $12,650
Christie's Oscar Dress Auction 3/18/1999

G GERNREICH, RUDI

BATHING SUIT, 1960S
Brown nylon, tank top.
est. $300–$500 sold: $460
William Doyle Galleries 5/12/1999

BATHING SUIT, 1960S
Brown nylon, tank top.
est. $300–$500 sold: $488.75
William Doyle Galleries 5/2/2000

BATHING SUIT, 1966
Top and bottom of bright red wool and
cotton knit petals lined in yellow.
est. $400–$600 sold: $2760
William Doyle Galleries 12/6/1995

BATHING SUIT, 1967
Wool knit, tan and white, with tan straps,
size 12.
est. $800–$1200 sold: $748
William Doyle Galleries 5/2/2000

BATHING SUIT, 1967
Wool knit, black and tobacco diagonal
stripes, black straps.
est. $800–$1200 sold: $862.50
William Doyle Galleries 5/2/2000

BATHING SUIT, 1967
Wool knit, with high waist, thin straps
sewn close together in front, farther apart
at back, yellow and white check with yellow straps.
est. $800–$1200 sold: $747.50
William Doyle Galleries 5/2/2000

BATHING SUIT, 1967
Wool knit, diagonal tan and purple stripes,
purple straps, size 14.
est. $800–$1200 sold: $690
William Doyle Galleries 5/2/2000

BATHING SUIT, 1967
Black and brown diagonal stripes with
black straps.
est. $800–$1200 sold: $2070
William Doyle Galleries 5/12/1999

BATHING SUIT, 1967
Brown herringbone.
est. $800–$1200 sold: $1495
William Doyle Galleries 5/12/1999

BATHING SUIT, 1967
Brown wool.
est. $800–$1000 sold: $1840
William Doyle Galleries 5/12/1999

BATHING SUIT, 1967
Lime green wool.
est. $800–$1200 sold: $1840
William Doyle Galleries 5/12/1999

BATHING SUIT, 1967
Orange wool.
est. $800–$1200 sold: $1610
William Doyle Galleries 5/12/1999

BATHING SUIT, 1967
Diagonal brown and purple stripes, purple
straps.
est. $800–$1200 sold: $2070
William Doyle Galleries 5/12/1999

BATHING SUIT, 1967
Gray wool.
est. $800–$1200 sold: $1725
William Doyle Galleries 5/12/1999

BATHING SUIT, 1967
Yellow and white checked wool knit with
high waist, thin straps sewn close together
in front and farther apart in back.
est. $800–$1200 sold: $1840
William Doyle Galleries 5/12/1999

BATHING SUIT, 1967
Brown herringbone tweed, high-waisted
with thin knit straps sewn closely together
in front, farther apart in back.
est. $2000–$2500 sold: $2875
William Doyle Galleries 11/10/1998

Bathing Suit, 1967
Wool knit, tan and white, with tan straps, size 12.
est. $800–$1200 sold: $805
William Doyle Galleries 5/2/2000

Bathing Suit, 1967
White with electric blue stripes and straps, labeled: Rudi Gernreich Design for Harmon Knitwear, with original paper hand tag, unworn.
est. $1200–$1600 sold: $1150
William Doyle Galleries 11/2/2000

Bathing Suit, 1968
Black wool knit one-piece with circular cut-outs on each side and patent leather belt.
est. $750–$1000 sold: $2300
Sotheby's 4/8/1998

Bathing Suit, 1970–1971
Cinnamon and black.
est. $400–$600 sold: $1150
William Doyle Galleries 4/24/1996

Bathing Suit, 1971
Black and brown wool knit, black straps wrap around body in crisscrossed manner.
est. $2000–$3000 sold: $2875
Sotheby's 4/8/1998

Bra, 1960s
For Exquisite Forms, black sheer soft cup, nude bra.
est. not available sold: $225
The Paper Bag Princess 1/8/1999

Coat, 1960
Black and ivory wool woven in a scrolling foliage pattern.
est. $125–$175 sold: $230
William Doyle Galleries 4/24/1996

Coat, 1960s
Black plush wool, single-breasted with stand-away neck, fastening down front with large buttons.
est. $200–$300 sold: $373
William Doyle Galleries 12/5/1996

Coat, 1969
Black cotton knit, quilted, ankle-length with industrial zippers.
est. $200–$300 sold: $287
William Doyle Galleries 4/24/1996

Coat, 1970s
Black fur felt, single-breasted button-front car coat.
est. not available sold: $895
The Paper Bag Princess 9/1/1998

Coat Dress, 1970s
Black wool knit maxi-length sweater coat/dress with synthetic leather trim and snap front.
est. not available sold: $1295
The Paper Bag Princess 3/1/1997

Cocktail Dress, 1970s
Black wool knit, floor-length with V neck, upturned V high waist and long sleeves.
est. $125–$175 sold: $431
William Doyle Galleries 5/6/1998

Cocktail Dress, 1972
Navy wool with zipper front, sleeves of transparent blue silk, navy belt.
est. $750–$1000 sold: $1725
William Doyle Galleries 9/30/1993

Dress
Navy knit A-line knee-length dress with flared sleeves.
est. not available sold: $495
The Paper Bag Princess 11/1/1996

Dress, 1960s
Rectangular checkerboard fabric of gold and gray, cap sleeves.
est. $300–$500 sold: $488
William Doyle Galleries 11/17/1994

Dress, 1960s
Long tank-top dress of pink and orange striped knit, faux sweater of smaller stripes sewn at back, sleeves wrapping around shoulders, tying in front.
est. $700–$900 sold: $1265
William Doyle Galleries 11/10/1998

G

DRESS, 1960s
Black-and-white-checked knit, sleeves of
red faux sweater tying in front.
est. $300–$500 sold: $1725
William Doyle Galleries 11/12/1997

DRESS, 1960s
Geometric design on front in lavender with
orange, back of dress is solid orange, boat
neck, long sleeves.
est. not available sold: $247
eBay Online Auctions 4/10/2000

DRESS, 1960s
Long black knit with randomly spaced
chartreuse and pink circle appliqués, long
sleeves, high neck, side slits.
est. $600–$800 sold: $920
William Doyle Galleries 11/10/1998

DRESS, 1960s
Red and white gingham wool knit, A-line
dress, cut-out shoulders and short sleeves.
est. $100–$150 sold: $316
William Doyle Galleries 4/24/1996

DRESS, 1960s
Wool knit, A-line red with white honeycomb print, above the knee, cap sleeves.
est. not available sold: $395
The Paper Bag Princess 2/17/2000

DRESS, 1963
Black and white checkerboard wool knit
with V neck and flared sleeves, obi of diagonally striped purple and red knit with
green tie.
est. $500–$750 sold: $4370
William Doyle Galleries 4/12/1995

DRESS, 1965
Wool knit woven with purple and pink
checks with bodice band and sleeve facing
of red with blue circles, green bodice tie,
kimono sleeves.
est. $300–$500 sold: $862
William Doyle Galleries 11/16/1999

DRESS, 1965
Wool knit woven with small purple and
black checks, bodice band and sleeve facing
of larger checks, red bodice tie, kimono
sleeves.
est. $300–$500 sold: $920
William Doyle Galleries 11/16/1999

DRESS, 1965
Knee-length, wool knit woven with diagonal black and white stripes, green bodice
band and sleeve facing, purple bodice tie,
kimono sleeves.
est. $300–$500 sold: $1955
William Doyle Galleries 11/16/1999

DRESS, 1966
Blue vinyl A-line with stitching around
neck, armholes, and hem, strategically cut-
out holes.
est. $700–$900 sold: $402
William Doyle Galleries 5/12/1999

DRESS, 1966
Purple and red checked wool knit, empire-
waisted with green ribbon around bustline
forming center bow.
est. $750–$1000 sold: $1265
Sotheby's 4/8/1998

DRESS, 1967
Silk printed with Op Art checkerboard in
navy, red, and cream.
est. $200–$300 sold: $747
William Doyle Galleries 4/27/1994

DRESS, 1968
Yellow wool knit inset down the front with
a band of clear vinyl.
est. $300–$500 sold: $431
William Doyle Galleries 12/5/1996

DRESS, 1968
Long-sleeved shift with draped funnel neck
of white Banlon printed with black letters
of the alphabet in various sizes and types.
est. $300–$500 sold: $690
William Doyle Galleries 11/16/1999

G

DRESS, 1968
Ivory wool knit inset with two horizontal bands of clear plastic.
est. $300–$500 sold: $460
William Doyle Galleries 12/5/1996

DRESS, 1968
See-through inset with clear plastic strips, matching bikini pants.
est. $150–$200 sold: $287
William Doyle Galleries 4/24/1996

DRESS, 1968
Black satin with turtleneck, zipper running from neck to sleeve and side seam.
est. $300–$400 sold: $345
William Doyle Galleries 9/30/1993

DRESS, 1969
Brown silk chiffon with elasticized neckline, high waist, puffed sleeves and tiered ruffled miniskirt.
est. $300–$500 sold: $575
William Doyle Galleries 4/24/1996

DRESS, 1970s
Long knit patterned in purple and red blocks and zebra stripes, leotard-style long-sleeved bodice and full skirt.
est. $200–$300 sold: $373
William Doyle Galleries 6/11/1997

DRESS, 1970s
Silver and gold Lurex, maxi-length, cross-your-heart neckline with silver Lurex trim, long-sleeved, empire waist and A-line skirt; side-seam pockets.
est. not available sold: $1295
The Paper Bag Princess 1/5/1999

DRESS, 1970s
Silver Lurex tank style with long sleeves.
est. not available sold: $895
The Paper Bag Princess 12/1/1996

DRESS, 1971
Black and gray/white wool knit worked with stripes for the jumper torso and belt, gingham checks for the collar, sleeves, and skirt.
est. $250–$400 sold: $345
William Doyle Galleries 4/24/1996

DRESS, 1973
Floor-length sheath of blue wool knit, appliquéd with psychedelic bull's-eyes and large daisy heads, marigold and pink band sleeve and neck trim.
est. $500–$700 sold: $1265
William Doyle Galleries 11/16/1999

DRESS, 1973
Knit floor-length dress with silver bands creating crisscross bodice, V neck, long fitted sleeves, A-line silhouette.
est. $400–$600 sold: $373.75
Skinner 9/14/2000

ENSEMBLE, 1960s
Olive and red diagonal striped wool, tapered-leg capri pants and two bandeau tops.
est. $300–$500 sold: $431
William Doyle Galleries 5/12/1999

ENSEMBLE, 1967
Wool knit knee socks, tunic with cream collar and red bow, hat with chin ties.
est. $500–$750 sold: $2300
William Doyle Galleries 4/24/1996

EVENING GOWN, 1960s
Long-sleeved, high neck, metallic Lurex knit, gold and silver alternating panels, zippered back, slit at one side, excellent condition, no flaws.
est. not available sold: $800.08
eBay Online Auctions 8/23/2000

EVENING GOWN, 1970
Patterned with triangle motif, straight sheath, long sleeves, off-the-shoulder neckline, side slit pockets, very good condition.
est. $500–$700 sold: $747.50
William Doyle Galleries 11/2/2000

JUMPSUIT, 1960s
Wool knit woven with immense white dots against a black background, two knit belts of yellow and red.
est. $300–$500 sold: $517
William Doyle Galleries 12/6/1995

G

MAILLOT, 1955
Black wool knit with Swedish flag blue midriff, buttons down the front, V neck.
est. $75–$100 sold: $287
William Doyle Galleries 4/24/1996

MAILLOT, 1962
Black wool knit with triangular midriff cut-outs.
est. $200–$300 sold: $230
William Doyle Galleries 12/5/1996

MAILLOT, 1963
Wool knit patches in bright geometric patterns and solids, with black vinyl tie belt.
est. $200–$300 sold: $258
William Doyle Galleries 12/5/1996

NIGHTGOWN, 1960
Full-length, orange and green baby-doll style, with puff sleeves and green satin ribbon tied at the empire waist.
est. not available sold: $395
The Paper Bag Princess 7/1/1998

NIGHTGOWN, 1960s
Baby-doll style with white puff sleeves, empire waist with a pink bow, blue skirt.
est. not available sold: $325
The Paper Bag Princess 7/1/1998

PANTS, 1967
Black wool knit tunic with tiered ruffled sleeves of black-and-white-plaid knit, matching ruffled pull-on pants with stocking feet.
est. $300–$500 sold: $402
William Doyle Galleries 12/5/1996

PANTS, 1967
Black wool knit tunic with ruffled sleeves of black and white plaid, matching ruffle on pants, stocking feet.
est. $600–$900 sold: $1840
William Doyle Galleries 11/17/1994

PANTS, 1970s
Shocking pink silk matte jersey, hip-huggers with two front slash pockets and three-inch zipper fly.
est. not available sold: $695
The Paper Bag Princess 6/1/1997

PANTSUIT, 1970
Black wool knit woven with nutmeg parallelograms, turtleneck tunic with zipper from neck down one arm, pants zipper down one leg.
est. $250–$400 sold: $345
William Doyle Galleries 4/24/1996

SUNSUIT, 1965–1966
Couture collection, cut-in camisole low-waisted bodice of cream silk printed with orange ribbon swirls, shorts of same print in violet.
est. $300–$400 sold: $258
William Doyle Galleries 4/24/1996

TOP, 1970s
Fitted, stretch metallic gold top with mock turtleneck, long sleeves, back zipper.
est. $75–$100 sold: $258
William Doyle Galleries 11/12/1997

GIGLI, ROMERO

EVENING COAT, 1989
Changeante brown silk, quilted pattern with sequins, swing coat with oversized shawl collar, narrow sleeves, labeled: Callaghan/Made in Italy.
est. $700–$900 sold: $977.50
William Doyle Galleries 11/2/2000

WRAP, 1980s
Gold metallic mesh, studded with simulated pearls and gold-toned chain tassel at both ends, reversible silk with tassels, floral pattern.
est. $200–$400 sold: $316.25
Skinner 12/16/1999

GIMBEL, SOPHIE

COCKTAIL DRESS, 1950s
Black and white chiffon.
est. $100–$150 sold: $258
William Doyle Galleries 9/30/1993

EVENING GOWN, 1940s
Blue silk net with blue sequins in spiderweb pattern with beaded dragonflies caught in web, skirt with six matching petticoats.
est. $800–$1200 sold: $1840
Sotheby's 4/8/1998

EVENING GOWN, 1950s
Red faille trimmed with orange floral cut velvet.
est. $100–$150 sold: $201
William Doyle Galleries 9/30/1993

GIORGIO OF BEVERLY HILLS

ENSEMBLE, 1970s
Brown silk bias-cut halter top and skirt with long bronze beading.
est. not available sold: $1295
The Paper Bag Princess 7/1/2000

ENSEMBLE, 1970s
Two-piece, silk pleated, strands of bronze beads, dangling top has open back with crossing straps, long pleated flowing skirt, excellent condition.
est. not available sold: $1200
The Paper Bag Princess 7/28/2000

GIORGIO DI SANT'ANGELO

BIKINI, 1970s
Cropped tank top and spare bottom of white stretch fabric studded with faceted white stones set in silver metal.
est. $300–$500 sold: $546
William Doyle Galleries 5/2/2000

BODY SUIT, 1970s
All-in-one knee-length leotard with round front neckline and triangular panel at bare back, black lace re-embroidered with jet beads over red satin.
est. $500–$700 sold: $747.50
William Doyle Galleries 5/2/2000

CAFTAN, 1970
Patchwork of various velvets, printed cottons, and brocaded lamé, edging at neckline, cuffs, and hem of silver and gold lamé ribbons.
est. $750–$1000 sold: $3450
Sotheby's 4/8/1998

CAPE, 1970s
Fur arranged to overlap like bird feathers, hem sewn with tails, brightly patterned wool challis lining, labeled: Sant' Angelo, very good condition.
est. $700–$900 sold: $1265
William Doyle Galleries 11/2/2000

COCKTAIL DRESS, 1970
Black cashmere with halter neck strap, back standing away from the body via an upward swag of back fabric attached to strap at neck, black fox hem.
est. $400–$600 sold: $1725
William Doyle Galleries 11/16/1999

COCKTAIL DRESS, 1970s
Fuchsia stretch jersey tube draped Austrian-style at sides, slim straps billowing into flowing back cape.
est. $75–$100 sold: $460
William Doyle Galleries 5/12/1999

COCKTAIL DRESS, 1970s
Tight black minidress with bare bodice sewn at top and bottom with bands of Mongolian lamb.
est. $300–$500 sold: $2300
William Doyle Galleries 11/16/1999

DRESS, 1960s
Turquoise form-fitting gauze with Lycra minidress.
est. not available sold: $395
The Paper Bag Princess 3/1/1998

DRESS, 1970s
Strapless tube of black lace re-embroidered with jet beads over copper satin lining, back extending into long scarf wrapping around neck to front.
est. $600–$800 sold: $805
William Doyle Galleries 5/2/2000

DRESS, 1970s
Black, long-sleeved, matte jersey dress, lace insert on sleeve. Excellent condition.
est. not available sold: $495
The Paper Bag Princess 9/21/2000

DRESS, 1970s
Ankle-length A-line dress of pieced and ap-pliquéd velvet depicting Native American–inspired motifs, white feather trim cuffs and hem, apron with beads.
est. $200–$300 sold: $747
William Doyle Galleries 12/5/1996

ENSEMBLE, 1970s
Sarong skirt, wrap bodice, cape of silk vel-vet tie dyed in rainbow colors and trimmed with bead fringe.
est. $1500–$2000 sold: $2990
William Doyle Galleries 5/12/1999

ENSEMBLE, 1970s
Black velvet A-line maxi-skirt and matching velvet jacket with multicolored "candy" buttons and colored trim.
est. not available sold: $595
The Paper Bag Princess

ENSEMBLE, 1980s
Cream silk camisole, straight-leg pants and matching beaded blouse-styled jacket.
est. not available sold: $495
The Paper Bag Princess

EVENING COAT, 1970s
Hanging full from shoulders, with Nehru collar, side slits, blue silk quilted with geo-metric pattern applied to sleeves and hem, silver trim on edges.
est. $300–$400 sold: $460
William Doyle Galleries 5/2/2000

EVENING ENSEMBLE, 1970s
Pink chiffon halter dress with flowing lay-ered skirt and integral stretch briefs.
est. $900–$1200 sold: $1725
William Doyle Galleries 5/12/1999

EVENING GOWN, 1970s
Black spotted net, strapless bodice a mere band tying at back, full skirt standing away from body by way of stiff black fox hem band.
est. $700–$900 sold: $1495
William Doyle Galleries 11/16/1999

GLOVER OF KENTUCKY

TEA GOWN, 1911
Ivory printed silk with pink, lavender, green, yellow floral pattern, empire waist, square neckline, lace and silk sleeves, asym-metrically cut skirt.
est. $200–$300 sold: $517.50
Skinner 9/14/2000

GOLDWORM

DRESS, 1960s
Leopard print wool jersey, knee-length, with long sleeves, round neck, zip up the back.
est. not available sold: $295
The Paper Bag Princess 6/15/1998

DRESS, 1960s
Wool jersey, yellow, blue, orange, and black geometric printed motif, long sleeves, knee-length with tie belt.
est. not available sold: $325
The Paper Bag Princess 5/9/1998

GORDON, BILLY

EVENING GOWN, 1954
Black chiffon and crepe floor-length halter dress, halter top embroidered with green sequins and rhinestones, fitted waist, tiered skirt.
est. $600–$800 sold: $489
Skinner 12/16/1999

GRAY, AMELIA

ENSEMBLE, 1960s
Black A-line dress and coat with jeweled
buttons, mink fur collar and cuffs.
est. not available sold: $595
The Paper Bag Princess 9/18/1998

GREER, HOWARD

COCKTAIL DRESS, 1950s
Black mousseline with underbodice of
black Alençon over beige satin, black satin
cummerbund and full mousseline skirt.
est. $60–$80 sold: $431
William Doyle Galleries 4/24/1996

COCKTAIL DRESS, 1950s
Ivory cotton dress with silver bugle beads
and rhinestones, sweetheart neckline, short
sleeves, slash pockets, narrow skirt, nylon
lining in bust.
est. $700–$1000 sold: $690
Skinner 12/16/1999

GRÉS, MADAME

COAT, 1960s
Baby blue lined with white knit and
trimmed with white mink.
est. $500–$750 sold: $258
William Doyle Galleries 9/30/1993

COCKTAIL DRESS, 1950s
Pink matte jersey, one-shouldered, fitted
torso intricately draped above ankle-length
tulip skirt.
est. $400–$600 sold: $920
William Doyle Galleries 4/12/1995

COCKTAIL DRESS, 1963
Purple and orange-red matte jersey with
matching purple matte jersey shawl.
est. $750–$100 sold: $517
William Doyle Galleries 4/12/1995

COCKTAIL DRESS, 1970s
Navy and blue silk crepe asymmetrical
sheath with pleating on the shoulder falling
into single cap sleeve, asymmetrical black
back panel.
est. $800–$1200 sold: $920
Sotheby's 10/29/1997

COCKTAIL DRESS, 1970s
Black silk jersey with open bodice, separate
back panel attaches to collar and flows
down back, open batwing sleeves gathered
into cuffs.
est. $1000–$1500 sold: $920
Sotheby's 10/29/1999

COCKTAIL DRESS, 1970s
Teal green silk crepe slip dress with spaghetti
straps, silk tunic with symmetrical seam at
left cowl neckline creating toga effect.
est. $800–$1200 sold: $920
Sotheby's 10/29/1997

COCKTAIL DRESS, 1975
Navy silk jersey finely pleated on halter
bodice, diamond cut-out midriff, straps
meet T-back.
est. $2000–$3000 sold: $4887
Sotheby's 10/29/1997

COCKTAIL DRESS, 1976
Black silk georgette bodice with knife
pleating in triangular pattern, two triangle
cut-outs below bust and abdomen, straight
skirt with fluted hem.
est. $2000–$3000 sold: $5175
Sotheby's 10/29/1997

DRESS, 1970s
Gossamer black chiffon, bodice bare, high-
waisted, low front V to waistband, skirt
with multiple pointed floating panels, long
scarf and satin belt.
est. $700–$900 sold: $3162.50
William Doyle Galleries 11/2/2000

DRESS, 1970s
Brown angora wool jersey cut in monastic
style with full elbow-length sleeves, self-
tying scarf at nape of the neck.
est. $300–$500 sold: $546
William Doyle Galleries 4/12/1995

G

ENSEMBLE, 1971
Coral tunic and pants.
est. $500–$750 sold: $373
William Doyle Galleries 9/30/1993

EVENING GOWN, 1960
Gray silk bodice, pink silk skirt, separate
gray apron.
est. $750–$1000 sold: $862
William Doyle Galleries 4/27/1994

EVENING SUIT, 1960s
Chine satin with blue, purple, and pink
paisley brocaded in gold and yellow with
floral scrolls, jacket has Nehru collar and
amethyst bead buttons.
est. $200–$300 sold: $431
William Doyle Galleries 12/6/1995

EVENING SUIT, 1960s
Chine satin with blue, purple, and pink
paisley brocaded in gold and yellow floral
scrolls, jacket has Nehru collar, amethyst
buttons.
est. $600–$900 sold: $345
William Doyle Galleries 4/27/1994

JACKET, 1950s
Beige mohair with four double-button and
loop closures, trimmed with tricolor fur at
collar, front, and cuffs.
est. $100–$150 sold: $373
William Doyle Galleries 11/12/1997

GRIFFE, JACQUES

CAPE, 1950s
Ivory silk with large, square black buttons.
est. $100–$150 sold: $345
William Doyle Galleries 12/6/1995

COCKTAIL DRESS, 1953
Navy silk faille has double-pleat boatneck
and cap sleeves, folded and appliquéd foliate motif at hips, multilayered taffeta-cov-
ered tulle skirt.
est. $1200–$1500 sold: $1380
Sotheby's 10/29/1997

GUCCI

BAG, 1970s
Doctor's style opening, burgundy leather
"G" logo print, hard-sided bottom, two fitted leather handles on top, gold-toned
hardware.
est. not available sold: $595
The Paper Bag Princess 12/18/2000

BAG, 1970s
Tan-colored ostrich skin, large travel size,
two handles, overflap with large "G" interlocking logo in gold-toned metal.
est. not available sold: $2225
The Paper Bag Princess 5/18/2001

BELT, 1970s
4-inch-wide leather and suede belt with
large gold-toned horse bit decoration, belt
and hardware stamped.
est. $200–$300 sold: $287.50
Skinner 9/14/2000

CASE, 1950s
Tan textured leather lined with burgundy
leather, fitted with silver metal containers,
brush, leather-backed mirror, and mani-
cure set.
est. $150–$200 sold: $920
William Doyle Galleries 6/11/1997

CASE, 1960s
Black lizard in the shape of an oversized
doctor's bag, double handles, trapezoidal
top portion hinged to bottom cosmetic
case.
est. $400–$600 sold: $373
William Doyle Galleries 5/12/1999

CASE, 1970s
Large, rectangular, hard frame overnight
bag, navy/white logo print, navy trim,
blue/red stripe, gold-toned hardware,
"Made in Italy by Gucci" inside.
est. $600–$800 sold: $632.50
Skinner 9/14/2000

Case, 1980s

Navy, white, and red toiletry case, camel leather lining with navy trim, interior pockets, bottle straps, mirror, stamped "Gucci Italy 067" in lining.
est. $600–$800 sold: $488.75
Skinner 9/14/2000

Clutch Bag, 1970s

Brown suede clutch with large central gold-toned double "G" motif, camel and brown leather lining, black patent leather clutch.
est. $200–$300 sold: $374
Skinner 12/16/1999

Coat, 1970s

Moss green suede, micro-ribbed pattern in suede, leather trimming, enamel and sterling silver tiger toggle on neck closure, pocket, and belt buckle.
est. not available sold: $2100
The Paper Bag Princess 12/19/2000

Coat, 1970s

Tan suede, collar, belt, pockets and sleeve trim of leather, metal leopard's-head ornament at waist.
est. $300–$400 sold: $1150
William Doyle Galleries 6/11/1997

Coat, 1970s

Light brown cobra, double-breasted trench coat with two patch pockets, double back vents, belt with gilt metal ornaments, detachable brown fox collar.
est. $1000–$1500 sold: $1380
William Doyle Galleries 5/12/1999

Coat, 1970s

Grayish/green suede, micro-ribbed pattern in suede, leather trimming, enamel tiger toggle on neck closure, and enamel belt buckle, excellent condition.
est. not available sold: $1900
The Paper Bag Princess 12/19/2000

Coat

Green leather, full length.
est. not available sold: $305
eBay Online Auctions 4/25/2000

Coat, 1970s

Double-breasted suede, red and green racing stripes running from pockets to hem, Gucci logo buttons.
est. not available sold: $1031
eBay Online Auctions 2/18/2000

Coat, 1973

Green suede and leather below-the-knee-length, gold-toned "G" insignia buttons.
est. $300–$350 sold: $920
Skinner 12/16/1999

Coat, 1975

Red suede below-the-knee-length, horseshoe insignia buttons.
est. $200–$250 sold: $431
Skinner 12/16/1999

Coat, 1980s

Baby blue leather car coat, with baby blue faux fur printed leopard cuffs and collar. Large gold-toned, ornate buttons.
est. not available sold: $1200
The Paper Bag Princess 12/1/1998

Dress, 1960s

Black suede shirtdress buttoning in front with self tie, solid vertical sections impressed with signature snaffle horse bits.
est. $200–$300 sold: $632
William Doyle Galleries 11/10/1998

Dress, 1970s

Printed canvas twill A-line fitted dress, knee-length, with brown "G"s, lace-up neckline, with sterling silver horse hooves and chain toggles.
est. not available sold: $1695
The Paper Bag Princess 3/1/1998

Evening Bag, 1940s

Black satin with petal-inspired design, three compartments, rhinestone clasp, rhinestone "vines" handle attachments.
est. $200–$300 sold: $373
Skinner 12/16/1999

Evening Bag, 1960s

Black silk charmeuse with sterling silver frame and rhinestone clasp.
est. $200–$300 sold: $632
Sotheby's 12/9/1998

G

HANDBAG, 1930s
Black suede with narrow black calf piping.
est. $200–$300 sold: $287
William Doyle Galleries 9/30/1993

HANDBAG, 1950
Brown embossed leather with square bottom, bamboo segments at base of handle.
est. $800–$1200 sold: $1495
Sotheby's 4/8/1998

HANDBAG, 1950s
Black crocodile with flat, oblong bottom, straight frame, ring clasp and crocodile coin purse.
est. $300–$500 sold: $1035
William Doyle Galleries 11/12/1997

HANDBAG, 1960
Black alligator with cylinder of lapis lazuli as closure.
est. $600–$800 sold: $2070
Sotheby's 4/8/1998

HANDBAG, 1960s
Brown leather with silver and enamel tiger's-head buckle.
est. not available sold: $695
The Paper Bag Princess

HANDBAG, 1960s
Black pebble-grain calf and red calf, gilt metal stirrup buckle with lock and key.
est. $200–$400 sold: $316
William Doyle Galleries 12/5/1996

HANDBAG, 1960s
Black alligator with fold-over snap closure, the handles attached with gilt metal buckles set with pink faceted stones.
est. $400–$500 sold: $316
William Doyle Galleries 6/11/1997

HANDBAG, 1960s
Brown lizard with rounded fold-over flap, bamboo pivot clasp and handle.
est. $150–$200 sold: $575
William Doyle Galleries 6/11/1997

HANDBAG, 1960s
Beige crocodile with single handle, gilt metal ring clasp.
est. $150–$200 sold: $460
William Doyle Galleries 11/10/1998

HANDBAG, 1960s
Black crocodile with single handle, gilt metal ring clasp.
est. $200–$300 sold: $632
William Doyle Galleries 11/10/1998

HANDBAG, 1960s
Black glazed alligator designed to be worn with a gold chain handle.
est. $300–$400 sold: $402
William Doyle Galleries 12/5/1996

HANDBAG, 1960s
Black structured leather with half circle black Lucite handle and toggle closure.
est. not available sold: $595
The Paper Bag Princess 3/14/2000

HANDBAG, 1960s
Black alligator, handles attached with gilt metal buckles.
est. $400–$600 sold: $1955
William Doyle Galleries 12/5/1996

HANDBAG, 1960s
Burgundy leather jewelry case with gold-plated hardware and decorative saddle stitching, four inner pockets, lockable jewelry compartment at bottom.
est. $600–$800 sold: $546.25
Skinner 12/16/1999

HANDBAG, 1960s
Bone leather with bamboo handle and pivot clasp, rounded fold-over flap.
est. $200–$300 sold: $373
William Doyle Galleries 5/6/1998

HANDBAG, 1960s
Black textured leather with bamboo handle and pivot clasp.
est. $100–$150 sold: $402
William Doyle Galleries 5/6/1998

HANDBAG, 1960S
Tan top-stitched calf with bamboo handle
and pivot clasp.
est. $200–$300 sold: $546
William Doyle Galleries 5/6/1998

HANDBAG, 1960S
Brown leather with soft sides, double bamboo handle.
est. $100–$150 sold: $402
William Doyle Galleries 11/12/1997

HANDBAG, 1960S
Crocodile, rectangular with flat top and
concave bottom, 18k gold square clasp and
chain mounts, gilt metal chain strap.
est. $1000–$1500 sold: $805
William Doyle Galleries 5/12/1999

HANDBAG, 1960S
Black crocodile with fold-over flap, side
gussets.
est. $400–$600 sold: $316
William Doyle Galleries 11/12/1997

HANDBAG, 1960S
Brown suede, rectangular with top handle,
geometric cut-out flap, gilt metal and
leather bar clasp.
est. $200–$300 sold: $402
William Doyle Galleries 5/12/1999

HANDBAG, 1960S
Burgundy alligator with black wooden
handle inset with a band of alligator.
est. $250–$400 sold: $632
William Doyle Galleries 12/6/1995

HANDBAG, 1960S
Black alligator with envelope flap and double handle.
est. $200–$300 sold: $373
William Doyle Galleries 11/17/1994

HANDBAG, 1960S
Bone calf with bamboo handle and toggle
catch.
est. $100–$150 sold: $373
William Doyle Galleries 12/6/1995

HANDBAG, 1960S
Red textured leather with bamboo handle
and bamboo pivot clasp.
est. $100–$150 sold: $373
William Doyle Galleries 11/12/1997

HANDBAG, 1960S
White grained leather with bamboo handle
and catch.
est. $50–$75 sold: $345
William Doyle Galleries 6/11/1997

HANDBAG, 1960S
Tailored, with rigid top frame, double handles, interior compartments.
est. $250–$350 sold: $748
William Doyle Galleries 5/2/2000

HANDBAG, 1960S
Brown glazed alligator with faux tortoise
chain handles, applied with a gold monogram.
est. $250–$400 sold: $517
William Doyle Galleries 12/6/1995

HANDBAG, 1960S
Black calf with handles of calf, gilt metal,
and bamboo.
est. $125–$175 sold: $373
William Doyle Galleries 4/12/1995

HANDBAG, 1970S
Burgundy leather handbag with rounded
top flap and bamboo toggle closure and
handle.
est. $250–$300 sold: $460
Skinner 12/16/1999

HANDBAG, 1970S
Black suede and calf with fold-over flap,
side gussets, double spring silver clasps and
gold-toned fittings.
est. $100–$150 sold: $345
William Doyle Galleries 11/12/1997

HANDBAG, 1970S
Black satin with four reversible covers:
red/navy calfskin; black patent
leather/white embossed leather; black calf-
skin/suede.
est. $800–$1200 sold: $920
Sotheby's 12/9/1998

G

HANDBAG, 1970s
Canvas with leather trim, printed with brown "G's, large gold-toned sliding ball clasp.
est. not available sold: $295
The Paper Bag Princess 1/1/2000

HANDBAG, 1970s
18k gold chain runs through four gold-ringed eyes, black crocodile.
est. $2000–$3000 sold: $2760
William Doyle Galleries 11/12/1997

HANDBAG, 1970s
Shoulder bag with double "G" print and double "G" gold-toned-metal closures.
est. not available sold: $325
The Paper Bag Princess 8/1/1999

HANDBAG, 1980s
Brown suede with plastic handle.
est. $400–$600 sold: $460
Sotheby's 12/9/1998

HANDBAG, 1980s
Black leather tailored bag with single handle and detachable shoulder strap, suitcase-style gilt metal clasp.
est. $400–$600 sold: $690
William Doyle Galleries 11/12/1997

HANDBAG, 1980s
Red and white logo print bag with red leather trim, blue/red striped handle, 10 × 9 in., with a white leather/gold hand close and black leather wallet.
est. $200–$400 sold: $632.50
Skinner 9/14/2000

HANDBAG, 1980s
Black patent leather, flap with geometric silver and gold clasp.
est. $100–$150 sold: $316
William Doyle Galleries 5/6/1998

HANDBAG, 1990s
Red patent leather handbag with triangular silhouette, short top handle, and silver closure and hardware, mustard leather lining.
est. $200–$300 sold: $230
Skinner 12/16/1999

JACKET, 1970s
Cropped shearling swing hip-length jacket with longer back hem, fur lining that forms shawl collar and cuffs.
est. $500–$700 sold: $977.50
Skinner 12/16/1999

JACKET, 1970s
Wool, single-breasted, printed with stirrups.
est. $125–$150 sold: $632
William Doyle Galleries 6/11/1997

JACKET, 1970s
Cropped brown shearling swing jacket with longer back hem, fur lining forms shawl collar and cuffs.
est. $500–$700 sold: $977
Skinner 12/16/1999

JEANS, 1970s
Red cotton twill flared jeans with gold-tone metal bit on each front patch pocket.
est. not available sold: $225
The Paper Bag Princess 5/1/1999

MINAUDIÈRE, 1960s
Patterned silver encrusted with clear and gray variously shaped rhinestones and gray faux pearls.
est. $150–$200 sold: $460
William Doyle Galleries 11/12/1997

MINAUDIÈRE, 1960s
Patterned gilt metal encrusted with faceted gold stones set in lattice pattern.
est. $150–$200 sold: $575
William Doyle Galleries 5/6/1998

PANTS, 1960
Camel-colored leather bell-bottoms with two front pockets, one back pocket, fly closure.
est. $400–$600 sold: $575
Sotheby's 4/8/1998

PANTS, 1970s
Hip-huggers, bell-bottom legs, canvas twill fabric, blue Gucci logo, lace-up front.
est. not available sold: $895
The Paper Bag Princess 12/8/2000

PANTS, 1970S
Beige cotton hip-huggers with gilt metal harness fittings at pockets.
est. $75–$100 sold: $373
William Doyle Galleries 6/11/1997

SHOULDER BAG, 1960S
Black leather with red and green surcingal stripe.
est. not available sold: $495
The Paper Bag Princess 9/1/1997

SHOULDER BAG, 1960S
Burgundy crocodile, small, with flap, rounded corners, closure tab with interlocking "G" logo, detachable self shoulder strap.
est. $500–$700 sold: $1265
William Doyle Galleries 11/10/1998

SHOULDER BAG, 1960S
Rust patent leather with sterling silver and enamel tiger's-head buckle clasp.
est. not available sold: $695
The Paper Bag Princess

SHOULDER BAG, 1970S
Large rectangular bag with darker camel overall "G" print, camel trim and piping, "Made in Italy by Gucci 14" on lining.
est. $400–$600 sold: $575
Skinner 9/14/2000

SHOULDER BAG, 1970S
Black suede with pivot clasp, green and red fabric strap.
est. $100–$150 sold: $373
William Doyle Galleries 6/11/1997

SHOULDER BAG, 1970S
Bag with rounded bottom, adjustable shoulder strap and gold-toned hardware, camel leather lining, stamped "Gucci."
est. $400–$600 sold: $546.25
Skinner 9/14/2000

SHOULDER BAG, 1970S
Brown lizard with lizard shoulder straps attached with bracelet link chains.
est. $200–$250 sold: $373
William Doyle Galleries 11/12/1997

SHOULDER BAG, 1970S
Brown lizard with rounded corners on body and fold-over flap, silver- and gold-toned metal pivot clasp and gold-toned shoulder chain with tiger's eye.
est. $200–$300 sold: $431
William Doyle Galleries 11/12/1997

TOP, 1970S
Cream silk with fitted ribbed waistband and printed flying duck motif on front.
est. not available sold: $125
The Paper Bag Princess 9/1/1999

TOTE BAG, 1980S
Rectangular tote bag with zipper top, round leather handles, gold-toned hardware, black suede lining with gold-toned plate stamped "Gucci."
est. $200–$400 sold: $230
Skinner 12/16/1999

GUERIN, GERMAINE

EVENING BAG, 1980S
Black crocodile with arched flap and rhinestone-set logo.
est. $100–$150 sold: $920
William Doyle Galleries 5/6/1998

HALLEE, JEANNE

EVENING GOWN, 1910
Ivory satin, train, allover bead and rhinestone embroidery, including bow and rose motif, vertical net insets, lace flounce sleeves with satin overlay.
est. $800–$1200 sold: $460
William Doyle Galleries 11/16/1999

HALLEY, GEORGE

COCKTAIL DRESS, 1960S
Lavender-checked wool, short-sleeved bodice embroidered with lattice pattern of white flower paillettes and rhinestones, circular skirt.
est. $500–$700 sold: $690
William Doyle Galleries 5/12/1999

HALSTON

BATHING SUIT, 1976
Black stretch satin with low V halter neck, bottom wrapping and tying in front.
est. $600–$800 sold: $1380
William Doyle Galleries 11/16/1999

BATHING SUIT, 1976
Black stretch satin tying at neck and wrapping around front at waist.
est. $400–$600 sold: $1495
William Doyle Galleries 5/12/1999

CAPE, 1970S
Greige, sewn at mid-back with gathered flounce, welt seam at edges.
est. $250–$350 sold: $575
William Doyle Galleries 5/2/2000

COAT, 1970S
Wide pointed lapels, large patch pockets, self belt.
est. $300–$500 sold: $374
William Doyle Galleries 5/2/2000

COAT, 1970S
Velvet tie dyed in marigold, green, and brown, shawl collar, patch pockets.
est. $800–$1200 sold: $1380
William Doyle Galleries 11/16/1999

COAT, 1970S
Black wool wrap coat with wide lapel, sloped shoulders, slash pockets, and self belt.
est. $200–$400 sold: $632.50
Skinner 12/16/1999

COAT, 1970S
Lavender Ultrasuede, double-breasted, belt, wide-brimmed soft rain hat.
est. $200–$300 sold: $488
William Doyle Galleries 11/12/1997

COAT, 1970S
Black wool with wide lapel, sloped shoulders, self belt.
est. $200–$400 sold: $632
Skinner 12/16/1999

COCKTAIL DRESS, 1960S
Knee-length, one-shouldered tube of red chiffon extending at left shoulder into a long scarf for wrapping or draping.
est. $600–$800 sold: $920
William Doyle Galleries 11/16/1999

COCKTAIL DRESS, 1970S
Strapless, four layers of black chiffon tying like a scarf in back over a keyhole opening.
est. $150–$250 sold: $402
William Doyle Galleries 12/6/1995

COCKTAIL DRESS, 1970S
Black silk jersey with maillot neckline.
est. $125–$175 sold: $632
William Doyle Galleries 12/6/1995

COCKTAIL DRESS, 1970S
Iridescent teal and black chiffon, one-shouldered, handkerchief hem and attached toga scarf.
est. $75–$125 sold: $373
William Doyle Galleries 11/17/1994

COCKTAIL DRESS, 1970S
Short slip dress of peach silk embroidered with iridescent clear sequins, blouson waist overdress of black sheer silk.
est. $200–$300 sold: $460
William Doyle Galleries 12/6/1995

COCKTAIL DRESS, 1970S
Metallic gray, sleeveless, bias-cut, low V front and back, sheer chiffon underslip, cape/jacket cut round and full.
est. $700–$900 sold: $1380
William Doyle Galleries 5/12/1999

COCKTAIL DRESS, 1970S
Strapless sheer bodice, full skirt with handkerchief ruffled hem, ruffled stole, labeled: Halston, good condition.
est. $600–$800 sold: $1035
William Doyle Galleries 11/2/2000

COCKTAIL DRESS, 1980S
Black floor-length wrap dress of pleated silk, V neck bodice with full bishop sleeves, skirt with ruffled hemline.
est. $100–$200 sold: $373
Skinner 12/16/1999

Dress, 1970

Green suede with scoop neck, zippered front and long bishop sleeves.
est. $80–$120 sold: $517
William Doyle Galleries 4/12/1995

Dress

Black, collar ties at one side, pleated bias crisscross panel that comes to a slit.
est. not available sold: $778
eBay Online Auctions 3/9/2000

Dress, 1970s

One-shouldered sheath of silk jersey, overlaid iridescent sequins, triangular scarf, labeled: Halston, very good condition.
est. $600–$800 sold: $862.50
William Doyle Galleries 11/2/2000

Dress, 1970s

Bib-front halter, gathered on a drawstring at neck, bare back, full skirt of multiple layers of chiffon in graduated tones, labeled: Halston.
est. $400–$600 sold: $977.50
William Doyle Galleries 11/2/2000

Dress, 1970s

Melon cashmere fashioned as a sport shirt with pointed collar, three-button placket, and short sleeves.
est. $200–$300 sold: $373
William Doyle Galleries 5/6/1998

Dress, 1970s

Peach Ultrasuede wrap dress with long sleeves, A-line skirt, two slash pockets, elasticized waistband, self belt.
est. $150–$300 sold: $374
Skinner 12/16/1999

Ensemble, 1969

Purple silk satin wrapping and tying in front over a top, stitched panel.
est. $100–$150 sold: $546
William Doyle Galleries 4/12/1995

Ensemble, 1970s

Tie-dyed chiffon bell-bottom pants, top with bell sleeves and scarf.
est. not available sold: $405
eBay Online Auctions 2/23/2000

Ensemble, 1970s

Brown silk jersey tank-style top and pant set, long sleeve brown and white tie-dyed chiffon tunic caftan.
est. not available sold: $895
The Paper Bag Princess 11/3/2000

Ensemble, 1970s

Beige cashmere maxi-length tank-style dress with matching maxi-cardigan.
est. not available sold: $995
The Paper Bag Princess 11/1/1996

Ensemble, 1978

One-shouldered tunic wrapping and tying at left shoulder, slim pants slightly tapered, labeled: Halston, very good condition.
est. $600–$800 sold: $1092.50
William Doyle Galleries 11/2/2000

Evening Gown, 1960s

Black velvet, strapless, tying at gathered back.
est. $250–$300 sold: $690
William Doyle Galleries 11/12/1997

Evening Gown, 1970s

Silk chiffon with cream and silver buggle beads, sequins, and pearls in a geometric motif.
est. not available sold: $1295
The Paper Bag Princess 1/8/2000

Evening Gown, 1970s

Dusty rose layered chiffon with plunging ruffled neckline, full shirt, poet sleeves, and matching sash belt.
est. not available sold: $895
The Paper Bag Princess

Evening Gown, 1970s

Pink chiffon, asymmetrical neckline below-the-knee top layer, with separate under-skirt, of tiered and layered chiffon.
est. not available sold: $1200
The Paper Bag Princess 1/8/1999

Evening Gown, 1970s

A-line jersey sheath, white bodice changing to gray in flame pattern at waist, covered in iridescent sequins.
est. $400–$600 sold: $1092
William Doyle Galleries 11/12/1997

H

Evening Gown, 1970s
Changeante aquamarine metallic gauze, bodice hugging to hip, skirt in multiple tiers descending in length from front to back, circular cape.
est. $700–$900 sold: $1265
William Doyle Galleries 5/6/1998

Evening Gown, 1970s
Green chiffon, bias-cut.
est. not available sold: $660
eBay Online Auctions 2/23/2000

Evening Gown, 1970s
A-line sheath of gray silk jersey printed with floating clouds, overlaid entirely with iridescent sequins.
est. $400–$600 sold: $1840
William Doyle Galleries 11/12/1997

Evening Gown, 1970s
Mint green three-ply cashmere, round neck, long sleeves, maxi-length.
est. not available sold: $695
The Paper Bag Princess 7/1/2000

Evening Gown, 1970s
Black jersey, draped front, plunging neckline, large dolman sleeves, high center front slit.
est. not available sold: $950
The Paper Bag Princess 3/1/1998

Evening Gown, 1980s
Ivory silk crepe sewn with silver bugle beads in honeycomb pattern, straight sheath with jewel neck, long, slightly flared sleeves.
est. $400–$600 sold: $1092
William Doyle Galleries 5/6/1998

Evening Jacket, 1970s
Cardigan-style, cream chiffon, embroidered with pearls and gold beads in swirling pattern.
est. $300–$500 sold: $431
William Doyle Galleries 11/16/1999

Evening Jumpsuit, 1970s
Red matte jersey, backless with plunging halter neckline, wide-legged skirt and self sash.
est. $200–$250 sold: $431
William Doyle Galleries 12/5/1996

Hat
Silver sequined beret style.
est. not available sold: $195
The Paper Bag Princess 10/1/1999

Jacket, 1970s
Knee-length and tie belt, tan Ultrasuede.
est. not available sold: $495
The Paper Bag Princess

Jumpsuit, 1970s
Violet cashmere with tank top and wide legs, top slit to waist, with four-cornered shawl.
est. $200–$300 sold: $373
William Doyle Galleries 5/6/1998

Jumpsuit, 1970s
Black sheer zebra-striped silk/chiffon, wide-legged jumpsuit, nude lining, with matching sash belt and trumpet sleeves.
est. not available sold: $1495
The Paper Bag Princess 9/1/2000

Jumpsuit, 1970s
Black sheer silk woven with black opaque zebra stripes over beige sheer silk, asymmetrical V neck, flared long sleeves, flared legs.
est. $100–$150 sold: $287
William Doyle Galleries 12/5/1996

Suit, 1970s
Tie-dyed velvet in green, purple, and yellow, three-quarter-length cardigan jacket with elasticized sleeve ends, wide-legged pants, separate scarf.
est. $800–$1200 sold: $517
William Doyle Galleries 11/16/1999

Sweater Set, 1970s
Apricot cashmere with self belt.
est. $200–$250 sold: $460
William Doyle Galleries 12/5/1996

Sweater Set, 1970s
Apricot cashmere.
est. $125–$175 sold: $258
William Doyle Galleries 12/6/1995

Top, 1970s

Gold and black zebra motif, sequinned, round-necked fitted bodice and sleeves.
est. not available sold: $395
The Paper Bag Princess 9/1/2000

Top, 1970s

Long-sleeved, gold and black star motif with buggle beads and sequins.
est. not available sold: $395
The Paper Bag Princess 9/1/2000

HARRIS, RED

Coat, 1960s

Red and gray plaid tweed, knee-length, single-breasted coat with fitted silhouette.
est. $150–$250 sold: $230
Skinner 9/14/2000

HARTNELL, NORMAN

Evening Gown, 1930s

Full-length, bias-cut oyster silk with slight train to skirt, embroidered with silver and gold bugle beads and sequins in feather design.
est. 600–800 pounds sold: 747 pounds
Sotheby's London 11/25/1998

HEAD, EDITH

Evening Gown, 1959

Pink georgette embroidered with silver glass bugle beads, stand-up collar and self belt. Janet Leigh, 1959 Academy Awards.
est. not available sold: $34,500
Christie's Oscar Dress Auction 3/18/1999

Evening Gown, 1969

Periwinkle blue and violet faille crepe dress with décolleté neckline, full skirt with asymmetrical double flounce of blue and violet fabric. Elizabeth Taylor, 1969 Academy Awards.
est. not available sold: $167,500
Christie's Oscar Dress Auction 3/18/1999

HEIM, JACQUES

Cocktail Dress, 1950s

Silver satin hand-embroidered with foliate design in blue silk, silver bugle beads, pink sequins.
est. $200–$400 sold: $345
Skinner 12/16/1999

Cocktail Dress, 1950s

Silver silk satin dress hand-embroidered, fitted camisole bodice with dropped waist-line, attached belt, below-the-knee skirt, in chiffon and flannel.
est. $200–$400 sold: $345
Skinner 12/16/1999

Evening Gown, 1961

Green silk, sleeveless with jewel neckline and plunging back trimmed with white ap-pliquéd flowers, rhinestones, crystal beads, and pendant crystals.
est. $600–$800 sold: $575
Skinner 12/16/1999

HERMÈS

Agenda, 1966

Black baby alligator with silver-toned me-chanical pencil and notebook fillers for 1966.
est. $75–$100 sold: $517
William Doyle Galleries 12/5/1996

Bag, 1990s

"Quelle Idole," serial #033391CK, 7″ × 6.5″, orange leather character purse, cutouts in flap (eyes), strips cross in front (arms), with brown "feet."
est. $499 sold: $1276
eBay Online Auctions 3/4/2001

Bathing Suit, 1950s

One-piece with side zipper of red Lastex woven with broken silver pinstripes and printed with double-winged flying insects (locusts or dragonflies).
est. $150–$200 sold: $316
William Doyle Galleries 5/2/2000

H

BATHING SUIT, 1950s
Red stretch Lurex printed with insects.
est. $300–$500 sold: $546
William Doyle Galleries 4/12/1995

BEACH BAG, 1970s
Terry cloth printed in black and white with a stirrup pattern.
est. $100–$150 sold: $345
William Doyle Galleries 4/24/1996

BELT, 1950s
Black calf with silver-toned metal slots run through with French coins.
est. $100–$125 sold: $402
William Doyle Galleries 12/6/1995

BELT, 1970s
Black leather with gilt metal "H" buckle.
est. $75–$100 sold: $345
William Doyle Galleries 5/6/1998

BELT, 1970s
Black calf with two-tone buckle inscribed "Hermès Sport."
est. $75–$125 sold: $373
William Doyle Galleries 12/5/1996

BELT, 1970s
Brown calf with gold metal "H" buckle.
est. $100–$150 sold: $287
William Doyle Galleries 11/12/1997

BELT, 1970s
Brown calf with gilt metal pyramid studs and sliding catch.
est. $100–$150 sold: $517
William Doyle Galleries 12/5/1996

BLOUSE, 1960s
Silk twill printed with show horses jumping and show ribbons on two-tone green ground, separate tie.
est. $100–$150 sold: $258
William Doyle Galleries 11/12/1997

BLOUSE, 1980s
"République Française" navy blue silk printed with symbols of freedom including an oak leaf wreath.
est. $200–$250 sold: $488
William Doyle Galleries 11/12/1997

BLOUSE, 1980s
Silk twill with gold uniform decorations and military document bags.
est. $200–$250 sold: $373
William Doyle Galleries 11/12/1997

CARD CASE, 1960s
Red calf containing two packs of cards signed by A. M. Cassandre for Hermès.
est. $75–$100 sold: $143
William Doyle Galleries 12/5/1996

CARDIGAN, 1980s
Blue wool knit with silk twill front depicting playing cards and Medieval figures.
est. $100–$150 sold: $230
William Doyle Galleries 11/12/1997

CARDIGAN, 1980s
Black cashmere button-up sweater, black, green, aqua, gold, and red front panels, mythological print.
est. $200–$400 sold: $575.00
Skinner 9/14/2000

CASE, 1930
Combination dressing case and portable desk, cobra-grained leather, blue velvet interior, gilt metal locks, keys, clasps, detachable carry strap.
est. $3000–$4000 sold: $3220
William Doyle Galleries 5/2/2000

CASE, 1955
Brown alligator lined with green morocco, fitted with gilt sterling soap box, another box, two bottles, brush, shoehorn, comb case, shaving kit.
est. $2000–$3000 sold: $2300
William Doyle Galleries 12/5/1996

CASE, 1960s
Black leather with top zipper, fold-over clip handle, red nylon lining, separate canvas cover.
est. $300–$400 sold: $632
William Doyle Galleries 6/11/1997

Clutch Bag, 1980s

Beige ostrich, small and rectangular with flap closing into loop ornamented with gilt metal buckle, beige topstitching.
est. $300–$400 sold: $690
William Doyle Galleries 11/16/1999

Coat, 1950s

White cotton, hand-painted with trompe l'oeil buttons, hooded.
est. $300–$400 sold: $2300
William Doyle Galleries 12/6/1995

Coat, 1950s

Gray, green, beige, and yellow wool plaid with cape sleeves and capelet.
est. $200–$300 sold: $747
William Doyle Galleries 12/6/1995

Coat, 1960

Oatmeal tweed, single-breasted with gold buttons.
est. $100–$150 sold: $431
William Doyle Galleries 6/11/1997

Coat, 1960s

Red wool with band collar, black leather zipper placket.
est. $200–$250 sold: $546
William Doyle Galleries 11/12/1997

Coat, 1960s

Below-the-knee-length coat with full silhouette, two patch pockets, welted seam detail, and bold orange and white "H" print lining.
est. $800–$1000 sold: $1380
Skinner 9/14/2000

Dress, 1930s

Black wool, top with V neck and cut-in-one elbow-length sleeves, A-line skirt with black suede band at center front.
est. $125–$175 sold: $575
William Doyle Galleries 12/5/1996

Dress, 1960s

Brown leather, fitted, knee length.
est. not available sold: $1800
What Comes Around Goes Around
2/20/2001

Dress, 1960s

Tan silk twill printed with swirling plumes and crowns, straight shift with front placket and long-cuffed sleeves.
est. $150–$200 sold: $373
William Doyle Galleries 6/11/1997

Dress, 1970s

Black silk jersey, long sleeve, A-line, knee-length, with gold scrolling motif.
est. not available sold: $1000
The Paper Bag Princess 7/1/1997

Dress, 1970s

Sleeveless, turtleneck, shift dress. Top portion is knit, skirt portion is leather.
est. not available sold: $1800
Vintage Designs Ltd. 2/20/2001

Dress, 1980s

Navy, gold, and red printed silk jersey dress, fitted silhouette with mock turtleneck, long sleeves, matching self-tie rope belt.
est. $250–$350 sold: $546.25
Skinner 12/16/1999

Dressing Gown, 1970s

Blue silk printed with rope-tied lattice pattern, round lapels, patch pockets, self belt.
est. $100–$125 sold: $373
William Doyle Galleries 5/6/1998

Ensemble, 1970s

Double-breasted coat and wrap skirt of green felted wool edged with leather, pewter-toned metal buttons.
est. $200–$300 sold: $373
William Doyle Galleries 5/12/1999

Envelope Bag, 1960s

Large, black calf, closing with strap run through leather "H."
est. $300–$500 sold: $690
William Doyle Galleries 11/12/1997

Gloves, 1930s

Fingers and thumbs of pink kid, the rest in scalloped-edged black suede.
est. $60–$90 sold: $161
William Doyle Galleries 11/17/1994

H

HANDBAG, 1930S
Patchwork of tan and black snakeskins with tortoise frame, double snake strap.
est. $300–$400 sold: $373
William Doyle Galleries 11/10/1998

HANDBAG, 1940S
Brown crocodile, box-shaped with two shaped strap handles.
est. $1200–$1500 sold: $1035
William Doyle Galleries 6/11/1997

HANDBAG, 1940S
Brown crocodile with round gilt metal push-button clasp.
est. $500–$700 sold: $977
William Doyle Galleries 6/11/1997

HANDBAG, 1950
Slightly trapezoidal, gilt metal slide locks, rigid hinged frame, single top handle, key sheath, decorative tab with gilt metal crown.
est. $2000–$3000 sold: $1840
William Doyle Galleries 5/2/2000

HANDBAG, 1950
Brown alligator with side pockets and zippered pocket.
est. $1000–$1500 sold: $6900
Sotheby's 4/8/1998

HANDBAG, 1950
Black alligator with jewelry compartment and taupe felt cover trimmed with alligator.
est. $2000–$2500 sold: $6325
William Doyle Galleries 12/6/1995

HANDBAG, 1950S
Rounded fold-over flap, rolled top handle, the handle fittings and clasp rope twisted gilt metal, arranged in a knot form at clasp.
est. $500–$700 sold: $1035
William Doyle Galleries 5/2/2000

HANDBAG, 1950S
Black calf with gold block letter monogram.
est. $200–$300 sold: $1610
William Doyle Galleries 12/6/1995

HANDBAG, 1950S
Wine crocodile, slightly trapezoidal with double handles, padded edging, front and back exterior compartments.
est. $700–$900 sold: $1380
William Doyle Galleries 5/6/1998

HANDBAG, 1950S
Brown crocodile with round gilt metal push-button clasp, separate coin purse.
est. $800–$1200 sold: $1495
William Doyle Galleries 6/11/1997

HANDBAG, 1950S
Black crocodile with gilt metal fittings and separate zippered jewelry case.
est. $1500–$2000 sold: $5060
William Doyle Galleries 12/5/1996

HANDBAG, 1950S
Brown calf with brass catch and lock.
est. $500–$750 sold: $862
William Doyle Galleries 11/17/1994

"KELLY" HANDBAG, 1950S
Black crocodile with gilt metal fittings and lock, key sheath.
est. $2500–$3000 sold: $5175
William Doyle Galleries 5/6/1998

"KELLY" HANDBAG, 1956
Black crocodile with lock and key.
est. $2000–$2500 sold: $2990
William Doyle Galleries 12/5/1996

HANDBAG, 1959
Black calf with brass fittings.
est. $150–$250 sold: $517
William Doyle Galleries 12/6/1995

"KELLY" HANDBAG, 1960
Black crocodile with brass fittings and lock, crocodile key sheath on cord.
est. $750–$1000 sold: $1265
William Doyle Galleries 11/17/1994

"KELLY" HANDBAG, 1960
Brown alligator with alligator-covered lock and key sheath, gilt metal fittings.
est. $2000–$3000 sold: $8625
William Doyle Galleries 12/5/1996

"KELLY" HANDBAG, 1960
Black crocodile with gilt metal fittings.
est. $1000–$1500 sold: $2990
William Doyle Galleries 12/5/1996

HANDBAG, 1960s
Black lizard with gilt metal fittings.
est. $1500–$2000 sold: $2300
William Doyle Galleries 5/6/1998

"KELLY" HANDBAG, 1960s
Black calf with gilt metal fittings and lock.
est. $2000–$2200 sold: $3162
William Doyle Galleries 5/6/1998

HANDBAG, 1960s
Black baby alligator handbag, rectangle-framed, three inner compartments, gold-plated hardware, black leather lining, stamped "Hermès-Paris 24 F. St. Honoré."
est. $2000–$3000 sold: $1840
Skinner 9/14/2000

HANDBAG, 1960s
Black crocodile with shaped flap, side gussets, oval gilt metal clasp.
est. $1000–$1200 sold: $1840
William Doyle Galleries 5/6/1998

HANDBAG, 1960s
Double handles, exterior compartments, rolled edging, 9k gold metal trim, key sheath, clasp marked.
est. $400–$600 sold: $805
William Doyle Galleries 5/2/2000

"KELLY" HANDBAG, 1960s
Black calf with gilt metal fittings and lock, calf leather key sheath.
est. $150–$200 sold: $1265
William Doyle Galleries 6/11/1997

HANDBAG, 1960s
Green canvas, large pouch shape, tan calf strap, handle, and trim.
est. $200–$300 sold: $920
William Doyle Galleries 6/11/1997

"KELLY" HANDBAG, 1960s
Black alligator with alligator-covered lock, gilt metal fittings.
est. $1000–$1200 sold: $2300
William Doyle Galleries 6/11/1997

HANDBAG, 1960s
Beige crocodile with gilt metal clasp.
est. $300–$500 sold: $920
William Doyle Galleries 12/5/1996

HANDBAG, 1960s
Toile bound with navy box calf.
est. $200–$250 sold: $747
William Doyle Galleries 12/5/1996

"KELLY" HANDBAG, 1960s
Black crocodile with gilt metal fittings, crocodile-covered lock.
est. $3500–$5000 sold: $5750
William Doyle Galleries 5/2/2000

HANDBAG, 1960s
Black lizard with gilt metal push-button clasps.
est. $200–$400 sold: $1150
William Doyle Galleries 12/6/1995

HANDBAG, 1960s
Toile and navy calf with gilt metal fittings and lock.
est. $500–$700 sold: $1495
William Doyle Galleries 6/11/1997

"KELLY" HANDBAG, 1960s
Black calf with gilt metal fittings and lock, key sheath.
est. $1200–$1800 sold: $2990
William Doyle Galleries 5/2/2000

HANDBAG, 1960s
Black calf box with detachable shoulder strap.
est. $500–$750 sold: $977
William Doyle Galleries 6/11/1997

"KELLY" HANDBAG, 1960s
Black crocodile with crocodile-covered lock and key sheath.
est. $2000–$3000 sold: $3450
William Doyle Galleries 6/11/1997

"KELLY" HANDBAG, 1960s
Black crocodile with gilt metal fittings and crocodile-covered lock.
est. $1200–$1500 sold: $1840
William Doyle Galleries 6/11/1997

H

"Kelly" Handbag, 1960s
Black calf with gilt metal fittings and lock.
est. $150–$200 sold: $805
William Doyle Galleries 11/12/1997

Handbag, 1960s
Black lizard with gilt metal pivot clasp.
est. $125–$175 sold: $460
William Doyle Galleries 12/5/1996

Handbag, 1960s
Black lizard with gilt metal ring clasp.
est. $400–$600 sold: $517
William Doyle Galleries 12/5/1996

"Kelly" Handbag, 1965
Black crocodile with gilt metal fittings and
crocodile-covered lock.
est. $1000–$1500 sold: $3450
William Doyle Galleries 12/5/1996

Handbag, 1970
Black crocodile with two gilt metal "H"
catches.
est. $800–$1200 sold: $2530
William Doyle Galleries 12/5/1996

"Kelly" Handbag, 1970
Black calf with gilt metal fittings and lock,
calf key sheath.
est. $300–$400 sold: $747
William Doyle Galleries 5/6/1998

Handbag, 1970
Black calf with adjustable strap and separate
extension strap.
est. $300–$400 sold: $747
William Doyle Galleries 5/6/1998

"Kelly" Handbag, 1970
Black calf with gilt metal fittings and lock,
calf key sheath.
est. $700–$900 sold: $1725
William Doyle Galleries 5/6/1998

Handbag, 1970s
Chocolate brown trim with change purse
attachment.
est. $300–$500 sold: $862
William Doyle Galleries 4/12/1995

Handbag, 1970s
Black lizard, envelope flap, gilt metal
twisted rope catch.
est. $400–$600 sold: $747
William Doyle Galleries 4/12/1995

Handbag, 1970s
Black calf and natural canvas trim.
est. $300–$500 sold: $747
William Doyle Galleries 4/12/1995

Handbag, 1970s
Burgundy lizard envelope with textured gilt
metal chain link catch and shoulder strap.
est. $400–$600 sold: $632
William Doyle Galleries 12/6/1995

"Kelly" Handbag, 1970s
Black calf with gilt metal fittings and lock,
calf key sheath.
est. $500–$700 sold: $1495
William Doyle Galleries 5/6/1998

Handbag, 1970s
White leather envelope with gilt metal "H"
and wooden button catch.
est. $200–$300 sold: $431
William Doyle Galleries 12/6/1995

Handbag, 1970s
Gray calf with gilt metal fittings.
est. $500–$750 sold: $805
William Doyle Galleries 12/5/1996

Handbag, 1970s
Toile and burgundy calf with leather "H"
clasp.
est. $300–$500 sold: $517
William Doyle Galleries 12/5/1996

Handbag, 1970s
Toile and tan calf with gilt metal fittings.
est. $500–$750 sold: $862
William Doyle Galleries 12/5/1996

"Kelly" Handbag, 1970s
Tan calf with soft sides and gilt metal
fittings.
est. $500–$750 sold: $1610
William Doyle Galleries 12/5/1996

"Kelly" Handbag, 1970s
Chestnut brown alligator bag with lock and
key and detachable shoulder strap, brown
leather lining.
est. $4500–$6400 sold: $9200
Skinner 12/16/1999

Handbag, 1970s
Brown canvas trimmed with tan pebble-
grained leather and gilt metal pyramid
studs.
est. $200–$250 sold: $431
William Doyle Galleries 12/5/1996

"Kelly" Handbag, 1970s
Black lizard with gilt metal fittings.
est. $750–$1000 sold: $3737
William Doyle Galleries 12/5/1996

Handbag, 1970s
Burgundy calf with red- and gold-plated
fittings.
est. $500–$750 sold: $1035
William Doyle Galleries 12/5/1996

"Kelly" Handbag, 1970s
Navy calf with gilt metal fittings.
est. $500–$750 sold: $1725
William Doyle Galleries 12/5/1996

"Kelly" Handbag, 1970s
Brown calf with gilt metal fittings.
est. $500–$750 sold: $1380
William Doyle Galleries 12/5/1996

"Kelly" Handbag, 1970s
White calf with gilt metal fittings, white
calf-covered lock and key sheath.
est. $800–$1200 sold: $862
William Doyle Galleries 5/6/1998

"Kelly" Handbag, 1970s
Tan calf with gilt metal fittings and lock,
calf key sheath.
est. $800–$1200 sold: $3450
William Doyle Galleries 5/6/1998

"Kelly" Handbag, 1970s
Green calf with gilt metal fittings and lock,
calf key sheath.
est. $800–$1200 sold: $4025
William Doyle Galleries 5/6/1998

"Kelly" Handbag, 1970s
Black calf with gilt metal fittings.
est. $500–$750 sold: $1725
William Doyle Galleries 12/5/1996

Handbag, 1970s
Black calf with shoulder strap.
est. $600–$800 sold: $805
William Doyle Galleries 4/12/1995

"Kelly" Handbag, 1970s
Brown calf with gilt metal fittings and lock,
calf key sheath.
est. $700–$900 sold: $1092
William Doyle Galleries 5/6/1998

Handbag, 1979
Black crocodile with interior gilt metal
monogram "BBB" and Hermès horse logo.
est. $1200–$1500 sold: $2070
William Doyle Galleries 6/11/1997

"Kelly" Handbag, 1980s
Black pebble-grained leather with black
leather interior with three inner pockets.
est. $700–$900 sold: $1840
Skinner 12/16/1999

Handbag, 1980s
Tan calf with long strap.
est. $300–$400 sold: $1495
William Doyle Galleries 5/6/1998

"Kelly" Handbag, 1980s
Wine calf with gilt metal fittings and lock,
calf key sheath.
est. $800–$1200 sold: $2530
William Doyle Galleries 5/6/1998

Handbag, 1980s
Green ostrich with adjustable strap, gilt
metal "H" clasp.
est. $1500–$2500 sold: $862
William Doyle Galleries 11/16/1999

"Kelly" Handbag, 1980s
Black crocodile with lock and key and detachable shoulder strap, black leather lining.
est. $4000–$6000 sold: $6900
Skinner 12/16/1999

H

"KELLY" HANDBAG, 1981
Toile and tan calf with gilt metal fittings
and lock, leather key sheath.
est. $500–$700 sold: $1725
William Doyle Galleries 6/11/1997

"KELLY" HANDBAG, 1981
Beige horsehair and tan calf with gilt metal
lock and fittings, calf key sheath.
est. $500–$750 sold: $3910
William Doyle Galleries 6/11/1997

"KELLY" HANDBAG, 1984
Navy calf with gilt metal fittings, lock and
key sheath.
est. $700–$900 sold: $2530
William Doyle Galleries 6/11/1997

"KELLY" HANDBAG, 1984
Wine calf with gilt metal fittings and lock,
calf key sheath.
est. $500–$700 sold: $2070
William Doyle Galleries 6/11/1997

"KELLY" HANDBAG, 1990
Gilt metal fittings, crocodile-covered lock,
key sheath.
est. $4000–$6000 sold: $8625
William Doyle Galleries 5/2/2000

"KELLY" HANDBAG, 1990
Gilt metal fittings, crocodile-covered lock,
key sheath.
est. $4000–$6000 sold: $6900
William Doyle Galleries 5/2/2000

"KELLY" HANDBAG, 1990
Black crocodile, gilt metal fittings,
crocodile-covered lock, and key sheath.
est. $2000–$3000 sold: $7475
William Doyle Galleries 5/2/2000

JACKET, 1980S
Brown nutria double-breasted jacket with
long sleeves, slit pockets, dark brown
leather trim at wrists, pockets, and lapel,
dark brown quilted lining.
est. $800–$1200 sold: $805
Skinner 12/16/1999

MALLETTE BAG, 1940
Wine leather with gilt fittings and velvet-
lined jewelry compartment.
est. $750–$1000 sold: $1265
William Doyle Galleries 11/17/1994

MALLETTE BAG, 1950S
Black crocodile travel case with burgundy
velvet-lined jewelry compartment.
est. $3500–$4500 sold: $6325
Sotheby's 12/9/1998

MALLETTE BAG, 1960
Black crocodile with gilt metal fittings and
"H" clasps, interior lined with sang de
boeuf leather, jewelry compartment lined
with wine velvet.
est. $5000–$7000 sold: $2875
William Doyle Galleries 6/11/1997

MALLETTE BAG, 1960
Red calf lined with red morocco, jewelry
compartment lined with burgundy velvet,
gilt metal fittings, "H" clasp.
est. $1500–$2000 sold: $2530
William Doyle Galleries 12/5/1996

MALLETTE BAG, 1960S
Black crocodile with gilt metal fittings,
sang de boeuf calf interior, jewelry case
lined in burgundy velvet.
est. $2000–$3000 sold: $4600
William Doyle Galleries 5/6/1998

MEN'S SHIRT, 1970S
Silk twill printed motif in black, gold, and
white.
est. not available sold: $300
What Comes Around Goes Around
2/20/2001

SCARF, 1945
Wool flannel printed with 16th-century
map of Paris.
est. $100–$125 sold: $460
William Doyle Galleries 12/5/1996

SCARF, 1950S
"La France" printed with map of France
and French castles.
est. $150–$250 sold: $316
William Doyle Galleries 11/17/1994

SCARF, 1950s
"Chateaux Historiques de la France en
1852" ivory silk twill printed in lavender,
gray, green, red, beige, chartreuse, and
black with a rust border.
est. $50–$75 sold: $230
William Doyle Galleries

SCARF, 1950s
"La Volière des Dames par Hermès Paris"
silk jacquard with hummingbirds.
est. $150–$250 sold: $258
William Doyle Galleries 11/17/1994

SCARF, 1950s
Cream satin printed and flocked with
feathers.
est. $100–$150 sold: $201
William Doyle Galleries 4/12/1995

SCARF, 1950s
"Paris Modistes" printed in pastels with
figures and hats.
est. $150–$250 sold: $103
William Doyle Galleries 11/17/1994

SCARF, 1960
Silk twill printed with a horse-drawn
flower cart surrounded by border of flowers against green.
est. $100–$150 sold: $230
William Doyle Galleries 6/11/1997

SCARF, 1960
Silk twill printed with a scene "at the
races" in orchid, olive, turquoise, white,
and gray against beige ground with black
border.
est. $100–$150 sold: $287
William Doyle Galleries 6/11/1997

SCARF, 1960
White silk twill printed in black with Dal-
matians and other dogs.
est. $100–$150 sold: $316
William Doyle Galleries 6/11/1997

SCARF, 1960
Silk twill, white ground printed in gray,
black, and navy with a navy border.
est. $100–$150 sold: $287
William Doyle Galleries 6/11/1997

SCARF, 1960
Silk twill printed with 18th-century horses
and grooms from Spain, Denmark, and
England.
est. $100–$150 sold: $172
William Doyle Galleries 6/11/1997

SCARF, 1960
Silk twill printed in tan and turquoise with
studies of dogs.
est. $100–$150 sold: $316
William Doyle Galleries 6/11/1997

SCARF, 1960s
"Les Figures d'Équitation" silk twill printed
in beige, gray, blue, and ocher with equestrian figures, brown and black border.
est. $80–$120 sold: $201
William Doyle Galleries 12/5/1996

SCARF, 1960s
By "Cassandre," silk twill printed in taupe
and pink.
est. $80–$120 sold: $201
William Doyle Galleries 12/5/1996

SCARF, 1960s
Silk twill printed with scene of sailors adjusting sails.
est. $80–$120 sold: $103
William Doyle Galleries 12/5/1996

SCARF, 1960s
By "de Linares," silk twill printed with
pheasants and other game birds, tan border.
est. $80–$120 sold: $115
William Doyle Galleries 12/5/1996

SCARF, 1960s
Silk twill printed with keys in gold, olive,
and beige with red border.
est. $80–$120 sold: $143
William Doyle Galleries 12/5/1996

SCARF, 1960s
Silk twill printed in winter colors with
sleigh-ride scene.
est. $100–$150 sold: $172
William Doyle Galleries 6/11/1997

H

SCARF, 1960s
White silk twill printed with 18th-century horses and grooms from Spain, Denmark, and England.
est. $100–$150 sold: $431
William Doyle Galleries 6/11/1997

SCARF, 1960s
Green and white "Les Cantinieres en 1860," illustrations of military costumes, printed with "Sculpt, Hermès, Paris."
est. $200–$400 sold: $115
Skinner 9/14/2000

SCARF, 1960s
White silk twill printed in gray and gold with blue border.
est. $100–$150 sold: $143
William Doyle Galleries 6/11/1997

SCARF, 1960s
Rectangular and double-sided silk twill printed with circus actors and animals in yellow, gray, gold, and pink.
est. $100–$125 sold: $431
William Doyle Galleries 5/12/1999

SCARF, 1960s
Silk twill printed with a micro-mosaic of ancient Greek horses and riders.
est. $100–$150 sold: $258
William Doyle Galleries 6/11/1997

SCARF, 1969
Large silk scarf printed with multicolored passementerie and tassels on an ivory ground, pink border.
est. $150–$200 sold: $316.25
Skinner 12/16/1999

SCARF, 1970s
Geometric stylized flowers in gold, brown, and caramel on black with yellow border.
est. $100–$150 sold: $201
William Doyle Galleries 11/12/1997

SCARF, 1970s
White silk twill, "Les Voitures à Transformation," printed with carriages and removable tops in maroon with gold latticework center.
est. $100–$150 sold: $115
William Doyle Galleries 11/12/1997

SCARF, 1970s
Astrological chart in greens and gold on blue background.
est. $100–$150 sold: $172
William Doyle Galleries 11/12/1997

SCARF, 1970s
"Frontaux et Cocardes" with horses' heads and multicolored cocardes.
est. $50–$75 sold: $230
William Doyle Galleries 9/30/1993

SCARF, 1970s
"Épisodes de la Chasse à Courre," white silk twill with hunting scenes presented as photos in an album, pink border.
est. $100–$150 sold: $258
William Doyle Galleries 11/12/1997

SCARF, 1970s
White silk twill printed with ironwork ornaments and fittings in brown with purple entwining ribbon, pink border.
est. $100–$150 sold: $201
William Doyle Galleries 6/11/1997

SCARF, 1970s
Winter with a snowy Renaissance hunting scene and snow-covered stone statues.
est. $100–$150 sold: $201
William Doyle Galleries 4/27/1994

SCARF, 1970s
White silk twill printed with golden saddle bags on coral ground.
est. $100–$150 sold: $115
William Doyle Galleries 11/12/1997

SCARF, 1970s
White silk twill printed with jockeys riding racehorses in a circle.
est. $100–$150 sold: $172
William Doyle Galleries 11/12/1997

SCARF, 1970s
"L'Hiver" printed with a snowy Renaissance hunting scene and with snow-covered stone statues, olive green border.
est. $100–$150 sold: $172
William Doyle Galleries 12/6/1995

SCARF, 1980
Cashmere and silk printed with game in shades of brown, beige, and rust.
est. $60–$90 sold: $172
William Doyle Galleries 11/17/1994

SCARF, 1980s
Silk twill printed with striped belts in red, green, gold, and brown against a blue background.
est. $100–$150 sold: $115
William Doyle Galleries 4/12/1995

SCARF, 1980s
"Post et Cavalerie," white silk twill printed with military insignia in gold, turquoise, and red with a red border.
est. $100–$150 sold: $57
William Doyle Galleries 4/12/1995

SCARF, 1980s
Chiffon printed in yellow, brown, and green orchids.
est. $60–$90 sold: $172
William Doyle Galleries 11/17/1994

SCARF, 1980s
Ancient sailing ships printed on peach and orange background.
est. $100–$125 sold: $143
William Doyle Galleries 11/12/1997

SCARF, 1980s
White chiffon with circular motif, horse, carriage, and driver in yellow and gray.
est. $60–$90 sold: $86
William Doyle Galleries 11/17/1994

SCARF, 1980s
White figured silk twill printed with wheel entwined with blue morning glories, pink peonies, and yellow daisies, green border.
est. $80–$120 sold: $287
William Doyle Galleries 6/11/1997

SCARF, 1980s
"Les Pivoines," white chiffon with brown, mauve, yellow, and aqua peonies.
est. $60–$90 sold: $86
William Doyle Galleries 11/17/1994

SCARF, 1980s
"Les Pivoines," white chiffon printed with pink, green, and yellow peonies.
est. $60–$90 sold: $143
William Doyle Galleries 11/17/1994

SCARF, 1980s
White silk twill printed with ceremonial bridles in gray and gold, pink border.
est. $100–$150 sold: $172
William Doyle Galleries 11/12/1997

SCARF, 1980s
White silk twill printed with large bouquet of flowers associated with the Queen of England in yellow, green, and orange with blue border.
est. $100–$150 sold: $201
William Doyle Galleries 6/11/1997

SCARF, 1980s
By F. Faconnet, scene of two repeats of the astrological chart design in yellow, black, and white.
est. $100–$150 sold: $230
William Doyle Galleries 6/11/1997

SCARF, 1980s
"Les Pivoines," white chiffon printed in orange, lavender, and beige peonies.
est. $60–$90 sold: $86
William Doyle Galleries 11/17/1994

SHOULDER BAG, 1960s
Tan calf with saddle-shaped flap and gilt metal ornament.
est. $100–$125 sold: $345
William Doyle Galleries 6/11/1997

SHOULDER BAG, 1970
Brown calf with gilt metal ring door-knocker closure.
est. $300–$400 sold: $402
William Doyle Galleries 12/5/1996

SHOULDER BAG, 1970s
Rectangular shoulder bag with front flap, circular gold-toned clasp and alligator shoulder strap, taupe leather lining.
est. $2000–$3000 sold: $1150
Skinner 12/16/1999

H

SHOULDER BAG, 1970s
Black calf with fold-over shaped flap, gilt metal stirrup buckle.
est. $300–$500 sold: $805
William Doyle Galleries 5/6/1998

SHOULDER BAG, 1970s
Tan calf with top-stitched shaped flap, gilt metal, stirrup-shaped buckle.
est. $300–$400 sold: $517
William Doyle Galleries 5/6/1998

SHOULDER BAG, 1978
Brown calf with flap and ring closure, adjustable shoulder strap.
est. $150–$200 sold: $1265
William Doyle Galleries 5/6/1998

SHOULDER BAG, 1978
Brown calf with flap and ring closure, adjustable shoulder strap.
est. $300–$400 sold: $805
William Doyle Galleries 6/11/1997

SHOULDER BAG, 1990s
Fold-over flap, corners of bag and flap cut on diagonal, center strap closing into gilt metal buttons, shoulder strap attached by gilt metal ornaments.
est. $400–$600 sold: $748
William Doyle Galleries 5/2/2000

SWEATSHIRT, 1960s
Orange and white surface and sundial print, silk with cream ribbed and knitted silk neckband, wrists, and waist.
est. $75–$100 sold: $103
William Doyle Galleries 4/27/1994

SWEATSHIRT, 1980s
Silk twill printed with fall leaves.
est. $100–$150 sold: $143
William Doyle Galleries 11/12/1997

HOBÉ

EVENING BAG, 1942
Clutch of blue silk brocade depicting cranes, pines, mountains, center with carved bone figure framed in gold-filled and sterling silver floral ground.
est. $800–$1200 sold: $1092
William Doyle Galleries 5/6/1998

HODE, HOWARD—WORTH OF BOSTON

HATS, 1960s
Red faux fur hat with high crown and army green suede band, and black velvet cloche-style hat with rhinestone embellishment.
est. $150–$200 sold: $172.50
Skinner 9/14/2000

HOLT RENFREW

EVENING BAG
Lunchbox-style gold-plated, set with rhinestone daisies throughout, U-shaped daisy and rhinestone handle, mirrored interior lid, black velvet lining.
est. $175–$200 sold: $170
Ritchie's 9/20/2000

HOUSE OF ADAIR

ENSEMBLE, 1920s
Brown velvet wrap coat edged with lamé and embroidered with black beads, long skirt edged in more velvet.
est. $125–$175 sold: $690
William Doyle Galleries 12/6/1995

HOUSE OF KUNEL

COCKTAIL DRESS, 1950s
Black taffeta woven with pink roses and green leaves.
est. $200–$400 sold: $460
William Doyle Galleries 11/17/1994

HULITAR, PHILIP

COCKTAIL DRESS, 1960s
Strapless, black silk organza, torso appliquéd with black velvet and organdy roses.
est. $100–$150 sold: $373
William Doyle Galleries 11/17/1994

EVENING GOWN, 1957
Strapless black velvet bodice, white tulle skirt with black velvet and organdy roses with black velvet stems.
est. $200–$300 sold: $488
William Doyle Galleries 11/17/1994

INGBER

HANDBAG, 1940s
Black fur with black leather handle.
est. $500–$700 sold: $575
Sotheby's 12/9/1998

IRENE

COCKTAIL DRESS, 1960s
Green silk tulle embroidered with flowers and sprigs in ribbon work, sequins, and metallic threads, sleeveless with dropped waist.
est. $500–$700 sold: $632
William Doyle Galleries 5/12/1999

EVENING ENSEMBLE, 1960
Ivory silk shantung sleeveless shell and wide-legged pants sewn with horizontal tiers of silver-beaded fringe.
est. $700–$900 sold: $1725
William Doyle Galleries 5/12/1999

EVENING GOWN, 1960s
Fleshtone chiffon, empire-waisted gown encrusted with rhinestone pinwheel flowers layered over ivory crepe.
est. $300–$500 sold: $4500
William Doyle Galleries 5/6/1998

EVENING GOWN, 1960s
Fleshtone silk chiffon, spaghetti straps, crossover-draped bodice, empire waist, multilayered full skirt with flying panels at back waist.
est. not available sold: $5600
The Paper Bag Princess 10/10/2001

SUIT, 1940s
Gray wool, jacket with curved and pointed lapels, straight skirt.
est. $200–$250 sold: $402
William Doyle Galleries 6/11/1997

SUIT, 1940s
Brown wool, single-breasted with straight three-quarter-length skirt.
est. not available sold: $795
The Paper Bag Princess 7/1/1997

SUIT, 1940s
Gray two-piece suit, straight skirt to knee, button-front jacket, slits in cuff and skirt.
est. not available sold: $995
The Paper Bag Princess 9/23/2000

SUIT, 1940s
Light brown wool tweed, single-breasted jacket.
est. $100–$150 sold: $402
William Doyle Galleries 12/6/1995

SUIT, 1940s
Raisin-colored, fitted jacket with curved seaming and buttons defining waist, white linen faux collar, straight skirt.
est. $200–$250 sold: $575
William Doyle Galleries 6/11/1997

SUIT, 1950s
Black wool, jacket with rectangular piecing at each side accented with three button tabs repeated at back waist, straight skirt.
est. $150–$200 sold: $575
William Doyle Galleries 11/10/1998

J., WILLIAM

HAT, 1950s
Sapphire velvet trimmed with mink, lined in silver lamé, with original box.
est. $75–$100 sold: $120
William Doyle Galleries 4/12/1995

JABLOW, ARTHUR

JACKET, 1960s
Cream tweed with cream braid.
est. $100–$150 sold: $201
William Doyle Galleries 9/30/1993

JAMES, CHARLES

BLOUSE, 1940s
Taffeta with a flat collar, V neck yoke seam continuing to form the underseam of curved sleeves.
est. $200–$300 sold: $1380
William Doyle Galleries 4/12/1995

BLOUSE, 1950
Black silk with stand-up collar framing a sweetheart neckline and curved sleeves.
est. $200–$300 sold: $1265
William Doyle Galleries 4/12/1995

BOLERO JACKET, 1952
Bronze silk faille, jewel neck, fan pleated at top, bodice cut-away at chest level.
est. $500–$700 sold: $862
William Doyle Galleries 11/12/1997

COAT, 1940s
Navy wool, short, A-line with asymmetrical shawl collar.
est. $900–$1200 sold: $2760
William Doyle Galleries 12/6/1995

COAT, 1945
Short, rust wool lined in amethyst silk faille.
est. $2000–$3000 sold: $9200
William Doyle Galleries 12/6/1995

COAT, 1945
Red wool woven with a large plaid of navy and green, lined in red satin.
est. $2000–$3000 sold: $19,550
William Doyle Galleries 4/24/1996

COAT, 1954
For William Popper, camel ribbed wool, single-breasted, hourglass shape with padded hip pockets, pleated back with curved half-belt.
est. $750–$1000 sold: $2300
William Doyle Galleries 4/12/1995

COAT, 1955
Ivory and green weave wool, double-breasted with lapels reaching to shoulders forming cape collar in back, empire half self belt with bow in back.
est. $750–$1000 sold: $1495
William Doyle Galleries 4/12/1995

COCKTAIL DRESS, 1940s
Brown silk satin with wide shelf décolletage with wings at back of neck, skirt curved at hips and narrowing toward hem.
est. $10,000–$15,000 sold: $8625
William Doyle Galleries 4/12/1995

COCKTAIL DRESS, 1940s
Navy silk faille with portrait neckline formed by asymmetrical panel, angled and fitted bodice, skirt wrapping at an angle.
est. $8000–$12,000 sold: $17,250
William Doyle Galleries 4/12/1995

COCKTAIL DRESS, 1944
Sheath of brown satin, skirt front draped in polonaise style.
est. $2000–$3000 sold: $3737
William Doyle Galleries 6/11/1997

COCKTAIL DRESS, 1945
Black silk satin woven with groups of seven pinstripes, sleeveless with cut-out halter neckline, draped at the front hip and back with a self bow.
est. $6000–$9000 sold: $49,450
William Doyle Galleries 4/24/1996

COCKTAIL DRESS, 1950
Blue gauze appliquéd and embroidered with faux pearls and beads.
est. $2000–$3000 sold: $1840
William Doyle Galleries 12/6/1995

COCKTAIL DRESS, 1950s
Ivory chiffon, sleeveless bodice with asymmetrical draping.
est. $2000–$3000 sold: $4887
William Doyle Galleries 12/6/1995

COCKTAIL DRESS, 1951
Claret silk faille, sleeveless sheath with asymmetrical neckline falling into cape effect in back, skirt gathered at waist on one side.
est. $3000–$5000 sold: $16,100
William Doyle Galleries 11/16/1999

Cocktail Dress, 1962
Black silk satin with sweetheart neckline with radiating tucks, short sleeves, narrow skirt arranged in folds at the sides and front, ducktail hem.
est. $1000–$1500 sold: $575
William Doyle Galleries 12/5/1996

Cocktail Suit, 1940s
Black wool, jacket lined with black Alaskan seal, long skirt.
est. $1000–$1500 sold: $1092
William Doyle Galleries 12/6/1995

Dress, 1940s
Pumpkin satin, fitted bodice with asymmetrical boned portrait collar.
est. $200–$300 sold: $1725
William Doyle Galleries 4/12/1995

Dress, 1940s
Navy faille, stand-up collar, slit neckline.
est. $1000–$1500 sold: $1035
William Doyle Galleries 12/6/1995

Dress, 1940s
Navy taffeta, wide flat collar, short sleeves.
est. $1000–$1500 sold: $1092
William Doyle Galleries 12/6/1995

Dress, 1950
Black wool jersey, stand-up collar, slit neckline.
est. $1000–$1500 sold: $4600
William Doyle Galleries 12/6/1995

Evening Coat, 1952
Silk ottoman, princess line with angled seaming, melon sleeves, skirt flaring outward in front and falling full at back, curved quarter belt.
est. $600–$800 sold: $2300
William Doyle Galleries 11/16/1999

Evening Gown, 1948
Changeante lavender taffeta overdress with short sleeves, opening in front to an ivory satin underskirt draped in polonaise fashion at front.
est. $1500–$2000 sold: $2760
William Doyle Galleries 11/10/1998

Evening Gown, 1950s
Dark gray velvet bodice, ivory organza woven with yellow and charcoal plaid over yellow silk taffeta.
est. $3000–$5000 sold: $4312
William Doyle Galleries 12/6/1995

Evening Gown, 1951
Burgundy velvet bodice, burgundy satin skirt, pleated muslin underskirt.
est. $20,000–$30,000 sold: $29,900
William Doyle Galleries 4/27/1994

Evening Gown, 1951
Crimson silk faille bodice, petals and skirt of ivory organza flocked with red dots.
est. $2000–$3000 sold: $1610
William Doyle Galleries 12/6/1995

Evening Gown, 1951
Green velvet bodice, petals of green satin, skirt of ivory organza over blue tulle over white tulle.
est. $7500–$10,000 sold: $4887
William Doyle Galleries 12/6/1995

Evening Gown, 1953
Formfitting sheath of ivory satin, strapless, sewn with ivory faille hoop flounce at bottom, decorated with two strips of silver bugle beads.
est. $2000–$3000 sold: $1610
William Doyle Galleries 11/10/1998

Evening Gown, 1953
Princess-line sheath of ivory satin with heart-shaped strapless neckline, fitted bodice, sculptured hip line, bow-shaped flounce, black petticoat.
est. $10,000–$15,000 sold: $18,400
William Doyle Galleries 5/2/2000

Evening Gown, 1954
Body-hugging strapless black velvet sheath sewn at bottom with immense ivory faille hooped flounce embroidered with gold and silver beads.
est. $10,000–$15,000 sold: $14,375
William Doyle Galleries 5/6/1998

J

EVENING SKIRT, 1940s
Ballet-length flared skirt of black fishnet
mesh over taupe taffeta.
est. $200–$300 sold: $258
William Doyle Galleries 12/6/1995

HAT, 1948
Burgundy silk velvet brimless hat with encircling band.
est. $200–$300 sold: $1035
William Doyle Galleries 4/12/1995

JACKET, 1951
Taupe artillery drill with dolman sleeves.
est. $1000–$1500 sold: $6325
William Doyle Galleries 12/6/1995

SCARF, 1940s
Navy silk faille and green tourmaline silk
satin.
est. $300–$500 sold: $2185
William Doyle Galleries 4/12/1995

SCARF, 1950s
Pale blue and brown satin.
est. $300–$500 sold: $632
William Doyle Galleries 4/27/1994

SCARF, 1950s
Pale blue satin.
est. $100–$150 sold: $690
William Doyle Galleries 4/27/1994

SCARF, 1950s
Pale blue and pale mauve silk satin.
est. $100–$150 sold: $287
William Doyle Galleries 4/27/1994

SUIT, 1950s
Gray flannel single-breasted jacket and
A-line skirt.
est. $1000–$1500 sold: $1380
William Doyle Galleries 12/6/1995

SUIT, 1976–1980
Plum wool lined in amethyst silk.
est. $100–$150 sold: $230
William Doyle Galleries 12/6/1995

SUIT, 1976–1980
Plum wool lined in amethyst silk, crossover
front jacket and long skirt.
est. $300–$500 sold: $575
William Doyle Galleries 4/27/1994

JANTZEN

BATHING SUIT, 1920s
Black wool, tank-style with red appliquéd
diver on leg.
est. $75–$100 sold: $172
William Doyle Galleries 5/12/1999

JENNY

COCKTAIL DRESS, 1920s
Embroidered with ethnic-inspired design
in gold bullion and crystal beads, sleeveless, slit front to reveal rhinestone buttons
on underdress.
est. $300–$500 sold: $575
William Doyle Galleries 12/6/1995

DRESS, 1920s
Ivory silk, embroidered top with sequins
and beads, chiffon cummerbund, skirt of
feathers.
est. $200–$400 sold: $431
William Doyle Galleries 9/30/1993

DRESS, 1927
Jacket trimmed in sheared beaver, bronze
braid skirt attached to silk underdress.
est. $600–$900 sold: $1840
William Doyle Galleries 9/30/1993

JERAN DESIGN

EVENING GOWN, 1980s
Long strapless gown with silver bugle
beading, white ground with multicolored
beading on bodice, slit from hem to knee.
est. $500–$700 sold: $1265
Skinner 12/16/1999

JOSEF

HANDBAG, 1930s
Black satin with jeweled clasp.
est. not available sold: $295
The Paper Bag Princess 12/1/1997

KAHN, BEN

SHOULDER BAG, 1980S
Large mink pouch with brown shoulder straps and brown silk satin lining.
est. $300–$500 sold: $373.75
Skinner 12/16/1999

KAMALI, NORMA

SHOES, 1980
High-heeled sneakers with black suede uppers and white rubber heels.
est. $100–$150 sold: $1265
Sotheby's 4/8/1998

KIESELSTEIN-CORD, BARRY

HANDBAG, 1990S
Black leather handbag with rounded bottom, flap closure with matte gold-toned dog closure and short leather handle, green suede interior with one pocket.
est. $400–$600 sold: $862.50
Skinner 12/16/1999

KLEIN, ANNE

COAT, 1970S
Velveteen woven in carpet pattern of burgundy, ivory, and black, edges trimmed in burgundy faux fur.
est. $200–$250 sold: $747
William Doyle Galleries 11/12/1997

KLEIN, CALVIN

EVENING GOWN, 1993
Champagne-colored bias-cut silk satin with shoulder straps wrapping around to a bare back, slight train. Goldie Hawn, 1993 Academy Awards.
est. not available sold: $13,800
Christie's Oscar Dress Auction 3/18/1999

EVENING GOWN, 1995
Brown satin-back organza, strapless, cut in a princess style, fitted waist, flared skirt. Sandra Bullock, 1995 Academy Awards.
est. not available sold: $7475
Christie's Oscar Dress Auction 3/18/1999

KORET

EVENING BAG, 1960S
Black crocodile with aquamarine jeweled clasp.
est. $600–$800 sold: $1840
Sotheby's 12/9/1998

HANDBAG, 1950S
Black alligator oblong bag.
est. $500–$700 sold: $1265
Sotheby's 12/9/1998

HANDBAG, 1960S
Brown alligator box with gilt metal handle, clasp, and fittings at four corners, tan leather interior with top mirror.
est. $150–$200 sold: $345
William Doyle Galleries 6/11/1997

MALLETTE BAG, 1950S
Black crocodile travel case with leather-lined jewelry compartment and change purse.
est. $1000–$1500 sold: $2300
Sotheby's 12/9/1998

MALLETTE BAG, 1960S
Black alligator with black leather interior and gilt metal fittings.
est. $400–$600 sold: $402
William Doyle Galleries 6/11/1997

KORSHAK, STANLEY

COCKTAIL DRESS, 1960S
Sleeveless, fitted dress with backless bodice and square neckline, fitted skirt with fishtail hem at back.
est. $200–$300 sold: $373.75
Skinner 9/14/2000

K

ENSEMBLE, 1960s

Black wool shift dress with matching jacket, rhinestone buckles on jacket bodice.
est. not available sold: $900
The Paper Bag Princess 9/9/2000

LACROIX, CHRISTIAN

COCKTAIL DRESS, 1968

Brown lace with black underlayers, bodice cut in sweetheart form, sewn to lace-edged black tulle scarf extending to neck and wrapping around back.
est. $700–$900 sold: $460
William Doyle Galleries 5/12/1999

EVENING GOWN, 1987

Red silk taffeta, strapless with crisscross lacing down side, bouclé shaped skirt randomly tufted.
est. $2000–$3000 sold: $2300
Sotheby's 10/29/1997

EVENING GOWN, 1996

Black organza, gazar, and gauze, draped, with décolleté and pleated flap bustle. Kristen Scott-Thomas, 1996 Academy Awards.
est. not available sold: $9775
Christie's Oscar Dress Auction 3/18/1999

LAGERFELD FOR FENDI

CAPE, 1970s

Cape with brown Native American–inspired geometric pattern on a natural buff hide. Very good condition, slight wear on collar, relined, leather added.
est. $2000–$2500 sold: $1380
William Doyle Galleries 11/2/2000

LAGERFELD, KARL

EVENING GOWN, 1980s

Strapless black princess gown with gored skirt, with beaded passementerie fans placed at bosom and center back, cord belt with tassels.
est. $300–$500 sold: $287.50
William Doyle Galleries 5/2/2000

LAGERFELD, KARL FOR CHANEL

EVENING GOWN, 1996

Halter bodice embroidered with silver paillettes, glass beads, icicle beading at midriff, asymmetrical hem train. Celine Dion, 1996 Academy Awards.
est. not available sold: $27,600
Christie's Oscar Dress Auction 3/18/1999

LANA OF LONDON

HANDBAG, 1980s

Black lizard with double flat self handles, top zipper, exterior pocket with bracket-shaped flap.
est. $600–$800 sold: $632
William Doyle Galleries 11/10/1998

LANGLOIS & JARGEAIS

EVENING BAG, 1933

Small evening purse adorned with red, gold, and silver, cut-steel beads in foliate pattern, gold-toned frame with rhinestone clasp, short beaded handle.
est. $400–$600 sold: $460
Skinner 12/16/1999

LANVIN, JEANNE

CAPE, 1920s

Black velvet, wide collar of brown fur.
est. $300–$500 sold: $575
William Doyle Galleries 12/6/1995

CLOAK, 1940s

Three-quarter-length green cape with double-breasted closure and rounded standaway collar.
est. $600–$800 sold: $805
Sotheby's 10/29/1997

COAT, 1920s

Black satin lined with pink satin, stand-up collar in folds and sewn with pink tabs, coat embroidered with silver stitch, cuffs with silver and pink.
est. $500–$750 sold: $575
William Doyle Galleries 4/24/1996

Coat, 1928–1929

Peach silk and silver metallic lace, embroidered with pink and green beads, edged with pink velvet and white fox.
est. $1000–$1500 sold: $977
William Doyle Galleries 12/6/1995

Cocktail Dress, 1928

Black silk velvet sewn with flounces of cordonnet and net lace, squared V neckline trimmed with wide lace bertha, double-tiered skirt.
est. $1500–$2000 sold: $1265
William Doyle Galleries 5/6/1998

Cocktail Dress, 1929

Two-piece, all bugle beads, skirt with woven signature pink tied bow and streamers, minor darkening, labeled: Jeanne Lanvin/Paris/Été, 1929, no. 22131.
est. $3000–$5000 sold: $6900
William Doyle Galleries 11/2/2000

Cocktail Dress, 1935–1936

Black Chantilly lace, sleeveless, empire V-neck bodice with two bands of silver leather, separate lace shawl.
est. $125–$175 sold: $632
William Doyle Galleries 12/6/1995

Cocktail Dress, 1950s

Apricot-colored silk twill, short-sleeved, double ruffle and scalloped organza outline neckline, hem and skirt front, self belt.
est. $800–$1200 sold: $920
Sotheby's 10/29/1997

Cocktail Dress, 1960

Cream gazar, sleeveless with firework beading, bursts of pink and orange crystals around scalloped V neckline.
est. $800–$1200 sold: $920
Sotheby's 10/29/1997

Cocktail Dress, 1967–1968

Magenta silk twill, crosses at breast wrapping around nape of neck, neckline and hem embroidered with silver lamé and paillettes.
est. $1000–$1500 sold: $1150
Sotheby's 10/29/1997

Cocktail Dress, 1970s

Black silk charmeuse and velvet, one sleeve, velvet band encircles top of bodice to bow on shoulder, bias-cut skirt flounce from hip to hem.
est. $600–$800 sold: $690
Sotheby's 10/29/1997

Cocktail Dress, 1979

Black silk flowered lace and silk taffeta, long-sleeved with rounded neckline and full skirt.
est. $1500–$2000 sold: $1150
Sotheby's 10/29/1997

Evening Gown, 1950s

Black satin, strapless, front double-breasted tuxedo-style, flared skirt in front and gathered at back forming full sweep to the floor.
est. $400–$600 sold: $575
William Doyle Galleries 5/12/1999

Evening Gown, 1960s

Ivory taffeta chine with long-stemmed roses, sleeveless bodice with scoop neck, dropped V waist in back, full skirt with hip rolls underneath train.
est. $200–$300 sold: $1092
William Doyle Galleries 4/24/1996

Evening Gown, 1970s

Floor-length dress of blue lace woven with silver metallic flowers with geometric bands below the hip, long puffed sleeves, changeante silk slip.
est. $200–$300 sold: $402
William Doyle Galleries 5/12/1999

Evening Suit, 1940s

Black faux pony quilted and tailored jacket and matching floor-length skirt, wool braid binds edges at lapel and turned-back cuffs.
est. $400–$600 sold: $1955
Sotheby's 10/29/1997

Evening Suit, 1970s

Black faille knit two-piece, open front placket surrounded by ornate garland of multicolored silk cord, paillettes, beads, and diamanté, black pants.
est. $800–$1200 sold: $1495
Sotheby's 10/29/1997

HAT, 1920s

Black straw with wide brim, wide crown trimmed with silver lamé band and lace veil.
est. $150–$200 sold: $862
William Doyle Galleries 11/12/1997

HAT, 1930s

Embroidered leaf design in black wool yarns and passementerie, labeled: Jeanne Lanvin/Paris/22. Faubourg St. Honoré, handwritten in ink no. 59HI.
est. $150–$200 sold: $805
William Doyle Galleries 11/2/2000

LANVIN-CASTILLO

COAT, 1950s

Beige grass cloth.
est. $150–$200 sold: $402
William Doyle Galleries 4/24/1996

COCKTAIL DRESS, 1950s

Two bodice pieces pleated and arranged diagonally forming an asymmetric neckline, pleated skirt, wide cummerbund and rhinestone brooch at waist.
est. $800–$1200 sold: $1610
William Doyle Galleries 11/12/1997

COCKTAIL DRESS, 1950s

Embroidered underneath top layer with copper sequins, top layer with gunmetal sequins and rhinestones, belt of white satin with sequins and beads.
est. $600–$900 sold: $345
William Doyle Galleries 4/24/1996

COCKTAIL DRESS, 1955

Blue taffeta, empire-line bodice with sash and ribbon flower decoration, A-line skirt over huge petticoats, simple wrap bolero.
est. 400–600 pounds sold: 1035 pounds
Sotheby's London 11/25/1998

EVENING BOLERO JACKET, 1960s

Short-sleeved cream faille embroidered with crystals, pearls, rhinestones, and silver braid.
est. $500–$750 sold: $402
William Doyle Galleries 11/17/1994

EVENING GOWN, 1950s

Black Chantilly floral lace, flowers re-embroidered with black horsehair tape, brown tulle skirt, black satin ribbon belt.
est. $750–$1000 sold: $402
William Doyle Galleries 9/30/1993

EVENING GOWN, 1955

Red organdy embroidered with red and gold flowers.
est. $2000–$3000 sold: $575
William Doyle Galleries 9/30/1993

LAROCHE, GUY

COCKTAIL DRESS, 1960s

Orange silk crepe pongee sheath with tulip skirt that gathers to bustline in coral bead sunburst.
est. $750–$1000 sold: $1265
Sotheby's 10/29/1997

LAYNE, HOMER

COAT, 1985

Homer Layne copy of a Charles James coat from 1946, high-waisted, brown wool bodice and bias-cut skirt of brown, olive, and cream plaid wool.
est. $300–$500 sold: $460
William Doyle Galleries 4/27/1994

LEDERER

HANDBAG, 1950s

Black crocodile rectangular handbag with front flap, gold-toned closures and hardware, round handle, and black leather interior.
est. $100–$200 sold: $373.75
Skinner 12/16/1999

HANDBAG, 1960

Black alligator.
est. $150–$250 sold: $345
William Doyle Galleries 12/5/1996

LÉGER, HERVÉ

Evening Gown, 1994

Sleeveless dress of horizontal ribbons of black jersey, bodice highlighted with clustered simulated pearl beading, diamanté beading on bust and open back. Rita Wilson, 1994 Academy Awards.
est. not available sold: $17,250
Christie's Oscar Dress Auction 3/18/1999

LEIBER, JUDITH

Clutch Bag, 1970s

White lizard with crystal-covered bar frame, two sizes gem-set faceted rhinestones.
est. $400–$600 sold: $488
William Doyle Galleries 11/10/1998

Clutch Bag, 1970s

Black lizard with black bar top frame, two sizes of gem-set faceted rhinestones.
est. $400–$600 sold: $747
William Doyle Galleries 11/10/1998

Clutch Bag, 1978

Blue kid with petit point inset.
est. $100–$125 sold: $373
William Doyle Galleries 6/11/1997

Clutch Bag, 1980s

Oval, with striated gilt metal ornaments set on self-covered curved frame, black cameo clasp set in similar ornament, slender shoulder strap.
est. $300–$500 sold: $431
William Doyle Galleries 5/2/2000

Clutch Bag, 1980s

Oval, with gilt metal bar ornaments on self-covered frame, tiger's-eye and carnelian clasp, coin purse.
est. $200–$300 sold: $488.75
William Doyle Galleries 5/2/2000

Clutch Bag, 1980s

Iridescent pink snakeskin gathered into double-sided bone and purple cabochon bar frame.
est. $100–$150 sold: $460
William Doyle Galleries 6/11/1997

Clutch Bag, 1980s

Black crocodile pleated in gilt metal shaped ridged frame, Art Deco–inspired clutch set with black cabochon stone, drop-in chain, comb, and mirror.
est. $300–$400 sold: $690
William Doyle Galleries 5/6/1998

Clutch Bag, 1980s

Oval with curved striated gilt metal frame, two self-covered clasps, slender self strap, coin purse, mirror.
est. $200–$300 sold: $460
William Doyle Galleries 5/2/2000

Clutch Bag, 1980s

Oval, with striated gilt metal curved frame set with two large tiger's eyes and small red carnelian stones, slender self shoulder strap, coin purse.
est. $400–$600 sold: $374
William Doyle Galleries 5/2/2000

Clutch Bag, 1980s

Multicolored pastel snakeskin with gold-toned ridged frame.
est. $150–$200 sold: $460
William Doyle Galleries 6/11/1997

Clutch Bag, 1980s

Blue karung, oval with silver and gold ridged frame set with blue stones, mirror, comb, and satin coin purse.
est. $250–$300 sold: $373
William Doyle Galleries 5/6/1998

Clutch Bag, 1980s

Green python with ridged gilt metal frame.
est. $150–$250 sold: $373
William Doyle Galleries 12/5/1996

Clutch Bags, 1980s

First, a small aubergine trapezoid with Art Deco–style velvet and leather, tiger's-eye frame with purple quartz stones; second, an olive oval shape.
est. $300–$500 sold: $546
William Doyle Galleries 5/2/2000

L

CLUTCH BAGS, 1980s
First, in turquoise, rectangular with rounded corners, karung gathered into gilt metal frame, clasp set with two lapis stones; second, in purple.
est. $300–$500 sold: $863
William Doyle Galleries 5/2/2000

CLUTCH BAGS, 1980s
First, in red, with double silver metal tubular frame, double teardrop clasp; second, in white with rounded silver metal frame set with gilt star shapes.
est. $400–$600 sold: $920
William Doyle Galleries 5/2/2000

ENVELOPE BAG, 1980s
Navy, fold-over front, cord quilted and re-embroidered with silk chain stitch, square clasp of textured gilt metal.
est. $150–$200 sold: $431
William Doyle Galleries 6/11/1997

EVENING BAG, 1960s
Gilt metal with birds, foliage, and small rhinestones.
est. $50–$75 sold: $373
William Doyle Galleries 4/27/1994

EVENING BAG, 1960s
Gilt metal in the shape of a coin purse, rhinestone-studded, lined in silver leather.
est. $75–$125 sold: $862
William Doyle Galleries 4/27/1994

EVENING BAG, 1960s
Rounded clutch of green leather studded with various-sized green crystals.
est. $100–$150 sold: $431
William Doyle Galleries 12/6/1995

EVENING BAG, 1960s
"Gift-wrapped" black crocodile tied up with gilt metal twisted wire.
est. $400–$600 sold: $1035
William Doyle Galleries 12/6/1995

EVENING BAG, 1967
Black satin with rhinestone strap closure and handle.
est. $200–$300 sold: $1265
William Doyle Galleries 6/11/1997

EVENING BAG, 1970s
Rounded bottom of brown suede, the dome top of gilt metal, rigid square handle with rounded corners, coin purse.
est. $200–$300 sold: $403
William Doyle Galleries 5/2/2000

EVENING BAG, 1972
Turbo shell and gold.
est. $2000–$3000 sold: $4600
Sotheby's 12/9/1998

EVENING BAG, 1980
Red karung, silver-toned metal frame set with rhinestones and faux rubies.
est. $200–$300 sold: $1035
William Doyle Galleries 12/5/1996

EVENING BAG, 1980s
Black karung with a black-tasseled cord shoulder strap, gilt metal catch set with carved black onyx and carnelian cabochons.
est. $200–$300 sold: $1495
William Doyle Galleries 12/5/1996

EVENING BAG, 1980s
Black karung gathered into shaped rhinestone-studded frame.
est. $300–$400 sold: $632
William Doyle Galleries 6/11/1997

EVENING BAG, 1980s
Beige karung with double-sided gilt and silver metal frame set with variously colored and shaped semiprecious stones.
est. $150–$200 sold: $460
William Doyle Galleries 6/11/1997

EVENING BAG, 1981
White lizard with Art Deco–style silver-toned metal mount set with frosted crystal scarab drop and rhinestones, silver-toned metal shoulder strap.
est. $200–$300 sold: $632
William Doyle Galleries 12/5/1996

EVENING BAG, 1990s
Bright gold, trapezoidal, with corrugated sides, karung gussets and frame, double handle of gilt metal, channel set with crystals and gold stars.
est. $300–$500 sold: $460
William Doyle Galleries 5/2/2000

HANDBAG, 1960s

Black beaded crocheted purse with faux
ivory handle.
est. $100–$150 sold: $316
William Doyle Galleries 4/27/1994

HANDBAG, 1960s

Black crocodile with accordion-pleated
sides and envelope flap, gilt metal snake
chain shoulder/hand strap.
est. $100–$150 sold: $287
William Doyle Galleries 4/12/1995

HANDBAG, 1960s

Pearlized pewter leather in shape of treas-
ure chest, edges ornamented with silver
studs.
est. $50–$100 sold: $316
William Doyle Galleries 9/30/1993

HANDBAG, 1960s

Black crocodile clasp and straps ornamented with black jet rhinestones.
est. $250–$400 sold: $977
William Doyle Galleries 12/5/1996

HANDBAG, 1960s

Black patent, double-sided.
est. $100–$150 sold: $431
William Doyle Galleries 12/5/1996

HANDBAG, 1960s

Black patent leather double-sided, frame
and catch studded with small jet rhinestones.
est. $200–$250 sold: $517
William Doyle Galleries 12/5/1996

HANDBAG, 1970s

Black lizard, two rhinestone ring handles
attached to exterior side compartments.
est. $300–$500 sold: $431
William Doyle Galleries 11/10/1998

HANDBAG, 1970s

With double handles, bottom half crystal-
covered, opening separately like jewel compartment, interior mirrored top, comb and
mirror.
est. $300–$500 sold: $460
William Doyle Galleries 11/10/1998

HANDBAG, 1970s

Black and white oversized retangular shoulder bag with thin double straps and gray
grosgrain interior with two pockets.
est. $200–$400 sold: $373.75
Skinner 12/16/1999

HANDBAG, 1970s

Rectangular brown, black, white, and gray
patchwork fur handbag with taupe leather
frame and handles. Four compartments
with gold-toned closures.
est. $300–$500 sold: $488.75
Skinner 12/16/1999

HANDBAG, 1980s

Green gathered into a gilt metal and
karung frame, catch set with a green
cabochon.
est. $100–$150 sold: $373
William Doyle Galleries 12/5/1996

HANDBAG, 1980s

Brown with gilt metal ribbed frame set
with tiger's eye and carnelian.
est. $100–$150 sold: $632
William Doyle Galleries 12/5/1996

HANDBAG, 1980s

Teal snakeskin gathered into a metal frame
set with cabochon quartz, carnelian, black
onyx, and fool's gold.
est. $125–$175 sold: $402
William Doyle Galleries 12/5/1996

HANDBAG, 1980s

White gathered karung, the straps and clasp
ornamented with gilt metal hearts set with
rose quartz cabochon stones.
est. $100–$150 sold: $373
William Doyle Galleries 6/11/1997

HANDBAG, 1980s

Lozenge-shaped hard-sided leather handbag with top closure and short round handle, black satin lining.
est. $500–$700 sold: $632.50
Skinner 12/16/1999

L

HANDBAG, 1980s
Taupe gathered into frame overlaid with
silver-toned and gilt metal bands, clasp set
with tear-drop tiger's eye and carnelian.
est. $100–$150 sold: $345
William Doyle Galleries 12/5/1996

HANDBAG, 1980s
Black crocodile, round gilt metal bangle
handle molded with two barrel-shaped ornaments set with rings of small pink and
green round stones.
est. $700–$900 sold: $575
William Doyle Galleries 11/10/1998

HANDBAG, 1980s
Black crocodile oval, skins gathered into
self-covered frame trimmed with gilt metal
ridged strips, clasp set with black onyx
cabochon, thin strap.
est. $500–$700 sold: $747
William Doyle Galleries 5/6/1998

MINAUDIÈRE, 1960s
Pouch-shaped of brushed gilt metal studded with graduated-sized crystals arranged
in flame pattern, gilt metal chain, silver kid
lining.
est. $500–$700 sold: $403
William Doyle Galleries 5/2/2000

MINAUDIÈRE, 1960s
Brushed gilt metal studded with rhinestones and lined with silver kid.
est. $750–$1000 sold: $1380
William Doyle Galleries 12/5/1996

MINAUDIÈRE, 1960s
Brushed gilt metal with rhinestones.
est. $400–$600 sold: $977
William Doyle Galleries 12/5/1996

MINAUDIÈRE, 1970s
Brushed gilt metal.
est. $100–$150 sold: $402
William Doyle Galleries 12/5/1996

MINAUDIÈRE, 1970s
Leopard pattern, rhinestone-studded with
change purse, mirror, and comb.
est. $800–$1200 sold: $2070
Sotheby's 12/9/1998

MINAUDIÈRE, 1970s
Silver-toned metal, eyes set with green
stones.
est. $800–$1200 sold: $488
William Doyle Galleries 11/10/1998

MINAUDIÈRE, 1980s
Gilt metal molded with ridges and pebbles,
ridges studded with rhinestones, catch set
with black onyx.
est. $250–$400 sold: $517
William Doyle Galleries 12/5/1996

MINAUDIÈRE, 1980s
Gilt metal molded in butterfly shape, outlined with white crystals and further decorated with semiprecious stones including
carnelian and lapis.
est. $700–$900 sold: $920
William Doyle Galleries 11/10/1998

MINAUDIÈRE, 1980s
Oblong gold-toned gilt metal incised with
rows of scrolling brackets, gold kid lining,
green, white, and gold silk tassels.
est. $300–$500 sold: $431
William Doyle Galleries 5/6/1998

MINAUDIÈRE, 1980s
Gilt metal set with clear and amber rhinestones, corners set with teardrop quartz.
est. $300–$500 sold: $862
William Doyle Galleries 12/5/1996

MINAUDIÈRE, 1980s
Rectangular, brushed gilt metal studded
with black, red, and gold rhinestone
stripes, drop-in chain, gold kid lining, silver kid coin purse.
est. $600–$800 sold: $517
William Doyle Galleries 5/6/1998

MINAUDIÈRE, 1980s
Rectangular with rounded edges, covered
with geometric pattern in gray, bronze,
white, and gold crystals.
est. $600–$800 sold: $920
William Doyle Galleries 11/10/1998

MINAUDIÈRE, 1980s
Rectangular with zigzag pattern in charcoal
and white rhinestones.
est. $700–$900 sold: $690
William Doyle Galleries 5/6/1998

MINAUDIÈRE, 1980s
Oblong silver-toned metal incised with
rows of scrolling brackets, silver kid lining,
comb, black, red, and gray silk tassels.
est. $300–$500 sold: $431
William Doyle Galleries 5/6/1998

MINAUDIÈRE, 1980s
Charcoal, semicircular, rhinestone-studded
with silver-toned edges and clasp set with
three stones: onyx, rose quartz, and jade,
with silver kid lining.
est. $400–$600 sold: $1495
William Doyle Galleries 6/11/1997

MINAUDIÈRE, 1980s
Gilt metal studded with amethyst rhinestones.
est. $300–$500 sold: $977
William Doyle Galleries 12/5/1996

MINAUDIÈRE, 1980s
Brushed gilt metal, clasp set with lapis
lazuli.
est. $200–$300 sold: $373
William Doyle Galleries 6/11/1997

MINAUDIÈRE, 1980s
Covered with white crystals with black
onyx cabochon spots, bow tied at neck,
padded silver kid bottom.
est. $800–$1200 sold: $1035
William Doyle Galleries 11/10/1998

MINAUDIÈRE, 1980s
Gilt metal molded with small pattern of
herons, frogs, and various leaves, surrounding space covered with white crystals.
est. $600–$800 sold: $862
William Doyle Galleries 11/10/1998

MINAUDIÈRE, 1980s
Cylindrical, covered with white crystals
and scattered with red, green, and blue
small flowers, green stone clasp.
est. $600–$800 sold: $632
William Doyle Galleries 11/10/1998

MINAUDIÈRE, 1980s
Crown-shaped set with white crystal, gilt
metal rims, jeweled "turban" clasp.
est. $400–$600 sold: $747
William Doyle Galleries 11/10/1998

MINAUDIÈRE, 1988
Brushed gold elephant's head adorned with
garnets, green onyx, and rhinestone trim.
est. $3000–$4000 sold: $2185
Sotheby's 12/9/1998

SHOULDER BAG, 1970s
Snakeskin accordion bag with gold horse's-
head closures and lock.
est. $600–$800 sold: $747
Sotheby's 12/9/1998

SHOULDER BAG, 1970s
Navy leather with rounded flap decorated
with carved rock-crystal lion's head set in
gilt metal.
est. $400–$600 sold: $460
William Doyle Galleries 5/6/1998

LELONG, LUCIEN

COCKTAIL DRESS, 1930s
Black wool crepe with shirred sweetheart
neckline.
est. $300–$500 sold: $862
William Doyle Galleries 4/12/1995

COCKTAIL DRESS, 1940s
Ivory cotton net dress, both the layered
skirt and neckline have black velvet appliquéd bows with gold star paillettes.
est. $2000–$3000 sold: $2300
Sotheby's 10/29/1997

COCKTAIL DRESS, 1940s
Black crepe, long sleeves and V neck, skirt
in two layers, top layer draped and gathered
to form peplum effect at hips and hem to
show underskirt.
est. $600–$800 sold: $2300
William Doyle Galleries 5/6/1998

LEONARD

DRESS, 1960s
Printed cashmere, knee-length with long
sleeves and jeweled tasssel belt.
est. not available sold: $395
The Paper Bag Princess 1/1/2001

DRESS, 1970s
Floral pink print, silk jersey, scoop neck,
long sleeves, A-line, knee-length.
est. not available sold: $345
The Paper Bag Princess 8/1/1997

DRESS, 1970s
Silk jersey knee-length, long sleeves,
printed pink and black geometric motif.
est. not available sold: $345
The Paper Bag Princess 8/1/1997

EVENING GOWN, 1960s
Black silk jersey floor-length, fitted bodice
printed with leaf patterns in pink, peach,
and gray, printed band at cuff of long sleeves.
est. $150–$200 sold: $690
Skinner 9/14/2000

EVENING GOWN, 1970s
Pink silk jersey with scoop neckline, empire
bodice, with full A-line skirt and floral motif.
est. not available sold: $695
The Paper Bag Princess 7/1/1997

HOSTESS GOWN, 1970s
Black jersey maxi-length, A-line, pink
floral print trim, long sleeves, excellent
condition.
est. not available sold: $575
The Paper Bag Princess 12/11/2000

SCARF, 1960s
Chiffon printed with colored geometric
shapes, in pink, green, white.
est. not available sold: $175
The Paper Bag Princess 1/1/2001

LESER, TINA

COCKTAIL ENSEMBLE, 1960s
Swing coat and bouffant dress of blue,
green, and turquoise printed silk, dress has
low square back to waist, coat reversible to
solid green shantung.
est. $400–$600 sold: $373
William Doyle Galleries 5/12/1999

DRESS, 1950s
Blue and white batiste with white eyelet
embroidery at collar.
est. $100–$150 sold: $316
William Doyle Galleries 4/27/1994

EVENING ENSEMBLE, 1960
Coat of red and green poppy chine taffeta,
ruffled cape sleeves, jumpsuit of green
crêpe de chine, sleeveless with scoop neck.
est. $150–$250 sold: $373
William Doyle Galleries 4/12/1995

LEVINE, BETH

BOOTS, 1969
Thigh-high, velvet dyed in gold, red,
orange, and green.
est. $100–$150 sold: $345
William Doyle Galleries 6/11/1997

BOOTS, 1970
For Herbert Levine, black stretch satin tie
dyed with multicolored fish.
est. $100–$150 sold: $345
William Doyle Galleries 4/27/1994

EVENING SHOES, 1950s
For Herbert Levine, black satin with Lucite
heels.
est. $100–$150 sold: $172
William Doyle Galleries 4/27/1994

SHOES, 1960s
For Herbert Levine, zebra-haired calf with
teak sole and heels.
est. $100–$150 sold: $230
William Doyle Galleries 6/11/1997

SHOES, 1960s
For Herbert Levine, silver stocking, clear
Lucite heels.
est. $200–$300 sold: $517
William Doyle Galleries 4/27/1994

SHOES, 1960s
For Herbert Levine, bone calf with slanted
block heels faced on each side with silver
kid, gold kid, rust suede, or gray suede.
est. $200–$250 sold: $345
William Doyle Galleries 12/5/1996

SHOES, 1960s
Red satin with shaped glossy black wooden
platforms.
est. $100–$150 sold: $575
William Doyle Galleries 4/24/1996

SHOES, 1962
For Herbert Levine, black satin with shaped
gold wooden soles.
est. $250–$350 sold: $373
William Doyle Galleries 4/27/1994

SHOES, 1969
For Herbert Levine, caramel calf sling backs
with rolled heels.
est. $150–$250 sold: $287
William Doyle Galleries 4/27/1994

LEVINE, HERBERT

SHOES, 1950s
Pink leather pumps with rhinestone toes.
est. not available sold: $195
The Paper Bag Princess

LIBERTY AND CO.

COAT, 1920s
Reversible blue velvet to silver silk crepe,
collar extending to long ties.
est. $100–$150 sold: $805
William Doyle Galleries 11/12/1997

COAT, 1920s
Black tulle embroidered in gold chain
stitch with leaves and flowers, tie-dyed lining shows through the net, fur collar, glass
beads on sleeves.
est. $400–$600 sold: $373
William Doyle Galleries 12/5/1996

LLEWELLYN

HANDBAG, 1950s
Gray marbleized plastic handbag with mirrored lid.
est. $500–$700 sold: $575
Sotheby's 12/9/1998

HANDBAG, 1950s
Beehive-shaped Lucite with brown hive
and clear gold top flap with incised vine
pattern and inset gold-toned metal bees.
est. $175–$200 sold: $201
Skinner 12/16/1999

LOEWE

HANDBAG, 1950s
Black crocodile with rounded envelope
flap, gilt metal ring clasp and handle
fittings.
est. $400–$600 sold: $1265
William Doyle Galleries 6/11/1997

HANDBAG, 1960s
Square, black suede with jeweled oval clasp
and wrist strap.
est. not available sold: $225
The Paper Bag Princess 8/10/1998

LOUIS, JEAN

COAT
Maxi-length pink brocade with white mink
trim, stand-up collar.
est. not available sold: $895
The Paper Bag Princess 4/12/2000

COCKTAIL DRESS, 1960s
Cream silk chiffon over chartreuse chiffon,
back with blouson panels with fringed
leaves in chartreuse and crystal.
est. $100–$150 sold: $230
William Doyle Galleries 12/6/1995

L

COCKTAIL DRESS, 1983

Designed for Marlene Dietrich, ivory bugle-beaded with cap sleeves and Nehru-style collar, knee-length skirt. Jamie Lee Curtis, 1983 Academy Awards.
est. not available sold: $9200
Christie's Oscar Dress Auction 3/18/1999

COCKTAIL SUIT, 1970S

Metallic gold crocheted jacket and skirt, fitted mid-thigh length unlined jacket, long sleeves, A-line mid-calf skirt lined with lamé.
est. $300–$500 sold: $431.25
Skinner 12/16/1999

LOWE, ANN

EVENING GOWN, 1955

Ivory silk taffeta, camisole bodice, skirt with long bow swag of bone taffeta faced with red taffeta.
est. $250–$400 sold: $287
William Doyle Galleries 12/6/1995

MACKIE, BOB

COCKTAIL DRESS, 1970S

Brown, gold, white, and silver-beaded, brown net beaded with bugle beads and rhinestones, high neck with trompe l'oeil necklace, sheer beaded sleeves.
est. $1000–$1500 sold: $747
Skinner 12/16/1999

COCKTAIL DRESS, 1970S

Bodice has bugle bead fringe yoke, flesh-colored mid-section with rhinestones in diamond pattern and gold coins, bugle bead fringe on zigzag fringe.
est. $1000–$1500 sold: $1840
Skinner 12/16/1999

COCKTAIL DRESS, 1972

Harem-style from a sheer silk fabric with borders embroidered with gold cord paillettes. Cher, 1972 Academy Awards.
est. not available sold: $27,600
Christie's Oscar Dress Auction 3/18/1999

COCKTAIL DRESS, 1979

Ivory silk crepe strapless dress, knee-length skirt, blouse with sequins, bugle beads; purple, pink, gold, ivory jacket. Sally Field, Academy Awards.
est. not available sold: $4025
Christie's Oscar Dress Auction 3/18/1999

DRESS, 1960S

Black chiffon sheath lined in silk, embroidered with purple, green, and pink beads, sequins and dangling strands in abstract cloud-like pattern.
est. $300–$500 sold: $431
William Doyle Galleries 11/16/1999

EVENING ENSEMBLE, 1980S

Cocoon coat and slip dress of black chiffon embroidered with red bugle beads and brilliants, coat trimmed with black fox.
est. $200–$300 sold: $862
William Doyle Galleries 5/6/1998

EVENING ENSEMBLE, 1980S

Cocoon coat and slip dress of nude chiffon worked with gold bugle beads and square brilliants, coat trimmed with champagne-toned fox.
est. $200–$300 sold: $862
William Doyle Galleries 5/6/1998

EVENING GOWN, 1970S

Gold beaded floor-length dress, upper bodice has high band collar, padded shoulders, bugle bead–fringed yoke, rhinestone mid-section.
est. $700–$900 sold: $920
Skinner 9/14/2000

EVENING GOWN, 1970S

Brown, gold, white, and silver beaded floor-length dress, high-necked bodice, twisted bead rope that forms a yoke above bust and across shoulders.
est. $1000–$1500 sold: $747.50
Skinner 12/16/1999

M

Evening Gown, 1970s

Black, sequined and beaded long gown with purple, fuchsia, red, gold, blue, and aqua stripes, fitted sheath, sweetheart neckline, spaghetti straps, front slit.
est. $600–$800 sold: $920
Skinner 12/16/1999

Evening Gown, 1970s

Strapless silk chiffon with beaded bodice of ivory net with white and gold bugle beads and pearls in "Taj Mahal" design on front, skirt of ivory chiffon.
est. $500–$700 sold: $575
Skinner 12/16/1999

Evening Gown, 1980s

Black strapless evening gown with beading in diagonal rows of black bugle beads and black sequins, sweetheart neckline.
est. $800–$1000 sold: $690
Skinner 12/16/1999

Evening Gown, 1980s

Spaghetti strap bodice of clear, gold, and silver bugle beads and diamanté beading, ostrich feather skirt and white ostrich feather jacket.
est. $800–$1000 sold: $747
Skinner 12/16/1999

Evening Gown, 1980s

Black, orange, and hot pink beaded floor-length evening gown, long-sleeved turtleneck bodice with flame pattern in sequins.
est. $800–$1000 sold: $690
Skinner 12/16/1999

Evening Gown, 1980s

Front zipper and elastic bottom band of black and silver denim sewn all over with blue, black, and silver sequins, collar, cuffs of chinchilla.
est. $200–$300 sold: $373
William Doyle Galleries 5/12/1999

MAD CARPENTIER

Cocktail Dress, 1950s

Strapless black silk satin.
est. $400–$600 sold: $2070
William Doyle Galleries 11/17/1994

MAGNIN, I.

Coat, 1950s

Below-the-knee-length cocoon day coat with wide-pointed collar, oversized center-front buttons, and black satin lining.
est. $500–$700 sold: $345
Skinner 12/16/1999

Coat, 1960s

Black peau de soie silk opera coat.
est. not available sold: $495
The Paper Bag Princess 12/20/1998

MAINBOCHER

Coat, 1960

Lavender silk lined in lime green silk.
est. $200–$300 sold: $287
William Doyle Galleries 9/30/1993

Coat, 1960

Oatmeal tweed with Peter Pan collar.
est. $300–$500 sold: $460
William Doyle Galleries 9/30/1993

Cocktail Dress, 1930s

Blouse bodice of the sheath of silk lamé printed in red, black, and metallic gold diagonal stripes, wool skirt.
est. $200–$300 sold: $1380
William Doyle Galleries 11/16/1999

Cocktail Dress, 1930s

Silk crêpe de chine printed with swirling ribbons in red, yellow, green, blue, and white against navy blue, forty-five small buttons down back.
est. $750–$1000 sold: $1495
William Doyle Galleries 4/12/1995

Cocktail Dress, 1950s

Ivory silk woven with dots, sleeveless bodice sewn with pearl pendants and beads.
est. $300–$500 sold: $287
William Doyle Galleries 6/11/1997

M

Cocktail Dress, 1950s
Strapless underdress with black lace over nude silk bodice and black silk skirt, black silk tulle overdress, silk cummerbund with two rhinestone clips.
est. $300–$500 sold: $316
William Doyle Galleries 4/12/1995

Cocktail Dress, 1950s
Sari-style of pink and gold silk, sleeveless with full-pleated skirt, self belt.
est. $400–$600 sold: $460
William Doyle Galleries 9/30/1993

Cocktail Dress, 1950s
Short, sheer navy lace over iridescent lavender/topaz shantung, strapless with self bow at one side of sweetheart neckline.
est. $400–$600 sold: $1265
William Doyle Galleries 4/12/1995

Cocktail Dress, 1950s
Green floral silk faille, fitted and draped bodice, full knee-length skirt.
est. not available sold: $1295
The Paper Bag Princess 1/12/2001

Cocktail Dress, 1960
Silver, blue, green, and yellow brocade.
est. $400–$600 sold: $230
William Doyle Galleries 9/30/1993

Cocktail Dress, 1960s
Fitted bodice with curved seaming at bust and low cowl neck cut-in-one with straps extending into long back streamers falling to floor to form train.
est. $800–$1200 sold: $1840
William Doyle Galleries 5/2/2000

Cocktail Ensemble, 1960s
Black brocaded silk sleeveless dress with bow at bustline, ivory brocaded silk jacket with Peter Pan collar.
est. $800–$1200 sold: $1840
Sotheby's 4/8/1998

Dress, 1950
Black silk crepe, short sleeves, front and side of skirt has Chinese-inspired self bands and braided ball enclosures.
est. $100–$150 sold: $345
William Doyle Galleries 11/17/1994

Dress, 1950s
Blue silk printed with a crosshatched gingham check in black, self buttons at collar, belt and pleated skirt.
est. $100–$150 sold: $373
William Doyle Galleries 4/24/1996

Dress, 1950s
Black and bone printed silk, flared bolero bodice with cut-in armholes, underdress, calf belt and barrel skirt.
est. $300–$500 sold: $402
William Doyle Galleries 11/17/1994

Dress, 1960s
Blue silk, sleeveless, A-line dress woven with pebbles and leaves, short jacket lined with white mink.
est. $200–$300 sold: $258
William Doyle Galleries 12/6/1995

Ensemble, 1960
Sweater bodice of black cashmere with satin buttons, edging and diagonal ribbon trimmed with bow, skirt of black wool with four floating panels.
est. $300–$400 sold: $345
William Doyle Galleries 5/12/1999

Evening Apron, 1950s
Blue silk taffeta with cowl neck bib, self bow at waist.
est. $150–$200 sold: $431
William Doyle Galleries 12/6/1995

Evening Ensemble, 1960s
Long sleeveless V-neck dress and single-breasted jacket of green metallic floral brocade, jacket lined in pink silk.
est. $400–$600 sold: $575
William Doyle Galleries 12/5/1996

Evening Gown, 1930s
Black satin two-piece with asymmetrically draped neckline and long bias-cut skirt.
est. $600–$800 sold: $1840
Sotheby's 9/30/1999

Evening Gown, 1948
Blue and white checked cotton.
est. $2000–$3000 sold: $3680
William Doyle Galleries 9/30/1993

EVENING GOWN, 1950s
Satin with fitted camisole bodice, poofed peplum sewn at natural waist, slightly flared skirt, very good condition, labeled: Mainbocher, Inc.
est. $600–$800 sold: $2587.50
William Doyle Galleries 11/2/2000

EVENING GOWN, 1950s
Lavender satin, camisole bodice sewn with faux bandeau centered with front bow, skirt augmented by back flowering panel, separate bolero jacket.
est. $300–$500 sold: $431
William Doyle Galleries 11/10/1998

EVENING GOWN, 1960s
Pale blue silk organza woven with gold metallic garlands of flowers, sleeveless bodice, skirt gathered and full-form, slightly dropped waist.
est. $800–$1200 sold: $1265
William Doyle Galleries 5/2/2000

EVENING TURNOUT, 1961
Pink brocade long dress, camisole bodice, long stole, lime green tweed jacket.
est. $750–$1000 sold: $460
William Doyle Galleries 9/30/1993

SUIT, 1940s
Green, navy, and yellow plaid wool suit.
est. $100–$150 sold: $258
William Doyle Galleries 9/30/1993

SUIT, 1965
Cream broadtail jacket and skirt.
est. $500–$750 sold: $345
William Doyle Galleries 9/30/1993

MANGONE

SUIT, 1940s
Navy wool gabardine, double-breasted into single-breasted closure.
est. $75–$125 sold: $431
William Doyle Galleries 12/6/1995

SUIT, 1950s
Brown and beige silk.
est. $75–$125 sold: $230
William Doyle Galleries 12/6/1995

MANGUIN

COCKTAIL ENSEMBLE, 1950s
Fawn satin draped cape jacket, gathered skirt, and taupe bowed belt ending in streamers.
est. $200–$300 sold: $287
William Doyle Galleries 11/10/1998

MARIMEKKO

DRESS, 1970s
Green, fuchsia, pink, and black printed cotton smock, elbow-length sleeves, two patch pockets, low round neckline, cap sleeves, full skirt.
est. $100–$200 sold: $201
Skinner 12/16/1999

MARKS, LANA

HANDBAG, 1980s
Beige lizard, briefcase-style with double handles, top zipper, exterior compartment with parenthesis-shaped flap.
est. $800–$1200 sold: $517
William Doyle Galleries 5/6/1998

HANDBAG, 1980s
Brown crocodile with soft sides, rigid top, rolled handle and frame, exterior pocket with bracket-shaped flap.
est. $1200–$1500 sold: $3910
William Doyle Galleries 11/10/1998

MASTERS, ADDIE

PANTS, 1950s
Black grosgrain long straight pants with horizontal rows of black silk fringe.
est. $200–$300 sold: $259
Skinner 12/16/1999

M

MAX, PETER

SCARF, 1960s
Purple central circle with a profile of a woman and "love" in green, bright pink border.
est. $50–$100 sold: $103
William Doyle Galleries 12/5/1996

SCARF, 1970s
Silk twill printed with astrological chart.
est. $50–$75 sold: $143
William Doyle Galleries 11/12/1997

SHORTS, 1970s
Avocado color cotton denim with red belt loops, blue, kelly green back pockets by Wrangler with original leather patch.
est. not available sold: $295
The Paper Bag Princess 9/2/2000

MCCARDELL, CLAIRE

BATHING SUIT, 1950
Purple and white plaid cotton with a piping-outlined gathered bodice and midriff, skirt and bloomers.
est. $250–$400 sold: $632
William Doyle Galleries 4/24/1996

BATHING SUIT, 1950s
Tunic, self belt, and cotton drawers woven with plaid of red, navy, and green, fastens at shoulder of tunic with brass buttons.
est. $200–$300 sold: $1955
William Doyle Galleries 4/24/1996

COAT, 1950
Black and brown small check wool, fitted with band at torso, cape collar, bishop sleeves gathered at wrist with band cuff.
est. $600–$800 sold: $345
William Doyle Galleries 11/16/1999

COAT, 1950s
Black waffle weave cotton piqué with cut-in-one shawl collar extending to the hem, kimono sleeves.
est. $150–$200 sold: $316
William Doyle Galleries 11/12/1997

COCKTAIL DRESS, 1940s
Pink satin, long full skirt gathered at the waist, bodice with V neck, brass hooks and eyes in front, wide sashes wrapping and tying at the waist.
est. $400–$600 sold: $460
William Doyle Galleries 6/11/1997

DRESS, 1940s
Pleated cherry wool knit, black leather belt with gilt metal buckle.
est. $200–$300 sold: $1265
William Doyle Galleries 12/6/1995

DRESS, 1940s
Blue rippled rayon, bodice pleated at low V, elasticized straps at shoulders converging on center back, full skirt, separate fishnet cape with ties.
est. $100–$150 sold: $1380
William Doyle Galleries 11/10/1998

DRESS, 1940s
Gray linen-textured rayon, outlined at neckline and higher of two waistlines with self piping, fastens at side of midriff with brass buttons.
est. $200–$300 sold: $287
William Doyle Galleries 4/24/1996

DRESS, 1940s
Black synthetic silk with V neck, padded shoulders, long dolman sleeves, draped neckline.
est. $100–$150 sold: $373
William Doyle Galleries 4/24/1996

DRESS, 1940s
Crepe tucked all over at half-inch intervals, long cut-in-one sleeves, bodice tucking diagonal and skirt tucking horizontal.
est. $300–$500 sold: $632
William Doyle Galleries 11/12/1997

DRESS, 1940s
Rust silk, front and back pleated surplice bodice with long sleeves cut-in-one with bodice, pleated skirt.
est. $150–$200 sold: $460
William Doyle Galleries 6/11/1997

DRESS, 1949

Windowpane check wool sewn in four quadrants in blue, red, and taupe, front placket with slanted buttonholes, separate boned black chiffon waist wrap.
est. $300–$500 sold: $575
William Doyle Galleries 11/16/1999

DRESS, 1950

Olive silk pongee, chemise dress with cut-in-one sleeves and diagonal points meeting to form points down the front.
est. $200–$250 sold: $373
William Doyle Galleries 12/5/1996

DRESS, 1950

Black jersey sleeveless gathered from the shoulders, spaghetti ties at the neck, midriff, and tying around the waist.
est. $200–$300 sold: $431
William Doyle Galleries 6/11/1997

DRESS, 1950s

Black crinkle cotton with brass tab closure at neck and spaghetti ties.
est. $100–$150 sold: $575
William Doyle Galleries 12/6/1995

DRESS, 1950s

Red cotton with burgundy and gray pattern, panels that cross at bodice front tie in back.
est. $300–$500 sold: $287
William Doyle Galleries 11/17/1994

DRESS, 1950s

Cotton printed with satin and textured ribbon, Southwestern color palette.
est. $750–$1000 sold: $460
William Doyle Galleries 9/30/1993

ENSEMBLE, 1950s

Coat of fuchsia wool tweed lined to match the dress in rose satin printed with roses in burgundy and violet, cummerbund sash and pleated skirt.
est. $400–$600 sold: $316
William Doyle Galleries 4/24/1996

GLOVES, 1950s

White and red gingham.
est. not available sold: $98
The Paper Bag Princess 5/10/2001

JACKET, 1940

Red and black houndstooth wool, single-breasted, flat collar.
est. $100–$150 sold: $460
William Doyle Galleries 6/11/1997

SUIT, 1940s

Navy blue wool gabardine with tan top-stitching, unstructured kimono-style jacket with deep V neck, shirt sewn with wide hip band fastening with hooks.
est. $150–$200 sold: $575
William Doyle Galleries 11/12/1997

SWIMSUIT, 1950s

Yellow and white gingham, matching swim dress, bloomers, and smock jacket.
est. $100–$150 sold: $1092
William Doyle Galleries 11/17/1994

MCCONNELL, JACK

HAT, 1950s

White wool with oversized lily flower trimmed in white rhinestones.
est. not available sold: $245
The Paper Bag Princess 4/8/1996

HAT, 1950s

Black wool with oversized black lily flower trimmed in white rhinestones.
est. not available sold: $245
The Paper Bag Princess 8/10/1998

MCFADDEN, MARY

EVENING GOWN, 1970s

Floral lace bodice embroidered with pearls, white sequins, seed beads, gold braid, beads, pleated skirt with fishtail train.
est. $600–$800 sold: $575
Skinner 12/16/1999

MCQUEEN, ALEXANDER FOR GIVENCHY

EVENING GOWN, 1997
Full-length dress of green silk crepe maro-cain and matching bolero of silk satin, both hand-embroidered with silk thread and crystal beads. Kate Winslet, 1997 Academy Awards.
est. not available sold: $57,500
Christie's Oscar Dress Auction 3/18/1999

MIGNON

COCKTAIL DRESS, 1960S
Fitted sheath, straight skirt, with iridescent sequins and embroidered with flower triplets and leaves, labeled:
Mignon/Paris/New York.
est. $400–$600 sold: $2587.50
William Doyle Galleries 11/2/2000

MILGRIM, SALLY

COCKTAIL DRESS, 1937
Sleeveless black satin dress with V neck and plunging V back, net overdress has gathered ruffles at neck, sleeves, and from hips to hem.
est. $150–$250 sold: $489
Skinner 12/16/1999

MILLER, I.

EVENING SHOES, 1920S
Crimson velvet and gold calf.
est. $80–$120 sold: $103
William Doyle Galleries 12/6/1995

SHOES, 1920S
High-heeled, T-strap, brown, teal, and chestnut suede.
est. $60–$90 sold: $201
William Doyle Galleries 12/6/1995

MILLER, NOLAN

COCKTAIL DRESS, 1986
Pleated silk taffeta ball skirt with train, sheer illusion bodysuit with foliate ap-pliqué and cap sleeves. Laura Dern, 1986 Academy Awards.
est. not available sold :$6900
Christie's Oscar Dress Auction 3/18/1999

EVENING GOWN, 1986
Pink silk taffeta with corset formed bodice, three-quarter-length sleeves, skirt has pleat between ruffles, pink silk stemmed roses at waistline. Elizabeth Taylor, 1986 Academy Awards.
est. not available sold: $25,300
Christie's Oscar Dress Auction 3/18/1999

MILNER, DEBORAH

EVENING GOWN, 1997
Lavender silk taffeta with strapless bodice, full gathered skirt. Helena Bonham-Carter, 1997 Academy Awards.
est. not available sold: $4600
Christie's Oscar Dress Auction 3/18/1999

MISSONI

COCKTAIL DRESS, 1966
Silver, pale blue, and gold metallic and rayon knit below-the-knee-length dress with V neck, long sleeves, and waist gath-ered with matching rope belt.
est. $400–$600 sold: $230
Skinner 9/14/2000

COCKTAIL DRESS, 1966
Multicolored rayon and metallic knit below-the-knee-length dress with low V neck, long bishop sleeves.
est. $400–$600 sold: $287.50
Skinner 9/14/2000

COCKTAIL ENSEMBLE, 1970
V-neck cardigan sweater, pleated skirt, and camisole in metallic knit dyed in purple, rose, and gray and shot with gold.
est. $150–$200 sold: $316
William Doyle Galleries 5/6/1998

Rhinestone and silver bugle bead
dress, redesigned by Daniela Kurrel for
The Paper Bag Princess Couture Collection,
original circa 1960s. ACTRESS ONNA HART

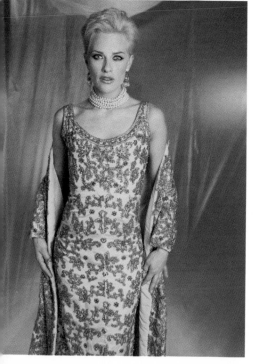

Couture cream satin evening gown with
relief beading and matching evening coat by
Roxanne for Samuel Winston, circa 1960s.
MODEL KELLY COLE

A champagne silk chiffon couture
evening gown by Irene, circa 1940s.
Platinum and diamond bracelet
courtesy of Harry Winston.
ACTRESS MARIA BELLO

A five-piece suit by Yves Saint Laurent,
circa 1960s. Hat by Yves Saint Laurent,
circa 1980s. Handbag by Josep, circa 1960s.
MODEL KELLY COLE

Couture silk chiffon evening dress with rhinestone
halter bodice. Redesigned by Daniela Kurrel for
The Paper Bag Princess Couture Collection,
original circa 1970s. MODEL KELLY COLE

Black-and-nude zebra print, silk chiffon jumpsuit
with sash and asymmetrical neckline by Halston,
circa 1970s. Gray wool felt hat with snake band
by Yves Saint Laurent, circa 1980s. Charles Jordan
satin cigarette heels, circa 1980s. ACTRESS MARIA BELLO

Black lace and tulle couture gown with rhinestone bodice, redesigned by Daniela Kurrel for The Paper Bag Princess Couture Collection, original circa late 1950s. Platinum and diamond necklace and earrings courtesy of Harry Winston.
ACTRESS MARIA BELLO

"Le Smoking" women's tuxedo by Yves Saint Laurent, circa 1970s. Hat by Yves Saint Laurent, circa 1980s. Rhinestone studded gloves from West Germany, circa 1950s. Rhinestone tie, Paste, circa 1970s. MODEL KELLY COLE

Sapphire matte jersey, Marilyn-inspired
halter-neck dress by Halston, circa late 1970s.
ACTRESS MARIA BELLO

Black jersey gown by Rudi Gernreich, circa
1973. Shoes by Charles Jordan, circa 1983.
Travel cases by Louis Vuitton.
ACTRESS ONNA HART

Black jersey with rhinestone jeweled arrow
details and collar by Karl Lagerfeld for Chlóe,
circa 1980s. MODEL KELLY COLE

Black silk gown by
Balenciaga, circa 1950s.
Actress Onna Hart

DRESS, 1970s
Multicolored space-dyed knit in orange,
yellow, and brown.
est. not available sold: $495
The Paper Bag Princess 1/1/1998

DRESS, 1980s
Silk jersey red, purple, and blue dots on
white background, draped bodice through
the waistline.
est. not available sold: $395
The Paper Bag Princess 3/14/1999

ENSEMBLE, 1970s
Striped knit dress in gray and burgundy, tan
cotton raincoat with gray, gray and green
stripes, belted, trimmed at collar and cuffs
with knit.
est. $150–$200 sold: $201
William Doyle Galleries 5/6/1998

ENSEMBLE, 1970s
Silk knit brown and blue check, long sleeve
top and A-line knee-length skirt.
est. not available sold: $425
The Paper Bag Princess 2/10/1997

ENSEMBLE
Pink and gold Lurex knit top and full knee-
length skirt.
est. not available sold: $445
The Paper Bag Princess 1/1/1997

ENSEMBLE, 1970s
Silk knit, space-dyed in rust, beige, gray,
and black, long-sleeved polo top in striped
pattern, crystal-pleated wide-legged pants
in chevron print.
est. $100–$150 sold: $316
William Doyle Galleries 12/5/1996

ENSEMBLE, 1970s
Glitter knit sleeveless blouson vest and top
with crystal-pleated long skirt with stripes
and squiggles multicolored against gold
background.
est. $75–$100 sold: $373
William Doyle Galleries 4/24/1996

ENSEMBLE, 1970s
Gold Lurex top and pants.
est. not available sold: $595
The Paper Bag Princess 4/1/1997

ENSEMBLE, 1970s
Rayon knit brown and blue checked blouse
and wide-leg, flared pant.
est. not available sold: $425
The Paper Bag Princess

EVENING GOWN, 1970s
Orange, red, and yellow space-dyed dress
with cowl neck, long sleeves, with matching oversized fringed wrap.
est. not available sold: $2000
The Paper Bag Princess 4/3/2000

SCARF
Green, gold, and brown knit with five-inch
fringe hem.
est. not available sold: $165
The Paper Bag Princess

SUIT, 1990s
Solid lavender tank with lavender and purple striped slim-cut flared pant, beaded
with clear sequins.
est. not available sold: $795
The Paper Bag Princess 4/1/1997

MIYAKE, ISSEY

DRESS, 1970
Loose dress of black and blue lattice pattern
weave composed of two vertical halves
crossing over diagonally from left shoulder
to hip (sack-like).
est. $300–$500 sold: $316.25
William Doyle Galleries 5/2/2000

DRESS, 1985
Cotton/wool blend asymmetric with modified caftan silhouette, diagonal buttons
across front, geometric cut-away sleeves,
two slash pockets.
est. $275–$375 sold: $690
Skinner 9/14/2000

M

MIZRAHI, ISAAC

EVENING GOWN, 1994
Pink georgette full-length dress with flowing skirt and held with silk ribbon halter, embroidered with sequins. Vendela, 1994 Academy Awards.
est. not available sold: $6900
Christie's Oscar Dress Auction 3/18/1999

MOLYNEUX

COAT, 1925
Black wool, cardigan-style with white fox collar and cuffs.
est. $200–$400 sold: $373
William Doyle Galleries 11/12/1997

COCKTAIL DRESS, 1950S
Navy satin with ballet-length skirt, strapless bodice embroidered with floral motif worked in pearlescent sequins and gold beads, streamers at back.
est. $150–$200 sold: $230
William Doyle Galleries 11/10/1998

ENSEMBLE, 1930S
Cream re-embroidered net lace, long-sleeved, skirt ends in pointed train, with silk tulle veil.
est. $600–$800 sold: $345
William Doyle Galleries 11/16/1999

EVENING GOWN, 1950S
Strapless, with fitted bodice and full skirt, ornamented with gold passementerie on gold satin, separate waist wrap and separate silk petticoat.
est. $600–$800 sold: $345
William Doyle Galleries 5/2/2000

EVENING GOWN, 1960S
Orange silk with metallic gold trapunto quilting in abstract pattern, floor-length dress with camisole bodice, empire waist, and back slit.
est. $600–$800 sold: $374
Skinner 12/16/1999

SUIT, 1930S
Blue mohair tweed with long cardigan jacket, self sash, long A-line skirt, sewn at the yoke of the shoulders and skirt with pin tucks.
est. $125–$175 sold: $316
William Doyle Galleries 12/5/1996

MORABITO

HANDBAG, 1950S
Brown ostrich gathered into sides of the hinged frame, interior of suede with two sections.
est. $150–$200 sold: $373
William Doyle Galleries 11/10/1998

HANDBAG, 1960S
Dark taupe alligator with pink quartz Buddha catch, seated on gilt metal pedestal.
est. $250–$400 sold: $258
William Doyle Galleries 12/6/1995

HANDBAG, 1970S
Beige alligator with adjustable strap and self-covered drawstring threaded through gilt metal ringed holes.
est. $800–$1000 sold: $460
William Doyle Galleries 6/11/1997

MORI, HANAE

COCKTAIL DRESS, 1970S
Navy blue silk chiffon floor-length dress with allover multicolored butterfly print, bloused bodice with round neckline and full skirt.
est. $200–$300 sold: $115
Skinner 9/14/2000

COCKTAIL ENSEMBLE, 1970S
Three-piece: pantsuit, overtunic, and wrap. Pantsuit with sleeveless bodice and chiffon palazzo pants, sheer orange overtunic, self-rope belt.
est. $200–$400 sold: $230
Skinner 12/16/1999

MOSCHETTI-GIAUBERT

COCKTAIL DRESS, 1950S
Strapless with double-breasted tuxedo-style bodice, silk faille skirt gathered at the hips.
est. $400–$600 sold: $460
Sotheby's 10/29/1997

MR. BLACKWELL

COCKTAIL DRESS, 1950S
Long slip dress embroidered in sequins, silver at bodice, black at skirt.
est. $100–$150 sold: $172
William Doyle Galleries 4/27/1994

COCKTAIL DRESS, 1950S
Black wool embroidered down front with flowers and leaves with black metal studs.
est. $80–$100 sold: $201
William Doyle Galleries 11/17/1994

EVENING GOWN, 1950S
Off-white silk chine with multicolored poppies.
est. $300–$500 sold: $230
William Doyle Galleries 4/27/1994

MR. JOHN

ENSEMBLE, 1970
Broadtail with long-sleeve tunic top slit in low front V, band collar, bell-bottom pants.
est. $700–$900 sold: $402
William Doyle Galleries 11/16/1999

HAT, 1950S
Green satin sewn with two black birds holding a green bow in their beaks.
est. $50–$75 sold: $201
William Doyle Galleries 12/5/1996

HAT, 1950S
Black satin with top knot and black organdy veil.
est. $50–$75 sold: $316
William Doyle Galleries 4/27/1994

HAT, 1970S
Zebra print, faux fur fedora.
est. not available sold: $495
The Paper Bag Princess 2/1/1999

MUGLER, THIERRY

DRESS, 1980S
Pleated silver lamé with wide stand-away shoulders, sleeves horizontally pleated, dress pleats converging in a sunburst below plunging V neck.
est. $800–$1200 sold: $3450
William Doyle Galleries 11/16/1999

MUIR, JEAN

DRESS, 1970S
Black jersey, long sleeves, full-length with crossover front bodice.
est. not available sold: $595
The Paper Bag Princess 8/31/2000

ENSEMBLE, 1970S
Green suede knee-length coat with kimono sleeves and matching angora dress with dolman sleeves.
est. $100–$150 sold: $460
William Doyle Galleries 11/17/1994

ENSEMBLE
Tangerine cashmere tie-front wrap sweater and silk jersey pants.
est. not available sold: $695
The Paper Bag Princess 8/21/2001

MUNN, CARRIE

COCKTAIL DRESS, 1950S
Black velvet with black tulle yoke, skirt has satin band with self bows.
est. $60–$90 sold: $201
William Doyle Galleries 11/17/1994

MYLES ORIGINALS

HANDBAG, 1950S
Olive green, red, and metallic gold Lucite handbag with top flap, gold-toned hardware and top handle, mirrored inner top and black interior.
est. $120–$250 sold: $431.25
Skinner 12/16/1999

M

NIK-NIK

SHIRT, 1970S
Fitted shiny black polyester, blond woman motif on the back of the shirt, with her hair flowing over onto the front of the shirt.
est. not available sold: $225
The Paper Bag Princess

SHIRT, 1970S
Polyester, rock and roll graffiti design, pinball player motif on back of shirt.
est. not available sold: $145
The Paper Bag Princess 9/1/1997

NORELL, NORMAN

BLOUSE, 1970
Black silk crepe sewn with flat silver sequins, long sleeves, jewel neck, cuffs and neckline encrusted with rows of rhinestones.
est. $400–$500 sold: $431
William Doyle Galleries 5/12/1999

CAPE, 1960S
Orange, red, and charcoal houndstooth wool, double-breasted short cape, skirt, charcoal jersey blouse.
est. $200–$300 sold: $258
William Doyle Galleries 4/27/1994

CAPE, 1960S
Circular cut, double-sided, raspberry reversed to turquoise with rectangular arm slits.
est. $300–$400 sold: $345
William Doyle Galleries 5/12/1999

COAT, 1960
Knee-length sewn with rows of coral red ostrich feathers.
est. $2000–$3000 sold: $4025
William Doyle Galleries 5/12/1999

COAT, 1960S
Oatmeal wool trimmed with black braid.
est. $200–$300 sold: $345
William Doyle Galleries 4/27/1994

COAT, 1960S
Black silk/wool ribbed weave, A-line, cuffed sleeves, patch pockets.
est. $400–$600 sold: $690
William Doyle Galleries 5/12/1999

COAT, 1960S
Beige wool with sable collar.
est. $600–$800 sold: $287
William Doyle Galleries 9/30/1993

COAT, 1960S
Black wool, double-breasted with rhinestone buttons.
est. $250–$400 sold: $488
William Doyle Galleries 4/24/1996

COAT, 1960S
Black wool, double-breasted, chrome plastic buttons.
est. $75–$125 sold: $345
William Doyle Galleries 11/17/1994

COAT, 1960S
Red wool, double-breasted ankle-length with four front patch pockets and gold buttons.
est. $300–$500 sold: $460
Skinner 12/16/1999

COAT, 1960S
White wool woven with red grid plaid, double-breasted with Nehru collar, red buttons.
est. $150–$200 sold: $402
William Doyle Galleries 4/24/1996

COAT, 1960S
Brown mohair, single-breasted, slightly barrel-shaped.
est. $200–$300 sold: $373
William Doyle Galleries 4/24/1996

COAT, 1960S
Black wool, double-breasted with rhinestone buttons.
est. $200–$300 sold: $287
William Doyle Galleries 11/17/1994

COAT, 1960S
Black wool, double-breasted, Peter Pan collar, black buttons.
est. $75–$125 sold: $287
William Doyle Galleries 12/6/1995

COAT, 1960s

Orange bubble-shaped, double-breasted with diagonal sleeve seams and white buttons.
est. $200–$300 sold: $258
William Doyle Galleries 5/6/1998

COAT, 1960s

Brown tweed, double-breasted with upper and lower flopped patch pockets.
est. $150–$200 sold: $345
William Doyle Galleries 11/10/1998

COAT, 1960s

Red double-breasted ankle-length coat with four front patch pockets and large gold-toned buttons, red lining.
est. $300–$500 sold: $460
Skinner 12/16/1999

COAT, 1967

Navy wool knit, floor-length with cuffed sleeves, jewel neckline, coat fastens at front with ten rhinestone-set round buttons.
est. $600–$800 sold: $402
William Doyle Galleries 11/10/1998

COAT DRESS, 1960s

Beige wool, wrap front, half-belt fastens with black buttons.
est. $125–$175 sold: $345
William Doyle Galleries 4/24/1996

COAT DRESS, 1970

Floor-length, flat collar, notched lapels, patch pockets, half-belt at back, front elaborate buttons, labeled: Norman Norell/Dayton's Oval Room.
est. $500–$700 sold: $575
William Doyle Galleries 11/2/2000

COCKTAIL DRESS, 1960

Slip dress of black silk sewn with randomly placed bugle beads.
est. $800–$1200 sold: $3220
William Doyle Galleries 5/12/1999

COCKTAIL DRESS, 1960s

Navy blue matte silk jersey embroidered with flat blue sequins, with turtleneck and long sleeves.
est. $250–$400 sold: $1265
William Doyle Galleries 12/5/1996

COCKTAIL DRESS, 1960s

Black wool, long sleeves and hem edged with wide crystal-sequined bands.
est. $300–$500 sold: $345
William Doyle Galleries 6/11/1997

COCKTAIL DRESS, 1960s

Gold matte silk jersey embroidered with flat gold sequins and across the shoulders with bands of faux rubies, sapphires, emeralds, and rhinestones.
est. $400–$600 sold: $258
William Doyle Galleries 12/5/1996

COCKTAIL DRESS, 1960s

Black wool, sleeveless, straight silhouette gathered at waist with silk satin bow at center back.
est. $300–$500 sold: $287
Skinner 12/16/1999

COCKTAIL DRESS, 1960s

Black wool knit kimono-inspired design, sash around waist fastening with three bows, bell-shaped skirt.
est. $500–$700 sold: $1725
Sotheby's 4/8/1998

COCKTAIL DRESS, 1960s

Short, sleeveless dress of olive silk damask, black organza underskirt.
est. $200–$300 sold: $373
William Doyle Galleries 4/24/1996

COCKTAIL DRESS, 1960s

Orange red wool jersey, sleeveless with high collar and self belt, buttons across one shoulder and down side with rhinestone buttons.
est. $200–$300 sold: $316
William Doyle Galleries 12/6/1995

COCKTAIL DRESS, 1960s

Yellow silk jersey sewn with gold sequins, long sleeves, round neckline.
est. $250–$400 sold: $747
William Doyle Galleries 12/6/1995

N

Cocktail Dress, 1960s

Black wool crepe empire-waisted overdress with low square neck and short sleeves, buttons down front with pink silk crepe underskirt.
est. $300–$500 sold: $747
William Doyle Galleries 11/10/1998

Cocktail Dress, 1960s

Strapless asymmetrical bodice and pleated skirt of white chiffon, skirt of red, white, and blue silk bands, flowing white scarf cape.
est. $200–$300 sold: $690
William Doyle Galleries 6/11/1997

Cocktail Dress, 1960s

Black wool crepe, one-shouldered with single short sleeve, self belt.
est. $100–$150 sold: $488
William Doyle Galleries 12/5/1996

Cocktail Dress, 1960s

Black crepe, sleeveless, high waist defined by satin sash tying in bow at front, bottom of skirt has black satin flounce.
est. $300–$500 sold: $230
William Doyle Galleries 11/16/1999

Cocktail Dress, 1960s

Black wool crepe, sleeveless, self belt, edged at hem with band of silk embroidered with beads.
est. $200–$300 sold: $345
William Doyle Galleries 12/6/1995

Cocktail Dress, 1960s

White silk crepe sewn with rhinestones, bracelet-length sleeves.
est. $250–$400 sold: $1092
William Doyle Galleries 4/24/1996

Cocktail Dress, 1960s

White A-line with band collar, wide black chiffon sleeves sewn with sequins and rows of rhinestones.
est. $150–$200 sold: $690
William Doyle Galleries 5/6/1998

Cocktail Dress, 1961

Sleeveless sheath with flowers in fuchsia, blue and silver sequins sewn in concentrated band at hem, beaded fringe at bottom.
est. $300–$500 sold: $488
William Doyle Galleries 11/12/1997

Cocktail Dress, 1965

Black wool crepe, sleeveless chemise, self belt with rhinestone buckle.
est. $75–$100 sold: $460
William Doyle Galleries 4/12/1995

Cocktail Dress, 1968

Black knit sleeveless A-line with band collar, skirt buttoned to the bodice at slightly raised waist with round rhinestone-set buttons.
est. $400–$600 sold: $632
William Doyle Galleries 11/10/1998

Cocktail Dress, 1968

Black wool, sleeveless, curved A-line shape, fastens down side front with rhinestone buttons.
est. $100–$150 sold: $230
William Doyle Galleries 12/6/1995

Cocktail Dress, 1968

Sleeveless, black, A-line with scoop neck, patent leather belt with rhinestone buckle.
est. $100–$150 sold: $345
William Doyle Galleries 11/12/1997

Cocktail Dress, 1970

Black matte jersey embroidered with paisley pattern in copper and white sequins and rhinestones, turtleneck and long sleeves, black satin ribbon sash.
est. $400–$600 sold: $345
William Doyle Galleries 12/5/1996

Cocktail Ensemble, 1960s

Wool crepe dress with fitted, sleeveless bodice and slightly flared knee-length skirt, matching hip-length jacket with Peter Pan collar.
est. $200–$400 sold: $517
Skinner 9/14/2000

COCKTAIL ENSEMBLE, 1965
Navy wool sleeveless double-breasted
overblouse trimmed with six rhinestone
buttons, dress with silk slip bodice and
knife-pleated skirt.
est. $700–$900 sold: $460
William Doyle Galleries 11/10/1998

DRESS, 1960s
Sleeveless sailor top of navy wool crepe
with tie of black ribbed silk, underdress of
black wool crepe.
est. $150–$250 sold: $287
William Doyle Galleries 4/24/1996

DRESS, 1960s
Burgundy linen, sleeveless with self belt.
est. $100–$125 sold: $316
William Doyle Galleries 4/24/1996

DRESS, 1960s
Blue linen chemise dress with Peter Pan
collar, short sleeves, fastening down front
with ivory plastic buttons.
est. $100–$150 sold: $345
William Doyle Galleries 4/12/1995

DRESS, 1960s
Black wool, straight shift, knee-length,
with scoop back and front slash pockets.
est. not available sold: $595
The Paper Bag Princess 2/1/1999

DRESS, 1960s
Black wool vest-style top. Back buttons,
with matching A-line knee-length skirt.
est. not available sold: $495
The Paper Bag Princess 9/9/2000

DRESS, 1960s
Black sleeveless chiffon with beaded fringe
and satin ribbon belt, underslip with wool
crepe skirt.
est. $300–$500 sold: $460
William Doyle Galleries 11/12/1997

DRESS, 1960s
Black wool crepe sleeveless dress with empire waist, front slash pockets and knee-
length, slightly A-line skirt.
est. $200–$300 sold: $258.75
Skinner 9/14/2000

DRESS, 1960s
Black wool with round neck, black calf
belt, slightly gathered skirt with two
pockets.
est. $100–$150 sold: $258
William Doyle Galleries 4/12/1995

DRESS, 1960s
Navy blue cotton knit three-quarter-length
sleeveless jumper, loose-fitting sheath,
round neckline, oversized patch pockets
below hips.
est. $200–$300 sold: $460
Skinner 12/16/1999

DRESS, 1960s
Hot pink wool crepe, long A-line dress,
sleeveless bodice, band collar, matching
belt.
est. $300–$500 sold: $287.50
Skinner 12/16/1999

DRESS, 1960s
Blue linen, sleeveless and double-breasted
with self belt.
est. $100–$150 sold: $402
William Doyle Galleries 4/24/1996

DRESS, 1960s
Pink wool crepe, A-line with sleeveless
bodice, band collar, and waist cinched with
matching belt.
est. $300–$500 sold: $287
Skinner 12/16/1999

DRESS, 1960s
Black wool, wide scooped neck, high waist.
est. $75–$100 sold: $316
William Doyle Galleries 4/27/1994

DRESS, 1960s
Red silk printed with long-stemmed pink
and purple flowers, sleeveless with slight
extensions at shoulder, skirt gently gathered at waist.
est. $200–$300 sold: $632
William Doyle Galleries 5/6/1998

DRESS, 1960s
Red silk crepe with cowl neckline continuing to form sleeves, dropped-waist skirt.
est. $75–$125 sold: $316
William Doyle Galleries 12/6/1995

N

Dress, 1960s
Navy wool knit with white linen collar, tied with red silk bow, buttoning down the front with mother-of-pearl buttons.
est. $150–$250 sold: $460
William Doyle Galleries 6/11/1997

Dress, 1960s
Black wool bouclé, sleeveless, wide scoop neckline.
est. $75–$125 sold: $373
William Doyle Galleries 12/6/1995

Dress, 1960s
Black wool with black faille necktie, sleeve-less top and narrow skirt.
est. $100–$150 sold: $402
William Doyle Galleries 12/6/1995

Dress, 1960s
Black wool, double-breasted, sleeveless with slightly raised waist and self belt.
est. $100–$150 sold: $402
William Doyle Galleries 12/6/1995

Dress, 1965
Strapless, with fully boned bodice, slightly gathered floor-length skirt with petticoats, and separate bolero jacket.
est. $400–$600 sold: $575
William Doyle Galleries 5/2/2000

Dress, 1967
Black knit sleeveless short shell top and dress with silk slip bodice, wide waistband, gathered skirt with two patch pockets.
est. $250–$350 sold: $431
William Doyle Galleries 11/10/1998

Dress, 1971
White knit shift with short sleeves, band collar, and patch pockets, trimmed with red and blue anchor at bodice front.
est. $200–$300 sold: $575
William Doyle Galleries 5/12/1999

Ensemble, 1960
Charcoal pongee blouse, gray tweed skirt.
est. $100–$150 sold: $431
William Doyle Galleries 11/17/1994

Ensemble, 1960s
Narrow coat and skirt of violet, beige, and cream wool tweed, coat lined in violet shantung to match the blouse.
est. $150–$250 sold: $316
William Doyle Galleries 4/24/1996

Ensemble, 1960s
Tangerine silk, midriff-length cropped sleeveless top, self belt and side-buttoning skirt.
est. $150–$200 sold: $316
William Doyle Galleries 6/11/1997

Ensemble, 1960s
Yellow wool, bouclé-breasted coat with white buttons, skirt slightly gathered.
est. $150–$200 sold: $402
William Doyle Galleries 6/11/1997

Ensemble, 1960s
Blue tweed, sleeveless dress with wide band above and below waistband, two-button jacket.
est. $125–$175 sold: $747
William Doyle Galleries 11/12/1997

Ensemble, 1960s
Navy wool crepe, boxy middy top, black silk bow, knife-pleated skirt.
est. $400–$600 sold: $345
William Doyle Galleries 11/10/1998

Evening Ensemble, 1960s
Blue chiffon with rhinestone-studded midriff top and full-legged pants sewn at waist with wide wrap sash.
est. $700–$900 sold: $1955
William Doyle Galleries 5/12/1999

Evening Ensemble, 1960s
Black wool jumpsuit and jacket trimmed with rhinestones.
est. $500–$750 sold: $345
William Doyle Galleries 9/30/1993

Evening Ensemble, 1960s
Black velvet floor-length gown with camisole bodice, satin belt, jacket trimmed at collar and cuffs with black fox.
est. $400–$600 sold: $1380
William Doyle Galleries 11/12/1997

EVENING ENSEMBLE, 1960s
Green organza blouse and bugle bead
pants, blouse has pussycat bow and full-
cuffed sleeves.
est. $250–$400 sold: $402
William Doyle Galleries 6/11/1997

EVENING ENSEMBLE, 1960s
Pink organdy blouse with self pussycat ties,
pants of pink silk embroidered with silver
beads.
est. $250–$400 sold: $575
William Doyle Galleries 12/5/1996

EVENING ENSEMBLE, 1960s
White organza blouse with self pussycat
ties, pants of tangerine silk embroidered
with orange beads.
est. $250–$400 sold: $345
William Doyle Galleries 12/5/1996

EVENING ENSEMBLE, 1970
Silk jersey blouse with long sleeves and
jewel neckline, sewn with sequins, neck
and cuffs rimmed with bands of round
rhinestones, black silk skirt.
est. $800–$1200 sold: $460
William Doyle Galleries 5/12/1999

EVENING GOWN, 1950s
Grecian-style halter top dress gathered
across waist and with full skirt falling from
knife pleats at waist, hemmed ivory silk
lining.
est. $400–$600 sold: $517.50
Skinner 9/14/2000

EVENING GOWN, 1960
Pink silk jersey sewn with flat sequins,
body-hugging sheath with low square
camisole neckline.
est. $2000–$3000 sold: $5175
William Doyle Galleries 11/16/1999

EVENING GOWN, 1960s
Cream silk jersey sheath embroidered with
gold sequins in various patterns, jewel
neckline.
est. $300–$500 sold: $460
William Doyle Galleries 6/11/1997

EVENING GOWN, 1960s
Orange and gold matelasse, ankle-length,
with empire waist tied with self belt, round
neck, short sleeves, bottom skirt with gold
bead fringe.
est. $800–$1200 sold: $690
William Doyle Galleries 5/2/2000

EVENING GOWN, 1960s
Black organza with sleeveless bodice, sprinkled with gold sequins sewn in rows to de-
lineate waistline and lower third of skirt.
est. $400–$600 sold: $977
William Doyle Galleries 5/6/1998

EVENING GOWN, 1960s
Silk jersey with green iridescent sequins,
sleeveless, round low back, self band defining waist.
est. $1000–$1200 sold: $2070
William Doyle Galleries 5/6/1998

EVENING GOWN, 1960s
Silk jersey sheath with long-cuffed sleeves
and high band collar, sewn with green sequins, mohair maxicoat.
est. $2000–$3000 sold: $7475
William Doyle Galleries 11/10/1998

EVENING GOWN, 1960s
Black sequined, sleeveless with boat neckline, low V-back, slightly flared skirt, satin
ribbon tying at waist.
est. $800–$1000 sold: $1610
William Doyle Galleries 11/10/1998

EVENING GOWN, 1960s
Sleeveless silk jersey sheath with jewel
neckline and V-back, embroidered with
blue sequins.
est. $300–$500 sold: $920
William Doyle Galleries 6/11/1997

EVENING GOWN, 1970
Sleeveless sheath of blush silk underlayer
with multicolored stones veiled by a black
tulle overdress studded with stones, hem
with beaded fringe.
est. $1000–$1500 sold: $1955
William Doyle Galleries 5/6/1998

N

Evening Gown, 1972
Green silk jersey sewn with iridescent green sequins, bodice cut away from jewel neckline, chiffon sash at waist, cardigan jacket.
est. $1000–$1500 sold: $2990
William Doyle Galleries 5/12/1999

Evening Gown, 1972
Green silk jersey sewn with purple/green iridescent sequins, dress cut away from high band collar, cardigan jacket collarless.
est. $800–$1200 sold: $3737
William Doyle Galleries 11/10/1998

Evening Pants, 1960s
Ivory silk flared pants embroidered with silver bugle beads arranged horizontally.
est. $500–$700 sold: $1265
William Doyle Galleries 5/12/1999

Hat, 1960s
Cream silk satin top-stitched in pale beige.
est. $100–$150 sold: $258
William Doyle Galleries 4/12/1995

Jacket, 1960s
Black knit, double-breasted with low self belt buttoning in front, large patch pockets slightly above hemline.
est. $300–$500 sold: $230
William Doyle Galleries 11/10/1998

Suit, 1960s
Black wool twill, one-button riding-style jacket and A-line skirt.
est. $150–$200 sold: $747
William Doyle Galleries 5/6/1998

Suit, 1960s
Black and white glen plaid wool, single-button jacket and A-line skirt.
est. $300–$500 sold: $287
William Doyle Galleries 5/12/1999

Suit, 1960s
Gray wool two-piece A-line skirt and jacket.
est. not available sold: $895
The Paper Bag Princess 3/1/1997

Suit, 1960s
Green tweed, three buttons, curved seam, skirt gathered at waistband with side slit pockets.
est. $100–$150 sold: $460
William Doyle Galleries 11/12/1997

NORTH, SYDNEY

Dress, 1960s
Green/gold Lurex, draped fitted bodice, scoop neckline and thigh-high side slit.
est. not available sold: $795
The Paper Bag Princess 12/15/2000

OFFENTHAL, LUCIENNE

Handbag, 1960s
Black crocodile, flat with top handle, rounded fold-over flap, two gilt metal rope twist clasp ornaments.
est. $400–$600 sold: $488
William Doyle Galleries 11/10/1998

Handbag, 1960s
Black crocodile with rigid hinged frame, gold-toned bar at top, single handle.
est. $300–$400 sold: $230
William Doyle Galleries 11/10/1998

OLDFIELD, BRUCE

Evening Suit, 1992
Black gabardine single-breasted jacket separating to long fringe at hip, matching black trousers. Vanessa Redgrave, 1992 Academy Awards.
est. not available sold: $4370
Christie's Oscar Dress Auction 3/18/1999

ORRIER, PAUL LOUIS

Cocktail Dress, 1980s
Ankle-length dress with fitted sheer black chiffon bodice, high neck and cuffs with beading, dropped waistline.
est. $600–$800 sold: $747.50
Skinner 9/14/2000

PAOLI, GINA

DRESS, 1960S
Black knit, sleeveless sheath with knotted satin cord fringed hem.
est. $100–$150 sold: $258
William Doyle Galleries 11/17/1994

PAQUIN, MME.

COAT, 1919
Black silk satin, hem and asymmetrical collar embroidered in French knot stitch with colored wools, tassel-trimmed triangular hanging panel at the back.
est. 500–700 pounds sold: 977 pounds
Sotheby's London 11/25/1998

COAT, 1920S
Cranberry velvet with shawl collar, lined with red wool inset with velvet points.
est. $100–$150 sold: $287
William Doyle Galleries 12/6/1995

COAT, 1926–1927
Black velvet trimmed with fur at the collar, sleeves, and hem.
est. 400–600 pounds sold: 747 pounds
Sotheby's London 11/25/1998

COAT, 1927
Black velvet with white fox shawl collar, puffed sleeves, pink lining with roses.
est. $200–$300 sold: $632
William Doyle Galleries 11/12/1997

COAT, 1933
Green velvet, cardigan-style with sable collar extending to waist level, Renaissance-style sleeves trimmed with double bands of fur.
est. $200–$400 sold: $1265
William Doyle Galleries 11/12/1997

DRESS, 1950
Beige silk organdy with narrow tucks, vertical for the sleeves and bodice, horizontal for the skirt, sleeves edged with Chantilly lace.
est. $300–$500 sold: $488
William Doyle Galleries 4/12/1995

EVENING GOWN, 1905
Two-piece black chiffon and velvet decorated with blue velvet grape clusters, cape collar and white lace stand collar.
est. $700–$900 sold: $3220
William Doyle Galleries 5/12/1999

EVENING GOWN, 1930S
Lilac/gray chiffon inset with lace dahlia-type flowers, long gown with short puffed sleeves, high neck with chiffon ties, skirt with tulle hem.
est. $200–$300 sold: $517
William Doyle Galleries 6/11/1997

EVENING GOWN, 1930S
Black and white chiffon flowers woven with satin accents, wide straps fastening at low back, self belt and short bolero jacket.
est. $200–$300 sold: $632
William Doyle Galleries 6/11/1997

EVENING GOWN, 1955
Backless white satin bodice, bead and paste embroidered, black skirt split to one side and trimmed with pleated bow.
est. 400–600 pounds sold: 402 pounds
Sotheby's London 11/25/1998

P

PARNIS, MOLLIE

COCKTAIL DRESS, 1950S
One-shoulder bodice of gray chiffon, silk skirt printed with gray leaves and orange blossoms, overlaid at left with orange and gray chiffon panel.
est. $250–$300 sold: $373
William Doyle Galleries 11/16/1999

DRESS, 1950S
Black and white gingham taffeta, black velvet piping at yoke.
est. $75–$100 sold: $345
William Doyle Galleries 11/17/1994

EVENING GOWN, 1950S
Satin floor-length evening dress with fitted, sleeveless bodice with jewel neckline that wraps around to back, A-line skirt, pink chiffon lining.
est. $400–$600 sold: $230
Skinner 9/14/2000

PATOU, JEAN

CAPE, 1920s
Black rayon faille with cape back and softly pleated rolled collar.
est. $200–$300 sold: $431
William Doyle Galleries 4/12/1995

COAT, 1930s
Black wool crepe, cardigan-style.
est. $200–$300 sold: $546
William Doyle Galleries 12/6/1995

COCKTAIL DRESS, 1925
Silvery tan silk velvet, inset front and back panels of gold lace, embroidered with flowers.
est. $2000–$3000 sold: $1150
William Doyle Galleries 4/27/1994

COCKTAIL DRESS, 1926
Brocade of floral pattern in blue, pink, and green, chemise dress with camisole bodice, skirt with front-draped scarf panel, waist and hem with beads.
est. $700–$900 sold: $1495
William Doyle Galleries 11/16/1999

COCKTAIL DRESS, 1930s
Black silk crepe with lace inset panels, embroidered with beads.
est. $3000–$5000 sold: $1725
William Doyle Galleries 9/30/1993

COCKTAIL DRESS, 1950s
Silk printed with pearls and other jewels in orange, yellow, and white, bodice has halter scarf straps, full-pleated skirt.
est. $300–$500 sold: $632
William Doyle Galleries 4/12/1995

EVENING ENSEMBLE, 1950s
Pink velvet sarong-draped dress, coat with shawl collar and brown mink cuffs.
est. $500–$750 sold: $287
William Doyle Galleries 9/30/1993

EVENING GOWN, 1930s
White silk satin bodice with chiffon long skirt.
est. $3000–$5000 sold: $2185
William Doyle Galleries 9/30/1993

EVENING GOWN, 1970s
Champagne chiffon with shoulder straps and off-the-shoulder cap sleeves, asymmetrical flounce from shoulder across bust, pleated skirt with train.
est. $2000–$3000 sold: $1725
Sotheby's 10/29/1997

HAT, 1950
Wired black velvet piping encrusted with pearls, beads, and paillettes in green, peach, purple, and black.
est. $200–$300 sold: $287
William Doyle Galleries 11/10/1998

SUIT, 1970s
Black sequined coat with band collar and flared wide-legged pants.
est. $300–$500 sold: $316
William Doyle Galleries 5/12/1999

PATRICK, HERMAN

COCKTAIL DRESS, 1930
Ivory organza appliquéd with large black velvet dots, long slip dress with petaled hem.
est. $200–$300 sold: $172
William Doyle Galleries 4/24/1996

COCKTAIL DRESS, 1930
Slip torso of black silk satin, tiered cut-away skirt of black tulle.
est. $600–$800 sold: $690
William Doyle Galleries 4/24/1996

PERETTE, SUZY

COCKTAIL DRESS, 1950s
Black velvet with center-front and back panels of black silk faille, sewn in poufs below hip, extending to back for bustle effect.
est. $300–$400 sold: $517
William Doyle Galleries 11/10/1998

COCKTAIL DRESS, 1950s
Black organza embroidered with roses and lily of the valley.
est. $60–$90 sold: $201
William Doyle Galleries 12/6/1995

P

DRESS, 1950S
Green cotton printed with French phrases,
fitted bodice dipping low in back, full
gathered skirt.
est. $100–$150 sold: $172
William Doyle Galleries 11/12/1997

PERETTI, ELSA FOR TIFFANY

EVENING BAG, 1980S
Sterling silver worked in a basket weave,
flat and rectangular with lift-off top.
est. $500–$700 sold: $1840
William Doyle Galleries 5/12/1999

PERTEGAZ

COAT, 1930S
Black heavy wool, silk-lined, six buttons,
double-breasted, shoulder to hemline pleat
in back, deep-cut folds over hip pockets.
est. $75 sold: $809.98
eBay Online Auctions 2/24/2001

COCKTAIL DRESS, 1951
Black paper taffeta and Chantilly lace cocktail dress, sleeveless taffeta bodice, full
skirt, lace shawl, boned bodice attached
at crinoline.
est. $700–$1000 sold: $460
Skinner 12/16/1999

PERUGIA FOR I. MILLER

EVENING SHOES, 1920S
Pink suede with silver floral appliqué.
est. $200–$300 sold: $402
William Doyle Galleries 12/6/1995

PERUGIA OF PARIS

EVENING SHOES, 1950S
Shantung printed with roses and leaves in
red and green against ecru, organdy bows
printed in same pattern.
est. $60–$90 sold: $57
William Doyle Galleries 4/12/1995

PICASSO, PALOMA

BOOTS, 1970S
Black suede with gold leather detail.
est. $400–$600 sold: $488
Sotheby's 12/9/1998

JACKET, 1963
The imagery from the painting printed in
original colors, on cotton, the jacket thigh-
length with ribbed neck, zipper front,
black sleeves, lining.
est. $200–$300 sold: $374
William Doyle Galleries 5/2/2000

POIRET, PAUL

DRESS, 1911
Empire-line ivory satin with powder blue
chiffon tunic-like overlay, silver rope tie
and tassels to the high waist.
est. 1000–1500 pounds sold: 1380 pounds
Sotheby's London 11/25/1998

DRESS, 1920S
Black satin with overblouse silk lace skirt.
est. $300–$500 sold: $1840
William Doyle Galleries 9/30/1993

DRESS, 1924
Black silk velvet painted silver and hand-
painted with flowers in black, red, and yellow, neckline and slit inset with ivory silk
crepe.
est. $3000–$5000 sold: $8050
William Doyle Galleries 4/24/1996

EVENING COAT, 1911
Purple damask patterned with floral pattern, collar and kimono sleeves of purple
crocheted lace.
est. $5000–$7000 sold: $19,550
William Doyle Galleries 11/16/1999

EVENING GOWN, 1910
Ivory satin with tunic overdress of blue
chiffon embroidered in wool with a row of
green, black, and white palm trees.
est. $3000–$4000 sold: $18,400
William Doyle Galleries 5/6/1998

P

EVENING GOWN, 1913

Yellow gauze damask patterned with phoenixes amidst foliage, green chiffon pleated front panel and sleeve ends, belt with sequins and embroidery.
est. $12,000–$15,000 sold: $36,800
William Doyle Galleries 11/16/1999

POLAND, G.

EVENING TOP, 1960S

Black and white mink diagonal-striped top.
est. $800–$1200 sold: $632
Sotheby's 9/30/1999

PORTER, THEA

COAT, 1970S

Shiny floss woven in a bargello pattern in peach, rust, blue, green, and white, jewel collar.
est. $100–$150 sold: $345
William Doyle Galleries 11/12/1997

ATTRIBUTED TO THEA PORTER

EVENING GOWN, 1968

Red, black, cream chiffon with Japanese cart and sumi brushstrokes motif print, embroidered with gold thread, sequins, edged with gold cord.
est. not available sold: $2250
The Way We Wore 1/1/2000

PRADA

EVENING GOWN, 1994

Full-length sleeveless dress with cinched midriff flaring into skirt of lavender chiffon overlaid with iridescent paillettes. Uma Thurman, 1994 Academy Awards.
est. not available sold: $9200
Christie's Oscar Dress Auction 3/18/1999

PRINCESS ZOLTOWSKA

COCKTAIL ENSEMBLE, 1970S

Hot pink raw silk printed with red and green foliate design, fitted sleeveless top with jewel neckline, matching pants with fitted waist.
est. $150–$200 sold: $345
Skinner 12/16/1999

PROFILS DU MONDE

CAFTAN, 1984

Ivory silk embroidered in a floral motif in reds, greens, and aquas, interwoven with gold lamé. Angela Lansbury, 1984 Academy Awards.
est. not available sold: $6900
Christie's Oscar Dress Auction 3/18/1999

PRUSAC, LOLA

COAT, 1960S

Three-quarter-length cardigan in black, silver, and gold brocade edged with silver and gold brocade.
est. $500–$750 sold: $575
William Doyle Galleries 4/12/1995

PUCCI, EMILIO

BATHING SUIT, 1960S

Cotton poplin bikini and empire-waist velvet-finish terry cloth cover-up with multicolored triangle pattern, underwire top with apron bottom.
est. $100–$150 sold: $201
William Doyle Galleries 11/17/1994

BATHING SUIT, 1970S

Orange, pink, ivory, and purple printed Lycra with brief-style bottoms and underwire top.
est. $50–$100 sold: $201
Skinner 12/16/1999

Beach Bag, 1970s
Peach, orange, yellow, pink, and white velveteen with tan leather handle, piping, and trim.
est. $150–$200 sold: $402
Skinner 12/16/1999

Bikini, 1960s
Abstract geometric design of turquoise, blue, mint, green, lilac, purple, black on white cotton twill, ruching on cups and bottoms, unworn in cellophane.
est. not available sold: $735
eBay Online Auctions 2/24/2001

Bikini, 1970s
Orange, pink, ivory, and purple printed Lycra bikini with brief-style bottoms and underwire top.
est. $50–$100 sold: $201
Skinner 12/16/1999

Bikinis, 1960s
Three bikinis with low-slung bottoms and underwire bra tops; first, pink and green; second, peach, green, and brown geometric print; third, stripes of purple and gray.
est. $200–$300 sold: $546
William Doyle Galleries 5/2/2000

Blazer, 1970
Flat collar and lapels, slightly fitted waist, textured gold buttons, printed with abstract foliate pattern. Labeled: Emilio Pucci/Florence-Italy.
est. $200–$300 sold: $345
William Doyle Galleries 11/2/2000

Blazer, 1970s
Printed cotton with striped chain pattern in navy, white, gray, aqua. Notched lapel, center-front button closure and two front slit pockets.
est. $150–$200 sold: $259
Skinner 12/16/1999

Blouse, 1950s
Silk twill, green on one half, blue on the other printed with snowflakes, fairy lights, and snowy village inside a giant snowflake.
est. $100–$125 sold: $316
William Doyle Galleries 6/11/1997

Blouse, 1950s
Silk twill printed in amethyst, red, and turquoise with Italian alpine and surreal scenes.
est. $75–$100 sold: $172
William Doyle Galleries 4/12/1995

Blouse, 1960
Silk twill printed with a trompe l'oeil scene of an Italian landscape viewed through the parted draperies of a tent in red, pink, green, and gold.
est. $100–$150 sold: $373
William Doyle Galleries 12/5/1996

Blouse, 1960s
Silk twill printed in orange, yellow, black, pink, tan, and white.
est. $75–$100 sold: $287
William Doyle Galleries 12/6/1995

Blouse, 1960s
Silk twill, front printed with daisy-shaped flower heads, back has inverted petal burst centered with a single flower.
est. $75–$100 sold: $230
William Doyle Galleries 6/11/1997

Blouse, 1960s
White silk twill printed with gold ornaments and jewels.
est. $100–$150 sold: $230
William Doyle Galleries 11/12/1997

Blouse, 1960s
Silk twill, pink and gray geometric printed, long sleeves.
est. not available sold: $395
The Paper Bag Princess 2/1/1997

Blouse, 1960s
Silk twill, pink, black, and white checked long-sleeved button-down.
est. not available sold: $495
The Paper Bag Princess 12/1/1997

Blouse, 1960s
Silk twill, long-sleeved, button-front, green and blue printed psychedelic motif.
est. not available sold: $325
The Paper Bag Princess 12/1/1999

P

BLOUSE, 1960s

Silk twill, gold and black with printed geometric design.
est. not available sold: $325
The Paper Bag Princess 1/1/2000

BLOUSE, 1960s

Silk twill man-tailored shirt printed with graduated rows of female figures wearing long robes and balancing jars on their heads, in pink, purple, and black.
est. $200–$300 sold: $345
William Doyle Galleries 5/2/2000

BLOUSE, 1960s

Silk twill man-tailored shirt with covered buttons printed with geometric circles, lozenges, flower heads, in shades of hot pink, celery, gray, and peach.
est. $200–$300 sold: $345
William Doyle Galleries 5/2/2000

BLOUSE, 1970s

Silk twill, magenta, pink, and brown tapestry motif.
est. not available sold: $395
The Paper Bag Princess 1/17/2001

BLOUSE, 1970s

Silk twill long-sleeved blouse, turquoise, gray, and lilac diamonds and ovals pattern.
est. not available sold: $450
The Paper Bag Princess 1/17/2001

BOLERO JACKET, 1970s

Cotton velvet printed with geometric pattern in gray, white, black, raspberry, lilac, and purple. Long sleeves, notched lapel, and fitted silhouette.
est. $150–$200 sold: $460
Skinner 12/16/1999

CASE, 1970s

Oversized bag with geometric pattern in purple, brown, white, green, and yellow, brown leather trim, frame studded, white vinyl lining, labeled Italy "EP."
est. $500–$700 sold: $1495
Skinner 9/14/2000

CHEMISE, 1960s

Silk jersey printed with vines and geometric shapes in brown, chartreuse, purple, and fuchsia.
est. $75–$100 sold: $201
William Doyle Galleries 4/24/1996

CLUTCH BAG, 1960s

Broad curved bands in gray, lilac, and brown, interior has three zippered compartments.
est. $125–$175 sold: $258
William Doyle Galleries 5/6/1998

COAT, 1960s

Olive velveteen printed with white Queen Anne's lace and magenta flowers, sleeveless A-line shift, cardigan coat.
est. $200–$300 sold: $517
William Doyle Galleries 5/12/1999

COAT, 1960s

Velvet printed in red, gray, navy and black, double-breasted with black velvet Chesterfield collar.
est. $100–$125 sold: $431
William Doyle Galleries 12/5/1996

COAT, 1960s

Cotton velvet, large round, purple, white, and green psychedelic motif.
est. not available sold: $895
The Paper Bag Princess 11/1/1996

COAT, 1970s

Maxi-length cotton velvet coat in geometric motif of white, blue, purple, and fuchsia. Silk lined, redesigned by The Paper Bag Princess.
est. $1295 sold: $2695
The Paper Bag Princess 1/1/2001

COCKTAIL DRESS, 1950s

Short, strapless white silk twill printed with island dancers and swirling ribbons in purple, turquoise, rose, gray, green, and black.
est. $150–$200 sold: $575
William Doyle Galleries 4/24/1996

Cocktail Dress, 1960s

Pink silk A-line, empire waist, spaghetti straps, beaded with rhinesones and pink crystals at neckline and hem.
est. not available sold: $1295
The Paper Bag Princess 1/4/2001

Cocktail Dress, 1960s

Blue, turquoise, and green floral and geometric print on white ground with beads, sequins, and colored stones.
est. $300–$500 sold: $632
William Doyle Galleries 11/12/1997

Cocktail Dress, 1970

Printed cotton velvet in white, green, blue, purple, aqua, below-the-knee-length, sleeveless, V neck and empire waist, A-line skirt, bias-cut.
est. $150–$300 sold: $316
Skinner 12/16/1999

Cocktail Dress, 1970s

Silk jersey dress with black skirt and printed bodice in black, white, gray, and pink. Fitted bodice, low round neckline, short sleeves, empire waist.
est. $150–$200 sold: $518
Skinner 12/16/1999

Cocktail Dress, 1975

Black silk jersey strapless sheath, bodice wraps to left and is finished with black satin bow.
est. $1000–$1500 sold: $1840
Sotheby's 4/8/1998

Cocktail Ensemble, 1960s

Shell blouse and skirt, silk printed with diagonal stripes and diaper pattern in pink, blue, yellow, and green overlaid with iridescent sequins.
est. $1000–$1500 sold: $920
William Doyle Galleries 11/16/1999

Cocktail Ensemble, 1960s

Magenta velveteen printed with swirling roses, camisole top, gathered wrap skirt and jacket.
est. $150–$200 sold: $316
William Doyle Galleries 11/12/1997

Cocktail Ensemble, 1970s

Printed silk jersey dress and bolero jacket with black, brown, pink, and orange vine and leaf pattern on beige ground, low V neck, spaghetti straps.
est. $200–$400 sold: $805
Skinner 12/16/1999

Dress, 1960s

Silk twill printed in peach, green, lavender, and pink, the dhoti panel wrapping through the legs, around the body, and fastening at the high waist.
est. $75–$100 sold: $201
William Doyle Galleries 4/12/1995

Dress, 1960s

Silk jersey, three-quarter-length sleeves, fuchsia, purple, chartreuse, and black, peacock feather print. Excellent condition.
est. not available sold: $850
The Paper Bag Princess 12/20/2000

Dress, 1960s

Silk jersey, long sleeves, slightly raised waist, geometric and curvilinear pattern. Labeled: Pucci/Florence-Italy. Very good condition.
est. $400–$600 sold: $920
William Doyle Galleries 11/2/2000

Dress, 1960s

Silk jersey, long-sleeved sheath in orange and brown with printed genie motif.
est. not available sold: $695
The Paper Bag Princess 12/1/1996

Dress, 1960s

Turquoise and yellow velvet sleeveless, V neck shift, with geometric motif.
est. not available sold: $595
The Paper Bag Princess 12/1/1996

Dress, 1960s

Silk jersey, long sleeves, yellow background with pink and violet geometic printed motifs.
est. not available sold: $595
The Paper Bag Princess 1/1/1997

P

DRESS, 1960s
Silk jersey, sleeveless tank-style with gray and yellow printed floral and geometric motif.
est. not available sold: $895
The Paper Bag Princess 7/1/1997

DRESS, 1960s
Black silk jersey, empire waist, A-line skirt, with large pink bird motif.
est. not available sold: $695
The Paper Bag Princess 6/1/1997

DRESS, 1960s
Brown silk jersey with black and white squares, long sleeves, crystal tassle rope belt.
est. not available sold: $595
The Paper Bag Princess 11/1/1999

DRESS, 1960s
Pink and black two-ply cashmere, sleeveless, with geometric swirl motif.
est. not available sold: $895
The Paper Bag Princess 8/8/1999

DRESS, 1960s
Silk jersey, tank-style V neck, with peach bodice and printed pink and peach straight skirt.
est. not available sold: $495
The Paper Bag Princess 1/1/2000

DRESS, 1960s
Silk jersey long-sleeved sheath with purple and black small geometric printed motif.
est. not available sold: $895
The Paper Bag Princess 10/1/1999

DRESS, 1960s
Silk jersey shift with three-quarter-length sleeves, in pink and gray with a geometric puzzle motif.
est. not available sold: $595
The Paper Bag Princess 8/1/1998

DRESS, 1960s
Silk jersey, straight knee-length sheath, with long sleeves in green and blue floral print.
est. not available sold: $495
The Paper Bag Princess 12/1/1997

DRESS, 1960s
Silk twill A-line shift with narrow straps, printed in pink, blue, and yellow.
est. $150–$200 sold: $287
William Doyle Galleries 11/12/1997

DRESS, 1960s
Silk jersey printed in lilac, pink, gray, and white.
est. $75–$100 sold: $258
William Doyle Galleries 4/12/1995

DRESS, 1960s
Silk jersey with low V neck printed in black, white, and pink design of phoenix-type birds set against large white discs suspended from chains.
est. $100–$125 sold: $230
William Doyle Galleries 6/11/1997

DRESS, 1960s
Cotton velvet, short-sleeved, printed black on one side of the front and white on the other, bisected by a single long-stem rose in brown, yellow, and green.
est. $125–$175 sold: $460
William Doyle Galleries 6/11/1997

DRESS, 1960s
Silk jersey with long sleeves printed in browns, grays, and white with scalloped sunburst on the skirt.
est. $75–$100 sold: $287
William Doyle Galleries 6/11/1997

DRESS, 1960s
Silk jersey, long-sleeved, printed with twirling ribbons and circles in purple, turquoise, gray, black, and white.
est. $75–$100 sold: $287
William Doyle Galleries 4/24/1996

DRESS, 1960s
Velvet panel in a rose window design in black, lavender, pink, blue, and green.
est. $60–$90 sold: $230
William Doyle Galleries 12/6/1995

P

Dress, 1960s
Silk jersey printed with checkerboards of varying dimensions, long sleeves with jewel neck.
est. $125–$175 sold: $316
William Doyle Galleries 11/12/1997

Dress, 1960s
Silk jersey, long-sleeved, printed in turquoise, purple, white, gray, and black with beaded tassel belt.
est. $60–$80 sold: $258
William Doyle Galleries 4/24/1996

Dress, 1960s
Cashmere silk knit straight, geometric-patterned stripes in purple and green, tasseled belt.
est. $80–$120 sold: $230
William Doyle Galleries 4/24/1996

Dress, 1960s
Silk jersey, V neck printed with butterflies amidst scrolls and strings of beads in aqua, periwinkle, orange, chartreuse, purple, and white.
est. $75–$100 sold: $287
William Doyle Galleries 4/24/1996

Dress, 1960s
V neck, silk jersey with printed geometric motif in purple, blue, and green, fitted waist and A-line skirt.
est. not available sold: $650
What Comes Around Goes Around 6/14/2000

Dress, 1970
Printed silk jersey with geometric pattern in white, tan, yellow, and pink, fitted, high round neckline, fitted long sleeves, flared skirt.
est. $150–$200 sold: $288
Skinner 12/16/1999

Dress, 1970
Silk jersey printed in white, black, tan, pink, and yellow, slit neckline, front zipper closure, matching tie belt with beaded tassel.
est. $150–$300 sold: $402
Skinner 12/16/1999

Dress, 1970s
Printed cotton velvet, V neck, empire waist, gathered full three-quarter-length skirt, colors of gray, white, black, red, orange, pink, and green.
est. $150–$300 sold: $489
Skinner 12/16/1999

Dress, 1970s
Gold Lurex turtleneck, fitted shift.
est. not available sold: $450
What Comes Around Goes Around 11/24/2000

Dress, 1970s
Printed minidress in black, white, lime green, and shades of gray and yellow, jewel neckline, long sleeves, self belt with tasseled ends.
est. $150–$300 sold: $374
Skinner 12/16/1999

Dress, 1970s
Printed silk jersey, round neckline, long sleeves, long straight skirt, matching belt with tassels. *Sunglasses to match.*
est. $200–$300 sold: $805
Skinner 12/16/1999

Dress, 1970s
Purple silk jersey with butterfly motif, empire waist, and long sleeves.
est. not available sold: $895
The Paper Bag Princess 2/1/1997

Dress, 1970s
Orange and pink silk jersey with V neck, butterfly motif, long sleeves, fitted bodice, and A-line skirt.
est. not available sold: $895
The Paper Bag Princess 11/1/1996

Dressing Gown, 1970s
Emilio Pucci for Formfit Rogers, turquoise, purple, white geometric print with long sleeves.
est. not available sold: $295
The Paper Bag Princess 11/1/1996

ENSEMBLE, 1960s
Sleeveless hip-length shell top with bottom
hem shaped to pattern and lined wide-
legged pants, each of sheer chiffon printed
with kite shapes.
est. $300–$500 sold: $288
William Doyle Galleries 5/2/2000

ENSEMBLE, 1960s
Lycra bikini, poplin miniskirt, and cotton
velvet terry cloth cover-up printed in coral,
pink, yellow, and white.
est. $75–$100 sold: $402
William Doyle Galleries 4/12/1995

ENSEMBLE, 1960s
Persimmon shantung pants and shirt.
est. $100–$150 sold: $373
William Doyle Galleries 6/11/1997

ENSEMBLE, 1960s
Gray cotton velvet maxi-shirt and fitted
jacket with scrolling geometric motif in
pink and black.
est. not available sold: $795
The Paper Bag Princess 5/1/1997

ENSEMBLE, 1960s
Shantung hip-hugger skirt and cotton voile
blouse printed with stylized roses and
irises with scrolling fronds in turquoise,
lavender, green, and black.
est. $100–$150 sold: $316
William Doyle Galleries 6/11/1997

ENSEMBLE, 1960s
Man-tailored silk twill blouse and velveteen
A-line skirt printed with suns and other
planetary motifs in purple, pink, black, and
gray.
est. $150–$200 sold: $287
William Doyle Galleries 6/11/1997

ENSEMBLE, 1970
Two-piece silk jersey tunic and silk pants,
tunic sun-patterned in white, chartreuse,
fuchsia, aqua, purple, and green, sheer
aqua palazzo pants.
est. $150–$300 sold: $575
Skinner 12/16/1999

ENSEMBLE, 1970
Top with wide round neck, front zipper,
slightly fitted waist, printed with geometric
pattern, one burn hole, labeled: Emilio
Pucci/Florence-Italy.
est. $200–$300 sold: $402.50
William Doyle Galleries 11/2/2000

ENSEMBLE, 1970s
White cotton man-tailored shirt and box-
pleated cotton duck skirt printed with
African ladies carrying vessels on their
heads.
est. $80–$100 sold: $258
William Doyle Galleries 12/5/1996

ENSEMBLE, 1970s
Printed cotton shirt and printed cotton velvet skirt in shades of aqua, purple, green,
bishop sleeves, and A-line skirt.
est. $200–$400 sold: $518
Skinner 12/16/1999

ENSEMBLE, 1970s
Silk twill long skirt and blouse printed in
amethyst, lilac, gray, black, and white.
est. $200–$250 sold: $230
William Doyle Galleries 6/11/1997

ENSEMBLE, 1970s
Printed silk jersey tunic and skirt, ethnic-
inspired print in pink and white on navy
blue ground, hip-length tunic with V neck,
long sleeves.
est. $150–$300 sold: $374
Skinner 12/16/1999

ENSEMBLE, 1970s
Velveteen shirt jacket with cuffed sleeves,
buttons, printed in grapevine pattern in
magenta, fawn, and turquoise with magenta wide-legged pants.
est. $150–$200 sold: $345
William Doyle Galleries 11/12/1997

ENSEMBLE, 1970s
Velveteen jacket printed in brown, white,
and periwinkle, wide-legged pants in
brown.
est. $150–$200 sold: $402
William Doyle Galleries 11/12/1997

ENSEMBLE, 1970s
Cotton duck skirt and voile blouse printed with palm leaves in pink, chrome, and yellow.
est. $100–$150 sold: $230
William Doyle Galleries 6/11/1997

EVENING BAG, 1960s
Silk twill printed in pink, green, and gray with two separate compartments, gold-toned rope chain handle.
est. $75–$100 sold: $373
William Doyle Galleries 6/11/1997

EVENING BLOUSE, 1960s
Silk shell with white, lavender, purple, pink, teal, and turquoise iridescent sequins.
est. not available sold: $405
eBay Online Auctions 12/15/1999

EVENING BLOUSE, 1960s
Sleeveless silk shell printed in pink and blue blocks with white swirling bands overlaid with iridescent sequins.
est. $300–$400 sold: $862
William Doyle Galleries 5/6/1998

EVENING BLOUSE, 1960s
Sleeveless silk shell printed in pink, lavender, and black with oval and rectangular framed mirrors, overlaid with iridescent sequins and stones.
est. $300–$500 sold: $1150
William Doyle Galleries 5/6/1998

EVENING ENSEMBLE, 1960s
Silk jersey printed with swirls and circles in blue, black, gray, and white, long-sleeved tunic top, pants, crystal bead belt.
est. $80–$120 sold: $230
William Doyle Galleries 11/17/1994

EVENING ENSEMBLE, 1960s
Strapless silk sheath and jacket printed with a floral grid joined by oval medallions in pink, green, and yellow, jacket with beads and sequins.
est. $2000–$3000 sold: $2530
William Doyle Galleries 5/6/1998

EVENING ENSEMBLE, 1960s
Wrap silk skirt and sleeveless shell top, printed with geometric pattern in purple, gold, black, and yellow with colored beads and sequins.
est. $3000–$4000 sold: $4312
William Doyle Galleries 5/6/1998

EVENING ENSEMBLE, 1970s
Long skirt of silk twill printed in fuchsia, peach, red, gray, black, and white, long-sleeved top of fuchsia silk jersey.
est. $150–$200 sold: $345
William Doyle Galleries 6/11/1997

EVENING ENSEMBLE, 1970s
Long skirt of silk twill printed with flames in amethyst, fuchsia, turquoise, gray, white, and black, long-sleeved top of turquoise silk jersey.
est. $150–$200 sold: $316
William Doyle Galleries 6/11/1997

EVENING ENSEMBLE, 1970s
Pink silk full ball skirt, with green silk button-front blouse and peach silk sash belt.
est. not available sold: $1295
The Paper Bag Princess 8/9/1998

EVENING ENSEMBLE, 1970s
Silk twill printed in pink, coral, gray, white, and black, sleeveless tunic top and palazzo pants.
est. $200–$250 sold: $316
William Doyle Galleries 6/11/1997

EVENING ENSEMBLE, 1970s
Silk twill printed with leaves in pink, chartreuse, gray-green, black, and white, tunic blouse with band collar, long sleeves and palazzo pants.
est. $200–$250 sold: $373
William Doyle Galleries 6/11/1997

EVENING ENSEMBLE, 1970s
Blue, green, ivory, and black chiffon hot pants with heavy beading at bust and pant hem.
est. $750–$1000 sold: $3795
Sotheby's 9/30/1999

EVENING GOWN, 1960s
Purple, green, and ivory silk organdy with
sequined and beaded bodice.
est. $750–$1000 sold: $2875
Sotheby's 9/30/1999

EVENING GOWN, 1960s
Sleeveless gown of silk chiffon printed with
scalloped pattern in pink, beige, and
brown, pattern outlined with beads and
rhinestones.
est. $400–$600 sold: $747
William Doyle Galleries 6/11/1997

EVENING GOWN, 1960s
Silk chiffon printed in fuchsia, chartreuse,
and blue with floral design embroidered
with pastel iridescent sequins and rhinestones.
est. $400–$600 sold: $345
William Doyle Galleries 12/6/1995

EVENING GOWN, 1960s
Pink, orange, yellow, and green printed silk
chiffon with beaded bodice and hem.
est. $750–$1000 sold: $1610
Sotheby's 9/30/1999

EVENING GOWN, 1960s
Orange and white, geometric motif, silk
jersey A-line, empire waist, with matching
wrap.
est. not available sold: $750
The Paper Bag Princess 2/1/1997

EVENING GOWN, 1960s
Silk jersey, green and purple geometric and
floral motif, long sleeves, empire waist
with full skirt.
est. not available sold: $995
The Paper Bag Princess 9/1/1997

EVENING GOWN, 1960s
Tank-style sheath, sleeveless, with jeweled
tassel rope belt, turquoise with white, blue,
lavender motif.
est. not available sold: $995
The Paper Bag Princess 4/1/1997

EVENING GOWN, 1960s
Black silk jersey A-line full skirt, fitted velvet bodice, with pink swirling geometric
motif.
est. not available sold: $995
The Paper Bag Princess 5/1/1997

EVENING GOWN, 1970s
Floor-length in starburst pattern in black,
white, jade, aqua, and purple, fitted V neck
bodice, long sleeves, A-line skirt.
est. $300–$500 sold: $747.50
Skinner 9/14/2000

EVENING GOWN, 1970s
Sleeveless fitted bodice and low V neck, silk
cord belt knotted at ends, cream crepe
pants under culottes, silk chiffon printed
with colored shapes.
est. $300–$500 sold: $230
William Doyle Galleries 5/2/2000

EVENING GOWN, 1970s
Strapless column of green and peacock blue
chiffon with paisleys and flowers, bodice
embroidered with peacock blue, green, and
sequins, self stole.
est. $400–$600 sold: $1035
William Doyle Galleries 5/2/2000

EVENING JACKET, 1960s
V neck and V back, silk beaded with bugle
beads, rhinestones, and sequins, purple lattice with white background and roosters.
Condition, fair.
est. not available sold: $599
eBay Online Auctions 4/30/2000

EVENING SUIT, 1960
Cardigan jacket with long sleeves, green,
magenta, and pink pattern.
est. $100–$150 sold: $172
William Doyle Galleries 9/30/1993

EVENING SUIT, 1960s
Velvet printed with tulips and morning
glories in blue, turquoise, lavender, and
green, single-breasted jacket and long slit
skirt.
est. $100–$150 sold: $373
William Doyle Galleries 12/5/1996

P

Evening Top, 1960s
Silk chiffon printed in chartreuse, purple, aqua, and cream in ribbon-tied-bows pattern emphasized by beading, sleeveless.
est. $200–$300 sold: $402
William Doyle Galleries 12/5/1996

Evening Top, 1960s
Sleeveless with scoop neck, silk chiffon printed in taupe, cream, black, lavender, orange, and green with sequins, beads, and rhinestones.
est. $300–$500 sold: $805
William Doyle Galleries 4/12/1995

Evening Top, 1960s
Sleeveless shell of silk printed in lavender, taupe, beige, black, orange, and green, pattern outlined in beads and sequins.
est. $200–$300 sold: $431
William Doyle Galleries 4/24/1996

Girdle, 1960s
Psychedelic print.
est. not available sold: $138
eBay Online Auctions 2/11/2000

Half Slip, 1960s
Formfit Rogers polyester with turquoise and purple geometric motif.
est. not available sold: $225
The Paper Bag Princess 11/1/1999

Half Slip, 1960s
Black nylon with turquoise and purple simple geometric print. Emilio Pucci for Formfit Rogers.
est. not available sold: $295
The Paper Bag Princess 3/2/2001

Handbag, 1960s
Silk twill edged with blue calf, with adjustable shoulder strap.
est. $100–$150 sold: $345
William Doyle Galleries 12/6/1995

Handbag, 1960s
Silk with multicolored pastel print, double gold ring handle.
est. $800–$1200 sold: $920
Sotheby's 12/9/1998

Handbag, 1960s
Small clutch with floral print in shades of lavender, coral, pink, lime, and olive green, with gilt metal chain handle secured with buckle.
est. $200–$300 sold: $460
William Doyle Galleries 5/2/2000

Handbag, 1960s
Casket-shaped with gold double handles, covered with silk twill printed in curvilinear pattern in brown, pink, and black.
est. $100–$125 sold: $460
William Doyle Galleries 11/12/1997

Handbag, 1960s
Blue, lavender, black, and white print on blue silk ground, white leather shoulder strap.
est. not available sold: $305
eBay Online Auctions 2/6/2000

Handbag
Pink, black, gray, and green velvet box bag with faux green crocodile handle.
est. not available sold: $610
eBay Online Auctions 2/6/2000

Handbag
Velvet and black leather trim, four inside compartments with black and red leather, four sides have flower print.
est. not available sold: $2025
eBay Online Auctions 3/15/2000

Handbag, 1960s
Earth-toned multicolored with double ring handle.
est. $800–$1200 sold: $920
Sotheby's 12/9/1998

Handbag, 1960s
Pink and blue print silk twill with leather trim and shoulder strap.
est. not available sold: $695
The Paper Bag Princess 9/1/1997

P

Handbag, 1970s
Blue, gray, white, and black silk bag with gold metal chain handle.
est. $300–$400 sold: $690
Sotheby's 9/30/1999

Jacket, 1960s
Velvet printed with exotic flowers in pink, burgundy, and green.
est. $100–$125 sold: $316
William Doyle Galleries 12/5/1996

Jacket, 1960s
Blue velvet with gray sun motif, long sleeves, button-up front.
est. not available sold: $895
The Paper Bag Princess 2/1/1997

Jacket, 1970s
Magenta cotton velvet, motorcycle style, zip up, with gray and black motif.
est. not available sold: $895
The Paper Bag Princess 11/1/1996

Jacket, 1970s
Cotton velvet in green, purple, and white, three-quarter-length with abstract geometric sun motif.
est. not available sold: $1295
The Paper Bag Princess 12/2/2000

Jacket
Printed cotton velvet with mandarin collar.
est. not available sold: $416
eBay Online Auctions 3/10/2000

Jacket, 1970s
Wool printed with turquoise, periwinkle, and black horizontal geometric pattern.
est. $200–$300 sold: $431
William Doyle Galleries 5/12/1999

Jacket, 1970s
Velveteen printed in geometric pattern in rust, brown, plum, and white.
est. $75–$100 sold: $402
William Doyle Galleries 11/12/1997

Jumpsuit, 1960s
Silk jersey printed with curved bands of zigzags in pink, chartreuse, and black with stripes accentuating the raised waist, deep V décolletage.
est. $75–$100 sold: $345
William Doyle Galleries 6/11/1997

Jumpsuit, 1960s
For Formfit Rogers, turquoise, blue, and white tank-style top and genie pant.
est. not available sold: $495
The Paper Bag Princess 9/1/1997

Jumpsuit, 1970s
Printed sheer silk pantsuit with psychedelic pattern in shades of orange and gold on black ground, fitted bodice, low round neckline, palazzo pants.
est. $200–$400 sold: $489
Skinner 12/16/1999

Leggings, 1960s
Three pairs of opaque tights in original packing: mosaic print, pebble print, and lozenge print.
est. $75–$100 sold: $431
Skinner 12/16/1999

Leggings, 1960s
Lycra turquoise with white and black geometric motif.
est. not available sold: $295
The Paper Bag Princess 11/1/1999

Leggings, 1960s
Lycra, black, beige, and pink geometric motif.
est. not available sold: $345
The Paper Bag Princess 3/1/1998

Men's shirt, 1970s
Pink polyester knit, long sleeves, with purple printed geometric motif.
est. not available sold: $250
What Comes Around Goes Around 5/6/1999

Nightgown, 1960s
Formfit Rogers, pink with white, lavender, and blue motif, short robe and nightie.
est. not available sold: $495
The Paper Bag Princess 5/1/1997

P

PANTS, 1960s
Black cotton velvet, wide-legged, flat front
with large pink rose-bud motif.
est. not available sold: $595
The Paper Bag Princess 9/1/1999

PANTS, 1970s
Velveteen printed with floral and lattice
pattern in chartreuse, lilac, and aqua on
blue ground.
est. $75–$100 sold: $201
William Doyle Galleries 11/12/1997

PANTS, 1970s
Two-toned velvet, one leg brown, the other
black, both with blue floral print on side.
Excellent condition.
est. not available sold: $595
The Paper Bag Princess 12/4/2000

PONCHO, 1970s
Printed cotton velvet with flower pattern in
black, white, red, green, pink, and orange,
ruffled collar, zipper closure, slit pockets.
est. $250–$400 sold: $863
Skinner 12/16/1999

SCARF, 1960s
Silk with geometric pattern, white, orange,
gold, pink, white seed-beaded handbag
with fleur-de-lis in glass seed beads and
pink gold top.
est. $100–$150 sold: $201.25
Skinner 12/16/1999

SCARF, 1960s
Silk printed with geometric pattern in
pink, citrine, and brown.
est. $75–$100 sold: $143
William Doyle Galleries 11/12/1997

SCARF, 1960s
Small silk twill with blue and green motif
and the word Portofino printed in middle.
est. not available sold: $225
The Paper Bag Princess 5/3/1997

SCARF, 1960s
Silk chiffon printed with green, brown,
and pink geometric motif.
est. not available sold: $325
The Paper Bag Princess 1/9/2001

SHIRT, 1960s
Cotton printed with flowers and geometric
shapes in green, purple, and blue.
est. $75–$100 sold: $316
William Doyle Galleries 4/24/1996

SHIRT, 1970s
Velveteen with pointed collar, cuffed
sleeves, concentric squares enclosing other
geometric forms in blue, green, and lilac.
est. $75–$100 sold: $373
William Doyle Galleries 11/12/1997

SHIRT, 1970s
Silk crêpe de chine printed in pink, mauve,
beige, and black against white.
est. $75–$100 sold: $316
William Doyle Galleries 12/5/1996

SHOES, 1960s
Turquoise leather, the toe and arch straps
ornamented with blue and green gem-set
marcasite stones.
est. $75–$100 sold: $373
William Doyle Galleries 6/11/1997

SHOES, 1960s
Bernardo turquoise leather thong sandals
with large blue jeweled ornamentation.
est. not available sold: $695
The Paper Bag Princess 9/1/1999

SHORTS ENSEMBLE, 1958
Green and white floral printed silk, long-
sleeved button-front shirt, matching shorts.
est. $500–$700 sold: $575
Sotheby's 4/8/1998

SHOULDER BAG, 1960s
Rigid, curved form covered with silk twill
printed in geometric pattern in black, pink,
and gray, black leather strap and lining.
est. $100–$125 sold: $460
William Doyle Galleries 11/12/1997

SHOULDER BAG, 1960s
Envelope covered with peau de soie printed
in green, blue, black, and white geometric
pattern, white calf lining.
est. $100–$125 sold: $201
William Doyle Galleries 11/12/1997

P

Shoulder Bag, 1970s
Silk day bag printed in pink and orange with brown leather and gold trim.
est. $800–$1200 sold: $920
Sotheby's 12/9/1998

Skirt, 1950s
Cotton, elasticized waist, brush-painted at bottom with scalloped stripes, hand-signed, Emilio, labeled: Emilio/Capri/Florence/Made in Italy.
est. $400–$600 sold: $287.50
William Doyle Galleries 11/2/2000

Skirt, 1960s
Black cotton velvet with gray floral print, zipper front, excellent condition.
est. not available sold: $695
The Paper Bag Princess 12/27/2000

Skirt, 1960s
Long printed velvet skirt.
est. not available sold: $600
Vintage Designs Ltd. 11/26/2000

Skirt, 1963
Printed cotton velvet skirt in black, white, pale aqua, and blue, floor-length A-line skirt slit at center from front hem to knee.
est. $150–$300 sold: $403
Skinner 12/16/1999

Skirt, 1970s
Printed cotton velvet skirt in white, black, lime green, purple, aqua, pink, fitted-waist, floor-length A-line skirt, white acetate lining.
est. $150–$200 sold: $374
Skinner 12/16/1999

Skirt, 1970s
Maxi-length, cotton velvet with printed geometric motif in vibrant purples and pink.
est. not available sold: $600
What Comes Around Goes Around 11/26/2000

Slip, 1960s
Formfit Rogers, blue and purple bubble print with bra top, maxi-length.
est. not available sold: $395
The Paper Bag Princess 6/1/1999

Slip, 1960s
Formfit Rogers, brown with lace trim, long A-line.
est. not available sold: $295
The Paper Bag Princess 1/1/1997

Suit, 1960s
Cotton, sheer, man-tailored blouse, short wrap skirt and long side-fastening shirt, printed in beige, brown, gray, black, and white.
est. $100–$150 sold: $517
William Doyle Galleries 6/11/1997

Sunglasses, 1960s
Oversized round plastic frames with aqua, purple, lilac, green, and blue pattern.
est. $100–$200 sold: $230
Skinner 12/16/1999

Sunglasses, 1960s
Aqua, purple, green, blue, and white Lucite over fabric round frames.
est. not available sold: $305
eBay Online Auctions 2/6/2000

Sunglasses, 1960s
Purple, blue, and white geometric pattern frames.
est. $75–$100 sold: $373
William Doyle Galleries 6/11/1997

Sunglasses, 1960s
Large round frames with geometric pattern in shades of blue, aqua, purple, and green, the box covered with similarly printed silk twill.
est. $200–$300 sold: $258.75
William Doyle Galleries 5/2/2000

Sunglasses, 1960s
Round plastic frames in purple and green.
est. $150–$200 sold: $115
William Doyle Galleries 11/10/1998

Sunglasses, 1960s
Geometric pattern in pinks, purples, and greens, silk case.
est. $200–$300 sold: $287
William Doyle Galleries 5/6/1998

P

SUNGLASSES
Pink, purple, blue, and black round plastic
frames.
est. not available sold: $405
eBay Online Auctions 2/10/2000

SUNGLASSES, 1970s
Plastic-covered fabric printed in turquoise
and purple.
est. $75–$100 sold: $172
William Doyle Galleries 12/5/1996

SWIMSUIT, 1960s
One-piece V neck black Lycra with pink,
orange, and green floral motif.
est. not available sold: $495
The Paper Bag Princess 1/8/1998

TIE, 1970s
Silk twill printed with squiggles in greens
and blues, purple, and pink on white.
est. $50–$75 sold: $103
William Doyle Galleries 11/12/1997

TOP, 1960s
Silk jersey, long-sleeved, purple, green, and
white geometric printed motif.
est. not available sold: $345
The Paper Bag Princess 10/1/1999

TOP, 1960s
Silk jersey, long-sleeved, pink and green
geometric motif.
est. not available sold: $395
The Paper Bag Princess 5/1/1998

TOTE BAG, 1970s
Peach, orange, yellow, pink, mustard, and
white velveteen tote bag with tan leather
handle, piping, and trim, white vinyl lining.
est. $150–$200 sold: $403
Skinner 12/16/1999

PULITZER, LILLY

HANDBAG, 1960s
Hard-sided box bag covered with patchwork of multicolored Pulitzer fabrics, gold-
toned frame, top closure, and clear plastic
handle, hot pink lining.
est. $100–$200 sold: $489
Skinner 12/16/1999

QUANT, MARY

BOOTS, 1960s
Yellow vinyl designed with zippers to the
sides and to the ankles, transparent heel
stamped with Mary Quant five-petaled daisy.
est. 400–600 pounds sold: 437 pounds
Sotheby's London 11/25/1998

BOOTS, 1960s
Black vinyl designed with zippers on out-
side, transparent heel stamped with Mary
Quant five-petaled daisy.
est. 300–400 pounds sold: 287 pounds
Sotheby's London 11/25/1998

RABANNE, PACO

COAT, 1960s
Rust velveteen overlaid with grid of cut-out
black leather with additional randomly
sewn dangling strips, dolman sleeves,
leather collar, cuffs.
est. $300–$500 sold: $1380
William Doyle Galleries 11/16/1999

COCKTAIL ENSEMBLE, 1960s
Metal disc miniskirt and halter top, matching shoulder bag of metal discs and white
alligator.
est. $700–$900 sold: $3450
Sotheby's 9/30/1999

HANDBAG, 1960s
Diamond-shaped bangle carrying handle,
pearlized buttons and pierced silver-toned
metal discs connected by metal links, lined
with black kid.
est. $75–$100 sold: $201
William Doyle Galleries 12/6/1995

HANDBAG, 1960s
Silver-toned metal-linked circular chainmail-
style, rectangular, with zip open top.
est. not available sold: $695
The Paper Bag Princess 7/1/1998

SHOULDER BAG, 1960s
Black plastic hexagons with silver-toned
metal links.
est. $50–$75 sold: $143
William Doyle Galleries 12/5/1996

R

RAPHAEL

SHOES, 1950s
Satin sewn with steel gray beads and faceted stones.
est. $100–$150 sold: $201
William Doyle Galleries 5/6/1998

SHOES, 1950s
Pink satin with stiletto heels and pointed toes, top decorated with jeweled butterfly and small pearls.
est. $250–$300 sold: $201
William Doyle Galleries 5/6/1998

RAYNE

SHOES, 1970s
Wedgwood Jasperware heels of yellow bisque china molded with winged sprite in white, sandals in yellow kid.
est. $75–$100 sold: $201
William Doyle Galleries 11/17/1994

REBOUX, CAROLINE

CAPE, 1920s
Cream satin with appliquéd flowers.
est. $400–$600 sold: $747
William Doyle Galleries 9/30/1993

REDFERN

EVENING JACKET, 1930s
Cardigan-style, black silk crepe top, stitched in a design of concentric oval scallops, elbow-length sleeves edged in silver fox.
est. $100–$125 sold: $201
William Doyle Galleries 12/5/1996

REIG, BEN

COAT, 1950s
Charcoal cashmere, robe-like, fabric draped from side pleats at waist seam, dolman sleeves, separate tie belt.
est. $600–$800 sold: $402
William Doyle Galleries 11/16/1999

REVILLON

COAT, 1980s
Dark brown mink three-quarter-length coat with brown shawl collar, center front closure, long sleeves, black silk lining.
est. $800–$1200 sold: $517.50
Skinner 12/16/1999

COAT, 1980s
White mink knee-length coat with full silhouette and white fox trim at collar, cuffs, shoulders, hem, white silk lining.
est. $600–$800 sold: $546.25
Skinner 12/16/1999

REVLON

CASE, 1960s
Black alligator with rounded top, fitted with container straps and two leather jewelry boxes, key sheaths, interiors lined with quilted sang de boeuf.
est. $1000–$1200 sold: $977
William Doyle Galleries 5/6/1998

RHODES, ZANDRA

CAPE, 1970
Beige wool, with pink and green inserted bands, printed with grids, doodles, and tassels, very good condition, labeled: Zandra Rhodes/Made in England.
est. $700–$900 sold: $862.50
William Doyle Galleries 11/2/2000

COCKTAIL DRESS, 1980s
Sequins and beading worked in peacock-feather tones on blue crepe, pouf skirt, net flower-head bow ornament in back.
est. $800–$1200 sold: $1150
William Doyle Galleries 11/16/1999

DRESS, 1970s
Bodice of stenciled cream chiffon, multi-layered ruffled skirt, sewn with pearls and one headdress feather hanging from each shoulder.
est. $500–$700 sold: $431
William Doyle Galleries 11/16/1999

R

DRESS, 1970s
White tulle printed with pink and gray abstract pattern, elasticized at top and at intervals to create pouf surrounding the body, white satin sash.
est. $700–$900 sold: $431
William Doyle Galleries 5/12/1999

DRESS, 1970s
Gray silk crepe de chine printed in lavender, black, and white with squares, squiggles, and other motifs, smocked shoulders, long draped sleeves.
est. $75–$100 sold: $431
William Doyle Galleries 4/24/1996

DRESS, 1970s
Gray chiffon printed in white with Persian-inspired motifs, jewel neckline and low-draped back, each outlined with pearls.
est. $200–$300 sold: $575
William Doyle Galleries 5/12/1999

DRESS, 1970s
Lavender chiffon printed with white line-drawn shells, folds of fabric gathered below the waist, neckline frills and hem trimmed with pearls.
est. $500–$700 sold: $517
William Doyle Galleries 5/12/1999

ENSEMBLE, 1970s
Two-piece, cardigan velvet jacket tie-dyed in teal, aqua and lavender, sleeves and skirt of teal chiffon printed with Persian motif.
est. $500–$700 sold: $575
William Doyle Galleries 11/16/1999

ENSEMBLE, 1970s
Green silk jersey chemise slip dress with satin straps and beading at bodice, printed chiffon coat tying at hip level, ruffled collar with rhinestones.
est. $300–$500 sold: $575
William Doyle Galleries 5/12/1999

ENSEMBLE, 1977–1978
Pink rayon jersey, long-sleeved sheath with matching sleeveless vest, trimmed with jeweled safety pins and rhinestones.
est. $500–$700 sold: $575
Sotheby's 4/8/1998

JACKET, 1970s
Red purple to purple synthetic satin, pleated and printed in turquoise and black circles, yoke has periwinkle faux pearls.
est. $75–$125 sold: $287
William Doyle Galleries 11/17/1994

JACKET, 1970s
Salmon, narrowly tucked satin ruffles with lavender stitched edging.
est. $150–$250 sold: $575
William Doyle Galleries 4/24/1996

JACKET, 1970s
Copper synthetic satin, pleated and printed in tangerine and off-white feathers.
est. $75–$125 sold: $201
William Doyle Galleries 11/17/1994

JACKET, 1970s
Peach synthetic satin, pleated with ruffled sleeves sewn with lavender faux pearls.
est. $75–$125 sold: $172
William Doyle Galleries 11/17/1994

SCARF, 1970s
Silk chiffon printed in orange, red, white, and amethyst with a design of scallops, conch, and other shells.
est. $75–$100 sold: $316
William Doyle Galleries 12/6/1995

RIALTO

HANDBAG, 1950s
Gray pearlized cocoon-shaped handbag with silver-toned metal floral band embellishing mid-section, top flap with interior mirror.
est. $175–$250 sold: $258.75
Skinner 12/16/1999

RICCI, NINA

COCKTAIL DRESS, 1940
Black silk satin, sweetheart neckline with asymmetrical collar, narrow ankle-length skirt draped to one side.
est. $250–$400 sold: $402
William Doyle Galleries 12/5/1996

COCKTAIL DRESS, 1950s
Green silk taffeta, sleeveless, surface covered with floral pattern steel gray silk embroidery with back beads, and gray-green diamanté beading.
est. $1000–$1200 sold: $1380
Sotheby's 10/29/1997

DRESS, 1930s
Black silk crepe trimmed with red and ivory printed silk, self scarf at neck.
est. $500–$750 sold: $287
William Doyle Galleries 9/30/1993

ENSEMBLE, 1932
Green wool bouclé long-sleeved dress, jacket with ruffled yoke of brown sheared fur and patch pockets with tucks, matching beret of quilted wool.
est. $200–$250 sold: $488
William Doyle Galleries 12/5/1996

ENSEMBLE, 1960s
Silk dress, cream with black polka dots, V neck, long-sleeved, rising hemline at front, matching cummerbund.
est. not available sold: $295
The Paper Bag Princess

EVENING ENSEMBLE, 1960s
Cream satin brocade coat woven with multicolored flowers, collar and front trimmed in white mink, lined in pink satin, cream satin sheath dress.
est. $600–$900 sold: $345
William Doyle Galleries 11/17/1994

EVENING GOWN, 1970s
Silk chiffon ankle-length dress with long, loose sleeves, jewel neckline, peach ostrich feathers extending from torso to hem, chiffon underdress.
est. $400–$600 sold: $230
Skinner 9/14/2000

SUIT
Tan wool short-sleeved dress with cropped fitted jacket.
est. not available sold: $495
The Paper Bag Princess

RIVOLIA

COAT, 1930s
Brown and cavalry twill, single-breasted with square brown leather buttons.
est. $150–$250 sold: $373
William Doyle Galleries 4/24/1996

ROCHAS, MARCEL

COCKTAIL DRESS, 1950s
Red and gold textured lamé with shoulder and hip-draped layers of chiffon, matching reversible jacket of lamé and velvet.
est. $500–$750 sold: $373
William Doyle Galleries 12/6/1995

JACKET, 1940s
Mint, peach, and brown plaid wool, single-breasted, fastening at neck with one and at the midriff with three woven tan leather buttons, padded hips.
est. $200–$300 sold: $230
William Doyle Galleries 6/11/1997

SUIT, 1930s
Green wool, single-breasted jacket with scalloped lapels, green celluloid buttons and self belt.
est. $200–$250 sold: $230
William Doyle Galleries 12/5/1996

RODRIGUEZ, NARCISO FOR CERRUTI

COCKTAIL DRESS, 1996
Ankle-length skirt of triangular panels in aqua silk satin, short-sleeved aqua knit cashmere shell. Claire Danes, 1996 Academy Awards.
est. not available sold: $3450
Christie's Oscar Dress Auction 3/18/1999

RODRIGUEZ, PEDRO

COAT, 1960
Champagne silk encrusted with faux pearls and sequins.
est. $150–$250 sold: $632
William Doyle Galleries 4/27/1994

COCKTAIL DRESS, 1950s
Black polished cotton twill embroidered
with colored puffed flowers on chain-
stitched stems.
est. $150–$200 sold: $575
William Doyle Galleries 11/10/1998

COCKTAIL DRESS, 1960s
Ivory organza underlaid with plain silk
worked all over, camisole bodice front, low
round neck, back bared to waist, skirt
slightly gathered.
est. $400–$600 sold: $431
William Doyle Galleries 5/2/2000

COCKTAIL DRESS, 1960s
White tulle embroidered with dome-
shaped pearls, white beads, and pearlescent
sequins.
est. $150–$250 sold: $517
William Doyle Galleries 11/10/1998

COCKTAIL DRESS, 1968
Ivory silk crepe sleeveless sheath, floral
beading in silver, red faux pearls, sequins,
crystal seed beads, white silk lining.
est. $400–$600 sold: $632.50
Skinner 9/14/2000

EVENING ENSEMBLE, 1960s
Floor-length sheath of silk shantung, wide
bodice with pink sequins, beads and pearls
in pattern, cardigan coat with cape sleeves,
same beading.
est. $1500–$2500 sold: $1380
William Doyle Galleries 11/2/2000

EVENING GOWN, 1960s
Sleeveless and princess-line, with high
bateau neck at front, keyhole-shaped bare
back, flower motif in sequins, gem-set
rhinestones, pearls, and beads.
est. $500–$700 sold: $287.50
William Doyle Galleries 5/2/2000

EVENING GOWN, 1960s
Short-sleeved sheath with jewel neckline,
silver and blue beads and swagged strands
of white bugle beads.
est. $600–$800 sold: $345
William Doyle Galleries 5/2/2000

ROSE, HELEN

COCKTAIL DRESS, 1950s
Changeante fuchsia/black taffeta woven
into a pink and blue chine floral pattern,
strapless dress with draped bodice and narrow skirt.
est. $150–$250 sold: $143
William Doyle Galleries 4/12/1995

ROSENFELD

HANDBAG, 1950s
Rectangular bag with rolled leather hinged
frame, gilt metal fittings, single black handle, lined in beige leather.
est. $200–$300 sold: $475
Ritchie's 9/20/2000

HANDBAG, 1950s
Red alligator, small sack shape folded at
sides, gilt metal frame and single tapered
strap.
est. $200–$300 sold: $230
William Doyle Galleries 6/11/1997

ROSENSTEIN, NETTIE

CLUTCH BAG, 1960s
Rectangular, silver lamé studded with large
gem-set rhinestones.
est. $400–$600 sold: $258
William Doyle Galleries 11/16/1999

COCKTAIL DRESS, 1958
Black silk sleeveless sheath, bodice of black
guipure lace over flesh-colored net, skirt
with silk flower at waist, flying panel at
back waist.
est. $200–$300 sold: $287
Skinner 12/16/1999

EVENING BAG, 1950s
Coral leather sewn with coral branches and
beads sprinkled with rhinestones, double
leather handle.
est. $300–$500 sold: $1610
William Doyle Galleries 5/6/1998

R

HANDBAG, 1940
Brown crocodile lined in tan leather.
est. $1000–$1200 sold: $1150
Sotheby's 9/30/1999

HANDBAG, 1950s
Brown with matching change purse.
est. $500–$750 sold: $460
William Doyle Galleries 4/27/1994

HANDBAG, 1950s
White with gilt metal studded faux amber
handle and catch.
est. $300–$500 sold: $230
William Doyle Galleries 4/27/1994

HANDBAG, 1950s
Black alligator gathered into a self frame.
est. $200–$300 sold: $517
William Doyle Galleries 12/5/1996

HANDBAG, 1950s
Off-white with gilt metal studded faux
amber handle and catch.
est. $200–$400 sold: $230
William Doyle Galleries 4/27/1994

HANDBAG, 1950s
Beige ostrich with accordion gussets, fold-
over flap, single handle.
est. $300–$500 sold: $373
William Doyle Galleries 5/6/1998

HANDBAG, 1950s
Straw and beige faille.
est. $100–$150 sold: $230
William Doyle Galleries 4/27/1994

HANDBAG, 1950s
Broadtail and black satin.
est. $200–$300 sold: $287
William Doyle Galleries 4/27/1994

HANDBAG, 1950s
Black crocodile box bag with short handle,
flap closure, and black leather three-
compartment interior, four inner pockets.
est. $300–$500 sold: $920
Skinner 12/16/1999

HANDBAG, 1960
Black with gilt metal corners.
est. $400–$600 sold: $402
William Doyle Galleries 4/27/1994

ROSSINO & ANGELA

COCKTAIL DRESS, 1970s
Black wool crepe sleeveless floor-length
dress, fitted silhouette with empire waist,
round neckline, seven rhinestone buttons,
wide straps.
est. $100–$200 sold: $172.50
Skinner 12/16/1999

ROUFF, MAGGY

COCKTAIL DRESS, 1930s
Black silk, halter slip neckline, self-ruffled
hem with black bows.
est. $200–$250 sold: $230
William Doyle Galleries 12/5/1996

COCKTAIL DRESS, 1930s
Black silk crepe embroidered at V neck and
down one long sleeve with gold and silver
braid and rhinestones.
est. $300–$500 sold: $316
William Doyle Galleries 12/5/1996

COCKTAIL DRESS, 1940s
Black faille, side-buttoning bodice.
est. $500–$700 sold: $287
William Doyle Galleries 9/30/1993

COCKTAIL DRESS, 1950s
Black silk net strapless bodice with pink
pleated cummerbund, pleated net rests over
skirt with two sprays of pink roses.
est. $1000–$1500 sold: $1150
Sotheby's 10/29/1997

COCKTAIL DRESS, 1950s
Pink silk jersey with spaghetti straps.
est. $150–$250 sold: $632
William Doyle Galleries 12/6/1995

COCKTAIL DRESS, 1960
Green, bodice ornamented with one strap,
skirt slightly flared, bodice top and side
middle of skirt gathered in large random
folds with side bows.
est. $500–$700 sold: $402
William Doyle Galleries 5/12/1999

R

DRESS, 1950
Navy wool, long sleeves, double collar of
ivory silk satin and wool.
est. $500–$750 sold: $460
William Doyle Galleries 4/27/1994

EVENING ENSEMBLE, 1957
Yellow silk-textured chiffon with halter
neck, yellow silk satin cummerbund.
est. $1000–$1500 sold: $6325
William Doyle Galleries 11/17/1994

EVENING GOWN, 1960
Cream silk twill, sleeveless, encrusted with
silver bugle beads sewn in vertical rows
and further trimmed with dangling bead
strands.
est. $300–$500 sold: $575
William Doyle Galleries 5/6/1998

JACKET, 1930
Garnet silk velvet with shawl collar, tie closure waist.
est. $100–$150 sold: $230
William Doyle Galleries 11/17/1994

SCARF, 1950s
Silk twill printed with a herd of zebras in
green, brown, and black against a lapis
lazuli background.
est. $75–$100 sold: $80
William Doyle Galleries 4/12/1995

SHAWL, 1950s
Pink satin woven with white-stemmed
flowers with yellow centers, fringed edges.
est. $100–$150 sold: $57
William Doyle Galleries 6/11/1997

SAINT LAURENT, YVES

BELT, 1970s
Wide brown suede with Art Nouveau–style
butterfly-shaped buckle in brass.
est. $60–$90 sold: $115
William Doyle Galleries 4/12/1995

BERMUDA SUIT, 1970s
Long jacket closing at left with antique
gold buttons, extends to lower thigh to reveal above-the-knee shorts.
est. $200–$300 sold: $1380
William Doyle Galleries 5/12/1999

BERMUDA SUIT, 1973
Navy twill double-breasted blazer and
white wool mid-thigh shorts.
est. $400–$600 sold: $690
William Doyle Galleries 5/12/1999

BERMUDA TUXEDO, 1970
Classic tuxedo jacket with Bermuda shorts
sewn with rhinestone straps.
est. $400–$600 sold: $1840
William Doyle Galleries 11/10/1998

BLOUSE, 1970s
Gold lamé, long full sleeves gathered into
wide three-button cuffs.
est. $80–$100 sold: $316
William Doyle Galleries 11/12/1997

CAPE, 1970s
Blue alpaca edged all around with brown
fox sewn in tufts.
est. $800–$1200 sold: $862
William Doyle Galleries 11/10/1998

CAPE, 1970s
Camel cashmere floor-length cape with
round neckline and welted seam detail at
collar and hem, center-front closure.
est. $600–$800 sold: $977
Skinner 12/16/1999

CAPE, 1970s
Black cashmere fastening at neck with
Byzantine-style buckle of copper metal.
est. $200–$300 sold: $690
William Doyle Galleries 12/6/1995

COAT, 1960s
Taupe wool, military-style double-breasted,
slightly tapered at the waist, silver buttons.
est. $150–$200 sold: $690
William Doyle Galleries 6/11/1997

COAT, 1970
Beige, double-breasted with tortoiseshell-
colored buttons, welt seaming around
edges, back inverted pleat with belt.
est. $300–$500 sold: $345
William Doyle Galleries 5/12/1999

S

COAT, 1970S
Chocolate brown velvet trimmed with black braid.
est. $100–$125 sold: $575
William Doyle Galleries 12/5/1996

COAT, 1980S
Black velvet, diamond-quilted in gold, hooded.
est. $100–$125 sold: $805
William Doyle Galleries 12/5/1996

COAT, 1980S
Rive Gauche navy wool three-quarter-length coat, slant side pockets, excellent condition.
est. not available sold: $725
The Paper Bag Princess 11/7/2000

COAT, 1980S
Lambskin, bodice fitted, stand-away collar, puffed shoulders, button and loop closure, dirndl skirt, collar and interior edges beaver, silk lining.
est. $700–$900 sold: $920
William Doyle Galleries 11/2/2000

COAT, 1986
Brown alpaca, three-quarter-length with stand-away collar and bishop sleeves with turned-up cuffs.
est. $500–$700 sold: $1150
Sotheby's 10/29/1997

COAT DRESS, 1966
Navy, double-breasted and high-waisted, hammered gold-toned dome buttons and white linen dickey.
est. $100–$150 sold: $690
William Doyle Galleries 6/11/1997

COCKTAIL DRESS, 1950S
Gray moiré silk with white chine polka dots, folds of the surplice bodice crossing over two self roses at waist, long sleeves, deep V décolletage.
est. $800–$1000 sold: $1035
William Doyle Galleries 5/6/1998

COCKTAIL DRESS, 1958
Black on black, gauffered silk woven with velvet floral pattern, bouffant dress princess-line with low V neckline, elbow-length sleeves, and crinoline.
est. $3000–$5000 sold: $3220
William Doyle Galleries 5/2/2000

COCKTAIL DRESS, 1958
Blue silk faille, sleeveless bodice with scooped neck, bow at waist, balloon skirt.
est. $1500–$2000 sold: $3450
William Doyle Galleries 5/6/1998

COCKTAIL DRESS, 1958
Yellow chine with fitted bodice and full flounced skirt sewn in three sections defined by ruched bands, bands repeated on shoulder straps, belt.
est. $3000–$3500 sold: $2185
William Doyle Galleries 11/16/1999

COCKTAIL DRESS, 1958
Black zibeline cap-sleeved gown trimmed at the waist with cummerbund and large bow.
est. 1000–1500 pounds sold: 9775 pounds
Sotheby's London 11/25/1998

COCKTAIL DRESS, 1958
Rose silk faille bouffant dress with stand-away camisole bodice, skirt with six layers of crinoline, roses at each side of skirt front.
est. $2000–$3000 sold: $6900
William Doyle Galleries 5/6/1998

COCKTAIL DRESS, 1959
Camisole bodice dress arranged in tiers of pink crystal-bead fringe looped over a ground of pink tulle with iridescent clear sequins, matching belt.
est. $750–$1000 sold: $10,350
William Doyle Galleries 6/11/1997

COCKTAIL DRESS, 1959
Black wool crepe bodice with cap sleeves and deep V décolletage, taffeta harem-style skirt.
est. 2000–3000 pounds sold: 3680 pounds
Sotheby's London 11/25/1998

COCKTAIL DRESS, 1959
Pleated black tulle with sleeveless bodice, full skirt, trimmed from neck to hem with black satin lace-edged center panel and satin-covered buttons.
est. 500–800 pounds sold: 517 pounds
Sotheby's London 11/25/1998

COCKTAIL DRESS, 1959
Two-piece, black faille, tulip skirt sewn to boned bustier, elbow-length sleeves, labeled: Christian Dior/Automne-Hiver/1959/#101237/Made in France.
est. $1200–$1800 sold: $1150
William Doyle Galleries 11/2/2000

COCKTAIL DRESS, 1959
Tangerine silk chine, skirt has double-bubble hem at front, separate strapless bustier with silk slip and garters, cummerbund belt and bouffant bow.
est. $300–$500 sold: $4370
William Doyle Galleries 11/10/1998

COCKTAIL DRESS, 1960s
A-line sewn with blue sequins.
est. $800–$1200 sold: $805
William Doyle Galleries 11/12/1997

COCKTAIL DRESS, 1960s
Ivory and navy Schiffli-style lace, slightly A-line mini dress edged at neck, sleeves, and hem with navy satin, hem also edged with white cotton.
est. $500–$750 sold: $977
William Doyle Galleries 12/6/1995

COCKTAIL DRESS, 1962
Strapless black silk crepe, narrow dress draped in a low pouf anchored by a self bow, hem with one curved panel and one weighted trailing panel.
est. $750–$1000 sold: $6325
William Doyle Galleries 6/11/1997

COCKTAIL DRESS, 1966
Nude silk organdy embroidered at neck, bust, hipline, and hem with beads, rhinestones, paillettes.
est. $1000–$1500 sold: $1495
William Doyle Galleries 4/27/1994

COCKTAIL DRESS, 1967
Ivory organdy embroidered with pearlized plastic, silver threads, rhinestones with silver beaded hem.
est. $1000–$1500 sold: $3910
William Doyle Galleries 4/27/1994

COCKTAIL DRESS, 1967
Ivory organdy over peach silk embroidered with geometric plastic pieces and rhinestones.
est. $1500–$2500 sold: $6670
William Doyle Galleries 9/30/1993

COCKTAIL DRESS, 1970
Short, flared black velvet dress edged at sleeves and hem with black feathers.
est. $600–$900 sold: $1725
William Doyle Galleries 4/24/1996

COCKTAIL DRESS, 1970s
Purple silk woven with gold dots, round neck, long sleeves, dropped waist, bias-cut skirt.
est. $300–$500 sold: $316
William Doyle Galleries 4/24/1996

COCKTAIL DRESS, 1970s
Long-sleeved bodice of red purple chiffon embroidered with flowers in multicolored sequins, skirt of red chiffon with side panel of green chiffon.
est. $500–$750 sold: $805
William Doyle Galleries 4/24/1996

COCKTAIL DRESS, 1970s
Sleeveless suede shift sewn with double-fringed hem and decorated with gold beads, pearls, and clusters of other colored stones.
est. $1500–$2000 sold: $4025
William Doyle Galleries 11/12/1997

COCKTAIL DRESS, 1979
White lace with plunging neckline surrounded by bias-cut white organza ruffles, ruffled cuffs and hem, black bow above fishtail train.
est. $2000–$3000 sold: $2300
Sotheby's 10/29/1997

S

COCKTAIL DRESS, 1980s
Coral silk chiffon, strapless, empire-waist
bodice has bow that ties at bust.
est. $600–$800 sold: $920
Sotheby's 10/29/1997

COCKTAIL DRESS, 1980s
Orange silk charmeuse with halter-style
bodice and V neckline, horizontal draping
on bodice contrasts vertical folds of skirt.
est. $1500–$2500 sold: $1150
Sotheby's 10/29/1997

COCKTAIL DRESS, 1980s
Black silk crepe knee-length dress, V neck
bodice, wraps to left and falls to form
asymmetrically draped front to hemline,
long bishop sleeves.
est. $200–$400 sold: $345
Skinner 12/16/1999

COCKTAIL DRESS, 1985
Red silk charmeuse wrap-style long dress
with asymmetrical neckline, skirt falls in
pleats, matching scarf used as sash.
est. $2000–$3000 sold: $1725
Sotheby's 10/29/1997

COCKTAIL DRESS, 1987
Cream silk taffeta printed with pink roses,
V neckline plunges in front and back, self
bow extends to form a train.
est. $2000–$3000 sold: $2800
Sotheby's 10/29/1997

DRESS, 1950s
Red wool, A-line, stand-up collar, slanted
pockets, long sleeves.
est. $750–$1000 sold: $402
William Doyle Galleries 9/30/1993

DRESS, 1957
Short, strapless, red velvet cut to red satin
in pattern of carnations.
est. $750–$1000 sold: $2530
William Doyle Galleries 6/11/1997

DRESS, 1957
Green silk satin, strapless, short, heart-
shaped bodice continuing to form faux
overskirt panels.
est. $750–$1000 sold: $2530
William Doyle Galleries 6/11/1997

DRESS, 1958
White satin, strapless dress with bodice
slightly draped and ornamented with self
bow, full-pleated skirt, matching stole.
est. $600–$900 sold: $345
William Doyle Galleries 4/12/1995

DRESS, 1958
Two-piece, skirt with slip top and a short
overblouse, of black nubbly wool, tulip-
shaped skirt with crinolines, short cropped
top, jewel neckline.
est. $800–$1200 sold: $2070
William Doyle Galleries 5/2/2000

DRESS, 1958
Trapeze dress, gray wool tweed with Peter
Pan collar, self bow.
est. $750–$1000 sold: $4140
William Doyle Galleries 11/17/1994

DRESS, 1958
Pink tulle embroidered with pearls, beads,
and rhinestones, pink tulle underdress.
est. $2000–$3000 sold: $1035
William Doyle Galleries 9/30/1993

DRESS, 1959
Camisole bodice dress arranged in tiers of
puffed black chiffon between bands of
black velvet, sewn at the bodice and at one
hip with silk roses.
est. $600–$900 sold: $3737
William Doyle Galleries 6/11/1997

DRESS, 1959
Short, strapless silk organza printed in
turquoise with a blurred abstract pattern,
ruffled skirt in tulip tiers.
est. $600–$900 sold: $8625
William Doyle Galleries 6/11/1997

DRESS, 1959
Green silk shantung with square neck,
sewn on both sides with large flower,
bracelet-length cuffed sleeves.
est. $1000–$1500 sold: $920
William Doyle Galleries 4/12/1995

S

DRESS, 1960s
A-line, ribbed silk wool with short sleeves
and square white re-embroidered lace bib
collar.
est. $100–$150 sold: $230
William Doyle Galleries 6/11/1997

DRESS, 1960s
For Neiman Marcus, black vinyl with
square cut-out armholes, embroidered
around neck with a trompe l'oeil necklace
in faux emeralds, pearls, and coral.
est. $500–$750 sold: $690
William Doyle Galleries 12/6/1995

DRESS, 1960s
Black wool crepe, sleeveless overdress with
jewel neck and self bow above inverted
pleat revealing underdress.
est. $300–$500 sold: $690
William Doyle Galleries 4/24/1996

DRESS, 1966
"Safari," beige cotton twill, lace-up front,
long-sleeved, mini-length, excellent condition.
est. not available sold: $2000
The Paper Bag Princess 12/5/2001

DRESS, 1970s
Black sheer silk woven with gold dots and
printed with red and turquoise concentric
circles, narrowly pleated collar, tiered skirt.
est. $200–$300 sold: $805
William Doyle Galleries 4/24/1996

DRESS, 1970s
Ribbed cotton mini-trenchcoat dress
printed with flowers in turquoise, lemon,
purple, and lime.
est. $75–$100 sold: $299
William Doyle Galleries 4/24/1996

DRESS, 1970s
Silver metallic silk quilted in a diamond
pattern, Nehru collar, single-breasted,
silver-toned metal buttons.
est. $100–$150 sold: $230
William Doyle Galleries 4/12/1995

DRESS, 1970s
Long-sleeved, wrap front, with orange
flowers on black background, lace at neckline and cuffs.
est. not available sold: $895
The Paper Bag Princess 10/9/2001

DRESS, 1980s
Rive Gauche yellow silk with fans, pearls,
and pink floral print. Knee-length with
long sleeves.
est. not available sold: $595
The Paper Bag Princess 3/2/2001

ENSEMBLE, 1958
Black shantung dress and jacket, dress has
short sleeves, full-pleated skirt, single-
breasted jacket.
est. $500–$750 sold: $460
William Doyle Galleries 11/17/1994

ENSEMBLE, 1959
Red wool bouclé cap-sleeved A-line shift
and jacket with black buttons.
est. $750–$1000 sold: $43,125
Sotheby's 4/8/1998

ENSEMBLE, 1959
Beige ribbed wool sleeveless dress and coat.
est. $300–$500 sold: $1495
William Doyle Galleries 6/11/1997

ENSEMBLE, 1960
Cream raw silk twill printed with charcoal
dots, sleeveless dress with halter armholes,
cardigan jacket with black grosgrain bow
at neck.
est. $300–$500 sold: $431
William Doyle Galleries 6/11/1997

ENSEMBLE, 1970
Denim midiskirt and coat with button-
down yoke flaps and pockets.
est. $150–$200 sold: $258
William Doyle Galleries 6/11/1997

ENSEMBLE, 1970s
Brown wool knit long button-front vest
and bell-bottom trousers.
est. $200–$250 sold: $460
William Doyle Galleries 11/12/1997

S

ENSEMBLE, 1970s
Black/red bolero jacket trimmed with faceted buttons, red changeante silk harem-pants and matching ribbed tie belt.
est. $200–$300 sold: $230
William Doyle Galleries 5/6/1998

EVENING ENSEMBLE, 1970
Blue and metallic gold woven crepe coat and harem pants, coat has gold piping along seams and edges.
est. $750–$1000 sold: $805
Sotheby's 9/30/1999

EVENING ENSEMBLE, 1980
Rose silk faille full skirt with black silk taffeta petticoat and black Chantilly lace ruffle at hem, black velvet wrap top with plunging back.
est. $1500–$2000 sold: $1840
Sotheby's 10/29/1997

EVENING GOWN, 1957
Blue satin with sweetheart neckline, sur-plice front, and bell-shaped skirt, sewn di-agonally from one shoulder to front of skirt with self bows.
est. $500–$750 sold: $1092
William Doyle Galleries 4/12/1995

EVENING GOWN, 1959
Black silk taffeta, strapless with interior boned bustier, bow at waist, full skirt gath-ered into waist, cut to knee-length in front.
est. $2000–$2500 sold: $2990
William Doyle Galleries 5/2/2000

EVENING GOWN, 1959
Pale blue short, strapless gown with fitted bodice and tiered skirt with black Chantilly lace hem.
est. $600–$900 sold: $2185
William Doyle Galleries 12/6/1995

EVENING GOWN, 1970s
Two layers of chiffon, gray underlaid with tan, bloused bodice with halter-shaped un-derbodice, cuffed sleeves, layered skirt, boa collar, self belt.
est. $500–$700 sold: $632.50
William Doyle Galleries 5/2/2000

EVENING GOWN, 1970s
Leopard print sheath of shimmering coated silk with long sleeves, deep V neck meeting inverted V waist seam.
est. $400–$600 sold: $460
William Doyle Galleries 5/6/1998

EVENING GOWN, 1970s
Long-sleeved A-line dress of gold/silver lamé, bodice has heartshaped cut-out hung with teardrop stone, neckline, cuffs, and hem sewn with jewel band.
est. $400–$600 sold: $747
William Doyle Galleries 5/6/1998

EVENING GOWN, 1970s
Green silk printed with black dots.
est. $300–$500 sold: $747
William Doyle Galleries 4/24/1996

EVENING GOWN, 1976
Forest green taffeta and black velvet floor-length gown, fitted black velvet bodice with taffeta ruffle at rounded neckline and cuffs, taffeta skirt.
est. $400–$450 sold: $460
Skinner 9/14/2000

EVENING GOWN, 1980s
Tea-length, layered full skirt, sheer bodice, draped long sleeves, jewel collar, loop and self-button back closure.
est. $500–$700 sold: $1150
William Doyle Galleries 5/2/2000

EVENING JACKET, 1974
Cardigan with V neck, button and loop front closure, embroidered with cable knit pattern in silver-toned sequins, beads, and metallic thread.
est. $5000–$7000 sold: $8050
William Doyle Galleries 5/12/1999

EVENING JACKET, 1980s
Red trapunto quilted silk waist-length jacket, cocoon-shaped with wide dolman sleeves and stand-up collar, black satin lining.
est. $150–$250 sold: $287.50
Skinner 12/16/1999

Evening Jacket, 1980s
Pink maribou-feathered long-sleeved jacket with front opening and pink ostrich feather trim at neckline, hem, and wrists, pink acetate lining.
est. $500–$600 sold: $977
Skinner 12/16/1999

Evening Skirt, 1980s
Long black wool crepe evening skirt, with side slit to knee.
est. not available sold: $250
The Paper Bag Princess 7/1/1999

Evening Suit, 1979–1980
Cardigan jacket and long skirt of black velvet, jacket trimmed with black cord embroidered epaulettes, gold patterned lamé blouse.
est. $500–$750 sold: $632
William Doyle Galleries 12/6/1995

Evening Suit, 1981
Black wool gabardine, double-breasted, tuxedo-style, jacket has satin lapels, skirt has rope belt of caviar beads.
est. $1500–$2000 sold: $1725
Sotheby's 10/29/1997

Evening Top, 1980
Sheer black top trimmed with rows of multicolored rhinestones beginning at bustline.
est. $600–$800 sold: $1840
Sotheby's 4/8/1998

Handbag, 1980s
Black square zip top, suede with gold heart studs.
est. not available sold: $195
The Paper Bag Princess 7/1/1999

Handbag, 1980s
Black silk, constructed rose shape, with painted red rose motif on front.
est. not available sold: $325
The Paper Bag Princess 7/1/1999

Handbag, 1980s
Large round bottom, gray suede and snake with drawstring.
est. not available sold: $225
The Paper Bag Princess 2/9/2001

Hat, 1963
Brown suede visor cap with side and neck flaps.
est. $60–$90 sold: $316
William Doyle Galleries 4/12/1995

Hat, 1970s
Large straw hat with fringe and gold metallic ribbon woven throughout.
est. not available sold: $295
The Paper Bag Princess 5/1/1997

Hat, 1980s
Rive Gauche black sailor's cap, gold bill, excellent condition.
est. not available sold: $225
The Paper Bag Princess 12/22/2000

Hat, 1980s
Green fur felt, with wide brim.
est. not available sold: $225
The Paper Bag Princess 12/1/1999

Jacket
Black velvet single-button dinner jacket.
est. not available sold: $225
The Paper Bag Princess 2/1/1997

Jacket, 1960
Camel suede with knit band cuffs and a sweep of lynx forming the collar and trimming the edges and hem.
est. $800–$1200 sold: $460
William Doyle Galleries 11/12/1997

Jacket, 1960s
Brown and black suede with fringe.
est. $500–$750 sold: $345
William Doyle Galleries 11/17/1994

Jacket, 1962
Camel wool, blouson-style ends below hip, narrow band centered with bow, bodice dissected by double seaming.
est. $300–$500 sold: $4025
William Doyle Galleries 11/16/1999

Jacket, 1969
Khaki wool gabardine with button-down patch pockets, leather-trimmed belt.
est. $200–$400 sold: $517
William Doyle Galleries 11/10/1998

S

Jacket, 1970s
Brown leather trench-style car-coat length, with tie belt with buckle.
est. not available sold: $600
The Paper Bag Princess 11/29/2000

Jacket, 1970s
Single-breasted faux astrakhan jacket with velvet lapels.
est. $150–$200 sold: $460
William Doyle Galleries 6/11/1997

Jacket, 1970s
Short green suede jacket with wolf collar and arrow belt at waist.
est. not available sold: $395
The Paper Bag Princess 11/1/1997

Jacket, 1980s
Boxy, mid-thigh length, stand-up collar, sleeves full at top and tapering to turned-back cuff, slit pockets, labeled: Yves Saint Laurent Fourrures.
est. $400–$600 sold: $345
William Doyle Galleries 11/2/2000

Pants, 1970s
Black satin, flat front, wide-legged with side pockets.
est. not available sold: $225
The Paper Bag Princess 2/1/1996

Pantsuit, 1969
Brown knit tunic with decorative placket covering front zipper, leather cord belt run through with silver grommets at waist, straight wide-legged pants.
est. $200–$300 sold: $345
William Doyle Galleries 5/12/1999

Skirt, 1960s
Black pleated crepe.
est. not available sold: $350
Vintage Designs Ltd. 11/24/2000

Skirt, 1970s
Silk wrap skirt printed with gold dots over stripes in red, orange, green, and turquoise.
est. $75–$100 sold: $345
William Doyle Galleries 4/24/1996

Suit, 1960s
Black crepe, straight ten-button double-breasted jacket extending below the hip, edged in grosgrain, straight skirt with taffeta yoke.
est. $200–$300 sold: $316
William Doyle Galleries 5/6/1998

Suit, 1960s
Cotton floral printed jacket and skirt.
est. not available sold: $450
Vintage Designs Ltd. 1/19/2001

Suit, 1962
Black and nutmeg plaid mohair and wool, pleated skirt, black silk shell trimmed in wool piping to match suit, single-breasted jacket.
est. $100–$150 sold: $517
William Doyle Galleries 12/6/1995

Suit, 1969
Black silk with red polka dots, jacket with wide lapels and scarf in pocket, straight wrap skirt.
est. $300–$500 sold: $345
William Doyle Galleries 11/10/1998

Suit, 1970
Black silk, long jacket with long row of buttons at side, bell-bottom pants slit at bottom and trimmed the entire length with soutache buttons.
est. $300–$500 sold: $1150
William Doyle Galleries 11/10/1998

Suit, 1970s
"Le Smoking," ladies' black tuxedo-style pants and jacket with satin lapels, three-button, single-breasted with patch pockets.
est. not available sold: $1295
The Paper Bag Princess 7/1/2000

Suit, 1970s
Navy blue wool, men's, with pinstriped jacket, vest, and trousers.
est. not available sold: $325
The Paper Bag Princess

SUIT, 1970s

Black wool pant and jacket, button-up front and long sleeves.
est. not available sold: $550
The Paper Bag Princess 4/12/2000

SUIT, 1973

Pinstripe classic blazer with wide-pointed lapels, pant legs cut wide and straight.
est. $300–$500 sold: $517
William Doyle Galleries 5/12/1999

SUIT, 1980

Burgundy velvet Edwardian-inspired jacket with high collar and taffeta neck ruffle, full peplum three-quarter-length skirt.
est. $200–$400 sold: $287
Skinner 12/16/1999

SUIT, 1980s

Gold kid jacket with black satin tuxedo lapels and short skirt.
est. $200–$300 sold: $230
William Doyle Galleries 5/6/1998

SUIT, 1980s

Gray wool and cashmere, jacket has gun-metal button closure, straight skirt with pleated front, matching suede belt.
est. $800–$1200 sold: $920
Sotheby's 10/29/1997

SUIT, 1980s

Gray pinstripe double-breasted jacket with gray pleated pants.
est. not available sold: $495
The Paper Bag Princess 7/1/1999

SUIT, 1980s

Gray pinstripe jacket with gray pants.
est. not available sold: $350
The Paper Bag Princess 7/1/1999

SUIT, 1986

Black ribbed wool, single-breasted, mandarin-style jacket and straight skirt.
est. $800–$1200 sold: $920
Sotheby's 10/29/1997

TUXEDO SUIT, 1980s

Two-piece black suit, pants with magenta stripe down side of leg, button-up front jacket with lapel. Excellent condition.
est. not available sold: $1295
The Paper Bag Princess 9/15/2000

WRAP

Oversized black and blue checked wool with black velvet trim.
est. not available sold: $265
The Paper Bag Princess 11/1/1996

SAKS FIFTH AVENUE

COAT, 1960s

Leopard-printed cotton velvet three-quarter-length, trench-style, fitted bodice and A-line body, with matching belt.
est. not available sold: $595
The Paper Bag Princess 2/5/1998

EVENING BAG, 1950s

Black alligator with black enameled frame and rhinestone-set catch.
est. $100–$150 sold: $316
William Doyle Galleries 6/11/1997

EVENING SHOES, 1950s

Black satin with gold-painted wooden soles.
est. $150–$200 sold: $402
Sotheby's 9/30/1999

SANT ANGELO, GIORGIO DI

ENSEMBLE, 1980s

Silk chiffon in shades of red, burnt orange, and beige, halter style with wrap skirt, and matching scarf.
est. not available sold: $462.99
eBay Online Auctions 3/4/2001

SARAFINI

EVENING BAG, 1970

Open work in foliate pattern over gray faille, closure in shape of a conch shell, overlaid with sterling silver in grid pattern.
est. $1500–$2000 sold: $2875
Sotheby's 4/8/1998

S

SARMI, FERDINANDO

EVENING ENSEMBLE, 1960s
Gray ombre silk chiffon dress with rhinestone and bugle bead embroidery, sleeveless tunic, mink-trimmed hemline, straight floor-length dress.
est. $500–$700 sold: $402.50
Skinner 9/14/2000

EVENING GOWN, 1950s
Black tulle embroidered with sequins, beads, and rhinestones, camisole bodice, full skirt.
est. $200–$300 sold: $287
William Doyle Galleries 9/30/1993

SCAASI, ARNOLD

COCKTAIL DRESS, 1950s
Short, chine taffeta woven with poppies in red and gray, short sleeves, bell-shaped skirt gathered in back with full underskirt.
est. $200–$300 sold: $488
William Doyle Galleries 4/12/1995

COCKTAIL DRESS, 1950s
Raw silk printed with abstract design in red and black.
est. $300–$500 sold: $345
William Doyle Galleries 4/27/1994

COCKTAIL DRESS, 1959
Red and black silk taffeta below-the-knee-length dress with fitted camisole bodice, full skirt, black taffeta lining.
est. $400–$600 sold: $431.25
Skinner 9/14/2000

COCKTAIL DRESS, 1960s
Short strapless princess-line dress of silk with peek-a-boo inset organza free-form hearts, bouffant skirt with tied bows.
est. $200–$300 sold: $230
William Doyle Galleries 5/2/2000

COCKTAIL DRESS, 1966
Pink silk and tulle strapless with empire waist, tulle overlay with ribbon, silver sequins, paillettes, and baubles. Mitzi Gaynor, 1966 Academy Awards.
est. not available sold: $12,650
Christie's Oscar Dress Auction 3/18/1999

ENSEMBLE, 1950s
Shantung organza printed with flowers in blue and white against turquoise, matching shawl.
est. $150–$250 sold: $230
William Doyle Galleries 4/12/1995

ENSEMBLE, 1960s
White organdy blouse with red ruffle, red and white check hot-pants, overskirt in tablecloth check with red plastic discs.
est. $400–$500 sold: $862
William Doyle Galleries 11/12/1997

EVENING ENSEMBLE, 1950s
Short, strapless crinoline dress printed with green flowers, yellow silk shantung self-lined cape.
est. $200–$300 sold: $460
William Doyle Galleries 6/11/1997

EVENING ENSEMBLE, 1960
Raw silk dress printed with multicolored flowers, long cardigan coat of cream silk, lining matches dress.
est. $2000–$3000 sold: $1725
William Doyle Galleries 4/27/1994

EVENING ENSEMBLE, 1960
Cocktail-length dress and full coat of silk taffeta, dress printed with large blossoms in red with strapless bodice and tulip skirt with back bustle.
est. $500–$600 sold: $977
William Doyle Galleries 11/16/1999

EVENING ENSEMBLE, 1960s
Long gown with fitted bodice, short sleeves, gathered skirt and waist-length fitted jacket with round collar, printed with bright-colored flowers.
est. $400–$600 sold: $403
William Doyle Galleries 5/2/2000

EVENING ENSEMBLE, 1960s
Dress and coat lining of pink and black velvet and satin broche, printed with Pop Art Nouveau tulip design, brown satin coat.
est. $200–$300 sold: $316
William Doyle Galleries 4/12/1995

SUIT, 1960s
Pink tweed woven with multicolored ribbons, jacket and flared skirt, short-sleeved blouse of white cotton with embroidered multicolored flowers.
est. $100–$150 sold: $345
William Doyle Galleries 4/12/1995

SCHIAPARELLI, ELSA

CARDIGAN, 1950s
Black lambswool with ribbed collar and trimmed with love knot worked in pearlescent and opalescent beads.
est. $100–$150 sold: $517
William Doyle Galleries 11/12/1997

CARDIGAN, 1950s
Black lambswool with ribbed collar and trimmed with rows of rhinestones.
est. $200–$250 sold: $546
William Doyle Galleries 11/12/1997

COAT, 1950s
Brown and white checkerboard, above-the-knee, wide-notched lapels.
est. $500–$700 sold: $632
William Doyle Galleries 11/10/1998

COAT, 1960
Mink strips in various brown tones, double-breasted, wide-notched lapels, full round collar, tiger's-eye round buttons, signature silk lining.
est. $600–$800 sold: $977.50
William Doyle Galleries 11/2/2000

COCKTAIL DRESS, 1940s
Black velvet, bodice arranged in reverse surplice, square neckline, short sleeves, trimmed with large domed black beaded buttons.
est. $300–$500 sold: $460
William Doyle Galleries 11/10/1998

COCKTAIL DRESS, 1940s
Sewn with alternating bands of black satin and faille that converge diagonally at back and form slight train, square-cut neck, short sleeves.
est. $500–$700 sold: $632
William Doyle Galleries 11/10/1998

COCKTAIL DRESS, 1950s
Black crepe sheath sewn in vermicular pattern with matte sequins overlapped to create surface texture.
est. $300–$500 sold: $575
William Doyle Galleries 11/10/1998

COCKTAIL DRESS, 1960s
Green silk trimmed with self band around edges.
est. $200–$300 sold: $287
William Doyle Galleries 11/17/1994

COCKTAIL JACKET, 1936–1937
Black wool embroidered with gold palm trees, gold embroidered buttons.
est. $2000–$3000 sold: $4715
William Doyle Galleries 9/30/1993

DRESS, 1935
Long black crepe sleeveless sheath fashioned to spiral around body like a sari, edged with fuchsia beads and gold paillettes.
est. $3000–$5000 sold: $10,350
William Doyle Galleries 11/12/1997

DRESS, 1947
Lavender silk shantung printed with line-drawn floral sprigs, pleated bodice wrapping across front obi-style to bouffant bustle bow at back.
est. $3000–$3500 sold: $4312
William Doyle Galleries 11/10/1998

EVENING BAG, 1935
Printed with a collage of newspaper clippings and headlines describing Schiaparelli fashions.
est. $500–$750 sold: $3105
William Doyle Galleries 12/5/1996

EVENING ENSEMBLE, 1931
Underdress with multicolored marbleized pattern, burgundy silk skirt, culotte skirt in same print, jacket of burgundy silk.
est. $1500–$2000 sold: $4887
William Doyle Galleries 4/24/1996

S

EVENING ENSEMBLE, 1933–1937
Sleeveless bias-cut gown of black silk
woven with undulating wire thread with
fishtail skirt, matching matador-style
capelet.
est. 1000–1500 pounds sold: 2070 pounds
Sotheby's London 11/25/1998

EVENING ENSEMBLE, 1937
Silk velvet, jacket with front edges embroidered with gilt metal thread and sequins
with blue and pink glass decoration, sleeveless halter-neck gown.
est. 5000–6000 pounds sold: 7475 pounds
Sotheby's London 11/25/1998

EVENING GOWN, 1930S
Rayon crepe printed with flowers in red,
blue, yellow, green, and black against an
ivory ground, straps of cut-out flowers,
slight train.
est. $2000–$3000 sold: $2070
William Doyle Galleries 4/24/1996

EVENING GOWN, 1937–1938
Wine silk velvet, jacket has sun face silver-
toned clips, front embroidered with gold
thread, rhinestones, and beads, V neck front
and back of dress.
est. $3000–$5000 sold: $6325
William Doyle Galleries 11/17/1994

EVENING JACKET, 1930S
Black silk velvet with surplice front and
turn-down collar revealing black silk crepe
lining.
est. $1000–$2000 sold: $1150
William Doyle Galleries 4/24/1996

FULL SLIP, 1950S
Black rayon with black lace trim and label.
est. not available sold: $225
The Paper Bag Princess 2/9/1999

GLOVES, 1950S
Black cotton, three-quarter-length with
scalloped edge, decorated with rhinestone
crescents.
est. $75–$100 sold: $230
William Doyle Galleries 11/12/1997

HANDBAG, 1950S
Black calf, upper half is a coin purse compartment sliding on double handles to
open bottom section, lined in buff leather.
est. $300–$400 sold: $1380
William Doyle Galleries 6/11/1997

HAT, 1930S
Dark green layered tulle, brimless with
green and orange bird-of-paradise plumes.
est. $300–$500 sold: $920
William Doyle Galleries 9/30/1993

HAT, 1950S
Green straw edged with silk flowers in
coral, yellow, green, and white.
est. $75–$125 sold: $201
William Doyle Galleries 4/12/1995

HAT, 1950S
Head-hugging form covered with pink
pleated chiffon decorated with bird-shaped
spangles and a black velvet mask at back.
est. $150–$200 sold: $258
William Doyle Galleries 6/11/1997

HAT, 1960
Black organdy, ruffled brim.
est. $50–$75 sold: $201
William Doyle Galleries 4/27/1994

HAT, 1960S
Pink fur felt with tassel and rhinestone,
with original pink logo box.
est. not available sold: $325
The Paper Bag Princess 9/10/2001

JACKET, 1950S
Yellow and brown spotted fur, below-the-
hip-length with wide black mink stand-up
collar.
est. $400–$600 sold: $747
William Doyle Galleries 11/16/1999

PEIGNOIR, 1950S
Pink nylon with gold dots, comprised of a
fitted top nightgown and double-layered
flowing robe with draped collar.
est. $400–$600 sold: $345
William Doyle Galleries 11/16/1999

S

Scarf, 1960
Rectangular, cobalt blue and white with gray and brown floral borders.
est. $60–$90 sold: $207
William Doyle Galleries 4/12/1995

Shirt, 1950s
Raspberry silk or rayon printed with white floral sprigs, pointed collar, short sleeves.
est. $100–$125 sold: $172
William Doyle Galleries 5/6/1998

Skirt, 1948
Red, green, yellow, and black plaid, three rows of taffeta form bustle and train.
est. $7000–$10,000 sold: $25,300
Sotheby's 4/8/1998

Stockings, 1950s
Three pairs, nude nylon printed with multi-colored spring bouquet border up the side.
est. $100–$125 sold: $103
William Doyle Galleries 5/6/1998

Suit, 1930s
Purple-blue herringbone tweed, single-breasted jacket.
est. $500–$750 sold: $632
William Doyle Galleries 4/24/1996

Suit, 1960s
Beige wool, jacket has sheared beaver shawl collar.
est. $500–$700 sold: $287
William Doyle Galleries 4/27/1994

Sweater, 1950s
Black orlon cardigan studded with rhine-stones and rhinestone buttons.
est. not available sold: $265
The Paper Bag Princess 9/1/1997

SCOTT, KEN

Bathing Suit, 1970s
Jersey hand-printed with an abstract coiled snake design in purple, green, turquoise, burgundy, and black.
est. $80–$120 sold: $80
William Doyle Galleries 4/24/1996

Coat, 1970s
Double-breasted plush linen printed with geometric shapes in purple, turquoise, and green.
est. $75–$100 sold: $345
William Doyle Galleries 11/12/1997

Evening Ensemble, 1960s
Nehru jacket and silk jersey tights, squiggle pattern of the fabric entirely worked in sequins and beads on the coat in pink, blue, mauve, and green.
est. $150–$200 sold: $575
William Doyle Galleries 6/11/1997

SIMPSON, ADELE

Dress, 1950s
Pink silk sleeveless A-line dress, with rhinestone jewel trim at neckline.
est. not available sold: $295
The Paper Bag Princess 1/1/2000

Dress, 1960s
Brown and ivory faux zebra below-the-knee-length coat dress, gold and brown buttons, long sleeves, flared skirt.
est. $150–$250 sold: $144
Skinner 12/16/1999

SLOAT

Ensemble, 1950s
Silk crystal pleated skirt and velvet camisole top.
est. $200–$250 sold: $373
William Doyle Galleries 9/30/1993

SPROUSE, STEPHEN

Cocktail Dress, 1980s
Sleeveless shift with scooped front and back neckline of magenta and gray knit, printed with lettering and overlaid with transparent sequins.
est. $300–$400 sold: $575
William Doyle Galleries 5/6/1998

S

Dress, 1985
Straight shift with scoop neck, pink top and orange bottom divided by industrial-style zipper.
est. $200–$300 sold: $316
William Doyle Galleries 5/6/1998

Jacket, 1980s
Red, white, and blue, sleeves striped, torso printed with photographic images, signature lettering, excellent condition, labeled: S and Made in Korea.
est. $200–$300 sold: $345
William Doyle Galleries 11/2/2000

Jacket, 1988
Printed with scrambled names and logos of rock bands in psychedelic colors on Day-Glo green ground, overlaid with layer of transparent sequins.
est. $400–$600 sold: $1092
William Doyle Galleries 11/16/1999

Jeans, 1980s
Hip-hugger bell-bottoms, each leg printed with the abstracted image of a man, round back pockets, labeled: Sprouse/Andy Warhol/Made in Italy.
est. $200–$300 sold: $172.50
William Doyle Galleries 11/2/2000

Leggings, 1985
Day-Glo camouflage.
est. $25–$40 sold: $90
William Doyle Galleries 4/27/1994

STARR, MALCOLM

Cocktail Dress, 1960s
Sleeveless shift of peach voile with gold and orange beads, orange beaded bands outlining neckline and arms.
est. $200–$300 sold: $230
William Doyle Galleries 5/2/2000

Dress, 1960s
A-line and sleeveless, silver and white matelasse patterned with swirls, covered with long tiers of shimmering silver beaded fringe.
est. $800–1200 sold: $862
William Doyle Galleries 5/2/2000

Evening Gown, 1960s
Flesh-colored silk chiffon floor-length dress, fitted sleeveless bodice with gold and crystal beading, empire waist and full chiffon skirt.
est. $400–$600 sold: $460
Skinner 9/14/2000

STERN BROTHERS

Evening Gown, 1905
Black point d'esprit trimmed with velvet bands, bodice with white lace yoke, skirt of layered black and white tulle.
est. $700–$900 sold: $2530
William Doyle Galleries 5/12/1999

SYBILLA

Coat Dress, 1980s
Wool, collarless, princess-line, single closure at waist, bottom half wired for individual shaping, labeled: Sybilla/Made in Spain.
est. $300–$500 sold: $3162.50
William Doyle Galleries 11/2/2000

TALBOT, SUZANNE

Hat, 1950s
Scullcap covered entirely with scarlet red bugle beads, the front-facing ponytail ending with a brush of cut black ostrich feathers.
est. $200–$300 sold: $862.50
William Doyle Galleries 5/2/2000

TEIL, VICKY

Evening Ensemble
Black silk with drop waist, floral scrolled sleeves, cobalt blue silk satin lining, matching black suede and blue silk satin opera-length gloves.
est. not available sold: $228
eBay Online Auctions 4/5/2000

EVENING SKIRT, 1980s
Black tulle decorated with sparkling ferns.
est. $100–$150 sold: $316
William Doyle Galleries 5/6/1998

THÉRÈSE, MARIE

COCKTAIL DRESS, 1950
Upper bodice embroidered in floral pattern
with beads, sequins, and diamanté beading, lower bodice has gathered midriff to
black silk gauze skirt.
est. $800–$1200 sold: $1725
Sotheby's 4/8/1998

COCKTAIL DRESS, 1950s
Black silk faille two-piece, diagonal pleats
on bodice emphasizing bustline, box-
pleated skirt, garter of silk organza, lace,
and ribbon.
est. $500–$700 sold: $1840
Sotheby's 10/29/1997

COCKTAIL ENSEMBLE, 1950s
Multicolored silk floral brocade in blue,
yellow, green, pink, purple, and metallic
gold on black ground, matching black silk
organza wrap.
est. $500–$700 sold: $460
Sotheby's 9/30/1999

THEYSKINS, OLIVER AND GAULTIER, JEAN-PAUL

COCKTAIL DRESS, 1997
Black silk robe redingote has train with
Chantilly lace, opens to reveal gray ball skirt
of multilayered tulle. Madonna, 1997 Academy Awards.
est. not available sold: $79,500
Christie's Oscar Dress Auction 3/18/1999

TIFFANY & CO.

EVENING BAG, 1920s
Petit point worked in a carpet design with
central facing birds in reds and greens on a
black ground, 14k gold frame and twisted
fringe.
est. $700–$900 sold: $2530
William Doyle Galleries 6/11/1997

EVENING BAG, 1930s
Frame of silver, pleated bag of burnt orange
Chinese silk brocade woven in garnet,
gold, periwinkle, and green against orange
ground.
est. $100–$125 sold: $373
William Doyle Galleries 12/5/1996

TOWNLEY

SUIT, 1950s
Gray tweed, jacket has collar and cuffs of
gray lamb, straight skirt gathered at waist.
est. $300–$400 sold: $488
William Doyle Galleries 11/16/1999

TRAINA-NORELL

COAT, 1950s
Black satin, swing-style.
est. $200–$300 sold: $373
William Doyle Galleries 12/6/1995

COCKTAIL DRESS, 1950s
Red satin, two-piece, camisole bodice sewn
with straps converging at center and hip-
length peplum, full skirt with crinoline.
est. $400–$600 sold: $488
William Doyle Galleries 11/12/1997

COCKTAIL DRESS, 1950s
Blue sequined mermaid halter dress with
plunging V neckline, skirt with slightly
flared hem.
est. $2000–$3000 sold: $2300
Sotheby's 4/8/1998

COCKTAIL DRESS, 1950s
Short, black silk with short sleeves, round
neckline.
est. $300–$500 sold: $862
William Doyle Galleries 4/27/1994

COCKTAIL DRESS, 1950s
Black wool jersey with stand-up collar,
cap sleeves, fastens across shoulder with
mirror-centered rhinestone buttons.
est. $150–$250 sold: $287
William Doyle Galleries 4/12/1995

T

COCKTAIL DRESS, 1955

Bodice with three-quarter-length raglan sleeves and V décolletage plunging to waist, full skirt pleated into cummerbund waistband.
est. $300–$500 sold: $575
William Doyle Galleries 5/2/2000

COCKTAIL DRESS, 1956

Black silk faille with halter neck and full skirt sewn in narrow pleats to a V yoke.
est. $200–$300 sold: $690
William Doyle Galleries 12/5/1996

COCKTAIL DRESS, 1957

Covered with cut bugle beads, beaded fringe, bodice high-waisted camisole, skirt straight, labeled: Traina-Norell/Style Exclusive with I. Magnin & Co.
est. $1500–$2000 sold: $2587.50
William Doyle Galleries 11/2/2000

COCKTAIL DRESS, 1959

Red satin with halter bodice cut in two petal shapes descending to bare back, gathered bouffant skirt with hooped petticoat.
est. $400–$600 sold: $1035
William Doyle Galleries 5/6/1998

DRESS, 1950s

Blue and white window-checked bodice and gingham check full skirt, bodice trimmed with bow and bands of skirt gingham.
est. $150–$200 sold: $431
William Doyle Galleries 5/6/1998

DRESS, 1950s

Black wool, puffed sleeves, pleated skirt over taffeta petticoat.
est. $300–$500 sold: $690
William Doyle Galleries 11/17/1994

DRESS, 1950s

Cream linen with round neck, short sleeves, pleated skirt sewn with three bands of Schiffli-lace.
est. $250–$400 sold: $373
William Doyle Galleries 4/24/1996

DRESS, 1950s

Black satin with fitted bodice, round neckline, straight skirt sewn at back with low flamenco flounce, belt with rhinestone buckle.
est. $300–$500 sold: $632
William Doyle Galleries 5/12/1999

DRESS, 1955

Black silk with white dots, kimono-cut gathered bodice with deep V ending at top edge of cummerbund waist, bouffant skirt, white silk rose at center.
est. $300–$400 sold: $1035
William Doyle Galleries 5/12/1999

DRESS, 1955

Blush satin woven with fawn and brown velvet roses, bodice with jewel neck, slit at center to waist, dolman sleeves and wide cummerbund.
est. $400–$600 sold: $230
William Doyle Galleries 11/16/1999

ENSEMBLE, 1960s

Black wool long sheath with two cropped knit tops, black silk taffeta camisole bodice, two coordinating black wool sweaters, first, long-sleeved and second, short-sleeved.
est. $300–$500 sold: $1610
Skinner 12/16/1999

EVENING GOWN, 1950

Black velvet, off-the-shoulder neckline, hem of tunic and skirt in black fox.
est. $800–$1200 sold: $1150
William Doyle Galleries 9/30/1993

EVENING GOWN, 1956

Silk jersey sewn all over with gun metal sequins, halter neck, low V front, bare back, very good condition, some wear, labeled: Traina-Norell/New York.
est. $2500–$3000 sold: $3737.50
William Doyle Galleries 11/2/2000

EVENING GOWN, 1960

Black satin fitted sheath with square neck, self bows at shoulders, back skirt hem sewn with full flounce.
est. $500–$700 sold: $690
William Doyle Galleries 11/12/1997

JACKET, 1940s
Black wool with Peter Pan collar.
est. $200–$250 sold: $431
William Doyle Galleries 6/11/1997

JACKET, 1950s
Navy cashmere trimmed at sailor collar,
flaps of pockets, turned-back cuffs of
sleeves with black faille, buttons molded
with eagles.
est. $150–$250 sold: $546
William Doyle Galleries 4/12/1995

SUIT, 1950s
Charcoal gray wool twill, straight jacket,
slightly flared skirt.
est. $125–$150 sold: $287
William Doyle Galleries 11/12/1997

SUIT, 1950s
Oatmeal tweed with a tan velvet collar,
long double-breasted hourglass jacket and
narrow skirt.
est. $250–$400 sold: $632
William Doyle Galleries 12/5/1996

TRAVILLA

DRESS, 1980s
Column of pleated peach satin, backed in
crepe. Pleats radiate from center of bustline, halter style.
est. not available sold: $309
eBay Online Auctions 2/18/2001

TRIGÈRE, PAULINE

CAFTAN, 1964
Brown silk chiffon A-line, embroidered
with stripes of diamond-patterned metallic
gold thread, long cape sleeves fall to hem.
est. $150–$200 sold: $356
Skinner 12/16/1999

COAT, 1960s
Black silk/wool, fastening at side, large
white V neck fox collar.
est. $400–$500 sold: $373
William Doyle Galleries 11/16/1999

COAT, 1960s
Blue wool, single-breasted, trimmed at
hem and cuffs with black soutache braid
and buttons.
est. $75–$125 sold: $258
William Doyle Galleries 4/12/1995

COAT, 1960s
Green wool knit knee-length shift dress
with loose silhouette, round neckline,
three-quarter-length sleeves, reversible
swing coat.
est. $200–$400 sold: $632.50
Skinner 12/16/1999

COAT, 1960s
Black wool, side closing with trapezoidal
front panel, wide flat collar, and waistband
set with round white rhinestones.
est. $400–$500 sold: $690
William Doyle Galleries 5/12/1999

COAT, 1960s
Gold brocade fitted three-quarter-length A-
line long skirt, jewel buttons down front
and back.
est. not available sold: $1295
The Paper Bag Princess 9/15/2000

COAT, 1960s
Pink, green, black, and beige tweed coat,
with wooden buttons down front. Excellent
condition.
est. not available sold: $850
The Paper Bag Princess 9/15/2000

COAT, 1970s
Black wool, one button at waist, long
sleeves, fitted bodice with a full A-line
skirt.
est. not available sold: $895
The Paper Bag Princess 12/2/2000

COCKTAIL DRESS, 1940s
Blue silk faille, double-layered bodice
"sculpted" high above the shoulders,
curved low V back, full skirt pleated at
waist, stole self-knotted.
est. $300–$500 sold: $1265
William Doyle Galleries 11/10/1998

T

Cocktail Dress, 1960s

Brown net sewn with gold beads and rhinestones in web pattern with separate brown wool crepe sheath underslip.
est. $200–$300 sold: $287
William Doyle Galleries 5/12/1999

Dress, 1950s

Gray pinstriped paper taffeta below-the-knee dress, fitted button-up bodice, taffeta rose at neckline, puffed elbow-length sleeves, full skirt.
est. $200–$300 sold: $517.50
Skinner 9/14/2000

Dress, 1950s

Black faille, bodice like bubble, ribbon sash, long skirt.
est. $200–$300 sold: $345
William Doyle Galleries 9/30/1993

Dress, 1960s

Navy and white striped knit sleeveless dress with belt, navy and white striped tweed jacket with Nehru collar and belt, striped bottom.
est. $200–$400 sold: $345
Skinner 12/16/1999

Dress, 1960s

Green wool knit shift dress with three-quarter-length sleeves and two pockets, self belt, reversible coat pink on one side, green on other.
est. $200–$400 sold: $632
Skinner 12/16/1999

Dress, 1960s

Brown and white wool tweed with stand-up collar, long sleeves, bodice buttoning in back and flared skirt edged with a band of fox.
est. $100–$125 sold: $258
William Doyle Galleries 12/5/1996

Ensemble, 1964

Black wool sleeveless shift, horizontal stripes in hot pink, green, orange; black coat, fitted bodice, striped shawl collar, oversized buttons.
est. $600–$800 sold: $862.50
Skinner 9/14/2000

Ensemble, 1970

Blue, green, red, black tartan plaid wool knit dress with long sleeves, mock turtleneck and one side pocket, taffeta-lined cape, and kerchief.
est. $300–$350 sold: $920
Skinner 9/14/2000

Ensemble, 1970s

Harlequin print of pink, blue, and yellow body top, royal blue linen wrap skirt, and matching bolero jacket.
est. not available sold: $495
The Paper Bag Princess 7/16/2000

Evening Coat, 1970s

Black, gold, green, and blue printed velvet late-19th century-inspired knee-length coat with brown fur trim at neck, opening lined with green taffeta.
est. $300–$500 sold: $1495
Skinner 9/14/2000

Evening Gown, 1960s

Princess-line sheath of black wool crepe, camisole bodice with trompe l'oeil bow in rhinestones, very good condition, labeled: Pauline Trigère.
est. $400–$600 sold: $402.50
William Doyle Galleries 11/2/2000

Evening Gown, 1960s

Strapless, bright red wool, silk lined, pointed front and back, built-in bra.
est. $60 sold: $372.12
eBay Online Auctions 1/14/2001

Evening Gown, 1979

Cream strapless, full-length dress, fitted bodice with jewel-toned diamanté beading, ivory jacket with puffed sleeves and jewel-toned buttons. Meryl Streep, 1979 Academy Awards.
est. not available sold: $6325
Christie's Oscar Dress Auction 3/18/1999

Evening Jacket, 1950s

Purple wool, swing-style, with circular hem descending in length from front to back, set all over with paired small and large rhinestones.
est. $400–$600 sold: $316
William Doyle Galleries 11/16/1999

SUIT, 1940s
Taupe wool trimmed at collar and cuffs
with black Persian lamb.
est. $80–$120 sold: $258
William Doyle Galleries 12/6/1995

TROY, HANNAH

COCKTAIL DRESSES, 1950s
First, navy silk faille dress with round neckline, short cap sleeves, fitted bodice; second, rose-patterned dress with fitted
bodice, cap sleeves, full skirt.
est. $200–$400 sold: $172.50
Skinner 9/14/2000

EVENING ENSEMBLE, 1960s
Metallic woven silver minidress and coat,
dress has crisscrossed neckline with two
rhinestone buttons at the back, coat with
brown mink cuffs.
est. $600–$800 sold: $1610
Sotheby's 9/30/1999

TYLER, RICHARD

COCKTAIL DRESS, 1993
Pleated silk taffeta ball skirt with high-rise
waist and train, sheer illusion bodysuit
with foliate appliqué and cap sleeves.
est. not available sold: $6900
Christie's Oscar Dress Auction 3/18/1999

EVENING GOWN, 1990
Black silk crepe fashioned after a man's tail-
coat, skirt has four vents and underpanels
of chiffon, hem with zigzag bugle beading.
Julia Roberts, 1990 Academy Awards.
est. not available sold: $9775
Christie's Oscar Dress Auction 3/18/1999

EVENING GOWN, 1996
Blue silk satin with empire bodice, square
halter neckline and straps that crisscross the
back, matching stole of black and blue panels. Frances McDormand, 1996 Academy
Awards.
est. not available sold: $4025
Christie's Oscar Dress Auction 3/18/1999

EVENING GOWN, 1997
Olive silk taffeta shirtwaist dress with
banded collar and button closure from
neckline to waist. Cloris Leachman, 1997
Academy Awards.
est. not available sold: $5175
Christie's Oscar Dress Auction 3/18/1999

TUXEDO SUIT, 1992
Three-piece ivory gabardine ensemble,
vest with silk-covered buttons, cuffed
trousers and jacket with silk satin lapels,
ivory silk satin tie. Diane Keaton, 1992
Academy Awards.
est. not available sold: $11,500
Christie's Oscar Dress Auction 3/18/1999

VALENTINA

COCKTAIL DRESS, 1940
Burgundy wool crepe with V neck and bias-
cut skirt with slight train, appliquéd piping
detail on front bodice and two pockets.
est. $1000–$1500 sold: $1840
Sotheby's 4/8/1998

EVENING GOWN, 1940s
Dress of black crepe, overlaid with black
net to form front V and long sleeves, layered black and gray net over skirt.
est. $300–$500 sold: $1840
William Doyle Galleries 11/12/1997

EVENING SUIT, 1950s
Black velvet cut to satin in pattern of scattered carnations, jacket with kimono-
bracelet sleeves, narrow skirt.
est. $300–$500 sold: $172
William Doyle Galleries 4/12/1995

HAT, 1950
Black and white woven raffia with black
crepe chin ties.
est. $75–$100 sold: $373
William Doyle Galleries 4/24/1996

HAT, 1950
Black felt with black cord chin ties.
est. $60–$90 sold: $201
William Doyle Galleries 4/24/1996

V

HAT, 1950
Black straw sewn at the crown and inside
the brim with pink silk flowers.
est. $100–$125 sold: $143
William Doyle Galleries 4/24/1996

HAT, 1950
Black sewn with black scrolls and beads.
est. $200–$250 sold: $143
William Doyle Galleries 4/24/1996

HAT, 1950
Black felt with black plush hatband and
chin ties.
est. $60–$90 sold: $115
William Doyle Galleries 4/24/1996

HAT, 1950
Plum straw with wide brim and shallow
crown, trimmed on the exterior and interior with bunches of lavender flowers.
est. $100–$125 sold: $172
William Doyle Galleries 4/24/1996

VALENTINO

CAPE, 1960s
Black cotton velvet, cape edged down
front with black satin, hooded scarf with
satin ties.
est. $200–$300 sold: $575
William Doyle Galleries 11/17/1994

COCKTAIL DRESS, 1960s
Pleated chiffon, sleeveless with V neck
edged in black faille, self belt.
est. $200–$300 sold: $345
William Doyle Galleries 11/10/1998

COCKTAIL DRESS, 1960s
Peplum jacket and tiered skirt of the underdress in black lace edged with black pleated
ruffles, belt of green velvet.
est. $400–$600 sold: $517
William Doyle Galleries 4/12/1995

COCKTAIL DRESS, 1960s
Salmon silk, double-layered, fitted sheath
under a sleeveless A-line shift gathered and
falling from jewel neck.
est. $200–$300 sold: $632
William Doyle Galleries 11/10/1998

COCKTAIL DRESS, 1970s
Ecru silk chiffon with embroidered and
beaded bands along the sleeves and lower
part of skirt, honeycomb-patterned waist,
neckline, and cuffs.
est. $2000–$3000 sold: $6900
Sotheby's 10/29/1997

COCKTAIL DRESS, 1980
Black paisley-pattern lace bodice lined
in taupe silk chiffon, lace sleeves with
beaded cuffs, black and red striped skirt,
velvet belt.
est. $2000–$3000 sold: $1150
Sotheby's 10/29/1997

COCKTAIL DRESS, 1980s
Olive silk chiffon and charmeuse with
pleated bodice and long chiffon sleeves,
chiffon overskirt gathered along straight
underskirt.
est. $1500–$2000 sold: $1150
Sotheby's 10/29/1997

COCKTAIL ENSEMBLE, 1960s
Two-piece aqua satin-sheen knit, sleeveless
jacket edged with jeweled bands and short
straight skirt.
est. $200–$300 sold: $632
William Doyle Galleries 11/10/1998

COCKTAIL ENSEMBLE, 1970s
Yellow silk, strapless dress and shawl sewn
with points of narrowly pleated ruffles,
corset interior.
est. $300–$500 sold: $977
William Doyle Galleries 4/12/1995

COCKTAIL ENSEMBLE, 1970s
Strapless fitted bodice of red silk satin trapunto, skirt of red silk edged with red
satin, matching silk shawl edged with satin.
est. $300–$500 sold: $1380
William Doyle Galleries 4/12/1995

COCKTAIL SUIT, 1980s
Jacket and skirt with allover sequined leopard and floral pattern, V neck short-sleeved
jacket with center-front closure, purple
satin lining.
est. $1000–$1500 sold: $575
Skinner 12/16/1999

DRESS, 1960s

Green georgette with short crystal pleated skirt, interior bustier, bare back.
est. $200–$300 sold: $316
William Doyle Galleries 11/10/1998

ENSEMBLE, 1960s

Wool coat and crepe de chine dress printed with same design in purple, black, turquoise, green, and white, both with high collars and long sleeves.
est. $300–$500 sold: $632
William Doyle Galleries 4/12/1995

ENSEMBLE, 1969

Black silk crepe edged with knotted fringes.
est. $100–$150 sold: $1035
William Doyle Galleries 4/24/1996

EVENING COAT, 1970s

Floor-length princess-line coat with hood, fabric sewn with red sequins, all edges and hood trimmed with marabou.
est. $400–$600 sold: $1725
William Doyle Galleries 11/10/1998

EVENING ENSEMBLE, 1960s

Black wool felt sleeveless A-line dress and jewel neck coat, embroidered at hem and sleeve ends with bands of rhinestones.
est. $400–$600 sold: $3220
William Doyle Galleries 11/10/1998

EVENING ENSEMBLE, 1960s

Chiffon long-sleeved blouse beaded and embroidered with Baroque floral and scrollwork pattern in olive and brown, olive silk skirt finely pleated.
est. $300–$400 sold: $345
William Doyle Galleries 11/10/1998

EVENING ENSEMBLE, 1969

Ivory dress, coat with white mink collar and trim around all edges, dress and coat embroidered with gold beads and rhinestones in paisley pattern.
est. $4000–$5000 sold: $6037
William Doyle Galleries 5/12/1999

EVENING ENSEMBLE, 1970s

Black and white polka dot silk satin dress and blazer, strapless dress with heavily beaded bodice, knee-length skirt, matching hip-length blazer.
est. $600–$800 sold: $460
Skinner 9/14/2000

EVENING ENSEMBLE, 1980s

Brown velvet and silk taffeta dress with brown velvet bolero jacket with mandarin collar, boned bodice, spaghetti straps.
est. $1000–$1500 sold: $2587
Sotheby's 10/29/1997

EVENING GOWN, 1960s

Colored chiffon panels sewn in kaleido-scope of colors, sleeveless bodice diago-nally pleated over interior boned bustier.
est. $400–$600 sold: $632
William Doyle Galleries 11/10/1998

EVENING GOWN, 1965

Full-length sheath of tangerine silk crepe trimmed with gold diamanté beading and leaf decorations.
est. 200–300 pounds sold: 632 pounds
Sotheby's London 11/25/1998

EVENING GOWN, 1967

Monastic-style dress of ivory silk hand-painted in one integrated pattern with coral branches, jewel neck, sweeping train in back.
est. $3000–$4000 sold: $3450
William Doyle Galleries 5/12/1999

EVENING GOWN, 1993

Dress with halter bodice embroidered with jet beading in a foliate motif, velvet coat with satin cuffed sleeves. Nicole Kidman, 1993 Academy Awards.
est. not available sold: $14,950
Christie's Oscar Dress Auction 3/18/1999

JACKET, 1960s

Black wool, single-breasted peplum jacket trimmed with large black fox collar and cuffs.
est. $200–$300 sold: $431
William Doyle Galleries 11/10/1998

V

SUIT, 1968
White cashmere double-breasted jacket with welt-seamed bands at neck, waist, and cuffs, A-line faux wrap skirt with welt-seam hem.
est. $400–$600 sold: $402
William Doyle Galleries 5/12/1999

SUIT, 1970s
Navy and red suede two-piece ensemble, fitted jacket with navy and red woven suede front, wide collar, faux flap pockets, navy knickers.
est. $150–$250 sold: $345
Skinner 12/16/1999

WRAP, 1980s
Dyed black fox fur boa with white fox fur inset down the center of the boa to look like a skunk. Hidden purse compartment at the tail. Fox tails ends.
est. not available sold: $950
The Paper Bag Princess 11/1/1996

VALOIS, ROSE

HAT, 1950s
Red velvet and coq feathers.
est. $50–$75 sold: $172
William Doyle Galleries 4/27/1994

VAN CLEEF & ARPELS

MINAUDIÈRE, 1940
Black enamel case with pink gold and diamond closure, interior trimmed with pink gold, mirror with pink gold and platinum frame.
est. $2500–$3000 sold: $3162
Sotheby's 4/8/1998

VANDEN AKKER, KOOS

EVENING COAT, 1970s
Straight line, with high collar, round shoulders, patterned patchwork form with faux broadtail, silk stripes, checkerboards, triangles, silk lining.
est. $800–$1200 sold: $575
William Doyle Galleries 5/2/2000

VENDÔME

COAT, 1950s
Black satin with fold-down collar and bracelet-length sleeves.
est. $100–$150 sold: $103
William Doyle Galleries 12/6/1995

VERSACE, GIANNI

DRESS, 1990
Red crepe, sleeveless bodice with abstract borders along neckline, exposed back and off-center jewel closure. Cindy Crawford, 1990 Academy Awards.
est. not available sold: $12,650
Christie's Oscar Dress Auction 3/18/1999

EVENING GOWN, 1993
Gold metal mesh, sleeveless with jewel neckline and rear vent. Ellen Barkin, 1993 Academy Awards.
est. not available sold: $6325
Christie's Oscar Dress Auction 3/18/1999

EVENING GOWN, 1996
Green crepe, flair at hem, strap is green sequin leaves crossing diagonally to back. Barbara Hershey, 1996 Academy Awards.
est. not available sold: $5750
Christie's Oscar Dress Auction 3/18/1999

EVENING TOP, 1990s
Couture, black beaded bodice with beaded fringe trim and spaghetti straps, side zipper.
est. not available sold: $1495
The Paper Bag Princess 3/2/2001

HANDBAG, 1990s
Rectangular handbag of black mesh with embroidered flowers, leather top handle.
est. $150–$250 sold: $184
Skinner 12/16/1999

TOP, 1980s
Patterned with stripes, each with a different texture, pointed short sleeves, velvet draped collar, labeled: Gianni Versace/Made in Italy.
est. $500–$700 sold: $805
William Doyle Galleries 11/2/2000

V

VIONNET, MADELEINE

DRESS, 1920s
Black satin-backed crepe, V neck, short sleeves.
est. $2000–$3000 sold: $1610
William Doyle Galleries 9/30/1993

DRESS, 1930s
Beige silk crepe with cowl-front neckline, elbow-length sleeves.
est. $300–$500 sold: $230
William Doyle Galleries 12/5/1996

EVENING GOWN, 1920s
Sheer salmon matte silk, high waist with applied pieces embroidered with gold beads and centered with cameo, gold lamé ribbon edging all around.
est. $3000–$5000 sold: $5750
William Doyle Galleries 11/16/1999

ENSEMBLE, 1935
Made of wool velvet and broadcloth, dress cut on the bias, long draping sleeves, wool coat loose, draped velvet collar, labeled: Madeleine Vionnet.
est. $3000–$5000 sold: $4312.50
William Doyle Galleries 11/2/2000

VIVIER, ROGER

SHOES, 1950s
Navy satin with square toes and spiked heels, embroidered at toes in navy silk with a stylized flower.
est. $100–$150 sold: $201
William Doyle Galleries 11/17/1994

SHOES, 1950s
Black leather with rhinestone buckle and low Sabrina heel.
est. not available sold: $195
The Paper Bag Princess 1/1/2001

SHOES, 1960s
Tie dyed in yellow, orange, and pink with square spiked heel and rounded double strap attaching at a covered button.
est. $100–$150 sold: $258
William Doyle Galleries 5/6/1998

SHOES, 1966
Crocodile.
est. $100–$150 sold: $230
William Doyle Galleries 11/17/1994

SHOES
Off-white satin with rhinestone buckle and low Sabrina heel.
est. not available sold: $195
The Paper Bag Princess 1/1/2001

VOLLBRACHT, MICHAELE

COAT, 1960s
Cardigan-style of black quilted silk appliquéd with multicolored circles and discs.
est. $150–$200 sold: $258
William Doyle Galleries 5/6/1998

ENSEMBLE, 1960s
Silk shift printed with red, white, green, and gray stylized feathers on black ground with a quilted cardigan coat.
est. $200–$300 sold: $230
William Doyle Galleries 5/6/1998

VON FURSTENBERG, DIANE

DRESS, 1970s
Cotton knit, wrap front with tie belt and winged cuff sleeves, printed white with orange star motif.
est. not available sold: $295
The Paper Bag Princess 8/1/1997

DRESS, 1970s
Black cotton wrap style with red piping.
est. not available sold: $295
The Paper Bag Princess 1/1/1997

DRESS, 1970s
Black cotton knit, wrap style with red flowers.
est. not available sold: $295
The Paper Bag Princess 2/1/1997

EVENING GOWN, 1970s
Polyester jersey baby blue snake print, silk wrap top and flared pants.
est. not available sold: $595
The Paper Bag Princess 10/1/1999

VUITTON, LOUIS

BACKPACK, 1990s
Flat backpack with outside zippered pocket, top zipper closure, adjustable straps, interior pocket, suede lining.
est. $300–$500 sold: $345
Skinner 12/16/1999

CASE, 1950s
Monogrammed canvas with top zipper opening, tan cowhide band trim and handle, cream flannel lining and elasticized pockets.
est. $60–$80 sold: $747
William Doyle Galleries 6/11/1997

CASE, 1980s
Monogrammed coated canvas with wide top-stitched calf handles, exterior zipper compartment and top zipper.
est. $150–$200 sold: $373
William Doyle Galleries 6/11/1997

ENVELOPE BAG, 1980s
Monogrammed canvas with tan leather trim on squared-off flap.
est. $150–$200 sold: $316
William Doyle Galleries 5/6/1998

HANDBAG, 1970s
Monogrammed canvas, rounded bottom, tan cowhide trim and shoulder strap, fold-over flap and buckle.
est. $60–$80 sold: $258
William Doyle Galleries 6/11/1997

HANDBAG, 1990s
Handbag with short handles, one exterior pocket, gold-toned padlocked zipper top closure and suede interior.
est. $400–$600 sold: $230
Skinner 12/16/1999

HANDBAG, 1990s
Sack-shaped shoulder bag with plain leather band encircling top, plain wide leather strap, suede interior, stamped "LV" on outside band.
est. $300–$500 sold: $258.75
Skinner 12/16/1999

HAT CARRIER, 1950s
Monogrammed canvas with "LV"-stamped leather trim, metal corner fittings, yellow center stripe, ivory silk moiré interior.
est. $300–$400 sold: $1840
William Doyle Galleries 5/6/1998

SHOULDER BAG, 1980s
Monogrammed canvas with textured leather interior and exterior trim with side gussets and flap closing at bottom with gilt metal clasp.
est. $300–$500 sold: $258
William Doyle Galleries 5/6/1998

WAKELY, AMANDA

EVENING GOWN, 1996
Silver/gray chiffon slip dress with thin shoulder straps and V neckline, asymmetrically tiered skirt. Emily Watson, 1996 Academy Awards.
est. not available sold: $2300
Christie's Oscar Dress Auction 3/18/1999

WALBORG

EVENING BAG, 1950s
Silver box-shaped handbag with mirrored lid.
est. $300–$400 sold: $517
Sotheby's 12/9/1998

HANDBAG, 1950
Suggestive of animal's face, composed entirely of black beads with loops defining areas of fur, yellow eyes, red nose and mouth, gold beaded collar.
est. $1500–$2000 sold: $4025
William Doyle Galleries 11/10/1998

WANAMAKER, JOHN

COAT, 1930s
Burgundy velvet with stand-up collar.
est. $100–$150 sold: $230
William Doyle Galleries 11/17/1994

W

COAT, 1940
Navy and pink embroidered wool crepe.
est. $800–$1200 sold: $1380
William Doyle Galleries 9/30/1993

WANG, VERA

EVENING GOWN, 1994
Sleeveless ivory illusion with silk piping at
neckline and arms, silk skirt with train,
buttons up side, sequin brassiere. Holly
Hunter, 1994 Academy Awards.
est. not available sold: $3220
Christie's Oscar Dress Auction 3/18/1999

EVENING GOWN, 1997
Navy blue silk jersey sheath dress with long
sleeves with soft points, flared hem, and
triangular neckline. Meg Ryan, 1997 Academy Awards.
est. not available sold: $10,925
Christie's Oscar Dress Auction 3/18/1999

WESTWOOD, VIVIENNE

HOOP SKIRT, 1980s
Red cotton with white polka dots, above
the knee, large circle, three-tiered hoop.
est. not available sold: $695
The Paper Bag Princess 4/15/1999

T-SHIRT, 1970s
Hand-silk-screened lettering with word
"Destroy" above an upside-down Christ
and swastika, picture of the Queen of
England, along with song lyrics.
est. not available sold: $355
eBay Online Auctions 7/25/2000

WHITING AND DAVIS

DRESS, 1980
Black metal mesh, straight, sleeveless chemise with narrow straps, low-draped front
and neckline, geometrically shaped armholes.
est. $600–$800 sold: $862
William Doyle Galleries 11/16/1999

TOP, 1970s
Gold metal mesh halter style with leather
ties.
est. not available sold: $395
The Paper Bag Princess 12/1/1999

TOP, 1980s
Black and red metal mesh halter with
leather ties at back.
est. not available sold: $495
The Paper Bag Princess 5/30/2000

TOP, 1980s
Gold and purple metal mesh halter neck,
gold leather tie straps.
est. not available sold: $495
The Paper Bag Princess 5/30/2000

WILARDY

HANDBAG, 1950s
Pearlized white, stepped Lucite with gold-
toned hardware, three compartments and
mirrored top.
est. $175–$250 sold: $258
Skinner 12/16/1999

HANDBAG, 1950s
Caramel-colored, hatbox-shaped Lucite bag
with mirrored top.
est. $175–$250 sold: $345
Skinner 12/16/1999

WORTH, CHARLES FREDERICK

CAPE, 1920s
Caramel silk velvet lined with black velvet,
two triangular front closures embroidered
with pearlescent bugles, gold sequins, and
beads.
est. $600–$900 sold: $345
William Doyle Galleries 4/24/1996

COAT, 1905
Black satin and lace.
est. $800–$1200 sold: $690
William Doyle Galleries 9/30/1993

W

Coat, 1920s

Black silk with chain-stitch floral pattern, pleated and honeycomb-padded collar, draped and pleated sleeves with banded cuffs.
est. $1000–$1500 sold: $1725
William Doyle Galleries 5/6/1998

Cocktail Dress, 1920s

Sleeveless with V neck, sewn with gold sequins, sash of green silk with tasseled ornament of silver bullion, green beads, and rhinestones.
est. $500–$750 sold: $1035
William Doyle Galleries 12/5/1996

Cocktail Dress, 1946

Dark brown silk bodice, straps sewn with multicolored gilt flowers.
est. $750–$1000 sold: $460
William Doyle Galleries 4/27/1994

Cocktail Dress, 1950s

Black lace re-embroidered with black glitter chenille, sheath dress with camisole top trimmed with black velvet bands and straps.
est. $125–$175 sold: $517
William Doyle Galleries 4/24/1996

Evening Gown, 1910

Empire-waisted gown of black chiffon over satin, cream chiffon panel with rhinestone swags and tassels, dangling ornaments on the bodice and shoulders.
est. $200–$300 sold: $1035
William Doyle Galleries 6/11/1997

Evening Gown, 1910

Gold brocade patterned with flower heads enclosed in vines, empire bodice of lace, green satin ribbon at bodice extending into long streamers.
est. $2000–$3000 sold: $3105
William Doyle Galleries 11/16/1999

Evening Gown, 1914

Pink satin floor-length gown with pink net, faux pearl, diamanté beading, empire waist, flesh net bust, pink net hanging sleeves, falling train.
est. $300–$500 sold: $977.50
Skinner 9/14/2000

Evening Gown, 1924

Pale pink satin sleeveless dress, blousy bodice with metallic lace underbodice, dropped waistline with sash, starburst pattern on sides of bodice.
est. $400–$600 sold: $1265
Skinner 9/14/2000

ZUCKERMAN, BEN

Coat, 1950s

Navy bouclé wool, wide collar, high waist.
est. $100–$150 sold: $201
William Doyle Galleries 12/6/1995

Cocktail Dress, 1960s

Black and white tweed wool sleeveless, knee-length sheath with rounded neckline and front slit pockets, matching hip-length jacket, fur collar.
est. $200–$400 sold: $345
Skinner 9/14/2000

ZUCKERMAN, RENE

Coat, 1960s

Black wool with long sleeves and jeweled buttons up the front.
est. not available sold: $495
The Paper Bag Princess 11/1/1996

Z

Glossary of the World's Most Collectible and Influential Fashion Designers

ADOLFO, F. SARDIÑA (1933-) Cuban from Cardenas, Cuba, naturalized in the USA in 1958. He began his career as an apprentice millinery designer for Bergdorf Goodman, 1948–1951, as well as at **Balenciaga** salon, Paris, 1950–1952. He introduced his first millinery label as **Adolfo of Emme** at Bergdorf Goodman, 1951–1958. He had worked as an unpaid assistant for a time with the house of **Chanel,** 1956–1957. He established his own millinery salon in New York in 1962 followed by the introduction of his women's custom clothing. He designed hats for **Norman Norell** to complement **Norell's** collections in the early 1960s. He introduced menswear in 1978 along with a line of scarves. He was known for his beautiful womenswear knits and millinery designs, often creating complete ensembles with matching handbags. His designs were popularized by Nancy Reagan's preference for his tidy little ladylike suits. He retired in 1993.

ADRI (ADRIENNE STECKLING) (1934-) American from Saint Joseph, Missouri. She began her career designing for **B. H. Wragge,** 1960–1967, then created her own line, **Clothes Circuit** for **Anne Fogarty, Inc.** In 1975 she introduced **Adri Clotheslab, Inc.** where she continued to design practical, interchangeable knit separates in mainly natural fabric until the 1980s.

ADRIAN, GILBERT (ADRIAN ADOLPH GREENBURG) (1903-1959) American from Naugatuck, Connecticut, of German-Jewish parents. The son of a milliner best known for his costume design work for MGM Studios, 1928–1939, resigning after a stormy confrontation with Louis B. Mayer over the costume designs for Greta Garbo in *Two-Faced Woman*. His successor at MGM Studios was his assistant, "**Irene**" **Lentz.** He successfully recruited assistant designer **Chris Ghiatis** away from **Irene Lentz's** ready-to-wear business in 1941–1951, making **Ghiatis** a very handsome offer to join him as an assistant designer. **Stanley Marcus** of Neiman Marcus referred to **Chris Ghiatis** as **Adrian's** "ghost designer." He opened his first expensive ready-to-wear and custom clothing salon in the Coreen Griffith Building on Shuterville Drive in Beverly Hills, California, but it closed shortly thereafter. His second location, on Wilshire Boulevard in Beverly Hills in 1942, was much more successful and produced beautiful ready-to-wear and custom garments which he sold in his salon, as well as in specialty departments in more than 46 retail businesses throughout the United States until 1952. A heart attack in 1952 caused him to retire abruptly and move with his wife to a plantation in Brazil. He died seven years later. His signature look was that of glamorous silk and chiffon gowns, as well as beautifully tailored women's suits with intricate use of inset fabric and unparalleled design.

AGNÈS B (1941-) Born **Agnès Troublé,** married **Christian Bourgois** in 1958, divorced, and married **Jean René Claret de Fleurieu** in 1980. She is French from Versailles, France. She began her career as a junior fashion editor at *Elle* magazine, Paris, 1964, then worked as a press attaché and buyer for **Dorothée Bis,** Paris, 1964–1965, then as a freelance designer for **Limitex, Pierre d'Alby, V de V,** and **Eversbin,** Paris, 1966–1975. She set up her company **CMC (Comptoir Mondial de Création),** and opened her first boutique in Les Halles, Paris, in 1975, specializing in generic women's sportswear and separates with a defined French flare. She also opened a secondhand shop in Les Halles, Paris, 1977, followed by her first American shop in the SoHo district in New York in 1980. Opened men's and children's boutiques in 1981. Has shops worldwide including four in the United States.

ALAÏA, AZZEDINE (1940-) Tunisian from Tunis, Tunisia, lives in Paris. He had been a design assistant for the house of **Dior, Guy Laroche,** and **Thierry Mugler,** 1957–1960. He introduced his first ready-to-wear in Paris, 1980, and his first show was held in New York at Bergdorf Goodman in 1982. Internationally known for his work in Lycra and knitwear, he fused his talent in sculpture with his design in knitwear creating an exquisite female form. He describes himself as a "bâtisseur," or builder, rather than couturier. Known as "The King of Cling" and a favorite designer among supermodels. Although his designs realized the height of their popularity in the mid-1980s, they saw a tremendous revitalization in the fall of 2000 with a major retrospective of his designs at the Guggenheim Museum in New York, which inspired an entire new generation of devotees, as well as many young contemporary designers to pay tribute to his design brilliance with derivative influences from his early work in the 1980s which appear in their new collections.

ALBINI, WALTER (1941–1983) Italian from Busto Arsizio, Italy. He began as a fashion illustrator for numerous Italian magazines. He joined **Krizia** in 1960 where he continued as a design consultant until 1963 when he joined **Basile,** where he produced several ready-to-wear collections prior to launching his own fashion business in 1965. **Rifat Ozbek** designed for **Walter Albini for Trell,** Milan, 1977–1980. Most noted for his glamorous designs from luxurious fabrics which were widely influenced by his passion for the looks of classic films from the 1930s and 1940s. His work was cut short by an untimely early death.

ALDRICH, LARRY (1906–) American, the son of Russians, born in America. He founded his own manufacturing company in 1927, in New York, hiring numerous designers, and in 1933 he introduced his own collection, taking over as head of design. His name did not appear on his label until the 1940s. **Marie McCarthy** began designing for the firm in 1957. Noted for his simple, sophisticated day dresses and suits throughout the 1950s and for his allover beaded dresses in the 1960s. An avid contemporary art collector, he commissioned **Julian Tomchin,** an American textile designer, to create an Op Art fabric based on a painting by **Bridget Riley** in 1960. In 1964 **Aldrich** was the silent partner behind ready-to-wear designer **Wilson Folman, Inc.** until **Wilson** closed the company in 1972. **Aldrich** closed his company in 1972 as well and opened the **Aldrich Museum of Contemporary Art** in Ridgefield, Connecticut. He also designed for **McCall's Patterns** from the 1960s to the early 1970s.

ALFARO, VICTOR (1965–) From Mexico, immigrated to the United States in 1981. Known best for his beautiful eveningwear which he established in New York in the early 1990s.

ALLARD, LINDA (1940–) American from Akron, Ohio, a design assistant to **Ellen Tracy,** New York, 1962–1964, then became design director in 1964 and has been the name behind **Ellen Tracy** ever since. They became known for their sportswear, blouses, jackets, and trousers. In 1984 the **Ellen Tracy** company added **Allard's** name to their label.

AMIES, HARDY (EDWIN HARDY AMIES) (1909–) He began his early career as a schoolteacher in Antibes, 1927, then became an office assistant in Bendorf, Germany, 1928–1930, and finally a trainee at W. E. T. Avery LTD, Birmingham, England, 1930–1934. He entered the world of fashion in 1934, succeeding **Digby Morton** as the managing designer for **Lachasse,** a quintessential English women's ready-to-wear manufacturer which specialized in refined wool and tweed suits and dresses. He became managing director/designer for **Lachasse** in 1935–1939, before serving in the British Army Intelligence Corps, 1939–1945; lieutenant colonel, head of Special Forces Commission to Belgium, 1944. He also worked for the house of **Worth** and for the British government Utility Scheme during World War II. After the war he established his own couture house, **Hardy Amies Ltd.,** 1946, introducing ready-to-wear in 1950. By 1955 he was awarded the Royal Warrant as Dressmaker to HM Queen Elizabeth II of England. He had already created numerous outfits for the then Princess Elizabeth's royal tour of Canada. Perhaps most notably, he created the gown for Elizabeth II's Silver Jubilee portrait that was seen all over the world and depicted on all sorts of tourist memorabilia, including beautiful English biscuit tins. He was the first women's couturier to introduce a menswear collection in 1959. His company, then famous for its finely tailored wool/tweed ladies' suits and impeccable menswear created for the individual customer, was purchased by **Debenhams, 1973–1981,** then reacquired by **Hardy Amies** in 1981. His menswear licenses, including licenses for small leather goods, ties, knitwear, and shirts in Canada, Australia, and Japan have been far more lucrative than his women's couture. In May 2001 the UK marketing group **Cardington** bought the house of **Hardy Amies** for an undisclosed amount, and it is speculated that they are likely to give the classic brand a makeover following the acquisition.

ANTHONY, JOHN (1938-) American from New York. He is recognized for his subtle, understated clothes. He established **John Anthony, Inc.** in New York in 1971, creating practical cardigans and pullovers teamed with skirts, as well as simple evening gowns which he designed by using alternative daywear fabrics. He also designed a less expensive ready-to-wear line of separates in the 1980s, **John Anthony for Friedricks Sport.** He also designed for **Vogue Patterns** from the 1970s–1980s. He is still in business today with this salon in New York, offering his classic eveningwear to his private clients.

ANTONELLI, MARIA (1903-1969) Italian from Rome. She is most noted for her suits and dresses of the 1950s. **André Laug** produced nine couture collections and five ready-to-wear collections for **Maria Antonelli,** 1964–1968.

ARDEN, ELIZABETH, AND ELIZABETH ARDEN COUTURE, NEW YORK Her real name was **Florence Nightingale Graham** (1878–1966), a Canadian from Woodbridge, Ontario, Canada, who immigrated to the United States in the early 1900s. She had worked as a beauty treatment girl for **Eleanor Adair,** New York, prior to founding **Elizabeth Arden, New York** in 1910 as a cosmetic company. The company name had been inspired by a Tennyson poem, *Enoch Arden,* and **Graham's** preference for the name Elizabeth. An original proponent of exercise, she opened a spa and health retreat in Maine in 1934 and developed a line of cosmetics for the film industry which would not run under the hot studio lights. As well as being a dominant force in the cosmetic and fragrance industry, the **Elizabeth Arden** salon/boutiques carried various designers including **Sarmi, Donald Brooks, John Moore,** and **Scaasi,** as well as manufacturing garments and accessories under the company's own label. From 1943–1945 **Charles James** was appointed to design for **Arden,** as well as to oversee the installation of her custom department. Prior to completing the collection, however, the two had a professional falling-out and the collection was never completed. **Antonio del Castillo** also designed for **Elizabeth Arden** (couture and ready-to-wear), **New York,** 1945–1950, as did **Oscar de la Renta,** 1963–1965.

ARMANI, GIORGIO (1934-) Italian from Piacenza, Italy, who designed for **Nino Cerruti** 1960–1970, then introduced **Armani** menswear collection in 1974 and womenswear in 1975. Barneys New York was the first store to carry the **Armani** line. **Armani** came to the forefront of fashion with the look he created for Richard Gere in *American Gigolo.* He is recognized for his impeccable tailoring and beautiful eveningwear, a look which is unmistakably **Armani.**

ARNOLD & FOX (SEE HERBERT KASPER) An American ready-to-wear manufacturer for whom **Herbert Kasper** designed, 1954–1964. Other divisions are known as **Kasper for Arnold & Fox Designs Inc.**

ASHPOOL, JOHN (DATES UNKNOWN) American ready-to-wear designer in 1970s through the early 1980s. He is credited with his creative hippie-look ensembles similar to contemporaries of the times such as **Scott Barrie** and **Stephen Burrows.**

ASSATLY, RICHARD (1960-) American from Brooklyn, New York, noted for his dignified eveningwear and his work for **Simplicity Patterns.**

ATWOOD, BRIAN (1968-) American from Chicago. After graduating from the Fashion Institute of Technology, New York, **Atwood** fell into modeling. Blessed with exceptional good looks and a charismatic smile, he was working in Milan in 1996 when hit with the epiphany that what he truly wanted was to be a designer. He handwrote his résumé and sent his portfolio over to his all-time design idol **Gianni Versace** who, in a stroke of fortune that young design hopefuls don't dare to dream of, hired him immediately to work on the **Versus** line. **Atwood** has worked with the house of **Versace** since 1996, initially designing the retail **Versus** collection before assuming the position of **Versace's** chief designer of women's footwear and accessories, creating alluring luxury accessories to complement the house's highly provocative collections. While continuing as the chief designer of accessories at **Versace,** in the spring of 2001 **Atwood** launched his first private collection of sinfully exotic women's footwear at Milan's exclusive Nilufar Boutique, which offers modern furniture and other rare and beautiful objects—not such an unusual venue when you understand **Atwood's** philosophy of design as one of fusing beauty, fashion, art, and functionality. His design approach harks back to the original work of such brilliant footwear designers as **Roger Vivier, Salvatore Ferragamo,** and **Edward Rayne,** considering each model as a single work of art. His seminal collection offered evening sandals in bleached frog skin with handpainted gold and silver spots and a jeweled brooch, a psychedelic tie dyed pony-hair stiletto boot with laser cut lace, a distressed crocodile mid-heel mod boot which was treated to look like denim, a patchwork suede boot handpainted by an Italian artisan, and a black sling-back stiletto called "Dangerous Blossom," accented with a lace flower handmade in Cantu, Italy, a town renowned for its exquisite lace work. The petals of the Dangerous Blossom's flower take over three hours to create, requiring as much as 30 hours for a single pair of shoes. **Atwood** combs the globe for beautiful antique and exotic inspiration, translating these foreign motifs and artifacts into edgy and sophisticated designs which remain true to the spirit of the times or place from which he borrows, yet supersede the present and transcend tomorrow so a woman will desire to wear them now and as much again in 20 years. The only thing missing from **Atwood's** fairy tale footwear collection is the glass dome which should accompany each design to place over them!

AUJARD, CHRISTIAN (1945-1977) A French designer who specialized in menswear and womenswear, as well as having **Christian Aujard Boutiques.** The house of **Guy Laroche** produced a licensed ready-to-wear collection for **Christian Aujard.**

AYTON, SYLVIA (1937-) British fashion teacher and freelance designer of ready-to-wear.

AZAGURY, JACQUES (1958-) Moroccan from Casablanca, Morocco, educated in England, he began his career working in a London clothing factory. He had a celebrated diploma show in 1978 and is recognized for his glamorous eveningwear.

BADGLEY MISCHKA A couture and ready-to-wear company of two partners, **Mark Badgley** (1961–) American from Burlington, Wisconsin, and **James Mischka** (1960–) American from East Saint Louis, Illinois. **Badgley** worked for **Donna Karan,** 1985–1988, and **Mischka** designed for **Willi Smith,** in New York, 1985–1988. In 1988 the two former Parsons School of Design, New York, classmates teamed up to launch **Badgley Mischka** which is internationally celebrated for their beautiful beaded eveningwear and has a tremendous Hollywood following. They were acquired by the German fashion house of **Escada** in the late 1990s.

BAILY, CHRISTIANE (1932-) Frenchwoman from Lyon, France. She began her career in the early 1950s as a model working for **Balenciaga, Chanel,** and **Dior** in 1957. By 1961 she had moved into fashion design working as a freelance designer with **Michèle Roseir** and **Chloé.** In 1962 she collaborated on a ready-to-wear collection called **Emma Christie** with friend and fellow model **Emmanuelle Khanh,** whom she had met while working at **Balenciaga.** The **Emma Christie** label received high critical acclaim and was considered by many to be revolutionary in the ready-to-wear markets in the early 1960s; however, it never received substantial commercial success.

BAKST, LÉON (1866-1924) Russian from St. Petersburg, Russia. He worked as a court painter and costume and scenery designer for the Imperial Academy of Arts in St. Petersburg. In 1908 he went to Paris as a scenery painter and costume designer for the Ballets Russes. In 1913 he did some design work for **Paquin** in Paris, and continued to produce plays for the Paris Opera, as well as founding a Liberal School of Painting in St. Petersburg. His costume designs for the stage were widely influential in the fashion world throughout the period.

BALENCIAGA, CRISTOBAL (1895-1972) Spaniard from San Sebastian, Spain. He established a tailoring business with sponsorship of the **Marquesa de Casa Torres,** San Sebastian, 1915–1921, then became the founder and designer of his second company, **Eisa Fashion House** in Barcelona and Madrid, 1922–1931, named after his mother's given name **Eisa.** He founded **Maison Balenciaga,** Paris, 1937–1940, and acted as its director. It closed as most couture houses did during World War II, opening again 1945–1968. He was respected for his proficient tailoring and his pictorial imagination. He created exceptional beaded eveningwear with a flare for the Spanish vernacular. **Maison Balenciaga** saw a tremendous revitalization in the late 1990s and in 2000 with the inventive and youthful design work of **Nicolas Ghesquière.** At the time of this writing it was reported that a deal was in the works for **Nicholas Ghesquière** to leave **Balenciaga** and launch his private collection with backing from **The Gucci Group NV.**

BALLERINO, LOUELLA (DATES UNKNOWN) American from California. She began her career teaching fashion history while working part-time as a salesclerk in a boutique where she occasionally sold some of her own creations. In 1938 she went into business for herself. Her designs were derivative of her art history background and ethnic-inspired prints and images. Her work was noted for her peasant dresses with bold prints, as well as her striped maillot in 1947. She was a contemporary of **Claire McCardell.**

BALLY, CARL FRANZ (1821-1898) Swiss from Schönenwerd, Switzerland. The son of a silk ribbon weaver/manufacturer, he began to manufacture shoes in the family company in the mid-1800s after purchasing a beautiful collection of shoes for his wife from one of his clients in Paris which had been buying the company's elastic tapes. The company is famous for its remarkable quality and it had become an important contributor to the ready-to-wear shoe industry by the early 1920s, and is still highly regarded today by connoisseurs of both men's and women's shoes.

BALMAIN, PIERRE (1914-1982) French from St. Jean de Maurienne. **Balmain** served as a freelance sketch artist for **Robert Piguet** in Paris, 1934; assistant designer **Molyneux,** Paris, 1934–1938; designer for **Lucien Lelong,** working alongside **Christian Dior** from 1939 to the early 1940s; founder and director of **Maison Balmain** in Paris, 1945–1982, and **Balmain Fashions** in New York, 1951–1955. The look of Balmain in the mid-to-late 1940s was very similar to that of **Dior's. Balmain** is celebrated for beautifully tailored, feminine silhouettes and exquisite eveningwear. **Eric Mortensen** worked with **Balmain** from 1948, and after **Balmain's** death in 1982 the business continued under **Mortensen's** design direction. French designer **Dominique Morlotti** was in charge of menswear for **Balmain** from 1980–1983. **Mortensen** was replaced by **Hervé Pierre** when French financier **Alain Chevalier** acquired the **Balmain** company in January of 1990. The ready-to-wear division was then headed by Scottish-born **Alistar Blair. Oscar de la Renta** is presently the design director and has designed for both couture and ready-to-wear since 1993. **Bernard Sanz** was named as the menswear designer. The company presently has over 150 licenses worldwide.

BAMBERGER, JEAN-PIERRE (MICHÈLE ROSEIR AND V DE V (VETEMENTS DE VACANCES) A French women's ready-to-wear and sportswear company founded in Paris by **Michèle Roseir** along with partner **Jean-Pierre Bamberger** in 1962.

BANKS, JEFF (BORN 1943-) Welsh from Ebbw Vale, Wales. A designer and retailer who opened his first shop called **Clobber** in London in 1964. The shop offered both his designs and those of other British designers. He went into business in 1974 with **Warehouse Utility,** a youth-oriented chain of shops in Britain that specialized in inexpensive women's ready-to-wear clothing. He also worked as a freelance designer for **Liberty of London** in the mid-1970s.

BANKS, JEFFREY (1955-) American men's sportswear designer who, after graduating from Parsons, New York, worked as an assistant to **Ralph Lauren** (1972–1974) and **Calvin Klein** (1974–1976) before becoming a designer for **Nik Nik,** 1976–1978, then for **Concorde International, Alixandre,** and **Merona Sport.** He launched his own men's ready-to-wear company in 1980, with the introduction of boyswear later in 1980. **Isaac Mizrahi** designed for him in 1984 before moving to **Calvin Klein.** He formed a joint venture with **Takihyo, Inc.,** Hong Kong, 1988, and became a design consultant for **Herman Geist,** New York, 1990. Over the years he has introduced numerous other products to his line including men's neckwear and licensed eyewear. Considered an all-American menswear designer in the tradition of **Ralph Lauren,** his customer demographic is still slightly more youthful and geared toward a broader mass market.

BANTON, TRAVIS (1894-1958) American from Waco, Texas. **Banton** began his career with a dress manufacturer in New York, then moved to Hollywood where he flourished as a costume designer in 1924 for **Paramount Pictures. Banton** moved to **20th Century-Fox** in 1939, then went on to work for **Universal**

Studios, 1945–1948. He continued designing his couture and ready-to-wear collections while working for the studios, and he was known for dressing women in men's clothing, as well as for his sensuous bias-cut satin gowns. He was likewise famous for his designs for Marlene Dietrich, Mae West, Claudette Colbert, and Carole Lombard, as well as for creating costumes for more than 200 films throughout his career.

BARRIE, SCOTT (1946-1993) American, from Philadelphia, Pennsylvania. He was a designer for **Allen Cole Boutique,** New York, 1966–1969. He launched **Barrie Sport, Ltd.,** New York, 1969–1982, **Barrie Plus,** and introduced a menswear collection in 1974. He moved to Milan, 1982, to form **Scott Barrie Italy Srl.,** 1986–1988, and was a freelance designer for **Krizia,** Milan. Recognized for his youthful approach to fashion in the 1970s and 1980s along with **Stephen Burrows** and **Giorgio di Sant' Angelo. Barrie** was awarded a Coty Award for his women's ready-to-wear designs.

BARTHEROTTE, BENOIR. (SEE ESTEREL, JACQUES)

BARTLETT, JOHN (1964-) American from Cincinnati, Ohio. He worked for **Ronaldus Shmask** and **Willi Wear** before establishing his own menswear line in 1992 and womenswear in 1995. His work is often compared to **Jean-Paul Gaultier** and **Vivienne Westwood,** along with the work of **John Galliano,** always exhibiting a flare for functionality.

BARTON, ALIX. (SEE GRÉS. MME "ALIX")

BASILE (BAH-SIL'-LEE) A ready-to-wear manufacturing corporation founded in the late 1950s, Italy. The company has played host to numerous designers over the years, including **Walter Albini** in 1963, who produced several ready-to-wear collections prior to launching his own fashion business in 1965, and **Angelo Tarlazzi** as a freelance designer in the late 1970s–early 1980s. Best known in the 1970s–1980s for their careerwear, blazers, suits, cocktail, and dinnerwear.

BASS, WALTER (WILLIAM) An American women's ready-to-wear manufacturer (1940s–1970s) founded by **Walter Bass. Rudi Gernreich** joined the company (1948–1951) designing ready-to-wear including **Bass's** client **Jax,** a Beverly Hills boutique. **Chris Ghiatis** worked as a freelance designer for the firm's sportswear collection, 1960–1962.

BATES, JOHN (1938-) English from Ponteland, Northumberland, England. He began designing for the British company **Jean Varon** in 1964 and stayed through the 1970s, known for youthquake designs such as micro minis and catsuits, empire-line, and embroidered eveningwear, as well as a bikini dress that featured two halves joined by transparent netting. **Bates** also designed the costumes for Emma Peel in the British series, *The Avengers.*

BECKERS, JEANNE (SEE PAQUIN, MADAME)

BEENE, GEOFFREY (1927-) American from Hynesville, Louisiana. Although he had originally intended to become a doctor, he has continued to celebrate an illustrious fashion career. He began his career as a display assistant at **I. Magnin, Los Angeles,** 1946; apprentice tailor, **Molyneux,** 1948–1950; assistant to **Mildred O'Quinn, Samuel Winston,** and **Harmay,** 1950–1951; and assistant designer for **Harmon** ready-to-wear, 1951–1958. He was appointed designer at **Teal Traina,** New York, 1958–1963, prior to founding his own fashion house, **Geoffrey Beene, Inc.,** 1963. He introduced menswear in 1970; **Beenebag Sportswear,** 1971; and opened his first boutique in New York in 1989. **Issey Miyake** designed for **Beene,** 1969–1970, before launching his own line. Considered to be one of the best *American* couture designers living today, his designs are always delivered artistically and are seamlessly simple and opulent in the same brushstroke. Famous for culling his inspiration from everyday life as well as historical references, his work continues to be innovative and surprising.

BELLVILLE SASSOON-LORCAN MULLANY British couture and ready-to-wear firm, founded by **Bellinda Bellville** in 1958. **Bellinda Bellville** retired from the company in 1983. **David Sassoon** (1932–) of London and **Lorcan Mullany** (1953–). Before joining **David Sassoon's** firm in 1987, **Mullany** had designed for **Bill Gibb, Ronald Joyce,** and **Hardy Amies.** The company was then renamed **Bellville Sassoon-Lorcan Mullany.** The collaborated efforts of this design firm is famous for beautiful evening and cocktail attire, which is known to London society ladies, including the late Diana, Princess of Wales.

BENENSON, FIRA (1900-1977) Russian, immigrated to the United States in the 1920s. Her father was a real estate, oil, and precious metals tycoon in Russia. She ran the **Bonwit Teller's Salon de Couture,** 1934–1940, overseeing the construction of Paris models of designs such as **Lanvin, Schiaparelli,** and **Chanel.** During the war when Paris fashion became inaccessible, she began designing two collections annually for **Bonwit Teller.** She opened her own salon, 1948–1954, in New York and gained a reputation for her dressmaking details such as shirring, tucking, and the use of appliqué.

BENOIT BARTHEROTTE (SEE ESTEREL, JACQUES) Originally the house of **Jacques Esterel,** renamed **Benoit Bartherotte** by **Esterel's** partner **Jean-Baptisle Doumeng** after **Esterel's** death in 1974.

BERETTA, ANNE-MARIE (1937-) Frenchwoman from Béziers, France. Her career began in 1955 while working for **Jacques Esterel** as a designer. She later joined the manufacturer **Pierre d'Alby** in 1965 designing a highly successful collection of brown linen garments. She established her own label in 1974. In addition to designing for **Ramosport, Macdouglas,** and outerwear for **Abe Schrader,** she also designs ski-wear and contributes to **Max Mara.**

BERIN, HARVEY (DATES UNKNOWN) American, **Berin** opened his manufacturing business in 1921, appointing **Karen Stark** as head designer with her name on his label. An avid follower of Paris fashion, he reinterpreted the looks of **Faith, Dior, Balenciaga, Lelong,** and **Patou. Berin's** designs by **Karen Stark** were classic, and favored by Pat Nixon, Bess Truman, and Lady Bird Johnson. Designer **Anne Fogarty** worked as a fit-model for **Berin** in the mid-1940s. Between 1940–1950, Berin was associated with the women's ready-to-wear manufacturer **Carolyn Modes** as a freelance designer. Renowned for embellished cocktail attire and dressy daytime ensembles, he closed his business in 1970.

BERKETEX (SEE NORMAN HARTNELL) A British women's ready-to-wear manufacturing company. **Norman Hartnell** designed for the company in the late 1940s.

BERNARD, AUGUSTA (AGUSTABERNARD) (DATES UNKNOWN) Frenchwoman from Provence, France. She was most famous for her beautiful bias-cut gowns which she cut on the cross-grain achieving a graceful fluid drape and great elasticity. A contemporary in the early and mid-1930s to **Callot Soeurs, Louisboulanger, Vionnet, Schiaparelli,** and **Chanel.** Noted for a neoclassic gown which was chosen by *Vogue* magazine as the most beautiful dress in 1932.

BESSIE, AVERADO (DATES UNKNOWN) An Italian who since the early 1960s has been recognized for his women's ready-to-wear designs in brightly printed silk jersey, often mistaken for the work of **Emilio Pucci** or **Leonard.**

BETSEY, BUNKEY, AND NIMI (SEE BETSEY JOHNSON)

BIAGIOTTI, LAURA (1943-) Italian from Rome, she originally joined her mother's small clothing company, but left in 1972 to establish her own design company specializing in knitwear.

BIBA (SEE BARBARA HULANICKI)

BIKKEMBERGS, DIRK (1962-) German from Flavorsheim, Germany. He formed his own company in 1985 after spending several years as a freelance designer for several European fashion houses. He specializes in men's ready-to-wear and launched a womenswear line in Paris in 1993. He is recognized for his military influences.

BIS, DOROTHÉE (DOH-ROH-TAY BEECE) A French designer/manufacturing operation founded in 1960 by manufacturer **Elie Jacobson** with his wife **Jacqueline** as the designer. It was highly successful in the 1960s and 1970s, specializing in colorful knitwear.

BLACKWELL, MR. (DATES UNKNOWN) American from Brooklyn, New York. He was a former child actor, turned designer and style-guru, and publishes his annual "**Worst-Dressed List**" in Hollywood. He did have his own designs during the 1960s through the 1970s which were primarily cocktail attire which favored black, and were somewhat on the garish side.

BLAHNIK, MANOLO (1943-) Spaniard from Santa Cruz, Canary Islands. An unparalleled shoe designer whose instantly recognizable style remains constant today. Discovered by **Diana Vreeland,** he was encouraged to open his first boutique in London in 1973. He has designed shoes for **Ossie Clark, Jean Muir, Perry Ellis, Calvin Klein, Zandra Rhodes, Yves Saint Laurent,** and **Rifat Ozbek,** as well as designing the **Jellies** sandals for **Fiorucci** in the early 1970s. He continues to design in the luxury category today, creating beautiful sexy women's shoes and handbags.

BLAIR, ALISTAR Scottish. Blair headed the ready-to-wear division of **Pierre Balmain** in 1990, prior to seceding to **Oscar de la Renta** in 1993.

BLASS, BILL (1922-) American from Fort Wayne, Indiana. He worked as a sketch artist for **David Crystal,** 1940–1941, and after World War II he designed for **Anna Miller & Co.** After the merger of **Anna Miller** and **Maurice Rentner, Ltd.** in 1962, **Blass** was appointed vice president, then bought the company in 1970 renaming it **Bill Blass,** where he continues to design today. He is revered for his fine tailoring and beautiful eveningwear.

BLOTTA, ANTHONY (1888-1971) From Italy, he immigrated to the United States, arriving in New York to open his first manufacturing business in 1919; however, he did not become recognized by the fashion press until the 1940s. Often compared to **Norell** for his use of intricate tailoring, ornamental pockets, and button details. He is noted for upscale day suits and evening attire with jeweled buttons and interesting décolletage.

BLUMARINE (ANNA MOLINARI) A ready-made house founded by **Anna Molinari** in 1977 is still very active today with **Anna Molinari** boutiques and departments in major shops around the world. It is known for its youthful upscale separates and beautiful marriage of vibrant colors, prints, and beadwork. It is known as the rich girl's **Betsey Johnson.**

BODY MAP A British design team, **Stevie Stewart** and **David Holah,** both born in 1958, British from London, England. The two met at Middlessex Polytechnic and forged a partnership which founded **Body Map,** 1982. The name was inspired by Italian artist Enrico Job's work known as a "Body Map," comprised of thousands of pictures of his anatomy in a two-dimensional collage. **Body Map,** 1982–1985, is recognized for their work in black, white, and cream jersey with bold design and oversized construction.

BOHAN, MARC (1926-) Frenchman from Paris, France, who between 1945 and 1958 worked for many prominent fashion houses—**Robert Piguet,** Paris, as assistant designer 1945–1949; **Molyneux,** Paris, 1949–1951; **Madeleine de Rauch,** Paris, 1952; and **Maison Patou,** Paris, 1954–1958. **Gérard Pipart** worked under **Bohan** while he was at **Patou.** He had briefly opened his own Paris salon in 1953, producing only one collection. He was head designer for **Dior** in London, 1958–1960, and head designer and art director for **Dior,** Paris, succeeding **Yves Saint Laurent,** 1960–1989. He was replaced at **Dior** by **Gianfranco Ferré** in 1989. **Bohan** became fashion director for **Norman Hartnell** in London, 1990, resigning in 1992.

BOSS, HUGO A German menswear company founded in 1923 by **Hugo Boss** which specialized in men's work clothes and raincoats. **Hugo Boss's** son **Siegfried Boss** and son-in-law **Eugen Holy** assumed direction of the company in 1948 and extended production to include uniforms, childrenswear, and men's suits. In 1972 **Hugo Boss's** grandchildren **Jochen** and **Uwe Holy** became chairmen of the company and began to export to Austria and Switzerland. Export was expanded throughout the 1970s to include Belgium, the Netherlands, Scandinavia, and England. By 1976 the company had begun to sponsor sports car racing events. **Hugo Boss Sarl, Paris** was created in 1977 and the company also began exporting to the United States and Canada. They introduced a men's shirt line in 1981, and by 1984 were sponsoring tennis and golf, followed by the introduction of their polo and sweatshirt collections. An American subsidiary was created in 1986 and by 1989 **Hugo Boss** had merged with **Joseph & Feiss,** an American manufacturing company. The new company then introduced numerous licenses including sunglasses and a fragrance. The company was acquired in 1991 by **Marzotto SPA,** a North Italian textile company. They opened a giant **Hugo Boss** flagship store in New York on Fifth Avenue in April 2001.

BOTTEGA VENETTA An Italian luxury leather goods manufacturer well-known for their expensive woven leather handbags, fine travel goods, and small leather accessories, as well as a limited collection of ready-to-wear leather garments.

BOUCHERON, CHARLES (SEE CHARLES JAMES)

BOUÉ, SYLVIE (1880-?) AND JEANNE (1881-?) (BOUÉ SOEURS) A French couture house founded in Paris, early 1910–1930, by **Sylvie** and **Jeanne Boué.** Like designers **John Redfern** and **Lucile, Boué Soeurs** moved their couture operations to New York during WWI. Contemporaries to **Paul Poiret, Callot Soeurs,** and **Mme. Paquin, Boué Soeurs** were renowned for their beautiful romantic tea gowns in luxurious fabrics such as silk organdies and lace which often culled their inspiration from classic costumes in historical paintings.

BOULANGER, LOUISE (1878-1950) Frenchwoman from Paris. She apprenticed with French couturier **Madame Madeline Chéruit** in 1891 at age 13, and founded her own couture house, **Louiseboulanger,** in 1923. Her designs were influenced by her early apprenticeship with **Madame Chéruit** and her deep appreciation for the designs of **Madeline Vionnet.** She became famous for her graceful bias-cut evening gowns and her above-the-knee dresses which cut long to the ankle in the back, as well as her finely tailored women's suits which were complemented by hats designed by **Caroline Beboux.**

BOUQUIN, JEAN (1936-) Frenchman from Paris, France. A luxury women's ready-to-wear designer and retailer, **Bouquin** opened his first shop in St. Tropez, followed by **Mayfair,** a boutique he opened in Paris after his tremendous success in St. Tropez. His opulent designs in silk panne velvets, embroideries, and feathers revolutionized the rich hippie chic movement in the late 1960s through the mid 1970s, and although he was only in business for approximately seven years he gained a tremendous reputation for capturing the true bohemian spirit of the European rich jet-set society.

BRIGANCE, TOM (DATES UNKNOWN) American who is famous for his work in women's sportswear in the 1950s–1960s. He was the head designer for **Frank Gallant,** as well as designing for **Sinclaire, Sportsmaker, Fonde,** and **Gabar.** He was one of the most important bathing suit designers of the 1960s.

BRIONI An Italian men's made-to-measure and off-the-rack design and manufacturing company founded in 1954 by **Nazareno Fonticoli** (1906–1981), Italian from Penne, Italy, and **Gaetano Savini** (1910–1987), Italian from Rome, Italy. The company is credited with presenting the first-ever men's catwalk show in 1952. Famous for their progressive tailoring and early designs including a futuristic space-age suit in 1954, Maharajah styles in the 1960s, as well as the now iconic look of actor Pierce Brosnan's portrayal of the ultimate secret agent in the *James Bond* series. Their expensive finely tailored men's suits became the must-have for those who could afford them in the 1980s and 1990s along with contemporaries **Giorgio Armani** and **Gianni Versace.** The company is still in operation today creating a complete line of men's suits, sportswear, and accessories.

BROOKS, DONALD (1928-) American from New York. He held a series of positions as a sketch artist and designer for undistinguished manufacturers in New York. By 1958–1964, **Brooks** had moved to **Townley Frocks** as the successor to **Claire McCardell,** after her untimely death in 1958. He debuted his own label in 1969 and continued to design for various other firms creating sleepwear for **Maidenform,** furs for **Coopchic-Forrest,** and **Bonwit Teller,** as well as fabrics and bedding for **Burlington.** In 1990, he became fabric and color consultant for **Ann Taylor** stores.

BROOKS BROTHERS Established in 1818, they are an American company revered for their distinctive British look, popularizing the button-down shirt collar in 1900, **Harris Tweed** jackets from Scotland, and the Polo Coat. They also introduced American women to the look of men's tailoring in 1950.

BRUYÉRE, MARIE-LOUISE (DATES UNKNOWN, EARLY 1900S) French couturier who trained with **Callot Soeurs** then apprenticed with **Jeanne Lanvin** before opening her own salon in the Place Vendrôme, Paris, 1937. A contemporary in Paris of **Chanel, Louiseboulanger, Vionnet, Patou** and **Schiaparelli;** her designs were available in the United States at Saks Fifth Avenue's Salon Moderne, New York, on a made-to-order basis in the late 1930s. Noted for her beautiful women's ready-to-wear and custom designed suits, day and eveningwear.

BUGNAND, BOB (DATES UNKNOWN) Frenchman from Paris, who in the 1960s designed for American ready-to-wear firm, **Sam Friedlander.** He also produced collections of his own from Paris. He was known in the 1960s for his beaded eveningwear.

BURBERRY, THOMAS (1835-1926) English, from Docking, England. He began his career as a drapery maker in 1856 and developed a waterproof fabric which he fashioned into a coat designed after an agricultural smock. He then designed the "trenchcoats" for the British Royal Flying Corps, creating the first trenchcoat which was later trademarked as "**The Burberry.**" The trademark beige, red, and brown check lining was introduced in the 1920s. The **Burberry Company** produces a complete line of fashion and accessories today. **Roberto Menichetti** resigned as creative director in March 2001 and was succeeded in May 2001 by **Christopher Bailey** (age 30) who had been a design director at **Gucci** since 1996.

BURROWS, STEPHEN (1943-) American from Newark, New Jersey. Often compared to **Halston** and **Giorgio di Sant'Angelo, Burrows's** work is recognized for his fluidity, color, and unexpected form. He is distinctly represented by his studded leathers, Native American and cowboy-inspired unisex clothing, as well as silk jersey silhouettes trimmed with contrasting zigzag machine-stitched edges, known as "Lettuce-edged." He began his career designing for **Weber Originals,** New York, 1966–1967; then **Anne Cole,** 1967–1968. In 1968 he co-founded "**O**" **Boutique** in New York with **Roz Rubinstein** (both were classmates at the Fashion Institute of Technology, New York (F.I.T.). In 1969, the two went to work for **Henri Bendel,** New York; **Burrows** as resident designer for **Stephen Burrows's World,** and **Rubinstein** as head accessories buyer until 1973. The team founded their own company in 1973 on Seventh Avenue, New York. They showed their first collection in Paris in November of 1973. Their design team was one of only five American designers to show in Paris that year. The two returned to **Henri Bendel,** 1977–1982. **Rubinstein** and **Burrows** dissolved their partnership and **Burrows** reintroduced himself with ready-to-wear in 1989, then a custom collection in 1990. He returned to Henri Bendel in 1993 with evening dresses and separates. In 1990, he resumed his custom designs, followed by designing a knitwear line for **Tony Lambert, Co.** in 1991.

BYBLOS Founded in 1973 by **Arnoldo** and **Donatella Girombelli** of **Genny SpA** in Ancona, Italy. It became independent of **Genny SpA** in 1983, creating both men's and women's ready-to-wear, with many notable designers including **Gianni Versace,** 1975–1976, and **Guy Paulin, Alan Cleaver,** and **Keith Varty** in 1981. More recently in 1996, American **Richard Tyler** was appointed design director.

CACHAREL, JEAN (JEAN LOUIS HENRI BOUSQUEST) (1932-) Frenchman from Nîmes, France. He adapted his name to **Cacharel** from the name of a Camargué native wild duck and founded **Cacharel,** a women's ready-to-wear company. He began as a designer and cutter for **Jean Jourdan,** Paris (1955–1957) before opening **Société Jean Cacharel** in the early 1960s, hiring **Emmanuell Khan** as a stylist and designer. The company began with a small collection of men's shirts before being contracted in 1965 to rescale and recolor the traditional floral prints of **Liberty of London** into softer, more feminine and contemporary designs for their ladies' shirt and separates departments. This venture proved very successful and a **Cacharel** shirt became a must-have for all fashionable young women. **Cacharel's** sister-in-law, **Corinne Grandval,** joined the company as a designer in 1966. The company introduced a children's line in 1970 and has since created licenses for jeans, socks, and bed linens, as well as numerous fragrances. The head designer today is **Clements Riberio,** whose second collection for the company was considered by the press to be confident and playful in the tradition established by the company. The company is most noted for their blouses and shirts made from **Liberty** fabrics.

CADWALLADER, BROOKE (1908-) **Cadwallader** was born in the Philippines before immigrating with his family to San Francisco, California. He designed fabrics and scarf prints for **Maison Tilly,** Paris, where his prints were used by renowned designers such as **Balenciaga, Schiaparelli, Molyneux, Nettie Rosenkin,** and **Paquin.** He left Paris due to the war, moved to New York and established his own design studio. His specialty scarves were manufactured as limited editions of no more than 1,600 per design. He also manufactured men's ties and silk bathrobes throughout the 1950s.

CALLAGHAN (SEE GIGLI, ROMERO AND ZAMASPORT SPA) A sophisticated, fine-tailored women's ready-to-wear manufacturer based in Milan which has hosted a series of designers including **Walter Albini, Romero,** and **Scott Crolla** throughout the 1990s. **Gianni Versace** had worked as a sketch artist from 1972–1974. **Zamasport SPA** is also a license for production and distribution for various design houses including **Norma Kamali, Romero Gigli, Helmut Lang, Katherine Hamnett,** and **Riccardo Piacenza.**

CALLOT SOEURS A French couture house founded in 1895 by three sisters, Mesdames **Marie Callot Gerber,** the eldest, **Marthe Callot Bertrand,** and **Regina Callot Chantrell.** Their mother had been a lace maker from a family of lace makers, and their father a painter. The house of **Callot Soeurs** originally specialized in creating shirtwaists and lingerie from fine antique lace and ribbon. The company had developed their small storefront into a thriving international couture business by 1914 when it moved to Avenue Matignon (until 1928), opening branches throughout the 1920s in Nice, Biarritz, Buenos Aires, and London. **Marie-Louise Bruyére** trained with **Callot Soeurs** then apprenticed with **Jeanne Lanvin** before opening her own salon in the Place Vendôme, Paris, 1937. **Madeleine Vionnet** also trained at the house of **Callot Soeurs** and credited her ability to create exceptional couture to her time spent at the house. B. Altman carried an exclusive line of seven dresses by **Callot Soeurs** which had originally been designed for actress Cecile Sorel in 1926. A contemporary of **Poiret** and **Paquin, Callot Soeurs** was famous for their one-of-a-kind embroideries, impeccable craftsmanship, perfection in detail, cut, and drape, and for taking inspiration from exotic artifacts, paintings, or places and interpreting these ideas and motifs into intricate beading and embroideries which they used to embellish their opulent evening and reception gowns. **Marie Callot Gerber** was the head designer as well as the director of the company and moved the house once again in 1928 to Avenue Montaigne, passing the house's direction over to her son **Pierre Gerber** in the late 1920s. **Marie Callot Gerber** retired in 1937 and the house merged with the house of **Calvet;** however, their designs continued to bear the **Callot** label until the house of **Calvet** closed in 1948.

CALVET (SEE CALLOT SOEURS) A French couture house which merged with the house of **Callot Soeurs** in 1937; however, their designs continued to bear the **Callot** label until the house of **Calvet** closed in 1948.

CAMERON, DAVID (DATES UNKNOWN) An American ready-to-wear designer who blazed a fast track in the fashion world during the mid-1980s along with contemporaries such as **Stephen Sprouse;** however, he had disappeared from sight by the beginning of the 1990s.

CAPASA, ENNIO AND CARLOS (SEE COSTUME NATIONAL)

CAPUCCI, ROBERT (1929-) Italian from Rome. After working for designer **Emilio Schubert,** he opened his own design studio in Rome at age 21, then moved to Paris, opening a couture salon in 1962. He returned to Italy in 1969 to capture the hearts of the Italian socialites, creating beautiful eveningwear noted for its extraordinary form and cut. He was considered on a par with the masters of cut and form, **Balenciaga** and **Charles James,** and was named the "Givenchy of Rome" by fashion writer Allison Adbueghan in 1957.

CAPRIATTI, CLAIRE (DATES UNKNOWN) American women's ready-to-wear designer and manufacturer who also operated a very successful retail operation in Beverly Hills, California, "**The General Store,**" that offered collections from some of the world's top designers.

CARDIN, PIERRE (1922-) French, born in San Biagio di Callalta, Italy. He began his career as a bookkeeper and tailor's cutter in Vichy, France, 1936–1940, apprenticed with **Manby,** a men's tailor in Vichy, 1939. He became a design assistant for the **Madame Paquin** and **Elsa Schiaparelli** fashion houses, Paris, 1945–1946; then the **House of Dior** as the head of the workroom in 1947, helping to design **Dior's** "New Look." He opened his own design house in 1950, presenting his first menswear collection in 1951, and womenswear in 1957. **André Oliver** joined **Cardin** in 1952. **Oliver** began at **Pierre Cardin** working on the company's first men's collection, eventually taking over men's and women's ready-to-wear collections. In 1987 **Oliver** was named artistic director for **Pierre Cardin** couture and was given complete artistic control under **Cardin's** direction. After **Oliver's** death in 1993, **Cardin** resumed his position as design director. **Jean-Paul Gaultier** handled **Cardin's** manufacturing for **Cardin's** United States Collections in the Philippines, 1974–1975. **Cardin** is known for his early work in costume design for Cocteau's film *Beauty and the Beast*, his Space Age collection, as well as his multitude of licensed products bearing his logo.

CARDINALI An American women's ready-to-wear manufacturer founded in the early 1960s by **Marilyn Lewis** (dates unknown), the wife of actor Harry Lewis and owner of the California-based restaurant chain Hamburger Hamlet. **Marilyn Lewis** named the company after her favorite baseball team, the Cardinals. She really liked the little red cardinal bird they had used as their symbol and had intended to use a similar bird motif on her label. She decided, however, that the silk-woven label with a small red cardinal on it would be too expensive to produce, so she opted to simply use the name of the cardinal with her own slant on the word, creating **Cardinali,** meaning "little cardinal." **Chris Ghiatis** had joined **Cardinali** as the head designer in 1962 after closing his Sunset Plaza custom salon. **Ghiatis** remained the head designer until the business closed in 1972. The company was most noted for their finely tailored suits, day dresses, and eveningwear, as well as for the costumes for Marlo Thomas on three seasons of *That Girl*.

CARNEGIE, HATTIE (HENRIETTA KANENGEISER) (1889-1956) From Vienna, Austria, she began as a hat maker in 1909, opening her custom dress salon in 1918, while still offering millinery. Her design house employed various other notable designers over the years such as **Claire McCardell,** 1938–1940, and later **Travis Banton, Gustave Tassell, Pauline Trigère,** 1940–1941, and **James Galanos** who worked briefly in the fabric department. She is celebrated for her French-inspired, beautifully tailored suits and matching accessories. The house of **Carnegie** continued producing designs after her death until 1965. The wholesale business was finally closed in the early 1970s.

CASHIN, BONNIE (1915-1999) American from Oakland, California. She began her career designing costumes for the Roxy Music Hall Dance Chorus, 1934–1937. In 1937 she designed sportswear for **Adler & Adler** New York. She moved to Hollywood to design costumes for more than 30 motion pictures at 20th Century-Fox, 1943–1949. She returned to New York, launching her own label with partner Philip Sills, 1953–1977. In 1960 **Miles** and **Lillian Cahn** asked **Bonnie Cashin** to design a now legendary, innovative collection of handbags for the company, which she finally had time to commit to in 1962–1974. Her designs included her hallmark striped linen, hand-woven madras plaid, raw silk, and canvas Indian jute or Mexican striped cotton lining, designed by **Dorothy Liebes,** as well as her famous brass toggles on her handbag designs for **Coach** and her outerwear designs for **Philip Sills. Cashin's** designs continue to inspire handbag designs today. **Coach** reissued a collection of four bags originally designed by **Cashin** after a highly successful exhibition of her early work appeared at the museum at The Fashion Institute of Technology, New York in September 2000. After **Philip Sills's** retirement in 1977 **Cashin** designed two lines for **Russ Taylor**—**"Weatherwear"** and **"Cashin Country."** She also created collections of fine cashmere sweaters for **Ballantyne,** Scotland, and handbags for **Meyers,** with the label **Bonnie Cashin for Meyers.** Her designs were in production until 1985 when she formally retired, turning her attention to her philanthropic ventures. She set up Innovative Design Fund to finance "impossible dreams" by providing funding for individuals to manufacture design prototypes in 1979, and in 1992 she set up the annual James Michelin Distinguished Visitor's Lecture Series at Caltech to foster creative interaction between the arts and the sciences.

CASSINI, OLEG (OLEG LOIEWSKI) (1913-) Russian, born in Paris, France. He began his career working in his mother's small dress shop in Florence, then created a small collection of custom-made dresses. His first job had been working as a sketch artist for **Patou** in Paris in the early 1930s. He moved to New York in 1936 working for various design houses until he headed for Hollywood to work for 20th Century-Fox, and in 1940 he became the head of the wardrobe department for Eagle-Lion Studios. He had been hired to replace **Omar Kiam** as **Edith Head's** design assistant. He married actress Gene Tierney and went on to design costumes for her films, most notably, *The Razor's Edge*. He moved back to New York in 1950, concentrating on his private label while still designing for television and the stage. He founded the ready-to-wear company **Casanova** with partner **Paul Portanova,** based on the two men's names. He created the look of Jacqueline Kennedy (Onassis), becoming the official designer of her wardrobe; although her pillbox hat which she wore to her husband's inaugural was actually designed by **Halston** and attributed to **Cassini.**

CASTELBAJAC, JEAN-CHARLES DE (1949-) Moroccan from Casablanca, immigrated to France in the 1950s. He started his career working in his mother's clothing business, then designed several collections for **Pierre d'Alby,** Paris. He opened his own design business in 1975 and became known for his modern, high-tech sportswear designs. He designed for **Max Mara's Sportmax,** Italy, in 1975, then **André Courrèges** in 1990. He is famous for his hand-painted designs and popularized the wearable art scene of the 1980s.

CASTILLO, ANTONIO DEL (ANTONIO CANOVAS DEL CASTILLO DEL REY) (1908-1984) Spaniard from Madrid, Spain. He began his career designing dresses, hats, and costume jewelry for **Paquin** and **Piguet,** 1936–1944. He joined **Elizabeth Arden** to design for the **Elizabeth Arden Salon, New York,** 1945–1950. During this time he also designed for the New York Opera and the Broadway stage. He was appointed head couturier of the house of **Lanvin,** Paris, in 1950 after the death of **Jeanne Lanvin.** He continued to produce designs based on her original "Robes de Style" design. **Oscar de la Renta** joined **Antonio del Castillo, Lanvin-Castillo** as assistant designer, 1961–1963. **Charles Kleibacker** also designed as a freelancer for **Lanvin-Castillo** in the late 1950s. **Antonio del Castillo** left **Lanvin-Castillo** in 1963 to open his own design house succeeded at **Lanvin** by **Jules-François Crahay** who remained at **Lanvin** until his retirement in 1984. **Oscar de la Renta** moved with **del Castillo** to design for **Elizabeth Arden Couture and Ready-to-Wear,** New York, 1963–1965, replacing **Sarmi. Del Castillo** continued to design beautifully elegant couture gowns for private clients, as well as elaborate theatrical costumes for film, including costumes for *Nicholas and Alexandra* in 1971.

CAT, ALLEY (SEE BETSEY JOHNSON) An American ready-to-wear manufacturer that **Betsey Johnson** designed collections for, 1970–1974.

CAUMONT, JEAN BAPTISTE (1932-) French designer of Italian ready-to-wear.

CAVANAGH, JOHN (1914-) From Ireland. He originally trained with **Molyneux,** followed by an apprenticeship with **Pierre Balmain,** prior to opening his own couture house in London, England, 1952, specializing in exquisite women's made-to-measure suits and day and evening dresses which catered to British society.

CELINE (SEE MICHAEL KORS) A French fashion house founded in 1947. The company originally only made top-of-the-line shoes; however, they launched a ready-to-wear collection in 1987 with trademarks such as a small gold chain at the neck of a lady's blouse, horse bit on the front of shoes, and a heel encircled in gold-toned metal detail. The company is headed today by **Michael Kors** who had his own label in 1980 prior to joining **Celine** in 1997. Respected for his classic tailoring, considered by many to be more than fashion, **Michael Kors** for **Celine** is an investment in style. Today **Celine** is owned by the luxury conglomerate **LVMH.**

CERRUTI, NINO (ANTONIO) (1930-) Italian from Biella, Italy. The **Cerruti Company** was founded by three brothers in 1881 as a textile business in Biella, a city in northern Italy. **Nino** took over the business from his grandfather in 1951 at the age of 21. **Giorgio Armani** designed for **Nino Cerruti,** 1960–1970. **Cerruti** debuted a knitwear line in 1963, his first men's ready-to-wear in 1967, and a women's collection in 1976. His elegantly classic tailoring is unsurpassed today and he is an undeniable leader in men's suits. He is a favorite designer of actor Harrison Ford, creating much of his film and personal wardrobe. Today **Narciso Rodriguez** is the head designer for women's collections at the house of **Cerruti.** The **Cerruti** company was acquired by the German fashion house of **Escada** in 2000.

CESARANI, SAL (1939-) American from New York City, the son of Italian immigrants. His introduction to the fashion world was as a fashion coordinator at **Paul Stuart,** a prestigious men's store in New

York, 1964–1969, then as the merchandising director for **Polo Ralph Lauren,** 1970–1972, followed by a position as designer at **Country Britches** and **Stanley Blacker,** 1973–1975. He established **Cesarani Ltd.** in 1976, which specialized primarily in finely tailored men's and women's wear. He sold licenses in the United States and Japan for his menswear and accessories in 1994. He no longer produces womenswear, instead focusing exclusively on his menswear collections.

CHANEL, COCO (GABRIELLE BONHEUR) (1883-1971) Frenchwoman from Saumur. She began by designing hats and opened her first small shop in Paris in 1910. In 1915 she was offering simple blouses and chemises, in 1916 she introduced jersey to her collections, and by 1918 she was designing cardigans and twinsets. Her breakthrough was with the wide-legged sailor pant she designed in 1920, followed by the "beach pajama." She commissioned **Fulco di Verdura** to design a collection of beautiful costume jewelry. She opened a shop in Paris in 1929 offering a selection of handbags and accessories. In 1930 she was in Hollywood designing costumes for Gloria Swanson in *Tonight or Never.* She was forced to close her boutique in Paris in 1939 due to World War II. She came back even stronger in 1954 and after that long absence, **Chanel** at 71 took the fashion world by a storm. The name **Chanel** is synonymous with that of the classically elegant woman. In 1983, **Karl Lagerfeld** was appointed head designer to the house of **Chanel** where he remains today.

CHAPMAN, CEIL (1912-) American from Staten Island, New York. She opened a dress business in the 1930s with **Gloria Vanderbilt** and **Thelma Furness** called **"Her Ladyship Gowns"**; however, this ventured failed and by 1940 she had gone into business with her husband producing ready-to-wear. She designed for the stage and television. She was popular in the 1950s for her version of "The New Look" which was affordable, elegant, and flattering day-to-evening dresses. Her eveningwear in the 1950s was strikingly glamorous and sexy, often embellished with beautiful beadwork which accentuated the necklines. By the 1960s she was designing evening pajamas and palazzo pant dresses with beautiful beadwork and lovely jeweled necklines. She was noted for her beautiful costume designs and was famous for being one of Marilyn Monroe's favorite designers.

CHARLES, CAROLINE (1942-) English, born in Cairo, Egypt. She began her career in the early 1960s when she moved London after graduating from Swindon Art School, and she went to work for **Mary Quant** for almost two years, branching out on her own in 1963. She was a popular designer with the entertainment industry celebrities of the times such as Barbra Streisand and Cilla Black, who favored her mini dresses of the 1960s, followed by her printed flowing peasant-style dresses of the 1970s.

CHERUIT, MADELEINE (DATES UNKNOWN) A French ready-to-wear designer who originally trained at the couture house of **Raudnitz,** Paris prior to opening her own ready-to-wear fashion house in the Place Vendôme, Paris, in the late 1890s. She was famous for her elaborate evening dresses of luxurious fabrics including taffeta, lamé, and gauze, which were often richly ornamented with sequins and beadwork. Her designs fell out of favor with the movement towards simpler dressing which was spearheaded by the designs of **Chanel.** She retired from designing in 1923, although the house remained in operation until 1935 when the premises were acquired by **Schiaparelli.**

CHEVALIER, ALAIN (DATES UNKNOWN) A French financier who acquired the **Pierre Balmain** company in January of 1990.

CHLOÉ French ready-to-wear house founded in 1952 by **Jacques Lenoir** and **Gaby Aghion.** The company was purchased by **Dunhill Holdings** in 1985, one of Britain's largest luxury products companies, then in 1993 it was acquired by Vendôme. They have been host to many notable designers such as **Karl Lagerfeld** along with **Graziella Fontana,** 1965–1972. **Lagerfeld** was the sole designer for **Chloé,** 1972–1984. In 1987 **Hervé Léger** was appointed designer for **Chloé** furs and **Martine Sitbon,** 1987–1991, with **Lagerfeld** returning for the Spring-Summer collection in 1993 and reintroducing many of his original designs from the 1970s. **Stella McCartney** was appointed head designer 1997–2001 and was celebrated for her feminine designs which harken back to the look which **Lagerfeld** popularized in the 1970s. **Stella**

McCartney was succeeded by her assistant designer **Phoebe Philo** in June of 2001 when her contract expired. **Stella McCartney** left to launch her own label with the **Gucci** company.

CIPULLO, ALTO (1936-1984) American born in Rome, Italy. A jewelry designer remembered for creating the "Love" bracelet with screw mechanism and accompanying screwdriver for **Cartier** in 1960.

CLAIBORNE, LIZ (ELIZABETH) (1929-) American born in Brussels, raised in New Orleans. Beginning her career as a sketch artist and model for **Tina Leser,** she became a design assistant in the late 1940s to **Omar Kiam for Ben Reig,** New York, before designing for **Youth Guild, Jonathan Logan.** She founded **Liz Claiborne Inc.** in 1976, taking it public in 1981. She is known as "The Wizard of the Working Woman's Wardrobe."

CLARK, OSSIE (RAYMOND CLARK) (1942-1996) British from Liverpool, England. He was discovered by **Alice Pollock** who owned **Quorum,** a fashionable youth-oriented boutique on the Kings Road, London, in the early 1960s. He began designing for **Quorum** while still attending the Royal College of Art in London in the 1960s, teaming with **Pollock** full-time in 1966. One of the most important designers of the time, his work with **Pollock** for **Quorum** made it the most popular boutique in Chelsea. He is famous for his work in printed crepe and jersey fabrics as well as leathers and exotic snakeskins. Many of his fabrics were designed by his wife **Celia Birtwell.** He designed for **Radley,** a dress manufacturer in London in 1975, and continued for several years. He had a brief comeback in 1983, continuing to design for a private clientele until his death in 1996.

CLEAVER, ALAN (SEE GENNY SPA)

CLERGERIE, ROBERT (1934-) Frenchman from Paris. The company was founded in 1895 by **Joseph Fenestrier** who had purchased a small shoe manufacturing firm in Romans, France. **Clergerie** acquired controlling interest in the firm in 1978 after seven years in management at **Charles Jourdan.** He is recognized today for shoes and handbags with clean architectural lines which fuse functionality with style.

COACH An American luxury leatherwear company specializing in handbags, footwear, and accessories which was founded by **Miles** and **Lillian Cahn** in 1941 as a family run workshop in a Manhattan loft. **Miles** and **Lillian Cahn** were first inspired by the distinctive markings he saw on a baseball glove and how the glove had become supple with use. In the beginning they introduced just 12 eloquently simple bags, and later their collections would include a large range of handbags and small leather goods, and eventually footwear. In 1960 **Miles** and **Lillian Cahn** asked **Bonnie Cashin** to design a now legendary, innovative collection of handbags for the company which she finally had time to commit to in 1962–1974. Her designs included her hallmark striped linen, handwoven madras plaid, raw silk, canvas Indian jute or Mexican striped cotton lining, designed by **Dorothy Liebes,** as well as her famous brass toggles on her handbag designs for **Coach. Cashin's** designs continue to inspire handbag designs today. **Coach** reissued a collection of four bags originally designed by **Cashin** after a highly successful exhibition of her early work appeared at the museum at The Fashion Institute of Technology, New York in September 2000. Today the company offers a full line of both men's and women's footwear, handbags, luggage, small leather accessories, and pet accessories which were introduced in the fall of 2000. **Lew Frankfort** is the chairman and CEO, and **Reed Krakoff** is president and executive creative director, with **Jack Gerson** as a head designer today.

COLCOBET (SEE CHARLES JAMES) A French textile manufacturer which **Charles James** designed for in Paris, 1934–1935.

COLE, ANNE (SEE COLE OF CALIFORNIA)

COLE, FRED (SEE COLE OF CALIFORNIA)

COLE OF CALIFORNIA (SEE ANNE COLE, FRED COLE) Originally an American drop-seat underwear company founded by the **Cole** family. In 1923 silent movie star **Fred Cole** was recruited by his mother to join the company. In the mid-to-late 1930s he began making knitted women's swimsuits. He renamed the company **Cole of California** in 1941. The company has hosted such noteworthy designers as **Christian Dior for Cole** and **Margit Fellegi.** They are most noted for the "scandal suit," in 1962. **Anne Cole** joined her father in the company after leaving UCLA; however, she left in 1960 when the company was sold to **Kayser-Roth.** She returned to the company to form the New York offices. **Bob Mackie** designed a collection of swimwear for **Cole of California** in 1976. **Anne** introduced the **Anne Cole Collection** in 1982. **Randolph Duke** designed for the company in 1984. The company was sold again in 1989. Presently **Anne Cole** is the company's executive vice president and chief design director.

COMME DES GARÇONS (KAWAKUBO, REI) (1942-) Japanese from Tokyo, Japan. After working in advertising for a Japanese textile company in 1964 then as a freelance designer, **Kauakubo** formed the company **Comme des Garçons** in 1969. She introduced her menswear line **Homme** in 1978. She opened her first boutique in Paris in 1981 and reached her zenith throughout the 1980s with her non-traditional designs, deconstructed forms, somber shades, and seemingly sexless style. She opened her flagship store in Tokyo, in 1989.

COMPLICE An Italian ready-to-wear company owned by **Genny SpA** which was founded by **Arnoldo** and **Donatella Girombelli** in Ancona, Italy in 1961. **Gianni Versace** was the chief designer for **Complice** in 1975 followed by **Claude Montana** in 1980.

CONNOLLY, SYBIL (1921-) Irish from Dublin, Ireland. She moved to London in the early 1940s to study fashion design, then returned to Ireland in 1943 and was appointed design director for **Richard Allan.** She worked primarily in fine Irish linen, wool, tweed, and lace. She opened her own fashion house in 1957 and continued to work with linens, designing fine blouses and dresses out of her trademark pleated linen. She was considered to be the Irish contemporary of American designers **Claire McCardell** and **Tina Leser** for her innovative, practical women's sportswear designs.

CONRAN, JASPER (1959-) Englishman from London, England, son of Sir Terence Conran, Conran's furnishing designs. He began designing for **Fiorucci,** New York, before designing for Henri Bendel, New York, in 1977. After consulting for the British firm, **Wallis,** he introduced his first collection in 1978. He is noted for simple, basic silhouettes for women.

COOPER, CHARLES (1905-) Canadian from Toronto, Canada; however, his professional career was initiated in California. **Morty Sussman** and **Hubert Latimer** once designed for his company. His dresses of the 1940s were typical of the period made mostly of rayon crepe; however, he implemented intricate design elements which were recognizably his. He introduced a ready-to-wear line, **Charles Cooper for Cooper Couture,** in the 1960s.

COPELAND, JO (SEE PATTULLO) (1900-1982) American from New York. She began working for **Pattullo Modes** as a fashion illustrator and assistant designer in the early 1920s through 1930 when she left to form a wholesale firm with partner **Anne Sadowsky.** Their venture lasted only four years and **Copeland** returned to **Pattullo Modes** where she resumed her design position until she was made partner four years later in 1938. Known as a master of details, she primarily produced ensembles consisting of jackets, blouses, and skirts which could move seamlessly from day to evening, as well as beautiful eveningwear which would utilize decorative effects of embroidery and ribbon trim. By the 1950s, her ready-to-wear designs were considered to be of couture caliber and sold as "Originals" in limited quantities in many major department stores across the United States. She also designed a line of costume jewelry for **Richelieu** in 1957. **George Halley** designed for her at **Patullo** in 1966. Her designs were similar to contemporaries of the day such as **Irene, Howard Greer, Norman Norell, Ceil Chapman,** and **Lilli Ann.** Most noted for her after-five designs and elaborate evening gowns. She closed the company in 1970.

COSTA, VICTOR (1935-) American from Houston, Texas. He started as a sketch artist for **Ceil Chapman, Oleg Cassini, Herbert Sondheim,** and **Philip Hulitar** prior to working for **Pandora** and the **Bride's World** designing bridal gowns. He moved to **Suzy Perette** in 1965 and was recognized for his French couture knockoffs until 1973. He then bought into **Ann Murray's** company in Dallas, Texas, producing one successful collection. While he was still teamed with **Murray,** prior to buying the company out and reopening under his own name, he continued to create affordable French-style eveningwear. At his height in the 1980s, his adaptations sold for a fraction of the original designs which had inspired him.

COSTUME NATIONAL, ENNIO CAPASA, AND CARLOS CAPASA. **Costume National** (named after a French book on uniforms) was founded by two brothers from Lecce in southeastern Italy. After graduating from Milan's Academy of Fine Arts in the early 1980s, **Ennio Capasa** traveled to Japan and stayed on to work for **Yohj Yamamoto** for three years. He returned to Italy in 1986 and founded **Costume National** with his brother **Carlos Capasa. Ennio** is the head of design and **Carlos** manages the business affairs. The two presented their first women's collection in 1987 and showed their first ready-to-wear collection in Paris in 1992. They introduced **Costume National Homme** in 1993 and their **Luxe Limited Collection** which uses rare fabrics, 1999–2000. Their head office today is in Milan with shops in Hiroshima, Hong Kong, Los Angeles, Milan, New York, Osaka, Rome, and Tokyo. They are most noted for their avant-garde silhouettes which closely follow the body, subtracting the emphasis on the shoulders. In 1998 the company became a PLC starting a partnership with the English investment bank 3i who now hold 15 percent controlling capitol.

COURRÈGES, ANDRÉ (1923-) Frenchman from Pau, Pyrénées Atlantiques, France. He started his career as a cutter for **Cristobal Balenciaga** in 1945 and continued with the company until 1961 at which time he founded his own fashion house. Throughout the 1960s he designed architectural silhouettes which were very futuristic with a functional forward focus on the "Space Age." **André Laug** freelanced and collaborated with **André Courrèges,** 1960–1963. He sold his company to **L'Oréal** in 1965, and resumed designing his own collection in 1967. His designs have been widely copied and continue to inspire other designers today. In the 1990s Courrèges presented a revival of his designs from the 1960s and continues to design.

COX, DOROTHY (DATES UNKNOWN) American. She began her career designing womenswear for **McMullen** in the 1940s. Her designs, including her eveningwear, were practical and affordable. She is noted as the designer for Miss and Mrs. Average America.

COX, PATRICK (1963-) Canadian from Edmonton, Alberta, Canada. He is a shoe designer whose talent brought him to the attention of **Vivienne Westwood,** who had him design the gold platform shoes for her first solo collection in 1982. He went on to design shoes for **John Galliano** and **Body Map.** He opened his first shops in Toronto in the prestigious Manulife Center, and in London in 1991. He cross-merchandises shoes and antiques in his London shop today. In April 2001 he was appointed design consultant to **Marc Jacobs** for **Louis Vuitton**'s shoe collections.

CRAHAY, JULES FRANÇOISE (1917-1988) Belgian from Liège, Belgium. He started by working in his mother's dressmaking shop in Liège, and became a salesman for the house of **Jane Regny,** Paris. He joined **Nina Ricci,** Paris, in 1951, working as her collaborator on collections, then later as her chief designer, prior to moving to the house of **Lanvin** in 1963, succeeding **Antonio del Castillo.** He remained at **Lanvin** until his retirement in 1985, succeeded by **Maryll Lanvin** who joined the company in 1982. He is recognized for his beautiful feminine eveningwear and was a leading designer promoting the peasant and gypsy styles of the 1960s. He formally retired in 1984, just four years prior to his death in 1988.

CREED, HENRY, SR., HENRY, JR., AND CHARLES (DATES UNKNOWN) Born in England, (1820–?) to a line of tailors dating back to the beginning of the 18th century, **Henry, Sr.** opened his first tailoring business in Paris in the 1850s. **Henry Creed, Jr.** (1863–?) was known for making riding habits for the British Royal family and producing women's tailored suits. **Charles Creed** (1909–1966) in Paris, son of **Henry Creed, Jr.** studied tailoring in Vienna before he joined his father's tailoring business in Paris in the 1930s. He opened his own business in London after World War II specializing in classically tailored tweed suits.

CROLLA, SCOTT (1955-) From Edinburgh, Scotland. He trained originally in art and sculpture, but found his true artistic expression in fashion and launched his first fashion venture with fellow artist

Georgina Godley in 1981. He worked as the design director throughout the 1990s for **Callaghan,** a sophisticated, finely tailored women's ready-to-wear manufacturer based in Paris before branching out on his own. Famous for his perfectionism and exquisite finely tailored women's ready-to-wear.

CRYSTAL, DAVID (SEE DAVIDOW) (DATES UNKNOWN) American, son of **William H. Davidow** of **Davidow,** an American design manufacturer founded in 1880. **David Crystal** took over the house of **Davidow** in the 1930s. **Bill Blass** designed for **David Crystal** in the 1940s. **David Crystal** was known primarily for his shirtwaisted dresses; **Davidow** also produced a line of suits and dresses with the label, "**A Christian Dior Junior Design for David Crystal.**" By 1968 **David Crystal** had partnered with **Lacoste** and produced shirtdresses which were essentially a longer version of the classic **Lacoste** sport shirt with the alligator motif.

DACHÉ, LILLY (1904-1989) Frenchwoman from Bègles, France, immigrated to New York in 1924. She began as a millinery salesperson at **Macy's** in New York, 1924, as well as the **Bonnet Shop** later that year. By the end of 1924 she had bought out the two owners of the **Bonnet Shop,** and christened her own shop **Lilly Daché.** She built the **Lilly Daché** building in 1937, offering hats, pocketbooks, and shoes; both custom-made and take-aways. The building was seven stories, housing her boutique, penthouse apartment, as well as manufacturing facilities for her 150 employees. She designed numerous hats for costume designer **Travis Banton** in Hollywood, including the towering turbans of fruit for Carmen Miranda. Noted as one of America's best milliners with contemporaries such as **Sally Victor** and **John Frederics,** (later known as **Mr. John**). She introduced costume jewelry and accessories in 1950, sensing the declining interest in women's hats. **Halston** designed hats for her in 1958 before moving to head the millinery department at **Bergdorf Goodman,** New York. She closed her business and retired in 1968.

D'ALBY, PIERRE (SEE DANIEL HECHTER AND ANNE-MARIE BERETTA) (DATES UNKNOWN) French ready-to-wear. **Anne-Marie Beretta** designed for the **Pierre d'Alby Company** in 1965.

DAVIDOW (SEE DAVID CRYSTAL) American design manufacturers founded in 1880 by **Wm. H. Davidow & Sons. David Crystal,** (dates unknown), the son, took over in the 1930s. **James Galanos** designed for the firm briefly in 1940, although found the conservative sportswear company contrary to his fashion sense. **Bill Blass** designed for **David Crystal** in the 1940s as well. Throughout the 1930s and 1940s they were renowned for their expensive wool, tweed, and gabardine suits and sporty dresses. In the 1960s they began to offer popular ensemble suits with blouses matching the jacket linings, in the same manner as **Chanel.**

DAVIS, JACOB (DATES UNKNOWN) An American tailor from Carson City, Nevada, who teamed with **Levi Strauss** in 1873 to create a patent for a pair of trousers which they had designed based on an earlier version of work trousers that **Levi Strauss** designed in 1850. The new design had copper rivets at various stress points on all of the pockets.

DE LA RENTA, OSCAR (1932-) From Santo Domingo, Dominican Republic. He began sketching for **Balenciaga's Elsa** branch in 1949, moving to **Antonio del Castillo, Lanvin-Castillo** as assistant designer, 1961–1963, then moved with **Castillo** to design for **Elizabeth Arden Couture and Ready-to-Wear, New York,** 1963–1965, replacing **Sarmi.** After teaming up with **Jane Derby Inc.** in 1965 he produced under the label **Oscar de la Renta for Jane Derby.** In 1967, after **Jane Derby's** death he took over the company renaming it **Oscar de la Renta** and continued producing luxury women's ready-to-wear. He introduced a fun, inexpensive **Something!** line in 1972. Appointed as head designer to the French couture house of **Pierre Balmain** in 1993, he succeeded **Alistar Blair** who had been head of ready-to-wear for **Pierre Balmain** since 1990. This was the first time in history that an *American* designer was to head a French couture house. He popularized the gypsy themes of the 1970s. He continues to design in New York today.

DE LUCA, JEAN-CLAUDE (1948-) French, from Paris, France. He began his career designing for **Hubert de Givenchy** in 1971 and for **Dorothée Bis** in 1972. In 1976 he developed a following on his own and is presently designing under his own label.

DE TOMMASON, CARMEN (CARVEN) (1909-) Frenchwoman from Châteauroux, France. After studying architecture she pursued fashion design out of her own desire to create beautiful clothing to fit her own petite proportions, which was an area in fashion which was left primarily to the custom designers or home sewers. Her foray into women's petite ready-to-wear would soon become a burgeoning success in the untapped petite market. She founded the house of **Carven** in Paris in 1937 (the name was a modified version of her given Christian name). Along with a very successful career in fashion she also licensed various fragrances including **Ma Griffe.**

DELL'OLIO, LOUIS (1948-) American, from Long Island, New York. He started working in the mid 1960s and 1970s with **Norman Norell, Dominici Rompollo** at **Teal Traina, Traina Boutique, Originala's Giorgini,** and **Ginori** divisions. In 1974 he was brought into **Anne Klein** as co-designer by his friend, **Donna Karan,** from Parsons School of Design in New York. **Karan** had been assistant designer at **Klein** and was appointed head designer after **Klein's** death in 1974. **Dell'Olio** took over as head designer at **Anne Klein** after **Donna Karan** left in 1985 to launch her own line. The last collection on which he collaborated with **Donna Karan** at **Anne Klein** was spring 1985. He continued to design for the **Anne Klein** company until 1993 when he was succeeded by **Richard Tyler.**

DEMEULEMEESTER, ANN (1959-) Belgian from Kortrijk, Belgium. She began as a freelance designer in 1981. Known as one of the influential Belgian designers to come out of the Royal Academy of Fine Arts at Antwerp, she continues to design monochromatic, cutting-edge, avant-garde men's and women's ready-to-wear collections today.

DENNIS, PAMELA (1960-) American from Newark, New Jersey. Without a formal design background she got her first break when she was asked by a commercial stylist to loan one of her personal creations that she was spotted wearing at a friend's wedding. The dress appeared in a diamond commercial. Her meteoric career took off with subsequent designs for television commercials, followed by her establishing her own ready-to-wear company in the late 1980s. Today she is known primarily for her Hollywood awards-style eveningwear, sexy sheaths with intricate bead and crystal work favored by many of the who's who in Hollywood.

DE RIBES, JACQUELINE (COMTESSE) (1931-) Frenchwoman from Paris, France. A wealthy French aristocrat who launched her first couture collection at the age of 52 in 1983. A designer known for her discreet grandeur, she had been on the International Best Dressed List by the age of 25, and had been written up in *Town and Country* magazine as the most stylish woman in the world in 1983. Famous for her eveningwear which catered to the affluent French social scene.

DERBY, JANE (JEANNETTE BARR) (1895-1965) American from Rocky Mount, Virginia. She opened her own retail business in 1936 in New York, and founded **Jane Derby, Inc.** in 1938, which she ran until her death in 1965, at which time **Oscar de la Renta** took over the company. Her wholesale womenswear company hosted many designers over the years including **George Halley** in the early 1960s and **Oscar de la Renta.** Recognized for her women's ready-to-wear with contemporaries of the 1940s such as **Ceil Chapman, Jo Copeland, Pauline Trigère, Harvey Berin, Norman Norell, Gilbert Adrian, Irene,** and **Howard Greer.**

DÉSIRÉ, MME. (SEE NORMAN HARTNELL) (DATES UNKNOWN) A British couturier who was the dressmaker to the Royal Family in the 1920s. **Norman Hartnell** designed for **Mme. Désiré** for a short period of time in 1923 before being appointed as a dressmaker to the Royal Family in 1938.

DESSÈS, JEAN (JEAN DIMITRE VERGINIE) (1904-1970) Greek born in Alexandria, Egypt. A contemporary of **Pierre Balmain, Christian Dior, Nina Ricci, Jacques Fath,** and **Balenciaga.** He designed for **Mme. Jane,** a couture house in Paris, 1925–1937; then opened his own house in Paris in 1937. He introduced **Jean Dessès Diffusion** line in America in 1950. **Valentino** studied fashion design at the Chambre Syndicale de la Couture, 1949–1951, while working as an assistant designer to **Jean Dessès,** Paris, 1950–1955. He closed his couture business in 1960 then his ready-to-wear business in 1965 due to ill health; however, he continued to freelance until his death five years later. He was celebrated in 1951 for his

Grecian- and Egyptian-style chiffon gowns which were similar to those beautifully draped columns of **Madame Grès.** His work was popularized by movie stars and royalty. Actress Renée Zellweger wore a beautiful, vintage 1950s couture, yellow chiffon **Jean Dessès** gown to attend the 2001 Academy Awards.

DIMITRI COUTURE (SEE GIGLI, ROMERO)

DIOR, CHRISTIAN (1905-1957) Frenchman from Granville, France. Undeniably one of the most famous designers of the 20th century. He began as an art dealer, 1928–1931; then a freelance sketch artist, 1934–1937, and assistant to **Robert Piguet,** 1937–1939; then worked for **Lucien Lelong,** Paris, 1941–1946, alongside **Pierre Balmain.** When French textile magnate and friend, **Marcel Bousac,** offered to finance him, he opened **Maison Dior** in 1947. His first collection was a revolution in fashion silhouettes of the times and heralded as the "**New Look**" (**originally called Corolle line**) which is still referenced today by many designers. He launched **Christian Dior-New York,** 1948, and **Miss Dior Boutique** in 1967. **Herbert Kasper** worked for him in the late 1950s. **Dior** sold many license agreements internationally including perfume, furs, scarves, lingerie, costume jewelry, and knitwear. **Davidow, David Crystal's** ready-to-wear company held a license and produced a line of suits and dresses with the label "**A Christian Dior Junior Design for David Crystal.**" **Hubert Latimer** became the first American designer to design for **Christian Dior-New York,** 1970–1973. **Dior** was succeeded after his death in Paris in 1957 by his design assistant, **Yves Saint Laurent,** who produced only one collection for **Christian Dior** in 1958 before leaving to establish his own couture house. **Marc Bohan** was head of **Christian Dior-London,** 1958–1960, then became head designer and art director, **Dior,** Paris, 1960–1989. **Marc Bohan** was replaced at **Dior** by **Gianfranco Ferré,** 1989–1996. French designer **Dominique Morlotti** handled **Christian Dior Monsieur** from 1983 through early 1990 succeeded by **Hedi Slimane.** The house of **Christian Dior** was acquired by French luxury conglomerate **LVMH** in 1984. **John Galliano** assumed the role of head designer of **Christian Dior** women's couture in 1996 and is presently at the helm of the house of **Dior** today, where he is responsible for a tremendous revitalization in the house with the reintroduction of the **Dior** logo print and a fantastic array of sexually provocative designs supported by a very strong ad campaign. **Hedi Slimane** debuted her Autumn/Winter collection for **Christian Dior Homme** at Colette, a luxury boutique in Paris, in May 2001.

DI CAMARINO, ROBERTA (GIULIANA COEN CAMERINO) (1920-) Italian from Venice, Italy. She began making handbags in Switzerland where she had gone to escape the war. After the war in 1945, she founded **Roberta di Camarino** in Venice. She is most known for her cut-velvet pocketbooks and satchels in signature Italian green and red, as well as for her accessories and ready-to-wear garments all bearing her initial "R" motif, fashioned from a looping belt with buckle. The company realized a tremendous rejuvenation in popularity in the late 1990s and has added expensive versions of many of their original designs to their collections.

DI SANT' ANGELO, GIORGIO (COUNT GIORGIO IMPERIALE DI SANT'ANGELO) (1933-1989) Italian from Florence, raised in Argentina, educated in Italy, immigrated to the United States in 1962. Interestingly he began his career as an animator at the **Walt Disney Studios,** Hollywood, 1962–1963, then became a textile and jewelry designer, 1963–1967. He moved to New York in 1967 initiating his own designs and **Giorgio di Sant'Angelo, Inc.,** 1968–1989. His work in the 1970s paralleled that of **Rudi Gernreich, Halston, John Ashpool, Scott Barrie, Betsey Johnson,** and **Stephen Burrows.** Many of his design inspirations were culled from hippie and street fashions. He popularized the romantic gypsy styles of the late 1960s, and is recognized for his brightly colored body-conscious womenswear designs based around a body stocking which truly inspired the silhouette of the 1970s and 1980s. He also designed a collection of Lucite jewelry and accessories in brightly colored geometric shapes.

DI VERDURA, FULCO (FULCO SANTOSTEFANO DELLA CERDA, DUKE OF VERDURA, PALERMO, SICILY) (1898-1978) In 1927, at the age of 29 he went to work for **Chanel** in Paris, designing both textiles and costume jewelry. He moved to New York ten years later in 1937 to design jewelry for **Paul Flato,** heading up his California division. He opened his own shop in New York in 1939. He is remembered for his mixtures of precious and semiprecious stones in the designs he created for **Chanel.** He sold his business in 1973 prior to his death in 1978.

DOEUILLET, GEORGE (?-1929) French couture designer who founded his own couture house in Paris in 1900. Famous for its magnificent fabrics and opulent designs, it was considered at the time to be one of Paris' most prestigious couture houses. The house of **Doeuillet** merged with the house of **Doucet** in 1929 upon the death of **Doeuillet** that same year.

DOLCE & GABBANA A design partnership formed in 1985 between **Domenico Dolce** (1958–) from Palermo, Italy, and **Steffano Gabbana** (1962–) from Milan, Italy. **Domenico Dolce** began by helping his father in the family's small clothing firm, whereas **Steffano Gabbana** attended art school in Venice before the two met at a dinner table and were introduced by a mutual friend and fashion designer. Both men shared a singular and extremely personal taste and intense desire to express it. They designed ready-to-wear for **Complice (see Genny SpA)** in the early 1980s. Self-produced and self-financed, they were chosen by Milano Collezioni in 1985 as one of three new names to present Italian fashion. After presenting their first womenswear collection in Milan in 1985, they have been creating sexy cutting-edge fashion ever since. The 1990s saw the team take lingerie out from underneath and present it as an acceptable, provocative outer-fashion worn by stars such as Madonna. Most noted for their sexy body-conscious designs, including a collection paying tribute to Madonna's "Blonde Ambition Tour," as well as a fall/winter collection for 2001 inspired by Deborah Harry of the rock band Blondie.

DOLCI, FLORA (SEE MANDELLI, MARIUCCIA) (DATES UNKNOWN) She teamed with **Mariuccia Mandelli** and founded the ready-to-wear fashion house **Krizia** in Milan (named from Plato's dialogue on the vanity of women) in 1954.

DOUCET, JACQUES (1871-1932) From Paris, France. **Doucet** opened his couture house in 1875 after inheriting his grandparents' lingerie shop. Inspired by 17th- and 18th-century paintings, his designs were the height of opulent femininity offering ivory chamois and opera coats lined in swan's down or chinchilla. He was credited with reviving the art of fashion in France, considered a highly respected couturier of the times, a contemporary of **Poiret,** and was popularized by royalty, socialites, and actresses for his beautiful tea gowns and eveningwear. **Doucet's** company merged with the house of **Doeuillet** in 1929 upon the death of **Doeuillet** that same year.

DRANELLA (SEE CATHY HARDWICK) A Danish ready-to-wear manufacturer located in Copenhagen. **Cathy Hardwick** designed for **Dranella** in the early 1960s.

DRÉCOLL, CHRISTOFF VON (DATES UNKNOWN) Founded the couture house **Drécoll** in Vienna in 1902 and specialized in dressing the ladies of the Viennese court. He opened a branch in Paris in the 1920s which was headed by **Monsieur** and **Madame Besançon de Wagner.** In the late 1920s, daughter **Maggie Besançon de Wagner** joined the company working with her mother designing sportswear until 1928 when she was appointed director of the company. In 1929 the house of **Drécoll** merged with the house of **Beer,** moving to a new location, and **Maggie Besançon de Wagner** with her husband took over the original premises of **Drécoll,** founding the house of **Maggy Rouff.** The house **Drécoll-Beer** merged once again in 1931 with the house of **Agnès,** known now as **Agnès-Drécoll. Jean Louis** worked with the new company **Agnès-Drécoll** in the early 1930s before he moved to **Hattie Carnegie,** New York, in 1935. **Agnès-Drécoll** finally closed their doors to business in 1963. They were notable for their eveningwear which was favored by the Viennese courts.

AGNÈS-DRÉCOLL (SEE CHRISTOFF VON DRÉCOLL)

DUFY, RAOUL (1877-1953) From Havre, France. A painter who in 1911 worked with **Paul Poiret** developing fabric dyeing techniques as well as fabric printing. He also worked with **Bianchini-Ferier,** a French textile company where he used his paintings to develop beautiful fabrics for garments as well as home decor.

DUKE, RANDOLPH (1958-) American sportswear designer who began in swimwear and exercise wear, working for **Jantzen, Cole of California,** and the **Anne Cole Collection** in 1984, then for **Gottex** in 1987. He opened his own retail establishment in New York, and established a wholesale business from 1989–1992. He worked for **CMT,** a private label where he designed and marketed ready-to-wear on the **QVC Television Network,** where he would often make personal appearances to boost sales. For a brief period of time in the late 1990s he was head designer behind the revitalization attempt at **Halston.** Presently he is designing under his own name in Los Angeles where he is incredibly successful in creating custom gowns for many notable celebrity clients for their personal appearances and award presentations.

ECHO An American scarf manufacturer established in the 1920s.

EISEN, MARK (1958–) From Cape Town, South Africa, he attended the University of Southern California and designed in the United States. He specializes in mid-range women's ready-to-wear separates. Popular for his first collection in 1988 of bleached denim, which was then re-dyed in various colors.

EISENBERG & SONS ORIGINALS a wholesale fashion company founded by **Jonas Eisenberg** in Chicago in 1914. **Irma Kirby,** whose name appeared on the label, was head designer in the 1930s. They were renowned for their suits and evening dresses which were beautifully embroidered with motifs which resembled real costume jewelry, and for their ornately jeweled buttons. In the mid-1930s they began to design and manufacture costume jewelry which was met with great acceptance through the 1940s. Using mainly **Swarovski** crystals, much of the jewelry they manufactured during the war years were set in silver because metal was commandeered by the government.

ELLIS, PERRY (1940-1986) American from Portsmouth, Virginia. He began his career in 1963 as a sportswear buyer for **Miller & Rhodes,** a conservative chain of department stores in Virginia. In 1967, he became a merchandiser for the company, eventually being appointed as a designer. **Ellis** left the **John Meyer** company after **John Meyer's** death in 1974 and joined **Manhattan Industries** assisting **Vera Neumann** for **Vera Sportswear.** Shortly after designing clothing for **Manhattan Industries** with **Vera's** beautifully painted fabrics, **Ellis** introduced his own line, **Portfolio,** with Manhattan Industries. Two years later he received tremendous acclaim when he launched his own label which is considered by many to be the quintessential look of American sportswear. **Isaac Mizrahi** became assistant designer to **Perry Ellis,** 1982–1983. **Andrew Corrigan** joined the **Perry Ellis** company as design director in 1988 under the direction of **Roger Forsythe.**

EMANUEL, DAVID AND ELIZABETH A husband and wife design team from Britain. **Elizabeth Weiner,** (1953–) from London, England, and **David Emanuel** (1952–) from Bridgend, Glamorgan, Wales. They opened a salon in Beauchamp Place, London, shortly after leaving college in 1974, and by 1979 were designing both ready-to-wear and couture for women worldwide at Harrods, Harvey Nichols, Bergdorf Goodman, Henri Bendel, and Neiman Marcus. They received international fame for the wedding dress they designed for Diana, Princess of Wales. After their divorce they closed their joint business in 1990 and continued to design under their own individual labels.

ERTÉ (ROMAIN DE TIRTOFF) (1892-1990) Russian from St. Petersburg, Russia. He worked as an illustrator for **Paul Poiret,** 1913–1914, and illustrated covers for *Harper's Bazaar,* 1916–1926. He designed sets for the Folies Bergère and the Ziegfeld Follies, also creating costume designs for Josephine Baker. The look of **Erté** is synonymous with the look of the twenties.

ESCADA (WOLFGANG AND MARGARETHE LEY) A German fashion house which is a privately held company originally founded by **Wolfgang** and **Margarethe Ley** (dates unknown); held solely by **Wolfgang** after **Margarethe's** untimely death in 1992. Their holdings have included, among others, **Escada, Cerruti, Crisca, Kemper, Laurel, Natalie Apriori, Seasons, Marie Gray, Acatrini, Schneberger,** and most recently **Badgley Mischka. Margarethe** was the chief designer until her death, when her place was taken by **Michael Stolzenburg,** who was succeeded after his death in the early 1990s by **Todd Oldham** as the head design consultant to **Escada** in 1994. Today **Escada** is under the design direction of **Brian Rennie.**

ESPRIT An American design company founded by a husband and wife team, **Susie Russell** and **Doug Tompkins.** Both **Russell** and **Tompkins** were born in 1943. **Esprit** was launched in 1968 from the **Plain Jane Dress Company** which specialized in pretty, simply cut 1940s-style dresses in the 1960s (**see Plain Jane**). By 1972 the company was renamed **Esprit de Corps.** They often used their own employees in their advertising, directing their moderately priced, colorful sportswear collections to real people. They were

The Gap of the 1970s and 1980s. **Susie Russell,** chief designer, left the company after divorcing **Doug Tompkins** in 1989. **Esprit** opened a flagship store in May of 2001 on Regent Street, London, in the old Warner Brothers' store in an effort to spearhead its return to the UK.

ESTEREL, JACQUES (1918–1974) Frenchman from Bourne-Argental. Originally he presided over a metal foundry and dealt in the import-export of metal tools before turning to fashion. He launched his own couture house in 1958 after securing the assistance of two salespeople from **Louis Féraud,** followed by two boutiques in Paris. By 1959 he had been commissioned by Brigitte Bardot to create her unconventional wedding dress out of Vichy check linen for her marriage to Jacques Charrier. He later partnered with multimillionaire **Jean-Baptile Doumeng** shortly after **Esterel's** endorsement by Bardot's wedding dress. He is most noted for his work in the 1960s and the early 1970s. **Anne-Marie Beretta** designed for him in 1955. **Jean-Paul Gaulthier** worked as a freelance sketch artist for **Esterel** in 1972–1974. **Jean-Baptile Doumeng** renamed the company **Benoit Bartherotte** after **Esterel's** death in 1974.

ESTÉVEZ, LUIS (1930–) Cuban from Havana, Cuba, living and working in the United States. He worked for two years in the early 1950s for **Patou,** Paris; then designed under his own name for a New York–based manufacturer, **Grenelle,** in 1955, where he was met with tremendous applause, and was considered to be one of the bright stars with contemporaries such as **James Galanos, Scaasi,** and **Sarmi.** He moved to California in 1968, designing as **Estévez for Neal,** as well as creating a slinky, jersey eveningwear line called **Eva Gabor for Estévez.** He produced a collection under his own name in 1974 and has continued to run his own company specializing in eveningwear since 1977. Noted for his feminine and sexy little black dresses which paid much attention to revealing necklines as well as halter backs.

ETA, MME. (ETA VALER HENTZ) (DATES UNKNOWN) Hungarian from Budapest, Hungary, immigrated to the United States and began designing a ready-to-wear collection in the early 1920s. She had a partnership with **Maurice Rentner** in the mid-1920s, known as **Ren-Eta.** She went into business in the 1930s with **Ann Sadowsky** who had left **Jo Copeland.** By the 1940s she was considered top-drawer with such contemporaries as **Norell, Adrian, Jane Derby, Irene, Harvey Berin,** and **Ceil Chapman.** She was distinguished by her Grecian-inspired toga-style featuring soft pleats and draping.

FABIANO, ALBERTO (DATES UNKNOWN) Italian from Tivoli. He began working in his family's retail clothing business in the mid-1940s, taking over the business five years later. By the 1950s he had established himself as a renowned tailor and creator of fine dresses and suits. He teamed with rival designer **Simonetta, (see Duchess Simonetta di Cesaro)** in 1953 and the two later married. In 1962 they debuted the house of **Simonetta e Fabiani** in Paris. Their designs were on a par with such contemporaries of the time as **Mainbocher, Sophie of Saks, Capucci of Italy,** and **Stiebel of London. Fabiano** and **Simonetta** returned to Rome in the mid-1960s and the two divorced shortly after, closing their joint business in 1965; however, the two continued to design under their own names. **Fabiano** retired in the early 1970s, **Simonetta** in 1973.

FABRICE, SIMON (1951–1999) Haitian from Haiti, immigrated to the United States at age 14. He began his career in New York working for two fabric designers before he ventured out on his own, creating a collection of hand-painted silk dresses in the mid-1970s. In the early 1980s he started to send his fabrics to his home of Haiti to have them embellished with intricate beadwork. He would then design beautiful 1920s- and 1960s-inspired gowns from the beaded fabric, which would become his signature throughout the 1980s. He branched out into menswear in 1985.

FALKENSTEIN, ARTHUR (DATES UNKNOWN) An American who opened an upscale boutique in the early 1930s in the Hotel Meurice, New York, which offered duplicates of the models he purchased in Paris. He began designing his own custom ready-to-wear in 1941 with comparable contemporaries of the time such as **Mainbocher, Sophie of Saks, Fira Benenson of Bonwit Teller & Co.,** and **Valentina.** He is most noted for an inspirational tent-shaped overcoat which became a prolific look after the war.

FATH, JACQUES (1912–1954) Frenchman from Maison-Lafitte, France. He began his career as a bookkeeper and stockbroker for the Paris Bourse. He opened his first salon in 1937 and rose to great popularity just after World War II. He is considered to have been the inspiration for **Dior's** 1947 **"New Look,"** as early as 1939. **Herbert Kasper** worked as **Fath's** assistant just after the war. In the late 1940s he was commissioned by **Joseph Halpert,** an American manufacturer to design ready-to-wear suits, as well as day and evening dresses based on his Paris models, in the same way as **Dior** had done at the time for his ready-to-wear originals for **Christian Dior-New York. Hubert de Givenchy** worked for **Fath,** 1945–1949, as did **Gustave Tassell** as a sketch artist in 1955 under the design direction of **Fath's** wife, **Geneviève,** who ran the company after her husband's death at age 42 in 1954. The company was sold in 1957.

FAY, LESLIE (SEE KASPER FOR JOAN LESLIE AND HERBERT KASPER) An American women's ready-to-wear manufacturer founded by **Fred Pomerantz** after World War II. **Herbert Kasper** was the head designer, 1965–1985. He was appointed vice president in 1980. Most noted for their moderately priced women's separates, dresses, and suits which had refined tailoring in affordable fabrics. The company went public in 1962.

FENDI An Italian fur and leather manufacturer founded by **Adele Casagrande** (1918–1978), Italian from Rome, Italy. The company changed its name to **Fendi** when **Adele** married **Eduardo Fendi.** They first produced high-quality fur and leather goods in 1925 in Rome. After the death of **Eduardo** in 1954, his five daughters have been at the helm of **Fendi**: **Paolo** (1931–), **Anna** (1933–), **Franca** (1935–), **Carla** (1937–), and **Alda** (1940–). **Karl Lagerfeld** has been designing their fur collections since 1967, and was also responsible for their logo design of the interlocking "**F**" which is as nationally recognized as the **Chanel** "**C**" and **Gucci** "**G**" logos. **Fendi** has been on the forefront of fashion since the introduction of their **Fendi** baguette, which was responsible along with **Chanel, Gucci,** and **Prada** for igniting the handbag wars of the mid-to-late 1990s. In 1999 the **Fendi** company sold 51 percent of their name to a joint venture between **Prada** and **LVMH.**

FENG, HAN (DATES UNKNOWN) Chinese from Hangzbou, China. She began designing scarves in 1980, and then worked with womenswear. Her designs have often been compared to those of **Issey Miyake.** Her organic shapes, softly pleated and weightless, wrap the body like a light sculpture. She has become noted for her home collections of table linens, pillows, and bedcovers.

FÉRAUD, LOUIS (1921-) Frenchman from Arles, France. He opened his first salon in Cannes, France, in 1955. It was in Cannes, during the festival, that attending celebrities discovered him. He has designed for many notables including Brigitte Bardot, Kim Novak, Catherine Deneuve, and Joan Collins. He moved to Paris in the early 1960s and worked extensively as a costume designer for film and television, designing for over 80 films. He opened a ready-to-wear house in Paris in the mid-1960s and introduced menswear in 1975. He launched a flagship store in New York in 1990 and today continues to design beautifully tailored, feminine ready-to-wear and couture.

FERRAGAMO, SALVATORE (1898-1960) Italian from Naples, Italy. He apprenticed as a shoemaker in Bonito, Italy, 1907–1912, then immigrated to the United States at the age of 16 in 1914, and opened a shoe repair shop with his brothers in Santa Barbara, California. He manufactured handmade shoes for the American Film Company, 1914–1923, moving to Hollywood, 1923–1927. He returned to Italy in 1929 where he established a shoe manufacturing business in Florence, which subsequently went bankrupt in 1933. The business was reestablished in the late 1930s. **Ferragamo** created shoe collections for the house of **Schiaparelli**, most notably, the "wedgie," a two-inch-soled shoe that became a major fashion trendsetter in the late 1930s. Noted for such important shoe designs as the Invisible Shoe, as well as platform and wedged-shaped heels as early as the late 1930s.

FERRÉ, GIANFRANCO (1944-) Italian from Legnano, Italy. He began his career with an education in architecture which he often referenced as a freelance jewelry designer, 1969–1973, for **Walter Albini, Lagerfeld,** and **Fiorucci.** He started designing sportswear for **Baila, Milan** in the early 1970s and by 1978 had launched his own womenswear collection, introducing menswear by 1982. He is known in the fashion industry as "The Frank Lloyd Wright of Italian Fashion." He is recognized for his practical yet opulent approach to beautifully tailored men's and women's suits, as well as for exceptional eveningwear.

FERRETTI, ALBERTA (1940-) Italian, a designer as well as fashion businesswoman who represented, produced, and distributed such designers as **Ozbek** and **Moschino.** She continues to produce her own collections of beautiful womenswear and eveningwear.

FIGUEROA, BERNARD (1961-) Frenchman from Montpellier, France. A shoe designer who in the early 1980s designed whimsical, avant-garde shoe collections for **Thierry Mugler, Christian Dior,** and **Claude Montana.** He moved to Boston in the late 1980s and designed sport shoes for **Rockport.** In 1992 he moved to New York and founded his own manufacturing company producing his own couture shoe line. He is recognized for his play with themes and hand-sculpted heels.

FIORUCCI, ELIO (1935-) Italian from Milan, Italy. **Elio Fiorucci** had inherited a shoe shop in Milan from his father in 1962. Throughout the 1960s the shop began to diversify and sell collections from other designers which **Fiorucci** had brought back from London, designers such as **Ossie Clark** and **Zandra Rhodes,** as well as many others which represented the Youthquake of the times. The **Fiorucci Boutique** became famous for their miniskirts, brightly colored graffiti T-shirts, and fluorescent "Jellies" sandals. In 1976 Fiorucci had launched a line of jeans, 1976–1978, which had become a jeans staple look more prevalent in youth fashion than **Levi's,** for their straight, tight cut. The **Fiorrucci Jean** was the crest of the designer jeans craze. The New York store opened in 1976 and others in Beverly Hills, Boston, Tokyo, Hong Kong, Zurich, London, and Rio de Janeiro soon followed.

FISH, MICHAEL (MR. FISH) (DATES UNKNOWN) British from London, England. A men's ready-to-wear designer and retailer he opened his boutique **Mr. Fish** in 1965 on Clifford Street in London, a fashionable district recognized for its classic tailor shops. The **Mr. Fish** boutique was unequivocally the hippest menswear boutique in London in the 1960s, playing host to an impressive roster of celebrity clientele including Lord Snowdon, the Duke of Bedford, and Mick Jagger who wore one of **Mr. Fish's** famous mini shirts for a performance with the Rolling Stones in Hyde Park. Famous for his flamboyant and colorful designs made out of beautiful floral printed fabrics, voile, sequins, and brocades, as well as suede, leathers, and fur.

FOALE AND TUFFIN, MARION FOALE (1939-) British from London, England, and **Sally Tuffin** (1938–), British from London, England. The two women met while studying at the Royal Academy of Art, London, in the late 1950s and joined forces to found their fashion company out of their own small flats in London in 1961. They sold their modest collection of brightly colored youth-oriented women's ready-to-wear dresses and separates to various London shops before opening their own boutique in the early 1960s on Carnaby Street, which was truly the pulse of the Youthquake movement in London. Along with the designs of both **Sally Tuffin** and **Marion Foale,** the boutique also offered designs by other fresh young British designers including **Mary Quant.**

FOGARTY, ANNE (1919-1980) Born **Ann Whitney,** American from Pittsburgh, Pennsylvania. She began her career as a drama major with an eye toward acting. Between auditions she worked as a fit-model for **Harvey Berin.** In 1948, she began designing for **Youth Guild,** introducing the "New Look" to the teenage market. In 1950, she designed coats, hats, shoes, jewelry, and lingerie for **Margot, Inc.** junior-size division. She was best known for her "Paper Doll" silhouettes and fitted bodices with full skirts throughout the 1950s. She continued to design for **Margot, Inc.** throughout the 1950s, as well as **Saks Fifth Avenue** in 1957. She introduced her own business, **Anne Fogarty, Inc.** in 1962. She produced various collections under her own label, such as **A.F. Boutique, Clothes Circuit,** and **Collector's Items.** She closed her business in 1970 and as a freelancer created a collection for **Shariella Fashions** just prior to her death in 1980.

FOLMAR, WILSON (1911-) American from Troy, Alabama. He began as a sketch artist for **Mabelle Manning,** a custom dressmaking shop on Madison Avenue, New York, in 1931. He started designing as well as sketching for **Manning** by 1935, then he moved from **Manning** to the **Jay-Thorpe Department Store,** New York, in 1936 when he was appointed as the head of the custom department. His ready-to-wear, custom work at **Jay-Thorpe, Inc.,** 1936–1939, was top-rung and comparable to contemporaries such as **Sophie of Saks, Muriel King of Stein & Blaine, Mainbocher,** and **Arthur Falken.** After World War II he resumed designing his custom work for **Jay-Thorpe, Inc.** and for **Ben Gam,** 1946–1956, as well as **Mau-**

rice Renter for a time in the early 1950s. In 1957, he designed for Edward Abbott, leaving in 1964 to launch his own business with silent partner Larry Aldrich, naming his business Wilson Folman, Inc. He continued to design beautiful evening and cocktail attire, as well as introducing a lesser line for juniors, Folman Fantasy. He closed his business in 1972 at the age of 61.

FONDE (SEE TOM BRIGANCE) An American ready-to-wear manufacturer whose head designer in the 1950s was Tom Brigance.

FONTANA An Italian fashion house in Rome, originally founded in 1907 in Parme, Italy, by the Fontana family and later inherited in 1944 by the three Fontana sisters, Zoe, (1911–78), Micol (1913–), and Giovanna (1915–). They are best known for their glamorous eveningwear and wedding dresses which they produced for the Italian aristocracy and film stars, most notably Ava Gardner for whom they created the voluptuous look in The Barefoot Contessa, 1954. They employed numerous designers including Princess Irene Galitzine from Russia, 1945–1948. They presented their first ready-to-wear collection in Rome in 1960. The company is still active today.

FONTANA, GRAZIELLA (DATES UNKNOWN) Designer for Chloé along with Karl Lagerfeld, 1965–1972.

FONTICOLI, NAZARENO (1906-1981) (SEE BRIONI) Italian from Penne, Italy.

FORD, TOM (DATES UNKNOWN) American from Austin, Texas, who spent most of his childhood in Santa Fe, New Mexico. In 1986 he joined the creative staff of the American designer Cathy Hardwick. In 1988, he worked with Perry Ellis where he became the design director. He moved to Milan in 1990 to join Gucci (see Gucci) as the company's womenswear designer. In 1992, he became design director and in 1994 he was appointed creative director of Gucci. He is responsible for the design of all product lines, from clothing to perfumes, and for the group's corporate image, advertising campaigns, and store design. Ready-to-wear was not an integral part of Gucci's history; however, when Ford joined the house in 1990 he developed it into a significant and profitable business. Not only is Ford a brilliant designer, he is also an adept marketer—his designs, ads, and the esthetics of all the Gucci boutiques are conceived with a keen continuity and a sharp focus, and are clean, cool, and sexy. In January 2000, following the acquisition of Yves Saint Laurent Couture (see Yves Saint Laurent, YSL) and Sanofi Beauté by the Gucci Group, Ford assumed the position of creative director of Yves Saint Laurent and Yves Saint Laurent Perfumes. In addition to his existing duties at Gucci, Ford works with all creative teams at YSL to define the overall image and positioning of the YSL brand including all product categories and communication activities. Ford's approach to his designs for the house of Yves Saint Laurent is very forward thinking without a glance to the past. Unlike Yves Saint Laurent, Ford will not labor arduously over a design detail, perfecting and exacting a cut or drape; he understands that today's customer doesn't care. In the house's tradition, his first collections have been clean and classic with an edge that reflects the moment with uncompromising quality.

FORTUNY, MARIANO (1871-1949) Spaniard from Granada, Spain. Initially he worked in a variety of disciplines: painting, sculpture, photography, lighting design, theater direction, set design, architecture, and costume design. Ultimately he developed his artistic abilities as a magnificent designer of fabrics and clothing. Best recognized for his pleated fabrics and Delphos gowns which he patented in 1909, as well as his printed velvets which he made into cloaks, capes, and jackets. He opened shops in Paris and Milan in 1920. He received tremendous success for his gowns which were extremely popular with ladies entertaining at home and for those traveling abroad because of the ease with which the pleated gown could be rolled up and tucked into a suitcase, thus eliminating the need for ironing. His creations and pleating process have inspired many subsequent designers such as Mary McFadden, Diane Fries, and Issey Miyake. After his death in 1949, his pleating process was purchased by Countess Gozzi (Elsie McNiel).

FOX, FREDERICK (1931-) Australian from New South Wales, Australia. A milliner who trained in Sydney prior to moving to London in 1958. He began working for Longee in Brook Street before launching his own line of hats in the mid-1960s in London. He designed hats for such notable British companies as Hardy Amies and John Bates. His label was appointed by Queen Elizabeth of England and he has created hats for many members of the British royal family and is a favorite at the royal enclosure at Ascot.

FOX, SEYMORE Founded in 1950, an American ready-to-wear manufacturer which specialized in better womenswear, suits, coats, and dresses made of fine fabrics such as tweeds, wool, and fleeces. Respected for their attention to detail and their excellent tailoring techniques such as bound buttonholes and bias self-fabric edging. The company continued operating until the early 1970s.

FOXBROWNIE (FOX-BROWNIE) An American manufacturer in the 1940s which specialized in better ready-to-wear women's late-day to eveningwear, as well as printed silk afternoon tea dresses made by the best fabric houses.

FREUD, BELLA (1961-) British designer who was originally an assistant to **Vivienne Westwood** in London. Popular for her quirky vision and **Westwood**-style influences.

FRIZON, MAUD (1941-) From Paris, France. She began her career in the fashion industry as a model and was a favorite of **André Courrèges**; she also worked for **Nina Ricci, Jean Patou,** and **Christian Dior.** She began by designing her own shoes to wear on her modeling assignments which she hand-cut and finished herself, and she launched her first collection of shoes in 1970, receiving overnight success. She designed for numerous luminaries such as **Alaïa, Missoni, Montana, Mugler,** and **Rykiel.** She introduced another line in the late 1980s known as **Miss Maud.** Her witty and whimsical designs were made of fine leather and exotic skins such as snake and lizard. One of her most noteworthy designs was a shoe covered in lip prints. A noted favorite designer of Brigitte Bardot, **Frizon's** designs have become widely inspirational to many designers that followed. The company was purchased by the **Sun family,** spearheaded by **Mary Sun** early in 2000.

GABAR (SEE TOM BRIGANCE) An American ready-to-wear manufacturer whose head designer in the 1950s–1960s was **Tom Brigance.**

GABOR, EVA (SEE ESTÉVEZ, LUIS) (DATES UNKNOWN) An actress most famous for her film roles as well as her character on the television series, *Green Acres*. She was a great customer of designer **Luis Estévez** and in the late 1970s the two collaborated on a line of slinky, jersey eveningwear called **Eva Gabor for Estévez.**

GABRIELLA A line of sports clothes which were knitted to measure in Milan and designed by **Countess de Robilant** for Bergdorf Goodman department store, New York, in 1931.

GALANDS, JAMES (1924-) American with Greek heritage, raised in New Jersey and Philadelphia. He began his illustrious career as a sketch artist for **Hattie Carnegie,** 1944–1945, then for **Jean Louis,** head of costumes for Columbia Pictures, 1945–1946. He worked as a nonpaid apprentice with **Robert Piguet** in Paris for a short period of time in 1946–1947, then worked in New York for ready-to-wear manufacturer **Davidow,** 1948–1949. He moved back to California, following fellow Philadelphian and designer, **Gustave Tassel,** whom **Galanos** met in Paris and advised to move to California to found his own line in the early 1950s. In 1951 **Galanos** opened his salon on Beverly Hills Drive in Los Angeles. Considered to be one of the brightest talents of the early 1950s with contemporaries such as **Estévez, Scaasi,** and **Sarmi.** In 1953 he brought his first collection to New York and was met with tremendous success; however, it wasn't until Nancy Reagan wore his evening dress to President Ronald Reagan's inaugural ball that he received international recognition for his couture-caliber collections. He is most noted for his beautiful chiffon gowns as well as intricate hand-beading and fine attention to details such as lovely silk linings. He retired his Los Angeles business in the late 1990s.

GALITZINE, IRENE, PRINCESS IRENE GALITZINE (1916-) Russian, princess able to trace her roots back to Catherine the Great of Russia. She moved to Rome to escape the revolution. She started as a design assistant to the **Fontana** sisters' design and manufacturing firm in Rome, 1945–1948. She established her own import business in Rome in 1949, then debuted her first collection in 1959. (**Valentino** worked for one year as an assistant to **Princess Irene Galitzine,** Paris, in 1959 before moving to Rome and founding his own small atelier in 1960.) In 1960, she introduced her most famous collection of silk, jeweled-neck, palazzo-pant jumpsuits which won the hearts of women the world over. Known for her princely, Roman-inspired eveningwear, she found great success throughout the 1960s. She closed her house in 1968, reopening briefly to show spring/summer 1970.

GALLAGHER, LOUISE BARNES (DATES UNKNOWN) American, designing women's ready-to-wear in the late 1930s through the 1940s. Recognized for her fabric known as **Gallagher Mesh,** a wool which had the look and feel of hand-knitted wool. Her designs were limited primarily to day and afternoon dresses, coats, and suits. A contemporary to **Irene, Howard Greer, Wilson Folman, Claire McCardell,** and others.

GALLANT, FRANK (SEE TOM BRIGANCE) An American ready-to-wear manufacturer whose head designer in the 1950s–1960s was **Tom Brigance.**

GALLIANO, JOHN (1960-) British from Gibraltar. His diploma collection in 1984 from St. Martin's School of Art in London which was called "Les Incroyables," *The Incorrigibles,* was an exaggerated fantasy expression of 18th-century France, flavored by the myth of the Scarlet Pimpernel. His designs are often shocking theatrical and thematic collections which are usually historically derivative. **Jorgen Simonsen** was a design assistant at **Galliano,** 1994–1996. He was appointed head designer at **Givenchy's** couture and ready-to-wear in 1995; however, he left the following year in 1996 to take over the house of **Dior. Jorgen Simonsen** worked with **Galliano** at **Givenchy,** 1995–1996. He continues to produce his own collection, **John Galliano** ready-to-wear and couture.

GARNETT, ELEANORA (DATES UNKNOWN) A designer with her own boutiques in New York and Rome in the 1950s, offering mid-range ready-to-wear suits, day dresses, and ball gowns. She is known for her intricate detailing on her gowns and dresses.

GARRATT, SANDRA (1951-) American ready-to-wear designer who worked for various designers in the early 1970s such as **Mary McFadden, Zoran,** and **Halston.** She revived a graduation collection she had created at the Fashion Institute of Design and Merchandising in Los Angeles in 1977, which was based on the simple idea of various one-sized knitted separates which could be worn interchangeably which she called **"Units."** The collection met with tremendous success for its ease of use and wear; however, after a legal dispute she renamed her collections **"Multiples"** in 1986. The collection was sold in department stores across North America by stylists (rather than sales staff), who would demonstrate to the buyer how to wear the interchangeable pieces. **Multiples** also employed the use of in-store video monitors in the 1980s to demonstrate the multiple ways the garments could be worn.

GATTINONI, FERNANDA (1909-) Italian from Cocquio, Italy. After training at the house of **Ventura,** Rome, **Gattinoni** launched her own couture salon in the early 1940s in Rome. Famous for her sophisticated, romantic, and often indulgent couture and custom designs including richly embroidered wedding gowns, as well as eveningwear and opera coats. The world developed an insatiable thirst for beautiful Italian couture in the 1950s spearheaded by the excitement of the film *Roman Holiday,* starring Audrey Hepburn. **Gattinoni's** fashion house celebrated tremendous success during this period and hosted an impressive list of celebrity clients including Audrey Hepburn, Ingrid Bergman, and Anna Magnani.

GAULTIER, JEAN-PAUL (1952-) He started working as a sketch artist for **Pierre Cardin,** 1972–1974, as well as for **Jacques Esterel** and **Jean Patou.** He handled **Pierre Cardin's** manufacturing for **Cardin's United States Collections** in the Philippines, 1974–1975; and then for **Majago,** Paris, 1976–1978. He founded his own ready-to-wear in Paris in 1977 and by 1980 was unequivocally the force behind the term *avant-garde* throughout the 1980s. His technical brilliance and innovative tailoring was always humorous, clever, and extremely showy! His designs, like **Galliano's,** are often historically derivative. Most noted for his corsets as outerwear which were immortalized by Madonna onstage during her World Tours in the 1980s through the early 1990s.

GENESCO CORPORATION (SEE GERNREICH, RUDI)

GENNY SPA An Italian manufacturing company founded in 1961 by **Arnoldo** and **Donatella Girombelli** of **Genny SpA** in Ancona, Italy, specializing in fine tailored ready-to-wear. Lines include **Genny Moda, Complice,** and **Byblos,** 1973–1983, as well as **Malisy** until 1993. **Gianni Versace** designed for **Genny** in

1974 before designing for their younger collection introduced in 1973, **Byblos,** 1975–1977; for their other holding, **Complice,** in 1975; prior to **Claude Montana** taking over the designs for **Complice** in 1980. **Guy Paulin** designed for **Byblos,** 1977–1980, as well as **Alan Cleaver. Dolce e Gabbana** designed for **Complice** in the early 1980s. **Keith Varty** has designed for **Byblos** since the 1980s. **Christian Lacroix** designed a collection of ready-to-wear for **Genny** in 1988. **Donatella Arnoldo** took over as the head of **Genny** after her husband's death in 1980.

GERNREICH, RUDI (RUDOLPH) (1922-1985) Austrian from Vienna, Austria. He fled Austria and the Nazis in 1938 and settled in California, becoming an American citizen in 1943. Initially he worked in his aunt's dress shop in Austria while a teenager. In California he was a dancer and costume designer, 1942–1948, for the **Lester Horton Company.** He was a freelance designer, 1948–1951, and then joined forces with **(William) Walter Bass's** manufacturing company where he designed ready-to-wear for **Bass's** client **Jax,** a Beverly Hills boutique. He designed swimwear for **Westwood Knitting Mills** from 1953–1959, and shoes for **Genesco Corporation** from 1958–1960. Along with his own more expensive collections, he designed for **Harmon's Knitwear** from 1960 through the late 1970s. He also created a lingerie line for **Lily of France. Pappagallo,** an American footwear manufacturer, created a line of shoes to complement **Gernreich's** collections in the early 1960s. In 1964 he scandalized the world by designing the "topless swimsuit." He continued to shock the design world with his forward-thinking designs such as the "no-bra" in 1964, as well as unisex dressing and the thong bathing suit for both men and women. His final venture prior to his death in 1985 was a line of designer soups which were available at various specialty shops in Beverly Hills, California. His designs continue to influence and inspire designers today.

GERSHEL, BEN An American garment manufacturing company whose head designer from 1927 to 1942 was **Adele Simpson. Simpson's** designs for **Ben Gershel** focused on soft feminine suits, day-to-evening dresses, as well as beautiful strapless evening gowns which she favored in chiffon. **Pauline Trigère** worked for the **Ben Gershel Company** in the late 1930s.

GERVAIS, NATALIE (DATES UNKNOWN) She began her career working with **Tom Ford** at the **Gucci Group** in 1994, designing ready-to-wear, before moving to **Valentino** in 1996 to supervise **"Diffusion"** collections. Today she is the head designer at the house of **Nina Ricci** where she continues the ultra-feminine tradition of the house, which was established in 1932.

GHESQUIÈRE, NICOLAS (1972-) Frenchman from Loudon. He began as a freelance designer for numerous design houses including **Trussardi, Thierry Mugler,** and **Jean-Paul Gaultier,** as well as **Balenciaga's** licenses prior to being appointed head designer for **Balenciaga** in 1977 at age 25. Most noted for his rigid, architectural, hard-core cool and forward-thinking designs in dramatic skintight leather which are startlingly sexy. In June of 2001 **The Gucci Group** acquired the French firm Balenciaga for an undisclosed amount, giving **Ghesquière** a 9 percent stake in the company. They plan to expand both retail and production.

GHIATIS, CHRIS (1917-) American born in New Hampshire of Greek immigrants and raised in Athens. His father owned a small department store in New Hampshire as well as in Athens, and two of his sisters were dressmakers. He worked with a custom dressmaker as a young man in Athens before he returned to the United States. In 1937–1941 he went to work as an assistant designer to **Irene Lentz, "Irene,"** when she had her own custom department for Bullocks-Wilshire. In 1941 he was recruited by **Adrian** to leave **Irene** and become the assistant designer, ready-to-wear collection, at the house of **Adrian,** 1941–1951. **Stanley Marcus** of Neiman Marcus referred to **Chris Ghiatis** as **Adrian's** "ghost designer," recognizing his tremendous contribution to the designs of **Adrian** at the time. When **Adrian** closed his business in 1952 after suffering a heart attack, **Ghiatis** accepted an offer from the **Neiman Marcus** department store to continue on in the tradition of **Adrian's** designs and create his own collection. **Ghiatis** created only one collection for **Neiman's** under the label **Chris Originals.** Financial mismanagement by the company controller caused the new venture to cease after only one collection, which reportedly sold out completely. In early 1951 **Ghiatis** opened his own women's custom shop on Sunset Plaza in Los Angeles, where he offered his custom designs under his new label, **Chris Limited,** having lost the rights to the use of his name **Chris Originals** after the dissolving of the former company. Under the label **Chris Limited,** the company enjoyed ten years of success creating beautiful custom work for many notable Hollywood celebrities and socialites. While with his company **Chris Limited, Ghiatis** freelanced for numerous other designers and manufacturers including **Jean Louis, Walter Bass,** and **Helen Rose.** By early 1961 **Ghiatis** had closed his Sunset Plaza location and gone to work with **Jean Louis,** with whom he collaborated on creating two collections before moving to work with **Helen Rose,** 1962. He worked with **Rose** for approximately one year before **Rose** sold her company to her sales manager on the insistence of her husband who wanted her to retire. After a short retirement, **Rose** teamed with **Ghiatis** again to create one final collection. In the fall of 1962 **Ghiatis** became the head designer for **Marilyn Lewis** who had just founded **Cardinali,** a women's ready-to-wear company, where he remained for the next ten years. In 1972 **Ghiatis** opened a small salon on Maple Drive in Beverly Hills and resumed his freelance work for numerous designers and manufacturers including **Gagliano, Inc., Lee Herman, Inc., and Olga, Inc.** He relocated his studio to San Vicentte Blvd. in Los Angeles in 1981 where he continued his design work until his retirement in 1999.

GHOST A British ready-to-wear company founded in 1984 by **Tanya Sarne,** British (1948–). Throughout the 1980s to the present they specialize in flowing viscose fabrics which are known as "Grey Cloth" prior to being constructed into the garments and to the shrinking and dyeing process which is employed in every garment. The shrinkage to the garments, which are originally cut oversized, causes the garments to reach their intended size, creating a clinging bias-cut fit to their feminine day and evening dresses. **Amy Rogers,** who trained at St. Martin's and was the assistant to **John Galliano,** is now the head designer at **Ghost.**

GIBB, BILL (1943-1988) From Fraserburgh, Scotland. Originally from a farming family in Scotland, **Gibb** was encouraged by his grandmother, a painter, to pursue his love of sketching historical costumes, which later greatly influenced his designs. While attending the Royal College of Art in London he sold a collection of his designs to Henri Bendel in New York, whereupon he shortly left the college without finishing to begin his career early in 1968. He worked for **Baccarat** for three years. By 1972 he had founded his own company and was highly acclaimed for his colorful, flamboyant, floating chiffon evening dresses, as well as his appliquéd and embroidered jersey gowns. He closed his company in the late 1970s due to financial mismanagement.

GIGLI, ROMERO (1949-) Italian from Castelbolognese, Faenza, Italy. After studying architecture he moved into fashion design creating his first collection for **Quickstep by Luciano Papini** in 1972. He designed for **Dimitri Couture,** New York, in 1978. He introduced his own label, **Romero Gigli,** in 1981 then **Romero Gigli for Zamasport** in 1984, which he continued until becoming a consultant to **Callaghan for Zamasport** through 1991. He introduced his **G Gigli** sportswear line in 1990. **Alexander McQueen** worked for him in the early 1990s. He is most known for his romantic womenswear knits in muted colors with sinuous cuts and soft sculptural forms, as well as for his relaxed approach to menswear throughout the 1980s. A contemporary to **Gaultier, Mugler,** and **Montana, Gigli** saw great success in the 1980s and was very influential in his designs, inspiring many who followed.

GIMBLE, SOPHIE (SOPHIE-GIMBLE, SOPHIE OF SAKS, SOPHIE ORIGINALS) (1901-1981) American, the wife of **Adam Gimble** who owned **Saks Fifth Avenue,** founded in 1924; she began by managing the "**Salon Moderne**" at **Saks,** in 1927, where she would oversee the manufacturing of models based on French imported couture. Each dress which was modeled after a French import was guaranteed to only have ten copies made before it was discarded as a model, assuring the buyer of an exclusivity which no other department store was offering. **Emmet Joyce,** in 1940, designed custom-made dresses for the **Saks Originals** ready-to-wear line. Sophie started designing under the name **Sophie-Gimbel,** in the early 1940s and was considered a top-rung designer with contemporaries such as **Irene, Mainbocher, Valentina,** and **Jean Schlumberger.** In 1950 she came to be known as simply **Sophie of Saks,** and **Sophie Originals.** Her designs sold exclusively at **Saks** for $1,000 in the 1960s. She retired in 1969.

GIVENCHY, HUBERT DE (HUBERT JAMES MARCEL TAFFIN DE GIVENCHY) (1927-) Frenchman from Beauvais, France. Early in his career he worked for **Lucien Lelong,** 1945–1946; **Robert Piguet,**

1946–1948; **Jacques Fath,** 1948–1949; and **Schiaparelli's** boutique line, 1949–1952. He opened his own business in late 1952 at age 25 offering couture and custom ready-to-wear. He invited **Philippe Venet** (whom he had met the previous year at **Schiaparelli**) to join him in his new venture, a collaboration which lasted ten years until 1962 when **Venet** left to found his own couture house. Throughout the early 1950s to late 1960s he designed for Audrey Hepburn both on and off the screen; most notably for her films *Sabrina* (1954), *Love in the Afternoon* (1957), *Funny Face* (1957), and *Breakfast at Tiffany's* (1961). She remained his muse for almost 40 years. He was very close to **Balenciaga,** in fact his boutique in Paris was across the street from **Balenciaga** on rue George V. Unlike any others' design relationships, the two shared each other's confidence and critiqued and influenced each other's sketches and collections regularly. He followed **Balenciaga** in his decision to boycott the press in 1957 and no longer allowed the press to view his collections until eight weeks after the buyers had seen them. When **Balenciaga** retired and closed his salon in 1968 he referred his clients to **Givenchy. Issey Miyake** worked as an assistant to **Givenchy,** 1968–1969. **Givenchy** sold his firm in 1988; however, he stayed on as head design director until his retirement in 1996. **John Galliano** was appointed head designer after his retirement in 1995; he moved to the house of **Dior** after his last collection autumn/winter 1996 and was succeeded by **Alexander McQueen. Jorgen Simonsen** worked with **Galliano** at **Givenchy,** 1995–1996, then remained under **McQueen's** design direction for one season, ready-to-wear, fall/winter, 1998. Today the **Givenchy** company produces haute couture and ready-to-wear and is owned by the luxury conglomerate **LVMH.** In March 2001, Welsh designer **Julien Macdonal** succeeded **Alexander McQueen** as head designer at **Givenchy.**

GOMA, MICHÈL (1932–) Frenchman from Montpellier, France. He started by working for **Lafaurie,** a French couture and ready-to-wear house, 1950–1958, at which time he purchased the company renaming it **Michèl Goma.** He closed his company in 1963 after only five years and subsequently joined the house of **Jean Patou** where he designed until 1973 before being replaced as head designer by **Tarlazzi.** He now works as a freelance designer.

GONZALÉS (SEE JEAN PATOU) (DATES UNKNOWN) A couture designer who worked at **Jean Patou,** 1977–1982.

GRAHAM, FLORENCE NIGHTINGALE (SEE ELIZABETH ARDEN) (1878–1966) Canadian from Woodbridge, Ontario, Canada; immigrated to the United States in the early 1900s. Founded **Elizabeth Arden** in 1910, New York.

GREER, HOWARD (1888–1974) American from Nebraska. He began working for **Lucile,** Paris (**see Lucile,** and **Lady Duff Gordon**) for her specialty shop in Chicago, as well as her New York branch of her Paris operation in 1916. He continued to work for **Lucile** after WWI, and then for **Molyneux** and for **Poiret** as a sketch artist. He returned to New York in 1921 to design costumes for the Greenwich Village Follies. Shortly thereafter he moved to Hollywood to design for Paramount Pictures, 1923–1928. He shared screen credit for costume design with his assistant **"Irene" Lentz** in 1932, before she replaced **Adrian** at Metro-Goldwyn-Mayer. He had opened a boutique in 1927 on Sunset Boulevard creating beautiful couture for his predominantly celebrity-based clientele such as Rita Hayworth, Greta Garbo, and Gypsy Rose Lee. His work was comparable to other Hollywood-based costume designers who crossed over into custom designs such as **Adrian** and **Irene.** He was most noted for his captivating late-day and eveningwear which commanded attention, befitting the demands of his notable clientele. He retired in 1962.

GRENELLE (SEE ESTÉVEZ, LUIS) A New York–based manufacturer in business in the 1950s.

GRÉS, MME. "ALIX," BORN GERMAIN EMILIE KREBS (1903–1993) From Paris, France. She began as a sculptor, and sold toiles (sample patterns out of muslin) to many couture houses in Paris. She apprenticed in the early 1930s to the house of **Premet** using the name **Alix Barton.** She opened the house of **Maison Alix** with private funding, 1934–1940, then sold the rights to her share and her name **Alix** in 1940. She opened her own house in 1940 adopting the name **Grés** which was an adaptation of her sculptor husband, **Serge Czerefkow's** given name spelled backwards. She had closed for a time during the 1940s, and in 1942 during the German occupation of France she reopened for approximately six months, then closed again until after the war. She is ranked by many with the great couturiers of the time such as **Vionnet** and her silhouettes are as characteristic of her style as those of **Halston, Gernreich,** or **Mc-Cardell.** She specialized in draped and molded jersey silks and wool using fluid asymmetrical shapes, bias cuts, and dolman sleeves resembling Greek sculptures. It wasn't until 1980 that she even considered the idea of ready-to-wear and was one of the last great couturiers to do so. She sold her business in 1986 then retired in 1987. The house of **Grés** continued under the design direction of **Frederic Molenac** until it went bankrupt in 1987. It was purchased by a Japanese company in 1988 and continues today in Japan primarily as a ready-to-wear company under the design direction of **Lloyd David Klein.**

GRIFFE, JACQUES (1917-) From Carcassonne, France. He began his career being trained as a tailor in his hometown in 1936. After his military training he became a protégé to **Vionnet** in Paris where he learned the brilliant technique of draping which was the genius behind **Vionnet's** designs. He opened his own couture and ready-to-wear house in 1946 and was appointed head designer for **Molyneux** in 1950, after **Molyneux** had closed all of his salons except Paris and retired to Jamaica leaving the Paris salon under the direction of **Griffe.** He continued throughout the 1940s, 1950s, and 1960s to specialize in beautiful fluid and draped designs influenced and inspired by **Vionnet** until his retirement in 1960.

GROULT, NICOLE (1887-1967) A French couturier active in the 1920s and 1940s who was the sister of another French couturier, **Paul Poiret.** Her father had been a cloth merchant in the late 1800s. American designer **Elizabeth Hawes** worked for her in 1928.

GUCCI An Italian luxury goods manufacturer whose founder was **Guccio Gucci** (1881–1953) an Italian from Florence, Italy. He began as a lift attendant in London's opulent Savoy Hotel at the turn of the 19th century. In 1921, after his return to Florence, he opened a shop at 7 Via della Vigna Nuova selling luggage and saddlery, as well as opening a small workshop that handcrafted them. He introduced the signature moccasin shoe with the extended tongue and gilt bit in 1932. He began to manufacture handbags as well as original equitation goods when he relocated to a larger space on Lungarno Guicciardini along the Arno River in 1937. By this time the iconic bit and stirrups, which were derived from the company's origins and denoted the sophistication of the products, had come to represent **Gucci's** success. In 1938, the business expanded to Rome with the opening of a shop on the prestigious Via Condotti. The one-man business became a family business when sons **Aldo, Vasco,** and **Ugo** joined the company in 1939. Another son, **Rodolfo,** later joined the company and in 1951 he opened a shop in Milan. The early 1950s saw the introduction of the intertwined double "**G**" logo which would later become a trademark and status symbol. The opening of the Manhattan store on 58th Street in 1953 launched the **Gucci** brand as one of the pioneers of Italian design in the United States. Due to a saturation of products through licenses, the brand had lost its appeal in the late 1970s and 1980s; however, American **Dawn Mello** restored the luxurious image of **Gucci** as executive vice president and creative director, 1989–1991. **Richard Lambertson** was with the company, 1989–1992. The **Gucci Company** was acquired by **Investcorp** in 1993. **Tom Ford** joined the company in 1993 (**see Tom Ford**). In 1999 **The Gucci Group NV** halted an uninvited takeover attempt by **LVMH** to take controlling shares of **The Gucci Group NV** by a $3 billion investment and alliance by **Pinault-Printemps-Redouts.** In January 2000, following the acquisition of **Yves Saint Laurent Couture** (**see Yves Saint Laurent, YSL, and Tom Ford**) and **Sanofi Beauté** by **The Gucci Group NV, Tom Ford** assumed the position of creative director of **Yves Saint Laurent** and **Yves Saint Laurent Perfumes.** In addition to **Ford's** existing duties at **Gucci, Ford** works with all creative teams at **YSL** to define the overall image and positioning of the **YSL** brand, including all product categories and communication activities. In April of 2001 **Domenico De Sole,** CEO of **The Gucci Group NV,** announced that they had finalized a deal to bring **Chloé's** head designer **Stella Mc-Cartney** into the company and have her create a collection under her own label. **McCartney** would finish her contract with **Chloé** through June 2001, succeeded by her assistant **Phoebe Philo.** The company also announced the acquisition of **Bottega Veneta, Sergio Rossi shoes,** Swiss watch designer **Christian Bédat,** and French jeweler **Boucheron,** as well as backing **Alexander McQueen's** private collections. In June 2001 **The Gucci Group** acquired the French fashion firm **Balenciaga** for an undisclosed amount, giving **Nicholas Ghesquière, Balenciaga's** head designer, a 9 percent stake in the company. They plan to expand both retail and production. **Ghesquière** is reported to be launching his own collection with backing from the **Gucci** group in May 2001.

HALLEY, GEORGE (DATES UNKNOWN) Designer of American women's ready-to-wear from Ohio. He designed for **Jane Derby** and **Charles James** in the early 1950s to 1960s and for **Jo Copeland for Patullo** in 1966 before opening his own design house in 1966 with his wife **Claudia,** who had been a model and muse to **Norman Norell.** He is most known for brilliance in his eveningwear which was simply shaped, empire-waisted with full skirts of romantic cut velvets and chiffons with bold floral prints or large silk flower embellishments at the bodices.

HALPERT, JOSEPH An American wholesale ready-to-wear manufacturer. In the late 1940s **Jacques Fath,** Paris was commissioned by **Joseph Halpert,** to design ready-to-wear suits, as well as day and evening dresses based on his Paris models, in the same way that **Dior** had done at the time for his ready-to-wear originals for **Christian Dior-New York.**

HALSTON, ROY HALSTON FROWICK (1932-1990) American born in Des Moines, Iowa, although he grew up in Evansville, Indiana. He began as a freelance milliner in Chicago, 1952–1953, and as a window dresser at **Carson-Pirie-Scott,** Chicago, 1954–1957. He moved to New York to design for **Lilly Daché** in 1958; however, shortly thereafter he became the head of the millinery salon at Bergdorf Goodman, New York. It was at Bergdorf's that he met and worked with many notable clients such as Jacqueline Kennedy (Onassis) for whom he would later design the pillbox hat which she wore with the outfit designed by **Oleg Cassini** for John F. Kennedy's presidential inauguration. **Halston** had the same head size as Jacqueline and would often simply custom design a hat for her by fitting it on himself. He had designed hats for **Norman Norell** to complement **Norell's** collection in the early 1960s. From 1959 through 1968 he designed ready-to-wear as well as hats for **Bergdorf Goodman,** and founded **Halston Ltd. Couture** with **Henry Pollack Inc.,** 1962–1973. He established **Halston International** ready-to-wear in 1970, then **Halston Originals** ready-to-wear with **Ben Shaw** in 1972. He renamed **Halston Ltd., Halston Enterprises** in 1973, selling the company design services and trademark to **Norton Simon.** In 1983 the company was sold to **Esmark** and they introduced the **Halston III** collection for **JC Penney.** During this time he created a line of lingerie for **Vassarette.** Then in 1986 they sold the company to **Revlon.** The company has been owned by **Halston Borghese, Inc.** since 1992. **Stephen Sprouse** worked for **Halston** in the early 1970s. Selling his lesser-priced line, **Halston III,** to JC Penney proved to be the downturn of popularity for **Halston** and Bergdorf Goodman canceled his higher-priced collections on the grounds that the association with JC Penney severely dissipated his cachet with Bergdorf's clients. Most noted for his simple yet chic designs favoring ivory, black, and red as well as his shirtwaisted Ultrasuede® dresses in the 1970s which were widely copied and sold over 60,000 copies. It was considered at the time as the most popular American dress. **Halston** was never able to regain the rights to his name and design custom and higher-priced ready-to-wear clothes under his own name. After **Halston's** death in 1990 there was a revitalization of the company's higher-priced designs by the company. The company has been owned by **Halston Borghese, Inc.** since 1992. **Randolph Duke** was with the company for a period in the mid-to-late 1990s and today the company is under the creative direction of **Craig Natiello.**

HAMNETT, KATHARINE (1948-) British from Gravesend, Kent, England. She co-founded **Tuttabanken Sportswear** in 1970 with a friend she met while studying at St. Martin's School of Art in London. When **Tuttabanken** folded she went on to freelance for many companies in London, Paris, Hong Kong, and Rome for almost ten years before founding **Katherine Hamnett Ltd.,** London, in 1979. She introduced menswear in 1982 and launched her flagship shop in London in 1986. Noted for her designs out of parachute silk, cotton jersey, and drill, her hallmark was unisex styles which were based on traditional workwear. Her political and environmental views were expressed in a collection of oversized T-shirts in 1984 with slogans such as "Stop Acid Rain," "Worldwide Nuclear Ban Now." Her designs were widely plagiarized in the early 1980s. She had been a major force throughout the 1980s in London along with **John Galliano** and **Vivienne Westwood;** however, her influences as a designer have certainly diminished in more recent years. **Hamnett** signed a licensing deal in the spring of 2001 with **Gibo Co. SpA,** an Italian manufacturer who produced a new main line collection for spring/summer 2001 with a strong focus on organic cottons.

HARBERGER, HANSI (SEE FREDERIC HIRST, JOHN-FREDERICK, AND MR. JOHN) (1906-1993) Austrian from Vienna, Austria. His mother opened a millinery shop on New York's Madison Avenue after WWI. **Hansi Harberger** partnered with **Frederic Hirst** in the mid-1940s naming the millinery company **John-Frederick.** They dissolved the partnership in 1948 and the two men continued to produce hats for their own companies: **Hansi Harberger** as **Mr. John** and **Frederic Hirst** as **John-Frederick. Hansi Harberger** as **Mr. John** went on to design less expensive lines for **Lilly Daché** known as **Dachettes,** as well as **Mr. John Juniors** in the mid-1950s. **Herbert Kasper** sold his Parsons School project designs to **Mr. John** in the early 1960s. **Stan Herman** designed hats for **John-Frederick** in 1954. **Hansi Harberger** continued to design for his company **Mr. John** until the late 1970s.

HARDEN, ROSEMARY (SEE ELIZABETH HAWES) (DATES UNKNOWN) American designer in business with **Elizabeth Hawes,** 1928–1930, producing couture.

HARDWICK, CATHY (1933-) Korean from Seoul, Korea, who became an American in 1959. She was a freelance designer and boutique owner, 1966–1970, and designed silk bikinis for the boutique in the late 1960s. She worked as a knitwear designer for **Alvin Duskin,** San Francisco, in 1960, and as ready-to-wear designer for **Dranella,** Copenhagen, and **Pranx,** New York, in the 1960s. She formed **Cathy Hardwick 'N' Friends,** New York, in 1972. Then she organized **Cathy Hardwick, Ltd.,** New York, 1975–1981, and formed **Cathy Hardwick Design Studio,** New York, from 1977. **Gemma Kahng** was a design assistant, 1981–1984. The company reorganized in 1988. **Tom Ford** worked for the company in 1986. She is most noted for her moderately priced ready-to-wear which fused her Eastern roots with the West. She designed ready-to-wear for **Sears, Roebuck Company** in 1990. **Cathy Hardwick's** company had been very successful throughout the early to mid-1980s with annual sales of $20 million, however, she declared bankruptcy in 1988 and closed the company.

HARMON KNITWEAR (SEE RUDI GERNREICH) An American knitwear manufacturer known primarily for its work with **Rudi Gemreich** in the 1950s–1960s.

HARP, HOLLY (1939-1995) American from Buffalo, New York. After dropping out of Radcliffe she found herself in Acapulco designing sandals in the early 1960s. After returning to the university and marrying her English professor, **Jim Harp,** she moved to Los Angeles and opened her first boutique, **Holly's Harp,** in 1968 on the Sunset Strip funded by a loan from her father. She opened a boutique at **Henri Bendel** in 1972 and launched her wholesale line in 1973. Her off-beat evening clothes, which favored matte jersey and airbrushed patterned chiffon adorned with feathers and fringe, were popularized by her celebrity and rock star clientele who frequented her Sunset Strip boutique. She also designed for **Simplicity Patterns,** as well as **Fieldcrest** bed linens.

HARTNELL, NORMAN, SIR (1901-1979) British from London, England. He began his design career as an assistant to court dressmaker **Mme. Désiré** in 1923 and worked briefly for **Lucile** in 1923 as well. He opened his own design house with his sister in London in late 1923, showing his first collection in Paris in 1927, followed by his second full collection in Paris in 1930, which received tremendous accolades. He quickly became the largest couture house of the times in London. In 1938 he was appointed dressmaker to the royal family in London, designing gowns for both the Queen Mother and Queen Elizabeth II, creating both her wedding gown and her coronation gown, while continuing to create all of their gowns for their overseas engagements. He is best remembered for his beautiful evening and ball gowns of satin and tulle, lavishly embellished with embroidery, sequins, and trimmings, as well as for his finely tailored fur-trimmed suits and coats of both French and British wool and tweeds. (He also produced a beautiful collection of fine costume jewelry.) He produced ready-to-wear in 1940 and designed for **Berketex** in the late 1940s. He received a knighthood from Queen Elizabeth II in 1977. French couturier **Marc Bohan** who had left the house of **Dior,** revitalized the house of **Hartnell** between 1990 and 1992. The firm is now no longer in business.

HATCH, MICHELLE (1961-) American from Bucks County, Pennsylvania. She had been discovered by a buyer from Henri Bendel when carrying one of her personal handcrafted handbags. Her first order for Bendel was for 24 handbags, followed by immediate additional orders. Her career was off and running. She continued her studies, enrolling in evening classes of accessory pattern making and design, and was contracted by her instructor to freelance for his company. This led to an opportunity to travel to Europe where she was offered a position to work for the prestigious fashion house of **Salvatore Ferragamo.** The company had been contracted in 1988 to outfit the Italian Olympic team and **Hatch** was appointed as the chief coordinator to dress all the members of the Italian Olympic team. Later that year she was hired by the **Donna Karan Co.** where she designed leathers, fabrics, accessories, and components for several divisions from late 1988 until early 1997. In the summer of 1997 she joined **Judith Leiber** as creative director. Two months later **Judith Leiber** retired after being at the helm of her company for over 35 years, leaving **Hatch** with the creative control. **Hatch** launched her own firm in the spring of 1999. Today her bags can be found in the luxury bag departments of Neiman Marcus, as well as other specialty salons of major department stores across North America. Most noted for her fine craftsmanship, signature details such as green silk lining in all of her bags, conveniently attached beveled mirrors, classic designs, and unique hardware which draws inspiration from beautiful handbags from the early collections of **Nettie Rosenstein** and **Koret,** as well as **Judith Leiber.**

HAWEIS, E. JAMES (SEE CHARLES JAMES)

HAWES, ELIZABETH (1903-1971) American from New Jersey. After graduating from Vassar College she left for Paris and in 1925 worked as a sketcher at fashion shows, as well as being a stylist collecting ideas to replicate and import for **Macy's** and **Lord & Taylor.** She also worked as a fashion writer and critic for various publications including the *New Yorker Magazine* and for a time for **Nicole Groult,** (**Poiret's** sister). In 1928 she returned to New York to found her own couture house with her partner **Rosemary Harden,** naming the business **Hawes-Harden.** It was a custom dressmaking business on Sixty-seventh Street. They were considered along with **Jessie Franklin Turner** to be one of the first authentic American couture houses and were fast becoming a household name in fashion at the time. **Rosemary Harden** left the company in 1930. **Elizabeth Hawes** showed her first collection in Paris in 1932, then in the Soviet Union in 1935. She began producing ready-to-wear, spearheaded by **Lord & Taylor's Dorothy Shaver** in 1932. During this time she continued to focus on her fashion writing and produced numerous books, including most notably, *Fashion Is Spinach.* She retired in 1940; however, she returned to fashion in 1948–1949 by opening another boutique offering up reintroduced versions of her original 1930s designs.

HEAD, EDITH (1899-1981) American from Los Angeles, California. Known primarily as a costume designer, she began her career working for **Howard Greer** at Paramount Pictures in 1923, and was later an assistant to **Travis Banton** in 1927. She was appointed head designer at Paramount when **Banton** left in 1938 and she remained as head designer until 1967. **Oleg Cassini** had been an assistant to **Head** for a time in the late 1930s and **Bob Mackie** worked under her as a sketch artist in the early 1960s. She worked as a freelance designer for Universal while at Paramount in the late 1960s, as well as for Metro-Goldwyn-Mayer, Columbia, 20th Century-Fox, and Warner Brothers and achieved over 1,000 screen credits and eight Academy Awards prior to her death. Many of her designs for the screen were very influential and inspired numerous American designers to replicate many of her creations, most notably the breathtaking strapless evening gown covered in white violets for Elizabeth Taylor in *A Place in the Sun.* She was quoted as saying that the restrictions imposed on the manufacturing of garments during WWII known as L-85 strengthened the costume design industry. Although she did design uniforms for the Coast Guard and Pan American Airlines, unlike her contemporaries in costume design, such as **Adrian, Irene, Greer,** or **Jean Louis, Head** did not cross over into producing ready-to-wear. She had no desire to produce garments for women outside of the film industry.

HECHTER, DANIEL (1938-) From Paris, France. He worked for **Pierre d' Alby,** 1958–1962, then he founded his own fashion house. His first collection was young women's ready-to-wear, including separates, suits, outerwear, and most notably a military style maxicoat. He introduced childrenswear in 1965, followed by menswear in 1970. In the early 1970s he sold numerous licenses to his ready-to-wear including an exclusive to **Fairweathers,** a moderately priced youth chain in Canada which sold his popular ready-to-wear throughout Canada.

HEIM, JACQUES (1899-1967) From Paris, France. In 1920, at the age of 21, he took over managing the furrier business of his parents, **Isadore** and **Jeanne Heim,** which was founded in 1898. He began designing womenswear in 1925 for the firm. He opened his own fashion house in 1930. The hallmark of his designs while at his family's business and independently in the 1930s focused on interpreting fur as a fabric, using fur accents and combinations of fur and wool in his designs. His designs were favored by Mme. Charles de Gaulle and he was a noted designer for Mrs. Dwight D. Eisenhower. He introduced a junior collection called **"Heim-Jeunes Filles"** in 1936 and is credited for the introduction and promotion of the French two-piece swimsuit and bikini, often using cotton in his beachwear. He opened a chain of sportswear boutiques in Biarritz and Cannes, 1946–1966. The company was taken over by his son, **Philippe Heim,** after his death in 1967. The house closed in 1966.

HEIM, ISADORE (DATES UNKNOWN) French, father to **Jacques Heim** and cofounder with his wife **Jeanne** of a furrier business in 1898. Son, **Jacques Heim,** began designing womenswear in 1925 for the firm until 1930 when he opened his own fashion house.

HEIM, PHILIPPE (DATES UNKNOWN) French, son to **Jacques Heim,** grandson to **Jeanne** and **Isadore Heim.** He took over running his father's ready-to-wear firm after his death in 1967; the house closed in 1966.

HEISEL, SYLVIA (1963-) American from Princeton, New Jersey. In 1981–1982 she designed and sold costume jewelry. She started designing women's ready-to-wear in 1982 and introduced her own label under her newly founded company **Postmodern Productions, Inc.** in 1983. She sold her first collection of coats to **Henri Bendel** in 1982 and then an exclusive line of ready-to-wear to **Barneys New York** in 1987. She held her first full-scale runway show in 1988. She is noted for her minimalist-construction, sportswear-inspired suits, separates, sophisticated dresses, and evening coats, as well as faux pony fur coats, lizard prints, and McFaddenesque dresses.

HELPERN, DAVID AND JOAN (DATES UNKNOWN) (SEE JOAN AND DAVID) An American men's and women's shoe manufacturing company in Italy founded in 1967 by husband and wife team **David** and **Joan Helpern.** They introduced handbags, belts, knits, and sportswear in 1986. The company remains in business today.

HERMAN, STAN (1930-) An American from New York. He designed hats for **John-Frederick** in 1954 and in 1961–1971 created sportswear, utility uniforms for corporations and airlines, as well as founding his own company with the label Mr. Mort, which produced eveningwear throughout the 1960s–1970s. Primarily a freelance designer working over the years for **Henri Bendel, Youthcraft, Charmfit, Slumbertogs,** and various uniform manufacturers. His uniform designs have included creations for Mcdonalds, United Airlines, Federal Express, TWA, and Avis. In the 1970s while working out of his **Henri Bendel** studio he campaigned against the use of real fur and introduced a collection of coats which used faux fur.

HERMÈS Founded in France in 1837 by **Thierry Hermès** who had specialized in saddle making. He opened a shop in Paris offering a number of handcrafted necessary and luxury leather items including moneybelts, gauntlet-gloves, and boots as well as saddles. His grandson **Emile Hermès** began designing garments from deerskin in the 1920s. The company became internationally renowned for their master-handcrafted handbags and silk scarves with equestrian themes, most notably the **Kelly bag,** introduced in 1935, which was an interpretation of an earlier saddle bag. The **Kelly bag** was renamed by permission of Grace Kelly who became **Princess Grace of Monaco,** after numerous press photographs of her appeared depicting her carrying the oversized handbag which she used frequently in many colors to disguise her early stages of pregnancy by holding the bag in front of her when in public. A **Kelly bag** is handcrafted by a single craftsperson who will work on the bag from beginning to end. If the bag is ever in need of repair it is said that as long as the craftsperson is still with the company, the bag is shipped back to the original person who constructed it. There is a small marking on every bag which identifies it to its maker. In

1997 **Hermès** appointed Belgian designer **Martine Margiela** design director of their ready-to-wear collections. The company is still privately held by the original descendants of the founding family.

HERRERA, CAROLINA, MARIA CAROLINA JOSEFINA PACANINS Y NINO (1939-) Venezuelan from Caracas, Venezuela. Considered by many to be a socialite turned designer, but who better to appreciate design than someone whose station in society and affluence took her to some of the finest couture houses in the world. She was on the International Best Dressed List for ten years and nominated to the Best Dressed Hall of Fame. Her inspiration is said to come from the work of a favorite couturier, **Balenciaga.** Spearheaded by supporter **Diana Vreeland** she introduced her first couture collection in 1981, often designing for many of her friends such as Estée Lauder, Nancy Reagan, as well as Jacqueline Kennedy Onassis. She introduced a collection for **Revillon** in 1984 and then a diffusion line of her own called **CH** in 1986. She followed with debuting a bridal line in 1987 and a sportswear line in 1989, followed by menswear in 1992.

HILFIGER, TOMMY (1951-) American from Elmira, New York. He opened his first store **People's Places** with three friends from high school selling bell-bottom jeans in Elmira, New York, in 1969. **Larry Stemerman** was one of the original investors in **People's Places.** In August 1977, **Hilfiger** and **Stemerman** filed for bankruptcy after almost a decade of tremendous success. **Hilfiger** with new wife **Susie Cirona** began to look for design work on Seventh Avenue. After a short time as a design team at **Jordache** they moved for a time to **Bonjour.** In 1983 they partnered with investor **Mohan Murjani,** an Indian entrepreneur who owned the license for **Gloria Vanderbilt** jeans, and **Coca-Cola** clothes. After five years of incredible growth in 1988 the **Mohan Murjani** empire imploded after overextending itself. **Silas Chou** was the financial savior and by 1989 **Hilfiger USA** had leapfrogged from $28 million a year to $50 million in 1990 and then to $100 million the following year. Founder, designer, and vice-chairman of **Tommy Hilfiger Corporation,** New York, **Tommy Hilfiger** took his company public in 1992 and is presently listed on the New York Stock Exchange. **Stephen Cirona,** a cousin to **Hilfiger's** wife **Susie,** was appointed as the principal designer of menswear and womenswear. Today his clothes are all-American in the tradition of **Ralph Lauren:** clean-cut, comfortable, and exuberant. Expansion plans include new stores in Europe including 20 stand-alone stores in Italy.

HIRST, FREDERIC (SEE HANSI HARBERGER, JOHN-FREDERICK AND MR. JOHN) (DATES UNKNOWN) **Hansi Harberger** partnered with **Frederic Hirst** in the mid-1940s, naming the millinery company **John-Frederick.** They dissolved the partnership in 1948 and the two men continued to produce hats under their own companies: **Hansi Harberger** as **Mr. John** and **Frederic Hirst** as **John-Frederick.** **Stan Herman** designed hats for **John-Frederick** in 1954.

HORN, CAROL (1936-) American from New York. Initially worked in retail as a fashion coordinator and then as a designer of junior sportswear for **Bryant 9.** She was the head designer for **Benson and Partners** for four years before designing the **Carol Horn Division** of **Malcolm Starr.** She started her own company in 1983, **Carol Horn Sportswear,** then introduced **Carol Horn Knitwear.**

HOWELL, MARGARET (1946-) British from Tadworth, England. She launched her men's and women's ready-to-wear collections in 1972, with inspirations culled from her love of the innovative sportswear looks of the early 1930s, and her affection for traditional British country clothes. Famous for her use of men's tailored tweeds for her womenswear, linen duster coats, shirtdresses, and raincoats. Her designs throughout the 1970s were very influential and widely replicated by many design houses.

HULANICKI, BARBARA (SEE BIBA) (1936-) From Warsaw, Poland, raised in Palestine, immigrated to England in 1948. She began as a freelance fashion illustrator for *Vogue, Women's Wear Daily,* London's *The Tattler,* and various other newspapers, 1961–1964. In 1963 she launched a mail-order business offering her ready-to-wear designs with her new husband **Stephen Fitz-Simon.** In 1964 she opened her first **Biba Emporium.** In 1968 she launched a larger mail-order catalog business. In 1969 she opened her High Street, Kensington, London store, as well introducing a line of footwear. Also that same year they sold 75 percent interest in the company to a consortium of investors. In 1970 they opened the **Biba Boutique** in

Bergdorf Goodman, New York. In a monumental move in 1972 they purchased the enormous beautiful Art Deco building which was the **Derry and Toms Department Store.** The Derry and Toms Building was transformed into a fabulous boutique completed by exquisite Art Deco decor which became the look of **Biba** in the early 1970s. It was an internationally known symbol of swinging London in the mid-1960s and people came from around the globe to experience its scene. In 1972 the control of **Biba** passed to **British Land,** and in 1973 they opened **Big Biba,** which closed just two years later in 1975. The company declared bankruptcy in 1976. Apparently the signature style of **Biba** in the 1960s, such as vamp dresses, floppy cut-out hats, and billowing crepe dresses with sweetheart necklines was not able to transcend the look of the 1970s. **Barbara Hulanicki** worked as a fashion designer in Brazil, 1976–1980. She relocated to Miami Beach, Florida, in 1987 to design hotel and nightclub interiors, as well as a line of children's ready-to-wear and theater costumes.

HULITAR, PHILIP (DATES UNKNOWN) American, began designing debutante, wedding, and maternity clothes for Bergdorf Goodman from 1935 until 1949. In 1949 he launched his own design company and specialized in beautiful, sexy, and romantic eveningwear which often offered an empire waist with a very flared skirt of silk, chiffon, or draping matte jersey in a sheath silhouette. **Victor Costa** sold design sketches to **Hulitar** in the mid-1950s. **Hulitar** continued to design beautiful eveningwear until his retirement in 1964.

IRENE (SEE IRENE LENTZ)

IRIS LINGERIE (SEE SILVIA PEDLAR) An American lingerie wholesale manufacturer founded by **Silvia Pedlar** in New York, in 1929.

JABLOW, ARTHUR (SEE DAVID KIDD) An American women's ready-to-wear manufacturer founded in the 1940s. Most noted for their feminine suits, coats, and day dresses. **David Kidd** joined the company in the 1950s and continued designing in the tradition of the company through the early 1960s. **Kidd's** designs in the 1960s borrowed heavily on influences derivative of **Balenciaga's** work of the period.

JACOBS, MARK (1964-) American from New York. He originally dreamed of becoming a veterinarian; a blessing to the fashion community was that he decided to study design instead. While at Parsons in New York, he designed sweaters for **Charivari,** a New York clothing store where he had worked as a stock boy. After graduating he went to work for **Ruben Thomas, Inc.** until 1985, designing for their **Sketchbook** label. His most memorable collection for **Sketchbook** was inspired by the movie *Amadeus*. He designed his own collections, 1986–1988, first with backing from **Jack Atkins** and later from **Onward Kashiyama.** He was appointed vice president for womenswear, **Perry Ellis,** in the fall of 1988. He went on to become head designer for **Perry Ellis,** 1989–1993. His work with **Perry Ellis** reestablished the firm as an exciting major fashion concern. He launched his own collection again in 1994. **Irene Chung** is presently his senior accessories designer. His work is always romantic, and remarkably sophisticated. Today, as well as continuing with his own collection, **Jacobs** as head designer has been the driving force behind the exciting revitalization of **Louis Vuitton,** a luxury holding of **LVMH** (Louis Vuitton, Moët, Hennessy).

JAEGER A British garment manufacturer founded in 1884 by **Lewis Tomalin** (dates unknown), who had purchased the rights to **Dr. Gustave Jaeger's** name in order to manufacture woolen ladies undergarments which **Dr. Jaeger** had decreed would be healthier for the wearer. The idea was tremendously successful until the 1920s when the style of dress for the period was no longer suitable for heavy undergarments. The company had branched off to manufacture numerous separates such as cardigans, jumpers, suits, and coats. **Jean Muir** designed there, 1956–1963, before producing her own clothing line under the name **Jane & Jane. Jaeger** is still recognized today as a company which manufactures good quality garments in an international marketplace.

JAMES, CHARLES (1906-1978) British, from Sandhurst, England, of Anglo-American parentage. Educated at Harrow, he moved to his mother's hometown of Chicago in the early 1920s and established a millinery business as **Charles Boucheron,** 1924–1928. He moved to New York and began to design custom dresses, 1928–1929. He moved to London, England, in 1929 and stayed through 1939 and produced a small couture collection using the name **E. James Haweis, London and Paris.** While in London he began to sell some of his original models to **Lord & Taylor** and **Saks Fifth Avenue** which used these models to make copies selling for approximately $200, about one-sixth of what the originals sold for. While in Europe he worked under **Paul Poiret's** patronage, as well as designing fabrics for **Colcobet,** a French textile manufacturer, 1934–1935. He relocated back to New York in 1940 and established his custom design business, **Charles James, Inc.** He designed a couture collection for **Elizabeth Arden Salon,** New York, 1943–1945. He was appointed to design for **Elizabeth Arden Salon,** as well as to oversee the installation of their custom department; however, prior to completing the collection they had a professional falling-out and the collection was never completed. In 1950 he experimented with ready-to-wear, but without much success due to his lack of a keen business acumen. **Arnold Scaasi** worked for him, 1951–1953, as well as **George Halley** in the early 1950s to early 1960s. **Linda Kinoshita** was the protégée of **Charles James** in the early 1950s and ran his atelier until she opened her own salon in 1957. In 1955 he signed a deal with American blouse manufacturer **Samuel Winston** to produce a line of clothes; however, like many of his deals, this ended badly, culminating in a lawsuit where **James** charged **Winston** with illegally pilfering his design ideas for their **Roxanne** division. He closed his custom design business in 1958 and in 1962 designed a ready-to-wear collection for **E. J. Korvettes. Antonio,** a brilliant illustrator, sketched and documented many of **James's** designs over a period of years from 1964. **James** also designed a maternity collection for **Lane Bryant,** as well as producing children's clothing. He is most noted for his ingenious asymmetrical, sculptural forms in lustrous fabrics such as heavy faille, slipper satins, and velvets. He spent the last part of his life living in the Chelsea Hotel in New York documenting his life's work. In his day he was a very formidable designer whose work continues to inspire designers today.

JAMES HAWEIS, E. (SEE CHARLES JAMES)

JANE, PLAIN, PLAIN JANE DRESS COMPANY (SEE ESPRIT) An American dress manufacturer which specialized in pretty, simply cut 1940s-style dresses in the 1960s. It was the company from which the **Esprit de Corps Company** was launched in 1968.

JAY-THORPE, INC. A deluxe specialty department store which specialized in avant-garde merchandise from the 1920s to the late 1960s. They had hats from top Paris designers, as well as exceptional lingerie in the early 1920s. **Harry Lichtenstein** was hired to set up his own custom-order department in 1929. Traveling to the shows in Paris he would purchase models from which he created as adaptations or exact versions. **Mrs. Hendrick Suydan** was head of the trousseau department, and **Renée Montaigue** was the in-house staff designer in the late 1920s through the 1930s. **Mollie Parnis's** designs were sold without her label on them at **Jay-Thorpe, Inc.** in 1933. **Wilson Folmar** was the custom designer, 1936–1939, and then again after the war in 1946. The business closed in the late 1960s.

JAX An American boutique in Beverly Hills, California, most noted for their cutting-edge fashions of the times. They were one of the first boutiques to showcase the designs of **Rudi Gernreich** in 1952 when he was teamed with **Walter Bass.** Famous for their narrow-legged, long pant with side zippers which were made more famous by Marilyn Monroe wearing them.

JOAN AND DAVID (SEE JOAN AND DAVID HELPERN)

JOHN-FREDERICK (SEE FREDERIC HIRST, HANSI HARBERGER, AND MR. JOHN) (DATES UNKNOWN) **Hansi Harberger** partnered with **Frederic Hirst** in the mid-1940s naming the millinery company **John-Frederick.** They dissolved the partnership in 1948 and the two men continued to produce hats under their own companies: **Hansi Harberger** as **Mr. John** and **Frederic Hirst** as **John-Frederick. Stan Herman** designed hats for **John-Frederick** in 1954.

JOHNSON, BETSEY (1942–) American from Weathersfield, Connecticut. After graduating from Syracuse University she was a young guest editor for *Mademoiselle* magazine, (summer college issue) in 1964. Shortly after working with *Mademoiselle* she became a freelance designer with the encouragement of many of her fellow workers who purchased her off-beat sweaters she made. She freelanced for **Paraphernalia,** a youth-oriented New York boutique, 1965–1969. In 1969 she opened her first boutique with three friends called **Betsey, Bunkey, and Nimi.** She continued to design for numerous other companies, including **Alvin Duskin Co.** of San Francisco in 1970 and ready-to-wear manufacturer **Alley Cat,** 1970–1974; then for **Gant,** 1974–1975. She designed for **Butterick Patterns** in 1971 and again in 1975. Throughout the 1970s she continued to work for various manufacturers, **Gant,** 1974–1975, as well as creating **Betsey Johnson's Kidswear,** a division of **Shutterbug,** 1974–1977, and **Tric-Trac** by **Betsey Johnson,** 1974–1976. She teamed with **Michael Miles** to create **Star Ferry,** 1975–1977. She founded her own company **Betsey Johnson Vines** in 1978 and remains head designer and president today. She opened her first **Betsey Johnson** boutiques in 1979. Most noted for her Youthquake designs, using unorthodox materials such as vinyl, sequin sheeting, and stretch fabrics. Her fun and flirtatious designs derive much of their influence from her dance background, her basic silhouette often a ballerina torso and tutu. She is considered to have been the anti–Seventh Avenue designer of the 1960s much like **Biba** and **Mary Quant** were in the London fashion movement at that time.

JONES, STEPHEN (1957-) British from West Kirby, Liverpool, England. A milliner whose first collection for **Fiorucci** in 1979 spawned a vibrant career which has included most notably being, in 1984, the first British milliner to work in Paris, designing for designers such as **Jean-Paul Gaultier, Claude Montana, Thierry Mugler, Rei Kawakubo** of **Comme des Garçons, John Galliano,** as well as for **Vivienne Westwood, Katherine Hamnett, Zandra Rhodes, Emanuel Ungaro,** and **Antonio Berardi.** He worked for **Lachasse** in 1980 just prior to opening his first salon, the boutique **PX,** in Covent Garden, London. He added **Stephen Jones Scarves** and **Miss Jones** lines in 1988, **Jonesboy** and **Stephen Jones Handkerchieves** in 1990, **Stephen Jones Kimonos,** in 1991, and handbags in 1993. He branched out of fashion as a color creator for **Shiseido Cosmetics** in 1988. He has also created millinery designs for many celebrities, including Boy George, Madonna, and George Michael.

JOOP, WOLFGANG (1944-) German from Potsdam, Germany. Originally a journalist, he worked as a freelance designer for **Christian Aujard,** as well as **Brecco** and others in the late 1970s. He introduced his first fur collection under his own label in 1978, followed by **Joop!** ready-to-wear in 1981, and a menswear collection in 1985. He opened his first boutiques in Hamburg and Munchin in 1986 and added a successful jeans collection in 1989. Along with **Jil Sander, Wolfgang Joop** is recognized as the most important and influential German designer.

JOURDAN, CHARLES (1883-1976) He began as a foreman at **Établissement Grenier,** a shoe leather cutting company in 1917 at the age of 30. He began manufacturing his own collection of shoes in Romans, France, in 1921. He began distributing his shoes to all of France by 1930. His sons **René, Roland,** and **Charles** took over the business after WWII in the mid-1940s. They launched their first Paris boutique in 1957, followed by London in 1959. They were contracted by the house of **Christian Dior** in 1959 to distribute a line of shoes for **Dior** worldwide. **Perugia** began to design for the company in the early 1960s. The first American store was opened in New York in 1968, followed by the launch of a ready-to-wear collection and handbags in the 1970s. The company sold numerous franchises and by 1975 there were 21 franchises in North America and Europe. After **Charles Jourdan's** death in 1976, the sons continued the company and launched a men's fragrance, as well as menswear in the 1980s. After the retirement of **Roland Jourdan** who had headed the company, the company was bought by **Portland Cement Werke** in 1981, appointing **Bernard Sucheras** as chief designer. The company had also commissioned **Hervé Léger** to design accessories in the 1980s and ready-to-wear in 1992. After 75 years in business, the **Jourdan** company continues to design luxury shoes, handbags, and accessories as well as international fashion.

JOYCE, EMMET (DATES UNKNOWN) American from Chicago. A women's ready-to-wear designer who established his wholesale manufacturing firm **Emmet Joyce,** New York, in 1928. His intricately detailed day and colorful evening designs were sold at Bergdorf Goodman and Jay-Thorpe Inc. **Claire McCardell** had worked as both a sketch artist and sales associate for him in 1928. **Joyce** closed his business in 1935 and worked for **Hattie Carnegie** and **Mme. Frances** in the mid-1930s prior to designing custom-made dresses with **Sophie Gimbel,** the **Saks Originals** ready-to-wear.

JULIAN, ALEXANDER (1948-) American from Chapel Hill, North Carolina. The son of a retailer, he designed his first shirt at the age of 12 and was managing his father's shop by age 18. By 21 he had opened his own shop and by 27 had moved to New York to pursue a design career. His menswear is uniquely classic and expensive, and he often designs his own fabrics. In the late 1980s and 1990s he sold licenses to various manufacturers who produce menswear, home furnishings, decorative fabrics, and small leather goods and accessories. In the early 1990s he and his partner purchased his company, **Colours by Alexander Julian,** back from **Cluett Peabody,** renaming the company **Collection Clothing Corp.**

KAMALI, NORMA (NORMA ARRAEZ) (1945-) American from New York. Began her career as a free-lance illustrator, then a reservation clerk at Northwest Airlines. She married **Mohammed (Eddie) Houssein Kamali** in 1967 and opened her first retail store with him in the same year on East Fifty-third Street in New York. She originally stocked the store with swinging looks from London which she was able to purchase there by way of her discounted airline tickets, an employee perk. She quit her airline job in 1971 to concentrate full-time on producing her own designs for her flourishing boutique. She relocated the boutique to a second story on Madison Avenue in 1974 and stepped up her designs to more sophisticated tailoring and soft feminine dresses. She divorced her husband in 1978 and ventured out with a new boutique and collection, **OMO (On My Own)** on West Fifty-sixth Street. By the early 1980s she ruled the youth-oriented markets with her widely copied sweatshirt fabric designs produced by **Jones Apparel Group** and was fast becoming a household name. She is most noted for her parachute and her big-shouldered sweatshirt designs, as well as her beautifully tailored suits and dresses which usually draw their inspiration from the 1930s and 1940s. She also designed the whimsical costumes for the motion picture The Wiz. She launched a website in 2000, and in 2001 announced that she has resurrected and reintroduced designs from her vast archives, as well as cross-merchandised her vintage pieces with her contemporary designs.

KARAN, DONNA (DONNA FASKE) (1948-) American from Forest Hills, New York. She began working as a sketch artist for **Anne Klein** prior to graduating from Parsons in New York in 1967. Her part-time job with **Klein** quickly escalated to design assistant and by 1973 when **Anne Klein** took ill she was appointed as head designer. She succeeded **Anne Klein** after her death in 1974 and brought **Louis Dell'Olio,** a friend from Parsons, in as her associate designer for **Anne Klein.** She left in 1984 to design her own collection and launched **Donna Karan New York** with her second husband **Stephen Weiss** and financial partner **Takihyo Corporation** of Japan, **Anne Klein's** parent company. **Louis Dell'Olio** remained as the chief designer for **Klein** until 1993. Most noted for her luxurious designs for women of status, throughout the late 1980s and 1990s: formfitting body tops with matching separates, clothes she said she herself would wear. In the years to follow she would add accessories, menswear, fragrances, a bridge line, **DKNY,** hosiery, lingerie, and swimwear. Today the company is perhaps the most formidable fashion manufacturer in America. Early in 2000 it was announced that luxury conglomerate **Louis Vuitton, Moët, Henesey (LVMH)** would buy the **Donna Karan** company, and on April 2, 2001 **LVMH** confirmed the acquisition of **Gabrielle Studio, Inc.** which owns the **Donna Karan** and **DKNY** brands, and other brands used by **DKI. LVMH** would be buying factories in Italy and moving the production for **Donna Karan** to Italy as part of their acquisition in the hopes of broadening the appeal of the company and to benefit from the Italian know-how. Her partner and husband, **Stephen Weiss,** died suddenly in the spring of 2001, just shortly after the sale of the company.

KASPER, HERBERT (1926-) American from New York. He worked for many design houses throughout the 1950s while living in Paris, including **Jacques Fath, Marcel Rochas, Christian Dior,** as well as Elle magazine. While in Paris he continued to sell sketches to the **Mr. John** millinery company. In 1954 he returned to America and worked for **Arnold & Fox,** New York, from 1954 to 1964, as well as for **Mr. John,** designing hats in 1960. His work at **Arnold & Fox** became known as **Kasper for Arnold & Fox Designs, Inc.** He also worked for a time with **Penart,** his designs distributed through **Lord & Taylor** as **Kasper of Penart.** He began working for **Leslie Fay,** a women's ready-to-wear manufacturer, in 1965 and established **Kasper for Joan Leslie** as a division of **Leslie Fay** in 1967, followed by **Kasper for JL Sport, Ltd.,** and **Kasper for Weatherscope.** He became vice president of the **Leslie Fay** company in 1980 and left the company in 1985 to launch his own label. Most noted for his moderately priced women's separates, dresses, and suits, which had refined tailoring in affordable fabrics.

KAWAKUBO, REI, COMME DES GARÇONS (1942-) Japanese from Tokyo, Japan. She began her career in 1964 in advertising for **Asahi Kasei,** a Japanese textile company. She worked as a freelance stylist and designer, 1966–1967, then founded **Comme des Garçons** in 1969, launching her first collection for the company in 1975. She introduced menswear in 1978. The 1970s and 1980s saw the height of her popularity with her non-traditional, avant-garde designs. Her first international exposure came in 1981 with the opening of her first boutique in Paris. Her minimal, monochromatic, and modern designs have influenced many other designers and continue to inspire them today.

KELLY, PATRICK (1954-1990) American from Vicksburg, Mississippi. His career had a staggered and varied beginning in Atlanta, from window dresser at **Yves Saint Laurent Rive Gauche** boutique, modeling school instructor, to vintage clothing proprietor in the 1970s. After failing to find his feet on Seventh Avenue in New York he moved to Paris and was discovered selling his own designs of cut-out cotton tub dresses in a Paris flea market. He worked as a costume designer for **Le Palais Club,** 1980–1981, and as a freelance designer, 1980–1990. He introduced his first ready-to-wear collection in Paris in 1985 and was a freelance designer for **Benetton** in 1986. The height of his fame was in 1987 when he opened his first boutique in Paris, launched a couture collection, and sold worldwide rights to his ready-to-wear collections. An untimely death tragically halted his work in 1990.

KEMPER, RANDY (1959-) American from Philadelphia, Pennsylvania. A ready-to-wear designer who began by designing for **J. G. Hook** in Philadelphia, 1980–1981; then for **Givenchy,** Paris, 1981–1982; followed by **Hanae Mori,** New York City, 1983–1984; and **Bill Blass,** New York City, 1984–1986. He established his own design firm, **Randy Kemper Corp.** in 1987 in New York. Noted for his graceful, low-key, sophisticated evening and leisure apparel. He gained tremendous attention in 1992 and 1993 when Hillary Clinton began to buy his designs through a Little Rock, Arkansas, dress shop.

KENZO (KENZO TAKADA) (1939-) Japanese from Kyoto, Japan. He began his career in Japan designing for **Sanai** department store and as a pattern designer for *Soen* magazine, 1960–1964. He moved to Paris in 1964 and sold sketches to **Louis Féraud,** as well as working as a freelance designer for many companies such as **Rodier** and **Pisanti.** He opened his first boutique **Jungle Jap** in Paris in 1970 receiving tremendous success for his women's ready-to-wear oriental-style blouses, tunics, smocks, wide-legged trousers, and printed velvets. He launched his menswear collection in 1984, and opened boutiques around the world, including New York, London, Milan, Tokyo, Saint-Tropez, and Copenhagen. He introduced **Kenzo Jungle** and **Kenzo Jeans** in 1986. His designs have been widely influenced by his international travels, assimilating specific costume elements from various parts of the world to create a harmonious multicultural expression. Today **Gillies Roseir** is in charge of women's ready-to-wear and **Roy Krejberg** is in charge of menswear. There are presently over 170 **Kenzo** boutiques worldwide. The **Kenzo** company was acquired by the luxury conglomerate **LVMH.**

KERR, PAT (DATES UNKNOWN) American custom designer who worked out of Memphis, Tennessee; most noted for her women's evening and romantic day dresses made from antique fabrics and jet beading. Her collection of Edwardian whites, lace-trimmed dresses with patchwork lace, was bought by **Neiman Marcus** in 1979. She continued to use the antique fabrics and lace which she purchased through European auctions and flea markets to create ensembles for brides, bridesmaids, flower girls, and ring bearers. Her elaborate one-of-a-kind eveningwear embellished with jet-embroidered panels sold for upwards of $25,000.

KHANH, EMMANUELLE (RENÉE MEZIÈRE) (1937-) Frenchwoman from Paris, she worked as a stylist and designer for **Jean Cacharel,** Paris, in 1955–1957 then as a model for **Balenciaga** and **Givenchy,** 1957–1963, before becoming a freelance designer for numerous fashion houses, 1963–1969, including **Belletête, Missoni, Dorothée Bis, Laura, Cacharel, Pierre d'Alby, Krizia, Max Mara,** and **Le Bistrot du Tricot.** She was also creating her own collections from 1962, notably her collaborated venture with fellow model **Christiane Baily** whom she had met at **Balenciaga,** called **Emma Christie.** The **Emma Christie** label received high critical acclaim and was considered by many to be revolutionary in the ready-to-wear markets in the early 1960s; however, it never received commercial success. **Khanh** launched her own company in 1971. Most noted for her edgy and sexy designs in the 1960s, **Khanh** was to France what **Mary Quant** was to London. Her designs emphasized the feminine form and were cut close along the curves of the body. Romanian hand-embroidery and peasant-style dresses of brightly colored Indian gauze fabrics were the signature of her look throughout the 1970s. She turned to retro looks in the 1980s and in 1990 she created collections for **Jet Lag Showroom** for whom she continues to freelance, producing women's ready-to-wear suits, jackets, and coats. She also produced a successful line of eyewear in the late 1970s–1980s.

KIAM, OMAR (ALEXANDER KIAM) (1894-1954) Mexican from Monterey, Mexico. He began designing for the millinery department for a Houston department store in 1912. During the 1920s he had worked in Paris and New York as a freelance designer, as well as creator of theatrical costumes. After working on Broadway in the early 1930s he was hired by **Samuel Goldwyn's** production company in Hollywood where he continued for many years to produce costume designs for various films, often designing specifically for Loretta Young and Merle Oberon. During this time he also worked for United Artists and Paramount Pictures. His most notable films were *A Star is Born* and *Stella Dallas*. He became the head designer for **Ben Reig,** a New York ready-to-wear manufacturer in 1941, under the label **Omar Kiam for Ben Reig.** He continued designing for the company throughout the 1940s and early 1950s, creating a line of costume jewelry for them in 1948. He was recognized for his expensive and elegant women's ready-to-wear which was often fur trimmed; a suit could sell for as much as $300 in the 1940s. He left the company shortly before his death in 1954 and was succeeded by **Eva Rosencrans** in 1961.

KIDD, DAVID (SEE ARTHUR JABLOW) (DATES UNKNOWN) American ready-to-wear designer for **Arthur Jablow,** a New York wholesale firm, throughout the 1950s and 1960s. His work in the 1960s was highly reliant on the look of **Balenciaga** at the time. His designer suits and separates were sold through better department stores.

KIESELSTEIN-CORD, BARRY (1948-) American from New York. A high-end jewelry, handbag, belt, gloves, and home furnishings designer. He founded his company in 1972. His signature look is that of heavy sculpted reptiles in fine sterling silver, coupled with exotic skins such as alligator, crocodile, and lizard.

KILPATRICK, BUD (DATES UNKNOWN) American ready-to-wear designer based in California whose designs throughout the 1960s were very luxurious and creative, usually from fine European fabrics. Most noted for his meticulously tailored suits and elegant eveningwear.

KING, MURIEL (1901-1977) American from Bayview, Washington. She began her career as a fashion illustrator in New York for *Harper's Bazaar* and *Vogue,* moving to Paris in 1927 to work for *Modes and Manners, Femina,* and *Vogue, France.* She began working as a freelance designer in the early 1930s, creating a collection in 1933 for **B. Altman.** She designed for films in 1935 creating costumes on and off screen for Katharine Hepburn, most notably for Hepburn's role in *Sylvia Scarlett.* She also designed for Ginger Rogers in *Stage Door.* She moved her custom salon to 49 East Fifty-first Street in New York in 1937 where she continued as a top-rung designer with contemporaries such as **Elizabeth Hawes, Jo Copeland,** and **Claire McCardell,** creating breathtakingly elegant eveningwear. After a short retirement at the end of the 1930s, she went back to designing and created a venture called **d'Armand King,** which was a collection of women's air force uniforms which were bought by **Boeing, Lockheed,** and Douglas. After World War II she freelanced for **Lord & Taylor** and became the head of the custom department for **Stein and Blaine** until she retired in 1957.

KINOSHITA, LINDA (DATES UNKNOWN) Japanese, born in California. She was the protégée of **Charles James** in the early 1950s and ran his atelier until she opened her own salon in 1957. Her designs drew their influences from her Japanese roots, often incorporating elements from ancient Japanese traditional clothing with contemporary couture design. Her most notable client was Babe Paley for whom she created a beautiful kimono ensemble. She also designed oriental-style eveningwear for the wholesale house **Dynasty** which manufactured out of Hong Kong. She continued to design into the early 1960s.

KIRBY, IRMA (SEE EISENBERG) (DATES UNKNOWN) American, she was the designer whose name appeared on the label for the **Eisenberg and Sons Originals** in the 1930s. They specialized in little black dresses at that time.

KLEIBACKER, CHARLES (DATES UNKNOWN) American from Alabama. He began as a journalist working for an Alabama newspaper, then moved to New York and worked as a copywriter for Gimbel's advertising department. He later took a job working for entertainer Hildegarde, traveling to Paris where he met many of her favorite couturiers. It was in Paris that he discovered his desire to design and took a position in the late 1950s working for **Antonio del Castillo,** who was with **Lanvin** at the time. He returned to New York in 1958 to work for **Eva Rosencrans** at **Nettie Rosenstein,** prior to opening his own company in 1963. His company remained a relatively small firm due to his strong desire to maintain the highest quality control on his masterfully bias-cut off-the-rack gowns which he produced from fine silk jersey, silk crepe, or taffeta, and sold through Bergdorf Goodman and Henri Bendel in New York. He continued to produce beautiful eveningwear until his retirement in 1984 when he moved to Ohio to become the designer-in-residence for the Department of Textiles and Clothing at the School of Home Economics and Curator of Historical Costumes at Ohio State University.

KLEIN, ANNE (HANNAH GOLOFSKI) (1923-1974) American from Brooklyn, New York. She began working as a sketch artist on Seventh Avenue in 1938 when she was just 15. She created a junior line for **Varden Petites,** 1938–1940. She married **Ben Klein** in 1939. She left **Varden** to join **Maurice Rentner,** 1940–1947. In 1948 she formed **Junior Sophisticates** with her husband **Ben Klein.** She designed coats and sportswear separates for **Mallory Leathers** in 1965, prior to forming **Anne Klein and Company** with **Sanford Smith** and her second husband, **Chip Rubenstein,** in 1968. She introduced a lion's head, her astrological sign, on her label in 1972. She is best known for her women's sport and ready-to-wear designs throughout the 1950s and early 1970s. After her death in 1974 her assistant, **Donna Karan,** was appointed head designer. **Donna Karan** appointed her friend and fellow student from Parsons in New York, **Louis Dell'Olio,** as her co-designer. The company introduced **Anne Klein II,** designed by **Maurice Antaya** in 1982. **Dell'Olio** became head designer when **Donna Karan** left to form her own company in 1984. **Dell'Olio** remained the head designer until 1993 when he was succeeded by **Richard Tyler.** The company introduced **A-Line,** a younger sporty line in 1993. **Tyler** remained for one year and was replaced in 1994 by **Patrick Robinson** who had formerly been with **Giorgio Armani-Le Collezione.**

KLEIN, BEN (DATES UNKNOWN) American, former husband of the late **Anne Klein.** Co-founder of **Junior Sophisticates** with **Anne Klein** in 1948.

KLEIN, CALVIN (1942-) American from the Bronx, New York. After graduating from F.I.T. at the age of 21 he worked for **Dan Millstein,** an American wholesale sportswear manufacturer, 1962–1964. He then worked as a freelance designer in New York, 1964–1968, prior to founding **Calvin Klein Co.** with longtime friend **Barry Schwartz** in 1968. In the beginning the company's primary focus was on women's coats. By the early 1970s the company had established a solid reputation in women's sportswear, designing man-tailored suits and separates. **Klein's** keen business acumen served to ignite a strong movement in sexually expressive advertising in the 1980s with the notorious campaign for his jean ads featuring Brooke Shields, as well as his underwear campaign for which the large bus shelter poster ads were continually stolen by admirers. **Gordon Henderson** worked as a design assistant for him in 1984, as did **Isaac Mizrahi,** 1985–1987. Fragrances were introduced: **Obsession,** 1985, **Eternity,** 1988, **Escape,** 1991, and **CK One,** a shared-gender fragrance in 1994. The company reorganized in 1991. In May of 2001 the company announced that they were restructuring and cutting their $50-million-a-year bridge line **CK.**

KLEIN, DAVID LLOYD (SEE GRÉS, MME. ALIX)

KLEIN, RONALD (1938-) From Rouen, France. After studying at the École de la Chambre Syndicale de la Couture Parisienne, he worked, 1960–1962, in the tailoring department at **Christian Dior,** then worked for **Patou,** and as an assistant to **Karl Lagerfeld.** In 1973 he worked for **Marcel Fenz** in London and became the managing director with his own label. He launched his own ready-to-wear business in

1979, specializing in beautifully tailored, well-cut, simple, elegant womenswear. He also designed for **MaxMara.**

KLIEN, MICHEL (DATES UNKNOWN) French couture designer who began designing for the house of **Guy Laroche** in 1993 after **Laroche's** death.

KOBAYASHI, YUKIO (DATES UNKNOWN) A Japanese menswear designer for **Matsuda.** Often described as having literal traits and propensities, and possessing audacious style eclecticism and dandy-like Beau Brummel exactness. His first collections were shown in 1984. His influences are early 20th-century designs from England and Scotland, capturing an unpretentiousness with comfortable tweed and rugged fabrics. Considered to be a casual, ready-to-wear designer dressing the modern, creative, intellectual man.

KORET An American handbag manufacturer established in the 1920s which by the 1940s had become a major producer of quality designer handbags similar to those of **Joseff's.** Noted for being the manufacturer who made most of Jacqueline Kennedy Onassis's handbags to match her shoes in the early 1960s.

KORS, MICHAEL (1959-) American from Long Island, New York. After graduating from F.I.T. in 1977 he worked as a sales assistant, buyer, and display director for **Lothar's Boutique,** New York, 1977–1980. His first collection, launched in 1981, consisted of only 16 pieces, all in black and brown. Most noted for his practical, minimalist approach in neutral colors which derive their inspiration from early **Claire McCardell** designs. He introduced his less expensive line, **KORS,** in 1990 while continuing to freelance for various companies including **Erreuno J.** and **Lyle and Scott,** a Scottish firm for which he created cashmere knits, as well as designing for various licenses for swimwear and shoes. He was appointed head designer for **Celine** in 1998. **Alex Shuman** is presently designing for **Michael Kors** ready-to-wear. Noted for his classic tailoring, considered by many to be more than fashion, **Michael Kors** is an investment in style.

KORVETTES, E. J. (SEE CHARLES JAMES) An American ready-to-wear wholesale manufacturer.

KRIZIA (SEE MARIUCCIA MANDELLI)

LACHASSE A British women's ready-to-wear manufacturer founded in 1929 under the design direction of **Digby Morton,** 1928–1933, which specialized in the quintessential "English" style, creating finely tailored women's tweed suits, sportswear, and country clothes. **Morton** was succeeded by **Hardy Amies** as managing designer in 1934, and then as managing designer/director from 1935–1939, followed by **Michael Donellan** in 1939–1953. **Peter Lewis-Crown** was appointed chief design director in 1974. The house is famous for their appointment to design for the British royals as well as for their work designing for British theater.

LACOSTE, RENÉ (1904-1996) French tennis star **René Lacoste** whose nickname was "Le Crocodile," began with a simple white tennis shirt with a small crocodile emblem on the breast of the shirt and founded a sportswear manufacturing company in 1934. The company branched into a complete line of sportswear; however, it continues to be most noted for its first polo shirt which at its height in the 1980s was synonymous with preppy affluence until its popularity was dwarfed by the new kid on the block, **Ralph Lauren,** with the introduction of the polo pony motif on his sports shirts.

LACROIX, CHRISTIAN (1951-) From Arles, France. He began as a freelance sketch artist, 1976–1978. He went to work as an assistant at **Hermès,** 1978–1980, then he assisted **Guy Paulin** at **Hermès,** 1980–1981. He worked for a short period of time for a Japanese designer in Japan prior to being appointed head of couture and artistic director at **Jean Patou,** Paris, 1981–1987. In 1987 with financial backing from French conglomerate **Financière Agache,** which also owned the house of **Dior,** he launched his own couture house. This was the first new couture house to open in Paris since the house of **Yves Saint Laurent** opened in 1961. He created a ready-to-wear collection for **Genny** in 1988. He is credited with revitalizing Paris couture in the 1980s. His designs continue to shock and astound; they are elaborate, irreverent, and witty with an eccentric sense in beautiful and exotic fabrics. His inspirations are often historically derivative as much as they are picked up off the pavement at the Paris flea markets. Today **Lacroix** is owned by the luxury conglomerate **LVMH.**

LAFAURIE (SEE GOMA, MICHEL) A French couture and ready-to-wear house, 1950–1963. **Michel Goma** was head designer, 1950–1958, at which time he purchased the company renaming it **Michel Goma.** He closed the company in 1963 after only five years.

LAGERFELD, KARL (1938–) Born in Hamburg, Germany, to a Swedish father and German mother. He immigrated to Paris in 1952. He won second prize for the International Wool Secretariat design contest for a coat design the same year **Yves Saint Laurent** won for a dress design. The coat design was bought and put into production at **Pierre Balmain** where he was appointed art director at age 20 and was a designer, 1955–1958. He left **Balmain** to join **Jean Patou,** 1958–1963. He left in 1963 and moved to Italy to study history, returning in 1965 to resume freelance designing for numerous firms including **Chloé, Krizia, Valentino, Ballantyne** sweaters, and shoes for **Charles Jourdan.** He remained designing for **Chloé,** 1965–1972, along with **Graziella Fontana,** and became the sole designer for **Chloé,** 1972–1984. He has worked as a design consultant for **Krizia** and joined **Fendi** in 1967 where he continues today to design their fur and coat collections. He was responsible for creating the interlocking "**F**" logo for **Fendi** in the late 1970s. He was appointed design director for **Chanel** in 1983 and continues to design both their ready-to-wear and couture collections today. **Hervé Léger** worked with **Lagerfeld** at **Fendi,** 1977–1980, and then for **Lagerfeld** at **Chanel,** 1982–1983. He launched his first collection under his own name in 1984. **Karl Lagerfeld's** private label was purchased by **Chloé's** parent company, **Dunhill,** in 1992. He returned in 1993 to design spring and summer collections for **Chloé,** which was then held by a new company, **Vendrome.** His collection for **Chloé** in 1993 was reminiscent of his designs for the company in the 1970s. **Jorgen Simonsen** worked as a freelance designer for **Lagerfeld,** 1996–1997. **Lagerfeld** is a prolific designer who has always maintained a successful freelance design status most noted for his hippie, romantic designs for **Chloé** in the 1970s and for his interpretive eye for street fashion and his ability to translate this into high-fashion couture for **Chanel.**

LAMY, MICHÈLE (SEE RICK OWENS) (DATES UNKNOWN) French ready-to-wear designer who specialized in women's knitwear and celebrated her height of popularity in the 1980s. **Rick Owens** worked for her in the early 1990s; however, she closed her design business in 1993 and in the late 1990s became a successful restaurateur with an exclusive restaurant, Le Deux Cafe, in Los Angeles.

LANCETTI, PINO (1935–) Italian from Bastia Umbra, Italy. Originally a painter, he began his fashion career as a freelance sketch artist in Rome in the late 1950s. He launched his seminal collection in 1963 based on military uniform dressing. Famous for his designs that catered to the wealthy Italian society ladies, offering them feminine empire-waisted eveningwear with matching wraps in luxurious fabrics, as well as his ready-to-wear day dresses which often culled their inspiration from his early years as a painter, taking expressions from various artistic movements and styles including those of Modigliani and Picasso.

LANE, KENNETH JAY (K.J.L.) (1932–) American from Detroit, Michigan. He began as an art staff member at *Vogue*, New York, 1954–1955, then became an assistant designer at **Delman Shoes,** New York, 1956–1958, moving to **Christian Dior Shoes,** New York, 1958–1963. He founded his costume jewelry company **Kenneth Jay Lane,** New York, in 1963. Because he was still designing shoes for **Delman's** he began designing his jewelry under just his initials **K.J.L.;** he would later use his full name. In 1969 his company became part of the **Kenton Corporation** whose holdings included **Cartier, Valentino, Mark Cross,** as well as other fashion companies. **Lane** purchased his company back in 1972. He introduced a less expensive line **K.J.L.,** licensed to **The Costume Jewelry Company,** and sold very successfully on the **QVC** network. His jewelry was regularly featured on various soap operas including *Another World*, *The Guiding Light*, and *Days of Our Lives*. Considered to be the undisputed king of costume jewelry, one of the greatest costume jewelry designers of the 20th century.

LANG, HELMUT (1956–) Austrian from Vienna, Austria. He grew up in the Austrian Alps and, although he claimed he dreamt of becoming a farmer and the best skier in the valley, he began his career working in a bar after studying business in Vienna. He became involved in the Vienna art scene in the mid-1970s and was encouraged by his associates to pursue designing. He opened a women's made-to-measure shop in Vienna in 1979, followed by developing his ready-to-wear, 1984–1986. He showed his first collection in Paris in 1986. He entered into a license agreement with **Mitsubishi,** Japan, in 1987 and introduced menswear that same year. He became a professor of Fashion Masterclass at the University of Applied Arts, Vienna, in 1993. He introduced a line of men's shoes in 1995, and men's underwear and jeans in 1996. Most noted for his deceptively simple, avant-garde, yet essentially understated and masterfully tailored men's and women's ready-to-wear in modern fabrics. **Helmut Lang** joined the **Prada** company in 1999 and has since expanded his line to include accessories, fragrance, and a number of new shops.

LANVIN, JEANNE (1867-1946) From Brittany, France. She began originally as a dressmaker then moved into millinery design. She opened a millinery shop in Paris in 1890, then began designing made-to-measure dresses for her younger sister and infant daughter. Later she began to create copies of these dresses for her millinery clients and eventually created a line of mother and daughter designs. Just before World War I, she introduced her famous "Robes de Style," which were based on 18th-century designs. Her simple chemise dresses which she introduced during World War I became the silhouette of the 1920s. **Antonio del Castillo** was appointed head couturier of the house of **Lanvin,** Paris, after her death in 1950. He continued to produce designs based on her original "Robes de Style" design. **Oscar de la Renta** moved to **Antonio del Castillo, Lanvin-Castillo** as assistant designer, 1961–1963. **Charles Kleibacker** also designed and freelanced for **Lanvin-Castillo** in the late 1950s. **Antonio del Castillo** left in 1962 to open his own design house and was succeeded at **Lanvin** by **Jules-François Crahay** who remained at **Lanvin** until his retirement in 1984. **Hervé Léger** joined the company in 1985, working with **Maryll Lanvin** on ready-to-wear and couture. The **Lanvin** company gave **Hervé Léger** a boutique under their name in 1985. **Léger** left in the late 1980s to launch his own collection and pursue other freelance work. French designer **Dominique Morlotti** designed for both men's and women's ready-to-wear, 1992–1993, and was replaced in womenswear by **Ocimar Versolato** in 1993, while **Dominique Morlotti** continued to design a men's ready-to-wear collection. **Claude Montana** began designing for the house of **Lanvin** in 1997. **Jeanne Lanvin** was known for her beautiful embroideries and use of a particular hue of blue which came to be referred to as "Lanvin Blue," as well as for her postwar designs which were the spirit of the time.

LAPIDUS, OLIVER (1959-) From Paris, France. Son to designer **Ted Lapidus, Oliver** began his career as a freelance designer and in 1984–1985 he signed on as designer of menswear collections for **Pierre Baliman,** followed by a very successful private collection in Japan under his label **Oliver Montagut.** In 1989 he joined his father's company **Ted Lapidus** and assumed the position of head designer for couture, as well as designing for his own label, **Oliver Lapidus, De Luxe** ready-to-wear.

LAPIDUS, TED (1929-) French from Paris, France. After studying technical engineering in Tokyo, Japan, he moved back to France and opened his first boutique in Paris in 1950, producing women's ready-to-wear. He opened numerous other boutiques, as well as franchises throughout the 1970s and 1980s in both North America and Europe. French designer **Dominique Morlotti** worked for Lapidus in the mid-to-late 1970s. He is renowned for his men's and women's ready-to-wear and unisex designs which were masterfully tailored with technical precision. He designed a safari jacket in the early 1960s which was widely popular and influenced many copies. **Ted Lapidus's** son **Oliver Lapidus** assumed the position as head designer for the house of **Lapidus** in 1989.

LAROCHE, GUY (1923-1990) Frenchman from La Rochelle, near Bordeaux, France. He began his career as a milliner in Paris before moving to New York to work as a milliner on Seventh Avenue, as well as a freelance ready-to-wear designer. He returned to Paris in the late 1940s to work as an assistant to **Jean Dessès** for some eight years. He established his own couture business in his apartment in the early to mid-1950s, followed by ready-to-wear in 1960. **Valentino** worked for **Guy Laroche,** Paris, 1956–1958, whom he had met while he was working at **Jean Dessès. Laroche** moved his establishment to Avenue Montaigne in 1961. **Issey Miyake** worked as an assistant to **Laroche,** 1966–1968. He is known for his simple cuts, delicate color palette, as well as for his bold colors. His designs were popularized by France's high society. The house of **Laroche** included many licensed ready-to-wear labels, including **Christian Aujard, Lolita Lempicka, Angelo Tarlazzi,** as well as a lower-priced collection by **Thierry Mugler.** In 1989 **Angelo Tarlazzi** was entrusted with designing the couture collections and was succeeded by **Michel Klien** in 1993 after **Laroche's** death. **Jean-Pierre Marty** was appointed ready-to-wear designer.

LATIMER, HUBERT (DATES UNKNOWN) American who took over as design director for the "**Irene**" **Lentz** company (1962–1970) after her death in 1962, and became the first American designer to design for **Christian Dior-New York,** 1970–1973. He also freelanced for **Charles Cooper.** In 1973 he designed the couture or higher-priced division for **Mollie Parnis.**

LAUG, ANDRÉ (1931-1984) Frenchman from Alsace, France. He moved to Paris in 1958 and in the early 1960s began freelance work for **Raphäel** fashion house, **Venet,** and **Nina Ricci,** as well as collaborating with **André Courrèges** until 1963. During 1964–1968 he produced nine couture collections and five ready-to-wear collections for **Maria Antonelli.** He opened his own couture and ready-to-wear house in Rome in 1968. Most noted for his undeniably beautiful, luxurious designs which possessed a reserved and discreet sense of good taste desired by his highly selective social clients. His house continued to produce both couture and ready-to-wear for a few years after his death at age 52 in 1984, before closing in the mid-1980s.

LAUREN, RALPH (1939-) His first job was working as sales assistant at Alexander's stores, New York, then assistant menswear buyer for Allied Stores, New York, 1958–1961. He worked for numerous companies in various capacities while attending night school, studying business at City College, New York. He later worked as a salesman at Brooks Brothers and Bloomingdale's, New York, in 1962. He became a road salesman in New England for A. Rivetz & Co., a neckwear manufacturer based in Boston. He moved to **Beau Brummell,** a menswear firm and began designing neckwear, then created the **Polo** line of exceptionally wide handmade ties of opulent silks with **Beau Brummell** in 1967. He entered into a contract with **Norman Hilton** with whom he established **Polo** in 1968, creating an entire line of menswear. By 1971 he had introduced womenswear, followed by the launch of the **Ralph Lauren** label in 1972. He was noted for his exceptionally popular "Prairie Look," which was full denim skirts with layers of white petticoats for women in 1978. Numerous other collections were added to the line in years to follow, including leather goods, luggage, **Polo Ralph Lauren,** and the diffusion line, **Chaps,** and the **Double RL.** He gained international acclaim in 1974 with his costume designs for Robert Redford in "*The Great Gatsby.*" **Maggie Norris** became senior design director for **Ralph Lauren Women Classic Collections** in 1983, building the **Ralph Lauren Classic Line** from its inception, 1983–1994. **Norris** was senior design director, 1995–1997, succeeded by **Max Wilson** as senior design director for women's collections in 1997 when **Norris** left to head the design team in Germany. **Wilson** is presently vice president in charge of women's collections. **Lauren** is most noted for his timeless, traditional, and classic American fashions which derive their romantic inspirations from the nation's past.

LÉGER, HERVÉ (1957-) Frenchman from Bapaume, Pas de Calais, France. He began his career as a hat and accessories designer for **Venus et Neptune, Pablo Delia,** and **Dick Brandsma,** 1975–1977. He apprenticed with **Tan Giudicelli,** couture and ready-to-wear, 1977–1980, before moving to work with **Karl Lagerfeld** for **Fendi,** Rome, for fur, ready-to-wear, swimsuits, and accessories. He then moved to Paris to work with **Lagerfeld** at **Chanel,** 1982–1983, then for **Cadette,** Milan, 1983–1985. He founded his own company **MCH Diffusion** in 1985 and began to work as an assistant at the house of **Lanvin** for couture and ready-to-wear. That same year the **Lanvin** company gave him a boutique under his name. He freelanced for **Diane von Furstenberg,** 1985; **Chloé** furs, 1987; accessories for **Swarovski,** 1988–1992; and **Charles Jourdan** ready-to-wear in 1992. He formed a partnership with **Mumm** in 1992 and introduced his first couture and deluxe ready-to-wear collection for **Hervé Léger SA** in 1993. He is best known today for his "Bender" dresses, which were composed of narrow strips of elastic material combined with rayon which were horizontally hand-sewn like bandages to form the garment, creating a shapely hourglass silhouette of the body within. In the late 1990s he sold his name and the **Léger** company to **Max Azzario (BCBG),** losing the rights to his name. In early 2000 he reorganized and formed a new company which today is called **Hervé Rouge.**

LEIBER, JUDITH (1921-) Hungarian from Budapest, Hungary. She started an apprenticeship with the Hungarian Handbag Guild in 1939. She met her husband **Gerson Leiber** during the war and married in 1946, immigrating to New York in 1947. She became an associate designer at **Nettie Rosenstein** in 1948 and stayed with the firm until 1960, when she moved to **Richard Kort,** 1960–1961. Her next stop was designing handbags for **Morris Moskowitz Co.,** 1961–1962. She opened her own firm with her husband **Gerson Leiber** in 1963. For 35 years she designed exquisite handbags and accessories with unparalleled craftsmanship from fine leather, exotic skins, and most notably her whimsical, rhinestone-studded evening bags which were crafted in the form of minaudières. She frequently turns to nature for her inspirations and has created a vast menagerie of crafted jeweled animal minaudières. In 1997, she appointed **Michelle Hatch** who had just left **Donna Karan** accessories, as creative director of the company in preparation for her retirement which she announced shortly after in fall 1997. **Hatch** continued in the tradition which **Judith Leiber** had established until she left to form her own company in the spring of 1999. The **Leiber** company continues to produce its famous and widely collectible handbags and accessories.

LELONG, LUCIEN (1889-1958) A French designer who launched his fashion house in Paris after the First World War, specializing in couture and ready-to-wear. **Christian Dior** worked there, alongside **Pierre Balmain,** 1941–1946, as well as **Hubert de Givenchy,** 1945–1946. He was highly noted as the president of the Chambre Syndicale de la Couture, 1937–1947, and for his efforts in resisting German occupation efforts to export couture to Berlin or Vienna, therefore keeping more than 100 French couture operations in France throughout the Paris occupation, 1940–1944. Highly regarded for his exquisitely elegant eveningwear which often possessed a surreal quality.

LEMPICKA, LOLITA (DATES UNKNOWN) A French designer who launched her first women's ready-to-wear and couture collections in 1984. She introduced a junior line, **Lolita Bis,** in 1987. The house of **Guy Laroche** produced a licensed ready-to-wear collection for **Lolita Lempicka.** She signed a deal with the Japanese group **Kashiyama** for her lines and the opening of 80 **Lolita Lempika** boutiques in Japan. She is noted for creating imaginative, naughty, sexy, and fun party dresses and feminine tailored daywear.

LENTZ, "IRENE" (MRS. ELIOT GIBBONS) (NOT TO BE CONFUSED WITH IRENE OF NEW YORK, THE MILLINER, OR IRENE SHARAFF) (1901 OR 1907-1962) American from Brookings, South Dakota. Her first husband **Richard Jones** encouraged her to open a small boutique on the campus of the University of Southern California in the late 1920s or early 1930s. It was a tremendous success until **Richard** died suddenly causing her to close her shop. She opened another boutique after taking some time off to travel abroad and recover from the tragic loss of her husband. In 1935 she was given her own custom salon in **Bullock's Wilshire Department Store,** becoming the first American designer to have a department devoted exclusively to them. In 1937 **Chris Ghiatis** went to work for **Irene** as assistant designer until 1941 when he was recruited by **Adrian** to become the assistant designer of ready-to-wear collections at **Adrian's** new ready-to-wear salon. **Irene** began designing costumes in 1938 for RKO under the direction of **Harold Greer,** before replacing **Adrian** at Metro-Goldwyn-Mayer (MGM) in 1942 when **Adrian** left to open his Wilshire Boulevard Salon. It is understood that she had an indirect and influential link to the MGM studios through her second husband **Eliot Gibbons,** the brother of MGM's brilliant art director, Cedric Gibbons. She produced costumes for over 260 films for RKO, Metro-Goldwyn-Mayer, Paramount, United Artists, and Columbia Pictures. In 1947 she established her ready-to-wear and had successfully licensed many major department stores around the country to carry her line, including **Bullock's Wilshire Department Store's Custom Salon** where she was the head designer. Most noted for her soft tailored suits of English worsted wool, as well as fabrics woven by **Pola Stout.** Her suits and dresses were complemented by custom hats designed by **Rex,** which were made in fabrics to match. Her eveningwear was always dramatic with elaborate trains or scarf panels, as well as being embellished with either embroidery or beautiful beading. She continued to design throughout the 1950s; however, a broken leg and signs of depression, compounded with the loss of a second marriage had taken their toll; she took her own life in 1962. Her company continued under the design direction of **Hubert Latimer** until 1970 when he left to become the first American designer to design for **Christian Dior-New York.**

LEONARD, JACQUES (DATES UNKNOWN) (SEE DANIEL TRIBOUILLARD) French founder of **Leonard Fashion** couture house, Paris, in 1958. **Jacques Leonard** appointed 20-year-old **Daniel Tribouillard** as designer and general director the same year. By 1960 **Tribouillard** introduced fully fashioned pullovers with printed designs for which he acquired an international patent for his revolutionary printing process, which always favors beautiful floral motifs including camellias, calla lilies, lilacs and orchids; however, it was orchids that became the symbol of **Leonard.** The fully fashioned **Leonard** sweaters were a celebrated success for more than ten years when in 1968 **Tribouillard** introduced his first collection of printed silk jersey garments. The company launched its first fragrance in 1969, followed by their first exclusive boutique in Paris in 1970, and New York in 1974. Various licenses were introduced in 1975, including scarves and ties, followed by a line of floral porcelain in 1979. In 1983 **Tribouillard** was honored by the Japanese government and granted the right to learn the age-old secrets of traditional kimono-making in Kyoto. He presented his first collection of kimonos in Japan in 1984. By 1985 the company had expanded its licenses to include smaller leather goods, glasses, watches, and jewelry. In 1987 **Tribouillard** became the company chairman and bought out **Jacques Leonard's Group,** and partner **Antonio Ratti,** one of the world's leading manufacturers of natural silk. Home furnishings were introduced in 1988 and an international expansion effort was launched which today holds more than 120 exclusive **Leonard** boutiques worldwide. Menswear was introduced in 1992 and a second boutique was opened in Paris in 1994. In 2000 the **Tribouillard Company** purchased the shares of the **Ratti Company,** making them the sole owner. They also bought back the fragrance line from the licenser. The company celebrated tremendous renewed interest for **Tribouillard's** vivacious **Leonard** designs after the International Press ran photos of Julia Roberts wearing a striking vintage **Leonard** dress at a recent movie premiere.

LESAGE, ALBERT (1888-1949) From Paris, France. A couture-caliber embroidery house founded in 1922 by **Albert Lesage,** who was later joined by his son **François Lesage.** Famous for their collaboration with **Schiaparelli** creating fantastic fantasy, jewel-studded embroideries on **Schiaparelli's** couture creations, most notably her evening jackets in the 1930s. The company is still in business today and most recently is noted for their beautiful embroideries which they created for **Maggie Norris's** seminal couture collection, based on equestrian inspired corsets, fall 2000.

LESER, TINA (CHRISTINE WETHERILL SHILLARD-SMITH) (1910-1986) American from Philadelphia, Pennsylvania. In 1931 after studying at the Sorbonne in Paris, she moved with her first husband **Curtis Leser,** whom she married in 1931, to Hawaii and opened a small dress shop which specialized in selling high quality ready-to-wear playclothes. In 1941 after the outbreak of World War II she moved to New York and formed her own company designing glamorous women's sportswear, including a playsuit which Saks requested in a quantity of 500 in their initial order. She freelanced for numerous firms, including **Edwin H. Foreman Co.,** New York, 1943–1945, **Signet** men's ties in 1949, **Stafford Wear,** men's sportswear in 1950, as well as designing industrial uniforms for **Ramsey Sportswear Co.** in 1953. She had divorced **Curtis Leser** in 1936 and married **James J. Howley** in 1948. She retired briefly, 1964–1966, returning again, 1966–1982, when she retired permanently. Having traveled extensively as a child with her family, then later with her first husband, her work had always revealed inspirations from her multicultural experiences which possessed a consistent sense of humor and intelligence in her choice of references. Her postwar collections contained relaxed day- and eveningwear which was eminently suited to most women's budgets, often using block-printed cottons for her sarong-style dresses which she favored from her years in Hawaii.

LESLIE, JOAN, KASPER FOR (SEE LESLIE FAY AND HERBERT KASPER) A division of **Leslie Fay,** an American women's ready-to-wear manufacturing company.

LESTER, CHARLES (1942-) AND PATRICIA LESTER (1943-) British from Banbury, England. A husband and wife design team who began experimenting with various fabrics in the 1960s. They are noted for their handpleated fabric designs in the early 1960s which were reminiscent of **Fortuny's** some

80 years earlier. They also perfected the devoré technique of creating patterns on velvet by chemically dissolving fibers with pattern plates, as well as creating beautiful handpainted designs which they interpreted into tunics, dresses, and robes. They created the costumes for Helen Bonham Carter's role in the film *The Wings of a Dove*, 1990.

LEVINE, BETH (1914-) American from New York. One of America's most renowned and innovative shoe designers who began designing shoes with little experience or training in the early 1940s, creating sexy little "Spring-o-lator" mules, and quickly became one of the most sought-after shoe designers of her time. Her designs throughout the 1940s–1970s were always inventive and imaginative, often whimsical, and always sexy. Famous for her use of unconventional materials such as frog skin and Astroturf, and for her high-heel topless shoe which was nothing more than a satin sole attached to the foot with spirit gum, as well as her all-in-one multicolored suede shoe-pant. Her designs were highly influential and many designers today derive inspiration for their collections from her early designs.

LICHTENSTEIN, HARRY (SEE JAY-THORPE, INC.) (DATES UNKNOWN) A New York tailor, custom order department at **Jay-Thorpe, Inc.** department store from the late 1920s to 1930s.

LIVINGSTON, LEON (ORIGINALLY LEVINSON) (SEE MOLLIE PARNIS) (DATES UNKNOWN) Originally a textile designer in the early 1930s. He married **Mollie Parnis** and they co-founded **Parnis-Livingston,** a women's couture and ready-to-wear manufacturer.

LOEWE A Spanish leather goods company founded in Madrid, Spain, in 1846. In 1872, **Enrique Loewe Roessberg** (1829–1913) a German craftsman, came to Madrid and joined the small leather factory. By 1892 the company was established as **E. Loewe** and was located on Principe Street in Madrid and gained mainstream popularity. By 1905 the company was being managed by **Enrique Loewe Hilton** and the company was granted the title of "Official Supplier to the Royal Court" from King Alfonso XIII. They opened their first store in Barcelona in 1910 followed by a new flagship shop at number 7 Barquillo Street in Madrid. **Enrique Loewe Knappe** assumed the management of the firm in 1934, and by 1939 had opened the shop at number 8 Gran Via, Madrid, which is still in operation today. Designer **Pérez de Rozas** created a special box calf handbag for **Loewe** in 1945, which soon became the most classic model of the firm. In 1947 the **Loewe** company acquired the rights to sell **Christian Dior's** "New Look" in Spain. By 1959 they had launched the impressive new store on Madrid's Serrano Street which broke with the standard stereotype of luxury stores. They followed this by opening a store in London, England, and began their international expansion. They introduced women's ready-to-wear in the early 1960s, as well as their first designer scarf in 1970. In the same year **Vicente Vela** created their legendary anagram logo which has become the international symbol of luxury in Spain. Today under the creative genius design direction of **Narcisco Rodriguez,** who joined the company in 1997, they produce leather goods, ready-to-wear apparel, accessories, and perfume. Today the **Loewe** company is owned by luxury conglomerate **LVMH.**

LOUIS, JEAN (JEAN LOUIS BERTHAULT) (1907-1997) From Paris, France. He first worked with the house of **Agnès-Drécoll,** (formerly the house of **Cristoff von Drécoll**) in the early 1930s before he moved to **Hattie Carnegie,** New York, 1935–1942. He became head designer at Columbia Pictures in 1944 where his beautiful black satin bias-cut designs for Rita Hayworth in *Gilda* were widely influential in mainstream fashion and represented in many designer's collections of the times. **Bob Mackie** received his start under him as a sketch artist in the early 1960s. **Jean Louis** moved to Universal Studios in 1958 where he continued to design costumes for major motion pictures until he opened his first ready-to-wear business in 1961 and successfully specialized in lovely eveningwear. **Chris Ghiatis** worked as a freelance designer for **Jean Louis** in the early 1960s and collaborated on two collections in 1961–1962. He closed the business in 1988 and continued to design for the silver screen on a freelance basis until his death in 1997. (Famous for the gown which he created for Marilyn Monroe when she sang "Happy Birthday to You" to President John F. Kennedy.)

LUCILE, LADY DUFF GORDON (BORN LUCY SUTHERLAND) (1863-1935) British from London, England. She began as a private dressmaker, opening her own house in 1891. She married **Sir Cosmo Duff Gordon** sometime around the turn of the century and was shortly dressing some of London's grandest ladies. She had branches in London and New York in 1909, Chicago and Paris in 1911. **Howard Greer** designed for her, 1916–1920, and **Norman Hartnell** designed for her briefly in 1923. **Molyneux** and **Travis Banton** were also noted designers who worked for her. She was most noted for her beautiful tea gowns, as well as for her reputation designing for such notable film and stage stars as Sarah Bernhardt and dancer Irene Castle. The looks she designed for Irene Castle were often emulated by her followers and were noted as the "Irene Castle look."

LVMH A French luxury conglomerate whose CEO **Bernard Arnault** bought the house of **Dior** in 1984. **Arnault** has methodically built an empire which originally consisted of **Louis Vuitton, Moët, Henessey,** and the **Duty Free** shops, into an empire of fashion's best known names, from **Givenchy, Donna Karan, Julien Macdonald** for **Givenchy, Marc Jacobs** for **Louis Vuitton,** to **Michael Kors, Christian Lacroix, Emilio Pucci, Loewe, Kenzo,** and London's luxury shirtmaker **Tomas Pink. LVMH** also acquired 20 percent of the **Gucci Group** making **LVMH** its second-largest shareholder. The **Fendi** company sold a half-stake to **LVMH** and **Prada** in 1999. The company also owns numerous fragrance and cosmetic companies including the highly successful chain of cosmetic stores, **Saphora.**

LYOLÈNE A French couture house in the 1930s and 1940s. In 1931, Bloomingdale's department store established the Green Room where they sold exact copies of **Lyolène's** French couture models made from imported French fabrics.

MACDONALD, JULIEN (1972-) Welshman from Merthyr Tydfil. A contemporary ready-to-wear and couture designer known for his flamboyant designs. **Macdonald's** first intention was to become an actor until he discovered his passion for fabrics and enrolled at Brighton University; he completed his master of arts degree at the Royal College of Art, London. He had worked as a freelance knitwear designer while at college for various designers including **Alexander McQueen** and **Koji Tasuno.** After college he was the head of knitwear designs at **Chanel** couture, prior to founding his own women's ready-to-wear company in 1997 at the age of 24. **Macdonald** was awarded the coveted title of head designer at **Givenchy** on the eve of the company's 50th anniversary (March 14, 2001) after collections, despite the widespread assumption that **Oliver Theysken** would succeed **Alexander McQueen** at **Givenchy.**

MACKIE, BOB (1940-) American from Los Angeles, California. He began his career as a sketch artist for various costume designers, including **Jean Louise, Edith Head,** and **Frank Thompson.** He was a design assistant to **Ray Aghayan** prior to partnering with him in 1963 to design for numerous television shows including the *Judy Garland Show, The Carol Burnett Show* (11 years) and most notably, *The Sonny and Cher Comedy Hour,* and later *The Sonny and Cher Show.* Cher was perhaps his most significant muse and he continues to design important ensembles for her today, including sensational, if not somewhat scandalous creations for her appearances at the Academy Awards presentations. He has also created beautiful designs for Raquel Welch, Marlene Dietrich, Barbra Streisand, as well as being a favorite of Nancy Reagan. He launched a small subdued ready-to-wear collection of primarily matte jersey dresses in the early 1970s which was unsuccessful. He designed a collection of swimwear for **Cole of California** in 1976 and launched his deluxe ready-to-wear business in New York in 1982, which offered his signature glamour look of fabulously beaded show-stopping eveningwear. His New York deluxe ready-to-wear business, which also produced swim and loungewear, was a big success. He closed his New York ready-to-wear business in 1993 and continues to design for Cher and work with other freelance ventures, as well as archiving his early designs.

MAD CARPENTIER (MAD MALTEZO AND SUZIE CARPENTIER) A French couture and ready-to-wear house founded by **Mad Maltezo** and **Suzie Carpentier** in 1940 after the two left the house of **Madeleine Vionnet** when she retired in 1939. **Suzie Carpentier** had began as a *vendeuse* at **Vionnet.** Most noted for their designs which mirrored their mentor's beautifully draped bias-cut gowns, as well as for their voluminous, romantically sweeping long coats in robust textured fabrics throughout the 1940s and 1950s. Their refined and beautiful yet traditional designs did not transcend the modern movement of the late 1950s and 1960s. The house closed in 1957.

MAINBOCHER (MAIN ROUSSEAU BOCHER) (1891-1976) American, he first moved to Europe in 1911 and continued to work and study in Paris, London, and Munich until 1914. He began his career as a sketch artist for **E. I. Mayer,** a New York clothing manufacturer, 1914–1917. In 1917 he moved back to Paris to work as an illustrator for *Harper's Bazaar,* Paris, until 1921 when he was hired by French *Vogue* to work as a fashion correspondent, then as editor-in-chief through 1929. In 1930 he became the first American designer to open a couture house in Paris. His business flourished through the support of his influential associates and the relationships which he nurtured while writing about fashion. He was most noted for his famous associations, including Mrs. Wallis Simpson for whom he created the wedding dress for her marriage to the Duke of Windsor in 1937. He left Paris, closing his couture business there, with the outbreak of World War II and moved back to New York and established a new couture salon there. He found equal success in New York when the desire for Paris couture was in great demand by devoted society matrons such as C. Z. Guest and the Vanderbilts who avidly patronized his American couture salon. Throughout the 1940s and 1950s he designed simple short or long black evening dresses which could be worn undetected, time and time again, by simply alternating accessories. He created beautiful cashmere evening sweaters which were embellished with intricate beadwork and lined in silk to match the fabrics of the dress underneath. He designed for numerous Broadway productions throughout the 1940s and 1950s. He opened **"La Galerie,"** a made-to-order department in his couture salon in 1950 which offered designs in standard sizes which were available within one week after ordering. He was considered to be the most expensive custom dressmaker and only New York designer to never produce off-the-rack, ready-to-wear garments. He created a wasp-waist corset for **Warners** in 1940. He designed women's uniforms for American WAVES (U.S. Navy) in 1942, American Girl Scout uniforms in 1946, Red Cross in 1948, as well as for the U.S. women's Marine Corps in 1951. By the 1960s and into 1970 his refined and elegant designs were considered to be somewhat staid by the new demands of the Youthquake movement and closed his business, retiring in 1971.

MAJAGO (DATES UNKNOWN) French couture designer most noted for his work in the late 1960s and 1970s. **Jean-Paul Gaultier** worked for him, 1976–1978.

MALISY (SEE GENNY SPA)

MANGONE, PHILIP (DATES UNKNOWN) An American custom ready-to-wear designer who was a seventh-generation tailor. As a young man he began working on garments his father brought home to finish, and later he went to work with him at **B. Altman, Julius Stein, Harry Rothenbergand Levy,** and **Charles M. Cohen.** He set up his own wholesale ready-to-wear business in 1917 and by the 1920s he had realized tremendous success and his designs were available in over 200 stores across the country. He was one of the very first designers to have his ready-to-wear garments bear his label and not the department store's, which was an unusual practice at the time. His top-rung designs included suits, short and long coats, as well as a cape in every collection, the capes being made exclusively from woolen fabric designed by **Pola Stout,** an American fabric manufacturer. He opened a subsidiary firm, **Greco Blouse Co.,** to produce blouses to complement his suits. He continued with his beautifully tailored designs into the early 1960s before closing his business.

MANHATTAN INDUSTRIES An American sportswear company which hosted many designers such as **Vera Neumann** and **Perry Ellis** throughout the 1960s and 1970s.

MANDELLI, MARIUCCIA (1933-) (SEE KRIZIA) Italian from Milan. She began as a teacher, then, frustrated by the fashions which were available to her, she created some garments for herself. She then teamed with **Flora Dolci** and shopped her garments around Milan selling them to various retail outlets. The two founded the ready-to-wear fashion house **Krizia,** Milan (named from Plato's dialogue on the vanity of women), in 1954. They showed their first collection in 1957. **Mariuccia's** husband, **Aldo Pinto,** became her business partner in 1957, as well as the supervisor of the knitwear company **Kriziamglia** which was founded in 1966 and celebrated tremendous success in the 1970s. The company began with separates including skirts and dresses, and in 1967 they introduced knitwear, as well as a complete line of ready-to-wear. **Walter Albini** joined **Krizia** in 1960 as a design consultant until 1963. **Karl Lagerfeld** was also a noted consultant to the firm. By the 1970s they were most noted for their signature animal motifs in their designs, as well as creative and clever designs in eveningwear. They introduced childrenswear with **Kriziababy** in 1968. **Krizia** boutiques have been opened in cities around the globe including Milan, Tokyo, London, New York, and Detroit.

MARGIELA, MARTIN (1957-) Belgian from Louvain, Belgium. After graduating from the Royal Academy of Fine Arts at Antwerp he worked as a freelance fashion stylist in Antwerp, 1982–1985. In 1985 he moved to Paris and went to work for **Jean-Paul Gaultier** through 1987 before venturing out on his own. In 1988 he showed his first collection, spring/summer 1989, to tremendous widespread acclaim. He launched a knitwear line manufactured by **Miss Deanna Spa, Italy** in 1992. Most noted for his unconventional, undeniably strange, deconstructed fashion in a wide range of fabrics including salvaged flea market finds. Despite his destroyed and dismantled approach to the traditions of fashion, he is unmistakably an expert tailor and his designs sincerely reflect his genius for his craft. True to his off-beat approach to his designs, he has chosen to express this in his shows as well, presenting them in alternative venues such as abandoned lots or a Salvation Army hall where the fashion press sat perched on secondhand furniture drinking wine out of plastic tumblers.

MARIMEKKO (SEE ARMI RATIA) A Finnish textile and clothing manufacturer cofounded in Helsinki in 1951 by **Armi Ratia** and **Viljo Ratia.** They are recognized for their brightly colored, oversized floral and abstract cotton and jersey printed fabrics and simple shift dresses, as well as their home furnishing designs. Their designs enjoyed a tremendous revitalization when **Celine** introduced their spring/summer 2002 collections with prints inspired by Marimekko's early floral prints.

MARTY, JEAN-PIERRE (DATES UNKNOWN) French ready-to-wear designer who was appointed head of ready-to-wear at the house of **Guy Laroche** in 1993 after **Laroche's** death in 1990.

MASON, ELIZABETH (1962-) Canadian from Toronto, Canada; immigrated to the United States in 1988 and became a citizen in 1994. Began designing at the age of 9 with a domestic Singer sewing machine creating eveningwear for her Barbie® doll, as well as creating miniature garments for her girlfriends' dolls. By age 12 she was creating most of her own wardrobe and taking small custom orders from school classmates. She launched her own private label at the age of 19 to subsidize her modeling and acting career, taking custom orders for club and eveningwear from fellow models. Throughout the early 1980s she continued her custom work, as well as designing costumes for television and theater, including the theatrical production of Mike Malet Private Eye and the television comedy series That's Funny. She moved to Madrid, Spain, in 1985 to work as a correspondent writer for a Spanish-based company and continued to work as an actor in Europe, moving to London in 1987. She arrived in California in 1988 continuing with her acting career and freelance design work, creating custom designs for private clients and various specialty boutiques. She began The Paper Bag Princess, vintage clothing business in 1993, authored her first book, The Rag Street Journal, in 1994 and opened **The Paper Bag Princess** vintage boutique in 1995. She introduced a collection of vintage redesigned garments in 1999 and appointed **Daniela Kurrel** as chief designer in 2000. In January 2001 she opened **The Paper Bag Princess Atelier** with **Daniela Kurrel** as chief designer and **Mason** as artistic director. Recognized for her custom reinterpreted designs of original vintage couture models. Today her designs are available through The Paper Bag Princess Atelier and various specialty boutiques.

MATSUDA, MITSUHIRO (1934-) Japanese from Tokyo, Japan. His father worked as a designer in the Japanese kimono industry and **Matsuda** believed he would follow in his father's footsteps as a kimono fabric designer. However, while he worked as a designer for the **Sanai Company,** Japan, 1961–1967, he and **Kenzo** (a fellow graduating classmate from Bunka College of Fashion) moved to Paris in 1965. He returned to Japan six months later and resumed his work for the **Sanai Company,** Japan, until 1967. He launched his first company, **Nicole,** in Tokyo, in 1971. The company was named after a model he had admired in Elle magazine. He launched **Monsieur Nicole** in 1974 and **Madame Nicole** in 1976 followed by numerous other divisions throughout the 1980s. In 1982, he formed the **Matsuda** company and opened boutiques in New York and Hong Kong, followed by Paris in 1987. Most noted for his innovative designs which apply Japanese principles to his Western designs.

MATTLI, GIUSEPPE (1907-1982) Swiss from Locarno, Switzerland. He began his career working for **Premet** in Paris in the early 1930s prior to moving to London to found his own fashion house which specialized in both couture and ready-to-wear in 1934. He was most noted for his cocktail dresses and evening attire, including dramatic theater coats. He closed his couture division in 1955; however, he continued to produce fine ready-to-wear through the early 1970s.

MAUD FRIZON (SEE FRIZON, MAUD)

MAXFIELD PARRISH, NIGEL PRESTON (1946-) A British leather garment design company founded by **Nigel Preston** in 1972. They are noted for the company's classically styled sheepskin, suede, and leather garments which were popularized in the 1970s and 1980s by celebrities and pop stars.

MAXWELL, VERA (VERA HUPPÉ) (1901-1995) American from New York with Viennese parents. She danced with the Metropolitan Opera Ballet in 1919 until she married her first husband **Raymond Maxwell** in 1924 and began modeling for a wholesale manufacturer in 1929. She had always designed and made her own clothing and by the early 1930s through the 1940s she worked for various manufacturers such as **Adler & Adler, Max Milstein, Glenhurst,** as well as designing sportswear and tailored clothes for **Brows** and **Jacobson & Linde** from 1937. She founded her own company **Vera Maxwell Originals,** New York, in 1947 specializing in innovatively tailored suits and slim-cut coats and capes of the finest fabrics— silks, tweeds, wool—and casual sportswear throughout the 1940s and early 1950s. She produced more dresses and eveningwear, as well as coat and dress ensembles in matching fabrics in the 1950s through the 1960s. She had a brief period of inactivity between 1964 and 1970. Noted for having taken a calculated risk in purchasing 30,000 yards of Ultrasuede® and introducing the fabric in her designs in 1971, followed by her one-piece "Speedy Suit" in 1974, which resembled a suit ensemble, but was actually a dress with an elasticized waist with polyester knit top which could be quickly pulled on over the head without the need of fasteners or zippers. She varied this design in both long and short versions for each subsequent collection. She closed her business in 1985 but did not formally retire, and continued to freelance, designing a collection for **Peter Lynne** division of **Gulf Enterprises** in 1986.

MCCARDELL, CLAIRE (1905-1958) American from Frederick, Maryland. She began her career as a salesperson and sketch artist in 1928 for **Emmet Joyce,** a wholesale manufacturer. After graduating from Parsons in New York, as well as studying in Paris, she worked as a fashion model and knitwear designer for **Robert Turk, Inc.,** 1929–1931. She moved with **Robert Turk** as a design assistant to **Towney Frocks, Inc.,** New York, 1931–1938. She was appointed **Turk's** successor after his untimely death in a freak sailing accident in 1931, just before the debut of the first collection for **Towney Frocks, Inc.** She remained at **Towney Frocks, Inc.** until it closed in 1938 when she moved to work for **Hattie Carnegie,** New York, through 1940. She returned to the reorganized **Towney Frocks, Inc.** in 1940 and launched her first collection under her label, **Claire McCardell for Towney Frocks,** 1941–1958. She introduced a line of childrenswear, **Baby McCardells** in 1956. She is best known as the inventor of American women's sportswear; her designs were comfortable, practical, versatile, and flattering. She used primarily simple wool jersey, cotton, and corduroy, as well as muted colored silks and taffetas which could be easily cared for. Her popover dress with attached oven mitt sold in the tens of thousands, and her simple wrap and shift dresses were widely influential at the time, creating and defining the American look that continues to inspire many contemporary designers, including **Betsey Johnson** who dedicated her first collection to her in 1978. Her hallmarks were top-stitching and spaghetti ties which could be wrapped around the waist allowing the wearer to determine their own waistline. She was succeeded at **Towney Frocks Inc.** in 1959 by **Donald Brooks** due to her untimely death in 1958.

MCCARTHY, MARY (SEE LARRY ALDRICH) (DATES UNKNOWN) American who designed for **Larry Aldrich,** 1957–1970s.

MCCARTNEY, STELLA (1971-) British from London, England; daughter of musician Paul McCartney. She had her own line out of Notting Hill, England, in the early 1990s and worked briefly for **Lacroix.** She also had a short unofficial apprenticeship with **Edward Sexton,** a Savile Row tailor, London, prior to being named head designer for **Chloé,** 1997–2001. Considered to be a saucy bohemian mix of vintage couture and secondhand kitsch, her designs are sexy and romantic throwbacks to the looks which popularized **Chloé** in the early 1970s when **Karl Largerfeld** was head designer. **McCartney** confesses to having a passion for antique and vintage shopping, and often culls inspiration from her treasured flea market finds. **McCartney** was succeeded at **Chloé** by her assistant designer **Phoebe Philo** in June 2001 when her contract expired. **McCartney** left **Chloé** to launch her own label once again with backing from the **Gucci Company.**

MCFADDEN, MARY (1938-) Born in New York; however, she was raised primarily in the South on a plantation. She began her career as director of public relations for **Christian Dior-New York,** 1962–1964. She married her first husband **Philip Harari,** an executive for De Beers diamond firm, and moved with him to South Africa where she went to work for South African *Vogue* as a merchandising editor, 1964–1965. She then worked for *Rand Daily Mail,* South Africa, 1965–1968. She moved to Rhodesia with her second husband **Frank McEwan** and founded **Vokutu** sculpture studio for native artists, as well as working as a freelance editor for *My Fair Lady,* Cape Town, and French *Vogue,* 1968–1970. She moved back to New York in 1970 after divorcing **McEwan** and went to work for *Vogue,* New York, as special projects editor, 1970–1973. She began designing jewelry in 1973, the same year that her hand-painted China silk dresses had been discovered and bought by **Geraldine Stutz** for Bendel. She patented her "**Marii**" pleated fabric technique in 1975, which was based on the **Fortuny** pleat; however, hers was created with satin-backed polyester so the pleating was washable and the pleats were permanent. She established **Mary Mc-Fadden, Inc.,** in 1976, and although she was producing ready-to-wear, much of the detailed elements were done by hand in her New York workshop. She introduced her lower-priced bridge line **MMCF** which was manufactured by **Jack Mulqueen** from 1980, followed by **Mary McFadden Knitwear** in 1981. Recognized for her columnar silhouettes, hand-painted and pleated silks with themes that have been culled from various cultures and her extensive travels, as well as intricate bead and embroidery work. She introduced various other lines such as scarves, lingerie, eyewear, furs, shoes, bed, bath, and upholstery designs, as well as designing for **Simplicity Patterns.** She is still in business today.

MCLAREN, MALCOLM (1946-) British from London, England. **McLaren** and his friend **Vivienne Westwood** assumed the management of a small vintage clothing shop, **Let It Rock,** in London in 1971 and quickly set about adjusting the focus of the shop which by 1974 was known for its bondage and fetish clothing and accessories. Both **Westwood** and **McLaren** in a collaborative effort are credited with spearheading the British punk movement in the 1970s with their anti-establishment, anti-couture, anti-fashion, anti-monarchy, pseudo-porn graphic images on fabrics created by **Jamie Reid,** which they interpreted into T-shirts and minidresses that were often embellished with chains, chicken bones, and metal studs. They changed the name of the shop to **Too Fast to Live, Too Young To Die** in 1974, then again to **Sex,** then to **Seditionaries,** 1977, and finally to **World's End** in 1980. **McLaren** was also managing the U.S. band The New York Dolls in 1975 and was deeply ensconced in the pre-punk music scene. As a publicity stunt for the **Sex** shop, **McLaren** decided to form his own punk band made up of various colorful clients of the shop, giving birth to the **Sex Pistols. McLaren** claims that the formation of the band was actually a public relations exercise which took off, and that his original intention was just to sell trousers. **Westwood** went on to launch her own ready-to-wear collection in 1981.

MCM A German luggage and handbag manufacturing company founded in 1976 in Munich by **Michael Cromer** who had a one-room office and virtually no experience or capital. He launched his line of handbags, luggage, and accessories all bearing his signature logo **MCM (Michael Cromer Munich,** or **Modern Creation Münich,** the official name). **MCM** also translates into the Roman numerals 1900 symbolizing the beginning of the era of modern travel. Famous for the classic cognac colored line with dark brown lettering and the summer white line with navy blue imprint, introduced in 1977, followed by the highly successful black line in 1979. Turquoise was introduced in 1992–1993. Numerous licenses were introduced throughout the 1980s and early 1990s including perfume, cosmetics, watches, glasses, golf equipment, pens, and ties.

MCQUEEN, ALEXANDER (1969-) British from London, England. He began working in the garment industry at the early age of 16 as a pattern cutter for a **Savile Row** tailor before moving to Milan to work for **Koji Tasuno** and **Romero Gigli.** He returned to London to enroll at St. Martin's and opened his own business in 1993. Like other British renegade designers before him, such as **Vivienne Westwood** and **John Galliano** who had already blazed a rebellious trail, **McQueen's** ability to shock with his disquieting clothing has established him as the archetype of the avant-garde designer. His designs throughout the early 1990s have been spotlighted by his perception of street style which translated into his "Bumster" pants which were cut to reveal cheek cleavage, as well as for his gray suit with the slashes just below the buttocks. His company found substantial backing in the mid-1990s from **MA Commercial.** He succeeded **John Galliano** at the house of **Givenchy** (which is owned by luxury conglomerate **LVMH**) after **Galliano's** last collection autumn/winter 1996. **McQueen** left **Givency** and the **LVMH** umbrella when he signed a deal giving him financial backing for his private collection from the **Gucci Group.** It was widely assumed that **Oliver Theysken** would succeed **McQueen** at **Givenchy;** however, in March 2001 after collections, it was announced that Welsh designer **Julien Macdonald** would take the coveted title.

MELLO, DAWN (SEE GUCCI) (DATES UNKNOWN) She restored the luxurious image of **Gucci** in 1989 to 1991 as executive vice president and creative director.

MEYER, GENE (1954-) American from Louisville, Kentucky. He worked as a design assistant at **Anne Klein Studio** in the mid-1970s, and then designed eveningwear and accessories including shoes for **Geoffrey Beene,** 1978–1989. He opened his own business in 1989 specializing in made-to-order womenswear. In 1991, he closed his made-to-order business and focused on designing scarves and eventually began to specialize in men's neckties, pocket scarves, boxer shorts, and men's ready-to-wear and accessories. He also licensed his designs for dinnerware and decorative ceramic tiles.

MEYER, JOHN AND ARLENE MEYER (JOHN MEYER OF NORWICH) (DATES UNKNOWN) An American sportswear company specializing in knits. **Perry Ellis** was head designer, 1967–1974. The company, **John Meyer of Norwich,** closed after **John Meyer's** death in 1974.

MILAN, JANICE (SEE MILDRED ORICK) (DATES UNKNOWN) American women's ready-to-wear wholesale designer who founded her own company in the early 1940s and teamed with women's sportswear designer **Mildred Orrick** whose name appeared on the company's label. The company closed in the early 1950s and **Orrick** moved to **Anne Fogarty.**

MILES, MICHAEL (SEE BETSEY JOHNSON) (DATES UNKNOWN) American, partnered with **Betsey Johnson** to create **Star Ferry** collection, 1975–1977.

MILLER, NICOLE (1952-) American with a French mother and American father, born in Lenox, Massachusetts. She began her career as a designer creating coats for **Rain Cheetahs,** New York, in 1975, before being appointed head designer for **Bud Konheim, at PJ Walsh** a women's ready-to-wear fashion house, 1975–1982. She formed a partnership with **Konheim's** company and they renamed it **Nicole Miller,** in 1982. She launched her line of menswear accessories in 1987, followed by footwear in 1992 and fragrances and cosmetics in 1993, as well as numerous licenses including socks, tights, jeans, handbags, and men's formal wear. Most noted for her iconic character and logo-driven creative bold prints which she transferred to her men's neckwear and boxer shorts. Each of her print designs are dated to the specific collection she presents. Her womenswear continues to be sexy, lighthearted, mid-priced dresses and separates.

MILLER, NOLAN (1935-) American from Burkbarnette, Texas. **Miller** exploded onto the fashion scene in the early 1980s with the now iconic designs which he created for the cast of characters on the television series Dynasty. A contemporary of **Bob Mackie, Miller's** designs, however similar, possessed a powerful distinction with his inspirational interpretations of the dramatic and exaggerated silhouette created for Joan Crawford in the 1940s. The opulent and glamorous broad-shoulder designs which he created for the notorious Alexis Colby, played by Joan Collins, coupled with the power of television, truly set the pace for the look of the 1980s. He launched his own ready-to-wear collection of women's power suits and eveningwear on the heels of the success of the television show. He was a favorite choice by many Hollywood luminaries throughout the 1980s for glamorous public appearances and award presentations.

MILLSTEIN, DAN An American contemporary ready-to-wear, wholesale manufacturer specializing in women's coats and sportswear. **Calvin Klein** designed for the company from 1962 to 1964.

MIRMAN, SIMONE (SIMONE PARMENTIER) (1920-) Frenchwoman from Paris, France. The daughter of a dressmaker who began her career at an early age working as an assistant to milliners **Rose Valois** and **Schiaparelli** in Paris. She moved to London in 1937 and worked for **Schiaparelli's** London salon. She launched the opening of her own millinery business in 1947, and by 1952 she was fulfilling orders for her beautiful hats for Princess Margaret, as well as numerous other British royals. As well as operating a flourishing millinery business, she also created designs for the house of **Dior, Yves Saint Laurent,** and **Norman Hartnell.**

MISSONI, OTTAVIO AND ROSITA An Italian knitwear design manufacturer founded in Varese, Italy, in 1953 by **Ottavio (Tai) Missoni** (1921–) from Dalmatia, Italy, and **Rosita (Jelmini) Missoni** (1932–) from Lombardy, Italy. **Ottavio** was a runner on the Italian Olympic team and was designing the team's knitted wool track uniforms when he met **Rosita,** who had been working as a seamstress in her parents' bedspread manufacturing company. The two founded their knitwear business with just four knitting machines in 1953, when they married, and it has proven to be a happy and fruitful union ever since. They began by creating knitwear fabric for other designers; however, they introduced their first collection in 1958, followed by their first showings in Florence and Paris in 1967. **Ottavio** handles the knit designs, colors, textures, and patterns; while **Rosita** handles the design of the silhouettes, draping the knitted fabric directly on the model. In spring 1967 at their first show in Florence a somewhat scandalous moment presented itself when **Rosita** had requested the models remove their bras which were visible under the delicate knits and when the spotlights hit the runway the thin garments appeared to be transparent. The subsequent reactions from an unforgiving press is perhaps what caused the **Missonis** to choose not to show their collections in Florence, opting instead for Milan which was closer to their home. They established the **Missoni SpA** factory in Sumirago in 1968, followed by boutique openings in Milan and New York in 1976. Most noted for their beautiful knits in timeless designs built around basic pieces which they present in each collection, including pants, long cardigan jackets, dresses, and skirts, as well as knit accessories, introducing variations of all the signature patterns and beautiful color combinations which since their inception have been their hallmark.

MIYAKE, ISSEY (1938-) Japanese from Hiroshima, Japan. He moved to Paris in 1965 to continue his fashion studies. He joined **Guy Laroche** as a design assistant, 1966–1968, before assisting **Givenchy,** 1968–1969. He moved to New York to work as a designer for **Geoffrey Beene,** 1969–1970, when he returned to Japan and founded **Miyake Design Studio, MDS,** in Tokyo. He presented his first show in New York in 1971 followed by Paris in 1973 which featured his hallmark layered wrap dressing. He introduced his **"Pleats Please Issey Miyake"** in 1988, as well as opening his first boutique in North America in New York. Aesthetically a visionary and an innovative genius recognized for his beautiful fabrics, kimono textiles, and incredible use of textures. Other lines include **Issey Sport** and **Plantation.**

MIZRAHI, ISAAC (1961-) American from New York, raised in Brooklyn. He began as an assistant to **Perry Ellis** while in his last year at Parsons in 1981. After graduation he went to work at **Perry Ellis** as a design assistant, 1982–1983, when he moved to **Jeffrey Banks** in 1984. He worked for **Calvin Klein,** 1986–1987, then launched his own women's ready-to-wear company in 1987, followed by menswear in 1990, accessories in 1992, and handbags in 1993. He is considered to be a classic New York women's ready-to-wear designer who has culled his influences from numerous American designers including **Claire McCardell, Norman Norell, Geoffrey Beene, Halston,** and **Rudi Gernreich.** His company skyrocketed to success in the late 1980s, and in the mid-1990s with backing from **Chanel** he became a household name; then for a myriad of reasons **Chanel** pulled the plug on his financing; **Mizrahi,** like many designers before him, had grown too fast and lost control of his company. He regrouped and returned to his second love which is performing and presented a one-man show in New York in 2000 which reflected his life in the fashion industry and his character which he portrayed in the documentary film, *Unzipped*, about his 1994 collection. Today he is in preproduction with Dreamworks Pictures on a screenplay which he sold based on a book he wrote about a supermodel.

MODES, CAROLYN (DATES UNKNOWN) An American, women's ready-to-wear manufacturer in the 1930s–early 1950s. **Harvey Berin** and **Lo Balbo** had both worked as freelance designers for the company for a time throughout the 1940s–1950s. She was recognized for her Paris-inspired suits, coats, cocktail dresses, and eveningwear throughout the late 1930s and early 1950s. Her rayon dresses in the 1940s would often be embellished with sequin motifs, and her expensive dinner suits often had beautiful beaded collars or rhinestone buttons.

MOLENAC, FREDERIC (SEE GRÉS, MME. ALIX)

ANNA MOLINARI (SEE BLUMARINE)

MOLYNEUX, EDOUARD (EDWARD) H. (CAPTAIN) (1891-1974) British from Hampstead, London, with Irish parents. He began his career as a sketch artist in advertising and at the age of 20 he was engaged by the house of **Lucile (Lady Duff Gordon)** as a sketch artist after he had won a competition she had sponsored in 1911. He worked in her salons over the next eight years in Paris, London, and Chicago until 1919, when he opened his own dressmaking salon in Paris. He followed up the opening of his Paris salon with salons in Monte Carlo, Cannes, Biarritz, and London, 1925–1932. **Pierre Balmain** had apprenticed with him in the mid-to-late 1930s. He moved his head office to London in the mid-1930s and remained in London until after World War II, returning to his Paris salon in 1946. By 1950 he had closed all of his salons except Paris and retired to Jamaica leaving the Paris salon under the design direction of **Jacques Griffe.** He is recognized for his refined aristocratic designs for the leisure class with exquisite fabrics designed by **Brooke Cadwallader.** His elegant little black dresses and bias-cut gowns were quite popular amongst the "Cafe Society" and he was openly embraced by the society he created for. His designs were carried at Henri Bendel and in the "Green Room" on the third floor at Bloomingdales, as well as the Eldridge and Garson shop in the 1930s. His reemergence from retirement was an unsuccessful one in 1965 due to the fact that the youth markets of the 1960s did not connect with his refined designs and he found himself forced to consider retirement once again; this time he chose to move to Biot near Antibes and appointed **John Tullis,** a South African designer, as his successor.

MONTAIGUE, RENÉE (SEE JAY-THORPE, INC.) (DATES UNKNOWN) In-house staff designer at **Jay-Thorpe, Inc.,** department store, New York, in the late 1920s through the early 1930s.

MONTANA, CLAUDE (1949-) From Paris, France. He began his career after studying chemistry and law in Paris when he moved to London in the late 1960s and created papier-mâché jewelry embellished with rhinestones which he sold in street markets and which was featured in various fashion publications. He returned to Paris in 1972 to work with **Michael Costas,** ready-to-wear and accessories for **Idéal-Cuir,** Paris. He then moved to **MacDouglas Leathers** as an assistant designer in 1973, then head designer in 1974. He succeeded **Gianni Versace** in 1980 as head designer for **Complice (see Genny),** as well as working as a freelance designer for **Ferrer y Sentis Knitwear,** Paris, from 1975. He launched his own collection in 1979, followed by **Hommes Montana** and his first boutique in 1983. **Claude Montana** began designing couture for the house of **Lanvin,** 1989–1992. Most noted as an artist-designer whose strong work in leather in the early 1980s often culled inspiration from military and biker influences expressing a strong aggressive edge.

MONTEIL, GERMAINE (DATES UNKNOWN) An American women's ready-to-wear designer, who began designing in the late 1920s for wholesale manufacturer **Anthony Traina,** who would later become **Traina-Norell.** By the early 1930s, she was considered one of the top American designers along with contemporaries including **Elizabeth Hawes, Nettie Rosenstein, Claire McCardell,** and **Jo Copeland.** Having established a successful wholesale manufacturing business, she also created a cosmetic company in 1935, which by 1940 had become so successful that she ceased designing clothing to concentrate on her flourishing cosmetics business which included skin care, face powders, lipstick, and perfumes such as "Laughter" and "Nostalgia." She was most noted for her feminine dressy day- and eveningwear.

MONTE-SANO & PRUZAN An American custom-tailoring house established in the 1920s by **Vincent Monte-Sano.** The company became known for their expertly tailored womenswear suits and coats throughout the 1940s, 1950s, and 1960s. French designer **Jacques Tiffeau** was appointed head designer in 1952 where he continued in the company's classic tradition until 1958 when he left to launch his own company. Most noted for their expensive hand-finished ready-to-wear suits, coats, and little black dresses which could move seamlessly from day to night, as well as for their eveningwear in the late 1950s and early 1960s.

MOORE, JOHN (1928-) American from Texas. After graduating from Parsons in New York he worked briefly for **Elizabeth Arden** before moving to **Jane Derby** in the late 1940s. In 1951 he went to work for **Matty Talmack** prior to opening his own company in 1964 which he ran successfully through 1975, specializing in women's ready-to-wear, dressy day- and eveningwear. He retired to Texas in 1975 where he opened an antique business in the town of Alice.

MORI, HANAE (1926-) Japanese from Tokyo. After studying literature she returned to school to study sewing, sketching, and designing. She began her career by opening her first boutique in Shinjuku, Japan, and was immediately discovered by the Japanese film industry which contracted her to design costumes. She moved her shop to the very fashionable Ginza district in Tokyo in 1955 and realized tremendous success. She presented her first New York fashion show in 1965, then Monaco and Paris in 1975, followed by the establishment of a couture house in Paris in 1977 and a boutique on Faubourg St-Honoré, Paris, in 1985, as well as Monte Carlo in 1989. Her husband **Ken Mori** who had come out of the Japanese textile industry manages her multimillion-dollar business which specializes in beautiful feminine cocktail and eveningwear from soft silky fabrics which she designs. The fabrics are woven, printed, and dyed exclusively for her using traditional Japanese symbols such as butterfly and flower motifs. She has also sold licenses to her fabric designs for bed and bath linens. She is best known for her beautiful ready-to-wear, as well as for her costume designs which she has created for La Scala in Milan and the Paris Opera Ballet. The company is still in business today.

MORLOTTI, DOMINIQUE (1950-) From Paris, France. He began his career as a freelance designer for **Ted Lapidus** in the mid-to-late 1970s prior to moving to **Pierre Balmain** menswear in 1980, and **Christian Dior Monsieur** in 1983 through the early 1990s. He introduced his own men's ready-to-wear label while still with **Dior** in 1990. In 1992, he was appointed designer of both men's and women's ready-to-wear at the house of **Lanvin;** however, he was succeeded in 1995 by **Ocimar Versolato** as the womenswear designer. **Morlotti** is recognized for his refined and expertly tailored men's and womenswear.

MORRIS, LESLIE (DATES UNKNOWN) American, in-house designer who attended the Paris shows and designed custom and ready-to-wear from the Paris models for Bergdorf Goodman department store, New York, in 1931, continuing with Bergdorf for over two decades.

MORTENSEN, ERIC (SEE PIERRE BALMAIN) (DATES UNKNOWN) **Mortensen** worked with **Pierre Balmain** since 1948, and after **Balmain's** death in 1982 the business continued under **Mortensen's** design direction. **Mortensen** was replaced by **Hervé Pierre** when French financier **Alain Chevalier** acquired the **Balmain** company in January 1990.

MOSCHINO, FRANCO (1950-1994) Italian from Abbiategrasso, Italy. He began his career while studying fine arts at the Accademia della Belle Arti in Milan with a dream of becoming a painter; he worked as a waiter, model, and as a fashion sketcher for various fashion houses, including **Giorgio Armani** and **Gianni Versace,** 1971–1977, as well as doing collections for **Beged'Or** and **Genny** before taking a design position at **Cadette,** 1977–1982. He founded his first company, **Moonshadow,** in 1983 followed by **Moschino COUTURE!** in 1983 and his diffusion line **CHEAP & CHIC** in 1988. He introduced the **UOMO** menswear collection in 1986, followed by **CHEAP & CHIC UOMO** in 1991. Other lines included underwear, swimwear, jeans, children's clothes, accessories, and fragrances. Recognized at his height in the mid-to-late 1980s for his irreverent approach to fashion. His designs were more often sexy, yet wearable basic silhouettes which were expertly tailored and decorated with surreal, provocative visual puns that parodied fashion, materialism, and capitalism. He coined amusing phrases with which he adorned his garments and belts such as "Ready-to-Where?", "Waste of Money," "Bull Chic," and "Expensive Jacket." He opened new stores in Paris, Milan, London, and New York in the summer of 2001, and licensed a menswear line to **Gruppo Forall** in order to strengthen its presence in the international market.

MOSKOWITZ, MORRIS An American accessories and handbag manufacturer recognized for their attractive, unique ladylike bags and accessories from the 1950s through the mid-1970s. **Judith Leiber** was designing handbags for **Morris Moskowitz Co.,** 1961–1962, prior to opening her own firm with her husband **Gerson Leiber** in 1963. **Moskowitz** handbags have a quality and sensibility similar to those of **Koret.**

MR. JOHN (SEE FREDERIC HIRST, JOHN-FREDERICK, AND HANSI HARBERGER) **Hansi Harberger** partnered with **Frederic Hirst** in the mid-1940s naming the millinery company **John-Frederick.** They dissolved the partnership in 1948 and the two men continued to produce hats under their own companies: **Hansi Harberger** as **Mr. John** and **Frederic Hirst** as **John-Frederick. Hansi Harberger** as **Mr. John** went on to design less expensive lines for **Lilly Daché** known as **Dachettes,** as well as **Mr. John Juniors** in the mid-1950s. **Herbert Kasper** sold his Parsons School project designs to **The Mr. John Co.** in the late 1950s and came to work for the company in the early 1960s. The company also created a line of hats with the label, **Mr. John, Caprice** in the 1960s and early 1970s. **Hansi Harberger** continued to design for his company **Mr. John** until the late 1970s.

MR. MORT (SEE STAN HERMAN) An American ready-to-wear manufacturer.

MUGLER, THIERRY (1948-) Frenchman from Strasbourg, Alsace. He began his career as a dancer for the Opéra de Rhin, Strasbourg, as well as working as a window dresser. He worked as an assistant designer for **Gudule Boutique,** Paris, 1967–1968; then as a designer for **André Peters,** London, 1968–1969. He continued to work as a freelance designer in Milan and Paris, 1970–1973, and produced a lower-priced ready-to-wear collection for the house of **Guy Laroche** in the early 1970s. He opened his own company under the name of **"Cafe de Paris"** in 1973, followed by his label **"Thierry Mugler"** in 1974. As well as being a wonderfully talented and innovative fashion designer, he continues to pursue his love for photography and has worked as a professional photographer since 1967, producing a book of his photography, *Thierry Mugler, Photographer,* published in 1988. In 1992 he launched his highly successful fragrance line, **Angel,** as well as introducing his first couture collection. He is celebrated for his powerful, sexy, and saucy ready-to-wear women's suits and dresses which draw upon influences from the sculpted silhouettes of the 1940s and 1950s, with nipped waists and extended shoulders.

MUIR, JEAN (JEAN ELIZABETH MUIR) (1929-1995) She began her career working in various departments at Liberty, London, including stockroom assistant, sales associate in the made-to-measure department, then as a sketch artist. She designed dresses and knitwear collections for **Jaeger,** 1956–1963, then worked as a freelance designer for **Courtauld's,** 1966–1969. With separate financing she formed her own clothing line under the name **Jane & Jane** with her actor husband **Harry Leuckertt** as co-director in 1966. The two formed **Jean Muir Ltd.** in 1967. They sold the controlling interest in the company to **Coats Paton Group,** then bought back 75 percent interest in 1989. **Jaeger** had a **Jean Muir** department in their original store on Regent Street in London. She is best known in the 1960s and 1970s for her women's ready-to-wear dresses, suits, coats, and separates with hallmark signature work in rayon jersey and suedes which she manipulated like jersey in fluid, refined designs. **Jean Muir Ltd.** is still in business today producing three collections a year, spring/summer, autumn/winter, and resort, as well as two small collections a year produced on the **Jean Muir Essentials** label to complement the spring/summer, autumn/winter collections. Collections today include various woven and jersey cloths, leathers, suedes, and knitwear.

MUNN, CARRIE (DATES UNKNOWN) An American women's ready-to-wear and custom designer who opened a shop on Madison Avenue in New York, 1942. She introduced an evening dress known as "**Adorable**" in 1949 which was in black lace, net, and pink taffeta with black bow sleeves that she continued to produce in varied designs every year for subsequent collections. Remembered from the 1940s and 1950s for her versatile evening separates, full-quilted evening skirts, and evening dresses with full skirts with narrowed waists that were often embellished with appliqué and embroidery.

NEUMANN, VERA (SEE VERA) (DATES UNKNOWN) An American fabric painter who created fabric designs for the women's ready-to-wear manufacturer **Manhattan Industries** in the 1960s. **Perry Ellis** joined **Manhattan Industries** in 1974 and interpreted **Neumann's** fabric designs into garments. She was known for her beautiful and colorful motifs on scarves, garments, and household linens and textiles. Her logo often had a small ladybug next to her signature.

NICHOLSON, JENNIFER (1967-) American from Hollywood, California. Although **Nicholson** was born in Hollywood, California, she spent her formidable years living in Hawaii. Daughter of actor Jack Nicholson and actress/artist Sandra Knight, **Nicholson** began her career as a young actress while pursuing her passion for painting, a talent which she had inherited from both her father and mother. In 1986 she worked as a set designer for film and television before venturing into her own interior design business, adding such notable names as Courtney Love to her list of clients. Recognized by the international and Hollywood press as an arbiter of style and glamour, known for her elaborate theme events, **Nicholson** has used her fame as a conduit to a burgeoning fashion business, launching her first line as a collaborative women's ready-to-wear venture with designer **Pamela Barish** in June of 2000. **Nicholson** also launched her first fragrance line, **June,** at the same time. In the spring of 2001, Saks Fifth Avenue, Beverly Hills, presented the **Barish-Nicholson** spring collection. **Nicholson's** hip, edgy, and sensual designs are favored by the "who's who" in the young Hollywood scene. **Nicholson** launched her own collection in the summer of 2001.

NIPON, ALBERT (DATES UNKNOWN) An American women's ready-to-wear designer recognized for his expensive, refined, and ladylike dresses and suits in the 1970s and 1980s. He introduced a secondary line, **Nipon Boutique** in the mid-1970s.

NORELL, NORMAN (NORMAN DAVID LEVINSON) (1900-1972) (SEE TRAINA-NORELL) American from Nobelville, Indiana. After attending Parsons in New York to study painting he returned to his hometown of Nobelville and opened a small tie-dyeing fabric shop which along with batik fabric was very popular in the 1920s. He returned to New York in 1920 to study design at the Pratt Institute in Brooklyn. In 1922 he went to work designing costumes for Paramount Pictures, New York, as well as for various Broadway productions and the **Brooks Costume Company.** He designed for **Charles Armour,** a women's ready-to-wear manufacturer, 1924–1927, moving to **Hattie Carnegie** in 1928 where he remained until 1940. In 1941, he teamed with businessman/financier **Anthony Traina** to form **Traina-Norell.** He had structured his deal with **Anthony Traina** to draw a lower salary from the company in exchange for his name on the label. The new company hired publicist Eleanor Lambert to promote its profile and designs, a practice that was new to the fashion industry and which proved to be very successful. **Norell** showed his first collection for **Traina-Norell** in New York in 1941, their first year of business. By 1943, **Norell** was given this first Coty Award and later became the first designer to be elected to the Coty Hall of Fame. Throughout the 1940s, 1950s, and 1960s the company thrived on its purity of line designs, precisely tailored ready-to-wear dresses, coats, and separates, as well as luxurious eveningwear of silk faille, wool jersey, and crepe. They had much of their fabric designed by famed textile designer **Brooke Cadwallader.** As with other top-rung American designers of the times, many of **Traina-Norell's** dresses were sold as "originals," which meant that they were made in the hundreds as opposed to mass-produced ready-to-wear and sold in selected specialty departments in various department stores across America. In the early 1950s, he had successfully achieved a solid pavé effect with his sequined jersey fabric which he used to create simple evening sheaths with matching wool coats. By

1952 these sparkling slinky formfitting gowns were named "Mermaid" dresses. He continued to offer these handsewn flat-sequined sheaths through the 1960s and early 1970s. Interestingly, these sequined dresses were constructed in New York by embroiderer **Madame Anri** with an overlock stitch by hand, so that if the stitch broke only one sequin would come off. **Anthony Traina** retired in 1960 and closed the **Traina-Norell** company. **Norell** had already left the **Traina-Norell** company to form his own company, **Norman Norell, Inc.** with private backing. When the private backing pulled out he brought the **Revlon** company on board, which proved to be a very profitable partnership when they launched the **Norell** fragrance. **Louis Dell'Olio** worked as a designer for a time in the early 1970s with **Norell** before moving to **Anne Klein** with **Donna Karan** in 1974. Both **Halston** and **Adolfo** had designed hats to complement **Norell's** designs in the early 1960s. He presented his first collection under his own label in 1960 and continued designing successfully until his death in 1972. **Michaele Vollbracht** designed for **Norell** in 1971–1972 just prior to Norell's death. **Gustave Tassel** was appointed head designer and president of the company by **Revlon** with the understanding that he would continue the **Norell** label, as well as the tradition which had been established by **Norell. Tassell** introduced a secondary line for the company in 1972, **Norell-Tassell,** and presented his first collection for **Norell** later that year. **Tassell** continued to design for the company until the board of directors decided to close the company in 1980. **Norell's** timeless, strikingly simple designs continue to influence many contemporary designers including **Zoran** and **Isaac Mizrahi.**

NORELL, TRAINA (TRAINA-NORELL, ANTHONY TRAINA, SEE NORMAN NORELL) (DATES UNKNOWN) The business partner behind the label **Traina-Norell** established with designer **Norman Norell.** He retired in 1960 and **Norman Norell** changed the company to **Norman Norell, Inc.**

NORRIS, MAGGIE, (DATES UNKNOWN) MAGGIE NORRIS COUTURE American from Louisiana. **Maggie Norris** began her design career with **Ralph Lauren** in 1983 as senior design director for **Ralph Lauren Women Classic Collections,** building the **Classic Line** from its inception, 1983–1994. She was senior design director, 1995–1997, working closely with **Lauren** on sportswear, eveningwear, outerwear, and sweater collections. She moved to head **Mondi,** Munich, Germany, as design director, 1997–1999. In early 2000, she debuted her first private collection, **Maggie Norris Couture,** which is available exclusively at **Bergdorf Goodman,** New York. Her collections are romantic, equestrian-inspired eveningwear incorporating exquisite vintage and antique fabrics. Her basic silhouette is centered around the corsets with fine beadwork and embroideries done at **Lesage,** Paris. Her designs have been popularized by the who's who in American society, and in April 2001, one of her incredible corset gowns was worn by Nicole Kidman on the cover of the *Vanity Fair* "Legends" issue.

NUTTER, TOMMY (1942-1992) British from London, England. **Nutter** began as a salesman at **G. Ward and Co.,** a Savile Row tailor, in the early 1960s before launching **Nutter's** in Savile Row, 1969–1976. More the entrepreneur than a tailor, **Nutter** hired the best master cutters and tailors to create his youthful, hip version of the classic Savile Row suit, with tight-crotched flared trousers, narrow waists, wide lapels, square shoulders, and waistcoats. This sexy new cut on the classic was popular with the fashionable youth movement in the late 1960s and 1970s, and catered to a variety of celebrity clientele including Mick Jagger, who wore a white three-piece **Nutter** suit to his marriage to Bianca Jagger in St. Tropez in 1971. **Nutter** left the company in 1976 to team up with **Kilgour French and Stanbury.**

OLDFIELD, BRUCE (1950-) Englishman from London, England. Raised in a foster home, **Oldfield's** foster mother was a seamstress and inspired him to pursue a career in fashion. He began as a freelance designer creating a collection for Henri Bendel, New York, in the early 1970s. He sold sketches to **Yves Saint Laurent** in the early 1970s while working as a freelance designer. He introduced his first private label collection under his own name in 1975. His clothing sold well throughout the 1970s in leading American department stores such as Saks Fifth Avenue, Bergdorf Goodman, and Henri Bendel. He opened his own boutique in Beachamp Place, London in 1984 where he specialized in custom work including luxurious, theatrical eveningwear he created for both his British royal customers, including Diana, Princess of Wales, as well as his celebrity clientele.

OLDHAM, TODD (1961-) American from Corpus Christi, Texas. He began his career working in the alterations department at the **Polo/Ralph Lauren** boutique in Dallas in 1980. With no formal training, he taught himself pattern making and sold his first collection of womenswear to Neiman Marcus, Dallas, in 1981, followed by the formation of his first company in Dallas in 1985. By 1988 he was in New York and had launched his "**Times 7**" line which was basic women's blouses with eclectic antique and unusual buttons designed by his brother, **Brad Oldham.** In 1989 he received backing from a Japanese firm, **Onward Kashiyama Company,** and he presented his first show with them in 1990, followed by a line of handbags in 1991, and footwear in 1993. He became the head design consultant to **Escada** in 1994, then launched a line of licensed jeans in 1995. He is recognized for his flamboyant, colorful, and sexy ready-to-wear and eveningwear. His playful, formfitting day suits were favored by actress Fran Drescher for her starring role on the television series *The Nanny* in the mid-to-late 1990s. He designed a line of patterns for **Vogue Patterns** in 1992. **Oldham** has closed his ready-to-wear business today to concentrate on interior design.

OLIVE, FRANK (DATES UNKNOWN) American from Milwaukee, Wisconsin. He began his career in New York with a dream to design costumes for the stage; however, with the encouragement of **Norman Norell** who viewed his early sketches, **Olive** moved into millinery. He worked in the custom hat department **Tatiana** at Saks Fifth Avenue and subsequently for **Emme** and **Chanda** before opening his own shop in Greenwich Village, New York, in the early 1960s. His hats bearing the label **Frank Olive** and **Private Collection by Frank Olive** were favored by society's who's who and a large list of celebrities. His hats were desired because of their skilled craftsmanship and supreme quality.

OLIVER, ANDRÉ (1932-1993) Frenchman from Toulouse, France. A colleague of **Pierre Cardin** who joined **Cardin** in 1952. He began at **Pierre Cardin** working on the company's first men's collection, eventually taking over men's and women's ready-to-wear collections. He was named artistic director for **Pierre Cardin** couture and was given complete artistic control under **Cardin's** direction. After **Oliver's** death in 1993, **Cardin** resumed his position as design director.

ORIGINALA An American women's ready-to-wear design manufacturer noted for their finely tailored suits and coats, they have hosted many freelance and in-house designers. **Louis Dell'Olio** designed for **Originala's Giorgini** and **Ginori** divisions in the 1960s, and **Jacques Tiffeau** created a beautiful coat collection in the late 1970s prior to his retirement.

ORRICK, MILDRED (DATES UNKNOWN) An American sportswear designer from Virginia. After attending Parsons in New York, she began her career as a sketch artist and model for the couture house of **Natacha Rambova.** After her marriage and birth of her three children, she resumed working as a freelance sketch artist as she raised her young children, working for a time at *Harper's Bazaar.* While working there, she met Diana Vreeland who had encouraged a design idea that she had presented to her. Upon Vreeland's recommendation, **Orrick** took her concept for leotard dressing to **Claire McCardell** who had manufacturing capabilities at the time. **McCardell** put the design into production and was subsequently credited for the design. **Orrick** began designing for **Joset Walker** in the mid-1940s, then in 1945 she introduced her own label on the heels of her success with **McCardell** at a company founded by **Janice Milan.** The **Janice Milan** company closed in the early 1950s and **Orrick** began to design freelance for **Anne Fogarty,** then **Townley.** She supervised collections at **Townley** as **McCardell,** while serving as head designer, had taken ill. She then assumed **McCardell's** position at **Townley** after **McCardell's** death in 1958. **Orrick** moved to work for **Villager** in the late 1950s through the early 1960s. She is known for her women's sportswear, swimsuits, play suits, and floor-length sundresses.

ORRY-KELLY (1897-1964) Australian from Sydney, Australia. He began his career as a costume designer joining Warner Brothers in Hollywood in 1932. Throughout his 30-year career he worked on over 100 films for all of the major studios including Metro-Goldwyn-Mayer, Universal, RKO, and 20th Century-Fox. Most noted for his designs for Marilyn Monroe in *Some Like It Hot* in 1959, as well as for *An American in Paris* in 1951.

OWENS, RICK (1961-) American from Northern California. His first job after leaving Otis Parson was working for a Los Angeles–based company which manufactured designer knockoffs. He then went to work for ready-to-wear designer **Michèle Lamy** in the early 1990s. It is difficult to say who was muse to whom once the two designers joined forces. **Lamy** closed her business in 1993. **Owens** sold a collection of designs he had produced for **Lamy's** personal wardrobe to a cutting-edge upscale boutique, **Charles Gallay,** in Los Angeles in 1994. Today **Owens** works much in the way **Charles James** did in his time, producing only what he wants and in very limited quantities. A mysterious architect of women's couture and ready-to-wear, his designs have the sensuality of **Azzedine Alaïa** meeting the heightened and exaggerated form of early **Christian Dior.** His bias-cut gowns of washed-out and secondhand fabrics combine cutting techniques which transcend those emulated designs of the 1930s and 1940s. Despite **Owens's** claim to inspiration derivative of **Vionnet, Fortuny,** and **Grés,** his techniques give his gowns an ethereal liquid drape which create a gloomy post-apocalyptic look which supersedes the future. He remains by choice a fringe designer whose work is available through his private atelier and in very limited venues such as **Jeffrey's** in New York and **Maxfield** in Los Angeles.

OZBEK, RIFAT (1953-) Turkish man from Istanbul, Turkey. He moved to England at age 18 in 1971 to begin his studies in architecture; however, by 1974 he had shifted his focus to fashion design and moved to St. Martin's School of Art, London. He began his design career working for **Walter Albini** in Milan in 1977, returning to London in 1980 to design for **Monsoon,** a ready-to-wear line manufactured in India, 1980–1984. He launched his first private collection in 1984 from his apartment. However, three years later in 1987, he moved to a fashionable studio off Bond Street in London. He introduced his second line, "**O,**" that was renamed "**Future Ozbek**" in 1987, followed by a licensed collection to **Aeffe SpA,** Italy, in 1988. He introduced his "**New Age Collection**" in 1989. He moved his production to Milan in 1991 where he continued to present his collections until he moved his shows to Paris in 1994. He is most noted for his work in the late 1980s and early 1990s, influenced by elements of design from the Far East and the Ottoman Empire. His early designs reflect his Turkish origins with his use of exotic brocades and rich ornamentations which he fuses with his interpretations of contemporary London street fashion.

PAPINI, LUCIANO, QUICKSTEP (SEE GIGLI, ROMERO)

PAPPAGALLO (SEE RUDI GERNREICH) An American shoe manufacturer active in the 1950s to present.

PAQUIN, MADAME (JEANNE BECKERS) (1869-1936) Frenchwoman from Saint Denis, France. A French couture house founded in 1891 by **Jeanne Beckers** and her husband **Isidore Jacobs,** a businessman who originally procured the financial backing for the company and assumed the administration. The two became known as **Monsieur Paquin** and **Mme. Paquin. Mme. Paquin** began her career working at the couture house **Maison Rouff** in the late 1880s before opening her first couture house in Paris in 1891, followed by branches in London in 1896, making her the first French couture designer to have a foreign division. In 1911 she worked with **Georges Barbier** and **Paul Iribe** to create designs for her couture collections and accessories, as well as collaborating with **Léon Bakst** and **Drian** on dress designs. She opened other foreign branches in Buenos Aires, Madrid, and New York throughout the 1920s. The New York branch was known as **Paquin-Joire.** She was also the first woman to be awarded the Légion d'Honneur in Paris in 1913. When her husband died shortly after World War I she relinquished her position as head of the company to **Mademoiselle Madeleine** who continued in **Mme. Paquin's** tradition throughout the 1920s, with **Mme. Paquin** overseeing the operations. **Madame del Pombo** became the design director in the 1930s and **Mme. Paquin** retired completely; however, the focus of the house changed considerably under its new direction and the company's original reputation was compromised. By the mid-1940s, shortly after World War II, the Paris house merged its operations with the London branch, as well as with the house of **Worth** in Paris, becoming **Paquin-Worth,** until it closed in 1956. The house of **Worth** continued and was bought and sold once again. The house at its height boasted an exclusive clientele of queens, duchesses, and notable actresses, as well as the who's who in French society of the times. Remembered for its luxurious couture designs and the use of sumptuous fur trim on coats which the company continued to produce until it closed.

Although the company began as a small storefront business it evolved into one of the most formidable couture houses in Paris.

PARACHUTE A Canadian men's and women's designer ready-to-wear manufacturer headed by **Harry Parnass** and **Nicola Pelly.** Known for their hip boutique in the Yorkville Village in Toronto and their work in the late 1970s and early 1980s. Their designs were inventive edgy street fashion coupled with fine cut and tailoring.

PARAPHERNALIA (SEE BETSEY JOHNSON) A New York youth-oriented boutique where **Betsey Johnson** designed collections, 1965–1969.

PARAY, LUCILLE A French couture and ready-to-wear house whose designs were available in America at B. Altman and Henri Bendel in New York throughout the 1930s. They were considered to be on a par with **Molyneux,** the house of **Worth,** and **Callot Soeurs.**

PARNASS, HARRY (SEE PARACHUTE)

PARNIS, JERRY (DATES UNKNOWN) American women's ready-to-wear designer and sister to **Mollie Parnis.** Her company was in direct competition with that of her sister in as much as both created feminine, refined women's daywear and eveningwear.

PARNIS, MOLLIE (SARA ROSEN PARNIS) (1902-1992) American from Brooklyn, New York, of Austrian immigrant parents. She began her career working in sales for a blouse manufacturer, then as a stylist for **David Westheim,** 1928–1930, when she left to marry **Leon Livingston (originally Levinson),** a textile designer. The couple founded **Parnis-Livingston** women's ready-to-wear manufacturing in 1933. Her designs were sold without her label as "attributed to" throughout the 1930s in major department stores including Henri Bendel, Saks Fifth Avenue, Jay-Thorpe, Vera San Ville, Bergdorf Goodman, Stein and Blaine, as well as Madame et la Jeune Fille. She launched her own label with the company in the early 1940s and moved the company to Seventh Avenue in New York. She closed the company for three months after her husband's death in 1964. She introduced a boutique line in 1970, designed by **Morty Sussman,** while her couture and higher-priced collections were designed by **Hubert Latimer** beginning in 1973. The company launched **Mollie Parnis Studio Collection** ready-to-wear in 1979. She closed the company in 1984 after more than 50 years in business; however, she did not retire for long and resumed designing at-home wear for **Chevette Lingerie** which had been founded by one of her sisters, **Peggy Parnis,** and is now run by her nephew **Neal Hochman.** Her top-rung designs were comparable to those of her contemporaries such as **Ben Zuckerman, Larry Aldrich, Adele Simpson, Malcolm Starr,** and **Harvey Berin.** She is most noted for her feminine dressy day- and eveningwear favored by numerous first ladies throughout the 1950s, 1960s, and 1970s, including Mamie Eisenhower, Lady Bird Johnson, Pat Nixon, Betty Ford, and Rosalyn Carter.

PARNIS, PEGGY (DATES UNKNOWN) American, sister to **Mollie Parnis** and founder of **Chevette,** a lingerie manufacturer. **Mollie Parnis** designed an at-home collection for the company in 1984.

PARNIS-LIVINGSTON (SEE MOLLIE PARNIS)

PARTOS, EMERIC (1905-1975) Hungarian from Budapest, immigrated to the United States. After serving in the French army during World War II, he went to work for **Alex Maguy** where he concentrated on designing coats, as well as theatrical and ballet costumes. He joined his friend **Christian Dior** at the house of **Dior,** 1947–1950, then he moved to work for **Maximilian Furs** until 1955. He was appointed head designer for Bergdorf Goodman's fur department where he continued to design sumptuous sables, mink, and broadtail coats until his death in 1975.

PATOU, JEAN (1887-1936) Frenchman from Normandy, France. His father was a renowned tanner in France at the turn of the century and his uncle owned a furrier business where **Patou** began his career in in 1907. By 1913 he was ready to branch out on his own and opened a small dressmaking business under the name **Maison Parry,** selling his first collection under the **Parry** name in 1914 to American importer **Jake Lichtenstein. Patou** closed his salon during World War I and served as an army captain of Zouaves.

He reopened his salon in 1919 under his own name, **Jean Patou.** By 1925 he had opened a shop which specialized in sportswear and dresses worn by tennis star Suzanne Lenglen, both on and off the court, as well as launching his very successful perfume house. In 1924 he was the predecessor to the "designer logo" trend by placing his monogram on his leisure and sportswear designs. In 1925 he catapulted French couture and ready-to-wear into American popular demand by bringing six American models back to Paris after a visit, to work as his fit-models and to show his collection. American models were both taller and less curvaceous than the French women, which gave **Patou** an important edge over other French designers who were hoping to capture the burgeoning American women's fashion market. A contemporary of **Gabrielle (Coco) Chanel, Edouard Molyneux,** and **Madeleine Vionnet, Patou** had all of his fabrics designed exclusively for him by **Bianchini-Ferier,** as well as by **Rodier.** Throughout the 1930s and 1940s he opened numerous additional boutiques in Monte Carlo, Biarritz, Deauville, and Venice. In the late 1920s, versions of his models were sold at **Gervais,** a small chic New York boutique, and ready-to-wear design manufacturer **Harvey Berin** also purchased models to reproduce in the United States under **Berin's** label. Throughout the 1930s, **Patou's** handbags could be found in the Little Shop in Lord & Taylor, and his millinery designs in the hat salon at Bergdorf Goodman, as well as his custom designs in Bloomingdale's Green Room and at Hattie Carnegie's salon. Numerous important designers have worked for **Patou** over the years, including **Oleg Cassini** as a sketch artist in the early 1930s, (and after **Patou's** death in 1936 under the direction of his brother-in-law, **Raymond Barbas**); **Luis Estevez** in the early 1950s; **Marc Bowan,** 1953–1957, prior to replacing **Saint Laurent** at **Christian Dior; Karl Lagerfeld,** 1958–1963; **Michèl Goma,** 1963–1974; **Andrea Pfister** (designed shoes), 1964; **Jean-Paul Gaultier** (freelance sketch artist), 1972–1974; **Angelo Tarlazzi,** 1973–1976; **Roy Gonzalez,** 1976–1981; and **Christian Lacroix,** 1981–1987. **Patou** is remembered for his beautiful couture designs, as well as his innovative women's sportswear in the early 1920s and 1930s.

PATTULO MODES (SEE COPELAND, JO) An American women's ready-to-wear wholesale manufacturer with **Jo Copeland** as head designer in the early 1920s. **Copeland** left to form her own company with partner **Anne Sadowsky** in 1930, which lasted only four years. **Copeland** returned to **Pattullo** in 1934 and was made partner in 1938. **George Halley** designed for **Pattullo** in the early 1960s. The company remained in business with **Jo Copeland** at the helm until she retired and closed the business in 1970. **Copeland** died in 1982.

PAULIN, GUY (1945-1990) Frenchman from Lorraine, France. He began his career working as a lift operator at Printemps department store in Paris. With no formal training he sold fashion sketches to the Printemps department store's design department, and later moved to their rival company Prisunic. Primarily a freelance designer throughout his career, he worked for numerous design houses, including **Jimper, Dorothée Bis, Paraphernalia,** New York, **George Edelman, Byblos,** 1977–1980, and **Alan Cleaver,** among others. He established his own house in 1970 which he operated until 1984 when he was appointed successor to **Karl Lagerfeld** as the design director at **Chloé,** 1984–1986. He created **S.A. Guy Paulin** design studio in 1990 with **Mic Mac** and **Byblos** becoming his main clients. He also signed two licensing deals with the **Kanematsu Gosho** and **Yoshida** groups, as well as becoming a freelance artistic director for French ready-to-wear manufacturer, **Tinktiner,** in 1990. Most noted for his refined women's ready-to-wear, as well as his feminine and sexy knitwear.

PAULETTE, MME. (PAULINE ADAM) (DATES UNKNOWN) A French milliner from Normandy, France. She opened a millinery shop in 1929 and quickly became one of France's most celebrated milliners, noted for her draped wool turbans in 1942 and for her celebrity clientele, including Gloria Swanson and Rita Hayworth. During her illustrious career, she designed millinery collections for various fashion houses, including **Emanuel Ungaro,** 1970–1980.

PEDLAR, SILVIA (1901-1972) American from New York, New York. She founded **Iris Lingerie** in 1929 and was known for her beautiful feminine designs using the finest quality fabrics and lace, as well as exquisite craftsmanship. The houses of **Christian Dior, Emilio Pucci,** and **Hubert de Givenchy** are noted for having purchased her models to introduce to their lingerie collections. She closed her business in 1970, retiring just two years prior to her death in 1972.

PELLY, NICOLA (SEE PARACHUTE)

PENART An American women's ready-to-wear manufacturer for whom **Herbert Kasper** designed in the late 1960s. The **Kasper for Penart** division was sold through Lord & Taylor.

PERETTI, ELSA (1940-) Italian from Florence, Italy. After teaching language in Switzerland and studying interior design in Rome, **Elsa Peretti** began modeling in Paris, London, and New York, where in the mid-1960s she worked for some of the top design houses, including **Oscar de la Renta** and **Halston.** During this time she began to design jewelry and presented some of her pieces to both **Halston** and **Giorgio di Sant' Angelo,** who subsequently featured her jewelry designs in their shows. A long and prosperous relationship with **Halston** was to follow, with **Peretti** designing numerous signature pieces to complement **Halston's** collections, including the packaging for his fragrances and cosmetics. In 1974, she signed a deal to create for **Tiffany and Co.,** where her designs are still a prominent feature, including her "Diamonds by the Yard." She is recognized for her use of silver, gold, horn, ebony, and in the early years, ivory (not used in her designs today). Her asymmetrical heart is her most famous design.

PERRIS, BERNARD (1936-) Frenchman from Millau, France. His mother owned a ready-to-wear boutique in the south of France which strongly influenced him as a young boy. He moved to Paris at age 16 and by his early twenties had secured a position as a couture assistant to **Guy Laroche,** Paris, as well as assistant to **Mark Bohan,** 1960–1961. He worked as a designer for **Jacques Heim,** 1961–1963, followed by a period of time at the house of **Dior** in 1963, then **Paul Bon,** 1964–1969. He launched his first ready-to-wear business, **Bernard Perris Nouvelle Couture,** in 1969. In 1986 he chose to open his first boutique in America rather than France, on Madison Avenue in New York, followed by two in Paris in 1988. A bridge line was introduced in 1989; however, the company had some financial troubles shortly after and closed for a period of time between 1989 and 1992. The company regrouped and resumed business in 1992. Noted for his haute couture and deluxe ready-to-wear, his designs in the 1980s were powerful, opulent, and in dazzling colors with strong lines which appealed to his big-spending flamboyant customers. Today the company has new financial backing and is primarily focused on producing practical women's career-oriented ready-to-wear.

PERTEGAZ, MANUEL (1918-) Spaniard from Aragon, Spain. He began his career as a tailor's apprentice in 1930 at the age of 12. His family moved to Barcelona in the early 1940s and he began to make custom dresses for his sister, as well as a few private clients. In 1942, he opened a small custom dressmaking business in Barcelona. His business flourished and he opened salons in many major cities throughout Spain including Madrid in 1968, which offered beautiful couture and ready-to-wear including millinery designs throughout the 1940s, 1950s, and 1960s. He launched his first ready-to-wear collection in 1970. Along with **Balenciaga** and **Pedro Rodriguez, Pertegaz** was considered to be one of Spain's foremost couture designers, favored by the who's who of Spanish society. He is recognized for his elegant eveningwear and expertly tailored ready-to-wear.

PERUGIA, ANDRÉ (1893-1977) Frenchman from Nice, France. The son of a shoemaker, he opened a shoe salon in Paris in 1911, offering his custom-designed, handmade shoes. He designed shoe collections for numerous couture and ready-to-wear designers in the 1920s through the 1960s, including **Schiaperelli, Poiret, Fath, Givenchy,** and the **Charles Jourdan** company in the 1960s.

PFISTER, ANDREA (1942-) Italian from Pesaro, Italy; raised in and educated in Switzerland. He studied art in Italy and in 1961 moved to Milan to study shoe design. He moved to Paris in 1963 where he worked designing shoe collections for both **Lanvin** and **Patou.** He introduced his first shoe collection in 1965, followed by the opening of his first shoe salon in 1967. He is known for both men's and women's shoes made from fine leather and exotic skins in vibrant colors and whimsical designs, including his martini-glass-heeled pump with a slice of lemon in 1970.

PHELPS, WILLIAM AND ELIZABETH (DATES UNKNOWN) An American husband and wife team who founded a handmade handbag and belt business in New York in 1940. Their skillful yet rustic designs were very popular with the country set and the new demand for sportswear dressing. They received a Coty

Award in 1944 and had been very instrumental in popularizing the use of the newly favored shoulder bag in the 1940s. They moved their operations from New York to Pennsylvania in 1947. They are famous for their handmade bags and belts which in the 1940s were decorated with military insignias and brass eagles which they salvaged from local flea markets.

PICASSO, PALOMA (1949-) From Paris, France, daughter of artists **Pablo Picasso** and **Françoise Gilot.** She began her career in costume design after attending the University of Paris, the Sorbonne, and the University of Nanterre where she studied jewelry design. She created jewelry designs for **Yves Saint Laurent** in 1969 and freelanced as a costume designer in theater, working with various companies including the Folies-Bergère. In 1975 she created theatrical costumes for her soon-to-be husband, **Rafael Lopez-Cambil (a.k.a. Lopez-Sanchez)** an Argentine playwright. **Rafael Lopez-Cambil** and **Paloma** married in 1978 and teamed to form the **Paloma Picasso** brand which included collections designed for **Tiffany and Co.** in 1980. Her career has included the launch of a successful fragrance and cosmetic line in 1984, men's and women's accessories, eyewear, bone china, crystal, as well as household linens. She is recognized for her strong presence as a fine jewelry designer who often uses bold shapes including her signature X's and O's.

PICONE, EVAN An American women's ready-to-wear manufacturing company most noted for their affordably priced, practical women's careerwear as well as sportswear.

PIGUET, ROBERT (1901-1953) Swiss from Yverdon, Switzerland. The son of a Swiss banker, it was expected that he would follow in his father's footsteps. After completing his training as a banker; however, he moved to Paris to train as a designer, taking assistant positions with two important French design houses, **Redfern** and **Poiret.** He founded his own couture house in 1933 and employed primarily freelance designers. **Pierre Balmain** was a sketch artist for him in 1934; then **Christian Dior** as designer, 1937–1939; followed by **Hubert de Givenchy,** 1946–1948; **Mark Bohan** as assistant designer, 1945–1949; as well as **James Galanos** as an unpaid apprentice for a short period of time in 1946. He had suffered from ill health throughout most of his life and closed his business at the age of 50 in 1951. He died two years later. Although it is somewhat difficult to pinpoint the hallmarks of the couture house specifically because of the work and influences of so many different freelance and in-house designers, the most influential work was created in the 1930s through the 1940s, noted for dramatic, romantic styles, softly tailored dresses, and perfectly cut suits and coats.

PINGAT, EMILE (DATES UNKNOWN) French, **Pingat** was a contemporary and rival couturier of **Charles Frederick Worth** who offered beautiful couture creations from his Paris salon from 1860–1896. Famous for his romantic fantasy gowns in luxurious fabrics including silk faille and velvet.

PIPART, GÉRARD (1933-) From Paris, France. He began his career at age 16 in 1949 working as a sketch artist for **Pierre Balmain, Jacques Fath,** and **Givenchy.** He later worked as an assistant to both **Balmain** and **Fath.** He worked as an assistant under **Mac Bohan** when **Bohan** was at **Patou,** 1954–1958, and produced his own line for a brief period during this time, prior to completing his mandatory military service. By the early 1960s he was working as a freelance ready-to-wear women's designer, followed by an unsuccessful venture into couture in 1963. He joined the house of **Nina Ricci** in 1963–present, succeeding **Jules-François Crahay** as chief designer. A sophisticated and elegant womenswear designer often compared to **Jacques Fath.**

PLAIN JANE DRESS COMPANY (SEE ESPRIT) The **Esprit de Corps** was launched in 1968 from the **Plain Jane Dress Company** which specialized in pretty, simply cut 1940s-style dresses in the 1960s. By 1972, the **Plain Jane Dress Company** was renamed **Esprit de Corps.**

PLATTRY, GRETA (DATES UNKNOWN) An American women's ready-to-wear designer in the 1940s whose contemporaries were **Claire McCardell, Clare Potter,** and **Tina Leser.** She created feminine day dresses as well as moderately priced women's active- and sportswear, including swimwear and playsuits which were popular at the time. She retired for a period in 1960; however, in 1966 she created a line of casual clothes for a division of **Teal-Traina.**

POIRET, PAUL (1879-1944) From Paris, France. Brother to **Nicole Groult,** French couturier. Their father had been a cloth merchant in the late 1800s. As a young boy he worked as an apprentice at an umbrella manufacturing company, while teaching himself to sketch fashion. He sold his first sketches to **Mme. Cheruit** at **Raudnitz Soeurs,** then joined **Jacques Doucet** in 1896–1900, followed by **Charles Frederick Worth,** 1900–1904. **Poiret** launched his own house with the assistance of **Doucet,** who introduced him to a wealthy patron, French actress Réjane, who helped **Poiret** to open his house. He introduced numerous influential silhouettes including kimono shapes in the mid-1900s, and his "hobble skirt" and harem trousers in 1909, followed by his "lamp shade" shape in 1912. Although he claimed to be credited with the freeing of women from their corsets and petticoats with the introduction of the first straight skirt, he continued to work with various forms derivative of the corset for many years. In 1911 he established a craft school named **École Martine** after his daughter, where he employed students to design fabrics and furnishings. **Raoul Dufy** worked with him designing fabrics for **Bianchini-Ferier,** a French textile manufacturer. By 1912 he was the first designer to have toured Europe with his models, presenting his collection to many major European cities, followed by traveling to America and showing his collection in New York. In 1912 he was the first couturier to introduce a perfume. He returned to New York around 1914 to discover that many of his designs had been pirated and were being sold without his permission with false labels in them, a common practice at the time. Back in Paris and along with **Worth, Paquin, Cheruit,** and **Callot Soeurs,** he established a regulatory association to protect the French dressmakers—Le Syndicat de Défense de la Grande Couture Française—becoming its first president. He joined the French army with the outbreak of World War I and closed his business by 1924. He was in financial ruin and his wife divorced him in 1929. **Charles James** had worked for a short period of time under **Poiret's** patronage, designing fabric for the textile manufacturer **Colcombet,** Paris, 1934. In 1934 he was also working again as a freelance ready-to-wear designer; however, financial mismanagement and an irresponsible attitude caused the business to fail. Over the next few years he would work taking small parts in films and writing his autobiography. He moved to the south of France and at the age of 65, after years of poverty, he died of Parkinson's disease in a charity hospital.

POLLACK, HENRY (SEE HALSTON) (DATES UNKNOWN) **Halston** formed **Halston Ltd. Couture** with **Henry Pollack Inc.,** 1962–1973.

POLLOCK, ALICE (1942-) A British retailer and designer who founded her own shop, **Quorum,** on the Kings Road, London, in the early 1960s. She was the first to discover **Ossie Clark,** and the two collaborated on the **Quorum** line which was sold in the boutique, often using fabrics designed by **Clark's** wife **Celia Birtwell.** Their trademarks throughout the 1960s were plunging necklines and wasp waists in crepe, chiffon, satin, and body-hugging jersey fabrics, as well as in printed rayon.

PORTANOVA, PAUL (DATES UNKNOWN) Partnered with **Oleg Cassini** in the ready-to-wear company **Casanova,** a name based on the combination of the last names of the two men.

PORTER, THEA (DOROTHEA NAOMI SEALE) (1927-) Born in Jerusalem to English parents, raised in Damascus, Syria. After studying French and English at London University in 1949–1950, she moved to Beirut and took up painting in 1953–1962. By the mid-1960s she had moved back to London and opened a shop, Greek Street, in Soho which sold antique Turkish and Arabian carpets, silk textiles, as well as antique caftans, 1967–1969. The business evolved over the next few years, and when the demand for her antique caftans exceeded her supply she began designing her own, inspired by the Eastern and Middle-Eastern textiles which she was importing. She began to design her own textiles and chose to work with rich silks, brocades, velvets, crepe de chine, and floaty chiffons, often embellished with metallic embroidery and sequins. She branched out with an in-store boutique at **Henri Bendel,** New York, in 1969 and Paris in 1976–1979. She was famous for her flowing, exotic caftans in luxurious fabrics, as well as her Gypsy dresses of colorful printed fabrics which were favored by her wealthy, international clientele including Elizabeth Taylor, Barbra Streisand, and the Empress of Iran.

POTTER, CLARE (CLARE MEYER) (DATES UNKNOWN) An American from New York. A women's sportswear and ready-to-wear designer who first worked in the 1920s as a research assistant for **Edward**

L. Mayer, Inc., sourcing bead patterns for the company to use in their beaded dress designs of the period. She was promoted to designer for **Edward L. Mayer, Inc.,** where she remained until 1923, at which time she left to take a sabbatical in Mexico. She returned to New York in 1930 to work for **Charles W. Nudelman,** a women's ready-to-wear manufacturer. By 1937 she was a featured designer at **Lord & Taylor** and had won the Women's Sportswear award, followed by a Neiman Marcus award in 1939. She was recognized throughout the 1930s and 1940s for her activewear and playclothes including shorts, skirts, bra tops, and backless sundresses. Much of her inspiration for her designs was culled from her years in Mexico, as well as her subsequent vacations in Mexico and Bermuda. Throughout the 1930s and 1940s her label used the elided lower-case version of her name, **clareporter.** A contemporary of **Claire McCardell, Tina Leser, Tom Brigance,** and **Hattie Carnegie, Potter** was credited with creating the swimsuit with a small bra built into it, as well as the beaded evening sweater in 1940, just shortly before **Mainbocher** debuted his. She was also favored for her perfectly cut ladies' pants. By the 1950s she had moved away from sportswear and focused primarily on dressier designs including evening separates, tailored day dresses, and casual suits. She founded **Nyack,** New York, a wholesale manufacturer in the early 1960s.

PRADA (FRATELLI PRADA) An Italian luxury leather goods manufacturer founded in Milan in 1913 by **Mario Prada.** The company had been producing high quality leather goods until 1978 when the control of the company passed to **Mario Prada's** granddaughter, **Miuccia Bianchi Prada** (1949–). After receiving a degree in political science, **Miuccia Prada** studied mime with an eye toward a career in acting. Instead, she turned her creative focus on her family business and proceeded to expand and infuse the company with a fresh, new, and youthful aesthetic. The first thing she introduced was a simple black nylon backpack with leather shoulder straps, followed by other handheld bags and nylon accessories including small luggage, all stamped with a small plaque with the **Prada** name. Her waterproof nylon bags were so influential in the 1980s that many companies introduced copycat designs, as well as counterfeit copies. **Miuccia Prada** married **Patrizio Bertelli,** a leather entrepreneur, in 1987 and introduced her first women's ready-to-wear collection in 1988 in Italy for fall/winter 1989, followed by the couple's first showing in New York in 1994. **Patrizio Bertelli** has led an expansion of the **Prada** company including the acquisition of a stable of labels including **Helmut Lang, Jil Sander, Church's English Shoes,** and a joint venture between **Prada** and **LVMH** for **Fendi** in 1999. **Miuccia Prada** ready-to-wear designs are minimalistic streamlined sportswear inspired by the northern Italian traditions of beautifully constructed clothes made by local tailors and seamstresses. **Miuccia Prada** introduced her namesake line **Miu Miu** in 1992, a collection inspired by eclectic and bohemian items in her own closet. Today the company is headed by **Miuccia Prada** and her husband/business partner **Patrizio Bertelli,** who oversees all aspects of the company. From their Milanese headquarters, they produce both men's and women's ready-to-wear, accessories, shoes, handbags, luggage, and the complete **Miu Miu** line. In May of 2001 **Prada** announced that they will acquire **Genny SpA,** although **Genny SpA's** other holding, **Byblos,** is not included in the deal.

PRANX (SEE CATHY HARDWICK) A New York ready-to-wear manufacturer. **Cathy Hardwick** designed for them in the early 1960s.

PREMET, HOUSE OF A French couture house in located in Paris. Both **Mme. "Alix" Grés** and **Giuseppe Mattli** apprenticed with the house in the early 1930s.

PUCCI, EMILIO (MARCHESE EMILIO PUCCI DI BARSENTO) (1914-1992) Italian from Naples, Italy, a descendant of Russian nobility, and an Italian aristocrat. He spent two years at the University of Milan, then two more years at the University of Georgia, Athens, Georgia, followed by receiving his masters in social science from Reed College in Portland, Oregon, in 1939. He returned to Italy and served as a bomber pilot in the Italian air force until 1942. While in high school he had been a member of the Italian Olympic ski team, 1933–1934. After World War II he resumed skiing and, while skiing the Italian slopes was discovered—by Toni Frissell, a photographer from *Harper's Bazaar*—wearing a pair of fashionable, form-fitting, stretch-fabric ski pants that he had designed for himself. The magazine requested that **Pucci** create a small collection of women's ski wear for a magazine layout, which subsequently generated a tremendous response, and he was encouraged to create more which were sold in various New

York shops. By 1948 he was designing ski wear for **White Stag** for **Lord & Taylor.** He established his first boutique in Capri, Italy, in 1949, followed by Rome, Elba, and Motecantini from 1950. His New York boutique followed in the early 1950s. He formed **Emilio Pucci Srl.,** Florence, in 1950. He was vice president for design and merchandising for **Formfit International** in 1960, producing collections of lingerie and lounge wear for their line **Formfit Rogers.** Pucci had anticipated the advent of the leisure culture and invented "cruise chic" fashion. Although his designs of the late 1940s and early 1950s—including "Capri" pants, shorts, and classic shirts worn outside the waistbands—were very popular, it was in the 1960s that he found his greatest success with his feminine silk knits with printed optical fantasy and cheerful psychedelic motifs, all of which bore his cursive signature **"Emilio"** in the pattern. His colorful, beautiful, and glamorous silk jersey knit dresses became the cachet of luxury and were worn by celebrities such as Marilyn Monroe, Jacqueline Kennedy, and Elizabeth Taylor. His beautiful whirling motifs have been widely influential and in the 1960s were copied internationally. **Pucci** produced a collection of printed polyester shirts for **Chesa**, an American, ready-to-wear manufacturer, 1960–1970s. The company saw a decline in popularity in the 1980s, although a tremendous revitalization occurred in the early 1990s. **Laudomia Pucci, Emilio's** daughter, had assumed the company's design direction in the early 1990s, and at the close of the decade luxury conglomerate **Louis Vuitton, Moët,** and **Hennessey (LVMH)** had acquired 67 percent of the company, with the remaining 33 percent held by the **Pucci** family. **Catherine Vautrim** was named managing director of **Emilio Pucci Srl.,** Florence, after heading **Louis Vuitton's** ready-to-wear department. Today **Julio Espada** is chief designer for the company, working closely with **Laudomia Pucci.**

PULITZER, LILLY (LILLIAN MCKIM) (DATES UNKNOWN, MOST PROBABLY MID-1930S) American from Roslyn, New York, married **Hubert (Pete) Pulitzer.** The legend of the "Lilly" dress began as a lark in 1959 when **Lilly Pulitzer,** a bored, rich housewife, had her dressmaker construct a dozen shift dresses from printed cotton chintz which she purchased from a local Woolworth department store, and then sold them off a pipe rack at a lemonade stand in Palm Beach, Florida. Within five years the perky, colorful dresses in bold tropical prints were a hit across America, as women of all ages and social stature clamored to buy them. Initially she produced simple a-line shifts, later branching out into other playclothes including ladies' golf pants and skirts, as well as other sportswear separates, all of which bore her cursive signature **"Lilly"** hidden in the pattern. She formed **Lilly Pulitzer, Inc.** in 1961 and was president of the company until 1984. She introduced children's dresses, called **"Minnies,"** in 1962, followed by **Pulitzer Jeans** in 1963, and **Men's Stuff** line in 1969, which included colorful printed sports jackets and golf and leisure pants. The business closed in 1984; however, after almost a ten-year hiatus **Pulitzer** reestablished the business in 1993 with backing from **Sugartown International** and discovered a whole new generation of fans.

QUANT, MARY (1934-) From Blackheath, Kent, England. After attending Goldsmith's College of Art, 1950–1953, she worked briefly for **Erik,** a London milliner in 1955 just prior to opening her first boutique, **Bazaar,** on the Kings Road in London with her future husband, **Alexander Plunket Green,** and **Archie McNair.** In the beginning the boutique offered a variety of fashions from various British designers, but **Quant** became increasingly frustrated by what was available on the market so she began to design her own avant-garde fashions by using revamped **Butterick** patterns and fabric from Harrods department store in London. Her designs were simple and had a strong appeal to the youth market. She is credited with popularizing the miniskirt in the 1960s, and for starting the beatnik Chelsea or Mod look in the mid-1950s, with dark stockings, flat shoes, and polo-neck jerseys. By the 1960s her collections included skinny-rib sweaters, hip-hugger pants, brightly colored dresses, and ensembles paired with colored opaque knit tights. The appeal of her designs was classless and bridged all generation gaps. In order to reach an even broader range of customers in 1963 she established a wholesale manufacturing company with U.S. manufacturer **Steinberg,** which offered the **Ginger** label of women's ready-to-wear. She followed this venture with a cosmetic line in 1966, recognizable by her familiar small daisy motif as a logo. The cosmetic business was later acquired by **Max Factor.** By the 1970s she had sold licenses for numerous products including jewelry, carpets, household items, men's ties, and eyeglasses. In 1983 she created collections for the U.S. markets **J.C. Penney, Puritan Fashions, Alligator Rainwear, Kangol, Dupont**

Europe, and **Staffordshire Potteries,** as well as for those involving home furnishings and even wine. Franchise boutiques in Japan were opened in 1983. Her designs were very influential in the fashion movement in the 1960s and continue to be an inspiration for many contemporary designers today.

QUICKSTEP, LUCIANO PAPINI (SEE GIGLI, ROMERO)

QUORUM (SEE POLLOCK, ALICE AND OSSIE CLARK)

RABANNE, PACO (FRANCISCO RABANEDA Y CUERVO) (1934-) Spaniard from San Sebastian. His mother had been the head seamstress at the house of **Balenciaga** in San Sebastian, Spain; however, the family moved to France in 1939 to escape the Spanish Civil War. **Paco Rabanne** attended École des Beaux-Arts in Paris where he studied architecture, 1952–1955. He began to make bold plastic jewelry and buttons while studying architecture which he sold to the house of **Balenciaga, Dior,** and **Givenchy,** and worked as a freelance designer of handbags, shoes, and plastic accessories. He presented his first haute couture collection of 12 experimental dresses of plastic discs laced together with fine wire in Paris, 1964. He opened his own design house in 1966 and continued to work with incongruous materials creating a series of bizarre, futuristic garments using pliers instead of needles and fine wire instead of thread, becoming famous for his metal and plastic disc minidresses as well as his creations in chain mail and crinkled paper or aluminum. Highly influential for breaking old couture traditions with his Space-Age garments and utilization of new materials throughout the 1960s, he also created costumes for film, theater, and the ballet. He introduced home furnishings in 1983, followed by women's ready-to-wear in 1990 and leather goods in 1991. He opened his first boutique in Paris in 1990. Perhaps most internationally recognized for his men's fragrance line in the 1970s and 1980s, he has also introduced over 140 licenses.

RAMBOVA, NATACHA (NATACHA VALENTINO) (DATES UNKNOWN) The ex-wife of **Rudolph Valentino,** she worked designing costumes at the Astoria Studios with **Norman Norell** in the early 1920s before debuting her custom and ready-to-wear collections. She had a boutique in the early 1930s near Fifth Avenue and Madison Avenue, New York, that specialized in theatrically inspired tea gowns and wraps of antique Persian brocades. **Mildred Orrick** designed for her in the late 1930s and early 1940s.

RAPHAEL (DATES UNKNOWN) A Canadian jewelry and accessories designer who saw the height of his popularity in the early 1970s and 1980s in Canada. He is most remembered for his designs of poured glass sculpture jewelry from metals such as brass and copper.

RAPHÄEL A French fashion house based in Paris. **André Laug** freelanced for the house in the late 1950s and early 1960s.

RATIA, ARMI (SEE MARIMEKKO) (1912-1979) Co-founded **Marimekko,** a Finnish textile and clothing manufacturer in Helsinki in 1951 with **Vilio Ratia.** They are recognized for their brightly colored, oversized floral and abstract cotton and jersey printed fabrics and simple shift dresses as well as for home furnishing designs.

RAYNE, SIR EDWARD (1922-1992) British from London, England. A shoe manufacturing company founded by **Rayne's** grandparents in London in 1889. **Rayne** joined the company in 1940 at the age of 28 and assumed complete control of the company in 1951. Awarded the Royal Warrant for Queen Elizabeth and the Queen Mother, **Rayne** designed Princess Elizabeth's trousseau in 1947. He designed collections for both **Hardy Amies** and **Norman Hartnell,** while **Mary Quant** and **Jean Muir** created a youth collection for the company.

REDFERN, JOHN (1853-1929) British from England. He began as a young apprentice tailor on the Isle of Wight. By the late 1870s he had established a women's dress business creating silk and mourning dresses, moving into women's sportswear which focused primarily on the popular yachting industry. In 1881 he opened businesses in both London and Paris, followed by branches in Edinburgh and New York. By 1888 he had been appointed dressmaker to Queen Victoria of England and was producing yachting and traveling suits, as well as riding habits. His son **Ernest Redfern** would later head the London and New

York branches, and **Charles Poynter** became head of the Paris salon. **Robert Piguet** trained as an apprentice in 1918. The company is noted for having created the first women's Red Cross uniform in 1916. The business closed in the early 1920s.

REIG, BEN (DATES UNKNOWN) An American women's ready-to-wear manufacturer founded in 1929 by **Ben Reig.** The company hosted numerous freelance designers and specialized in women's higher priced ready-to-wear suits, coats, and dresses. **Omar Kiam** was appointed head designer, 1941–1950, continuing to design elegant, expensive women's ready-to-wear suits, coats, and day dresses, as well as short evening dresses and fur-trimmed suits. His suits sold for as much as $300 in the 1940s. In 1948 **Kiam** produced a line of costume jewelry for **Ben Reig. Liz Claiborne** worked as a design assistant to **Omar Kiam** at **Ben Reig** in the late 1940s. By the early 1950s the collections **Kiam** created for **Ben Reig** included day dresses, full-skirted and fitted suit dresses, as well as cocktail and short evening dresses. **Omar Kiam** retired from the company just shortly before his death in 1954, and was succeeded as head designer by **Eva Rosencrans** when she left **Nettie Rosenstein. Rosencrans** continued in the design tradition established by **Kiam** for **Ben Reig,** creating beautiful day and evening dresses, coat ensembles, and evening pantsuits. Her designs, like her predecessor's, were also considered expensive at the time, ranging as high as $1,000 for a fur-lined suit.

REN-ETA (SEE ETA. MME. ETA VALEZ HENTZ AND MAURICE RENTNER)

RENTNER, MAURICE (1889-1958) He was born in Warsaw, Poland, and immigrated to the United States at the age of 13. In his boyhood he began working briefly for his father's button making company, then worked as an errand boy, advancing to traveling salesman for childrenswear and a shirtwaist company by 1906. He teamed with his brother in purchasing a glove manufacturing company, forming **M. & H. Rentner,** where they manufactured women's ready-to-wear, 1912–1923. The company purchased Paris models by designers such as **Molyneux** and sold copies of these designs as ready-to-wear. He partnered with **Mme. Eta** in the mid-1920s, and the company became known as **Ren-Eta. Mme. Eta** left to build a new company in the 1930s with partner, **Ann Sadowsky. Anne Klein** designed for **Maurice Rentner,** 1940–1947. He died in 1958. In 1962 **Maurice Rentner, Inc.** merged with **Anna Miller & Co.,** which was owned by his sister and **Bill Blass,** who had been the house designer, was appointed vice president. **Blass** then bought the **Rentner Company** in 1970 renaming it **Bill Blass** where he continues to design today. The company is recognized for their uncomplicated yet innovative classic women's ready-to-wear designs including suits, day dresses, and eveningwear.

RESTIVO, MARY ANN (1940-) American from South Orange, New Jersey. As a young girl she dreamed of being a designer, creating clothing for her dolls and accompanying her father, who ran a local boutique, into New York on buying trips. She studied retailing at the College of St. Elizabeth, Morristown, New Jersey, 1958–1960, before studying design at the Fashion Institute of Technology, New York, 1960–1961. She apprenticed at **Abby Michael,** junior sportswear house, New York, 1961, before designing for **Bernard Levine, Petti for Jack Winter, Something Special, Sports Sophisticates,** and forming her own label **Mary Ann Restivo for Genre,** from 1962–1974. She designed for **Crisco Casuals** and was appointed head designer for the women's blouse division of **Christian Dior-New York,** 1974–1980. She launched her own women's ready-to-wear firm, **Mary Ann Restivo, Inc.,** in 1980, specializing in fashionable, sensible career clothes with an emphasis on a good fit using wool jersey, cashmere, and other fine fabrics which target women in middle- and upper-management positions. Her designs were favored by career women because of the ease with which the designs seamlessly move from office to evening. Her company was acquired by the **Leslie Fay Corporation,** 1988–1992. Although the company dropped the **Mary Ann Restivo** line, she continued to have a loyal following of customers and continued to work as an independent design consultant.

REVILLE AND ROSSITER A British couture house founded in 1906 by designer **William Reville** and **Miss Rossiter,** who handled the business operations. Both **Reville** and **Rossiter** had previously worked for a London department store, **Jay's,** before forming their company. Patronized for their formal gowns by members of the British royal family, as well as British aristocracy, the company was appointed court dressmaker to Queen Mary in 1910. The company merged with the London branch of the house of **Worth** in 1936.

REVILLON (REVILLON FRÈRES TRADING CO. LTD.) A fur and leather manufacturer founded in Paris, France, in the late 1700s by **Count Louis-Victor d'Argental,** who changed his name to **Revillon** during the French Revolution, which saved his life. His sons **Théodore** (–1920), **Albert** (–1887), **Anatole** (–1916), and **Léon** (–1915) took over the control of the company after their father's death and renamed the company **Revillon Frères.** The company has been operating in Canada and the United States since 1875. **Fernando Sanchez** created collections as a freelance designer for **Revillon,** Paris and New York, 1961–1973, then re-joined the company to produce a collection for the United States, 1984–1985. Today, **Revillon Inc.** is based in Paris, France, and is part of the **Cora-Revillon** group of companies, one of the largest privately held conglomerates in France with sales of $10 billion and over 30,000 employees in various fields such as luxury products, furs, perfumes, cosmetics, and accessories. Owner and chairman **Philippe Bouriez,** along with vice president **Claude Potier,** reported that their sales for the year 2000 reached approximately $25 million, ranking them the second largest fur manufacturer in the United States after **Evans, Inc. Revillon** fur salons have been in **Saks Fifth Avenue** for over 32 years and more recently at **Bloomingdale's** fur salons under the label **Maximillian. Revillon Inc.** recently dissolved its relationship with **Saks** and is scheduled to open free-standing fur boutiques in various cities throughout the United States, with stores presently in New York and Chicago. **Revillon Inc.** is recognized as one of the world's leading fur manufacturers and has hosted numerous freelance designers over the years, including **Carolina Herrera's** collection for **Revillon** in 1984.

RHODES, ZANDRA (1940-) British from Chatham, Kent, England. Her mother had been the head fitter at the house of **Worth,** Paris, and later taught fashion at Medway College of Art, Kent, England. **Rhodes** had originally intended on becoming a textile designer and studied lithography at Midway College of Art, 1959–1961, followed by studying fashion at the Royal College of Art, London, graduating in 1964. She established a dressmaking firm with **Sylvia Ayton,** London, 1964, and a textile design studio with **Alex McIntyre,** 1965. She became a partner and designer in the **Fulham Clothes Shop,** 1967–1968, then worked as a freelance designer, 1967–1975. She founded **Zandra Rhodes UK Ltd.,** and **Zandra Rhodes Shops Ltd.** by 1975, followed by women's ready-to-wear in Australia in 1979 and in Britain in 1984. She is recognized worldwide for her beautiful, romantic, and extravagantly feminine, fantasy designs of soft, floating chiffons, silks, and tulles, all handscreened with her signature prints including art deco motifs, stars, geometric squiggles, lipstick, and teddy bears motifs. Today her womenswear designs can be found in fine department stores and specialty boutiques around the world, as can her other designs in sportswear, sleepwear, textiles, sheets, and rugs.

RICCI, NINA (MARIA NIELLI) (1883-1970) Italian from Turin, Italy, moved to Florence with her family at age five, then to Paris when she was 12. She lost her father prematurely, and by age 13 she apprenticed as a dressmaker in Paris. By age 18 she was the head of an atelier, and by 22 she was chief designer. She married jeweler **Louis Ricci,** and in 1905 at the age of 22 had a son, **Robert Ricci** (1905–1988). With her husband's encouragement she founded her own design house at the age of 49 with her son **Robert,** then 27, in 1932. The house of **Nina Ricci** started as a one-room operation at 20 Rue des Capucines, which by 1939 had expanded to occupy 11 floors in three buildings on the same street. **Robert Ricci** assumed management of the company by 1945 and introduced the company's first fragrance **Coeur-Joie** in 1946, followed by **L'Air du Temps** in 1948. The house of **Nina Ricci** was considered a contemporary of **Christian Dior, Pierre Balmain, Jean Dessès, Jacques Fath,** and **Balenciaga** throughout the 1950s. **Fernando Sanchez** interned with **Nina Ricci** in the mid-1950s, and **Jules-François Crahay** became **Mme. Ricci's** collaborator on collections in 1951 and assumed the position of head designer in 1954, taking over complete design responsibilities by 1959. **Nina Ricci** retired in the early 1950s, leaving the business to her son **Robert. André Laug** freelanced for the house in the late 1950s and early 1960s. **Jules-François Crahay** was succeeded by **Gérard Pipart** as head designer in 1963. In 1993 **Christina Astuguevielle** became artistic director of the accessories department, launching new lines of accessories, handbags, and scarves. Today the house of **Nina Ricci** is under the design direction of **Natalie Gervais.** The company is recognized for its understated elegance and intoxicatingly feminine, yet classic designs which continue to appeal to wealthy society women worldwide.

RICHMOND, JOHN (1960-) British from Manchester, England. He began his career as a freelance designer working for **Lano Lano, Ursula Hudson, Fiorucci, Joseph Tricot,** and **Pin Up for Deni Cler,** 1982–1984, followed by becoming a partner and designer with **Maria Cornejo, Richmond-Cornejo,** London, 1984–1987. He introduced **John Richmond Man** and **John Richmond Woman** in 1987, and his lower priced **Destroy** collection in 1990, then his **Destroy Denim** collection in 1991. He opened his first boutique in London in 1992. Known initially for his biker chic and rebellious rock music themes in his collection, incorporating fetish motifs, bondage chains, zippers, and leather inserts with their roots in punk fashion, **Richmond's** designs, although brazen, are still strikingly well designed, sexy, and feminine. Favored by pop stars and celebrities who wish to make a definitive statement, his **Destroy** line was often emblazoned with his mottoes—Destroy, Disorientate, and Disorder. His later collections evolved and matured into more mainstream influences and offered unique cut and elegant refinements.

ROBERT (DATES UNKNOWN) An American in-house milliner at Saks Fifth Avenue in the early 1930s who thrilled the customers by designing custom hats for them directly on their heads.

ROBINSON, PATRICK (DATES UNKNOWN) American ready-to-wear designer who replaced **Richard Tyler** in 1994 as head designer at **Anne Klein.** He had formerly been with **Giorgio Armani-Le Collezione.**

ROCHAS, MARCEL (1902-1955) From Paris, France. He had originally intended on pursuing a career in law, but claims he opened his couture house so that he could provide his beautiful young wife with lovely clothes. He opened his couture house in 1924 at the age of 22, in Rue Faubourg St-Honoré, Paris, moving to Avenue Matignon in 1931. By the early 1930s he was already a tremendous success, and in 1942, a predecessor by five years to the post-war look and **Dior's** "New Look," **Rochas** created a new waist-cinching corset called the "*guêpière*" (French for wasp). He had also laid claim to having invented the word "slacks" in the early 1930s, no longer a fashion merely for recreation or informal lounging, but part of a lady's day or evening wardrobe. He was fond of accenting his designs with found objects from local Paris flea markets and antique stores. In 1937 he opened a New York salon offering ready-to-wear as well as made-to-order Paris designs. He was noted for his grand use of dramatic appliqués, often using large calla lilies at a neckline, taxidermist's blue birds on shoulders, and realistic seagulls on a bodice. His designs had a strong graphic sense and frequently used stripes to form geometric patterns. **Herbert Kasper** worked for the house of **Rochas,** Paris, in the late 1950s. He introduced his first fragrance **Femme** in 1944, dedicating it to his third wife **Hélène** as a wedding present. Possessing a keen business acumen he often predicted changes in popular demand and offered calculated silhouettes to meet the public shift. In 1951 he published *Twenty-five Years of Parisian Elegance, 1925–50.* As well as being highly recognized for his couture designs he was also a respected costume designer having created designs for numerous films. He closed his business in 1953 and died the following year, survived by his wife **Hélène** who inherited the **Rochas** perfume empire. The company introduced the fragrance **Madame Rochas** in 1960, and **Mystère** in 1978. The company announced in 1990 that designer **Peter O'Brien** would head up the house and introduce a new ready-to-wear collection which would be the first venture back into the apparel business since the death of **Rochas** in 1955.

RODGERS, SHANNON (SHANNON ROGERS FOR JERRY SILVERMAN) (DATES UNKNOWN) An American women's ready-to-wear designer. After receiving his degree in architecture from Western Reserve, Ohio, he was a costume designer in Hollywood before serving in the navy in World War II. After the war he went to work for **Martini,** a ready-to-wear manufacturer in New York. It was while working at **Martini** that he met **Jerry Silverman,** a lawyer and graduate of Harvard Law School, who was the business manager of **Martini.** In 1959–1970 the two founded their women's ready-to-wear manufacturing firm with **Silverman** handling the business affairs and **Rogers** as the head designer under the label **Shannon Rogers for Jerry Silverman.** The company specialized in copies of Paris dress designs, which **Rogers** would source on his trips to view the Paris collections, selecting simple details which he would reinterpret in their designs. Although the company closed in 1970, the two founded the School of Design and

Merchandising of Kent State University and the costume collection at the Kent State Museum. **Silverman** died later that year, and **Rogers** continued as the museum's curator.

RODRIGUEZ, NARCISO (1961-) American of Cuban descent, raised in Kearny, New Jersey. A women's ready-to-wear designer who originally dreamed of becoming an architect; throughout the early 1990s he worked for numerous design houses including **Anne Klein, Calvin Klein,** and **TSE** before being appointed head designer of women's ready-to-wear for **Loewe** and **Cerruti,** as well as launching his private collection in 1997. His 1998 collection was a combination of sensual separates in somber hues of moss green, burgundies, and grays, and was accessorized with cashmere-covered Birkenstock shoes, the ultimate in casual luxury. His third collection offered very feminine layered separates in colors derived from water—deep blue, turquoise, green, white, and silver—with materials such as Lycra and polyester fused with traditional linen. Famous for the bias-cut wedding dress which he created for friend Carolyn Bessette for her marriage to John F. Kennedy Jr. in 1996.

RODRIGUEZ, PEDRO (DATES UNKNOWN) Spanish women's custom and ready-to-wear designer who was active in the 1950s–1960s. A contemporary and friend of **Balenciaga, Rodriguez** is famous for his beautiful, elaborately beaded eveningwear as well as his architecturally inspired tailored suits and brilliantly sculptured coats.

ROEHM, CAROLYNE (JANE CAROLYNE SMITH) (1951-) American from Kirksville, Missouri. After studying fashion design at Washington University, she went to work designing polyester sportswear for **Mrs. Sportswear by Kellwood Co.** for **Sears, Roebuck & Co.** in 1973 before becoming an assistant and fit-model for **Oscar de la Renta,** 1974–1984. She married **Alex Roehm** in 1978 and divorced in 1981. She apprenticed under **de la Renta** for many years, learning the techniques of classic couture, and went on to design the **Miss "O"** line for **de la Renta** before launching her own deluxe ready-to-wear collection in 1985. With backing from her second husband, financier **Henry Kravis,** she formed **Carolyne Roehm, Inc.** A member of the privileged class without the need to work, she focused her designs on her own social demographics, designing for women with demanding social calendars who required beautiful, glamorous eveningwear. Her collections also included sporty separates, dresses, coats, hats, and shoes, always with a directive of the highest quality and fit. **Roehm** was her own fit-model and appeared in all her advertising campaigns. After her divorce from **Henry Kravis,** for personal reasons **Roehm** closed her ready-to-wear and couture business in 1991, but returned to designing with an upscale catalog business, as well as producing holiday and boutique catalogs for **Saks Fifth Avenue,** 1993.

ROSE, HELEN (1904-1985) American costume and ready-to-wear designer. She started her career by designing for nightclubs at age 15 and went on to design for the **Ice Follies.** She began to work for 20th Century-Fox in the early 1940s before she moved to Metro-Goldwyn-Mayer where she remained for almost three decades. Much like her contemporary **"Irene," Rose** crossed over from costume design to introduce a ready-to-wear collection in the late 1950s. She retired from costume design in the early 1960s after being nominated for ten Academy Awards and winning twice. She designed Grace Kelly's wedding dress in 1956. Rose is celebrated for the wrap-front cocktail dress she designed for Elizabeth Taylor in *Cat on a Hot Tin Roof* in 1958. She made a ready-to-wear version of the dress to satiate the demands of her clients and it sold extremely well. **Chris Ghiatis** had been a freelance designer collaborating on various collections between 1960–1962 when **Rose** finally retired and closed her business.

ROSEIR, MICHÈLE (1929-) From Paris, France, however spent her childhood in the United States with her mother, publisher Hélène Gordon-Lazareff. **Roseir** followed in her mother's footsteps and began her career in journalism writing for *New Woman* and *France-Soir* before moving into design. Noted as a pioneering women's sportswear and ready-to-wear designer who began designing in the early 1960s. **Christiane Baily** had worked with her in 1961 prior to forming her own company the following year with **Emmanuelle Khanh. Roseir,** along with partner **Jean-Pierre Bamberger,** founded **V de V (Vêtements de Vacances)** in 1962, specializing in innovative and youthful sportswear including a complete line of ski wear. **Agnès Troublé** worked as a freelance designer for the company in the late 1960s. Famous for her foil quilted all-in-one ski suits in the mid-1960s.

ROSENCRANS, EVA (SEE NETTIE ROSENSTEIN) (DATES UNKNOWN) **Eva Rosencrans** had partnered with her sister-in-law **Nettie Rosenstein** (Nettie Rosencrans) and **Charles Gumprecht** in a women's ready-to-wear wholesale manufacturing business in 1931. **Charles Kleibacker** designed under **Eva Rosencrans** for **Nettie Rosenstein** in 1958. The business flourished until **Nettie Rosenstein** decided to close the business and begin designing luxury handbags in 1961, at which time **Eva Rosenstein** went to design for **Ben Reig.**

ROSENSTEIN, NETTIE (NETTIE ROSENCRANS) (LATE 1800S?-) Austrian, immigrated to Harlem, New York, with her parents in 1890. She began designing clothing when she was just eleven creating garments for her friends and family and establishing a small dressmaking business in her family's home in Harlem. She established her own company in 1917 and by 1921 she had created a flourishing business with more than 50 employees. She closed her women's ready-to-wear manufacturing design business in the mid-1920s to pursue a wholesale business with a contract to I. Magnin, an American West Coast department store chain in California. She discontinued her wholesale business to design for **Corbeau et Cie** in 1929. In 1931 she partnered in another wholesale venture with her sister-in-law, **Eva Rosencrans,** and **Charles Gumprecht.** Her couture-caliber designs which were made by one seamstress from start to finish were sold around the country in America in various upscale department stores; however, only one department store in each city was authorized to sell her designs with her label, the others would use their own store label without the added cachet of the **Nettie Rosenstein** name. She had exclusive fabrics designed for her in Europe by **Brooke Cadwallader,** a prominent textile designer. She also designed a line of costume jewelry to complement her garments. **Charles Kleibacker** designed under **Eva Rosencrans** for **Nettie Rosenstein** in 1958 before launching his own company. She discontinued her ready-to-wear business in 1961 to pursue her interest in designing luxurious handbags. **Eva Rosencrans** also left the business and designed for **Ben Reig.** Today **Nettie Rosenstein** is remembered for her early womenswear designs and for her beautiful handbags from the 1960s.

ROTH, CHRISTIAN FRANCIS (1969-) American from New York City, New York. Considered a fashion prodigy, by age 11 he had his sights on becoming a designer, and by 16 was studying at the Fashion Institute of Technology at night and apprenticing with designer **Koos Van Den Akker** by day. He would later become a full-time employee with **Van Den Akker** while attending Parsons, New York, in the evenings. He produced his first small collection out of **Van Den Akker's** studio in 1988, followed by his first full showing in 1990 at the age of 21 with the assistance of **Van Den Akker.** A consummate technician, his designs cull their inspiration from a multitude of mediums including pop art concepts, cartoon motifs, Matisse's découpages, sunny-side-up eggs, and whimsical ideas such as pencil shavings and M&M candy.

ROUFF, MAGGY (MAGGY BESANÇON DE WAGNER) (1896-1971) From Paris, France, of Viennese parentage. In the late 1920s she joined the Paris branch of the couture house **Drécoll,** which was founded by **Christoff von Drécoll** in Vienna in 1902 and specialized in dressing the ladies of the Viennese court. **Drécoll's** Paris branch in the 1920s was headed by **Maggy Besançon de Wagner's** parents, **Monsieur** and **Madame Besançon de Wagner. Maggy Besançon de Wagner** began working with her mother designing sportswear at **Drécoll** until 1928 when she was appointed director of the company. In 1929 the house of **Drécoll** merged with the house of **Beer,** moving to a new location, and **Maggy Besançon de Wagner,** with her husband **Pierre B. de Wagner,** took over the original premises of **Drécoll** at 136 Avenue des Champs-Elysées, founding the house of **Maggy Rouff. Rouff** became the head designer of the new house with her husband acting as the financial director. In the 1930s her designs were available in the United States in **Macy's** "**Little Shop,**" and exact copies of her designs were offered at **Bonwit Teller,** New York. The house of **Maggy Rouff** moved to Avenue Matigon in the late 1940s. **Maggy Rouff** retired from the company in 1948, succeeded by her daughter who remained with the company throughout the 1960s. **Fernando Sanchez** was a design assistant at the house of **Maggy Rouff,** 1953–1956. The company had made one final move in 1965 to Avenue Marceau before closing in 1971, just shortly before **Maggy Rouff's** death. She is recognized for her finely tailored women's ready-to-wear, as well as her beautiful couture designs which were often embellished with witty touches including bird and cupid motifs. She often embroidered monograms on her scarves and jacket pockets throughout the 1920s–1950s. She is also noted for publishing *America Seen Through a Microscope* and *The Philosophy of Elegance.*

ROWLEY, CYNTHIA (1958-) American from Barrington, Illinois. After studying art at Arizona State University, she attended the Art Institute of Chicago, graduating in 1981. While still attending the Art Institute she sold an 18-piece collection to **Marshall Fields.** She moved to New York in 1983 and incorporated the business **Cynthia Rowley** in 1988 offering witty, playful women's ready-to-wear, specializing in dresses which often cull their inspiration from the 1950s and 1960s. Aside from her highly successful ready-to-wear business she has also designed costumes for dance troupes and for film. More recently she has launched free-standing boutiques as well as a line of footwear.

RUBENSTEIN, CHIP (DATES UNKNOWN) American ready-to-wear manufacturer. He was the second husband to **Anne Klein.** He co-founded the **Anne Klein and Company** with **Anne Klein** and **Sanford Smith** in 1968.

RUBENSTEIN, ROZ (SEE STEPHEN BURROWS)

RUFFIN, CLOVIS (DATES UNKNOWN) American women's ready-to-wear designer who freelanced for numerous boutiques in the late 1960s and early 1970s before launching his own ready-to-wear company **Ruffinwear** in 1972. The Coty Award–winning designer specialized in simple inexpensive day dresses, most notably a T-shirt dress which was in matte jersey, slightly flared, scoop-necked, with capped sleeves. The dress was manufactured in the thousands and proved to be a widely influential design in the early 1970s.

RYKIEL, SONIA (1930-) From Paris, France. She began designing her own maternity clothes in the mid-1950s, continuing to design for herself and her friends. She freelanced for her husband, **Sam Rykiel's** boutique **Laura,** Paris, in the late 1950s–1962, before opening her first boutique in the Paris department store **Galeries Lafayette,** and then a free-standing boutique on the Left Bank, Paris, in 1968. Her designs were available in the United States by the mid-1960s at **Henri Bendel** and **Bloomingdale's,** New York. She followed up the success of her boutique in Paris and her women's ready-to-wear line with a household-linens boutique, Paris, in 1975, and a children's boutique in 1987, as well as a cosmetic line in Japan, 1987. Menswear and a menswear boutique were introduced in 1989, followed by a new flagship boutique in Paris in 1990, footwear in 1992, and **Sonia Rykiel** fragrance in 1993. Famous for her formfitting, sensual knitwear, she was referred to as "The Queen of Knitwear" by the mid-1960s. She introduced her casual lines of soft cotton velours in the early 1980s and has continued to offer her dedicated followers two collections of this highly successful leisure line every year.

SACHS, GLORIA (1927-) An American women's ready-to-wear designer noted for her luxurious, finely tailored separates, dresses, suits, coats, and leathers, as well as her sportswear, knitwear, and sweater designs in the late 1970s and early 1990s.

SAINT LAURENT, YVES (YVES HENRI DONAT MATHIEU SAINT LAURENT) (1936-) From Oran, Algeria, of Alsatian descent. **Saint Laurent** left Oran to study art in Paris in 1953 at age 17. He worked as an independent clothing stylist while studying at l'École de la Chambre Syndicale de la Couture, Paris, in 1953–1954, and won first prize for his sketches in a fashion contest sponsored by the International Wool Secretariat. Two years later at age 19 he was introduced to **Christian Dior,** who hired him immediately as his design assistant in 1954–1957. When **Christian Dior** died unexpectedly in 1957, **Saint Laurent** was appointed head designer at the house of **Christian Dior.** At age 24 in 1960, **Saint Laurent** was called upon to do his mandatory military service for the Algerian army, however he was discharged three months later due to an illness. When he returned to the house of **Dior** to resume his position, which was to be held for him, he discovered that he had been replaced by **Marc Bohan,** who had been head designer for **Dior** in London, 1958–1960. **Saint Laurent** teamed with business partner **Pierre Bergé** and founded **Yves Saint Laurent,** Paris, in 1962. **Bergé,** who is considered the business genius behind the company, has been partnered with **Saint Laurent** for over 43 years now. In 1966 the two introduced the ready-to-wear line **Yves Saint Laurent Rive Gauche,** and set up the company's own free-standing franchise boutique chain to sell the collections. Menswear was introduced in 1974. **De La Falaise** had been a design assistant to **Saint Laurent** in the early 1970s, and **Jacques Tiffeau** supervised collections from 1971–1976, while **Bergé** concentrated on building the business by adding more perfumes and licensing to the company. **Saint Laurent** as the designer is brilliant at visualizing things early with a heightened awareness, interpreting the mood of the world, not just the street, and turning his vision into designs that people want. Drawing influences from history, art, and literature, he is famous for his 1958 trapeze line for **Christian Dior,** then under his own company; the "Mondrian" dress; "the smoking" (le smoking) suit, based on a man's tuxedo with satin lapel; the safari look; military styles; the costumes he designed for actress Catherine Denuve in *Belle de Jour;* the 1976 collection inspired by the Ballets Russes; and the ready-to-wear collections based on *Carmen,* 1976, which included 300 numbers and ran for over three hours. In the early 1990s **Saint Laurent** reprised many of his greatest designs. The company had been purchased by **Elf-Sanofi SA** in 1993; however, in January 2000 the company was sold again. Following the acquisition of **Yves Saint Laurent** ready-to-wear and **Sanofi Beauté** by the **Gucci Group, Tom Ford** assumed the position as creative director of **Yves Saint Laurent** and **Yves Saint Laurent perfumes.** In addition to his existing duties at **Gucci, Ford** works with all creative teams at **Yves Saint Laurent** to define the overall image and positioning of the **Yves Saint Laurent** brand, including all product categories and communication activities. **Saint Laurent** and **Bergé** retained the haute couture division that is owned by **Pinault-Printemps-Redoute,** which runs it at an estimated $11 million loss annually, as well as the retail boutique on the Rue du Faubourg St.-Honoré. **Loulou Klossowski, Saint Laurent's** longtime muse and design assistant, launched a project in the fall of 2000 introducing a few signature white blouses available exclusively at the boutique on Faubourg St.-Honoré, and followed the success of the blouses in the spring of 2001 by reintroducing a limited collection of a few of **Saint Laurent's** greatest hits including a shantung blazer, a silk raincoat, his first women's tuxedo or "le smoking," and his ultrasexy lace-up safari dress from the 1960s. Prices are steep—about $6,300 for a smoking suit and $2,500 for a safari dress. They are all numbered pieces and if one is not available in a customer's size it can be made ready for them in approximately one week. The offering of these vintage collections at the boutique is a noted political thorn in the side of the **Gucci Group. Bergé** also had the foresight to structure the deal with the **Gucci Group** in such a way as to require that they set up **The Centre de Documentation Yves Saint Laurent,** a $5 million archive facility which **Bergé** opened in 2000, and requires the **Gucci Group** to support in perpetuity. Today the look of the house of **Saint Laurent** under the design direction of **Tom Ford** is not lost in the past, not looking back, but focused clearly on the moment, functioning with its accustomed status, clean, cool, and sexy.

SANCHEZ, FERNANDO (1934–) Born in Spain of a Spanish father and Flemish mother, he moved to Paris and studied fashion at the École de la Chambre Syndicale de la Couture Parisienne, 1951–1953. He interned with **Nina Ricci** and had worked as a design assistant to **Maggy Rouff,** Paris, 1953–1956, as well as worked as a designer for **Hirsh of Brussels,** 1956–1958, before joining the house of **Christian Dior** to design lingerie and knitwear for **Dior** boutique licensees, Paris, Germany, Denmark, and the United States, 1960s. He became a freelance designer for **Revillon** furs, New York and Paris, for 12 years, 1961–1973, and worked as a design assistant at **Yves Saint Laurent** before starting his own lingerie company in 1973. He introduced his ready-to-wear collection in 1980, followed by menswear in 1983. He returned to **Revillon** in 1984–1985 to produce a collection for the markets in the United States. He is recognized primarily for his lingerie, as well as his forays into the high fashion ready-to-wear market. His trademark in his lingerie designs in the 1980s was a fan motif, as well as his extensive use of lace appliqués.

SANDER, JIL (HEIDEMARIE JILINE SANDER) (1943–) German from Wesselburen, Germany, raised in Hamburg. After graduating in textile design from Krefeld School of Textiles, Düsseldorf, 1963, she was a foreign exchange student at the University of Los Angeles, California, 1963–1964; she became a fashion journalist for *McCall's,* Los Angeles, and for *Constanze* and *Petra* magazines, Hamburg, 1964–1968. She then began working as a freelance women's ready-to-wear designer, 1968–1973, and opened her first boutique in Hamburg, 1968. She showed her first collection in Milan in 1973, followed by founding **Jil Sander GmbH,** 1978. In keeping with a strong linear progression, she launched her first fragrance and cosmetic line in 1979, furs, 1982, and leather and eyewear collections, 1984. By 1989 she had offered her first public stock in the company in 1989, converting the company to **Jil Sander AG,** a public corporation. The new company opened its first Paris boutique in 1993 and showed its first menswear collection in the same year. **Sander** is considered to be one of the most important women's luxury ready-to-wear designers working today, famous for her refined, tailored, minimalist designs, with a neutral color palette in luxurious wool, cashmere, suede, and leather. Much of her inspiration for her collections combines her simplified interpretation of male tailoring with an intelligent appreciation for soft feminine sensibilities. **Jil Sander** sold her label to the **Prada** company in 1999 and then resigned. **Milan Vukmirovic** presently oversees the label.

SARMI, FERDINANDO (COUNT SARMI) (DATES UNKNOWN) Italian from Ravenna, Italy. He had originally intended on becoming a lawyer, but began working in Italy for **Fabiani** in the early 1950s before being discovered by *Harper's Bazaar* editor Carmel Snow while showing his designs at the Pitti Palace in 1951. Snow referred him to **Elizabeth Arden,** who had been looking for a new couture designer at the time, and he was hired immediately. Considered to be one of the great new American designers with **Scaasi, Estevez,** and **Galanos** in the 1950s, **Sarmi** worked for **Arden** for eight years from 1951–1959 and was succeeded by **Oscar de la Renta** when he left to establish his own design house, 1959. Pat Nixon wore a **Sarmi for Elizabeth Arden** gown to the 1957 inaugural ball for her husband Richard Nixon. By 1960 he had already won the coveted Coty Award and was highly recognized for his expensive grand eveningwear in opulent materials such as silk chiffon, brilliant brocades, damask, and lace, which were often embellished with large flowers or mink and ermine trim.

SARNE, TANYA, TANYA GORDON (1948-) (SEE GHOST) British designer and founder of British ready-to-wear manufacturer **Ghost** in 1984. Prior to founding **Ghost** she had been the sales manager for **Entrepais,** an ethnic women's ready-to-wear company, 1976–1978, followed by chairman and designer for **Miz,** 1979–1984.

SAVINI, GAETANO (1910-1987) (SEE BRIONI) Italian from Rome, Italy.

SCAASI, ARNOLD (ARNOLD ISAACS) (1931-) Canadian from Montreal, Canada. The son of a furrier, after high school he moved to Melbourne, Australia, to live with a wealthy aunt who dressed with **Chanel** and **Schiaparelli,** and proved to be a profound influence on him. He returned to Montreal to study couture fashion, at École Contnoir Capponi, Montreal, and then to Paris to continue his studies at École de la Chambre Syndicale de la Couture Parisienne in the late 1940s. He became an apprentice to **Paquin** for one year prior to moving to New York and working for **Charles James** for just over two years from 1951 to 1953. He then worked as a freelance designer for **Dressmaker Casuals** and **Lilly Daché,** 1955–1957, before opening his own wholesale business on a shoestring. He named his company **Scaasi,** which is the reverse version of his surname. From the beginning he focused on beautiful women's evening and cocktail attire, specializing in the use of luxurious fabrics such as floral brocades, sari, and silk fabric adorned with oversized sequins or all-over crushed cellophane, as well as exotic skins such as crocodile which he made into evening pants. His signature was cut and shape as opposed to the embellishments of trim or appliqués, although he was very fond of bugle beads. His silhouettes were often fitted torsos, trumpeted or pouf skirts, and often he would combine both the trumpet skirt and the pouf together, which he referred to as "Brioches," rendering a look very reminiscent of his early experience with **Charles James.** His necklines were usually stand-away, off-the-shoulder portrait collars. Throughout the late 1950s and early 1960s he created couture, ready-to-wear, knitwear, costume jewelry, childrenswear, and, in 1969, pocketbooks. He was the first designer to present an above-the-knee cocktail dress in 1958, prior to its popularity generated by the youths in the 1960s. He also popularized the costume suit dress with beautiful evening coats designed to go over his evening dresses that were lined with fabric matching the dress. He introduced ready-to-wear in 1962–1963 and then again in 1984. He took an abrupt sabbatical in 1963, returning to concentrate on his custom designs. The company saw a diminished popularity for its flamboyant designs throughout the 1970s, but found a renewed interest with the demands for opulent dressing and flourished once again in the 1980s. A noted favorite of Nancy Reagan, his ready-to-wear collections ranged upwards of $1,000, whereas his couture designs sold for around $5,000.

SCHERRER, JEAN-LOUIS (1936-) From Paris, France. He began his career as a dancer after studying ballet at Conservatoire de Danse Classique, Paris, then moved into fashion after a fall ended his dancing career in 1956. He worked as a freelance sketch artist, then apprentice for **Christian Dior** at the house of **Dior,** 1955–1957, then with **Yves Saint Laurent** while **Saint Laurent** was at the house of **Dior** in

1957–1959. He then designed for **Louis Féraud,** 1959–1961, prior to launching his own design house in 1962. He introduced his first fragrance in 1979 and a ready-to-wear collection in 1971, then his diffusion line **Scherrer City** in 1992. He was famous for his sophisticated, restrained, yet sexy deluxe ready-to-wear which catered to wealthy society ladies throughout Europe, as well as celebrities. The house of **Scherrer** celebrated the height of its success and saw the greatest demand for its opulent designs throughout the 1970s and early 1980s when their designs could be found in over 100 department stores and specialty boutiques in the United States, as well as over 25 countries around the world. Popular were his beautiful chiffon evening dresses with beaded sequin bodices and his evening suits embroidered at **Lesage,** Paris. He often culled his inspiration from Eastern cultures, creating beautiful chinoiserie and Mongolian-inspired coats and jackets. He was fired from the fashion house he once founded in 1992, and despite the house's financial difficulties due to the loss of its founder it remained in business.

SCHIAPARELLI, ELSA (1890–1973) Italian from Rome, Italy. After studying philosophy she married Comte William de Wendt de Kerlor in 1914. She moved to New York and worked as a scriptwriter and translator, 1919–1922, before moving to Paris in 1923. She had begun designing gowns for herself and a few friends in 1915 and received tremendous support and influence from friend **Paul Poiret.** She showed her first collection in 1925 and was a contemporary of **Chanel,** with both designers beginning their careers with designing sweaters—**Schiaparelli's** trompe l'oeil black sweater with a large white bow knitted in at the neckline. **Schiaparelli** opened her first boutique, **"Pour le Sport,"** in 1927, followed by her first boutique **Schiaparelli** on Rue de la Paix, Paris. This was on the heels of the tremendous success of her first sweater designs in 1935, as well as the opening of a branch of the house of **Schiaparelli** in London and her girls' debutante department that same year. She introduced her iconic "Shocking" pink color as a major hue in her collections, which would later become the name of one of her most successful fragrances. She was very savvy in creating a collection of sophisticated, expensive working-class designs which became highly popular in polite society. She was also famous for her circus collection in 1938 which showed buttons designed by **Jean Schlumberger** in the shape of acrobats diving down the front of a silk brocade jacket which was elaborately embroidered with carousel horses by **Lesage,** Paris. Likewise, she was known too for her numerous other wildly witty and eccentric designs, including her "Rhodophane," a cellophane material which she created tunic dresses from; her suit with pockets which simulated a chest of drawers; and her military, zodiac, and insect themes and motifs. She collaborated with some of the most celebrated artists of the times including **Salvador Dali, Jean Cocteau,** and **Christian Bérard** who designed various concepts and fabrics for her collections. **Salvatore Ferragamo** created shoe collections for the house of **Schiaparelli,** most notably the "Wedgie," a two-inch-soled shoe which became a major fashion trendsetter in the late 1930s. She returned to New York during World War II and lectured on fashion, as well as working as a volunteer for the French war effort, 1941–1943. **Herbert de Givenchy** worked for her from 1949–1952, as well as **Philippe Venet,** 1951–1952, before leaving to join **Hubert de Givenchy,** who had left **Schiaparelli** to open his own couture house in 1952. **Schiaparelli** is unequivocally one of the world's most influential fashion designers whose work continues to influence contemporary fashion today.

SCHÖN, MILA (MARIA CARMEN NUTIZIO) (1919–) Yugoslavian, from Trau, Dalmatia, Yugoslavia; raised in Trieste and Milan. Having been raised as a wealthy Yugoslavian whose family fled to Italy to escape the communist regime, **Schön** grew up with an appreciation of expensive couture clothing and had been a client of **Balenciaga.** When the family fortune was lost she ventured into fashion design to earn a living, having had no design training or experience other than that of being a keenly observant couture customer. She opened her first atelier in 1958 and showed her first custom collection in 1965, followed by opening her first boutique in 1966 in Milan. The hallmark of her designs is her faultless attention to cut, and although her first collections were basically adapted copies of her favorite designers—**Balenciaga, Dior,** and **Schiaparelli**—she soon established a sophisticated reputation within the Italian fashion world for her high standards, demanding the best quality craftsmanship in her work. She is considered a contemporary of **Genny, Fendi,** and **Valentino,** and in the early 1960s catered to an impressive list of luminaries including Jacqueline Kennedy (Onassis) and Babe Paley. She launched several diffusion lines including **Mila Schön Due, Mila Schön Uomo, Aqua Schön, Schön Ottica,** as well as licenses for ties, scarves, fabrics, handbags, belts, and fragrances.

SCHNURER, CAROLYN (CAROLYN GOLDSAND) (1908-) American from New York. She originally trained as a teacher, but when she suggested an innovative women's sportswear design to a friend and buyer at Best & Co. which was a great success, she was encouraged to move into fashion. She would later study fashion at Traphagen School of Design, New York, 1939–1940, before going to work for her husband, **Harold Teller (Burt)** and his two partners' company **Burt Schnurer Cabana,** a women's ready-to-wear sport and swimwear manufacturer. Her designs for **Burt Schnurer Cabana** were available throughout the 1940s at Best & Co., Franklin Simon, and Peck & Peck. A contemporary of **Claire Mc-Cardell** and **Tina Leser, Schunrer's** innovative although mass-produced and inexpensive women's sportswear was highly influential in shaping the look of American women throughout the 1940s and early 1950s. The company was renamed **Carolyn Schnurer,** and after a trip to Peru sponsored by **Franklin Simon, Schnurer** introduced her ethnic-inspired collection "**Serano**" based on the traditional costumes and jewelry which she discovered in Peru. The most successful design of her "**Serano**" collection was a "**Cholo**" coat in 1946. She was noted for having popularized the one-piece swimsuit and introduced a very successful, very brief bikini in 1947. The bikini had become the latest trend in fashion and had been named after Bikini Island where the atom bomb had been tested. **Schnurer** divorced her husband in the late 1950s, leaving the company and fashion design to become a consultant to **J.P. Stevens,** a fabric manufacturer, then later worked as an executive placement agent specializing in the fashion industry.

SCHUBERTH, EMILIO (1904-1972) Italian from Naples, Italy. Considered to have been one of Italy's top couturiers of the 1950s, **Schuberth** opened his own salon with little training at the age of 28 in 1932. He was one of the first couture designers to present his collections on the Italian catwalks in 1952. Famous for his unique approach and attention given to his convertible evening skirts which were often double-sided and reversed to become wonderful capes, beautifully appliquéd. His elaborate, multitiered evening dresses were layered with crinolines embellished with baroque embroidery and silk flowers.

SCHWARTZ, BARRY (DATES UNKNOWN) American co-founder of **Calvin Klein Co.** with longtime friend **Calvin Klein** in 1968.

SCOTT, KEN (1918-1991) American from Fort Wayne, Indiana. He began painting in Guatemala after studying at Parsons, New York. A fabric designer noted for his beautiful Op Art patterns and use of color. **Rudi Gernreich** used many of his fabrics in his designs in the 1960s. He moved to Milan in 1950 and opened a salon where he used his beautiful fabrics to design swimsuits, caftans, tunics, silk jersey body stockings, as well as brilliantly colored printed scarves, which often favored circus and floral motifs. He often beaded his beautiful fabrics with bugle beads and sequins for his eveningwear collections.

SHAW, BEN (SEE HALSTON) (DATES UNKNOWN) **Halston** formed **Halston Originals** ready-to-wear with **Ben Shaw** in 1972.

SILVERMAN, JERRY (SEE SHANNON RODGERS, SHANNON ROGERS FOR JERRY SILVERMAN)

SIMON, NORTON (SEE HALSTON) (DATES UNKNOWN) **Halston Enterprises** was sold to **Norton Simon** in 1973.

SIMONETTA (DUTCHESA SIMONETTA COLONNA DI CESARO) (1922-) Italian from Rome, Italy. She launched her first collection in 1946 called **Simonetta Visconti,** named after her husband **Count Galaezzo Visconti.** Recognized throughout the 1940s, 1950s, and 1960s as one of Rome's top women's ready-to-wear and couture designers and one of the best known names in Italian fashion in America. After her divorce from **Count Galaezzo Visconti** she teamed with rival designer **Alberto Fabiani** in 1953, and the two later married. In 1962 they debuted the house of **Simonetta et Fabiani** in Paris. The new company was not as successful in Paris as **Simonetta's** had been in Rome; however, their designs were on a par with such contemporaries of the times as **Mainbocher, Sophie of Saks, Capucci of Italy,** and **Stiebel of London.** Famous for their youthful and elegant debutante and cocktail dresses, daywear, sportswear, suits, and coats with minimal detail, yet precision tailoring. Her list of clientele included Audrey Hepburn, Clare Booth Luce, Eleanor Lambert, Lauren Bacall, and Jacqueline Kennedy Onassis. **Fabiano** and **Simonetta** returned to Rome in the mid-1960s and the two divorced shortly after, closing their joint business in 1965; however, they continued to design under their own names. **Fabiano** retired in the early 1970s, **Simonetta** in 1973. **Simonetta** traveled to India in the early 1970s and after her retirement devoted herself to philanthropy and spirituality, establishing a colony for the care of lepers and a craft training program in India.

SIMONSEN, JORGEN (1974-) Dane from Struer, Denmark. After graduating in 1995 from Esmod, Paris, completing a three-year degree in only two, he began his design career working at **John Galliano,** 1994–1996, while also working with **Galliano** at **Givenchy** from 1995–1996. He then freelanced with **Karl Lagerfeld,** 1996–1997, followed by one season, fall/winter, 1998, for ready-to-wear at **Givenchy** under **Alexander McQueen.** He moved to **Versace** under **Donetella Versace,** 1997–2000, then to **Valentino,** 2000, as first assistant in the creative studio.

SIMPSON, ADELE (1904-1995) American from New York. After finishing her four-year degree in fashion at the Pratt Institute, New York, in two years, 1921–1922, she became design assistant at the age of 19 for **Ben Gershel Company,** a women's ready-to-wear manufacturer in New York, 1923–1926. **Simpson** was appointed head designer for **Ben Gershel,** 1927–1942. She moved to **William Bass,** New York, as chief designer, 1927–1928, followed by **Mary Lee Fashions,** 1929, where she began to design under her own name for the fashion house. She married **Wesley William Simpson,** a textile manufacturer in 1930, and bought out **Mary Lee Fashions** in 1949, renaming the company **Adele Simpson, Inc.** She produced **Givenchy's** special collections for Bloomingdale's in 1964 and had by then solidified an important position for herself in the American fashion industry as a designer creating practical interpretations of current fashion trends. She culled much of her inspirations from her world travels, particularly from Eastern cultures and traditional costumes and fabrics. Many of her fabrics were designed exclusively for her by **Galey & Lord,** often favoring simple cotton as a choice for both day- and eveningwear. A contemporary of **Hattie Carnegie, Pauline Trigère, Nettie Rosenstein,** and **Scaasi,** her designs had widespread appeal. Besides being favored by notable politicians' wives, they appealed to working women in the public eye who required the flexibility of garments which would not only travel well but also move seamlessly from day to evening as their schedules demanded. She produced a collection of costume jewelry in the 1960s which complemented her collection of costume suits, coats, and separates as well as day and evening dresses. Although her collections were predominately moderately priced in the 1950s at approximately $100 per dress or ensemble, to $200 in the 1960s, they rose as high as $500 in the 1970s. She donated her extensive collection of artifacts and costumes which she had collected during her world travels to the Fashion Institute, New York, and unofficially retired in 1978, but continued to oversee production and design until her death in 1995. **Donald Hobson** was appointed the official designer for the company in 1978.

SINCLAIRE (SEE TOM BRIGANCE) An American ready-to-wear manufacturer whose head designer in the 1950s was **Tom Brigance.**

SMITH, SANFORD American ready-to-wear manufacturer. In 1968, he co-founded **Anne Klein and Company** with **Anne Klein** and **Chip Rubenstein,** her second husband.

SMITH, WILLI (1948-1987) American from Philadelphia, Pennsylvania. A graduate of Parsons, New York, **Smith** began his professional career working as a freelance designer for various companies including **Arnold Scaasi** and **Bobbie Brooks,** New York, 1965–1969, then **Digits, Talbots,** and **Bonnie Brooks,** 1967–1976. In 1976 he partnered with **Laurie Mallet** and founded the ready-to-wear company **Willie Wear Ltd.,** which specialized in youthful, moderately priced, innovative, and relaxed sportswear. The company introduced men's ready-to-wear in 1978. With an inexhaustible appeal to the mass-market youth, in just 10 short years the company saw its profits soar from $30,000 in its first year to over $25 million by 1986. Famous for designing suits for Edwin Schlossberg and his groomsmen at his wedding to Caroline Kennedy, as well as the uniforms for the workers on Christo's Pont Neuf, Paris, wrapping exhibit in 1985. The company opened its first store on Fifth Avenue, New York, and in Paris posthumously in 1987, however is no longer in business today. He also designed for **McCall's Patterns.**

SOPHIE OF SAKS (SEE SOPHIE GIMBEL)

SPOOK, PER (1939-) Norwegian from Oslo, Norway. After studying art at the School of Fine Arts at Oslo he moved to École de la Chambre Syndicale, Paris to study fashion design in 1957. He apprenticed at the house of **Dior,** then worked for almost 20 years as a freelance designer for **Dior, Louis Féraud,** and **Yves Saint Laurent** before opening his own couture house in 1977. His initial approach to couture design never faltered and remained true to his original philosophy of beautiful, practical, down-to-earth designs which were graceful and polished with a flare for being fanciful and witty. He was famous for his distinctive innovations, including a versatile gown which included a device which would alter the length of the gown, shortening it for day wear, a collection of "Crumple" clothes which facilitated the wearer to pack them away in a small bundle without creasing for ease of travel, as well as collections which could be mixed and matched to move from day to evening use. His inspirations for his collections were often taken from the wealthy French leisure life of the 1920s and 1930s. He is also an accomplished painter, sculptor, and photographer. Although his business opened and closed a few times over its 25-year history due to the high cost and financial risks involved in producing couture, he finally closed the business permanently in 1996.

SPORTSMAKER (SEE TOM BRIGANCE) An American ready-to-wear manufacturer whose head designer in the 1950s was **Tom Brigance.**

SPROUSE, STEVEN (1953-) American from Ohio, raised in the backwaters of rural Indiana. After attending the Rhode Island School of Design for less than one semester, he arrived in New York with the dream of becoming a rock-and-roll photographer. After meeting Debbie Harry of the rock band Blondie in his New York, Bowery district apartment, he began to design stage costumes for Harry who would later introduce him to Andy Warhol, who in turn introduced him to **Halston.** He went to work for **Halston,** a fellow Indianan, as an apprentice for a period of time in the early 1980s, followed by a short stint with **Bill Blass,** prior to launching his first collection in 1983. It can be said that **Sprouse** blasted into the fashion spotlight with his widely popular clubwear which was inspired by the early work of **Courrèges** and **Gernreich,** and culled its inspiration from the nostalgia for New York's underground rock-and-roll scene in the 1960s mixed with **Sprouse's** New-Wave sensibilities and the punk movement of the late 1970s. He was famous for his expensive men's and women's ready-to-wear collections of motorcycle and sports jackets, tank style mini dresses, trench coats, and jeans in Day-Glo and fluorescent hues of hot punk pink, yellow, sky blue, and vibrant reds and greens. Also notable were his signature graffiti scribble prints by **Keith Haring,** 1983, and pop art prints by **Andy Warhol,** which were often embellished with oversized palettes. As well as producing his luxe line which was priced around $1,000 a garment, he also offered a bridge line of less expensive separates priced around $100 called "**SS.**" The turbulent rise and fall of **Sprouse** saw his business close in 1984, but was relaunched in 1987 with new backing, a new collection, and a new store in SoHo, New York. He was out of business again by 1988, and he created a new "**Cyber Punk**" line for Bloomingdale's in 1992. With famous rock star clients such as Debbie Harry, Iggy Pop, and Mick Jagger, it was a natural choice to appoint **Sprouse** in 1995 as costume curator for the opening of the Rock-and-Roll Hall of Fame Museum in Cleveland, Ohio, where he re-created the fashion scene of the late 1970s and early 1980s. In 2000–2001 he was back on the fast track again collaborating with **Louis Vuitton** to create a collection of handbags and accessories including over-the-elbow-length gloves with his signature graffiti scribble prints by **Keith Haring.** Despite his tidal rise and fall in the fashion world his design influences have been extensive.

STARR, MALCOLM An American women's ready-to-wear manufacturer on par with numerous design manufacturers including **Ben Zuckerman, Harvey Berin, Shannon Rogers, Jerry Silverman, Larry Aldrich,** and **Mollie Parnis. Elinor Simmons** was chief designer for **Malcolm Starr** and designed under the label **Elinor Simmons for Malcolm Starr** during the 1960s and 1970s. The company specialized in beautiful eveningwear, day dresses, and costume suits, often created out of draped chiffon, silk, and rayon crepe. Their evening gowns were lavishly beaded and embroidered in Hong Kong, with designs offering intricate clustered relief beading on net, organza, and satin. **Carol Horn** created the **Carol Horn Division** of **Malcolm Starr** in the mid-1970s.

STAVROPOULOS (1920-1990) Greek from Tripoli, Greece, he opened his first couture salon in Athens in 1949 offering beautifully tailored suits and coats. He married Nancy Angelakos, an American from New York, in 1960 and followed her back to New York, closing his Athens couture business. By 1961 he had launched his first luxury ready-to-wear collection in New York and by 1962 he was heralded by the fashion press as a bright young star. His ready-to-wear collections which he presented twice annually throughout his 30 years in business were always considered to be the caliber of Paris couture, and in the 1970s and 1980s prices for his exceptional eveningwear ranged from $2,000 to $7,500. Central to his collections were his elegant chiffon gowns which he offered year after year in a variety of reworked models, often with multiple layers of chiffon with free-floating panels in varying hues, halter necklines, and Grecian-inspired toga styles. His designs favored the use of chiffon, silk jersey, lamé velvet, woven lace, wool, and embroidered organdy. His work was often compared to that of his contemporary **Halston** in the 1970s and early 1980s for its minimalist approach. A favorite choice of wealthy American socialites and politician's wives, including Lady Bird Johnson who wore a **Stavropoulos** dress for her official White House portrait.

STIEBEL, VICTOR (1907-1976) British from Durban, England. After studying architecture at Cambridge he was encouraged to consider fashion by a friend, designer **Norman Hartnell.** He worked as an apprentice at **Reville et Rossiter** prior to founding his own ready-to-wear and custom fashion business in the mid-1930s. Recognized for his soft feminine day dresses favored by high society ladies, **Stiebel** became one of London's finest custom and ready-to-wear designers along with contemporaries **Hardy Amies, Edward Molyneux,** and **Norman Hartnell,** as well as an esteemed member of the Incorporated Society of London Fashion Designers. He also produced millinery collections.

STOUT, POLA, (SEE "IRENE" LENTZ) (DATES UNKNOWN) An American fabric designer.

STRAUSS, LEVI (MID-1800S-1902) Originally from Bavaria, **Strauss** arrived in San Francisco, California, as many did during the California gold rush in 1850s; however, he found a very unlikely gold mine of his own when he designed his first pair of work trousers for the miners out of brown tent canvas. He later used a French woven cotton fabric which he dyed indigo. He received a patent for his trousers in 1872. **Jacob Davis,** a tailor from Carson City, Nevada, teamed with **Strauss** in 1873 and together they created another patent for a pair of trousers which they designed with copper rivets at various stress points on all of the pockets. The company continued to carve out an impressive legacy after **Strauss's** death in 1902, creating numerous variations of the original trousers which were favored by workmen, cowboys, and sportswear enthusiasts. The fashion world has never matched the collectible market created by the demand for **Levi Strauss's** early designs, from sought-after details such as "hidden copper rivets," early cotton labels, and later versions known as "red lines"; collectible markets have witnessed a single pair of important early **Levi's** jeans selling for as much as $46,000 on eBay online auctions in the spring of 2001.

SUCHERAS, BERNARD (DATES UNKNOWN) Appointed the chief designer for the **Charles Jourdan** company in 1981, after the company was acquired from the **Jourdan** family by **Portland Cement Werke.**

SUI, ANNA (1955-) American from Dearborn Heights, Michigan. After spending two years at Parsons, New York, she began her career working as a design assistant for **Bobbie Brooks,** a women's junior sportswear firm, then later for numerous other firms designing sportswear and swimwear including **Glenora,** a hip, young ready-to-wear company. While pursuing a freelance design career she also worked as a stylist with friend and fellow Parson's graduate, fashion photographer Steven Meisel. **Sui** launched her first ready-to-wear collection in 1980 spearheaded by Meisel's encouragement and the decision to move her line into the Annette B showroom, owed by Annette Breindel who encouraged her to concentrate on her young women's dress designs, coupled with the sale of her first six dresses to Macy's department store. She followed with her first runway show in 1991, moving her business from her Manhattan apartment to a Seventh Avenue location that same year. She introduced her menswear collection the following year in 1992, and opened an in-store boutique in Macy's as well as a free-standing boutique in New York's Soho district, as well as other boutiques in Hollywood, California, 1993, and Los Angeles on the fashionable Sunset Plaza, 2000. She also launched a line of cosmetics and fragrances with beautiful hip packaging that recalls the innovative 1960s Youthquake style of **Barbara Hulanicki** for **Biba.** Noted for her cross-culture influences which she fuses with inspiration she culls from her passion for unique vintage designs, her collections are always surprisingly sexy, fresh, youthful, and distinctive.

SUSSMAN, MORTY (DATES UNKNOWN) American ready-to-wear designer who designed the boutique line for **Mollie Parnis** from 1970.

SUYDAN, HENDRIK, MRS. (SEE JAY-THORPE, INC.) (DATES UNKNOWN) She was the head of the trousseau department at **Jay-Thorpe, Inc.** in the early 1920s through the early 1930s.

TALBOT, SUZANNE (DATES UNKNOWN) A French custom and couture women's designer who produced elegant and feminine designs during the 1930s throughout the 1950s. Considered a contemporary of other French designers, including **Patou, Paquin, Schiaparelli, Norman Hartnell,** and **Lelong,** her dresses and hats were available in America in **Lord & Taylor's Little Salon.**

TAM, VIVENNE (1962-) Chinese-born from Canton, China, raised in Hong Kong, and worked in London, England, before moving to New York in 1981 and becoming a naturalized American. She launched her first collection in 1983, founding her company **East Wind Code Ltd.** Her collections are committed to medium-priced women's ready-to-wear with cross-cultural influences and idealistic globalism which transcends politics, offering whimsical motifs, including her most famous in 1994 of Chairman Mao with a bee perched on his nose, as well as often exploring Impressionism and Op Art. Her designs are always modern, although nostalgic and rooted in her love of beautiful vintage designs and unique objects which she passionately searches for the world over. Her creations are a favorite of the "who's who" of the young Hollywood celebrities.

TAPPÉ, HERMAN PATRICK (DATES UNKNOWN) American. Primarily an ultra-feminine custom wedding and bridesmaids designer based in New York, active in 1910–1940s. He was considered to be America's version of **Poiret** and was famous for the wedding dress which he created for Mary Pickford for her marriage to Douglas Fairbanks and its photograph in American *Vogue* in 1920.

TARLAZZI, ANGELO (1945-) An Italian couture and ready-to-wear designer who, after studying political science, began working as a design assistant to a couture house in Rome at the age of 19. He left Italy in 1965 for Paris and went to work as an assistant to **Jean Patou** from 1965 to 1968. From 1968–1972 he worked as a freelance designer in Paris, Rome, Milan, and New York before returning to **Jean Patou** as the artistic director, 1972–1977 designing for couture, ready-to-wear, and accessories. He became famous for his "handkerchief dress" which was constructed of fabric knotted together directly on the model. He left **Patou** in 1977 to launch his own ready-to-wear collection and by 1989 **Guy Laroche** appointed **Tarlazzi** as his successor just prior to his death. The house of **Guy Laroche** produced a licensed ready-to-wear collection for **Angelo Tarlazzi.** Today **Tarlazzi** divides his time between his ready-to-wear collections, his bridge line, **Tarlazzi II,** menswear, his Japanese licenses, and his Parisian boutiques.

TASSELL, GUSTAVE (1926-) American from Philadelphia, Pennsylvania. After studying art at the Philadelphia Academy of Art, he moved to New York and went to work as an assistant window dresser at **Hattie Carnegie.** Inspired by all that he saw at **Hattie Carnegie,** he returned to his hometown of Philadelphia and opened a small custom dress business working from his town house. Encouraged and promoted back to **Hattie Carnegie** by retailer Nan Duskin, he signed on as a designer at **Hattie Carnegie** in the late 1940s, as well as at **Elfreda Fox** for custom clothes. Dissatisfied creatively at **Carnegie** after only six months with the firm, he offered his resignation. He received **Hattie Carnegie's** blessings and assistance to move to Paris in the early 1950s, and worked as a freelance sketch artist for various couture houses including only two days at the house of **Jacques Fath,** (due to the language barrier), under **Fath's** wife **Geneviève Fath.** Even **Tassell** could not say for sure if **Jacques Fath** was still alive at the time of his employment because of the secrecy around the time of his passing for fear of the house's clients losing interest in the designs. While in Paris **Tassell** also sold sketches to American manufacturer **Jane Derby,** and worked closely with her to develop them as designs. She had been planning to open a licensed division of her company in Italy at the time. **James Galanos** met **Tassell** in Paris and supported **Tassell's** work by buying his sketches. After two years in Paris he moved to Los Angeles, California, and went to work for **Edith Washington,** a wholesale manufacturer whose major client was Ameilia Gray, an upscale Beverly Hills boutique. With the encouragement of friend and fellow Los Angeles–based designer **James Galanos, Tassell** opened his own small design manufacturing in 1957, in Los Angeles, later with a showroom in New York. Along with **Oleg Cassini** and **Donald Brooks, Tassell** had been a favorite designer of Jacqueline Kennedy (Onassis) in the early 1960s. He was awarded the Coty Award in 1961. He was chosen by the board of directors of Revlon who owned the **Norell** company to succeed **Norman Norell** as head designer and become president in 1972 after **Norell's** death. He moved to New York and settled in the Gotham Hotel for five years as he continued in the design tradition established by **Norman Norell,** until the company was closed by the directors in 1976. In 1976–1977 he designed a line of furs for **Michael Forrest.** Although **Tassell** is retired today, he continues to create, producing a design collection in 1997 for an exhibition at the Los Angeles County Museum's Costume Council, as well as sitting on their board.

TIFFEAU, JACQUES (1927-1988) Frenchman from the Loire Valley in France. He began his career working as a tailor's apprentice in the Loire Valley before moving to Paris and working as an assistant to **Christian Dior** in 1945. He moved to New York in 1952 and worked originally as a pattern maker for **Sano & Pruzan** before being appointed head designer for the company, which was now **Monte-Sano and Pruzan.** He continued in the company's classic tradition of expensive women's ready-to-wear coats, dresses, and suits until 1958 when he launched his own company **Tiffeau and Busch,** a ready-to-wear line of younger, lower-priced coats, dresses, and sportswear separates with **Max Pruzan's** daughter, **Beverly Busch.** He continued to design for both companies producing six collections a year between the two fashion houses for nearly a decade. He is credited for introducing a popular "midi"-length dress in 1966 which was echoed in **Galanos's** version of a below-the-knee length in 1967. He reorganized his company **Tiffeau and Busch** in 1966 by dropping **Beverly Busch's** name and adding his first name, creating **Jacques Tiffeau;** however, the company closed a few years later in 1971. He returned to Paris where he taught fashion design and worked for a time at **Balmain,** then supervised collections for **Yves Saint Laurent,** 1972–1976. He returned to New York briefly to create a collection of coats for **Originala** and **Bill Blass's Blassport.**

TOWNLEY FROCKS, INC. (SEE CLAIRE MCCARDELL AND ROBERT TURK) An American wholesale women's ready-to-wear manufacturer from the 1930s throughout the 1950s.

TRAINA, ANTHONY (SEE NORMAN NORELL) A women's ready-to-wear, wholesale manufacturer. **Germaine Monteil** designed for the company in the late 1920s prior to opening her own wholesale design business. He was also the businessman-financier who teamed with **Norman Norell** in 1941 to form **Traina-Norell.** He had structured his deal with **Norell** to have **Norell** draw a lower salary from the company in exchange for his name on the label. **Norell** left the company in the late 1950s to form his own company; **Traina** closed the company and retired in 1960.

TRAINA, TEAL (DATES UNKNOWN) The nephew of businessman **Anthony Traina** who partnered with **Norman Norell.** He produced a collection of women's active and ready-to-wear and eveningwear under the name **Teal-Traina** in the 1950s and early 1960s. Ready-to-wear designer **Greta Plattry** had retired from designing for a period in 1960; however, in 1966 she created a line of casual clothes for a division of **Teal-Traina. Louis Dell'Olio** had worked with **Dominic Kompollo** at **Teal-Traina** in the mid-1960s.

TRAVILLA, WILLIAM (UNKNOWN-1990) American from Los Angeles, California. Originally a costume designer, most famous for the Grecian-style adaptation, pleated halter-neck white dress he designed for Marilyn Monroe in *The Seven Year Itch*, 1955, as well as for creations for 11 of Monroe's films. He created his own often elaborate, expensive ready-to-wear collections which were sought after by society ladies and celebrities alike in the late 1970s and 1980s. He enjoyed a career which spanned more than 40 years, including creating the icon looks for the cast of characters on the highly popular television series *Dallas* in the 1980s. A contemporary of **Edith Head, Adrian,** and **Irene** in the 1940s–1950s, and later of **Nolan Miller** and **Bob Mackie** in the 1980s.

TRIBOUILLARD, DANIEL (SEE JACQUES LEONARD) (DATES UNKNOWN)

TRIGÈRE, PAULINE (1912-) Born and raised in Paris of Russian immigrant parents; her mother a dressmaker, her father a tailor who arrived in Paris in 1905. She had learned to operate a sewing machine by the age of ten and worked as an apprentice cutter in her father's tailoring business from a very young age, continuing until his death in 1932. She then worked for **Martial et Armand,** a couture house located in the Place Vendôme, Paris. While traveling from Paris to Chile with her family, stopping in New York, she chose to remain in New York where she eventually found work as an assistant designer for **Ben Gershel & Co.** in 1937, then later as an assistant to **Travis Banton.** She then designed for **Hattie Carnegie,** leaving in 1941. In 1942 she produced a small collection of a dozen styles and launched her own business, producing a complete ready-to-wear collection by the late 1940s. She appointed her son, **Jean-Pierre Radley,** president of **Pauline Trigère, Inc.,** designating the running of the business to him while she handled all aspects of design. Famous for her unmistakably feminine, simple elegance and timeless designs which were often compared to those of **Balenciaga** and **Vionnet, Trigère** preferred to create by draping the fabric directly on a dress form or live model as opposed to sketching out an idea. She is recognized for her beautiful dresses, coats, and capes which she often offered in reversible designs, and her dresses with attached jewelry, using a turtle as one of her favorite motifs which she interpreted in various costume jewelry designs. She kept her production small and manageable, producing in the 1960s approximately 1,000 garments a year which ran on average about $300 per garment. By the early 1970s her prices had climbed to over $1,000 for an evening coat. She created a collection of coats for **Abe Schrader** in the 1980s which were more moderately priced than her private ready-to-wear collections which ran as high as $5,000 a garment. She formally retired and closed her company in 1993, however returned to the design front creating a new line of costume jewelry for her dejected fans in 1994. In 2001 she announced that at 89 she had embarked on an entirely new design venture creating luxury accessories for the elderly, including beautiful walking sticks and bags which attach to a walker, for **Golden Violin,** an online storefront which caters to seniors.

TROUBLÉ, AGNÈS (SEE AGNÈS B)

TURKINE, VALENTINE (DATES UNKNOWN) From Paris, France. In-house designer of fine ready-to-wear for **Bergdorf Goodman** department store, New York, in the early 1930s.

TURK, ROBERT (ROBERT TURK INC.) A wholesale manufacturer for whom **Claire McCardell** had designed knitwear, 1929–1931. He moved to **Townley Frocks, Inc.** in 1931 with **McCardell** as his assistant designer; however, he died in a freak sailing accident just prior to the introduction of the first collection and was subsequently succeeded by **McCardell.**

TURNER, FRANKLIN JESSIE (DATES UNKNOWN) American custom couture designer who originally began working for **Bonwit Teller** prior to opening her own custom salon in the early 1920s in Greenwich Village, New York, moving her operations to 410 Park Avenue in 1923. Famous throughout the 1920s–1940s for her beautiful, sinuous tea gowns and eveningwear, she created by draping fabric which she also designed for her collections directly on the dress form. Noted as a reclusive person, as a designer she apparently never met any of her custom clients personally, instead working through her staff. A contemporary in the 1920s and 1930s in the caliber of **Elizabeth Hawes, Charles James, Valentina, Jo Copeland, Muriel King, Claire McCardell, Tom Brigance, Hattie Carnegie,** and **Lilly Daché.** By the late 1930s her designs often featured Chinese motifs, and she was so influenced by the Eastern aesthetic that she redecorated her salon in red, black, and chartreuse.

TUTTABANKEN SPORTSWEAR (SEE KATHARINE HAMNETT)

TULLIS, JOHN (DATES UNKNOWN) A South African women's ready-to-wear designer who had taken over the design direction of the house of **Molyneux** in 1965 when **Edouard Molyneux** retired for the final time and moved to Biot.

TYLER, RICHARD (1948-) Australian from Sunshine, Australia, immigrating to the United States in 1978. The son of a factory foreman and dressmaker/costumer at the Melbourne Ballet. **Richard Tyler** began his career as an apprentice for a Savile Row–trained tailor in Australia. By the age of 18 in 1966, and with his father's financial assistance, he opened a small store called **Zippity-Doo-Dah** in a run-down part of town in Melbourne, Australia. **Tyler** did the designing while his mother sewed up his creations in the back room. By the 1970s the shop had attracted an impressive list of celebrity clientele who had found **Zippity-Doo-Dah** while on tour in Melbourne including Cher, Elton John, Diana Ross, Alice Cooper, Super Tramp, Bee Gees, Go-Go's, and Rod Stewart. Rod Stewart had commissioned **Tyler** to create costumes for his 1978 "Blondes Have More Fun" tour and took him on the road with him. The tour brought **Tyler** to Los Angeles where **Tyler** fell in love with the city, chose to remain, and continued to design rock costumes for his numerous clients. When demands for rock costumes moved away from **Tyler's** unique style and began to become more outlandish, he dropped his costume design. He moved to Oslo, Norway, for two years, returning to Los Angeles in 1987 with no funds and a mind to return home to Australia. However, as luck would have it, he met **Lisa Trafficante,** an actress and businesswoman, who convinced him to remain in Los Angeles and pursue his strength in men's tailoring. **Trafficante** developed the business plan and raised the capital which launched the couple's first collection of tailored menswear in late 1987. They opened their Los Angeles showroom and manufacturing facility with financing from **Trafficante's** sister, **Michelle,** and investor **Gordon DeVol** in an Art Deco building in an off-the-beaten-path area on Beverly Boulevard in Los Angeles, which is still their flagship store today. **Tyler** and **Trafficante** later married in 1989. They launched their first womenswear show in New York in 1992 to incredible reviews which brought an offer of chief designer to **Tyler** from **Anne Klein.** **Tyler** designed at **Klein** for one year from 1993–1994 but was terminated for undisclosed reasons, with a reported $2.1 million buyout of his contract. It was speculated that although **Tyler's** designs for **Klein** were met with tremendous critical acclaim and saw store orders rise by 30 percent, his vision was too forward for the traditional **Klein** customer. In 1996 he was appointed chief designer to **Byblos.** He is famous for his impeccable tailoring in both his men's and women's collections, with entire garments completely finished by hand, the inside of which were finished equally as beautifully. His expensive luxury designs in fine wool, silks, and linens are favored by a "who's who" in society, as well as by an impressive lists of celebrities including Julia Roberts, Sigourney Weaver, and Oprah Winfrey.

UNGARO, EMANUEL (BORN 1933–) Frenchman of Italian parents, from Aix-en-Provence, France. He began his initial training at a very young age under the tutelage of his father who was a tailor and taught him the art of cut, fit, and sewing of men's clothing. In 1955 at the age of 22 he left Provence for Paris and took a job as a stylist for **Maison Camps** tailors, followed by joining the house of **Balenciaga,** Paris in 1958–1964. He was appointed head of the house of **Balenciaga,** Madrid, 1959–1961, moving to **Courrèges,** 1964–1965. He left **Courrèges** to establish his own fashion house in 1965, introducing **Ungaro Parallèle** ready-to-wear in 1968. He would later introduce menswear, 1975, a sportswear line **Emanuel,** 1991, as well as various fragrances. He is credited with being the design mind behind much of the Space Age designs which came out of **Courrèges** during his tenure there, and much of his work there carried over into his first private collections. The hallmark of his designs throughout the 1970s were the rich boldly printed fabrics with impressionistic floral and abstract motifs designed by **Sonja Knapp,** which he draped beautifully into soft feminine dresses. Throughout the 1970 and 1980s **Ungaro's** designs played with varying influences including the Far East (with chinoiserie patterned tunics) and Baroque (with Gypsy-inspired bouffant skirts). His luxurious designs always convey a refined sex appeal and offer the wearer an expression of confidence and independence. As well as his women's ready-to-wear, his collections today include menswear, furs, sheets, wallcoverings, curtains, knitwear, and fragrances.

UNITS (SEE GARRATT, SANDRA)

VALENTINA (VALENTINA SANINA) (1904-1989) Russian from Kiev, Russia, where she first studied drama. She met her husband **George Schlee** who founded a free university and newspaper in Sevastopol. The two fled Russia during the revolution in 1920 to Greece, then to Italy, and finally settled in Paris, setting up a small theater company, 1922–1923. It was in Paris where theater designer Léon Bakst met **Valentina** and encouraged her to pursue her talent in fashion design, for up until then she had only been creating lovely clothes to complement her own beauty. **Valentina** and her husband moved from Paris to New York in 1923 and two years later opened **Valentina's** first couture salon with outside financing. Her backing left two years later and she and her husband **George Schlee** founded **Valentina Gowns, Inc.** in 1928. They celebrated immediate success, selling more than $1,400 the first day and forcing **Valentina** to sell some of her personal wardrobe to meet the opening demands. A top-rung designer, she was considered a contemporary throughout the 1930s and 1940s to such designers as **Charles James, Mainboucher, Jo Copeland, Claire McCardell, Clare Potter,** and **Elizabeth Hawes.** By 1940 the company had moved its operations to a four-story building which had recently been vacated by **Elizabeth Hawes's** operation and was managing over 65 employees. **Valentina** did all the fabric buying, designing, employee management, sales, and client fittings, as well as modeled all of her collections for fashion editorials. Noted for her theatrical designs in the 1930s and 1940s including those for Judith Anderson in 1933 and Katharine Hepburn in *The Philadelphia Story*, 1939. During the 1940s her beautiful couture dresses ran around $250 and climbed as high as $600 in the mid-1950s. She considered fashion to be timeless and thought that a design should not be seasonal; therefore she produced collections which were seasonless and many of her ensembles were convertible and consisted of interchangeable separates. She often culled inspiration from classic European fine art, as well as adapting Eastern ideas including the use of obi sashes and Indian embroideries. Famous for her bias-cut silk or wool crepe dresses and suits which featured sable trims throughout the 1930s and 1940s. She purchased a fragrance manufacturing business and introduced a perfume called **My Own** in 1950. She formally retired and closed her business in 1957, however returned in 1964 to design costumes for Margaret Leighton in the play *The Chinese Prime Minister*. She was considered among the very top couturiers working in America.

VALENTINO, MARIO (VALENTINO GARAVANI) (1932-) After studying French at Accademia dell'Arte, Milan, 1948, **Valentino** then studied fashion design at l'École de la Chambre Syndicale de la Couture Parisienne, 1949–1951, while working as an assistant designer to **Jean Dessès,** Paris, 1950–1955. He later worked for **Guy Laroche,** Paris, 1956–1958, followed by one year as an assistant to **Princess Irene Galitzine,** Paris, 1959, before moving to Rome and founding his own small atelier in 1960. It was his first collection which he presented in Florence which caught the eye of the international press, and on the heels of this success he was soon able to move his tiny operation to its present location. He gained even greater notoriety when Jacqueline Kennedy (Onassis) wore a lace-trimmed two-piece ensemble with a short pleated skirt from his famous all-white collection in 1968 for her marriage to Aristotle Onassis. The first ready-to-wear boutique was established in Paris in 1968, then Rome (1972 and 1988), followed by Milan in 1979 and London in 1987. The company was acquired by **Kenton Corporation,** 1968–1973, and repurchased by **Valentino** in 1973. Menswear was introduced in 1972. Working with his partner and business manager **Giancarlo Giammetti, Valentino** has built a fashion empire based on lavish evening designs with magnificent details including opulent bead and embroidery work and meticulous attention to cut and drape. **Natalie Gervais,** who began her career working with **Tom Ford** at the **Gucci Group** in 1994 designing ready-to-wear, moved to **Valentino** in 1996 to supervise the house's **Diffusion** collections before leaving to become the head designer at the house of **Nina Ricci. Jorgen Simonsen** joined **Valentino** in early 2000 as his first assistant in the creative studio. Today **Valentino** is owned by **di Partecipazioni Industriali SpA (HdP),** a publishing fashion conglomerate which also owns **Fila.** The company today produces women's couture and ready-to-wear, men's ready-to-wear, **Valentino Piu** for gifts, interiors, bed linens and drapery fabrics, as well as a full line of fragrance products. The fashion world experienced a tremendous renewed interest in **Valentino's** designs when actress Julia Roberts wore an incredible black and white vintage **Valentino** gown to accept her Academy Award in March of 2001 for her role in the film *Erin Brockovich*. With vintage styles in such demand, the house of **Valentino** has begun to bring back popular styles and accessories from their archives much in the same way as **Yves Saint Laurent** did in the early fall of 2000 and then again in the spring of 2001.

VAN DEN AKKER, KOOS (1932-) From Holland. He began making dresses when he was just 11 years old. After studying at the Netherlands Royal Academy of Art, he worked briefly in a few department stores in The Hague and in Paris. He was noted for having completed a two-year study course at l'École Guerre

Lavigne in Paris in just seven months. He apprenticed at **Christian Dior** in the late 1950s before moving back to The Hague and opening his own boutique where he sold his custom designs. He moved to New York in 1968 and is said to have set up as a street vendor next to the fountain in Lincoln Center taking commissions for designs he would create with his portable sewing machine. He designed lingerie for **Eve Stillman** prior to opening his own boutique, selling his women's ready-to-wear, as well as running a wholesale business in New York. He later introduced menswear and in 1992 teamed with **Peter DeWilde** forming **Koos & DeWilde.** Most noted for his work in the early 1980s, simple silhouettes with his signature graphic collages with lace and beadwork. He also designed furs, home furnishings, and theater costumes. His early work in the 1980s has been exhibited through numerous museums and design institutions.

VARDEN PETITES (SEE ANNE KLEIN)

VARTY, KEITH (SEE GENNY SPA)

V DE V (VÊTEMENTS DE VACANCES) (SEE MICHÈLE ROSEIR) A French women's ready-to-wear and sportswear company founded in Paris by **Michèle Roseir** along with partner **Jean-Pierre Bamberger** in 1962.

VENET, PHILIPPE (1929-) Frenchman from Lyon, France. He apprenticed with a men's tailoring business at the age of 16, learning the rudiments of perfect cut and fabric drape. In 1945 he was hired as a tailor at **Pierre Court** in Lyon, which at the time held the exclusive right to manufacture for the **Balenciaga** label. After serving his mandatory military service he moved to Paris and went to work for **Elsa Schiaparelli** in 1951. While at **Schiaparelli** he met **Hubert de Givency,** and when **Givency** opened his own couture house in 1952 he invited **Venet** to join him, a collaboration which lasted ten years until 1962. **Venet** opened his couture house in 1962 on the Rue François, and by 1985 he had received the coveted Dé d' Or Award in France. **André Laug** freelanced for the house of **Venet** in the late early 1960s. The house's hallmark was exquisite tailored suits and coats, as well as feminine day dresses in floral themes. **Venet** shows collections annually in both Paris and New York and celebrates a tremendous following in the United States.

VENETTA, BOTTEGA Italian, luxury leather goods and ready-to-wear manufacturer founded by **Vittorio Moltedo** and his wife **Laura** in the early 1960s. Noted for their expensive woven leather handbags in the 1970s and 1980s, as well as fine travel and small leather goods. Today the company is considered to be a major fashion force with their "Britpack Dream Design Team," including **Giles Deacon** and **Stuart Verers,** who are creating youthful designs with an edgy vibe. In May of 2001 the company was acquired by the **Gucci Company,** an Italian fashion conglomerate.

VERA (SEE NEUMANN, VERA) (DATES UNKNOWN) An American fabric painter who worked for **Manhattan Industries** in the 1960s. Her designs were interpreted into garments for the company by newly appointed head designer **Perry Ellis** in 1974. She was recognized for her beautiful and colorful motifs on scarves, garments, household linens, and textiles. Her logo often had a small ladybug next to her signature.

VERSACE, DONATELLA (1955-) Italian from the small town of Reggio, Calabria, Italy. The sister of the late **Gianni Versace.** She originally studied foreign languages, receiving her degree before joining her brother's fashion house of **Versace.** She worked as both his muse and creative overseer for all of **Versace's** image campaigns, shaping a unique identity for the **Versace** brand by working with the world's leading photographers and supermodels. In addition to directing the house's advertising, she was involved in all aspects of the company and was her brother's consultant for most of the important decisions. In the early 1990s she began designing the **Versace** accessories collections and some of the clothing licenses such as **Young Versace.** In 1993 she started designing the **Versus** line, appointing **Brian Atwood** as her design assistant in 1996. Upon the unfortunate and untimely death of her brother **Gianni Versace,** the founder of the company, **Donatella** assumed total control of the company, taking over designing women's ready-to-wear. She presented a triumphant, loud, and proud collection in October of 1997, just a few short months after her brother's murder. **Jorgen Simonsen** worked with **Donatella** on women's collections, 1997–2000. Liz Tilberis once said that "If **Donatella** was to be anything else, she would have been a painter or a heavy metal rock star," and Anna Wintour declared her "the Bill Gates of Fashion." Likewise, André Leon Talley described **Donatella** as "Cinderella meets Barbarella on another planet, and that ultimately **Gianni Versace** and **Donatella** are the ethos of couture, creating their own universe." **Gianni** invented the **Versace** story; he was the tradition and **Donatella** is the future.

VERSACE, GIANNI (1946-1997) Italian from the small town of Reggio, Calabria, Italy. Although he began his career studying architecture while working with his mother in her couture dressmaking business, he eventually became the buyer for her atelier in the late 1960s prior to finishing his architectural studies and moving to Milan in 1972. He worked for various firms including **Genny** in 1974, creating beautiful suede and leather designs before designing for their younger collection introduced in 1973; **Byblos,** 1975–1977; and **Genny's** other holding, **Complice,** in 1975 where he created luxurious eveningwear prior to **Claude Montana** taking over the designs for **Complice** in 1980. **Franco Moschino** worked as a sketch artist for **Versace** while he designed for **Complice** and **Genny** from 1974 through 1977. **Versace** opened his first business in 1978. He showed his first collection of women's ready-to-wear in 1978 and menswear in 1979. He began designing costumes for Teatro Alla Scala and for Richard Strauss's ballet "Josephlegende" in 1982. He opened **Versace Atelier,** Milan, in 1989, followed by showing his first **Atelier** collection in 1990. Throughout his career **Gianni Versace's** designs always expressed an intense sexuality, an exuberance, and often audacious approach to the female form, celebrating its beauty through his sophisticated and elegant approach to hugging the body with technical perfection in his formfitting designs brilliantly employing a bias cut or asymmetrical drape. He introduced home furnishings in 1993 and his diffusion line **Versus** in mid-1993 with his sister and lifelong muse **Donatella Versace** as head designer. **Donatella Versace** also designed the highly successful accessories collections for **Gianni Versace (see Donatella Versace).** **Brian Atwood** joined the house of **Versace** in 1996, initially designing the retail **Versus** collection before assuming the position as **Versace's** chief designer of women's footwear and accessories, creating alluring luxury accessories to complement the house's highly provocative collections. On July 23, 1997 **Gianni Versace** was gunned down outside his South Beach home in Miami Beach, Florida. In October of that same year, **Donatella Versace** presented a triumphant first collection for **Versace's** women's ready-to-wear collections. The house of **Versace** remains a powerful fashion force with **Donatella Versace** now the chief designer continuing in the tradition which her brother had forged, while infusing her own intensely unique approach.

VIONNET, MADELEINE (1876-1975) Frenchwoman from Chilleurs-aux-Bois, France. **Madeleine Vionnet** began working as a dressmaker's apprentice in Aubervilliers when she was just 12 years old in 1888–1893, first for the house of **Vincent,** Paris, 1893–1895, before moving to London and working as a cutter, then as head of the workroom for **Kate Reilly,** London. While in London she also worked for **Callot Soeurs,** London, prior to returning to Paris and working as a saleswoman for **Bechoff David,** Paris, 1900–1901. She joined the house of **Callot Soeurs,** Paris, under **Marie Gerber** in 1901–1905. She moved to the house of **Doucet,** Paris, 1905–1911, before establishing her own fashion house in 1912–1939, closing during the First World War from 1914–1919. Considered by the fashion world to be amongst the greatest couturiers, she was a brilliant technician who perfected the art of the bias cut and even commissioned her fabrics two yards wider to facilitate her graceful and sensuous draping effect. The house of **Vionnet** employed numerous designers over the years including **Marcelle Chaumont,** who worked as her assistant for years, **Jacques Griffe,** and **Maltezos** of **Mad Carpentier** who left the house when **Vionnet** retired in 1939. **Vionnet** was known for using miniature mannequins with articulated joints, draping fabric directly on these small-scale forms, then translating her designs into full-scale models. She did not rely on any inner structures such as binding corsets, instead allowing her fabric to drape and flow, following the natural curve and form of the figure; by today's standard her designs would be referred to as having "no hanger appeal," but springing to life on the female form. She was instrumental in popularizing the use of crepe de chine, which up until then had been relegated strictly as a fabric suitable simply for linings. Much of her design influence was culled from neoclassic Greek sculpture and medieval influences, and she was a designer whose work and influence could be seen in such designers from the past as **Claire McCardell** and **Halston,** as well as in contemporary fashion designers including **Geoffrey Beene, John Anthony, Azzedine Alaïa, Issey Miyake,** and **Rei Kawakubo.**

VIVIER, ROGER (1913-1998) From Paris, France. After studying sculpture at the Ecóle des Beaux-Arts in Paris, he went to work as a sketcher for Belleville Theater and later began to design shoes for the theater before founding his own boot and shoe making business in the mid-1930s. By 1937 he had opened his first shop in Paris on Rue Royale that offered his often elaborate creations, most famously his reversed "comma"-shaped heeled shoe. After an introduction to **Christian Dior** in 1947 he began a ten-year collaboration with him, creating beautiful collections for him up until **Dior's** death in 1957. He also designed for numerous shoe manufacturers including **Delman, Rayne,** and **Bally,** as well as collections for numerous designers such as **Elsa Schiaparelli, Yves Saint Laurent, Guy Laroche, Nina Ricci,** and **Pierre Balmain.** He had chosen to semi-retire in 1970 and moved his operations to the French countryside in Toulouse; however, he opened a shop on Madison Avenue, New York in 1985, followed by one in Japan in 1991, and accepted the position of artistic director for **Myrys,** a highly recognized French shoe manufacturer, in 1997 just one year prior to his death. Considered by many to be the "Fabergé of Footwear," it is true that **Vivier** revolutionized women's footwear from the 1930s–1970s, and his creations continue to inspire many contemporary designers today. His work attracted many luminaries including the Beatles, Brigitte Bardot, Elizabeth Taylor, Marlene Dietrich, Sophia Loren, Josephine Baker, and Queen Elizabeth, who wore a gold kid-leather-studded-in-garnet design by **Vivier** to her coronation in 1953.

VOLLBRACHT, MICHAELE (1947-) American from Quincy, Illinois. After graduating from Parsons, New York, he went to work for **Geoffrey Beene,** 1967–1969, moving to **Donald Brooks,** back to **Geoffrey Beene** and **Beene Bazaar,** then back to **Donald Brooks** between 1969–1971, followed by one year with **Norman Norell** just prior to **Norell's** death in 1972. He then went to work as an illustrator for numerous department stores including **Henri Bendel,** 1972–1974, and **Bloomingdale's,** 1975, before launching his own fashion house in 1977. **Vollbracht's** designs centered around his graphic hand-screened silk fabrics created by **Belotti** which were vibrant abstract and painterly prints often embellished with sequins and beadwork and always bore **Vollbracht's** signature in the print. In 1979 he designed swimwear for the **Sofere** company, and by 1981 he had launched **Vollbracht Too,** a division of **Manhattan Industries,** followed by a **Vollbracht Sports** line, and **Overs by Vollbracht** in 1983. He closed his business in 1985 after his backers pulled out of his company and resolved to focus on his illustration and portraiture work

VON FURSTENBERG, DIANE (DIANE MICHELLE HALFIN) (1946-) Belgian from Brussels. After marrying **Prince Egon Von Furstenberg** in 1969 the couple immigrated to the United States and hit the New York social scene, becoming the aristocrats to be seen with among the party-going jet set of the late 1960s and early 1970s. **Von Furstenberg** fell into designing with no training, yet possessed a degree in economics from the University of Geneva and a desire to create practical, flattering, simple dresses to counter the flourishing jean-wearing culture. In 1970 she had a small collection made up in Italy, and basically peddled the line around herself to various New York department stores. Her first designs culled their inspiration from **Claire McCardell,** a women's sportswear designer icon in America throughout the 1940s and 1950s. Her universally flattering, simple, cotton jersey wrap dress with fitted bodice and A-line knee-length skirt featuring feminine prints was an immediate success; however, having a title attached to your name was certainly an added cachet which was considerably instrumental. She produced her famous wrap dresses from 1970–1977. She established a couture house in 1984–1988 and introduced a cosmetic and fragrance line in 1977–1983. **Hervé Léger** designed for **Von Furstenberg** in 1985. She reintroduced versions of her famous wrap dresses in the mid-1990s, this time finding an entirely new market by selling them through the QVC Television Network, as well as through various department stores throughout North America. Her lines over the years have included women's ready-to-wear, couture, cosmetics, fragrances, handbags, footwear, jewelry, table linens, furs, stationery, wallpaper, and designs for **Vogue Patterns.**

VUITTON, LOUIS (1811-1892) **Louis Vuitton** came to Paris in 1827 at the age of 16 and apprenticed with various luggage makers. He began working as a "layetier," or luggage packer, for various prominent households and was eventually appointed by Napoleon III as *layetier* to the Empress Eugénie. With **Vuit-ton's** expertise in packing and his understanding of the demands for travel by the privileged class, he began to design luggage to suit the new requirements of travel due to the opening of the first railway lines in France from Paris to St. Germain. He is credited with designing the first flat trunk as opposed to the traditional iron hooped trunks that had been used by the horse-drawn coaches until then. The new flat trunks were easily stackable in railway carriages and the holds of ocean liners. His first design was made of wood covered in canvas, referred to as "**Trianon Grey.**" However, his designs became so widely pop-ular that other manufacturers copied them, forcing him to introduce a striped design in beige and brown in 1876. He changed it once again in 1888 due to persisting imitators, introducing the "**Daumier**" checkerboard pattern with the interwoven words "**marque déposée Louis Vuitton.**" George Vuitton as-sumed control of the company after his father's death in 1892, and in an effort to halt the piracy of the company's designs once and for all he acquired a worldwide patent for a new design which incorporated his father's initials, stars, and a small French wildflower motif which is still in use today. Unfortunately, the world patent has never completely deterred the copying of the **Louis Vuitton** designs and it is a pre-vailing problem which continues today. The checkerboard motif was reintroduced in the late 1990s to the company's handbag and accessories collections. Today the company is at the core of the fashion and lux-ury conglomerate **LVMH (Louis Vuitton, Moët, Hennessy)** and offers a complete line of handbags, footwear, and women's ready-to-wear by head designer **Mark Jacobs.** For fall/winter of 2000, **Jacobs** collaborated with **Steven Sprouce** to create a collection for **Vuitton** of handbags and accessories includ-ing over-the-elbow-length gloves with **Sprouce's** signature graffiti scribble prints by **Keith Haring.**

WEINBERG, CHESTER (1930-1985) American from New York City. After graduating from Parsons, New York, he went on to receive his B.S. degree in Art Education from New York University at night while working as a freelance sketch artist by day. He worked as a freelance designer for various ready-to-wear manufacturers in New York during the early 1960s before creating his own line in 1966, and founding his own company in 1971. His focus was primarily on beautiful women's ready-to-wear evening attire; however, he also created collections of formal day ensembles and costume suits. A contemporary of **Bill Blass** and **Geoffrey Beene** in the 1960s, his designs favored big, bright, bold prints, and in the 1970s fea-tured silk tie-dye. He is credited with showing the first maxi lengths in 1965 and popularizing the "Baby Doll" look in 1969. His company became a division of the **Jones Apparel Group,** 1977–1981, and when it closed he moved to **Calvin Klein Jeans** as design director in 1981 while continuing to teach fashion at Parsons, New York, where he had been teaching since 1954, shortly after his own graduation. He con-tinued teaching up until his death in 1985.

WESTWOOD, VIVIENNE (VIVIENNE ISABEL SWIRE) (1941-) British from Glossop, Derbyshire, England. After studying for one term at Harrow Art School before training as a teacher, **Westwood** began her professional career as a teacher in the late 1960s prior to moving into fashion. **Westwood,** along with friend **Malcolm McLaren,** assumed the management of a small vintage clothing shop, "**Let It Rock,**" in London in 1971 and quickly set about adjusting the focus of the shop which, by 1974, was known for its bondage and fetish clothing and accessories. Both **Westwood** and **McLaren,** in a collaborative effort, are credited with spearheading the British punk movement in the 1970s with their anti-establishment, anti-couture, anti-fashion, anti-monarchy, pseudo-porn graphic images on fabrics created by **Jamie Reid,** which they interpreted into T-shirts and minidresses that were often embellished with chains, chicken bones, and metal studs. They changed the name of the shop to "**Too Fast to Live, Too Young to Die**" in 1974, to "**Sex**" in 1974, to "**Seditionaries**" in 1977, and finally to "**World's End**" in 1980. McLaren was also managing the U.S. band The New York Dolls in 1975 and was deeply ensconced in the pre-punk music scene. As a publicity stunt for the **Sex** shop, **McLaren** decided to form his own punk band made up of various colorful clients of the shop, giving birth to the **Sex Pistols. McLaren** claims that the for-mation of the band was actually a public relations exercise which took off, and that his original intention was just to sell trousers. **Westwood** went on to launch her own ready-to-wear collection in 1981 and opened a second shop, "**Nostalgia of Mud,**" in 1982, and a third shop in Mayfair, London, in 1990. She is most famous for her "**Bondage**" collection in 1976, "**Pirates**" in 1981, "**Savages**" in 1982, and her "**Mini-Crini**" based on the Victorian crinoline in 1985. From the beginning her designs have always impacted the fashion world and have been widely reinterpreted by many who followed. She recently signed a five-year license deal to release the "**Anglomania**" men's and women's line for spring 2001.

WORTH, CHARLES FREDERICK (1825-1895) British from Bourne, Lincolnshire, England. **Worth** began his career in London at the age of 12 when his lawyer father had lost all the family money gambling and apprenticed his son for 7 years at **Swan & Edgar,** a haberdashery, before he joined **Lewis & Allenby,** a silk mercer. He moved to Paris in 1845 and took a job at **Maison Gagelin** where he convinced them to allow him to make up some designs which they sold, resulting in **Worth** having his own department in the shop within five years. In 1858 **Worth,** with partner **Otto Bobergh,** a Swedish businessman, founded **Worth et Bobergh** on Rue de la Paix. The company closed in 1870 during the Franco-Prussian War and re-established itself in 1874. **Otto Bobergh** sold his interest in the company and returned to Sweden in 1870. **Worth** was considered an arbiter of taste, a designer whose work was aesthetically and technically perfect. He specialized in the copious use of opulent and lavish fabrics, frills, ribbon, lace, braids, and tassels, and his designs were greatly sought after by high society ladies throughout Europe and America, as well as ladies of the court, most notably the Empress Eugéneie of France and Empress Elizabeth of Austria, and actresses Sarah Bernhardt and Eleonora Duse. He was erroneously credited with the use of the collapsible steel frame crinoline and for making the crinoline obsolete in 1867 by flattening the front of his designs and sweeping the fullness to the back of the garment. He was also the first couturier to use live models to present his collections, using his young French wife and muse **Marie Vernet** as a house model, and the first to sell authorized models to be copied by fashion houses in America, although piracy was already a major issue in fashion. Most significantly **Worth** was the first couturier to put his label on his garment, not only physically but metaphorically, by establishing a strong, immediately identifiable style, culling much of his influences from master painters including Van Dyke, Gainsborough, and Velázquez. **Paul Poiret** designed for the house from 1901–1904, and **Hardy Amies** also worked for the house and for the British government Utility Scheme during World War II. He opened a London branch on New Burlington Street in 1911, moving to Hanover Square in 1922, followed by a second location on Regent Street in 1930. He also had locations in Cannes and Biarritz in 1930. **Worth's** sons **Jean-Philippe** (as the couturier) and **Gaston** (as the financial director) assumed control of the company upon his death in 1895, which then was passed to his grandsons in 1922 with **Gaston's** sons **Jacques** as the financial director and **Jean-Charles** as the couturier. By 1936 the company ultimately was passed to **Charles Frederick Worth's** great grandsons **Roger** and **Jacques.** The company was forced to close during World War II, and after the war closed the Paris operation and merged with the London branch. **Roger** retired in 1952, with **Jacques** remaining active until he sold the company, merging it with the London branch of **Paquin** and renaming it **Paquin-Worth** which it closed in 1954. At that time the **Worth** company was sold to a perfume manufacturer. The **Worth** company today only produces fragrances; however, the fashion name has reportedly been secured by a new investor.

WRAGGE, B. H. (SIDNEY WRAGGE) (1908-1978) An American ready-to-wear women's sportswear designer who bought a men's shirt manufacturer in 1931 and named the company **B. H. Wragge.** He expanded the company by the late 1930s to include women's shirts and eventually a full range of separates and coordinates. In the 1940s the company was recognized as one of the leading American women's sportswear design firms specializing in bright, feminine, inexpensive, and carefully coordinated separates and interchangeable wardrobes which were directed at students and young active professional women. One of the keys to the company's success were the ad campaigns which presented themes with each collection, much in the way **Tommy Hilfiger** and **Ralph Lauren** have marketed their companies to create brand awareness and lifestyle concepts today. By the 1950s **Sidney Wragge's** designs for his company remained moderately priced; however, he moved away from the college-aged client to a more sophisticated, professional woman or homemaker. The company was considered on par with contemporaries including **Claire McCardell, Vera Maxwell, Clare Potter, Anne Fogarty, Fred Picard & Bobbie Yeoman,** and **Tina Leser.** Although the primary focus of the company throughout the 1930s, 1940s, and 1950s was primarily women's sports and activewear, by the 1960s the company was also offering collections of relaxed and simple evening silhouettes in wool jersey, organza, and Lurex fabrics. **Adri (Adrienne Steckling)** began her career designing for **B. H. Wragge** from 1960 to 1967 before launching her own line. The company closed with **Sidney Wragge's** retirement in 1971.

ZAMASPORT (SEE GIGLI, ROMERO AND CALLAGHAN)

ZUCKERMAN, BEN (DATES UNKNOWN) A Romanian who immigrated to the United States and began working as a teenager in the garment district in New York City prior to being involved as a partner with the company of **Zuckerman & Kraus,** founded in 1929, as well as **Zuckerman & Hoffman.** He founded his own company, **Ben Zuckerman,** in 1950, specializing in women's ready-to-wear coats, suits, costume suits, and dresses with prices ranging from $150 to $300 in the early 1950s. Famous for his superb and exacting cut and meticulous tailoring, he was considered to be a top-rung ready-to-wear designer on par with **Adel Simpson, Harvey Berin, Shannon Rogers for Jerry Silverman, Larry Aldrich, Malcolm Starr,** and **Mollie Parnis.** He was most noted for his dress and coat ensembles with printed silk linings and faceted jeweled button details.

Resources

There are literally thousands of vintage clothing dealers all over the world. However, I have chosen to list a very select group of sources based on my personal dealings with them and their well-established reputations as purveyors of important, high-end designer vintage clothing and accessories.

DEALERS

CANADA

BLACK MARKET
24 Kensington Ave.
Toronto, Ontario
Canada M6K 1W3
416-599-5858
Focus on 1940s–1970s

SECOND LOCATION:
319 Queen Street West
Toronto, Ontario
Canada M6K 1W3
416-599-5858

WAREHOUSE
39 Moutray Street
Toronto, Ontario
Canada M6K 1W3
416-599-5858
By *appointment only.*

BLACKROSE VINTAGE
Antiques at the St. Laurence
92 Front Street East
Toronto, Ontario
Canada M5E 1C43.
416-350-8865
Blackrosevintage@aol.com
Focus on 1940s–1960s

COURAGE MY LOVE
14 Kensington Ave.
Toronto, Ontario
Canada M5T 2J9

416-979-1992
Focus on 1940s–1970s

DIVINE DECADANCE
Manulife Center
55 Bloor Street West
Toronto, Ontario
Canada M4W 1A5
416-324-9759
Focus on 1920s–1970s

EPHEMERA
Antiques at the St. Laurence
92 Front Street East
Toronto, Ontario
Canada
416-350-8865
Focus on 1940s–1960s

ROZAMEH
799 "B" College Street
Toronto, Ontario
Canada M6G 1C7
416-534-8303
Focus on 1900–1980s

STELLA LUNA
1627 Queen Street West
Toronto, Ontario
Canada M6R 1A9
416-536-7300
Focus on 1940s–1980s

VIBES
45 Kensington Ave.
Toronto, Ontario
Canada M5T 2J8
Focus on 1960s–1980s

UNITED STATES

CALIFORNIA

560 HAYES VINTAGE
BOUTIQUE
560 Hayes Street
San Francisco, CA 94102
415-861-7993
Focus on 1960s–1970s

ALICE AND ANNIE
11056 Magnolia Blvd.
North Hollywood, CA 91601
818-761-6085
Focus on 1920s–1960s

ANIMAL HOUSE
66 Windward Ave.
Venice, CA 90291
310-392-5411
Focus on 1960s–1970s

COME TO MAMA
4019 West Sunset Blvd.
Los Angeles, CA 90029
323-953-1275
Focus on 1960s–1970s

DADDYO'S
5128 Vineland Ave.
North Hollywood, CA 91601
818-769-8869
Focus on 1950s–1960s

DECADES
8214 Melrose Ave.
Los Angeles, CA 90046

323-655-0223
www.decadesinc.com
Focus on 1960s–1980s
Also available at Barneys in
New York

FINERY, THE
1611 Montana Ave.
Santa Monica, CA 90403
310-393-5588
Focus on 1940s–1970s

GOLYESTER
136 La Brea Ave.
Los Angeles, CA 90036
323-931-1339
Focus on 1930s–1960s

INTERNATIONAL SILKS
AND WOOLENS
8347 Beverly Blvd.
Los Angeles, CA 90048
323-653-6453
Intlsilk@aol.com
Focus on 1930s–present day

JET RAG
825 North La Brea Ave.
Los Angeles, CA 90034
323-939-0528
Focus on 1960s–1980s

JULIAN'S VINTAGE
CLOTHING
8366 West 3rd Street
Los Angeles, CA 90048
323-655-3011
Focus on 1900–1960s

LILY ET CIE
944 Burton Way
Beverly Hills, CA 90211
310-724-5757
Lily et cie@aol.com
Focus on 1920s–1980s

MEOW
2210 East 4th Street
Long Beach, CA 90814
562-438-8990
Focus on 1940s–1960s

MONICA DICKERSON
ANTIQUE GUILD
3225 Helms Ave.
Los Angeles, CA 90034
310-838-3131
Focus on 1960s–1980s

PAPER BAG PRINCESS, THE
8700 Santa Monica Blvd.
West Hollywood, CA 90069
310-358-1985
www.ThePaperBagPrincess.com
Focus on 1920s–present day

PLAYCLOTHES
11422 Moorpark Street
North Hollywood, CA 91602
818-755-9559
Focus on 1950s–1970s

REPEAT PERFORMANCE
318 North La Brea Ave.
Los Angeles, CA 90036
323-938-0609
Focus on 1930s–1940s

RESURRECTION
8006 Melrose Ave.
Los Angeles, CA 90046
323-651-5516
www.stylebyte.com
Focus on 1960s–1980s
See three other locations in
New York.

SHABON
7617½ Beverly Blvd. West
Los Angeles, CA 90036
323-692-0061
Focus on 1960s–1980s

SLOW
7474 Melrose Ave.
Los Angeles, CA 90046
323-655-3725
Focus on 1970s deadstock

SQUARESVILLE
1800 North Vermont Ave.
Los Angeles, CA 90027
323-669-8464
Focus on 1960s–1970s

SECOND LOCATION:
7312 Melrose Ave.
Los Angeles, CA 90046
323-525-1425

VER UNICA
148 Noe Street
San Francisco, CA 94114
415-431-0688
www.ver-unica.com
Focus on 1960s–1980s

VINTAGE SILHOUETTES
1301 Pomona Ave.
Crockett, CA 94525
800-636-1410
www.vintagesilhouettes.com
Focus on 1900s–1940s

WASTELAND, THE
1660 Haight Street
San Francisco, CA 94117
415-863-3150
www.thewasteland.com
Focus on 1960s–1970s

SECOND LOCATION:
428 Melrose Ave.
Los Angeles, CA 90046
323-653-3028

THE WAY WE WORE
1094 Revere Ave.
Suite 29
San Francisco, CA 94124
415-822-1800
www.thewaywewore.com
Focus on 1920s–1980s
By appointment only.

GEORGIA

REVAMPED RESALE BOUTIQUE
114 North Avondale Road
Avondale Estates, GA 30002
404-292-9770
Focus on 1960s–present day

ILLINOIS

FLASHY TRASH
3524 North Halsted
Chicago, IL 60657

773-327-6900
Focus on 1950s–1980s

HUBBA-HUBBA
3338 North Clark Street
Chicago, Illinois 60657
773-477-1414
Focus on 1960s–1970s

STRANGE CARGO
3448 North Clark Street
Chicago, IL 60657
773-327-8090
Focus on 1960s–1980s

NEW YORK

ALICE'S UNDERGROUND
481 Broadway
New York, NY 10024
212-431-9067
Focus on 1960s–1970s

ALLAN AND SUZI
416 Amsterdam Ave.
New York, NY 10024
212-724-7445
Focus on 1950s–1970s

MARY CATALINA, VINTAGE
LOFT
117 West 26th Street
Suite 3W
New York, NY 10001
212-529-6925
Focus on 1920s–1980s
By appointment only.

CHERRY
185 Orchard Street
New York, NY 10002
212-358-7131
Focus on 1960s–1980s

FAN CLUB, THE
22 West 19th Street
New York, NY 10011
212-929-3349

HOLLYWOOD AND VINE
32 Westchester Ave.
Pound Ridge, NY 10576

203-852-0649
Focus on 1940s–1970s

LORRAINE WOHL, ANTIQUE
SALON OF
870 Lexington Ave.
New York, NY 10021
212-472-0191
Focus on 1920s–1930s

LOVES SAVES THE DAY
119 Second Ave.
New York, NY 10003
212-228-3802
Focus on 1920s–1970s

PATINA
451 Broom Street
New York, NY 10013
212-625-3375
LN1120@aol.com
Focus on 1930s–1970s

PATRICIA PASTOR VINTAGE
FASHIONS
19 East 71st Street
New York, NY 10021
212-734-4673
Focus on 1920s–1970s
By appointment only.

RESURRECTION VINTAGE
CLOTHING
217 Mott Street
New York, NY 10012
212-625-1374
Focus on 1960s–1980s

SECOND LOCATION:
123 7th Street
New York, NY 10009
212-228-0063

THIRD LOCATION:
Henri Bendel Department
Store
712 Fifth Avenue
3rd Floor
New York, NY 10019
212-247-1100

STELLA DALLAS
218 Thompson Street
New York, NY 10012
212-647-0447
Focus on 1940s–1970s

TATIANA
860 Lexington Ave.
New York, NY 10021
212-717-7684
Focus on 1980s–present day

KENI VALENTI, RETRO
COUTURE
247 West 30th Street
5th Floor
New York, NY 10001
212-967-7147
www.kenivalenti.com
Focus on 1920s–1980s
By appointment only.

VINTAGE BY STACEY LEE
305 Central Ave.
White Plains
New York, NY 10606
212-352-0275
Focus on 1900s–1960s
By appointment only.

WHAT COMES AROUND GOES
AROUND
351 West Broadway
New York, NY 10013
212-343-9303
www.nyvintage.com
Focus on 1960s–1980s

OREGON

TORSO VINTAGE
64 South West Second Ave.
Portland, OR 97204
503-294-1493
Focus on 1960s–1980s

VINTAGE RE VU
232 South West Ankeny
Portland, OR 97204
503-241-1876
Focus on 1960s–1980s

EUROPE

ENGLAND

ANNIE'S VINTAGE COSTUME AND TEXTILE
10 Camden Passage
Islington, London
England N1 8ED
020-7359-0796
Focus on 1880s–1950s

BLACKOUT II
51 Endell Street
Holborn, London
England WC2H 9AJ
020-7240-5006
Focus on 1960s–present day

CORNUCOPIA
12 Upper Tachbrook Street
Westminster, London
England SW1 1SH
020-7828-5752
Focus on 1880s–1950s

ORSINI GALLERY
76 Earl's Court Road
London W8
England
020-7937-2903
Focus on 1850s–present day

STEINBERG AND TOLKIEN
181–183 King's Road
Chelsea, London SW3 5EB
England
020-7376-3660
Focus on 1920s–1980s

VENT
178A Westbourne Grove
London W11 2RH
England
09-5629-5568
Focus on 1920s–present day

VINTAGE CLOBBER
874 Christ Church Road
Boscombe, Bournemouth
England BH76DJ
44 (0) 1202429794

www.vintageclobber.com
Focus on 1940s–1980s

FRANCE

BOURIQUE LYDIA
Marché Dauphine
138-140, Rue des Rosiers
Saint-Ouen, Paris
France 93400
Stand 101
01-40-11-49-51

C! BYZANCE
Marché Dauphine
140 Rue des Rosiers
Saint-Ouen, Paris
France 93400
Stand 65
01-40-10-81-66

DIDIER LUDOT
Jardins du Palais Royal
24 Galeries Montpensier
Paris, France 75001
01-42-96-06-56
Didier Ludot.com
Focus on 1930s–1970s

SECOND LOCATION:
Barneys New York
575 Fifth Ave.
New York, NY 10017
www.Didier Ludot.com

THIRD LOCATION:
1 Setan Co., Ltd.
3-14-1 Shinjukku-
Shinjuku-Ku
Tokyo 160 Japan
www.Didier Ludot.com

FOURTH LOCATION:
Laisser Faire
Toshio Suenaga
Nagasaki 850 0852
Japan
www.Didier Ludot.com

FIFTH LOCATION:
Teresa Shop 210 Galliera
9 Queen's Road Central
Hong Kong, China
www.Didier Ludot.com

SIXTH LOCATION:
La Petite Robe Noire
Palais Royal
Galerie de Valois
01-40-15-01-04
www.Didier Ludot.com
Couture vintage designs by
Didier Ludot

KILLIWATCH
64 Rue Tiquetonne
Paris, France 75002
01-42-21-17-37
Focus on 1960s–1970s

RAGTIME
23 Rue Échaudé
Paris, France 75006
01-56-24-00-36
Focus on 1900s–1970s

CATHERINE ARIGOI
14 Rue de Beaune
Paris, France 75007
01-42-60-50-99
Focus on 1900s–1960s

SPAIN

MARMOTA
Calle Mira el Rio Baja, 13
(El Rastro)
Madrid, Spain 28005
914672452
Focus on 1960s–1970s

MATUSALEN
Calle Mira el Rio Baja, 11
(El Rastro)
Madrid, Spain 28005
619685019
Focus on 1900s–1960s

AUCTION HOUSES

CHARLES A. WHITAKER AUCTION CO.
7105 Emlen Street
Philadelphia, PA 19119
215-844-8788

CHRISTIE'S
20 Rockefeller Plaza
New York, NY 10020
212-636-2000
www.christies.com

CHRISTIE'S SOUTH
KENSINGTON
85 Old Brompton Road
South Kensington, London
England SW7 3LD
020-7581-7611

WILLIAM DOYLE GALLERIES
Doyle New York
175 East 87th Street
New York, NY 10128
212-427-2730
e-mail: info@doylenewyork.com
www.doylenewyork.com

DROUOT RICHELIEU
Drouot Hôtel des Ventes
9 Rue Drouot
Paris, France 75009
01-48-00-20-20

DURAN
Subastas de Arte
Serrano, No. 12
Madrid, Spain 28001
915776091
www.duran-subastas.es
duransubasta@internet.es

ERIC COUTURIER,
COMMISSAIRE-PRISEUR
ASSOCIÉ
8 rue Drouot
Paris, France 75009
01-47-70-82-66
www.etudecouturier.com

PHILLIPS AUCTIONEERS
101 New Bond Street
London W1Y 0AS, England
020-7629-6602
www.phillipsauctions.com/uk/

PHILLIPS NEW YORK
406 East 79th Street
New York, NY 10021
212-570-4830

D. & J. RITCHIE
288 King Street East
Toronto, Ontario
Canada M5A 1K4
416-364-1864
www.ritchies.com

SKINNER
357 Main Street
Bolton, MA 01740
978-779-6241

SKINNER
63 Park Plaza
Boston, MA 02116
617-350-5400
www.skinnerinc.com

SOTHEBY'S
1334 York Ave.
New York, NY 10021
212-606-7000
www.sothebys.com

SOTHEBY'S LONDON
34–35 New Bond Street
London WIA 2AA
England
020-7293-5000

VINTAGE CLOTHING EVENTS, NEWSLETTERS, AND ASSOCIATIONS

THE APPRAISER INSTITUTE
OF AMERICA, INC.
386 Park Ave. South
Suite 2000
New York, NY 10016
212-889-5404
www.AppraiserAssoc.org

ART DECO SHOW AND SALE
The Concourse Exhibition
Center
8th and Brahnan Street
San Francisco, CA

415-599-deco
www.artdecoto60s.com
Show held twice a year, first
weekend in June, and first
weekend in December; ap-
prox. 200 vendors with a large
number of fashion dealers.

ANTIQUE TEXTILE &
VINTAGE FASHIONS
EXTRAVAGANZA
Brimfield Show
Sturbridge Hotel
Route 20
Sturbridge, MA
207-439-2334

LINDA ZUKAS SHOW
ASSOCIATES
P.O. Box 729
Cape Neddick, ME 03902
www.vintagefashionandtextile
show.com
Vintage clothing show held
in Brimfield, Massachusetts,
three times a year.

THE CHICAGO O'HARE
VINTAGE CLOTHING AND
TEXTILE SHOW AND SALE
Bob Smith & Dolphin
Promotions, Inc.
Donald E Stevens Convention
Center-Hall B
P.O. Box 7320
Fort Lauderdale, FL 33338
954-563-6747
www.antiqnet.com/dolphin

CASKEY LEES
Textile, Costume, and
Clothing Show
P.O. Box 1409
Topanga, CA 90290
310-455-2886
Vintage clothing show held
in Burbank, California, three
times a year.

CAT'S PAJAMAS
The Midwest Antique Clothing and Jewelry Show and Sale

Hemmens Cultural Center
125 West Main Street West
Dundee, IL 60118
847-428-8368
Info.: P.O. Box 392
Dundee, IL 60118
www.catspajamasproductions.net
Vintage clothing show held
twice a year.

THE NEW YORK VINTAGE
FASHION AND ANTIQUE
TEXTILE SHOW
718-783-9736
AntiqueTextiles@aol.com
Sheila Feeney

TRIPLE PIER SHOW
Stella Management
147 West 24th Street
New York, NY 10011
212-255-0020
Vintage clothing and an-
tiques show held at the New
York Pier twice a year.

VINTAGE FASHION EXPO
Two locations:
Santa Monica Civic
Auditorium
and
San Francisco Concourse
Head Office: P.O. Box 883773
San Francisco, CA 94188
707-793-0773
Vintage clothing show held
in Santa Monica, California,
twice a year, as well as twice
a year in San Francisco.

ASSOCIATIONS AND MUSEUMS

BROOKLYN MUSEUM OF ARTS
AND SCIENCES
200 Eastern Parkway
Brooklyn, NY 11238
718-638-5000
Housing a permanent collec-
tion of the fashions of
Charles James.

COSTUME COUNCIL
Los Angeles County Museum
of Art
5905 Wilshire Blvd.
Los Angeles, CA 90036
323-857-6013

COSTUME INSTITUTE AT
THE METROPOLITAN MUSEUM
OF ART
1000 Fifth Avenue
New York, NY 10028
212-570-3908
www.metmuseum.org

COSTUME SOCIETY OF
AMERICA
55 Edgewater Drive
P.O. Box 73
Earleville, MD 21919-0073
800-CSA-9447, 410-275-
1619
www.costumesocietyamerica.
com

NATIONAL COSTUME SOCIETY
OF AMERICA
55 Edgewater Drive
P.O. Box 73
Earleville, MD 21919-0073
(410) 275-2329

THE MUSEUM AT THE
FASHION INSTITUTE OF
FASHION TECHNOLOGY
(F.I.T.)
Seventh Avenue at 27th Street
New York, NY 10001-5992
212-217-5970
www.fitnyc.suny.edu/museum

THE TEXTILE SOCIETY
OF AMERICA
P.O. Box 70
Earleville, MD 21919-0070
410-275-2329
www.textilesociety.org
Newsletters and associate
programs available.

VICTORIA AND
ALBERT MUSEUM
Cromwell Road
South Kensington, London
England SW7 2RL
44(0)2079422000

THE TEXTILE
CONSERVATION GROUP
5 Moraine Street
Andover, MA 01810
978-474-8069
e-mail: tcg@clearsailing.net

THE COSTUME AND TEXTILE
GROUP OF NEW JERSEY
12 Cedar Street
Keyport, NJ 07735
732-335-1648

CANADIAN CONSERVATION
INSTITUTE
1030 Innes Road
Ottawa, Ontario
Canada K1A 0M5
613-998-3721
www.cci-icc.gc.ca

NARTS, NATIONAL
ASSOCIATION OF RESALE
AND THRIFT SHOPS
P.O. Box 80707
St. Clairshores, MI 48080
www.narts.org

THE OLD CLOTHING SHOW
Automotive Building
Exhibition Place
Toronto, Ontario
Canada
Held in April and September
Info.: Bonnie Meacham
416-657-2156

IMPORTANT VINTAGE CLOTHING, AUCTION, AND REFERENCE WEBSITES

Whenever possible, I have indicated the websites of boutiques which host their own sites. The following listings are for businesses which strictly operate on the Internet.

WWW.AMAZON.COM
An online auction website which has a moderate amount of vintage clothing offerings.

WWW.AUCTIONBYTES.COM
A guide to online auctions for buyers and sellers.

WWW.AUCTIVA.COM
A powerful resource of solutions for online auction sellers.

BEVERLY BIRKS
www.camrax.com/pages/birks0.htm
A private collector with items on view and a selected few for purchase.

WWW.BOOKFINDER.COM
A fantastic search engine to source out-of-print books.

WWW.COSTUMESOCIETYAMERICA.COM
A reference and newsletter as well as associate programs are available.

DECO-ECHOE.COM
Art Deco Society of California magazine. 20th-century modern designs from furniture to fashion.

WWW.EBAY.COM
An online auction website which has a tremendous amount of vintage clothing offerings.

WWW.FASHIONDIG.COM
An online fashion mall.

WWW.FLEAMARKETGUIDE.COM
A state-by-state listing of local flea markets.

WWW.FLEATIQUE.COM
An online thrift site.

KENT STATE MUSEUM
www.Kent.&Du/Museum/Index.html-ssi

WWW.NARTS.ORG
The National Association of Retail and Thrift Shops, this site provides education, service, and resources to resale shop owners.

WWW.RETROACTIVE.COM
A resource for information on retro and vintage fashions and collectibles.

WWW.SECONDTIME.COM
The Internet resale directory to secondhand.

WWW.SECONDHAND.COM
A resource for surplus and salvage, as well as a listing of thousands of businesses from antiques stores, thrift and consignment shops, and flea markets.

WWW.SHOPGOODWILL.COM
An auction website for Goodwill Industries.

WWW.TEXTILEWEB.COM
A textile industry resource for all aspects of the textile industry.

WWW.TEXTILESOCIETY.ORG
The Textile Society of America site that has newsletters and associate programs available.

WWW.TROVENET.COM
A site which lists approximately 1,400 books, including many topics on antiques.

WWW.VINTAGECOUTURE.COM
Vintage Couture, an online site for the sale of consigned couture, and designer vintage apparel.

WWW.WGSN.COM
The Worth Global Style Network, an online subscription-based site for international fashion news and trends.

CONSERVATION SUPPLIERS AND RESOURCES

ACME DISPLAY FIXTURE CO.
1057 South Olive Street
Los Angeles, CA 90015
213-749-9191
or 800-305-9907
www.acmedisplay.com
Commercial display fixtures such as mannequins, hangers, and professional steamers.

CHERISH
205 West 86th Street
New York, NY 10024
P.O. Box 941
New York, NY 10024-0941
212-724-1748

Padded hangers and acid-free materials.
By appointment only.

LAMB'S REWEAVING
Claudette Hill
3717 South La Brea Ave.
P.O. Box 135
Los Angeles, CA 90016
323-931-4249
Mail-in inquiries and orders only.
Services available through Montavo's Tailoring and Reweaving, Los Angeles, CA.

CONSERVATION RESOURCES INTERNATIONAL
8000-H Forbes Pl
Springfield, VA 22151
800-634-6932
www.conservationresources.com
Acid-free materials, conservation supplies, and books.

LIGHT IMPRESSIONS
P.O. Box 940
Rochester, NY 14603-0940
800-828-6216
www.lightimpressionsdirect.com
Acid-free materials, conservation supplies, and books.

METAL EDGE
6340 Bandini Blvd.
Commerce, CA 90040
800-862-2228
www.metaledgeinc.com
Acid-free materials, conservation supplies, and books.

MONTAVO'S TAILORING AND REWEAVING
1624 Montana Ave.
Los Angeles, CA 90403
310-828-7748

RICHARD'S HOMEWARES
230 Fifth Avenue
Suite 1700
New York, NY 10001
212-889-0932

Order desk and customer service:
800-446-3880
100% breathable cotton frameless hanging, garment storage bags.

TALAS
568 Broadway
Room 107
New York, NY 10012
212-219-0770
Acid-free materials, pH test paper, and conservation supplies.

TEST FABRIC
415 Delaware Street
P.O. Box 26
West Pittston, PA 18643
570-256-3132
Padded covers for hangers, archival fabrics, conservation, exhibits, and storage services.

TEXTILE CONSERVATION WORKSHOP
3 Main Street
South Salem, NY 10590
914-763-5805
www.rap-arcc.org
(Regional Alliance for Preservation and the Association for Regional Conservation Center.)

UNIVERSITY PRODUCTS
517 Main Street
Holyoke, MA 01041-0101
800-336-4847
www.universityproducts.com
Acid-free materials, conservation supplies, and books.

CONTEMPORARY FASHION WEBSITES

www.Annasui.com
www.badgleymischka.com
www.betseyjohnson.com
www.celine.com
www.chanel.com
www.coach.com
www.colehaan.com
www.costumenational.com
www.christian-lacroix.fr
www.dianevonfurstenberg.com
www.dior.com
www.donnakaran.com
www.elsaperetti.com
www.firstlook.com
www.giorgioarmani.com
www.givenchy.com
www.goldenviolin.com
www.gucci.com
www.hanaemori.com
www.helmutlang.com
www.hermes.com
www.isabeltoledo.com
www.issseymiyake.com
www.jeanmuir.com
www.jilsander.com
www.jpgualthier.com
www.kenzo.com
www.loewe.com
www.lvmh.com
www.manoloblahnik.com
www.metrofashion.com
www.michaelkors.com
www.milashon.com
www.missoni.com
www.ninaricci.com
www.nicolemiller.com
www.normakamaili.com
www.normakamailivintage.com
www.pacorobanne.com
www.polo.com
www.prada.com
www.ralphlauren.com
www.soniarykiel.com
www.stephensprouse.com
www.valentino.com
www.versace.com
www.viviennewestwood.com
www.yvessaintlaurent.com
www.Zandrarhodes.com

Terms

1) ATTRIBUTED TO: Indicates through the characteristic look or history that a garment which is missing its label is designed by a specific noncredited designer working for a design house at the time of the garment's creation; made in the style of; or is a licensed replica of an original.

2) PICKER: A person who does business within the vintage clothing or antique and collectibles market by purchasing items through rag houses, thrift shops, flea markets, yard and estate sales, then sells the items for a higher price to another individual.

3) DEALER: A person who professionally engages in the buying and selling of vintage clothing or antiques.

4) RESERVE PRICE: The starting price set forth by the auction house on a particular item. This price is set by both the consignee and the auction house. This is usually a mutually agreed upon reserve price between the auction house which will have an estimate as to what they believe the piece should sell for, and the consignee who will have a price they wish to receive.

5) REALIZED PRICE: This is the price that the auction item ultimately sells for including the buyer's premium.

6) GOOD: This is a condition rating given to an item which would normally indicate that the item is not in perfect condition, and it may in fact have some damage to it, although the item is still considered to be in a salable condition.

7) EXCELLENT: This is a condition rating given to an item which would normally indicate that the item is in perfect or excellent condition, and without flaws or damage. This is the optimum condition to purchase.

8) FAIR: This is a condition rating given to an item which would normally indicate that the item is not without some problems. This condition is considered to be a less desirable than "Good" condition, while still being acceptable.

9) FAIR TO GOOD: This is a condition rating given to an item which would normally indicate that the item is better than "Fair," however not considered to be an advisable purchase unless you are well aware of the flaws in the item and are prepared to restore it, or use it as is.

10) POOR: This is the lowest condition rating given to an item which would normally indicate that the item is very badly flawed and is not advisable to purchase unless you are well aware of the flaws in the item and are prepared to restore it, or use it as is.

11) HAMMER PRICE: This is the price an item sells for at auction, excluding the "buyer's premium." Once all bids are in, it is the final price that is offered by the buyer.

12) BUYER'S PREMIUM: This is the percentage added to the "Hammer Price" at auction by an auction house which is paid by the buyer, and goes directly to the auction house. This percentage is not shared by the consignor and in most cases is approximately 15 percent.

13) WHOLESALER: This is someone who sells to a dealer or boutique owner at

a volume discount. This term can also be interchangeable with the terms, "Picker" or "Dealer."

14) FEEDBACK FORUM: This is an area on eBay's online auction site where the buyers and sellers can voice their opinions and experiences with each other. This is where you can place positive, negative, or neutral feedback on the seller or buyer if you have completed a transaction through eBay with them. This forum is designed to regulate the professional decorum of both the buyer and seller.

15) PROVENANCE: This is the history of ownership of a particular item. This can also refer to the history of the original designer of a garment when not indicated. It includes anything that may be of important historical significance, such as the person's title or social notoriety, that may increase the desirability of the item and ultimately its value.

Acknowledgments

Some people come into our lives, then go quickly, others leave footprints in our souls and we are never ever the same.   —FLAVIAN

This book is a culmination of a lifetime of pursuing, pestering, probing, searching, scouting, scrutinizing, elbowing, examining, and emphatically questioning every aspect of vintage clothing collecting, and as such draws insights, information, and inspiration from many different people. I have sought every possible authoritative source in an effort to make this a truly complete and accurate work, useful in every phase of collecting and selling vintage designer and couture wear.

I'd like to start by thanking all the thrift store clerks, flea market dealers and vintage clothing sellers around the world who recognized my gentle "haggling" as my passion for getting the *best possible price*. And, a special warm thanks to the closet which recently surrendered my first Charles James gown!

To my brilliant literary manager, mentor, and friend, Dr. Kenneth Atchity, who once told me over drinks many years ago, "You know you may be able to build a cottage industry out of this stuff, Elizabeth." (It's all your fault, Ken!) And to my faithful editor at Clarkson Potter, Margot Schupf, for her enthusiasm in unleashing me on the world and surviving my late-night calls.

Now, to the following kindred friends and family I send my love and deepest appreciation with these thoughts:

My very special friend, Richard Hankins, without whose love and encouragement I may never have found the time to write this book.

My sincere appreciation to my entire staff at The Paper Bag Princess, who filled my shoes in my absence to write this book, for their enthusiasm, loyalty, and devotion.

A very special thank-you to the beautiful ladies who donated their time to adorn these pages: actress Maria Bello, Kelly Cole, and Oona Hart.

My lifelong friend, Peter Meech, who over breakfast with me one summer morning in a Manhattan Beach diner told me that perhaps I was on to something and encouraged me to write my first book.

My devoted and loving family for suffering my interminable tales of thrift store bargains. My mother, Katherine Macdonald, for genetically passing on to me her passion for collecting, as well as her valuable time when she stepped in to fill my shoes in my business so that I could steal away and work on this book. My grandmother, Agnes Mason, for taking me to my first "penny sale" and blessing this world with her gentleness for 91 years. My father, Malcolm Mason, and his wife, Mary, for taking my exhausted cellular calls every other Saturday, giving me a patient ear to vent and the strength to keep working so hard. My brothers, Ian and Grant, for supplying me with nieces and nephews, Colin, Mark, Janette, and Alexander, to inundate with all of the amusing treasures I have found along the way. Sister Katherine for lightening my load and my overflowing closets by helping herself to my fabulous castoffs over the years, and my twin brother, Derek, who humored me with accepting the Warren Cook sports jackets I found for him in the thrift stores of Toronto so many years ago.

Laura Sewell, who was of inestimable help in reading the second draft and making suggestions for its improvement.

Finally, to all out there in the vast vintage clothing frontier who selflessly gave of their time and knowledge, without whose help this book would not have been possible. (You know who you are.) It is a delicate business eliciting information from these professionals. Fortunately for this book they recognized my sincerity in my search for the truth. Thank you all.

Index